SOCIAL RESEARCH

THEORY AND METHODS

R. GUY SEDLACK
JAY STANLEY
Department of Sociology
Towson State University

ALLYN AND BACON
Boston London Toronto Sydney Tokyo Singapore

Executive Editor: Susan Badger
Series Editor: Karen Hanson
Series Editorial Assistant: Deborah Reinke
Production Coordinator: Marjorie Payne
Editorial-Production Service: Chestnut Hill Enterprises, Inc.
Cover Administrator: Linda Dickinson
Cover Designer: Suzanne Harbison
Manufacturing Buyer: Megan Cochran

A NOTE FROM THE PUBLISHER

This book is printed on recycled, acid-free paper.

Library of Congress Cataloging-in-Publication Data

Sedlack, Richard Guy,
    Social research: theory and methods / R. Guy Sedlack and Jay Stanley.
      p. cm.
    Includes bibliographical references and index.
    ISBN 0-205-13187-5
    1. Social sciences—Research—Methodology. 2. Sociology—Research—Methodology. I. Stanley,
Jay. II. Title.
H62.S412 1992
001.4'2—dc20
                                                          91-14022
                                                           CIP

Printed in the United States of America
10 9 8 7 6 5 4 3 2 1   96 95 94 93 92 91

Contents

PREFACE

After teaching an introductory course in research methods collectively for over thirty years, we have a good deal of experience with the needs of students. We believe that the study of research methods is a vital and integral part of a student's intellectual development, and that the skills acquired in this course will serve the student in life after college, whether the student pursues a graduate degree or not.

A number of premises underlie this text. This is a book about doing science in the social sciences. It is written for the junior or senior majoring in the behavioral or social sciences or in a related field, such as health research, market research, or consumer behavior. We encourage students to take an introductory statistics course before using this book. The statistics here are not especially difficult, but a solid understanding of the basics is necessary. While a computer background is not necessary to understand the material, we encourage students to pursue computer studies as these skills will be demanded of the well-trained social scientist of the future. One of the special features of this book is our Chapter 15, Computers, Statistics, and SPSS. This next-to-final chapter serves as a summary example of much of the preceding material, bringing in topics of statistical analysis, computer technology, and the SPSS statistical package only as needed to fully understand the example.

The overall objective of any research methods book is to communicate the essential procedures. To achieve this objective, we have divided the text into four major parts. Part I includes chapters on (1) The Scientific Method, (2) Key Terms in the Scientific Language of Conceptualization, (3) Key Terms in the Scientific Language of Hypothesis Testing, (4) Causation and the Probability Model, and (5) the Conceptual Model. Part II is divided into chapters on (6) The Theory and Logic of Sampling, (7) The Characteristics and Techniques of Drawing Probability and Nonprobability Samples, (8) The Construction of Schedules and Guides, and (9) Issues in Measurement and Operationalization. Part III examines (10) Surveys: Interviews and Questionnaires, (11) Experimental and Quasi-Experimental Study Designs, (12) Content Analysis and Secondary Analysis, and (13) Observation, Unobtrusive Measures, and Exploratory Research. The final section looks at (14) Data Presentation: Individual Scores and Cross-Tabulations, (15) Computers, Statistics, SPSS^x, and a Summary Example, and (16) Ethical Considerations.

SUBSTANTIVE GOALS

Our primary concern is that the reader understand the connections between theory, research, and analysis. Each area functions to accomplish a different piece of an overall research project. However they do not and cannot happen in isolation from one another, as suggested by the way that these courses are scheduled in most colleges and universities. Since the student normally takes a single subject—e.g., statistics or methods—in any one semester and is advised not to double up on these courses, in this book we try to reinforce the relationships between theoretical models, research methods, and statistical analysis wherever possible.

Second, we discuss key issues in the philosophy of science throughout the text. Our hope is that the student will see the need for scientific rigor and for caution when using the specific tools and skills discussed herein.

Third, in the case of more advanced theoretical subject matter, we encourage the student to adopt a *multivariate* (three or more variable) analysis over the more simple *bivariate* (two or more variable) analysis that characterized earlier, less sophisticated research in the social sciences. This objective overlaps our concern with the relationship between research methods and conceptualization.

Finally, it is our goal to provide the reader with a high level of conceptual clarity. We have been careful to use technical language in a clear, consistent manner throughout the text.

STUDENT ACHIEVEMENT GOALS

After working with this text, the student should be able to accomplish three general goals.

First, this book is intended to be an initial exposure to research methods for the student. It is written with an eye toward meeting the needs of an undergraduate who requires a solid foundation upon which to build the more advanced skills in graduate or professional school.

Second, if the student does not plan to attend graduate school, our hope is that he or she will be a critical consumer of other people's research. The student should be able to discern strengths and weaknesses of a given project, as well as be able to identify quality research from substandard research.

Finally, we hope the reader has acquired sufficient research skills to be able to execute modest research projects for a non-technical audience. Businesses, church groups, local community groups, and similar organizations have research questions and needs that the well-trained undergraduate can address.

COMMUNICATIVE AND STYLISTIC CONCERNS

We would like to make a few points about the style of the material presented.

First, the material is directed to those interested in any of the social or behavioral sciences. We argue strongly that science is science and that there is no such thing as "sociological statistics," only statistics as applied to sociological topics. Much of the material and information presented can be used in a variety of disciplinary contexts: sociology, political science, market research, consumer behavior, health science, to name a few.

We seek to transcend the boundaries established by disciplinary lines.

Second, we illustrate as many important issues as possible through the use of the same example. We also try to construct examples that are conceptually easy to understand so as to focus attention on the difficult tasks of research design and statistical analysis.

Third, where possible, we present the material in the sequence in which one is likely to find it in a formal research proposal or final research report. This goal overlaps and reinforces our desire to meet the needs of students planning on graduate or professional training in which the preparation of a research proposal and report will be expected.

Finally, the order of topics suggested is that which the knowledgeable researcher might pursue in *communicating* the research results to the reader. This is not necessarily the order in which the study will be conceived or executed. Indeed, we disagree with those who argue that there is a series of well-formulated steps that must be scrupulously followed from beginning to end of a scientific study. While it is true that one cannot analyze any data until some have been collected, it is equally true that one must think how the data are to be analyzed to insure that the proper data are gathered in the most appropriate form. The execution of any scientific research project is often this type of careful working back and forth throughout the entire study.

Each academic discipline is likely to emphasize a different order of presentation, reflecting disciplinary preferences. We have had long discussions, while teasing our colleagues in other areas of study, about the peculiar ways in which they formulate their research problems. On a serious note, however, we are not concerned that other styles omit relevant material; they rarely do. Ultimately, there is a logical sequence for the presentation of one's research or results. The order in this book reflects, in our opinion, the maximization of communicative logic and efficiency.

ACKNOWLEDGMENTS

This work reflects the development and evolution of our thoughts regarding the scientific investigation of sociology through the last 25 years. Many persons have been important to our thinking and in our preparation of the manuscript. Our editor, Karen Hanson, and her staff have been exceptional in their work with us. Many helpful suggestions were offered by the reviewers, who worked diligently to sharpen and expand our original draft. We appreciate the contributions of Kathleen McKinney, Department of Sociology, Illinois State University; Obi N. I. Ebbe, SUNY at Brockport; Victoria L. Swigert, Department of Sociology, Holy Cross College; Michael P. Massagli, Center for Survey Research, University of Massachusetts—Boston; and William Kelly, Department of Sociology, University of Texas at Austin. Of course, the final decisions and their discussions remain the responsibility of the authors.

We acknowledge important contributions in our graduate training and especially recognize Professors Ramon Henkel, who instilled in us a respect for quantitative principles and concerns; the late Robert W. Janes, whose conceptual models illustrated the importance of clear theoretical thinking; and Robert K. Hirzel, who taught and encouraged us to be serious and professional sociological colleagues.

We recognize Dean R. Esslinger, associate dean of Faculty Development and Research, and his committees at Towson State University that have supported us with the valuable gift of time. We recognize Ida Ward, who provided valuable secretarial services and Alcie Cooper, whose office gave us word processing assistance in the beginning of this project. We are also grateful to Professor Irwin Goldberg, who, as our valued colleague and former chairperson, provided encouragement and manipulated what small departmental resources he had to assist us in this text's preparation.

Finally, we recognize our families, Marilyn, Sandi, Witt, Jeff, Douglas, and Hart, who have inspired and supported us in ways that they cannot fully know.

—R. Guy Sedlack and Jay Stanley

I would like to thank Dan Dinkin, Manager of Network Services, and Joseph Callahan, Operations Manager of Towson State University's Academic Computing Service, for their help in using the VAX mainframe and the SPSS^x software package.

—R. Guy Sedlack

In addition to the above, I wish to recognize the substantial contributions to my education of quantitative and substantive issues made by the late Professor Louis Dotson of the University of Tennessee at Knoxville; Professor Monroe Lerner of the Johns Hopkins University School of Hygiene and Public Health; and Professors Larry Hunt and, more recently, David R. Segal of the University of Maryland at College Park.

—Jay Stanley

—to our parents

PART I

SCIENCE

In this first section, we have incorporated the basic notions of the nature of science so that the reader will, first, understand what type of knowledge system science is and, second, will have enough material or background in the general system of science to be able to understand the reasons behind some of the more technical and specific issues that are endemic to the social and the behavioral sciences.

We believe that all of the material contained in Part I is material that is relevant to any substantive science. That is, the ideas and issues discussed are notions of equal importance and of equal relevance to the social sciences (e.g., sociology, psychology, political science), the biological sciences (e.g., botany, zoology), and the physical sciences (e.g., chemistry, physics, geology). Indeed, one of the central points to be made in Part I is that the differences among the various scientific disciplines are differences of subject matter, not differences of methodology.

In Chapter 1 we focus on the meanings implied in a formal definition of science. Chapter 2 is devoted to some of those ideas that are relevant to the language of conceptualization. Attention is drawn to the material that composes the theoretical aspects of any substantive science. In Chapter 3 we concentrate essentially on those concepts relevant to empirical testing, which collectively form the language of hypothesis testing. In Part I, we argue that both of these languages are necessary because they perform different functions for the scientist. In Chapter 4 we focus on some of the issues that underlie the scientist's notion of causation, probability, and chance fluctuation. Finally, in Chapter 5 attention is given to the concerns necessary to a productive review of the existing literature and the framing of a workable conceptual model to guide theoretically one's research efforts.

In sum, our basic objective in Part I is to present enough of the material that comprises the philosophy of science so that the reader will be sufficiently knowledgeable about the general structure of science to see the larger issues that underlie much of the seeming minutia with which the social and the behavioral scientist must contend. Further, we hope to sensitize the reader to the power of the scientific method as well as some of its limitations. After reading Part I, the reader should make a significant step toward the goal of becoming an intelligent and critical consumer of scientific knowledge.

1

CHAPTER 1

THE SCIENTIFIC METHOD

INTRODUCTION

Kuhn's Notion of Paradigms in Science

A *paradigm* is a set of ideas, assumptions, concepts, and relationships which helps the scientist focus or direct his or her attention toward the subject matter being studied. Quite simply, it is a particular way of perceiving the substantive material. Thomas Kuhn argues that paradigms are of critical importance to the scientist since they function to identify and to organize what is important.[1]

Science progresses in two basic ways. First, there are occasional shifts or changes in these basic paradigms. For example, after the critical work of Sir Issac Newton, physicists thought about matter using the Newtonian paradigm. However, this paradigm was discarded when the Einsteinian paradigm burst upon the scene. Thus, an occasional great scientist emerges who has the intellectual imagination to suggest a whole *new* set of ideas, concepts, and relationships that are more useful than the previous paradigm. Indeed, Kuhn argues that major advances in scientific knowledge are accomplished when such *paradigmatic shifts* occur.

Second, in the absence of a period of paradigmatic shift, *normal science* occurs where most, if not all, of the practicing scientists accept the major principles of the reigning paradigm and proceed to fill in the details between the major ideas and refine the basic concepts contained within the paradigm through scientific testing and research.

In sum, science progresses through the cyclical stages of refinement of the reigning paradigm, followed by the emergence of an occasional new paradigm and the subsequent refinement of this new paradigm. Kuhn argues that in the case of the social sciences, the various disciplines are in the preparadigmatic phase; i.e., each social science is waiting for its guru to emerge who will present the first paradigm.

Whether or not one shares Kuhn's interpretation of the work of the social and behavioral sciences is less important than seeing that scientific progress occurs in two rather different ways. The assumption in this book is that Kuhn is basically correct in arguing that science changes in these two ways. Further, since a vast majority of the scientists in the world are not developing new paradigms, the assumption here is that we will be talking about the conceptualizations and methodological strategies which characterize normal science. However, scientific knowledge is not the only type of information that people strongly believe, so we turn briefly to a consideration of other knowledge bases.

Types of Knowledge

We begin our discussion with the premise that there is some kind of absolute or ultimate truth in the universe. That is, there is some type of order which exists and that there are facts which describe this order. This does not necessarily mean that one knows what all the facts are or that we will ever know, for sure, what they are. Only, that we believe it is reasonable to pursue the accumulation of knowledge. While it is not our purpose to inventory all that which has or could be classified as sources of human knowledge, it is illustrative to mention a couple of types.

Intuition. Some have relied in the past upon intuition as a source of knowledge. *Intuition* is the very strong feeling that what one believes to be the case is indeed true. Thus, sometimes we accept as truth that which we strongly believe or strongly feel is truth.

Indeed, intuition is largely behind the notion of W. I. Thomas' concept of the "definition of the situation." Thomas argued that "[i]f men define situations as real, they are real in their consequences."[2] For example, if little Johnny thinks there are monsters under his bed at night, then for him there really are monsters under the bed. However, the scientist will have an impossible task of empirically demonstrating that this is true. For little Johnny, however, there is no reason to doubt their existence, because he strongly feels this is true.

Authority. A second type of knowledge is that which emanates from an authority. When little Johnny, aged five, tells his friend that something is true because his father said so, we have an appeal to an authority. When a teacher informs students that Columbus landed in America in 1492, this is a fact because teachers are authority figures and should, therefore, know these kinds of things. *Authorities*, then, are persons who function as sources of information that we come to believe because these persons occupy positions which command our respect.

Revelation. A third type of knowledge is that which comes from revelation. *Revelation* is the presentation of a set of ideas from some supernatural source, such as a deity. Thus, in response to the question, "Well how do you know?", one might reply, for example, that God told me so, or that the information is in a holy book, such as the *Bible*, the *Torah*, or the *Koran*.

What we are arguing is that many people have accepted the premise that there is absolute truth.

In their responses to their curiosity as to its nature, several different answers have emerged—appeals to intuition, authority, revelation, logic, and sense experience, to name but a few. While we recognize the presence of different sets of knowledge or beliefs that have been arrived at through different means, we will focus almost exclusively upon the scientific approach. This does not mean that we are right, and all those who espouse a nonscientific procedure for accumulating knowledge are wrong. Rather, we prefer a more conservative approach to this issue: we suggest that we are comfortable with the scientific procedure while recognizing the value of other approaches for potentially discovering some aspects of the "truth." The need for all of this seeming vacillation is because the scientific approach has been an eclectic one in that subsets or portions of many other systems of thought have been synthesized to frame the scientific approach.

SCIENCE DEFINED

In this section we will begin our formal discussion of science with the definition offered by Carlo Lastrucci:* "(S)cience may be defined, quite accurately and functionally, as an objective, logical, and systematic method of analysis of phenomena devised to permit the accumulation of reliable knowledge."[3]

This definition is deceptively simple. The words used to define science are in themselves complicated sets of ideas. Therefore, let us separately examine some of the central ideas contained in this definition, which distinguish science from other modes of thought.

Objectivity

Objectivity has been an often used and often abused notion in this context. There are those who have an image of the scientist as a person who is totally

*Parenthetically, we acknowledge a major debt to Lastrucci as a major source of input into this chapter. While we do not attempt to paraphrase all of the points in his excellent book, some are presented, some have been expanded, and some have been changed. Nevertheless, his book remains an impetus to our thinking.

value-free—an image of the scientist in a white laboratory coat who is somehow separated from and above all the more pedestrian affairs that characterize the world of most of us. The scientist is thought of as pure, nonmortal, living (if not in an ivory tower) in a pristine laboratory working endlessly in the search of truth. Depending upon one's perspective, fortunately or unfortunately, such ideal objectivity does not exist.

So what does objectivity mean here? *Objectivity* is a characteristic which should be a part of the scientist's attitudinal structure. It is an attitudinal characteristic of the scientist qua scientist wherein he is not to be biased or prejudiced or subject to personal whims. To be objective is to evaluate phenomena from a dispassionate, apolitical, atheological, nonideological viewpoint. It is the ability to deal strictly with the empirical facts in the analysis of data that have been gathered.

This does *not* mean that the scientist *never* exercises any personal judgments. It does not mean that the scientist is forever detached from the societal factors and current interests that exist at the time. Clearly, the scientist is not required to be objective when attending a professional football game on Sunday afternoon, if she is there as a fan. The scientist may scream, yell, and be as biased as anyone else because he or she is not there as a scientist. Additionally, when the scientist selects an issue for serious study, he or she does not reach into the hat of as yet unsolved problems and randomly pick out an issue. Of course not. The scientist will exercise personal interest or bias or whim and select a topic in which he or she is personally interested. This is as it should be. No one should be expected to devote serious study to an issue about which one has little or no interest.*

Thus, objectivity is required by the scientist when the data are being analyzed. After one has collected information and is in the process of trying to determine whether to reject the hypothesis being investigated, then it is crucial to be objec-

tive. The attitude of objectivity or professional detachment, if you will, is crucial when the scientific activities are analysis and evaluation.

Logic

Three basic points need to be made regarding logic: (1) following basic rules; (2) logical reasoning; and (3) maintaining a healthy attitude of skepticism.

Following the Rules.   The scientific approach necessitates following certain rules. There are certain assumptions, premises, and proper procedures to which the scientist must adhere. For example, there are certain legitimate forms of deductive and inductive inference and different kinds of mathematical formulas in statistics which assume that certain kinds of numbers are placed in those formulas. To put it another way, while various procedures have been discovered for the processing of information, any one procedure has been put together under a specific set of assumptions. If one does not meet the assumptions that underlie a particular procedure, then we would argue that the results of the procedure will be extremely hard, if not impossible, to interpret in any meaningful and correct fashion.

For example, if one were to play the Parker Brothers' game of Monopoly in accordance with the rules of Parcheesi (assuming one could), then we would argue it would be difficult to determine a winner. It simply can't be done in any meaningful way. In this sense, science is similar to a game. There are certain rules that have been established to help one reach the goals of science. To circumvent or change the rules will not prevent reaching some result. (Maybe it would be better if such were the case, because one would know an error had been made.) However, violating the rules will prevent you from knowing that the normal or usual or anticipated *interpretation* of the result is

---

*For additional discussion of this issue, one is referred to Alvin Gouldner's important article. See Alvin W. Gouldner, "Anti-Minotaur: The Myth of a Value-Free Sociology," *Sociology on Trial,* Maurice Stein and Arthur Vidich, ed., (Englewood Cliffs, New Jersey: Prentice-Hall, Inc., 1963), pp. 35–52.

accurate and acceptable to the community of scientists.

For example, let us assume that we measured the weight of each football player on last year's winning team in the Rose Bowl on New Year's Day in Pasadena, California. Next, we added all these weights together and divided by the total number of players, thereby getting the average (called the statistical mean) weight of 243 pounds. Next, we measured the weights of all the football players on your college team, added them, divided by the total number of players, and got an average (statistical mean) of 192 pounds. If the Rose Bowl winning team averages 243 pounds per player and your school's team averages 192 pounds per player, then you could conclude, and conclude legitimately, that all other things being equal (motivation, handling the pressure of a big game, constructing a really good game plan, for example), your team is likely to be outmuscled by the Rose Bowl winner because of their greater weight advantage.

So far, so good. But, let's do another calculation. Let's compute the average or mean football jersey number of both the Rose Bowl winner and your school's team. After we did the necessary calculations, assume that your team's average football number was 46.5, while the Rose Bowl winner had a mere 42.3. Do we now conclude that all other things being equal, your school's football team would defeat the Rose Bowl winner? No, because there's nothing in our understanding of football that suggests that football jersey numbers have anything to do with winning football games. Size of the players, degree of proficiency in football skills, stamina, amount of time spent practicing, degree of experience in playing the game, player motivation to win, degree of fan support, playing conditions on the field appropriate to the team's skills, the accuracy of the scouting report's assessment of the opposition's strengths and weaknesses, whether or not there are any pro scouts in the stands, and a whole host of other variables *are* relevant. However, the number of one's jersey isn't. Further, even if the football jersey number were important in some way, its importance could not be assessed using the arithmetic mean formula

from statistics. The proper use of this formula necessitates putting continuous data, not discrete data, into it. Football jersey numbers do not reflect degrees of anything; they are not those kinds of numbers. Rather, they reflect two things. First, they reflect the general position of the player; a number in the 60s or 70s generally identifies a lineman, while a number in the 20s, 30s, or 40s generally identifies a back. Second, from an historical point of view, numbers have been used for the identification of the player rather than his name, although recently both are sometimes used. Thus, instead of putting *Komachowski* across the player's shoulders, *62* is used instead. After all, it is a lot easier to see a *62* from the upper deck than it is to see a *Komachowski*. Therefore, the designer of the arithmetic mean statistic assumed that only a certain kind of number would go into this formula. To make the kind of interpretation that you were taught in your statistics course assumes that you play according to the established rules of the game when using this statistic. It's not that you can't put all the jersey numbers into a computer and then calculate the mean. You can calculate anything. The trick, however, is to be able to interpret the value that emerges when the calculations are completed. It is here that the scientist must adhere to the established rules and procedures so as to make interpretations that can be understood by others who are interested in the scientist's results.

Logical Reasoning. The term *logical* also refers to logical reasoning, which is a cornerstone of the scientific method. *Logical reasoning* is the ability to think in a reasonable fashion, and it takes on two faces—deduction and induction. Rather than include deduction and induction under the subheading of "following the rules," we have elected to single them out because they are so crucial to the enterprise of science.

Deduction is rational thought which allows one to move from a general idea to a more specific idea. For example, if one argued that large groups generally tend toward a bureaucratic orientation, then one could logically argue through deduction that large universities would tend to be bureaucratic. Deduction involves taking the essence of a general idea and applying that same essence to a more restrictive or limited situation.

At the beginning of the researcher's work, i.e., when one reviews the relevant literature, one is usually trying to find from previous research a number of general ideas that have some validity and to focus these ideas on the researcher's current, usually more specific, piece of research.

Induction is rational thought in which inferences are made from a specific situation to a more general situation. For example, if one studied a large university and found it to be bureaucratic, then one might conclude that all large organizations are bureaucratic on the basis of the evidence of this specific situation. Inductive reasoning is usually found at the conclusion of a piece of research, as the researcher attempts to generalize the findings of the specific research by stating the results in the form of more general principles.

Most good research contains both deductive and inductive reasoning. One usually starts with the deductive phase in that general ideas from the relevant scientific literature are translated into specific ones as they relate to the specific research project. Data are gathered and analyzed to investigate empirically the relevance of these general ideas to the specific context of the research. The empirical results next lead to inductive reasoning as one moves from the specific research conclusions to more general substantive principles.

In sum, both deductive and inductive reasoning play significant roles in the development of scientific knowledge, and we will have occasion to illustrate further these two essential mechanisms of thought in subsequent chapters.

One final point deserves mention here. Induction and deduction more specifically illustrate the general proscription to think logically in science. As we shall see later in this chapter, rationality and reasonableness are part of the criteria for scientific truth.

Attitude of Skepticism.   The third point noted earlier is that of maintaining a healthy attitude of skepticism. Because the scientific approach is made up of a series of rules and relies strongly on induc-

tive and deductive logic, it can also be self-critical. One of the basic notions of science is that the results of any study should be results that can be replicated. Thus, the procedures should be clearly explained so that they can be followed by any other scientist. Further, the analysis of the data should be explained so it too can be redone. Quite simply, any research should be public, with the procedures and the interpretations fully explained, so it can be repeated. In doing so, scientists cross-check their results. As others do essentially the same study, the procedures are checked to see that the originator's method has not been something that only the originator could do. Also, the results are compared to ensure that consistency is evident. Only then should the results begin to have credence.

Thus, along with objectivity, the scientist must have the healthy attitude of skepticism. This skepticism is tantamount to saying to one's colleagues, "Let me see you do it again," or "Here, let me see if I can get the same results. Now, how did you do it?" By constantly questioning the results, the scientist demands of himself and his colleagues that they become self-conscious about what they are doing. In this way, they can report to interested others how the studies were done and how the results were interpreted. In so doing, the community of scientists cross-checks themselves to make sure not only that their studies are public but also that their results are the same as can be obtained by other members of their own scientific community.

One of the consequences of the healthy attitude of skepticism is that it leads to a higher degree of caution in doing research. In addition to being careful, a researcher should know that others are ready to critique or cross-check the results. We would argue that some reported research that has potential social consequences has not been subjected to sufficient peer scrutiny. For example, in medical research, researchers have often rushed into print with results that have not been sufficiently self-criticized. Surely, the motives for publication are pure and laudable. There has been a sincere desire to eradicate a killer disease. Yet, the results may not have been sufficiently established so that they generate false hopes which are quickly dashed to ruin, largely because the scientific community has not pursued the healthy attitude of skepticism. As we shall illustrate in this and subsequent chapters, there are many good reasons for this note of caution. It is not merely a protection against the occasional mistake of a single scientist; it is crucial to the entire enterprise of science.

Systematic

The pursuit of science is systematic. That is, the information that is generated in the normal scientific stage is built upon previously established information. The systematic nature of science is one reason for doing a review of the literature at the beginning of any research project. The researcher will canvas the existing literature to find out at what stage our knowledge is. Other than satisfying a healthy attitude of skepticism by replication, there is little reason to keep testing the same hypothesis. Because research is not done in a purely random fashion, the scientist does not dip into the pot of as yet unsolved problems and randomly pick one to investigate. The review of the literature stage involves a curious tension between the need to be cautious, as typified by the healthy attitude of skepticism, and the need to take the next logical step into the frontier of the unknown, so as to advance the knowledge in one's field.

Method

Science is a method. "Science is a systematized form of analysis."[4] Science is a procedure for the accumulation, analysis, and evaluation of concrete evidence. It is our position that science, other than knowing how to do science, is *not* a body of knowledge. We are all interested in the product of science; we all want to know what the results of the scientific method are. That, after all, is the justification and motivation for using the scientific method in the first place. When asked what science is, we must reply that it is a method—a particular means for generating information.

Consider the following situation. There is a table in one of our classrooms on which the lec-

tern sits. Let us assume that as a class exercise, we asked you to measure its width. First, you need something with which to measure the table, so you may dig around at home until you uncover the previously forgotten meterstick that you got from the We-Clean-Everything dry cleaners. You know the kind of thing we're talking about. It's the stick with the name, location, and telephone number of the business that is handed out free as a gesture of good will and as a reminder that the cleaner exists. Using the measuring instrument, you will, if you are a good scientist, stretch that meterstick out over the width of the table *three times*. (Unless you are as unfortunate as one of your authors, you will remember that chemistry course dealing with quantitative analysis in which such a premium is placed on accuracy that you were asked to take three independent readings.) So let us assume that three independent readings, as indicated in the first column of Figure 1.1, were made. The best estimate of the width of the table would be the mean of the three readings made. So we would add 142.34, 142.36, and 142.33 together, divide by 3, and the result would be 142.343 centimeters.

After having explained your exercise to your friend from the physics department, her reaction might be one of great peals of laughter. "Let's get serious," she says. "What kind of measuring instrument is that? It's made of wood and cheap wood at that. When they put the calibrations on it, the ink seeped into the wood and spread out sort of like a blotter. Also, the wood itself expands and contracts with temperature changes and changes in humidity. Why, that thing is so inaccurate you don't know what you really have. Why not at least use a metal tape measure? After all, they are made with greater care and not as influenced by atmospheric temperature and humidity changes." Since your friend's argument seems to make sense, you borrow an expensive metal tape measure and redo the measurements getting the figures shown in column two of Figure 1.1. After explaining our second procedure and its results to the chairperson of the Department of Physics, Professor Groskovitch tells us that if we are truly serious about the width of the table, then we should have used a pair of calipers, since these are the best

READING/INSTRUMENT	METERSTICK	TAPE	CALIPERS
First reading	142.34	142.34	142.35
Second reading	142.36	142.36	142.35
Third reading	142.33	142.35	142.36
Mean reading = $\overline{X}$	142.343	142.350	142.353

FIGURE 1.1   Hypothetical Readings of the Width of a Table Reported in Centimeters Using Three Different Measuring Instruments

linear measuring devices available. Therefore, with some degree of discouragement that is tempered by the confidence in knowing that we see the light at the end of the tunnel, we trudge off to the classroom to take a third set of three independent readings, as shown in the third column of Figure 1.1.

A really interesting question emerges here—how wide is the table: 142.343 centimeters, 142.350 centimeters, or 142.353 centimeters? In other words, what is the truth? Notice that the product of science—the result—is subject to almost constant revision. However, what doesn't change and what remains constant throughout is the *procedure* through which the scientific result is generated. No matter how many different occasions arise during which the table is to be measured and no matter how many different types of measuring instruments are to be utilized, the procedure stays the same: take three independent readings, and determine the mean of the results. Science is a method; it is an invariant set of general procedural rules for the generation of a particular kind of information.

Analysis

Analysis can be a multifaceted concept and at the same time a nebulous one. In a very real sense a major portion of this book is devoted to an explanation of how the scientist analyzes the subject matter. All we need to say at this point is that the scientific method is a procedure designed to provide descriptive, predictive, and explanatory knowledge, all of which are discussed later.

Phenomena

Again, we have a complicated notion that can be only partially explained here. We will make a distinction later between what have been called the two languages of science. At this point, we will concentrate on scientific measurement and measurement alone. By way of introduction, scientists generally assume that the world is made up of two types of things—objective and subjective. *Objective phenomena* are those phenomena that can be understood through one's senses; one can see, taste, touch, hear, or smell these tangible, concrete items. For example, books, automobiles, hotels, and specific people are all objective items. *Subjective phenomena* are those phenomena that cannot be understood through one's senses. Subjective phenomena are intangible, not concrete items, such as attitudes, feelings, dreams, and the like. With this in mind, the scientist can *measure* "any kind of behavior or event that has objectively demonstrable attributes or characteristics."[5] Put simply, if you can see it, hear it, feel it, smell it, or taste it, then science can measure it. Conversely, anything that is inherently subjective, anything that is not capable of being apprehended by the senses, cannot be directly measured through the scientific method.

Let us explore this further. Consider the measurement of hunger. Let us presume that the National Science Foundation has asked us to think about measuring hunger and is not too fussy about how sophisticated the measurement has to be. For example, we could suggest that John and Fred both be invited to a buffet dinner, and we could measure the amount of time each person spent eating. If John ate for one hour and 15 minutes while Fred ate for only 45 minutes, then we could conclude that John was more hungry than Fred. Alternatively, we could weigh the food that John and Fred eat, thereby switching the dimension from the amount of time spent eating to the amount of food ingested. After all, Fred might just be a much faster eater than John. Perhaps we could measure the decibels of each person's stomach growls over a fifteen minute period prior to dinner. We could also take a sample of each person's blood and test it for sugar content per cubic centimeter.

Now, if we really pursue each and every one of these suggestions, what will we have? We will have measures on the amount of time spent eating, the weight of food ingested, the number and volume of stomach growls, and blood sugar. But will we have measured hunger? No! We did measure blood sugar, and we did measure amount of food eaten. And, then, we *assumed* that blood sugar was the same as hunger. We *assumed* that quantity of food eaten could be equated with hunger. Science does a very good job of measuring concrete, tangible, sense experience types of phenomena. However, if the thing in which we are interested is not amenable to sense experience, then the scientist must measure something else and assume it to be equivalent.

For example, if one asked little children what love was, they would most likely say something such as, "It's Mommy kissing Daddy." Well, what would you say? How do you measure love? We could stake out the parking lot behind the dorm and measure the number and duration of kisses between Pamela and Richard. That is, after all, what can be observed. However, while this may be a part of what one means by love, it isn't all of what is meant. There is, additionally, the affective, emotional, feeling component that accompanies the observable, tangible behavior of hugging and kissing. Love is all of the above, only part of which is amenable to sense experience.

The scientific method demands that concrete, tangible evidence be gathered. However, much of what we want to investigate, much of what we need to know, is not tangible. It cannot be *directly measured*. At this point, we have a true dilemma. On the one hand, we have a method that requires the scientist to gather empirical or sense experience data. On the other hand, much of what we need to know we believe to be essentially subjective or nonempirical. Suffice it to say that the scientific method *deals with or incorporates* in its subject matter all kinds of phenomena—both empirical and nonempirical. However, it can *measure* only the empirical data. In this case the epistemological requirements of science create a dilemma that the scientific community has not been fully able to satisfactorily resolve. Caution is often necessary because scientific conclusions are not as clear-cut as they may appear to be on the surface of things.

Again, the scientist assumes that all phenomena in nature fall into two broad categories: (1) objective and (2) subjective. Both types of phenomena are of interest to the scientist. Yet, in one sense only one type can be directly measured. In another sense, yet to be discussed, one could argue that *neither* phenomenon is measurable. It is truly a confusing series of interlocking issues but at the same time a series of ones that are vital to our full understanding of science. We shall return to this in the next two chapters.

Devised Strategy

The scientific method is not something that was sent to us from the heavens. It is a man-made strategy for gathering, interpreting, and explaining data. Since people make mistakes, you should not come to accept the scientific method as something that necessarily must generate truth. It should be questioned, studied, and evaluated, just as anything else that is important to you. Thus, we need the healthy attitude of skepticism here as well.

The scientific method was devised by putting bits and pieces of other systems of thought together to formulate the scientific method. In this subsection, we look briefly at some of the major epistemologies from which ideas were borrowed to frame eclectically the scientific method.*

Well, we have now used the term *epistemology* three times. So what does it mean? What is *epistemology*? Ledger Wood writes that this is "(t)he branch of philosophy which investigates the origin, structure, methods, and validity of knowledge."[6]

In the study of epistemology, we are concerned with the assumptions and criteria for knowledge that underlie any process which we believe generates knowledge. In other words, since science is a method for generating a certain type of knowledge, then what are the criteria for accepting something as a piece of scientific information? What must we do as scientists before anyone will accept the result of our work as a legitimate outcome of science? What assumptions, premises, or axioms do we accept as true without proof when we use the scientific method? In what ways is scientific information different from information that has been generated through other methodologies? The study of epistemology tries to get at the answers to these and similar questions.

The scientific approach has taken some ideas from rationalism. *Rationalism* is the notion that "human reason is both the chief instrument and the ultimate authority in man's search for the truth."[7] The rationalists believe in the absolute power of the mind, which is thought to be the sole source of knowledge. In other words, the rationalist contends that the human mind, operating in a reasonable and logical fashion, is capable of determining the truth. The scientist most definitely uses various logical forms of argument. Further, the scientist believes that the mind should operate in a reasonable and logical fashion. However, the

scientist is unwilling to place all faith in the power of the rational mind. So while borrowing from the rationalist the need to think in a reasoned, logical fashion, the scientist has been unwilling to put all the eggs in the rationalist's basket.

The scientist has also borrowed from the empiricist position. Lastrucci writes of *empiricism* that it is the notion that "sensory experience should be regarded as the most reliable source of knowledge."[8] The empiricist relies upon the information that can be apprehended through sense experience. Here, one is concerned only with that which can be seen, heard, smelled, felt, or tasted. The scientist would always like to have concrete, tangible, objective, sense experience data in the test of hypotheses. However, some phenomena of interest to the scientist are not objective and cannot be apprehended through the senses. Thus, although empirical data are important to the scientific approach, just as with rationalism, they cannot be relied upon as the sole source of knowledge. Therefore, sense experience or empiricism alone seems incapable of providing for all of the needs that the scientist has.

Science has also borrowed from pragmatism. As Lastrucci writes, *pragmatism* is the notion that "the ultimate test of the value of an idea is its usefulness in the solution of practical problems."[9] There are really two different parts to this quotation. First, there is the notion of usefulness, a notion that the scientist embraces wholeheartedly. Scientists are interested in information that they believe is useful in the sense that it provides answers which are acceptable to their questions. In one very real sense, the scientist cannot know for sure whether or not the truth has ever been discovered. The scientist begins using the scientific method with an assumption that there is an ultimate truth in nature. The task is to seek to discover, to understand, and to explain this supposed order. Should any conclusions about this order be

---

*We would be the first to acknowledge less than full comprehension of epistemological knowledge as presented by our colleagues in philosophy. Yet, since science has borrowed from a variety of other systems of thought, we must touch upon this. What follows is a somewhat oversimplified and selective presentation. In our discussion of the other epistemologies presented here, we will discuss their characteristics only as much as needed to illustrate an essential characteristic or notion of science.

reached, then at best it can only be argued that the conclusions are appropriate at the time of study. In other words, while we assume there is an overall order, we cannot be sure of this. Failing to achieve such certainty, the scientist settles for second best, which is that which is useful—that which works. We shall return to this point in a subsequent chapter when we discuss the nature of the validity of the information that the scientific method generates, but for now we need only to see that science borrowed from pragmatism the notion that one should seek that which is useful.

The second part to the definition of pragmatism is that pragmatism not only seeks that which is useful but also that which relates to a practical problem. Here, the scientist would reject this idea as too limiting. Rather, the scientist seems to ask two different types of questions about the subject matter. On the one hand, the scientist asks some questions that may be identified as problematics. A *problematic* is a question that is motivated solely by the scientist's desire to seek an answer to the question. It is a question that is motivated solely by the researcher's curiosity. When such problematics are answered, we refer to the information that results as *basic knowledge* or knowledge that has no practical utility except that it satisfies the questioner's need to know.

For example, during medieval times a group of philosophers called the medieval scholasticists debated for approximately a century and a half the problematic of the corporeal existence of angels. More popularly, this problematic has been paraphrased into the question, "How many angels can sit on the head of a pin?" This is a good example of a theological-philosophical problematic. Should research be able to determine that 1,743 angels can sit on the head of a pin, we would argue that this is a piece of basic knowledge. The fact that 1,743 angels can sit on the head of a pin is a piece of information that is of no practical utility except that it satisfies one's curiosity and represents knowledge for its own sake.

On the other hand, the scientist asks some questions that may be identified as problems. A *problem* is a question about a situation that has been defined as pejorative or detrimental to the general well-being of the society. Here, one is motivated beyond a simple desire to satisfy one's curiosity. A problem is a situation one wishes to understand because one wants to ameliorate the problem. Quite simply, information that results from the investigation of a problem can be used (or it is believed that it can be used) to help eradicate the situation. Such knowledge is called *applied knowledge* and can be used for the general benefit of society. For example, to discover a more efficient and less expensive way to extract oil from shale would be called applied knowledge in the pursuit of an energy problem.

In sum, the scientist asks two kinds of questions: (1) problematics, which are simply an outgrowth of one's natural curiosity to know and to understand and which lead to basic knowledge and (2) problems, which are perceived difficulties one is motivated to try to eliminate and which lead to applied knowledge. The scientist is interested in both kinds of knowledge and hence asks both types of questions. As we argued above, scientists are interested in getting useful answers to all questions, be they problematics or problems. If one means by *pragmatism* that which is useful, then of course the scientist pursues that which is useful. However, if one means by *pragmatism* that which will benefit society by leading to changes that help eliminate problems, then much of what the scientist does is not pragmatic.

Perhaps, you feel we have been a bit too strong in making the distinction between a problematic with its basic knowledge and a problem with its applied knowledge. Sometimes the pursuit of one type of question has led to the discovery of valuable information relevant to the other kind of question. That is, the pursuit of practical solutions to applied problems does not preclude the discovery of major insights into basic knowledge. Similarly, the search for basic knowledge has often led to practical, applied results as well. For example, the base two number system (the binary system) in mathematics began as a piece of basic knowledge that resulted from pure research only to become applied knowledge with the invention of the electronic computer. Given the right technology, a piece of basic knowledge can be transformed into applied knowledge.

Finally, science has borrowed from the epistemology of *determinism*. Again, we quote from Lastrucci who wrote "that nothing takes place in nature without natural causes."[10] Thus, if something exists in the natural world, the determinists believe that it must have been caused by something else. This idea is a basic premise that the scientist uses in studying the relationship between and among variables. Thus, our essential notion of causation in science has been taken from the epistemology of determinism.

However, we should pause to recognize, if not to resolve, what appears to us as a growing dilemma within the scientific perspective. The scientist has recently found the probability model to be a more useful model than the deterministic model. That is, when we find a relationship between, say, two variables, we argue that there is a high probability that the independent variable will be the cause of the dependent variable.

Consider the following situation. If Mr. Jones were speeding down a country road, failed to make a sharp curve, and ran into a brick wall at 92 miles per hour, an observer using the probability model would say that there is a high probability that Mr. Jones would die. On the basis of similar past empirical cases, we would argue that people who hit any brick wall at 92 miles per hour have little chance of survival. The determinist would argue that the driver would certainly lose his life, while the probability thinker would modify the above to say simply that there was a high probability that the driver would die. We know from our investigations of matter under the electron microscope that all matter is made up of small subatomic particles that have spaces between them. Thus, both the car and the brick wall are made up of tiny little pieces. So, also, is Mr. Jones. If Mr. Jones were to lose his life when he hits the wall, it will be because a sufficient number of the most crucial of Mr. Jones' pieces hit either the pieces of the brick wall or the pieces of the car. However, suppose that none of the pieces that compose Mr. Jones were to hit any of the pieces of the car or the

brick wall; then Mr. Jones will go flying right on through the car and the brick wall completely unscathed to end up laughing, relieved, and quite surprised to have survived the crash. It's all a matter of probability. There is a chance—a likelihood—that this could happen. Understand that the chances are very remote or, if you will, highly improbable. After all, there are a very large number of pieces to both Mr. Jones and the wall and the car. However, there is a slim chance that the above scenario could happen as described. The probability model says that relationships are a matter of chance—that all relationships have a higher or lower probability of occurring.

It appears to us, then, that the scientist is currently working with an internal contradiction. We begin by assuming that there are such things as cause and effect relationships. We start with the premise that X can be and is a cause of Y. However, we are willing to settle for the empirical reality which indicates that we *usually* find Y, when we find X. In other words, the scientist frames a proposition or hypothesis that suggests a specific relationship 100 percent of the time and then fails to reject as false empirically derived evidence that is less than 100 percent supportive. Not only will the scientist do this, he or she *does not expect* 100 percent accuracy. While the resolution of this contradiction is beyond the scope of this book (and the philosophers of science at the present time), we feel obliged to note its existence.

In sum, the scientific method is really an eclectic collection of bits and pieces of already well established epistemological positions. Rather than relying solely upon one system of thinking, the scientist has built a more cautious system involving what is believed to be the better components of rationalism, empiricism, pragmatism, and determinism.

Reliable Knowledge

The final concept in our formal definition of science is reliable knowledge. While we do not disagree with Lastrucci's basic orientation, we do feel that it is limited and needs expansion. *Reliable knowledge* focuses on the product of the scientific method. Essentially, the scientific method creates three different types of information. First, *descriptive knowledge* is information that posits the distribution or occurrence of a given variable. Here, there is no attempt to relate, in any sense of this term, one variable to another. Quite simply, one presents a specific characteristic that is relevant to some class or category of elements. For example, if we found that the mean age of a sample of college students was 24.2 years, then this would be a piece of descriptive knowledge. We are simply attributing one characteristic—that is, 24.2 years of age—to one sample of college students. A major proportion of the statistical formulas you were exposed to in your statistics course function to provide descriptive information about categories of phenomena studied.

Second, the scientific method also generates *predictive knowledge*, which leads to a reasonably accurate prognostication or forecast of some future event. This is knowledge that is useful in foretelling some future happening. For example, the major television networks all have voter profile analysis techniques with which they are able to predict the outcome of each election race with considerable accuracy. Admittedly, such predictions are occasionally wrong, sometimes by a rather large margin. Once again, we remind the reader of the relevance of the probability model. Nothing works with 100 percent accuracy. However a vast majority of the time the predictors are right on the money. Thus, scientists are also interested in being able to forecast future events.

Third, scientists are interested in explanatory knowledge. Explanatory knowledge is that which allows the scientist to understand why and how something happens. *Explanatory knowledge* is information that provides acceptable answers to the questions that the scientist raises about the subject matter. It is not enough for the scientist to describe phenomena and to be able to predict their occurrence. The scientist is a curious person who systematically seeks answers to how and why certain relationships occur.

In sum, scientists search for three types of information: (1) that which is descriptive of reality, (2) that which is predictive of the future, and (3) that which is explanatory in that it satisfies our curiosity or our desire to know.

TYPES OF EXPLANATION

Before we leave our discussion of scientific knowledge, we must entertain one further notion. When seeking to explain phenomena, the scientist will attempt to do so within a certain level of acceptance. To put this more clearly, there are two rather different types of explanation: (1) the idiographic model of explanation and (2) the nomothetic model of explanation.

Idiographic Explanation

The *idiographic explanation* is an attempt to fully account for all of the factors that are involved in a specific problem. The goal in an idiographic explanation is to present a total accounting of the variables related to a single instance of behavior. This type of explanation is that which separates the historian from the other social and behavioral scientists. We are not talking about whether or not this goal can be or ever is achieved. Rather, we are suggesting that such is the goal. For example, an historian may quite easily devote an entire lifetime of study, research, and scholarship to trying to fully understand, say, the Civil War.

Nomothetic Explanation

On the other hand, the *nomothetic explanation* does not attempt a full or total accounting. In the nomothetic explanation, the scientist is seeking to uncover the major factors that will account for a majority of the situation. The goal is to present a partial explanation—not a full one. Furthermore, the partial explanation will contain only the major factors. This is similar to the notion of Occam's razor or the rule of parsimony,[11] both of which suggest that if one has two or more explanations that function equally well, the simplest explanatory scheme should be adopted.

Thus, by definition, the nomothetic explanation will not be as fully explanatory as the idiographic model, but it will be more parsimonious. Further, the advocates of the nomothetic approach recognize what may be called here the law of diminishing returns. That is, will there be an appreciable increase in our understanding if one includes additional factors? If the answer to this question is "No!", then the nomothetic advocate will cease to pursue further analysis.

One final point separates the two strategies. While the idiographic explanation applies to a specific case, the nomothetic explanation tends to be more general in that it is applicable to a number of situations. Perhaps a simple example would be helpful. As indicated above, the idiographically oriented scholar would be interested in identifying all of the factors relevant to understanding the Civil War. However, the nomothetically oriented person would be more interested in finding a limited number of factors that would appear relevant to the understanding of wars in general, although such a person would recognize that all aspects of any one war would not be explainable or even identifiable using the nomothetic approach.

What does all this mean to the scientist? Well, when we argue that the scientist is interested in understanding or explanation, then it is within the limits imposed by the nomothetic model that such explanation is sought. The scientist is interested in a less than total explanation that will be relevant to more than one empirical situation. This doesn't mean that the single-case analysis is never done or that, if it is done, it is a waste of time. Certainly not. Rather, if one chooses to focus upon a single case, it is always with the idea of what that single case has to suggest to us generally in a broader framework.

SUMMARY

We began this chapter with an introductory section in which we identified the notion of a paradigm, Kuhn's idea of how science progresses and what normal science is. Making the assumption that some sort of absolute truth does indeed exist, we further recognized several different types of knowledge that have emerged from various systems of reasoning: that which comes from intuition, from authority figures, and through religious revelation. We argued, however, that in this book attention and emphasis would be placed on the scientific system of analysis.

A majority of this chapter, then, is devoted to a discussion of the central terms in a definition of science as an objective, logical, and systematic method of analysis of phenomena devised to permit the accumulation of reliable knowledge. While it is not possible nor even necessary for the scientist to be value-free, we feel that an unbiased, objective attitude toward the *analysis of collected data* is warranted. By logical, we mean that the scientist is guided by and must adhere to procedural rules which are a part of the scientific process, that the logical processes of deduction and induction are crucial components to the scientific method, and that the scientist must be more skeptical about the results and the truthfulness of this process than has certainly been the case for the social scientist (if not the biological or physical scientist) in the past. Further, science is systematic in the sense that the mandatory review of the literature after the selection of a general problem area prevents too much repetitious study of the same situation and encourages topic selection in those gray areas of informational chaos surrounding the selected subject matter. Very importantly, science is a method; it is a procedure for gathering and analyzing sense experience. As such, the rules that govern this mechanism are applicable regardless of the particular subject matter under investigation. Thus, while the scientist is very much interested in the information that emerges from scientific investigations, what remains the same about science through time is the set of rules for executing a scientific study.

Also of great importance is the subject matter to which the scientific method is directed. The scientist believes that reality is composed of two basic types of phenomena: objective and subjective phenomena. Objective phenomena can be directly apprehended through the use of one's senses, while subjective phenomena cannot. Therefore, science can measure objective, concrete items directly, while it cannot measure subjective, intangible items directly—a fact that causes the scientist some considerable difficulties.

Further, science is made up of an eclectic combination of bits and pieces of previously existing philosophical positions. The scientist borrows from rationalism the need to present arguments according to reasonable principles and in some cases through the expression of the formal rules of logic. However, the scientist refuses to accept the power of the rationally operating mind as the sole criterion for the demonstration of truth. Similarly, the scientist borrows from empiricism the need to provide sense experience evidence in the formal test of hypotheses. However, as with rationalism, such sense experience alone is deemed insufficient as a sole criterion for truth. From pragmatism, the scientist borrows the notion that scientific information should be useful in the sense of providing the scientist with acceptable answers to questions, but the scientist rejects the notion that only practical problems were worthy of study. Rather, the scientist focuses on two types of questions about the subject matter: (1) problematics that result, if answered, in basic knowledge or knowledge for its own sake, the study of which is motivated solely by the questioner's curiosity or desire to have an answer; and (2) problems that result, if answered, in applied knowledge or prac-

tical knowledge, the study of which is motivated by a desire to eliminate the existence of the situation that has been defined as a problem. Thus, the scientist does not wish to be restricted to the study of problems but also continues to have an interest in problematics as well. Finally, the scientist borrowed from determinism the notion that cause and effect relationships exist.

Lastly, while we argued that science is a method or procedure, the scientist is interested in the substantive product that emerges from scientific investigations. As such, the scientist recognizes three different functions of reliable knowledge: (1) descriptive knowledge, which presents the distribution or occurrence of specifically stated variables; (2) predictive knowledge, which allows a reasonably accurate forecast of some future event; and (3) explanatory knowledge, which provides acceptable answers in general terms to those questions the scientist raises about how and why something happens. Finally, there are two possible kinds of explanations: (1) idiographic explanations, which purport to fully explain a single situation and (2) nomothetic explanations, which purport to handle more than one situation in a general fashion with a limited number of factors that admittedly fall short of a total or complete explanation. The scientist is more oriented to the nomothetic explanatory goal than with the idiographic explanatory goal.

KEY TERMS

Applied knowledge	Idiographic explanation	Pragmatism
Attitude of skepticism	Induction	Predictive knowledge
Authority	Intuition	Problem
Basic knowledge	Logical reasoning	Problematic
Deduction	Nomothetic explanation	Rationalism
Descriptive knowledge	Normal science	Reliable knowledge
Determinism	Objective phenomena	Revelation
Empiricism	Objectivity	Science
Epistemology	Paradigm	Subjective phenomena
Explanatory knowledge	Paradigmatic shift	

REVIEW QUESTIONS

1. What is the notion of objectivity presented in this chapter, and how does it relate to the possibility of a value-free scientist?

2. Discuss any three reasons why the healthy attitude of skepticism is important to the work of the scientist. Can you anticipate any additional reasons that did not appear in this chapter which you think are likely to emerge in subsequent chapters?

3. What is the nature of the contradiction in the scientific method between the need to develop concrete measurements and the nature of the scientist's subject matter?

4. What are the four principle systems of thought from which the scientist has borrowed? What ideas has the scientist incorporated within the scientific process, and what ideas have been rejected?

5. Distinguish between an idiographic explanation and a nomothetic explanation. Which of these two types characterizes most of the work of the scientific community? What are the implications of this choice for determining and understanding the truth?

CHAPTER 2

KEY TERMS IN THE SCIENTIFIC LANGUAGE OF CONCEPTUALIZATION

INTRODUCTION

In the preceding chapter we concentrated on Lastrucci's definition of science by paraphrasing some of his ideas and by revising and expanding on others. In this chapter and the next, we continue our discussion of the nature of science by focusing on several terms often used by the scientist. We seek definitions that are mutually exclusive and present several relatively simple but powerful classifications that will help the reader to be a more critical evaluator of both the research process and the research product.

These two chapters are not perfunctory sections in which terms are quickly defined and then forgotten. It is our opinion that the terms discussed in these chapters have been so variously used that their meanings have become somewhat obscured and clouded. For example, we have seen essentially the same declarative sentence containing two factors described by different writers as a proposition, an hypothesis, and a theory. We feel that there has been a certain looseness in the use of technical terminology in science. Therefore, we want to remove any confusion about the meanings of certain key terms by consciously dealing with them and by using them in a consistent fashion.

SCIENCE'S TWO LANGUAGES

In "The Measurement Problem: A Gap Between the Languages of Theory and Research"—a very important article in our opinion—Hubert Blalock discusses the nature of and the interrelationship between (or, rather, the difficulties of creating an interrelationship between) the two languages in science.[1] He begins his article by paraphrasing a discussion presented by the physicist F. S. C. Northrop who asks us to imagine a visit to the planet earth from a Martian. Our Martian friend is quite intelligent (after all, she was able to get here from Mars) but she is at the same time totally unfamiliar with the state of the art of earthly physics. Having settled on the campus of a major research center, our Martian visitor observes a cyclotron experiment in progress. What her sense experience tells her is that there are people in white laboratory coats running around with clipboards who copy down at regular intervals pointer readings indicated on dials and gauges. When the experiment is over, Northrop wonders if our Martian friend will now understand that the existence of electrons has just been empirically verified. Both Northrop and Blalock conclude that she will probably not.

Blalock goes on to argue that there are two rather different languages in science.* The idea is that in creating an eclectic synthesis of various elements from previously known epistemological positions to formulate this thing called science, the scientist has created an, as yet, insurmountable difficulty—i.e., two languages.

---

*The two things referred to here have been variously identified. Northrop calls them concepts. Blalock, and we, call them languages. Others have called them definitions. It really does not matter what they are called. Rather, what matters is that we recognize the difficulty that the scientific method creates for us here.

Language of Conceptualization

One language is the *language of conceptualization*, or a theoretical language. This is the language of communication that the scientist uses when talking to others. It is a language of concepts and constructs that are used to summarize the actual empirical findings gathered by the scientist. In this language, words are used as general symbols of the ideas that the scientist wishes to communicate.

Language of Hypothesis Testing

The other language is the language of empirical testing. It is the language in which the ideas mentioned above are transformed into concrete, tangible, sense-experience entities. It is the language that can be apprehended solely through one's sense experience. Quite simply, it is the *language of hypothesis testing*.

Thus, the scientist utilizes two quite different languages. One is the language of words necessary for communicating one's ideas to others. The other is a redefinition or translation of the first into empirical terms so that hypotheses can be contrasted against sense-experience data. This contrast is made necessary by the requirement that, as scientists, we must substantiate our claims through the demonstration of concrete, objective evidence. We shall return to this issue at the end of Chapter 3. For now, we merely *introduce* it as a basic dilemma and suggest that the necessity for two languages will generate a number of more specific difficulties for us later on.

In Figure 2.1, we list the terms that will be discussed and show their correspondence to one another. Note that the left-hand column of terms

DIMENSION / ATTRIBUTE	ATTRIBUTE	ATTRIBUTE
Types of languages	Conceptualization	Hypothesis testing
Purpose of the language	Communication	Testing
Type of definition	Theoretical	Operational
Nature of the factors	Concept = Objective Construct = Subjective	Variable Constant = Controlled Var.
Nature of the statement	Proposition	Hypothesis
Total explanation	Theory	Simulation
Partial explanation	Conceptual model	Empirical model
Types of statements	Descriptive and analytical with concepts/constructs	Descriptive and analytical with variables
Factor relationships	Causal and associational among concepts/constructs	Causal and associational among variables
Types of associational relationships	Positive and negative	Positive and negative
Scientific truth	Axiom	Fact = verified

FIGURE 2.1   Categorization of Scientific Terms by Type of Language and by Equivalence Between Languages as Developed in This Book*

*The scientist makes the assumption that reality, or that which truly exists, is presumed to be either objective (i.e., concrete, such as a table) or subjective (i.e., abstract, such as an idea).

are those that relate to the language of conceptualization, while the right-hand column contains those terms germane to the language of hypothesis testing. If any of the theoretical or conceptual terms has an operational component (and most do), such will be listed across the row in Figure 2.1. We hope that Figure 2.1 will serve as a quick overview of the main categorization with the language equivalents of the scientific terminology used in this book.

SCIENCE'S LANGUAGE OF CONCEPTUALIZATION

Introduction

The remainder of this chapter focuses on a number of ideas that we have classified as belonging to the language of conceptualization. Attention is given to the notions of a concept, construct, dimension, attribute, proposition, theory, and model.

In Chapter 1 we argued that the scientist assumes that there are two types of phenomena: objective phenomena, which have characteristics or representations that are amenable to sense experience, and subjective phenomena, which have characteristics that are not directly amenable to sense experience. When talking about these two types of phenomena, the scientist uses two different words—one is called a concept and the other is called a construct.

Concept

A *concept* is a generalized idea about an entire class of objective phenomena.[2] The word *table* would be a good example. This concept is a *general* notion. The word *table* refers to the object that is in front of your sofa at home. It also refers to the thing on which you put your plate when you eat a meal. Further, it refers to the object on which you put your paper when you are writing some sort of report. It also describes the object on which the computer rested when this line was typed. Your classroom may have a table on which a

small lectern is placed for your instructor. The word *table* is a general thing in that it refers to all of these objects. Concepts are general in that they refer to whole collections of tangible objects.

A concept is also an idea. That is, it is an *abstraction*. It does not exist in the world of sense experience. However, didn't we just argue that concepts deal with classes of objective phenomena? Yes, we did, but consider this. Do you have a dog at home? If you do, or if a couple of your friends have dogs, what are their names? Suppose that you know three dogs whose names are Ruffie, Spot, and Prince. Well, Ruffie, Spot, and Prince are real, concrete, objective, tangible dogs. You can watch Ruffie eat; you can weigh Spot; and you can try to give Prince a bath. These are concrete dogs. Further, one can summarize or collect together all three of these objects with the word *dog*. However, when we do, *dog* does not exist; Ruffie exists, Spot exists, and Prince exists, but not *dog*. The concept *dog* is an idea. It exists only in the mind. The symbol itself is abstract.

Perhaps another example will make this point clearer. We've known many college students who are employed as well as enrolled in school. When asked what they do, students mention such jobs as counter operator at McDonald's; salesclerk in the sporting department at Sears, Roebuck; and desk clerk on the night shift at the local Quality Inn motel. These are real jobs held by real people, who are doing real work for which they are being paid real money. However, we summarize all of these jobs with the general concept *occupation*. The concept *occupation* does not exist. There is a job description for desk clerk; there is a list of duties and expectations for a salesclerk. If one is not honest, efficient, and pleasant, one may be fired from the position at McDonald's. However, there is no job description for *occupation*. There isn't any real person who does *occupation*, because occupation does not exist. It is an abstraction. It is an idea and ideas, by definition, are abstract, intangible things. Thus, concepts *refer* to collections of tangible objects, but the word itself is an intangible idea.

Finally, a concept is an idea about *concrete* objects. The word *table* refers to all those tangible things we normally picture in our minds when we hear the word. The word *dog* refers to Ruffie, Spot, Prince, and to Browny, Muffin, Brandy, Rusty, or whatever other real, concrete, four-legged, barking animals of the family Canidae live in your area. The word *occupation* refers to all the concrete things people do for employment. Concepts, then, are generalized ideas about entire classes of objective phenomena.

Construct

A *construct* is a generalized idea about an entire class of subjective phenomena.[3] The idea of a construct is very similar to that of a concept. Both are general, both are ideas, and both refer to classes of things. The only difference is that a construct refers to things that we believe are intangible. For example, think about love. As we argued earlier in Chapter 1, love is more than hugging and kissing between John and Mary. It is also an intangible—a feeling—an affective component that cannot be directly measured through empirical means. Thus, while concepts refer to tangible entities, constructs refer to intangible entities.

In sum, the theoretical or conceptual language of science is made up of two different kinds of words: concepts and constructs. While it is probably more important to understand the commonalities that these two ideas share, we have chosen to emphasize that there are really two different entities. The reader should recognize that both concepts and constructs are ideas and general abstractions in and of themselves and that they represent whole classes of things. Indeed, they are only distinguished by one dimension, and that is the nature of the phenomena they represent. The idea that phenomena can exist in two forms—the tangible and the intangible—when coupled with the notion that all conceptual language as language is symbolic and not concrete is crucial to some of the major limitations of the scientific approach. However, we must postpone a discussion on limitations until we have dealt with some of the other words in the lexicon of science.

Attributes and Their Dimension

An *attribute* is a specific characteristic that can be associated with a self-contained, definable entity and that describes a subset of a larger dimension. A *dimension* is the totality of logically related attributes. Consider a person named Mary. If asked to describe Mary, we might say that she is female, Caucasian, divorced, and working hard as an accountant. We will have identified four attributes that characterize Mary. However, any one of these attributes is not equivalent to Mary. It is not correct to say that Mary is only a female because she is at the same time a number of other things. The reader is encouraged to see that the subject matter or the unit of analysis (in this case, Mary) is something that is greater than any one attribute which she possesses. Thus, Mary is a person who happens, among other things, to be a carrier of the attribute of femaleness. Further, this attribute of being female is but one of two such attributes that combine logically to form a dimension. Thus, the attribute of being female and the attribute of being male combine to form the dimension of sex. While any object may possess one or another attribute or some degree of a dimension, no entity of study will possess the dimension. Rather, the subject may possess one or the other of a number of attributes within a single dimension. Thus, any human being could possess the attribute of being a female or the attribute of being a male, but no one possesses the dimension of sex. In the same way, Mary possesses the attribute of being a Caucasian on the dimension of race and the attribute of being divorced on the dimension of marital status.

In sum, any definable object of study could be characterized by any number of different attributes from respectively different dimensions. The definable object of study, however, is not synonymous with the attribute, and the dimension cannot be represented logically or empirically within the object of study. Finally, since words are used to identify attributes and dimensions, then attributes and dimensions are examples of concepts or constructs that have been presented at different levels of generality.

Propositions

If your professor were to list 10 concepts and/or constructs on the chalkboard during a lecture, you would only have a list of those 10 words. The scientist does more than present lists of concepts and constructs. The next step involves the creation of propositions. A *proposition* is a statement that describes some characteristic or that posits some relationship between or among concepts and/or constructs that has been written in the language of conceptualization. The essential function of a proposition is to communicate some sort of idea to the reader. It is written in the theoretical or conceptual language of the discipline.

While any scientific proposition may contain some number of concepts from a seemingly infinite number of concepts, there are only two types of propositions that may be suggested. It is to these types which we now turn.

Types of Propositions

Propositions possess two basic attributes if one focuses on the dimension of the number of concepts or constructs that appear within the proposition.

Descriptive Proposition. A *descriptive proposition* suggests some characteristic or some number of characteristics of the unit of analysis.[4] For example, if we were to say that all ducks were white, then all ducks are white would be a descriptive proposition. By making this statement, we are identifying some unit of analysis (in this case, ducks) and suggesting that on the dimension of color, ducks possess the attribute of being white. Similarly, if we said that the proportion of Hispanics in Miami, Florida, is growing, we would have presented a descriptive proposition. That is, when

looking at the unit of analysis (in this case, the population of Miami, Florida), the percentage of persons of Hispanic culture is growing.

Descriptive propositions are much more likely to emerge as conclusions in the results section of a research study. Generally speaking, researchers do not formally specify descriptive propositions in their studies. Therefore, when you read that all ducks are white or that the proportion of Hispanics is growing in Miami, what has clearly been implied, if not formally stated, are a number of descriptive propositions that were later transformed into hypotheses (we deal with the difference between propositions and hypotheses later), tested for their accuracy on certain units of analysis, and reported in the results section of the formal research report.

Analytical Proposition. An *analytical proposition* posits a relationship between two or more concepts and/or constructs.[5] Here one would be interested in discussing how changes in one or more concepts or constructs affect one or more other concepts or constructs. Analytical propositions are what most people think about when the word *proposition* is used. For example, if we argued that an increase in one's income is likely to be followed by an increase in one's social prestige, we would have suggested an analytical proposition.

Types of Relationships

One can classify *analytical* propositions according to two attributes on the dimension of the nature of the relationship suggested—be it causal or associational.

Causal Relationship. A *causal relationship* is one in which some presumed factor (or series of factors) is thought to be deterministic of another factor (or series of factors). For example, if we said that a person's income caused that person's social status, we would have not only offered an analytical proposition because we suggested a relationship between income and social status but also presented a casual proposition because we suggested that income was the factor responsible for the degree of social status also present. Obviously, one may suggest any number of factors that are causally related to any other number of factors. Which factors to select as causally related to which other factors will depend on the substantive literature relevant to one's research topic. In a word, one's conceptual model is important in suggesting which factors to choose to relate and in suggesting how they will be so related.

Associational Relationship.   A second type of relationship is an *associational relationship,* which posits that a change in either the direction or the magnitude of one factor (or series of factors) will be accompanied by a change in either the direction or the magnitude of another factor (or series of factors). For example, one might propose that an upward change in a person's income will be accompanied by an upward change in that person's federal income taxes. An associational analytical proposition is what one would call a *correlational relationship* in statistical terminology.

Several additional points remain concerning associational propositions. First, the degree of association can be determined for any number of factors. Thus, the Pearson product-moment correlation statistic can measure the association between one factor and one other factor. A partial correlation can measure the association between one factor and one other factor, holding one or more additional factors constant. A multiple correlation can measure the association between one factor and two or more other factors. And, a canonical correlation can measure the association between two or more factors and two or more other factors.

Second, we do not wish to imply that an association between, say, two factors needs to be a one

to one relationship. That is, a one unit change in factor A does not necessarily have to result in a one unit change in factor B. Let us go back to the proposition concerning income and federal income taxes. To find an association between income and taxes does not mean that a one dollar increase in income will be accompanied by a one dollar increase in federal income taxes. This one to one relationship does not have to exist for one to find a strong association between two factors.

Third, to find an association among a number of factors is not the same as saying that one has found evidence that there is a cause-and-effect relationship. We pursue this matter further in Chapter 4 when the issue of causation is more fully discussed. Clearly, however, the causal proposition and the associational proposition suggest different types of relationships.

Finally, the reader needs to consider the direction of the association. If one can argue that there is a linear association,* we can further subclassify associational propositions into two types based on the direction of the association. For the sake of simplicity, let us only think about the association between two factors or about that which would be measured through the use of the Pearson product-moment formula rather than the partial, multiple, or canonical techniques. If one looks at the association of two factors, then two possibilities emerge: (1) they can be associated positively, or (2) they can be associated negatively.

Positive Association.   A *positive association* between two factors is one in which an increase in the value of one factor is always accompanied by an increase in the value of the other. Alternatively, if there is a decrease in the value of the first factor, there will be a decrease in the value of the second. Again, remember that the degrees of change in the two factors don't have to be equal; the degrees of change only have to move in the same direction.

---

*A linear association, say, between two factors as indicated in a Pearson product-moment correlation (Pearson's r) is one in which a one unit change in one factor is accompanied by a constant (although not necessarily one unit) change in the other factor. To put it another way, for a given degree of change in one factor, there would be a constant unit of change in the other factor.

For example, there would be a positive association between income and social status. All other things being equal or held constant, an increase in one's income would be accompanied by an increase in one's social status. Similarly, a decrease in income would be accompanied by a decrease in social status.

Negative Association. A *negative association* means that as one factor increases in value, the other factor decreases in value. Alternatively, as the first factor decreases, the second factor increases. For example, there would be a negative association between one's income and one's degree of poverty. Thus, making more money would increase a person's income, and this in turn would reduce or decrease that person's degree of poverty. Similarly, loss of job and the resulting decrease in income would cause a person to experience a concomitant increase in the level or degree of poverty.

Summary. There are only two possible types of linear associations.* Factors may be associated either positively or negatively. While there are many different substantive propositions, there are relatively few *types of relationships*, which are listed in Figure 2.2.

Theory

Again, we borrow from Lastrucci who defines a *theory* as "a generalized, synthetic, explanatory statement" that interrelates a set of other more specific propositions.[6]

Composition of Theories. First, what do theories have in them? Concepts and constructs appear in theories, but a simple listing of these would most certainly not be a theory. Rather, these concepts and constructs have to be related to one another or put together into a series of propositions.

For example, consider the germ theory of disease. The germ theory of disease contains a number of concepts, only some of which are cited here and whose definitions are briefly given. (While this is not a biology text, the germ theory is widely known and a very good example with which to work.) Thus, the concept *germ* refers to some type of organism that leads to debilitating or discomforting illness. A *host* is a person who has been inflicted with the germ and, therefore, has the disease, while a *carrier* is a person who is capable of spreading the germ to others but is not suffering from the negative effects of the disease itself. The target tissue is the particular part of the host that is

---

I. Descriptive = contains only one concept or construct
II. Analytical = contains two or more concepts or constructs
   A. Causal = independent factor(s) cause(s) dependent factor(s)
   B. Associational = correlational
      1. Positive = X increases and Y increases or
                     X decreases and Y decreases
      2. Negative = X increases and Y decreases or
                     X decreases and Y increases
      3. Curvilinear = changing degrees of association

FIGURE 2.2   Types of Propositions and the Nature of the Relationships Among Their Factors

---

*If one investigates curvilinear associations, then there are a number of different possibilities: a geometric increase or decrease, an oscillation of some type, an S-curve, a U-curve, or no persistent pattern of any type, for example.

suffering the consequences of the disease. Remember that while you may have felt that your whole body had collapsed when you last had a head cold, in truth, only your sinuses and your bronchial passages were mainly afflicted. The concept *antibody* refers to a substance that the body fabricates on the initial introduction of a particular germ; the antibody subsequently functions to protect that person from incurring the consequences of that same germ again. And so it goes. But this theory is more than a simple listing of concepts and their definitions. The concepts are related to one another in propositional form. For example, there are the simple descriptive propositions that inventory the general characteristics of any germ. And then there are the analytical propositions; for example, germs cause disease. Thus, theories contain concepts and constructs that are put together into statements called propositions.

Theoretical Generality.   Any theory is general; that is, a theory applies to more than one instance or situation. The germ theory of disease is relevant to whooping cough, Rocky Mountain spotted fever, malaria, and a whole host of other diseases. Of course, you could have deduced that theories are general, because they contain concepts and constructs, which are *general* ideas about whole classes of things. Therefore, if a theory contains concepts and constructs, it must be applicable to more than one situation.

There is another characteristic that carries over to theories from our discussion of concepts and constructs. If concepts and constructs are ideas, then they are abstractions. Since theories are made up of propositions composed of concepts and constructs, theories are also abstractions. We discuss the consequences of all this in the next chapter after we have presented the notion of an hypothesis and when we entertain the differences between verifying and proving statements in science.

Synthetic Nature of Theory.   One should realize that theories are synthetic. We use this term here as we used *devised* when discussing the scientific method in Chapter 1. The scientific community is responsible for the construction of its theories, which may be correct or incorrect. Just because theoretical statements are often complicated is not sufficient reason to accord theoretical statements greater status than they deserve. On the other hand, because theories are abstractions is no reason to deprecate such statements as the murmurings of a bunch of eggheaded, ivory-tower academic types. Theories should be taken seriously for what they are: general, abstract statements that are relevant to classes of phenomena and that are explanatory. But when is a theory "explanatory"?

Theoretical Explanation.   When a theory is explanatory, it functions to answer all the questions the scientist *knows to ask* to the scientist's *satisfaction*. Let's repeat that because it is a deceptively simple statement. Something is explanatory when it provides satisfactory answers to all the questions scientists know to ask. Several clarifying comments are necessary here. First, a theory may not provide answers to all the questions that could be asked. Rather, if a theory is explanatory, it will provide answers to only those questions that scientists are knowledgeable enough to ask. Second, the answers that are given need not necessarily be the truth. Of course, scientists assume that truth exists, and they are interested in discovering what that truth is, but as we argued earlier when we discussed pragmatism, the scientist will settle for that which works. This may or may not be the truth. At this point, we must simply say that a theory is explanatory when the answers that are subsumed under it are satisfactory to the scientist. Therefore, a theory is that which provides answers that the scientist is willing to accept as truth because they are believed satisfactory and they address all those questions the scientist was insightful enough to recognize as relevant to the subject matter.

Perhaps further discussion of our example will help to clarify this rather difficult notion of an *explanatory* theory. We would argue that at a certain point in the history of modern medical practice, the germ theory of disease could be thought of as a completely explanatory theory. At one point it presented satisfactory answers to all the questions that physicians, biologists, and related medical personnel knew to ask about the nature of disease. The germ theory of disease explained, in general terms, what caused disease: germs. It gave answers to how the body prevented the recurrence of disease: through the formation of antibodies. It suggested how one could prevent getting the disease again: through vaccination. In essence, it answered all the questions physicians and others knew to ask, and they were satisfied with the answers.

You'll recall the statement that a theory doesn't necessarily give us the truth. Rather, it presents that which we are willing to accept as true. Consider the following. The germ theory of disease might actually have postponed the discovery of a preventive for poliomyelitis. Polio was (and is) a disease. In the research to discover some way to prevent its occurrence, the germ theory of disease suggested that one needed to isolate the specific organism that was associated with the disease of polio, but which also possessed the general characteristics of a germ, since germs cause disease. The medical research community had a difficult time isolating the polio germ—and for a very good reason. Polio was not caused by a germ. The causal agent for polio did not possess the general characteristics of a germ, as suggested by the germ theory. Rather, polio was caused by a virus, and viruses have different properties than do germs. Thus, in this instance, the germ theory of disease slowed down the process of finding a preventive for polio. More important for our discussion is the idea that with the discovery of viral diseases, the germ theory of disease *ceased* to be explanatory. It ceased to answer *all* the questions about the nature of disease. It didn't account for polio, the common cold (which turns out not to be so common), or cancer, for example. These were surely diseases, but the causal agents were different than the agents suggested by the germ theory.

Understand we are not saying the germ theory of disease is useless today. Rather, we have found

it is limited to a certain category of diseases. It has lost its status as a general, *explanatory* theory of *all* disease, which the scientific community had once given it. It is still relevant to whooping cough and a whole host of diseases. However, it does not answer all the questions we *now* know to ask about the nature of disease, because we now know to ask more questions than we did when the germ "theory" of disease was believed to be a theory.

Permit us another point here. Relative to the truth of the matter, we never did possess the total truth. While we have always *wanted* to know all there is about disease and while we at one time *thought* we knew, we never really did have *all* the information. Such is the tentative nature of scientific knowledge. We assume an absolute truth exists, but we can't be sure that we have discovered it. On the other hand, when we do discover a set of ideas that fits our definition of an explanatory theory, we can't assume that we *haven't* discovered the truth *either*. Does this sound difficult? We're sure it does, but go back to our understanding that the way scientists put the scientific method together has created a situation wherein we assume an absolute truth and we search for it, but we can never be positive that we have discovered it. This being the case, we have another reason why one needs that healthy attitude of skepticism in science.

Given the notion that a theory must be explanatory, one might ask if there are any conceptualizations that we call theories today. We will have to answer honestly that we don't think so. We believe that in other systems of thinking there are conceptions that could be called theories, but not in science. For example, in mathematics the base ten number system is, we would think, a mathematical theory. However, in science there are no theories that are explanatory today. We have some conceptualizations that come close. Our notions of embryology in the study of human development come close to being completely, if not totally, explanatory, but we really can't point to one example of that which we'd call a pure scientific theory today. Rarely would one expect to find something which has been totally explained; nor would one find many instances about which we knew absolutely nothing. Rarely are things dichotomous; instead we prefer to suggest that in science conceptualizations of things offer varying degrees of understanding.

Finally, what good is this definition when part of it suggests that we are searching, first, for that which is very elusive and, second, that if and when we find it, we won't know for sure if we have gotten it? Why suggest that a central component of science is something which is that hard to achieve and for which the procedure cannot guarantee that you know you have, if and when you do? Well, quite simply, let's call this a goal. As scientists, when we study some phenomenon, we are searching for a coherent set of propositions that will provide general and acceptable answers to all the questions we know to ask. That is our goal.

Conceptual Models

Since we rarely have theories in science, what do we call these substantive conceptualizations that you have been struggling to understand in your scientific courses? We would like to offer the term *conceptual model*. A *conceptual model* is a working conceptualization in which there are acceptable answers to some of the relevant questions. In other words, a model is a partial theory. Here, we have done sufficient research and analysis to frame what we believe are some of the major concepts and constructs and put some of them together into propositions that are somewhat supported by the empirical evidence. However, some of the known questions have no answers, or some of the answers that we have are unsatisfactory because they do not give us the full understanding we seek.

For example, we know that in competitive sports there are a number of factors responsible for any team's won-lost record: the amount of time spent practicing, the degree of talent that the team possesses, the degree of expertise presented by the opposition, the presence of playing conditions favorable to the team's abilities, a game plan that capitalizes on the team's strengths and on the

opposition's weaknesses, the team's morale and desire to win, the nature of the fan's support, and the perceived rewards to be gained through winning, to suggest but a few of the relevant factors. While we could continue the list, we doubt that we would have listed all the concepts necessary to fully explain a competitive team's won-lost record. Yet, we can frame a conceptual model. We do have some confidence that the concepts mentioned above are relevant and that they can and do function as independent causal factors in determining the won-lost record. Thus, while such a conceptual model may not explain everything we'd like to know, such a model does provide some degree of insight into the world of competitive sports.

In sum, science is filled with a number of conceptual models that are partial explanations of our subject matter and that will continue, hopefully, to be expanded and refined on the way to becoming theories.

Function of Theory

Introduction.   Earlier we argued that there were no existing examples of a scientific theory today. While we do not wish to change our posture here, we do want to discuss the function of theory and conceptualization in more detail than we have. Therefore, for the sake of this objective, our use of Max Weber's substantive definition of the city for illustrative purposes is *assumed* to meet the definitional characteristics of a theory mentioned earlier.

We will focus on two different circumstances: (1) the situation when the scientist knows little or nothing about the subject matter of interest and (2) the situation in which the scientist truly possesses a theory that provides satisfactory answers to all the questions he or she knows to ask. Of course, these two situations are extreme, and the vast majority of our conceptual material at this point in time is partially explanatory.

The Difficulty in Beginning.   Consider that the sociologist wishes to explain cities but knows nothing about these human aggregations. We assume here that the researcher is in a position similar to those who discovered the existence of AIDS in the middle 1980s—that is, the subject is of interest, but the literature is appallingly, although understandably, sparse. This is, of course, the situation in which one would be doing exploratory research, a topic we discuss in more detail in Chapter 13.

The first step would be to check the existing conceptual literature for help, but we will assume, for purposes of this example, a lack of literature on cities that would render this effort fruitless. In this situation, the researcher must begin by observing the subject matter, attempting first to describe the city and to identify key variables and their potential relationships.

After selecting what is believed to be a typical city, the researcher would observe this city. But what is being sought? What characteristics are important to a community's being urban? What characteristics can be safely considered irrelevant? Think for a moment of the incredible number of descriptive characteristics that could be identified in any metropolitan area. If one were to inventory them, the task would be staggering, if not impossible. Thus, in the beginning of scientific research into a completely new research topic, one is confronted with the situation of "looking for the needle (or needles) in the haystack," except that the researcher knows neither whether one or more than one needle is being searched for nor in which of the innumerable haystacks to look.

In sum, the researcher does not have a theory (or a conceptual model) to assist in identifying important concepts and constructs and their relationships. While such a position is, of course, extremely exciting when one discovers factors deemed important, one must also recognize the frustrations that accrue from hours of careful attention to detail, work, thought, speculation, and creativity that must be invested in the collection and analysis of data—much of which will turn out to be irrelevant. This is tantamount to the experience of Mr. Bayer, who initially named his formula for aspirin "606" after purportedly finding 605 other formulas that did not provide the positive results of 606. Perseverance and a high tolerance for frustration are among the critical characteristics demanded of the exploratory researcher who lacks a theory or conceptual model.

How is this situation different from the one in which a researcher has a theory? As an example, we focus in the next section on Max Weber's definition of an ideal, typical city.

The Meaning of a Theory.   An *ideal type* is a listing of the characteristics considered crucial to the situation being described. It is considered to be a list of characteristics that compose the essence of something. The great German sociologist Max Weber did much of his analytical work after having constructed ideal types by using them in his investigation of real, concrete situations.

For example, Weber constructed an ideal type of the city that identified five characteristics of a pure case of the city: "(1) a fortification; (2) a market; (3) a court of its own and at least partially autonomous law; (4) a related form of association; and (5) at least partial autonomy and autocephaly."[7] Armed with this ideal type,* the sociologist may return to the metropolitan community that was the subject of an exploratory research effort alluded to in the preceding section. Of the millions of observable descriptive characteristics that exist in the city, the ideal type suggests that five of them are relevant to making the community a city. Thus,

---

*Two points need to be mentioned. First, these characteristics are very difficult to understand partially because Weber used the social action theoretical paradigm. Thus, Weber was concerned with the existence of an objectively demonstrable characteristic and the meaning or function that this characteristic had for social interaction. For example, the presence of a marketplace and a money economy is an overt, empirical characteristic of a city, but its more important consequence is in the way that such a structure organizes human activity. Thus, the marketplace and the money economy provided a structure that permitted strangers to interact. Business transactions can be accomplished between strangers, because there was a defined place, the marketplace, where such could go on and because money, an impersonal medium of exchange, allowed a person to complete such business transactions, assuming the buyer's willingness to purchase and the seller's willingness to sell at a mutually agreeable price. Thus, people interact in the city in a way that differed significantly from interaction in nonurban societies. For example, in nonurban societies the goods and services in the economy were not distributed in the marketplace according to agreed-upon prices. Rather,

this ideal type functions as a set of intellectual blinders; that is, it tells the researcher that to understand a city, it is necessary only to understand these five factors and their consequences. The degree to which the community under investigation is an example of a city can then be determined by looking for the degree to which the five characteristics are present in this metropolitan community.

In a word, a theory functions to identify the relevant factors, their relationships, and their meanings. Conversely, a theory functions to identify—by their omission—the usual multitude of accompanying factors that are deemed irrelevant to the topic being studied. We can do no better than to paraphrase a favorite theory professor of ours who always maintained that theory is the best single summary of what we think we know.

SCIENCE'S TWO DEFINITIONS

To this point, we have discussed the terms that belong to the language of conceptualization, i.e., those terms that we use when communicating with one another. In the next chapter, we discuss the terminology that would be appropriate to hypothesis testing.

To make this transition, we now focus on science's two types of definitions: (1) the theoretical definition and (2) the operational definition. Our discussion of theoretical definitions will serve as a summary statement for the preceding material that was subsumed under the heading of "Science's Language of Conceptualization." The discussion of operational definitions will serve to introduce the language of hypothesis testing that follows in the next chapter.

Theoretical Definition

A *theoretical definition* is a definition of a word given in terms of other words. It is the kind of definition you've been reading and memorizing throughout your formal educational career. If we defined *duck* as "an animal of the family Anatidae," we would have defined *duck* theoretically. If we defined *social class* as a "stratum in an open system of social stratification that contains persons who have been accorded similar or equivalent social prestige," we would have theoretically defined *social class*. When we defined *science*, we presented a theoretical definition. These, then, are definitions of words or symbols in terms of other words or symbols.

In science, a theoretical definition is neither true nor false. Rather, a theoretical definition is a stated intention to use a word in a specified way. In philosophy there is a type of definition called a real definition. A *real definition* attempts to capture the essence of whatever one is trying to define. However, scientists do not deal with real definitions in their conceptual language. Instead, the scientist is concerned with a clear articulation of the particular meaning when using specific technical language. It is for this reason that one is exhorted to define one's terms. Why? The reason is that theoretical definitions are neither true nor false. If they are simply intentions to communicate the writer's specific ideas, then the writer must be clear what these ideas are. For example, if we define a *table* as "a piece of furniture with a flat surface," this is what *we* mean when we use the word *table*. However, if this definition is what you—the reader—mean by the word *framis*, it is certainly your decision to use *framis* in this way.

---

the group's food supply (say, the results of the day's fishing expedition) was distributed on the basis of one's relationship within the kinship structure of the society. Rather than charge prices for food in the marketplace, the nonurban community would divide the food supply according to the network of blood or kinship relationships. Thus, many small, isolated societies had ways of handling the dispersal of the economic system's products that differed from the city and, therefore, should not—according to Weber—be considered urban.

Second, because this is not a text in urban sociology, we will not further explicate these five characteristics. The interested reader is referred to Weber's book, *The City*.[8] For our purposes, the reader only needs to know that there are five such characteristics and that they have clear (and complex) meanings to Weber. Some caution is necessary in using these five characteristics since some urban sociologists may not agree with Weber's substantive position. To illustrate the function of theory, we assume no such difficulties.

Since theoretical definitions are neither true nor false, this is not wrong for either you or us to do. You and we just decided to assign different words to the same definition. (However, it would be confusing to readers of our respective manuscripts. That is why scientists are supposed to define their respective terms carefully for the reader.)

Finally, a few additional points about theoretical definitions. As with the concepts and constructs they define, theoretical definitions are *general* in the sense that they apply to more than one case. They are also *abstractions* because they contain ideas. Lastly, these definitions are *selective*. That is, when a scientist defines a thing theoretically, the scientist focuses on some dimensions of the situation and not others. In the preceding paragraph, we defined a *table* as "a piece of furniture with a flat surface." We decided to focus on the dimension of the general category of the thing (in this case, furniture) in which tables fall and on one structural dimension of tables (in this case, the nature of the surface). In doing so, we neglected to describe the other attributes that tables have on various other dimensions. For example, our theoretical definition indicated nothing about the composition of tables; that is, are they glass, wood, metal, plastic, bamboo? It said nothing about their finish, that is, wood-grained, natural, painted. It did not focus on the function to which tables are put, that is, for decoration (as an antique), for dining, for work, for entertainment. We may have neglected these dimensions for good reasons. The point is that we did *not* describe the specific attributes which any one table might possess on *all* the dimensions that are characteristic of tables. It is in this sense that one's theoretical definitions are selective, thereby resulting in the conclusion that theoretical definitions are neither true nor false.

Operational Definition

Among other things, the scientific method demands that we generate some degree of empirical support for our ideas. To generate such support, it is necessary to gather concrete, tangible evidence. That presents a major problem. One can't directly measure an idea. If propositions are made up of concepts and/or constructs that are abstractions, it is impossible for us to measure in terms of sense experience that which is intangible. Therefore, we need to translate these concepts and constructs into a different kind of language by offering what is called an operational definition. An *operational definition* is a definition offered in terms of the actual procedures that will be used to measure the factor so defined. Thus, when something is defined operationally, the actual steps taken to measure or to recognize the thing empirically must be specified.

AN EXAMPLE OF A THEORETICAL AND AN OPERATIONAL DEFINITION

Let us concentrate on the difference between theoretical and operational definitions and some of the implications of these differences by thinking through an example. Consider the concept of a duck. When we define a duck as an animal of the family Anatidae, the concept *duck* has been defined theoretically in terms of other concepts: animal, family, Anatidae. However, as we argued earlier, one *cannot* measure *duck*, because it is only a word and an abstract, general idea at that. Thus, if we asked you to gather up 10 animals of the family Anatidae, we don't think you could do it. You might reply that, of course, you could. Why, you'd just go to the pond and trap ten ducks. However, you would not round up Anatidae because Anatidae do not exist empirically. *Anatidae* is a concept—a name—which is similar to *occupation*, which we used in an earlier example. You can't collect Anatidae any more than you can collect occupation. Further, if we asked you to pick out some Anatidae from a group of animals, for what would you look? Can you *see* an Anatidae? No. Could you *hear* an Anatidae? No. What does an Anatidae smell like? Quite frankly, an Anatidae doesn't have any smell, because it is impossible for it to possess such a characteristic. It is impossible because it is something that is abstract.

Therefore, if we are to gather 10 such specimens, our theoretical definition has to be translated from the language of conceptualization into the language of hypothesis testing as an operational definition. We have to translate "duck as an animal of the family Anatidae" into terms that are amenable to sense experience. Let us suggest as the operational definition that a duck has two wings, two webbed feet, waddles on the land, and quacks. This is a definition of a duck in concrete, empirical, sense-experience terms that will permit anyone to recognize a duck through that person's senses. You can see those two wings flapping in the air. You can see those funny-looking webbed feet as the duck waddles awkwardly about on the shore. You can actually hear the duck quack and, through your senses, recognize it as a duck because an operational definition of it has been offered.

Let's approach this another way. Let us assume that you were born and raised in the heart of the city and are totally unfamiliar with the nature of a duck, much like our Martian friend was totally unfamiliar with the state of earthly physics. When asked, a friend tells you that a duck is a species of bird of the family Anatidae. You tell your friend that you would like to see one sometime and ask further what an Anatidae would look like. But your friend is puzzled. Your friend replies that one can't see an Anatidae because it is only a word or symbol used as equivalent to the symbol *duck*. Rather, if you wanted to *see* one, it would have wings, webbed feet, waddle on the land, and quack. The characteristics of this last list are those which you could see or hear. Armed now with both definitions, you ask your friend for one more piece of information. You ask him where you might find some ducks, and he replies that if you start walking in a direction to which he points, you can't miss them. So, off you go. On the way to the ducks, you cut across a field, and there you find an animal with four legs, hooves, a mane, which occasionally gallops around the pasture neighing. Well, it didn't have wings or webbed feet, and it most assuredly wasn't waddling or quacking. While it would be impossible for you to say what this thing is, it is surely not a duck. Why? Because it did not possess the observable characteristics that your operational definition of duck said the

duck should have. In sum, when you went to gather your concrete evidence, you did not look for an Anatidae because this doesn't exist. What you looked for were the characteristics of your operational definition which allowed you to recognize an example of the thing conceptualized empirically.

SUMMARY

We introduced this chapter with a discussion of the two languages that scientists have developed. One language is the language of hypothesis testing, where the subject matter is defined in concrete, tangible, sense-experience terms so that hypotheses may be framed and tested against empirical data. The vocabulary and presentation of the issues germane to the language of hypothesis testing are the subject matter of the next chapter. In this chapter we discussed the other language—the language of conceptualization—with which the scientist communicates ideas in general and in theoretical terms. As such, this entire language of conceptualization subsumes such terms as concept, construct, attribute, dimension, proposition, theory, conceptual model, theoretical definition, and conceptualization itself.

It was argued that both concepts and constructs are the basic building blocks of that which is conceptual. Concepts and constructs share several properties: they are general in that they refer to whole groups of things; their definitions are selective in that they only focus on some of the dimensions that these things possess; and they are abstractions or ideas on which the scientist wishes to focus. Concepts and constructs differ in terms of that to which they refer: concepts refer to whole classes of tangible, sense-experience things, such as dogs and cats, while constructs refer to whole classes of intangible things, such as love and self-esteem.

We argued that these concepts and constructs could be used as symbols to identify dimensions and their attributes. Thus, a dimension refers to a particular property that the scientist's units of analysis would possess (such as sex or weight or race), while an attribute refers to some particular subset of the dimension (such as male or 182 pounds or Caucasian). Further, concepts and constructs could be related to one another in sentences called propositions. We argued that propositions could be classified on the basis of the number of concepts or constructs within the proposition into either descriptive propositions, which contain only a single concept or construct, or analytical propositions, which relate two or more concepts and/or constructs together in some way. Additionally, the relationships within analytical propositions could be classified into two major types of relationships: those which were causal and those which were associational. In causal relationships, some supposed concept (or construct) or series of concepts (or constructs) are identified as independent factors that are deterministic or responsible for the occurrence of some other supposed concept (or construct) or series of concepts (or constructs) identified as dependent factors. On the other hand, in associational relationships, one factor or combination of factors is thought of as correlated with another factor or series of factors. This association may be, if it is a linear one, either a positive one in which both sets of factors change in the same direction or a negative one in which one set of factors changes in one direction while the other set of factors changes in the opposite direction. Mention was also made of various associational measures that accommodate different numbers of variables.

We argued further that a series of propositions could be strung together to form either a theory or a conceptual model. Theories were defined in such a way that they function more as goals for the scientist than as existing conceptualizations. Thus, a theory is a series of propositions that function to provide satisfactory answers to all the questions we are smart enough to ask about our subject matter. They have been presented in general terms and, therefore, are relevant to more than one single, empirical case. While the construction of theories is a laudable goal for the scientist, what occurs in practice is the formation of what we have called conceptual models. Conceptual models are essentially partial theories. They are general notions that provide some answers or partial answers to the questions we raise about our subject matter, but other questions remain unanswered.

Finally, we concluded this chapter with a discussion of the two types of definitions that the scientist uses. First, theoretical definitions are definitions of concepts or constructs given in terms of other concepts or constructs. Almost any definition read in an academic book is an example of a theoretical definition. These are the definitions that emerge from the language of conceptualization. Second, by way of contrast, operational definitions are definitions of concepts or constructs given in terms of the actual procedures through which the scientist will gather concrete, tangible, sense-experience evidence of the factors being studied. The consideration of the nature and function of an operational definition is an appropriate concluding section for the present chapter because it provides the contrast with the notion of a theoretical definition and it serves to introduce and to make a partial transition to the next chapter, which deals with the language of hypothesis testing.

KEY TERMS

Analytical proposition	Correlational relationship	Negative association
Associational relationship	Descriptive proposition	Operational definition
Attribute	Dimension	Positive association
Causal relationship	Ideal type	Proposition
Concept	Language of conceptualization	Theoretical definition
Conceptual model	Language of hypothesis testing	Theory
Construct	Linear association	

REVIEW QUESTIONS _____

1. What are the two languages of science, and how do each of them function?

2. Discuss the similarities and the difference between a concept and a construct.

3. Define *dimension* and *attribute*. What is the difference between them? Create an example other than those given in the text to illustrate both ideas.

4. What is a proposition, what types exist, and what types of relationships are found in propositions?

5. Define the concept of theory. List four characteristics that theories have.

6. What does it mean when we argue that a theory is explanatory? How is an explanatory theory sometimes different from scientific truth?

7. What is a conceptual model, and how is this relevant to the healthy attitude of skepticism mentioned in Chapter 1?

8. How do theories and conceptual models function for the scientist?

9. Define, illustrate, and discuss the significance of theoretical and operational definitions.

CHAPTER 3

KEY TERMS IN THE SCIENTIFIC LANGUAGE OF HYPOTHESIS TESTING

INTRODUCTION

At the end of Chapter 2, we argued that the two languages which compose science have created the need for theoretical and operational definitions. Further, we began to make the transition from those ideas relevant to the language of conceptualization to those ideas relevant to the language of hypothesis testing.

Now that you are aware of this contrast, we can complete the transition by starting the present chapter with the general problem of making some sort of equivalence between a concept or construct defined theoretically and a variable defined operationally.

EQUATING THEORETICAL AND OPERATIONAL DEFINITIONS

Since science demands that we use both the language of conceptualization with its theoretical definitions and the language of hypothesis testing with its operational definitions, how do we equate the two? Would you argue that your last paycheck could serve as an accurate operational measure of what you would mean if you were to speak of your theoretical wealth as that which has monetary value? Consider the happy circumstance of a modest deposit in your local bank plus a reasonable amount of previous savings safely invested in a number of well-chosen stocks. Would your salary be equal to your wealth? Alternatively, think about a survey in which you are asked to choose one response from among 5 selections (ranging from strongly agree to strongly disagree) to 25 statements relative to a given social concern. Would those 25 choices really reflect your feelings about that concern, e.g., the political situation in the United States or your future career plans? Maybe, but clearly you would recognize that the suggested operational and theoretical definitions are not easy to equate. In sum, the equation of any one theoretical definition and its operational counterpart is not a simple task.

First, not all theoretically defined concepts or constructs are equally easy to operationalize. For example, income may be easier to measure accurately than intelligence. The different degrees of difficulty in deciding what operationally equates with a theoretical statement may be due to the complexity of the item that has been theoretically defined or the clarity of our perceptions of the dimensions on which we have chosen to concentrate.

The second major point concerns the procedure that scientists use to make the connection between any theoretical definition and its concomitant operational definition. One of the primary functions of the review of the literature stage in any research project is to determine if the literature that has already been produced on one's topic can be used by the researcher in some fruitful way. The reviewer of this literature will come to see, among other things, how the community of scientists has grappled with the theoretical definitions of their concepts and constructs and the operational definitions of their variables.* In the development of a science, definitions of basic concepts have often been subject to change, as the scientist's thinking about the subject matter became more sophisticated. Such is also true of the scientist's attempts to measure or operationalize variables.

Indeed, as the community of scientists struggle with both the theoretical and operational notions of their ideas, through time and with the help of the previous literature, they frequently arrive at a greater degree of consensus. This tendency, along with conscious attention to the issues of reliability and validity, affords scientists a connection between the languages of conceptualization and of hypothesis testing.

We encourage you to think about this point carefully. It is the two languages that, as we see it, present a recurring difficulty for the scientist. The language of communication with theoretical definitions of abstract concepts and constructs just does not relate easily to the language of hypothesis testing with its operational definitions of variables. Understand that the difficulty is making the connection rather than the differences between the languages per se.

Throughout this book, this issue will take on a number of different nuances and faces, but it will still be the problem of equating a theoretical definition with its operational equivalent.

LANGUAGE OF HYPOTHESIS TESTING

Introduction

For the balance of this chapter, we focus on the language of hypothesis testing. While not all of the terms discussed earlier under the heading of the language of conceptualization have operational analogues, many do. We concentrate on these operationally defined terms and expand some of the

broader principles and characteristics that the scientific model possesses.

Constant

A *constant* is some factor that does not change during the course of one's study. By definition, this is a factor that either does not vary inherently or is not permitted to vary either by chance or by conscious research design on the part of the scientist. For example, you may recall *pi* as a mathematical constant: 3.14159265. This is a quantified factor whose value does not change from case to case or through time. In the behavioral sciences, however, constants of this nature do not exist. We can recall no factor in the subject matter of the social sciences that remains the same regardless of what happens.

That does not mean that some factors aren't *held* constant in the behavioral sciences. Indeed, one of the major concerns in any research study would be those factors that are to be manipulated purposefully by the researcher so that they will not fluctuate.

Variable

A *variable* is something that can change. Variables can fluctuate in one of two ways in the behavioral sciences. First, they may change through time. For example, if one measured a person's income in 1980 and that person's income at the present time and if these measurements were different, then income would be a variable. An entity can be a variable in a second sense. With very few (and most certainly notable) exceptions, if a person is born a male, he will die a male; if a person is born a female, she will remain a female. Thus, one's biological sex is not a variable in the sense that this characteristic can or will fluctuate through time. Yet, in the social sciences we treat sex as a

---

*One of the problems of textbooks is that they often leave the impression that definitions of concepts have been "chiseled in concrete." Such is not the case. See, for example, William R. Catton, Jr., "The Development of Sociological Thought," *Handbook of Modern Sociology*, Robert E. L. Faris, ed., (Chicago, Illinois: Rand McNally & Company, 1964), pp. 912–950.

variable because any subsequent person's gender category could be different from that of the previously investigated person. Thus, variables in the behavioral sciences may be such because they fluctuate, not within any one case, but as one moves from case to case. Variables are entities that can change either through time or from case to case.

There's another way to look at variables, which we believe is more important. Permit us to offer a *second definition* of a *variable* as the operational definition of any concept or construct. Recall that we discussed concepts and constructs in the previous chapter in part as general ideas that were crucial building blocks in the formation of propositions and, subsequently, of theories. Recall, further, that the language of conceptualization is important to thinking and to the communication of ideas. But we cannot *test* ideas because testing requires concrete, empirical evidence that cannot be gathered because ideas are abstractions by definition. Therefore, we need to translate a concept with its theoretical definition out of the language of conceptualization and into a variable with an operational definition in the language of hypothesis testing.

Earlier, when we theoretically defined a concept and a construct, we differentiated between them because the former *referred* to classes of tangible entities, while the latter *referred* to classes of intangible entities. When both definitions are translated into operational ones, the need to distinguish between them becomes mute since both become concretely identified entities. It is for this reason that we see little need to separate concepts from constructs and refer to both as variables in the language of hypothesis testing.

Values

A *value* is a specific category or a number descriptive of the degree to which the case studied possesses the variable being assessed. Perhaps a simple example will help to clarify all of this.

Let us theoretically define *income* as any person's salary. *Income* is a concept that is a general term and refers to a dimension which Mr. Groskovitch, you, and we all possess to one degree or another. Before we can measure your income, however, we have to translate this theoretical definition into an operational definition. Let us do that by saying that income may be operationally defined as the number of dollars cleared on your paycheck. If you made $300 and I made $400, both of these would be values—specific numerical entities of the degree to which you and I had income defined by our operational definition of take-home pay. Thus, the *concept of income* refers to the general notion in the language of conceptualization that we may use in our conversations with one another, while the *variable of income* refers to that entity in the language of operationalization that may take on any number of different numerical values as it is applied to one person after another.

Kish's Classification of Variables

Leslie Kish published an important article on some of the statistical issues in research design in which he presented a brief, but, in our estimation, very powerful, classification of different types of variables.[1] The following subsection is a paraphrase, with some amplification, revision, and expansion, of some of Kish's ideas. He discusses two general categories of variables—explanatory and extraneous.

Explanatory (Class I) Variables. *Explanatory variables* are those that are the objects of the research or those on which the researcher is specifically interested in focusing. Kish also calls the explanatory variables *class I variables*. These two terms are synonymous. Further, class I (explanatory) variables can serve as both independent or dependent variables.

Independent Variable. An *independent variable* is one that is presumed to be the cause of some other variable or series of variables. Thus, if one has posited a causal relationship, the independent variable would be the one doing the causing. However, if one is interested in the function of prediction, the independent variable is the one for which a meaningful value has been given or is already known; it is the one that the researcher will use to make a prediction on some other variable or series of variables. Thus, an independent variable is already known to the researcher, will be used as a predictor, or is believed to be the (or a) cause of another variable.

Dependent Variable.   On the other hand, the *dependent variable* is the variable that is presumed to have been caused by the independent variable. The dependent variable is also the one that is to be predicted or the one for which a value is not known to the researcher.

For example, consider the hypothesis that income causes social class position. Let us argue that income is the independent variable causing the dependent variable of social class position. Assume that we want to predict the value of the dependent variable from the value of the independent variable. Thus, we need to have some value of the independent variable with which to start. Could we use $5,000? Yes. Could we use $45,000? Yes. Indeed, we can use any value, which is why the independent variable is called the *independent* variable. It matters only that the selected value is known and that the value is meaningful and accurate.

Let us assume the value of $28,000 for the independent variable of income, and let us use this information to make a prediction on the value of the dependent variable. We are not likely to argue that the value of the dependent variable is lower class. Nor would a person making $28,000 be likely to be a member of the upper class. One would not randomly pick a social class position but would likely make an educated guess that one believes will be correlated with the value of the independent variable. Thus, if told someone made $28,000 per year, you would use this information to make a very specific prediction on the value of the dependent variable. Your educated guess would probably suggest the person's social class position

is at the lower end of the middle class. Clearly, whatever the predicted value of the dependent variable is, it *depends upon* the information given on the independent variable, which is the reason the dependent variable is so labeled.

In sum, one can start with any reasonable value of the independent variable, but once that value has been specified, the researcher will use it to make a very definite and limited prediction of the specific value of the dependent variable.

Extraneous Variables.   *Extraneous variables* are all the remaining variables that are *not* the objects of the research. The extraneous variables are the thousands of things that may fluctuate within the empirical universe but have not been treated as class I explanatory variables. Kish goes on to identify three categories or types of extraneous variables: (1) those which are controlled; (2) those which are uncontrolled and confounding; and (3) those which are uncontrolled and assumed to be irrelevant.

Class II Variables.   First, class II, or *controlled*, *variables* are those that have been manipulated by the researcher so that their effects upon one or more of the class I variables have been eliminated. They have been treated so that if they do affect one or more of the class I variables, they affect each case of the class I variables to the same degree. Therefore, the class II, controlled, variables have been manipulated in the research design to ensure that their effects on the objects of the research will not be variable effects. There are numerous strategies for controlling on variables, but we defer our discussions of these techniques for a later section of this chapter.

Class III Variables.   Second, *class III*, or *uncontrolled and confounding*, *variables* have three characteristics. First, as with the class II variables, they are not the objects of the research. Second, unlike the class II variables, they are not controlled. Thus, the researcher has made no attempt to manipulate the effects of the class III variables on any of the class I variables. Quite simply, the class III variables have been neglected in the research design. Finally, the class III variables are confounding in the sense that, at least theoretically, they have some differential effect on the values of one or more of the class I variables. Ideally, because they are confounding variables, they should be treated either as class II controlled variables or as class I objects of the research.

Class IV Variables. The final category of extraneous variables are *class IV variables.* Unlike class II but like class III variables, the class IVs are not controlled. They have not been manipulated so that their effects upon the class I variables have been eliminated or neutralized. Finally, unlike the class III variables, the class IVs are either irrelevant in their effects on the objects of the research or they are *assumed to be irrelevant.* Our argument is that the more proper conclusion is that the

class IV variables are assumed to be irrelevant. (See Figure 3.1.)

An Example. Let us look at an example to better grasp the nature of Kish's classification of variables. First, we must create a situation (a research project, if you will), because none of this makes sense if it is not related to a specific research interest. No variable can be classified until one has proposed some sort of relationship between two or more variables. After the relationship has been proffered, the classification of types of variables can begin. With this in mind, let us create a scenario.

Assume that one is interested in studying student grades in the research-methods course. If course grade is the dependent variable, intelligence quotient (IQ) readily comes to mind as an independent variable and the following relationship could be hypothesized: the greater one's in-

NAME OF THE VARIABLE	DESCRIPTION
Explanatory: Class I	The objects of the research; what the researcher is interested in testing.
a. Independent	The given, one whose value is known, the predictor, the causal one.
b. Dependent	The unknown, not given, to be predicted, the caused, the effect.
Extraneous	Not the objects of the research.
a. Class II: controlled	Manipulated so that they do not exert a varying influence on the class I objects of the research.
b. Class III: uncontrolled	Do influence differentially one or more of the class I objects of the research.
c. Class IV: assumed irrelevant	Believed by the researcher to have no effects on any of the class I objects of the research.

FIGURE 3.1 Identification and Brief Description of Kish's Types of Variables[*]

[*]See Leslie Kish, "Some Statistical Problems in Research Design," *American Sociological Review*, Vol. 24, No. 3 (June 1959), pp. 328–338.

telligence, the higher one's course grade ought to be. However, whether one performs well in the methods course will depend on a number of other factors besides the student's intelligence. Some of these factors would be suggested through a review of the relevant literature. For example, one might learn, first, that the student's interest in the course will influence the degree to which the student concentrates on the subject matter. Second, the student's overall course load during the term will be a factor. A student taking 12 credit hours will have more time to apply to the methods course than one taking 18 credit hours. Third, skill in note taking will influence one's performance on examinations and other written work. Fourth, time devoted to study the subject matter is an obvious factor. Finally, class attendance will influence the degree to which one is capable of meeting the requirements of the course. These are just some of the factors that would be expected to bear upon the student's ability to master the course.

As we indicated, however, the researcher is primarily interested in the influence of IQ on the course grade. Hence, IQ and course grade would be the class I variables. These are the objects of the research. Suppose that we decided to control or hold constant the remaining five factors mentioned above. We would then present the following hypothesis: IQ varies positively with course grade, holding constant interest in the course, overall course load, skill in note taking, time spent studying, and class attendance. The five factors identified as controlled would be the class II variables—their differential effects on one or more of the class I variables will be eliminated through the research design.

To summarize, the researcher is interested in the dependent variable of course grade and has chosen to focus on the independent variable of IQ with an additional five factors that have been controlled as class II variables. Additionally, there are an untold number of factors that have not been considered in the research design so far. For example, there is Brazil's annual rainfall and its gross national product. These two factors are variables, but the researcher would classify them as

class IV variables—factors that, while they do change, presumably have no influence on either the student's IQ or course grade. As such they can be disregarded as irrelevant to *this* study. There are a great number of such factors that have not been treated as class I variables or as class II variables, but which can safely be assumed to be irrelevant in their effects upon the class I variables of IQ and course grade.

After specifying the class I variables of IQ and course grade, after eliminating the effect of those additional five factors that the literature suggests are relevant to one or more of the class I variables, and with the knowledge that some factors, although variables, are of no significance or relevance to this research project, is the hypothesis a reasonable one? Consider the class III variables— those that are not the objects of the research, have not been controlled, and are confounding.

A number of additional factors could seem to be related logically to one's course grade. For example, the students may have a number of outside activities or commitments that impinge on their available study time: employment commitments, family responsibilities, or extracurricular activities such as participation in a sports program. Second, the available study environments may not be conducive to academic achievement. For example, dorms may be too noisy for any serious student. Third, it may be that some students do not have a clear career focus, so that commitment to the course is less than for students who do have such a focus. Fourth, not all students have the same degree of physical stamina. Some require more sleep than others, thereby having less time to devote to study. Fifth, achievement will be related to the background which one brings to the course. For example, if you have presumably taken a number of courses in your major area of study and perhaps a good course in statistics prior to your method's course, you would be expected to do better than a person who lacked such academic preparation. (We encourage you to continue to develop the list of the class III variables in this particular research context.) If the relationship between IQ and course grade is not as strong as one might expect, it may be because one or more class III variables, such as those that were noted, have influenced IQ or course grade, thereby obscuring the relationship between the class I variables.

Interaction Among Variables.   We hope our example is clear. In reality, empirical situations are usually more complicated than the situation constructed above. Are there any other considerations that would help us utilize more effectively the classification Kish has presented? Of course.

First, let us examine interaction. *Interaction* is the notion that the combined effect of two or more variables may be greater or less than the simple accumulation of the individual contributions of the isolated variables. It refers to the fact that there may be an *overlap* in the effects of two or more variables so that their combined effect is less than their simple accumulation or that there may be a *reinforcement* such that the combined effect is greater than the sum of the individual effects. It would be a dangerous notion to assume that multiple causal factors are mutually exclusive in their effects upon the dependent variable or variables.

For example, if two people—John and Frank—could lift 200 and 250 pounds, respectively, it is doubtful they could collaborate to lift the simple sum of 450 pounds. Together, they might be able to lift more than 450 pounds or, perhaps, they would be able to lift only 400 pounds. This is the nature of interaction among the variables. Such interaction is more likely to occur in the subject matter of the social sciences. With the biological and natural sciences and nonscientific systems of thinking, interaction may not be a major consideration. For example, in the base ten number system in mathematics, $2 + 4 = 6$. It is the simple accumulation of scores, and it never changes. In the social sciences, however, interaction is a complicating fact of life.

Second, when the researcher controls on class III, confounding, variables by treating them as class II variables, distortion will have, by definition, been introduced. This doesn't mean, however, that the researcher shouldn't control on

variables in order to isolate a single independent variable's contribution to some dependent variable. If we return to the example of the relationship between course grade and intelligence, the truth is that course grade *is influenced* by the intelligence of the student, by the remaining five variables that appear in the hypothesis, by the factors mentioned as class III variables, *and* by the additional factors about which you thought. When the researcher tries to isolate the influence of intelligence on course grade and controls on the class II variables already mentioned, the act of controlling on these variables will create a situation that differs somewhat from the reality.

Third, in all likelihood we won't have a complete inventory of all the independent causal variables that are determining the dependent variable. In the example given, we posited five variables as controlled and then "discovered" five additional variables as class III, uncontrolled and confounding, variables. Have we exhausted all the extraneous variables that affected the class I objects of the research? There may be more variables that are assumed to be irrelevant but which are, in truth, class III, confounding, ones. Consider sex. Would an argument that males or females may be more concerned with grades because a respectable grade point average (GPA) is essential if they are to achieve their career plans have any merit? What about racial identity? or ethnicity? or social background?

There may be some variables that were class IV but which in the current climate of opinion have turned into class III variables or have been unrecognized class III variables all along. Again, we point to the importance of the conceptual model that functions to alert the researcher to those variables that have been shown to be related, or are thought to be, so that one may judiciously select the class I objects of the research. Having made this selection, the model functions further to identify the class III variables that the researcher will decide to change into class II, controlled, variables or leave as class III, confounding, variables.

Because we are using a conceptual *model* rather than a conceptual *theory*, the model will, by definition, be but a partial explanation of the nature of the situation. While we have made this point earlier, the idea we want you to see here is that if the conceptual model is really a model, then some of those class IV, assumed-to-be-irrelevant, variables may well be class III, uncontrolled and confounding, variables. All other things being equal, one's study must rely upon a conceptual model to identify which relevant factors should or could be treated as the objects of the research or as controlled variables. In general, it is reasonable to argue that the better the conceptual model is, the better will be the propositions that guide the research.

However, it should not be assumed that a poorly done study is poor just because the conceptual model was inadequate or the researcher did not follow the information that was contained in an adequate conceptual model. While either of these difficulties may be relevant criticisms, there are other factors that could lead to erroneous conclusions. Indeed, it may be that the conceptual model identifies more important concepts than can be comfortably managed by the researcher methodologically. For example, assume that a researcher has identified 52 different class I variables on the topic of success in college. If success in college was selected as the dependent variable and one other class I variable as the independent one, we would argue that the researcher would experience difficulty in treating all the remaining 50 class III variables as class II, controlled, variables.

Summary of the Discussion of Kish's Variables.   At the conclusion of Chapter 1, we discussed the notion of the nomothetic explanation. You will remember we said that the scientist is interested in generating the greatest amount of understanding about the subject matter while using the fewest number of factors and while staying within a somewhat rigid set of rules. Indeed, for the scientist the goal is to simplify otherwise complex situations to a level where they can more easily be understood. In providing such simplifications, some information is, of course, lost, but the trick remains one of retaining that which is

most important while trying to make matters easier. In our opinion, Kish has done just that. Of all the things one could say about variables, Kish has managed to get at the essence of their differences with a limited number of mutually exclusive categories, which are inclusive of all such differences. All one needs in order to use this classification is a well-developed conceptual model.

For example, if one offered the hypothesis that income varies positively with social class, holding constant race, sex, and occupation, then Kish's classification is simple yet powerful. There are only two class I variables: income and social class. There are three class II, controlled, variables: race, sex, and occupation. Thus, all of the remaining variables in the universe must fall into one of the two remaining categories. Either they are class IV, irrelevant, variables or class III, uncontrolled and confounding, variables. What a simple, yet powerful and insightful, categorization! Just as Robert Merton's designation of a latent function sensitized the functionalist to look for hidden factors that didn't readily come to mind,[2] Kish warns us that there may be variables in the real situation that are class III, confounding, ones. He is saying, among other things, that we should be sensitized to look for variables that are or may be muddying the relationship (or relationships) among the class I variables. Here, in our opinion, Kish has made an important contribution to the theory of methodology. (See Figure 3.2.)

The Hypothesis

Earlier we argued that concepts and constructs were related to one another in statements called propositions within the language of conceptualization. Further, we argued that one cannot test these propositions because of the criteria for verification required by the scientific method. Therefore, the propositions that one so carefully framed after reviewing the relevant literature must be translated into the operational language of hypothesis testing.

QUESTION/TYPE OF VARIABLE	CLASS I	CLASS II	CLASS III	CLASS IV
1. Is the variable an object of the research? Does the scientist specifically want to focus on it?	Yes	No	No	No
2. Has the variable been held constant or controlled in the research design?	No	Yes	No	No
3. Would this variable appear in a formal statement of the hypothesis appropriate to the study?	Yes	Yes	Never	Never
4. If the research on the hypothesis as formally stated leads to erroneous conclusions based solely on the content of the hypothesis, which class or classes of variables are the culprits?	No	No	Yes	Maybe
5. If one's conceptual model is inaccurate, the trouble will lie with which type of variable?	No	No	Yes	Maybe
6. To be absolutely sure of the nature of the effect that a supposed independent variable has on a supposed dependent variable, one must *eliminate* the effects of which class of variable?	No	No	Yes	Yes

FIGURE 3.2   Responses to Some Questions That Could Be Asked About Kish's Classification of Variables as They Appear in Analytical Hypotheses

A *hypothesis* is a statement that can be empirically or scientifically tested.[3] Hypotheses are essentially propositions that have been translated into the language of hypothesis testing. That is, the descriptive and analytical propositions with their concepts and constructs have been translated into hypotheses containing operationally defined variables. Quite simply, we argue that these two terms are synonymous with one exception: propositions are written in the language of conceptualization, while hypotheses are written in the language of operationalization.

McGinnis's Types of Hypotheses

Just as we found Kish's discussion of different types of variables useful, we have similarly discovered a complementary discussion of different types of hypotheses offered by Robert McGinnis.[4] We have altered McGinnis's definitions to be consistent with Kish's types of variables. McGinnis identified three types of hypotheses: (1) the absolute hypothesis; (2) the finitely conditional hypothesis; and (3) the infinitely conditional

hypothesis. These represent different degrees of control over extraneous variables, but they are all analytical hypotheses. Thus, in using any of the three, one will be attempting to show a relationship between two or more class I objects of the research.

Absolute Hypothesis.   An *absolute hypothesis* contains only class I objects of the research. To be analytical, it must have at least two class I variables: an independent variable and a dependent variable. Parenthetically, this might be an appropriate time to reinforce an important aspect of proposition or hypothesis construction. As we suggested in the earlier IQ versus course-grade example, most dependent variables have more than one contributing causal, independent variable. We could have suggested a hypothesis with more than one independent and one dependent variable. For example, we could have suggested that IQ and time spent studying were the causal, independent variables that were related to the single dependent variable of course grade. If we had done so, the hypothesis would still have been an absolute hypothesis, because it contained only class I objects of the research variables. While an absolute hypothesis must have at least two class I variables (one independent and the other dependent), it may have as many objects of the research as the methodological state of the art permits. However, while an absolute hypothesis may contain any number of class I variables, it must contain only class I variables.

Finitely Conditional Hypothesis. A *finitely conditional hypothesis* contains some number of class I variables and one or more extraneous class II, controlled, variables. Here the researcher has taken steps to guarantee that some limited number of extraneous variables have been eliminated from affecting the class I objects of the research.

Let's return to our last example, the relationship between income and occupation, on the one hand, and social prestige, on the other hand. If we expand this absolute hypothesis into a finitely conditional one, we could suggest that income and occupation vary positively with social prestige, holding constant education. Education would be a class II, controlled, variable, and the revised hypothesis would be a finitely conditional one. Of course, one could control on more than one extraneous variable, if advisable and if the technological or procedural wherewithal were available.

Infinitely Conditional Hypothesis. McGinnis's final category is the *infinitely conditional hypothesis,* which again contains some number of class I objects of the research, and *all* the remaining extraneous variables would be class II, controlled, variables. Every remaining extraneous variable that is not an object of the research has been treated in such a way that its variable impact upon the objects of the research has been eliminated.

For example, holding constant every remaining variable in the empirical universe, if we hypothesized that income and occupation varied positively with social prestige, this would be an infinitely conditional hypothesis. However, such is impossible to attain empirically and reflects a theoretical completeness to McGinnis's classification.

There are two reasons for this impossibility. The first is a technical problem. Quite simply, even if we could write an infinitely conditional hypothesis, we do not possess the technical means to design a research study to accomplish this degree of control.*

The second point is theoretical. As we have argued, the substantive conceptualizations we find in the literature are really models. That is, they are partial rather than total explanations. Therefore, our models will be, by definition, missing some of the additional variables and relationships necessary for a full explanation of the phenomena we study. Hence, a thorough review of the literature will necessarily identify only some of the relevant concepts and constructs in the situation. Since this is true, a well-framed hypothesis that suggests controlling on all of these extraneous variables as class II variables will in all likelihood miss some relevant confounding factors because those which are missed will be erroneously classified as class IV, irrelevant, variables. An infinitely conditional hypothesis is one where *all* the class III, confounding, variables *and all* the class IV variables have in actuality been manipulated into class II variables. Thus, an infinitely conditional hypothesis is one in which there are only two classes of variables within the study—class I and class II.

If this cannot be accomplished, why discuss it? All three types of hypotheses mentioned by McGinnis focus on differing degrees of control

---

*In one sense this first point rests on the issue of the social scientist's ability to randomize the effects of extraneous variables, since randomization is one of the techniques for controlling variables. Opinion is divided on the degree to which randomization actually achieves the objectives claimed by its proponents. Since we count ourselves on the side of randomization's detractors, we argue that the social and behavioral scientist has a number of procedures through which only a limited number of variables may be controlled. We defer a more thorough discussion of randomization to a later point in this chapter.

over extraneous variables. An absolute hypothesis posits no empirical control over any extraneous variables, the finitely conditional hypothesis suggests control on some extraneous variables, and the infinitely conditional hypothesis posits control over all of the extraneous variables. While the latter is not achievable empirically at this time, it is still the next logical possibility on the continuum of one's degree of control over extraneous variables.

The notion of an infinitely conditional hypothesis is the ultimate in hypothesis construction. If one were to want to know income's contribution to social prestige and if a study were designed to eliminate all the other possible variables, we would have conclusive evidence of income's effect at that one moment in time. This, in a sense, is what we are striving for in science, i.e., to design our research with sufficient precision to be able to isolate the relationship between two variables. Therefore, if for no other reason, we want this notion in our theory of methodology to sensitize us to a goal that we hope to achieve.

Finally, one could argue that until we can actually design studies suggested by infinitely conditional hypotheses, our knowledge of phenomena will always be somewhat suspect and our conceptual models will remain models, i.e., incomplete explanations of our subject matter.

What utility does McGinnis's classification of hypotheses have? The reader will surely recognize that there are few situations in the social sciences that are single-factor causal situations. Thus, we should expect more than one independent variable and that one or more of the important variables may not yet be known to us. For these reasons, most current research is based on the use of finitely conditional hypotheses. In exploratory research or in situations where we know very little about the subject matter, however, we must rely upon relatively simple absolute hypotheses. Clearly, we are far from the capacity, either methodologically or theoretically, to frame meaningful infinitely conditional hypotheses. We are capable, however, given the current techniques for controlling on variables and our substantive

knowledge, of framing solid, finitely conditional hypotheses.

Types of Controlled Variables

Earlier in this chapter, we discussed controlling on extraneous variables. In this subsection, we focus on a classification of types of controlled variables. The concern here is not with the actual procedures through which the researcher controls these variables but with the different strategies for controlling on variables and their advantages and disadvantages.[5] Five different types of controlled variables are presented: (1) one-category control; (2) block variable control; (3) randomized variable control; (4) matching control, for both precision and frequency-distribution; and (5) statistical formula control.

One-Category Control. A *one-category control* of a class II variable is one in which the subjects studied are restricted to a single attribute of the dimension being controlled. For example, if the researcher used a one-category control of the dimension of sex, one's sample would contain only males or only females. Thus, all participants in the study would belong to the same category regarding the controlled variable.

The major advantage of a one-category control is that it is relatively simple to accomplish. Of course, the major disadvantage is that one's findings must be restricted to that category which has been studied.

Block Variable Control. When *block variable control* of a class II variable is used, the subjects are divided into two or more categories of the controlled variable and the class I variables are assessed for each of the subdivisions of the controlled variable (or variables). For example, if the variable of sex were block variable controlled, the sample would be divided into female and male participants and the class I variable analysis would be separately performed on both gender identity attributes. Block variable control is more sophisticated than one-category control and allows for a

NAME	AGE	SEX	EMPLOYMENT STATUS
1. Frank Smith	40	Male	Working full-time
2. William James	40	Male	Working full-time
3. Louise Jones	32	Female	Working part-time
4. Mary Anderson	32	Female	Working part-time
5. Ruth Simpson	72	Female	Retired
6. Lillian Johns	72	Female	Retired
7. Joshua Evans	16	Male	Not working
8. Jeff Williams	16	Male	Not working

FIGURE 3.3   Illustration of Precision Matching Control on Three Class II Variables for the Assignment of Subjects to Two Separate Study Groups

broader generalization of the results. The disadvantage is that one must increase the sample size by the multiple of the number of subcategories on which the block variable control has been done. For example, if 100 persons would be adequate for a one-category control, a block variable control with two categories would require 200 persons.

Randomization of Variables.   *Randomization* is the assignment of individuals or cases to different groups or the sample on the basis of chance. Here, one follows a probability model in determining which subjects would be studied or placed into which groups should a multiple group research design be used.

Randomization is an important consideration in that it *theoretically* permits control on *all* of the remaining extraneous variables. If randomization worked perfectly, each group would possess the same mean, same standard deviation, and distribution on any extraneous variable selected for evaluation. Unfortunately, randomization does *not* work perfectly. It is subject to the same restrictions imposed on any procedure that is arrived at through the probability process. (See Chapters 6 and 7 for a more thorough discussion of the nature

of probability.) It is a technique, however, to consider after one has elected to control on one or more variables through other means.

Matching Control.   *Matching control* involves the equation of a number of groups of cases on a limited number of variables. Given that one would like to set up experimental and control groups in an experimental research design and given that one wanted to control on sex and age, one could control the assignment of subjects through matching so that both groups would have an identical age and sex distribution. There are two types of matching controls: (1) precision control and (2) frequency-distribution control.

Precision control involves pairing individuals on several variables and then randomly assigning one of each pair to the experimental group and the other to the control group.[*] Figure 3.3 shows four *pairs* of people precision matched on the variables of age, sex, and employment status. Smith and James are the first pair, and they possess identical values on the variables that are to be controlled. If we randomly assigned Smith to one group and James to the other, each of the two groups would have a person who was 40, male, and working full-time. Similarly, if the people in the second

---

[*]The assumption here is that one would only want to form two groups. If one needed four groups, one would precision match on the controlled variables four similar people.

pair were randomly assigned to the two groups, each group would possess a person who was 32, female, and working part-time. When precision matching, it is not necessary to ensure equal values for all pairs. That is, if Smith and James are both male, this does not mean that Jones and Anderson have to be male also. Only the *pair* has to match for the variables that are being controlled. Obviously, if the study required the formation of three groups, one would need an additional male who was 40 and working full-time.

Precision control is one of the stronger techniques for controlling on variables. Its major advantage is to guarantee that the variables have been controlled. Its major disadvantage is that the researcher will need a larger number of individuals from which to select. This number will grow substantially when the researcher, first, adds additional variables and, second, when the variables to be controlled are quantified and have a large range of meaningful values. It is for these reasons that precision control is only a viable strategy when the researcher needs to deal with a limited number of variables.

Frequency-distribution control is a second matching technique. *Frequency-distribution control* involves the matching of *groups* of persons in terms of the overall *distribution* of a given series of variables. One equates groups on the basis of similar mean values on the controlled variables.

Consider the data presented in Figure 3.4. Group I and Group II have been frequency distribution controlled because each group has the same mean age and the same mean income. Yet, if one studies the data in Figure 3.4, one will see that the individuals are rather badly mismatched. In Group I there is a negative association between income and age; that is, as age increases, income decreases. In Group II there is a positive association between income and age; as age increases, income also increases. While the mean figures for each separate variable are identical, the groups are mismatched on *combinations* of variables. This is the major difficulty with frequency distribution control. Its major advantage over precision matching is that frequency distribution control requires a substantially smaller pool of cases from which to select.

Statistical-Formula Control. *Statistical-formula control* means that one eliminates the effects of one or more variables through the data calculations in one's statistical analysis. For example, the partial correlation measure of association allows one to measure the association between two class I variables, while eliminating the effects of one or more class II, controlled, variables through the mathematical manipulations of the formula. Thus, one may be able to control on variables through the data-analysis procedures used to measure the class I variables.

CASE/GROUP	GROUP I		GROUP II	
	AGE	*INCOME*	*AGE*	*INCOME*
Individual 1	20	$12,000	10	$ 5,000
Individual 2	30	10,000	20	7,000
Individual 3	50	8,000	60	11,000
Individual 4	60	6,000	70	13,000
Means ($\overline{X}$)	40	9,000	40	9,000

FIGURE 3.4 Illustration of Frequency Distribution Control for Two Variables and Two Groups of Subjects

Summary.   Of the various strategies of control mentioned, the one-category, block variable, and precision-matching strategies guarantee that the researcher has controlled on the differential effects of all included class II variables. Therefore, they are strongly recommended procedures of control. Frequency-distribution control is not as powerful, and statistical-formula controls, as with partial correlation, make other demands on the researcher (such as using data that has been measured at the appropriate level of analysis—see Chapter 9). Randomization works, but only in terms of probability, and is only recommended after having exhausted the more guaranteed strategies.

Proof Versus Verification

When we began to discuss hypotheses, we said that their outstanding or essential characteristic was that they could be scientifically tested. We focus attention now on the issue of scientific hypothesis testing with a concentration on the nature of the information that emerges. We begin by noting the distinction between proof and verification.

The Nature of Proof.   By *proof,* we mean to turn some notion into an absolute statement which will forever be true. Some systems of reasoning permit us to generate such statements. For example, in the base ten number system in mathematics, $2 + 3$ will always equal 5. We can define the nature of 2, 3, 5, the process of addition, and the notion of equality and then proceed to prove that $2 + 3 = 5$. This relationship was true 50 years ago, it is true today, and it will be true in the future.

The Nature of Verification.   In the process of proving a relationship, one reaches a point where sufficient evidence has been collected so that a relationship or incident can be said to be verified. The *verification* of a relationship is the collection of enough empirical evidence so that one has confidence that the relationship is probably true, but not enough evidence to state definitely that the relationship is an absolute truth.

Comparison of Proof and Verification.   When something is verified, sufficient evidence has been accumulated to lead the investigator *to think* the truth has been discovered. When a situation has been proven, enough evidence has been presented to *know* the situation is, and will be forever, true. Let us look at an example of scientific hypothesis testing.

An Example.   Consider again the hypothesis concerning the relationship between one's IQ and one's course grade. Assuming we had a representative sample of adequate size selected from our university and assuming an adequate operational definition of intelligence and course grade, we could measure these two variables and correlate the measurements with an appropriate statistic. If the results showed that the hypothesis was correct, can we say we have now proven the hypothesis? The answer is no. There may be something that is atypical about our university, which makes our students different from students at your college or university. Therefore, let us repeat the study using a representative sample of students from your school. If the results are the same, have we now proven the hypothesis? Again, the response is no. Assume we have done all that it is possible to do. After such a thorough study we will be in a position only to suggest verification of the hypothesis.

We would argue that the nature of science and our subject matter are both such that conclusive permanent evidence is an impossibility. There are two reasons for this. First, there is the practical fact that the scientist can rarely, if ever, investigate all the cases. With this example, we would be unable to study all of the college students currently enrolled in undergraduate programs in all of the accredited colleges and universities that exist in the world. Even if such a study were desirable, we rarely would have the time or financial resources to study all the cases of anything. Nor does such make much sense, especially in light of the second reason.

Second, social conditions change. As the norms and values of the culture fluctuate, the relationship between these two variables may also change. Consider that 40 years ago one could safely argue that most females were not as academically achievement-oriented as were their male counterparts, all other things being equal. Before the advent of the women's movement, a large majority of women accepted the supportive role of helper to the wage earner role, which was generally occupied by the adult male of the family. Therefore, because of the norms that governed one's "proper" role within the family, the association between IQ and course grade for women was not as strong as it was for men. We are not saying that women couldn't compete in college on the same level as men, but rather that the norms of the culture did not encourage women to do so. Clearly, the culture has undergone dramatic change, with strong pressures for an equalization of the relationship between males and females. Therefore, there is every reason to believe that what might have been true of the relationship between IQ and course grade for women in the 1940s is considerably different today.

Therefore, first, for the practical reason that scientists never investigate every situation and, second, for the reason that the world may change, the scientist can never prove any hypothesis. The best the scientist can do is to verify hypotheses.

Scientific Fact

A *scientific fact* is a verified hypothesis. When the scientist has replicated a study and found consistent, supportive evidence of the hypothesis, the hypothesis has become a scientific fact. We emphasize the point that facts are verified hypotheses and not proven hypotheses. This distinction signals a major difference between the scientific method and some other methods of investigation.

A Note on Different Levels of Generality

Statements in science—whether they be propositions or hypotheses—exhibit different levels of generality. *Generality* refers to the scope to which a piece of information can be applied. A simple example can serve to clarify this point. Different concepts may indicate different levels of abstraction. The concept *pediatrician* refers to a subset or

specialty within the profession of medicine. The concept *physician* refers to all the practitioners in the field of medicine, which would include not only pediatricians but also surgeons, urologists, cardiologists, gynecologists, and others. Finally, the concept *occupation* refers to all those persons who are currently employed, not simply physicians.

The social and the behavioral scientist has grown accustomed to rather quick and radical shifts in the level of generality in their conceptual language as usage of *pediatrician*, *physician*, or *occupation* suggests, and these shifts are reflective of a switch from one unit of analysis to another. When a proposition is presented, it may contain concepts that represent a range from narrow to extensive scope. Attention to the degree of generality is warranted, especially as one extrapolates and interprets one's actual data in light of the conclusions made from these data.

Inductive and Deductive Reasoning

We discussed inductive and deductive reasoning in Chapter 1. We are reintroducing these concepts because they are two important mechanisms that are germane to these levels of generality.

Deduction. *Deduction* is the logical process of moving from a more general to a more specific level of interest. For example, if we said that all candy is sweet, then we could logically use deductive reasoning to conclude that Reese's Pieces are also sweet, since Reese's Pieces are a subcategory of the more general category of candy. If a statement is true of the entire category, it must also logically follow that it would be true for a subset of the larger category.

Induction. *Induction* is the logical process of attributing some descriptive characteristic or relationship determined from a more specific and limited area of interest to a general and more comprehensive area of interest. For example, assume that the president of your college or university wants to know what proportion of the student body is gainfully employed, and your research-methods class draws an adequate sample and determines that 62.8 percent of the student body has either a part-time or full-time job. If one concludes, from these data, that over half of *all* college and university students work on either a part-time or full-time basis, one will have used inductive logic. On the basis of a subset of the population (i.e., the students at your school), an inductive conclusion will have been reached about *all* students everywhere.

Use of Induction and Deduction in Science. When reviewing the appropriate literature at the beginning of a research project, a researcher is looking for relevant general propositions in the substantive area of interest that have been discovered and argued as relevant by the community of scientists in earlier research. One might find such statements as: (1) income varies positively with social class; (2) size of the organizational structure varies positively with occupational specialization within the organization; or (3) the labeling process functions to increase recidivism among deviant persons. All three of these examples are general statements. The first suggests that *everyone's* income and social class position are related positively. The second speaks to a characteristic of *all* organizational structures. The third refers to *all* deviant persons.

As the development of the conceptual model begins, (see Chapter 5), the general propositions noted in the literature review process will orient the researcher through the process of deductive logic and will be applied to the more specific research context. Deduction, then, is often used in the initial stages in the construction of one's conceptual model.

However, when the results and conclusions are being presented, the researcher is more likely to use inductive logic. One of the goals of the scientist is to create general explanations. The scientist will, therefore, use inductive logic or reasoning to go from the evidence of the scientist's specific study in a specific context to a more general context.

Two Notes of Concern Regarding the Use of Deductive and Inductive Reasoning. The first concern is with deduction. If performed properly, deduction will never fail to produce a *logically* sound conclusion. For example, if ripe apples are sweet, Granny's ripe apples have to be sweet, because Granny's apples are subsumed under the more general category of *all* apples. However, Granny's apples may *not* be sweet—not because one's logic is bad or because one's use of deduction is poor—but because the more general statement—ripe apples are sweet—is not *empirically* true. The logic is fine, but the statement on which one makes a logical deduction is *not* a true statement. It may be that only some ripe apples are sweet and that some varieties of ripe apples are, instead, rather tart. Thus, the problem with deductive logic is not the logical process itself; instead the more general statement, which is assumed to be true when one used the process of deduction, may—in fact—not be true.

The second concern relates to the use of inductive logic, which always goes beyond the empirical evidence that the scientist has collected. If the scientist concludes that *all* students do something on the basis of what a sample of students do on *your* campus, the researcher is clearly overgeneralizing from the empirical data. However, the careful use of the proper sampling design and the considerations of probability theory in statistical reasoning will allow one to make such "leaps" on more solid ground than one might think.

In sum, while the process of deduction sometimes suffers because the broader statement may not be true and the process of induction suffers because the scientific goal of seeking more general principles encourages the researcher to overgeneralize from the data, these two logical mechanisms are important to the work of the scientist and are used in any research study. We shall return to induction and deduction, when we discuss the nature of the conceptual model in Chapter 5. Indeed, the inductive and deductive processes will emerge in a variety of different contexts: the formation of the conceptual model, the sampling design, the statistical analysis and interpretation of the data, to name but a few.

Simulations

A *simulation* is the attempt to replicate, in operational terms, some real world situation. While there are not a great number of current examples that meet the requirements of this definition, the development and growth of computer technology may lead to a greater emergence of some. A number of years ago some urbanologists at Michigan State University began to create a simulation of East Lansing, Michigan. If and when they are able to complete this, it will be a real example of a simulation. Marine biologists at the Chesapeake Bay Institute on the eastern shore of Maryland are creating a small-scale replication of the Chesapeake Bay on the East Coast of the United States. This simulation, when the bugs have been eliminated, will behave as does the real Chesapeake Bay, so that tidal changes and other phenomena can be studied in the laboratory. Similarly, there are flight simulators that are used by both the military and the commercial airlines in the training of pilots.

Thus, a simulation is an exact replica of some real empirical situation except that it is usually on a smaller scale than the real thing. Simulations are important to scientists because they allow the testing of differential consequences of various policy decisions before one introduces these decisions to the real situation.

Empirical Models

An *empirical model* is a partial simulation or a laboratory replication of some situation that is analogous or similar to some aspects of the real world. For example, you have played with an empirical model if you ever played the Parker Brothers' game of Monopoly. Think of the many aspects of this game that are analogous to the reality of treating the real estate industry as an investment opportunity. As in the real world, different properties have different monetary values. It costs $400 to buy Boardwalk, but only $40 to purchase Mediterranean Avenue. Further, the greater initial purchase price exacts a greater rental return, so that Boardwalk generates a $50 rental, while Mediterranean Avenue generates only $2 rent. Similarly, the construction of housing is more expensive on Boardwalk than on Mediterranean Avenue, although the return for such investment is commensurate with one's greater initial outlays. Did you stop to think that Luxury Tax is nestled over there between Park Place and Boardwalk, while the Jail is located adjacent to the lower rent areas of Vermont, Oriental, and Connecticut and the more modest "working-class" neighborhood of St. Charles, States, and Virginia?

As in reality the railroad usually separates neighborhoods by providing a boundary that impedes "cross-tracks" interaction. The four railroads do not divide properties of similar color. The Pennsylvania Railroad runs next to St. James, Tennessee, and New York, but it does not run between any two of these properties. As in reality, properties of different values are not randomly interspersed about the playing board but are pretty much segregated by a value gradient. While money can be made through the ownership of property, it also takes money to make money. To some degree, chance fluctuation is a determining factor. Thus, while the players of the game can bargain and barter to the maximum of their rational and persuasive abilities, the dice still have to be rolled and the resultant value, hence the course of each player, is still left partially to chance.

All these characteristics result in an empirical model. The game of Monopoly is not a laboratory replica of the empirical world of real estate. The base value of houses and hotels does not change through time as it would in the real world as recessions and depressions decrease the real estate industry and as recoveries, growth, and changes in consumer attitudes inflate the value of property empirically. Similarly, the empirical model does not incorporate changes in land use; e.g., Marvin Gardens never changes from residential property to public service property to accommodate the expansion of the Water Works as the "metropolitan area" grows, creating a need for additional water lines in the hitherto undeveloped or underdeveloped residential areas. Further, no player can "persuade" the local zoning board to grant some sort of exemption so that an essentially very low value property such as Mediterranean Avenue becomes a gold mine because its low-rent residential possibility is discarded in favor of a high-rent industrial or manufacturing function.

The difference between a simulation and an empirical model should be clear. A simulation is a scaled-down replica of some real situation that may function as an entity upon which hypotheses are tested and further relationships and consequences probed without incurring the possibly negative consequences of experimenting on the real thing. While an empirical model functions similarly to a simulation, the empirical model is but a *partial* replication of the reality. Hence, the results of such investigations using empirical models must be viewed with a greater degree of caution than that which is taken when using a simulation. Finally, notice that the terms *simulation* and *empirical model* are the empirical operationalization of the terms *theory* and *conceptual model*, respectively, as presented in Figure 2.1 in the preceding chapter.

SUMMARY

We began this chapter by finishing the transition between the language of conceptualization and the language of hypothesis testing by discussing the mechanism through which the scientific community agrees on the theoretical definitions, operational definitions, and their relationships. We noted the need to equate both languages but recognized that the scientific community has yet to crystallize firm procedures for meeting this challenge. Thus, the bridge, or link, between the two languages of science remains less than firm and is a cause of several difficulties that will concern us in subsequent chapters.

We next focused on those concepts found in the language of hypothesis testing beginning with

the notion of a constant, which was defined as a factor that does not change during the course of one's study. Constants include those items that simply don't change at all—for example the mathematical value of pi ($\pi = 3.14159265$), and those items that are in reality variables but which have been manipulated by the researcher so that they are not allowed to vary in the context of the research design. By way of contrast, a variable is an item that can change either through time or as one moves from case to case. Finally, a value is defined as a specific category or numerical amount that is descriptive of the degree to which some unit of analysis possesses the variable being measured.

While it made theoretical sense to distinguish a concept from a construct, both are treated as variables in the language of hypothesis testing. Quite simply, a variable is a concept or construct whose definition has been translated into characteristics that can be apprehended by the senses. Kish's simple classification of different types of variables was shown to be a conceptually powerful analytical tool. Kish distinguishes two basic categories of variables: those which are explanatory and those which are extraneous. The explanatory variables are those that the researcher treats as the objects of the research. There are two subcategories of explanatory variables: (1) an independent variable, which is responsible for the occurrence of another factor or from whose value predictions are made; and (2) a dependent variable, which is the effect or result of the causal process or one whose value is not known and whose value is to be predicted or intelligently guessed from the information about the independent variable. *All* of the remaining variables are, by definition, extraneous variables, which are *not* the objects of the research, and they fall into one of three subcategories. The class II variables are extraneous variables that have been purposely controlled or held constant through some research design procedure within the context of the research itself. The class III variables are extraneous variables that have not been controlled and are known to be confounding in the sense that these variables do differentially affect the values of one or more of the class I objects of the research. The class IV variables are extraneous variables that have not been controlled and are assumed to be irrelevant in their differential effects upon the class I, explanatory, variables. Finally, one must recognize that Kish's classification is a relatively limited, mutually exclusive but inclusive set of objective categories of some analytical power and usefulness to the researcher, but only so if one begins with some formally stated conceptual proposition. Also, the importance of interaction is noted as some variables overlap in their consequences rather than simply add together to affect situations. Finally, we cautioned the reader that the direction which any conceptual model provides will not be totally accurate and/or all inclusive because it is a *model* and not a *theory*. Thus, the treatment, for example, of the class IV variables as irrelevant *may* be, in the case of some of these variables, an error due to an incomplete conceptualization.

A hypothesis is a statement that can be empirically tested. If one translates the concepts and constructs that have been put together into propositions from the language of conceptualization to the language of hypothesis testing, one will have created hypotheses. McGinnis produced a useful classification of hypotheses based on the number of class II, controlled, variables that are contained in any analytical hypothesis. First, an absolute hypothesis is one which contains *no* class II variables. Second, a finitely conditional hypothesis is one in which *some* of the extraneous variables have been held constant as class II variables. Finally, an infinitely conditional hypothesis is one in which *all* of the extraneous variables have been held constant as class II variables. While a theoretical possibility, the infinitely conditional hypothesis is not an operational possibility at present.

Since one major objective in the test of hypotheses is to amass knowledge about the subject matter, we discussed the nature of proof and verification. Recognizing that information or knowledge may be presented with different levels of certitude, we defined proof as evidence that supports the truthfulness of some fact for all time. If something has been verified, sufficient concrete evidence has been presented to lead us to think seriously that the relationship or thing in question is most likely correct, true, and accurate. However, because of the nature of the scientific method, one can't be sure *beyond* that one moment during which the evidence was collected. We argued that science was such a procedure, that the scientist can only hope to verify hypotheses, and that he will never be able to prove them.

Next, a scientific fact is a verified hypothesis or that which the scientist is willing to accept as correct after repeated verification but that which falls short of proof. Attention was given to the different levels of abstraction or generality that the scientist encounters, and this led to a discussion of the logical processes of deduction and induction. We argued that deduction was the movement from a general statement to a more specific statement, and this was done quite often in the design of one's conceptual model in the beginning stages of one's research project. On the other hand, induction is the logical movement from a specific statement to a more general one, and this is usually done when the research study has been completed and the researcher seeks to summarize the major points that have been found. In both the use of induction and deduction, certain cautions are necessary.

Finally, simulations refer to operationalized total explanations of some phenomenon. While simulations are pretty rare in the social and behavioral sciences, empirical models abound. Empirical models are operational expressions of partial explanations of some phenomenon.

KEY TERMS _____

Absolute hypothesis	Class II variable	Constant
Block variable control	Class III variable	Deduction
Class I variable	Class IV variable	Dependent variable

Empirical model
Explanatory variable
Extraneous variable
Finitely conditional hypothesis
Frequency-distribution control
Hypothesis
Independent variable

Induction
Infinitely conditional hypothesis
Interaction
Matching control
One-category control
Precision control
Proof

Randomization
Scientific fact
Simulation
Statistical-formula control
Value
Variable
Verification

REVIEW QUESTIONS

1. What are science's two types of definitions, and how do they relate to the two languages of science discussed in the preceding chapter?

2. What are Kish's four types of variables? What do *explanatory* and *extraneous* mean in this context? How do the four types of variables relate to one another?

3. What is the difference between an independent and a dependent variable? Clearly illustrate this with an example.

4. Cite one reason why the class IV, assumed-to-be irrelevant, variables may complicate the researcher's attempt to demonstrate precise relationships? [Hint: there is some connection between this question and the idea of a conceptual model discussed in Chapter 2.]

5. What are McGinnis's three types of analytical hypotheses, and how do these types relate to Kish's class II variables?

6. Of the five ways to control class II variables cited in this chapter, which one technique would you argue is the best way? Cite the reasons for your choice.

7. What is the difference between proving and verifying an hypothesis? What does the scientist do and why is this so? How does the scientist's criteria for testing hypotheses impact on scientific knowledge (scientific truth)?

8. What is meant by different levels of generality? How does induction and deduction relate to these different levels? Cite one reason why one should be cautious in logically inferring between levels of generality for both deduction and induction.

9. Define *simulation* and *empirical model*, and create one example of an empirical model that is different from the text.

CHAPTER 4

CAUSATION AND THE PROBABILITY MODEL

INTRODUCTION

In this chapter we present an overview of causation in science and some remarks about the probability model. While a complete discussion of causation and probability is impossible in a beginning text on research methodology, we will present some of the more important issues and reasons they are issues. In so doing, we will add to our list of reasons for maintaining a healthy attitude of skepticism. Let us begin with a reasonably straightforward example. We will be working with the data in Table 4.1 and with a limited number of new concepts: population, sample, simple random sample, parameter, and descriptive statistic. Although we offer a brief definition of these terms, our focus in this chapter is on the notions of causation, probability, and chance.

An Example

Table 4.1 contains the midterm scores of 20 of our students.* You will note a lot of numbers, and as you scan the twenty percentages listed it may be difficult to determine how the class as a whole performed. There is a score in the 90s, several in the 80s, about the same number in the 70s, and so forth, but a review of this nature provides only an imprecise and vague picture. To get a better feeling, we might choose one of a number of mathematical measures that summarize and describe empirical data. Suppose, for example, that we added the percentage scores together and divided

by the total number of scores available. That is, μ (mu) equals the average value of the total

$$\mu = \sum_{i=1}^{N=20} \frac{X_i}{N}$$

population of 20 scores, which is arrived at by taking the sum (Σ) of the individual scores (X_i) and dividing that sum by the total number of population scores (N). Thus,

$$\mu = \frac{X_1 + X_2 + X_3 + \cdots + X_{20}}{N}$$

or, making the numerical substitution

TABLE 4.1 Percentage Scores of 20 Students on a Methodology Midterm

PERSON	SCORE	PERSON	SCORE
1	84	11	69
2	78	12	83
3	62	13	80
4	72	14	89
5	70	15	63
6	90	16	72
7	66	17	76
8	92	18	85
9	70	19	68
10	83	20	80

---

*We have kept the total numbers to be dealt with small in these examples. The focus in this chapter should be on the issues and problems suggested and not on the distractions that might arise from a large data base.

TABLE 4.2 Scores and Mean Values of Four Simple Random Samples of Five Students Who Took a Methodology Midterm

CASE	PERSON	SCORE	CASE	PERSON	SCORE
1	15	63	1	18	85
2	03	62	2	02	78
3	05	70	3	04	72
4	20	80	4	19	68
5	09	70	5	09	70
Sample I mean		69.0	Sample II mean		74.6
1	04	72	1	01	84
2	06	90	2	18	85
3	04	72	3	15	63
4	15	63	4	11	69
5	14	89	5	03	62
Sample III mean		77.2	Sample IV mean		72.6

$$\mu = \frac{84 + 78 + 62 + \cdots + 80}{20}$$

which calculates to

$$\mu = 76.6 \text{ percent}$$

Note a number of points here. First, we chose a summarizing descriptive measure because we had difficulty making sense of the total number of pieces of information at our disposal. Second, we dealt with the *population* scores; that is, we used all of the pieces of information (20 scores) that were available. Finally, the mathematical information that we calculated is the truth about the whole class of students, assuming that we didn't make any computational errors or misgrade anyone's examination. Thus, we have the TRUTH! We *know* that the 76.6 percent is the mean value or the *population parameter* of all the possible cases.

Social and behavioral scientists are rarely able to measure the value of a variable for all of the cases that exist. While the 76.6 percent is the average score of the population of our 20 students, you may argue that you are not interested in just our 20 students. Rather, you would like to know how well all of the undergraduate students in all of the colleges and universities who ever took research methods did. Therefore, let us change our research focus—conceptually.

Suppose there were too many students to measure directly. Suppose that it is important for you to have the mean value of the midterm grade, but you don't have the time or the assistance to determine *everyone's* midterm score. You would be forced into using a *sample*, which is some part of the population. Let us then draw four simple random samples* of five students each. The results are shown in Table 4.2.

---

*A simple random sample assumes an accurate list of elements (where each relevant element is listed once and only once) from which the researcher selects the desired number of elements while adhering to two criteria: (1) equal probability of selection and (2) independence of choice. See Chapter 7 for a more complete discussion of these criteria and their implications for social research.

As we did earlier, we can compute the mean value of the sample scores by using the formula

$$\overline{X} = \sum_{i=1}^{n=5} \frac{x_i}{n}$$

Note that the only difference between these two formulas is that earlier we used the symbol *mu* (μ) to indicate the mean of the population, while the symbol $\overline{X}$ is used to indicate the mean of the sample, *n* is the number of values in the sample, and x_i refers to the *i*th sample case. These are standard statistical distinctions, and, while they may appear trivial, the values obtained for each of the four samples are *different* from the mean value of the population parameter. Thus, while the population parameter was 76.6, the sample statistics were 69.0, 74.6, 77.2, and 72.6. Clearly, it is important for the scientist to distinguish summary statistics computed for the population from those computed from samples. Second, the sample means are not only different from the population parameter but also different from each other. Third, we used the *same* sampling procedure to draw all four samples. Finally, we used the same population data base (that is, set of values) for each of our samples, but we didn't get the same mean values.

Obtaining different values, however, does not mean we did anything wrong. We drew samples because of the practical necessity for saving time and money. Second, we used an appropriate sampling procedure. Yet, the fact that we were forced to use sample statistics as estimates of population parameters raises a number of difficulties for the scientist, some of which we will entertain in this chapter.

CAUSATION

We argued in Chapter 1 that the scientist has borrowed, in part, from the epistemology of determinism. We said the scientist assumes that there are cause and effect relationships. *Causation* is a process or mechanism wherein one factor or set of factors is the determinant of another factor or set of factors. Thus, if X is the cause of Y, then X is thought to be the determinant of Y. As we argued in Chapter 3, the factors doing the causing are the independent variables, while those that result or are being caused are the dependent variables. If X is really the cause of Y, then each time one finds an occurrence of X, it will be followed by the occurrence of Y. This is the logic of causation.

However, the scientist will not settle for the rational mind as the sole source of evidence for truth. The scientist also demands concrete, tangible evidence supportive of one's assertions. This is why propositions must be converted into hypotheses and subsequently tested. But a funny thing happens. There may be hundreds of times when one could demonstrate that Y follows X, but every now and then, one may discover Y and find that X did not precede it. Consider the following situation.

Remember Mr. Jones, who took his car out on the nearest highway and accelerated to 92 miles per hour, failed to make a curve, and headed straight for a brick wall that was close to the highway? The scientist could frame the proposition that crashing into a brick wall at 92 miles per hour would be the cause of our friend's demise. Such would be a causal proposition. Indeed, such a relationship would be so obvious logically that there would seem to be no need to test it. That is, the logical and empirical results are likely to be congruent.

But think about the following. We know from the research of the physical and biological scientists that all matter is made up of subatomic particles. With the aid of an electron microscope, one can see these little pieces with spaces between them. Thus, the car, the wall, and Mr. Jones are composed of billions of little pieces of matter. Suppose that when the car hit the brick wall, none of the pieces that compose Mr. Jones hit any of the pieces of the brick wall or the car. What would happen? Mr. Jones would go through the car and the brick wall to end up sitting, laughing, and, we're sure, much relieved on the other side, while the car would be a crumpled mess on the impact side of the wall. Will this happy result ever occur? Probably not. On the other hand, can the scientist guarantee that your friend will die? No, the scientist can not do that either. It is more accurate to say that there is a very high probability that the driver of the car will die. While such a conclusion cannot be guaranteed, the weight of empirical evidence would lean strongly toward such a conclusion.

Logically causation is deterministic. If one argues that there is a causal relationship between X and Y, then when X occurs, so will Y. On the one hand, if the empirical evidence leads us to say that Y has a high probability of occurring when X occurs, then *we are saying something different.* That is, if hitting the brick wall is a *cause* of death, then death *must* happen. On the other hand, if the empirical evidence points to a few exceptions to the rule, we are on much shakier grounds in proclaiming a causal relationship.

Let us put this another way. If the truth is that X causes Y, how can there be any exceptions to this "causal" relationship? If we mean by cause that one thing is responsible for another thing—and we believe this is the sense in which the word is used—, how can the thing that is responsible for something else happen *without* the something else happening? How can there be any exceptions to a causal relationship if that relationship is truly a causal one?

In sum, we believe the philosophers of science have not yet completely clarified the concept of causation. Maybe it is that the relationships between the formal definition of causation and the criteria, especially the empirical ones, are not congruent. Currently, we make the assumption that there are causal relationships in reality, but we assess these relationships with the probability model that admits that certainty is impossible.

Let us probe further the example of the 20 students and their midterm grades. Again, the truth is that the mean population parameter was 76.6 percent. Yet, the descriptive statistics of the mean of each of the samples drawn and presented in Table 4.2 were other than 76.6 percent each time. Why? Because of *chance*.

CHANCE

The scientist and the statistician would argue that random chance factors were responsible for the

fluctuation in the descriptive values of the various samples. *Chance* is the variation from what is expected to happen or what is due to all the factors that we have not yet discovered and/or been able to measure. L.H.C. Tippett wrote, "Events that follow exact laws can be described or predicted precisely; but we can only specify probabilities that chance events will occur or specify limits within which chance variations will probably lie."[1]

Further, he said, "Statisticians attribute to chance, phenomena (events or variations) that are not exactly determined, or do not follow patterns described by known exact laws, or are not the effects of known causes. That is to say, the domain of chance varies with our state of knowledge—or rather of ignorance."[2]

Tippett is not saying that chance fluctuations do not have causes, but that the scientist does not understand what they are in the present state of the discipline. Therefore, the scientist attributes these variations of unknown origin to chance, sometimes called pure chance or randomness. Again, why should the same sampling procedure from the same population data result in four mean statistics that are different among themselves and the population parameter? Because of chance, or, more frankly, because we do not understand those factors that would lead to the generation of a sample that would be totally representative of the mean population parameter.

PROBABILITY

Let's look at this from another perspective. As we have said, scientists use the probability model. Generally, *probability* is the likelihood that something may happen. More specifically, probability is the proportion of times that something could occur. For example, if we had a completely fair coin and a completely fair tosser of the coin, the *expected occurrence* of a toss in the coin resulting in a heads outcome would be one out of every two tosses. Similarly, the expected occurrence of a tails outcome would be one out of every two tosses. If nothing other than chance fluctuation is operative, we would *expect* to get an equal number of heads and of tails upon repeated tossing of the coin. However, what we expect to get and what we do obtain may not be the same.

The expression of probability occupies a range from zero to one. For example, the probability that each of us will die *some time* is one. Conversely, we can safely say the probability that we will swim from New York City to London, England, is zero. Thus, there are some things that must happen and other things that will never happen. In the realm of empirical events, the majority of events are believed to have probabilities of occurrence that range between zero and one. One can't be entirely accurate because, by definition, there are some random, chance, or unknown causal independent variables that result in the dependent variable's not following a totally predictable path. Finally, the notion of probability and of chance are inexorably related. If the probability of some event is zero or one, it is because chance factors do not operate.

Hence, we are brought back to our original discussion of causation. Remember that causation is the notion that one factor or set of factors is responsible for another factor or set of factors. However, if the posited causal relationship has an empirical probability that is greater than zero and less than one, some *other* unknown chance factor or series of factors must be operating as independent causal forces. As a result, we have a contradiction between the causal model and the probability model. Candidly, this should not surprise us. In Chapter 2 we made a distinction between a theory and a model. While a theory was a complete explanation that satisfied our curiosity, a model was recognized as a partial explanation that left some known questions without answers or answers that were not totally acceptable. If we are using models that have pieces missing, there must be chance factors operating about which we know little.

In sum, the scientist assumes that causal relationships exist. At the same time, the scientist recognizes that knowledge is limited in most instances to a partial understanding, which prevents the scientist from a totally precise prediction of expected outcomes. There is, therefore, a need for

the use of probabilities and the recognition of the function of chance fluctuations.

We shall have more to say about probability and chance when we discuss sampling designs and data analysis, but for now the basic definitions of the concepts of causation, probability, and chance should be clear. In the remainder of this chapter, we discuss some of the logical and empirical strategies for demonstrating cause-and-effect relationships.

SOME CRITERIA FOR DEMONSTRATING CAUSAL RELATIONSHIPS

Introduction

In all analytical situations, one must be aware of the assumptions that underlie legitimate analysis of empirical situations. The legitimate use of some of the criteria for causal relationships that are presented below rests upon conditions that are unrealistic and that are rarely, if ever, experienced in the social and the behavioral sciences. We give attention to them because they illustrate the logic of causation, even though they are more applicable to the subject matter of the physical and biological sciences. It is hoped that this juxtaposition will illustrate why the social and behavioral scientists are, in most cases, less sure about the causal relationships in their investigations.

To begin this discussion, we assume that a certain situation exists empirically—that X causes Y: that is, X and only X is the sole cause of Y and only Y.

Necessary and Sufficient Conditions

If X is the sole and only cause of Y, the criteria of a necessary and sufficient condition are applicable. The characteristics of a necessary and sufficient condition are potential characteristics of the independent variable.

Necessary Condition. A *necessary condition* is a condition that *must happen* if its supposed consequences are to happen. For example, experimentation with drugs is a necessary condition for drug addiction. It is impossible to become a drug addict without putting drugs into one's system. Similarly, registration in a formal program of collegiate instruction is a necessary condition to securing a baccalaureate degree. One cannot be certified as having an undergraduate degree without formally enrolling in a degree program.

Sufficient Condition. A *sufficient condition* is one that, when it happens, *will always result* in its supposed consequence. It is one that will guarantee that the dependent variable will occur. For example, destruction of the optic nerve will always result in blindness. Similarly, unplugging an electric lamp will always result in the lamp's going off.

Discussion. If *X* really is the one and only cause of *Y*, *X* will be both a necessary and a sufficient condition for *Y*. Hence, *X* is a necessary condition because it must happen prior to the emergence of *Y*, and *X* is a sufficient condition because when it does occur, it will guarantee the emergence of *Y*. One can be sure that one variable causes another variable when the independent variable has the property of both a necessary condition and a sufficient condition.

While we can be positive that some independent variable causes some dependent variable if the independent variable meets the criteria of both necessary and sufficient conditions, such circumstances are hard to find. Consider the examples cited earlier. While experimentation with drugs may be a necessary condition for drug addiction, it is not a sufficient one. While we can not imagine how one could become drug dependent without taking drugs, we could very well imagine how a person who experiments with drugs may stop the experimentation prior to the development of drug dependency. Similarly, the act of registering for a course of collegiate instruction, while a necessary condition for a college degree, is not a sufficient one. Registration does not guarantee that one will amass a sufficient number of academic credits to graduate.

Consider the sufficient condition of the destroyed optic nerve resulting in blindness. While this is surely a sufficient condition, it is not a necessary one, since there are any number of other independent variables which could precede blindness. One could have a detached retina or a serious viral disease resulting in blindness. A capillary explosion in the eye or serious injury to that portion of the brain connected with sight could likewise result in blindness, so that when blindness occurs one cannot know that it was for the reason of a destroyed optic nerve. We have a sufficient condition but not a necessary one. Similarly, while pulling the plug on an electric light will be a sufficient condition for the light not to burn, it is not a necessary condition. It is not something that must occur for darkness. After all, the switch on the lamp may not be in the on position or an electrical thunderstorm may have severed the power line.

Let us be clear. When a person's optic nerve is destroyed, that person will become blind. The key is to uncover some situation wherein one independent variable is linked with only one dependent variable. Given such a situation, the criteria of a necessary and sufficient condition will present conclusive evidence of an invariant cause-and-effect relationship. Unfortunately, this situation is rarely characteristic of the subject matter of the social and behavioral sciences. While we can not see how hydrogen chloride (HCl) could be fabricated except by the combination of a hydrogen and a chlorine atom, it is possible to get to New York City by way of a number of different routes. So one's emergence in New York is no guarantee that one travelled the New Jersey Turnpike. In sum, while the logic behind the notion of a necessary and sufficient condition of the independent variable is sound, the empirical situation in the social and behavioral sciences does not cooperate.

Mill's Canons of Evidence for Causality

John Stuart Mill presented four canons of evidence for the demonstration of a causal relationship.

TABLE 4.3   Hypothetical Characteristics of Five Automobiles, All with Good Gas Mileage or Fuel Economy

CASE/ CHARAC- TERISTIC	MAKE OF AUTO	COLOR	SIZE OF ENGINE	AGE OF AUTO	PASSENGER CAPACITY	OVER- DRIVE	WEIGHT (IN POUNDS)	ODOMETER READING	TYPE OF TIRES	GOOD GAS MILEAGE
1	Ford	Red	200 cc	5 yrs.	8	Yes	2,000	94,523	Goodyear	Yes
2	Buick	Blue	230 cc	2 yrs.	6	Yes	3,000	36,121	Goodrich	Yes
3	Dodge	Green	450 cc	1 yr.	5	Yes	2,200	15,097	Michelin	Yes
4	Mazda	White	376 cc	7 yrs.	4	Yes	1,800	152,123	Atlas	Yes
5	Saab	Brown	298 cc	4 yrs.	2	Yes	1,700	125,978	Sears	Yes

Method of Agreement.   The first canon is the *method of agreement* and can be presented either positively or negatively. The *positive canon of agreement* states that if two or more cases of a phenomenon have only one factor in common, there is a causal relationship between the factor and the phenomenon.[3] If after doing an inventory of several instances of some situation, one finds that all the cases of the situation possess only a single factor in common, then one would argue a cause-and-effect relationship between the factor and the phenomenon. For example, consider five automobiles all of which get good gas mileage. The data for this illustration are presented in Table 4.3. Let us assume that the ten characteristics listed in Table 4.3 exhaust all the possible characteristics of automobiles.*

Note that there are five automobiles and that each was made by a different manufacturer, each is a different color, each has a different engine size, each is a different age, each accommodates different numbers of passengers, each weighs a different amount, each was driven a different number of miles, and each was equipped with a different make of tires. Indeed, all five automobiles were different in every way except for sharing the capacity of overdrive and for receiving a good rating when tested for gas mileage. That is, these five cases possessed in common one factor—overdrive capability—and one phenomenon—good gas

mileage. On the basis of Mill's positive canon of agreement, we would conclude that overdrive capability and the good gas mileage were causally related. Thus, if, after a complete inventory of all the factors comprising two or more situations, these situations evidence only two factors in common, then the two factors are causally related.

The *negative canon of agreement* states that if two or more cases of the absence of some phenomenon are accompanied by the absence of only one factor, there is a cause-and-effect relationship between the factor and the phenomenon.[4] From the data presented in Table 4.3, we could argue that if the five automobiles had in common the absence of overdrive capability and the lack of good gas mileage, Mill's negative canon would suggest a causal relationship between good gas mileage and overdrive capability.

In short, if X is the cause of Y, one would expect that every time X happens, so will Y. Indeed, the positive canon states that if every appearance of Y is accompanied by the appearance of X and if all the other characteristics of the cases are variable, there is a causal relationship. Given that X and Y are causally related, the negative canon states that in each and every case where Y is missing, X also has to be missing. While the negative canon seems to be the logical obverse of the positive, the negative canon of agreement is not very practical without the positive canon. That is,

---

*Assume that the information given in Table 4.3 is accurate, reasonable, and exhaustive of the situation.

it is the positive canon that will isolate the single factor and its phenomenon for the researcher's attention. The negative canon asks the researcher to look at a number of cases where something is missing for some factor that is also missing. This is the proverbial search in the haystack for the missing needle, only in this case one doesn't know if there is a needle to be found.

Does this mean the negative canon of agreement, while a logical possibility, is an empirical waste of time? Well, yes and no. We would argue that the negative canon is virtually useless by itself. The negative canon is useful, however, *after* one has used the positive canon. For example, if the use of the positive canon resulted in the emergence of the relationship between the overdrive capability and the good gas mileage, *then* one could use this information to cross-check the results of the positive canon by using the negative canon. That is, one could purposely select several cases of automobiles without overdrive and posit that they would also not have good gas mileage. Confirmation of this hypothesis would lend additional support to the results obtained from the positive canon.

Limitations with the Method of Agreement. There are several disadvantages to the use of Mill's first canon. First, in the social and the behavioral sciences it is virtually impossible to find two or more cases of any phenomenon that have only a single factor in common. Let us return to Table 4.3. While we constructed the data to illustrate the use of the positive canon of agreement, think of the more typical situation. It is more likely that a number of different makes of automobiles will be produced with many more than two characteristics in common. For example, is it not the case that the larger automobiles are likely to have the same types of tires, reasonably equivalent engines, the same type of transmission, and fairly equivalent weights? Therefore, in any situation characterized by three or more commonalities, it is impossible to pinpoint the nature of the causal relationship solely through the use of either the positive or the negative canon of agreement.

A second problem is that even if only one factor and one phenomenon could be identified in common in a number of cases, one couldn't be *sure* that they were in a causal relationship. Remember we assumed that *X* really did cause *Y*, but as we shall see later in this chapter, the truth may be that both *X* and *Y* are caused by a third factor, *A*. (See Figure 4.1.) Even if one meets all the conditions of the positive or negative canons, conclusions of causality will be correct *if and only if* the model of *X*'s causing *Y* is appropriate.

A third problem is that this canon is not appropriate if the phenomenon under investigation is caused by more than one independent variable. Thus, if the dependent variable is influenced by several independent variables, then the method of agreement canon will not work.

A fourth difficulty is that the canon can not distinguish between the independent and dependent variables. Thus, while the method of agreement provides some evidence for a causal relationship, it does not indicate which variable is the cause and which is the effect.

A final difficulty has to do with the condition for the proper use of the method of agreement, that is that one must be able to separate the causal factor and the phenomenon from other factors. Realize that sometimes two or more categories of different variables are linked so that they can not be separated. For example, a professional football player is likely to be male, have attended a college

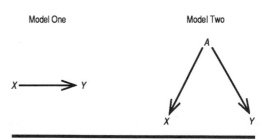

FIGURE 4.1   Two Causal Models: Model One with One Independent Variable and One Dependent Variable and Model Two with One Independent and Two Dependent Variables

or university, and be between 21 and 40 years of age. Thus, sex, level of education, and age are linked together so that it is impossible to separate these three factors.

Method of Difference. The second canon of evidence for causality presented by Mill is called the *method of difference*, which states that given only two cases, if one case contains a factor and a phenomenon while the other case does not contain either the factor or the phenomenon and if both cases have all other factors in common, then there is a causal relationship between the factor and the phenomenon.[5] Returning to our example, think about two almost identical automobiles. Both cars are Buicks, painted blue, have 230 cubic centimeter engines, are two years old, and seat six people. Further, they both weigh 3,000 pounds, have been driven an equal amount of miles, and are on their second set of Goodrich steel-belted radial tires. On all dimensions that characterize an automobile, these two cars are identical in every way except for one factor and one phenomenon. That is, one car has overdrive and gets good gas mileage, while the other doesn't have overdrive and fails to achieve good gas mileage. This situation is appropriate for the use of Mill's method of difference canon of evidence for causality. We have two cases that are identical with the exception that in one case there is a factor (overdrive) and a phenomenon (good gas mileage), while in the other case there is an absence of this factor (no overdrive) and an absence of the phenomenon (poor gas mileage). In such a case, using Mill's method of difference, we could conclude that there is a causal relationship between the factor and the phenomenon.*

Limitations with the Method of Difference. Most of the difficulties encountered with the method of agreement are also characteristic of the method of difference. First, the method of difference is not appropriate if the real situation is characterized as a multiple-factor causal one. For example, while overdrive would be a contributing factor to good gas mileage, so would be adequate tire pressure, a properly tuned engine, proper driving procedures on the part of the car's operator, road conditions influenced by weather, and the nature of the terrain. Thus, it is not so much that overdrive isn't a factor but that some of these factors may be of greater consequence to good gas mileage. That is, while overdrive may result in a 2 percent gas saving, a properly tuned engine may result in a 10 percent gas saving. (This may be more a function of an inadequate conceptual model or the selection of class I variables of lesser importance, than it is a problem with the method of difference per se.)

Second, as with the method of agreement, the method of difference does not differentiate between the independent and dependent variables. As with the first canon, however, this difficulty is easily rectified by using other criteria to be mentioned later in this chapter.

Third, as with the method of agreement, one often has difficulty separating causal factors. For example, for people in the Northern Hemisphere, the Christmas holiday is accompanied by the coldest weather of the year. Similarly, the Christmas season is accompanied by the hottest weather experienced by those living in the Southern Hemisphere. If we focus on those living in the United States, with the exception of those who reside in the Sun Belt, it may be that seasonal shopping in December increases because of the Christmas holiday, or it may increase because of the cold weather—in that cold weather may serve to restrict people to their homes, causing cabin fever, which could result in the desire to get out. Since cold weather generally precludes swimming, picnicking by the lake, watching Little League baseball, and other favorite summertime diversions, one turns to shopping as a means of escaping the house. We are not saying cold weather is respon-

---

*As we shall see in Chapter 11, this canon of evidence for causality is the logical foundation for the causal interpretation in an experimental research design.

sible for Christmas shopping, but we are suggesting such a conclusion is reasonable using the method of difference.

The fourth difficulty with the method of difference is that while the logic of it is sound, it is difficult to discover empirically any two cases of some phenomenon that differ in only one factor. As you will learn in Chapter 11, many experimental research designs are attempts to structure the data-gathering mechanism to be able to use the interpretative power of Mill's canon of the method of difference.

Finally, there is the *post hoc, ergo propter hoc* fallacy. Literally translated from the Latin, this means "after this, therefore because of this."[6] The *post hoc fallacy*, as it is identified in its shortened form, is the idea that because a phenomenon occurs after some other factor, it does not provide sufficient evidence to conclude that a cause and effect relationship exists. Again, think about the simple causal model, where X is the independent variable responsible for the dependent variable Y. If this is the truth, Y must happen after the occurrence of X. While this is the case, we must recognize that if Y comes after X, then Y could be caused by X, but it doesn't have to be caused by X. Y could have been caused by any number of other factors such as A, B, C, or D, which all occurred, along with X, prior to the emergence of Y. This problem is, after all, one of the reasons we presented the criteria of a necessary and sufficient condition earlier. Any independent variable has to happen prior to its consequence, but it must also meet the necessary and sufficient condition criteria.

We have presented two of Mill's four canons. We need to reinforce, at this point, that the methods of agreement and difference can only work when the empirical situation is a simple one; that is, when one factor (X) *is* the *only* cause of one phenomenon (Y). If X is the sole cause of Y, then we could offer conclusive evidence of a causal relationship, assuming we could meet the other stipulations of these two canons and if we could demonstrate a necessary and sufficient condition for X. However, in the social and the behavioral sciences, many dependent variables are not be-

lieved to be caused by a single factor. Therefore, we need a canon of evidence that recognizes multiple factor causation. Mill's third canon permits such, and it is to this one we now turn.

Method of Residues.   The *method of residues* states that if all the factors causing some phenomenon are known, if the total impact of all these factors is known, and if the combined contributions of all but one of the factors to the total is known, then one can figure out the contribution of the remaining unknown factor from the total impact.[7]

For example, consider an inept driver who parked an automobile partially on the sidewalk adjacent to one of San Francisco's hilly streets. Our objective is to discover the amount of the car's weight that is supported by the left rear tire. We could determine this by using Mill's method of residues if we knew several pieces of information. First, we have to know how many causal factors there are in the phenomenon. In this case we know that the total weight of the car is supported by four tires. Second, we have to know the total impact of all these causal factors. In this case, we know that the automobile weighs about 3,200 pounds. Third, we have to know each causal factor's contribution to the total impact except for one factor. Thus, let us presume that we know that the left front tire supports 700 pounds, the right front tire supports 500 pounds, and right rear tire supports 900 pounds. That is, these three tires are responsible for supporting 2,100 pounds of the car. Given all this information, the method of residues suggests that we can determine the remaining amount of weight that the last tire supports. In this case, the left rear tire must support 1,100 pounds.

$$\begin{matrix} \text{Total} \\ \text{consequence} \end{matrix} = \begin{matrix} \text{combined effect of} \\ \text{all but one factor} \end{matrix} + \begin{matrix} \text{the remaining} \\ \text{unknown factor} \end{matrix}$$

Thus,

3,200 lb. = 2,100 lb. + weight on the left rear tire

or

Left rear tire = 3,200 lb. − 2,100 lb. = 1,100 lb.

Limitations with the Method of Residues. With the methods of agreement and difference, as with the necessary and sufficient conditions criteria, we assumed a very simple causal model of one independent variable and one dependent variable. With the method of residues, however, we are assuming a quite different causal model that presupposes more than one independent variable. Further, it assumes that the researcher has discovered *all* the causal factors. That is, in fact, the problem. While the social and behavioral scientist has progressed in the study of most substantive areas beyond the simple one independent-factor and one dependent-factor type of statement, the point of an almost total understanding of the subject matter has not been reached. That is, the legitimate use of the method of residues presumes a greater degree of knowledge about causal relationships than has been achieved. For example, while we recognize more than one causal factor responsible for, say, juvenile delinquency, the writers doubt that the criminologist would claim to have discovered them all. Even if we have uncovered all the causal factors, we have not been able to measure adequately the individual contributions to delinquent behavior that we have identified.

In short, current knowledge clearly indicates that the method of difference and the method of agreement require a too naive causal model to be of major use in the social and the behavioral sciences. On the other hand, the method of residues presumes more knowledge than is currently possible. Therefore, it too is not of major significance in its impact. In truth, our knowledge of substantive situations lies somewhat beyond the naive and primitive gropings of a fledging science and somewhat short of a theoretical science. Consequently, the social and behavioral scientist needs a canon that presumes a moderate level of substantive sophistication, which is reflected in Mill's final canon of evidence for causality to which we now turn.

Method of Concomitant Variation. The final canon of evidence presented by Mill is the *method of concomitant variation*, which states that if a change in a factor in two or more cases is accompanied by a change in a different factor, then the two factors are in a causal relationship.[8] Thus, if a particular variable changes and a second variable also changes, one has some evidence of a causal relationship. Actually, the preceding sentence is true and false.

Let us assume that in reality *X* really is the only cause of *Y*. If it is true that *X* is solely responsible for *Y*, it must also be true that some change in the value of *X* must result in some change in the value of *Y*. If *X* and *Y* are causally related, they *have to be* correlated or associated with one another as well. To have causation is to have association.

Measuring Association with Pearson's r. To better understand that which follows, as well as several sections to come, we need to take a short look at one associational, descriptive statistic. Karl Pearson is responsible for originating an associational, descriptive statistic that has been formally labeled Pearson's product-moment correlation, or *Pearson's r*. This measure is useful because of its superior interpretative power as compared to many other measures of association. The following is not a thorough presentation but contains some of the interpretive aspects of Pearson's *r* so that the reader will more clearly understand the examples. As in most cases, for a more thorough discussion we direct your attention to Hubert Blalock.[9]

Pearson's *r* is an associational measure that will accommodate two variables. One can put any number of values of the two variables into the formula and calculate the degree of statistical association between them. For example, if you knew the height and weight of 100 persons, you could measure the association between height and weight by following the specifications in the formula. Barring any type of mechanical error, Pearson's *r* has an interesting mathematical property. The value of the association between two variables measured by Pearson's *r* cannot be larger than +1.0 or smaller than −1.0. That is, the calculated values must fall within the numerical range of −1.0 to 0.0 to +1.0.

This theoretical, numerical range has a number of interesting properties. First, if the value of the correlation is close to 1, there is a strong correlation. If the value is close to 0, there is a weak association. Second, if the sign is positive (+), the association is a positive one; i.e., an increase in the value of one variable will be accompanied by an increase in the value of the other variable. If, however, the sign is negative (–), the association is negative, whereby an increase in one variable will be accompanied by a decrease in the other variable. For example, given a correlation value of $r_{xy} = +0.982$, we could argue that the association between X and Y is very strong (since 0.982 is close to 1.000) and positive (that is, an increase in X is accompanied by an increase in Y). Similarly, given the correlation of $r_{ab} = -0.821$, we would argue a strong negative association between A and B.

Note that the interpretation of the sign (i.e., the direction) of the correlation value and the magnitude or strength of the correlation value are independent interpretations with one exception. The exception is when one secures a weak correlation, e.g., –0.101 or +0.121. Because the magnitudes of both values are so small, which virtually indicate there isn't any association between the two variables, it makes little sense to interpret the sign or direction of the correlation. Quite simply, the magnitude of the association in both cases is too small to argue any meaningful interpretation of the sign of either correlation value.

Conversely, a correlation value between X and Y of 0.982 or between A and B of –0.821 are strong correlations because of their large magnitudes. Thus, the sign (i.e., direction) of the statistic does not reflect the strength (i.e., the numerical value) of the association. Both of the above values are strong because they are close to unity.

A final point is that because the magnitude of the correlation between X and Y ($r_{xy} = 0.982$) is larger than the correlation between A and B ($r_{ab} =$ –0.821), one can say the association between X and Y is stronger than that between A and B. While both associations are strong, the one between X and Y can be interpreted as stronger because the magnitude is greater.*

Limitations with the Method of Concomitant Variation. A significant question to pose is whether an association between two variables indicates a causal relationship. The answer is that one can't be sure. To find a correlation between two variables does not constitute sufficient evidence to conclude conclusively that the relationship is causal. It *is* possible empirically to obtain a strong association between two variables and not have a causal relationship. For example, many years ago we noted a tongue-in-cheek piece in the journal literature that focused on just this issue. In this piece the author said that he had, while spending the summer in a small Texas town, taken daily measurements of the degree to which the tar in the main street had melted from the heat of the noonday sun. Using the Pearson product-moment correlation technique, he had correlated the degree of melting tar and the polio rate in the continental United States, securing a perfect correlation of 1.0. Using a companion statistic, he proceeded to make a number of predictions on Y, the polio rate, on the basis of the known value of X, the amount of melting tar. Thus, for a mean value of, say, 0.76 inches of melting tar for the month of July, he predicted that the continental polio rate for the United States would be, say, 552. When the Public Health Service reported some months later the polio rate for July, it was 552! He had been able to predict the polio rate from the information on the amount of melting tar in the small Texas town.

Now you would laugh if we tried to argue that melting tar *caused* the polio rate. This is absurd, and that was one of the points communicated in this hypothetical article. Although he was able to *predict* the polio rate from the value of the melting

---

*How much greater the association is cannot be determined through the information given here, although such a determination is possible. We encourage you to consult your textbook on statistics and figure that one out yourself. We do not really need that information here.

tar because of the strong association, we repeat our earlier argument that predictive knowledge is not the same as explanatory knowledge. A correlation does not prove (or even verify) that the associated variables are in a causal relationship.

So where does this leave us? If one starts with a causal relationship between two variables, a measure of association must logically indicate a correlation. In this case, the correlation could be interpreted accurately to mean a causal relationship. But if one first obtains a correlation without knowing there is a causal relationship (which is generally the case in an empirical study), the correlation can only be interpreted as *a* piece of evidence but not as *the* definitive evidence for causality.

A second difficulty with the method of concomitant variation is a problem that it shares with the methods of agreement and difference. Of the two variables that have been correlated, it is impossible to determine from the canon which variable is independent and which is dependent.

Summary of Mill's Canons.   All four of Mill's canons of evidence for causality work *if one meets the conditions that Mill requires.* Meeting these conditions, however, is the problem. The method of agreement assumes that when all the factors in several situations are inventoried, they will all end up being different except for one factor and one phenomenon. While the logic of the interpretation is sound, social and behavioral scientists rarely find an empirical reality to fit this circumstance. The method of difference assumes that when all the factors in the situation are inventoried, they will all turn out the same except for the presence of one factor and one phenomenon in one case and the absence of that factor and that phenomenon in the other case. Again, the logic is beautiful, but

reality does not cooperate. The method of residues presents a different problem. Here, its proper use depends upon the identification of all the independent variables that result in some situation. In this case the empirical reality is not contrary to the logical prerequisite, but *our knowledge* is inadequate to use this canon accurately. Thus, we must reject or postpone our use of these three canons.

However, the social and behavioral scientist can employ the method of concomitant variation, which is the one most frequently used. While we assume the existence of *causal* relationships in the empirical world, we most often test for these relationships with a *correlational* model. Because our subject matter makes the use of the other canons of evidence for causality largely inappropriate, we must use the one that provides the *least* rigorous evidence.*

Correlational Magnitude and Correlational Consistency.   Recognizing that the method of concomitant variation is the least capable of Mill's four canons in securing proof of a causal relationship, this problem can be mitigated through consideration of two additional criteria. The first is the *correlational magnitude.* All associational statistics give some measure of the strength of the association measured. Therefore, if X is the only cause of Y, one should expect a strong correlation between the value of X and the value of Y. Assuming no measurement error (see Chapter 6), one would expect to obtain an associational value that is the strongest possible. Therefore, given two correlations, one weak and one strong, one is on safer ground in interpreting the stronger correlation rather than the weaker one as a causal relationship. We emphasize "safer" ground; not necessarily "safe" ground! Remember our earlier discussion of the difference between correlation

---

*The method of difference, which buttresses the notion of an experimental research design, has a logical underpinning contrary to this claim. While we have some misgivings about the applicability of experimental research designs in the social and behavioral sciences, the existence of experimental designs and their legitimation through the method of difference is noted at this point. Essentially, the student of human mental behavior is stuck with the method of concomitant variation; if not all the time, then at least most of the time.

or association and causation? Even the strongest associational value is not a guarantee that a causal relationship exists.

The second supportive criterion is that of *correlational consistency*, which is the achievement of the same result upon repeated measures of the same variables under a variety of conditions. For example, assume we found a correlation between *X* and *Y* when we studied teenagers. We repeated the same study and found a correlation between *X* and *Y* for senior citizens and for middle-aged persons and for young adults. Further, if this association held up for samples of Americans, French, and Germans and if it held up for rural residents and urban residents, then we have greater reason to believe that we have uncovered a causal relationship.

Time-Priority Considerations

We have addressed two general categories of criteria that may be invoked in support of a causal relationship in an analytical proposition: (1) necessary and sufficient conditions and (2) Mill's four canons of evidence. With the exception of the method of residues, the canons presented by Mill share a common difficulty in that they are unable to differentiate between independent and dependent variables. This deficiency is not critical because there are procedures that can be used to rectify this problem. They are: (a) a logical or commonsense determination; (b) an observational determination; and (c) a cross-lagging procedure.[10]

Logic.   If one has amassed enough evidence using the method of concomitant variation to make a causal interpretation between two variables, logic can sometimes be used to separate the independent and dependent variables. By logic, we mean in this context a commonsense determination. The researcher can decide on the basis of logic, after considering what each variable entails, that one of the two variables must occur before the other. For example, if one had empirical evidence for a causal relationship between the mathematical skills of addition and multiplication, how would one decide which skill was the independent variable and which was the dependent variable? Logic or common sense suggests that addition precedes multiplication because the process of addition is not as complex as that of multiplication. Similarly, we would argue that the mathematical knowledge of algebra would precede knowledge of calculus.

Sometimes, then, it is possible to think about the relationship and then argue on the basis of one's common sense that one variable just has to come before another and, thereby, identify the independent and dependent factors.

Observation.   Logic or common sense does not always work. For example, given that the attainment of formal education is strongly associated with one's occupational prestige, which variable should be considered independent and which dependent? One can make a strong logical argument that attainment of formal education equips the individual with skills that are valuable to the business community and therefore leads to securing an important job. Thus, education should be the independent variable and occupation should be the dependent variable. However, we could offer an equally logical argument that when one has an important job, the conscientious employee will seek to upgrade these skills by acquiring additional formal education. In this case, occupation would be the independent variable and education would be the dependent variable.

When two logical explanations render one unable to suggest which is correct, one may be able to use observation. Here, *observation* means the use of one's sense experience to make an *empirical* determination of the time sequence. If the researcher observes that people go to school before they begin a career, then, on the basis of observation, one would conclude that education is the independent variable and occupation is the dependent variable. If, on the other hand, one observed that people work a few years and then go back to school for training, one would conclude that occupation was the independent variable and education was the dependent variable.

In sum, if logic or common sense fail to give a satisfactory determination of the independent and dependent variables, then perhaps some empirical sequence can be observed.

Cross-Lagging. What if neither technique provides a satisfactory answer? What if the researcher has found a persistent association between two variables and the use of logic has resulted in two equally reasonable explanations, and upon switching to the observational criterion, the researcher finds that neither variable is amenable to empirical observation? In this case, the cross-lagging technique is used.[11] *Cross-lagging* involves the computation of two associational statistics between two variables measured at two different times but on the same sample of cases.

For example, after repeated tests of the positive association between a student's grade point average (GPA) and intelligence quotient (IQ) on male students, female students, students in sex-segregated schools and in coed educational institutions, students in private institutions as well as public institutions, students in institutions on the West Coast and in institutions on the East Coast, and students in large as well as small educational institutions, one comes to offer a causal proposition. The magnitudes were always substantial, if not overpowering, and the association was consistently positive. Now, which variable causes which? Does IQ cause GPA? Or does GPA cause IQ?

Using the criterion of logic or common sense, we would argue that two equally reasonable explanations are possible. First, IQ is a measure of basic intellectual skills and the ability to manipulate symbolic information. Thus, high ability to perform analytical tasks should cause one to achieve a higher GPA. However, there's another logical possibility. Have you ever wondered why your high school counselor advised you to take the SAT examination in your junior year in high school and again in your senior year? If you experienced a measurable improvement in your SAT score, it was probably because you became more test-wise. The SAT examination is, after all, a different type of test than one is usually asked to

take. Repeated submissions are likely to result in higher scores because the student learns how to better budget time and to proceed through an atypical testing situation. It is unlikely that your analytical abilities increased much over a one-year period or that one year of additional study resulted in sufficient additional knowledge to make a substantial difference in your score. Therefore, we could argue that increased GPA causes high IQ, because an increased GPA indicates the ability to perform well in testing situations and an IQ test is, after all, a test!

We now have two equally plausible common-sense or logical notions of the causal relationship between IQ and GPA. As we have noted, when the logical procedure fails to produce a clear choice, one may be able to invoke an observational time sequence to determine which variable seems to happen first. While one can determine when GPA "happens"—that is, when your school's academic office computes it at the conclusion of each academic term—, one cannot observe IQ in the empirical world. In short, neither the logical nor the observational criterion is applicable to this particular problem. Hence, the researcher is forced into the cross-lagging technique.

To implement the cross-lagging procedure, the researcher must do a longitudinal study using the same sample of persons. By a *longitudinal study* we mean two or more measurements of the same variables taken at different times. Let us draw a sample of 100 first-year students and measure the two variables of IQ and GPA at the end of the first collegiate academic year. We will remeasure the same variables for the same sample of people at the end of their senior year. We now compute two Pearson product-moment correlations using these two sets of data. First, we correlate GPA for the *first* year with IQ for the *senior* year. If we had been using the method of concomitant variation, we would have assessed GPA and IQ, but we would have used values of these variables that were both drawn at the same moment in time. In the cross-lagging procedure, one crosses over time periods by correlating one variable measured at time one with the other variable measured at time two. This forms the basis for one correlation value. Then, one correlates the remaining variable at time one with the remaining variable at time two. This forms the basis for the second correlation value. (See Figure 4.2.)

One then compares the correlation values obtained and selects the stronger correlation of the two. In our example, let us assume that correlation II was the greater. The researcher then determines which of the two variables *occurred first* in time. In this case, it would be IQ, since IQ was measured at the end of the first year while GPA was measured at the end of the fourth year. The variable that was measured first in time in the stronger correlation is said to be the independent variable. In this hypothetical situation we would conclude that IQ is the independent variable that caused the dependent GPA.

Conclusion.   When a researcher has evidence for a causal relationship but is unable to determine which variable is the cause and which is the effect, one may use the time-priority considerations of logical determination, observational determination, or cross-lagging procedure. The first two mechanisms are the easier to do. The logical procedure assumes one can recognize the independent and dependent variables through rational thought. If the logical assessment fails to produce a clear causal pattern, one can search for an empirical pattern that can be observed in the natural world.

Neither of these first two procedures requires the execution of an additional research design. If the logical and empirical procedures fail to produce satisfactory results, one must embark on the cross-lagging procedure. This last procedure does necessitate securing more data and the use of a longitudinal design with the same sample of people. As we shall discuss later, longitudinal studies that require maintaining the same sample are not easy to do since the researcher is often plagued by *sample mortality,* or the fact that some of the sample cases, for a variety of reasons, drop out or disappear from the study. In sum, the time-priority considerations present the researcher with an important set of tools for distinguishing an independent variable from a dependent variable.

The Conceptual Model

In Chapter 2, we argued that a theory was a total explanation of some phenomenon in that a theory provides answers to all the questions we are knowledgeable enough to ask and that the answers provided are satisfactory to the scientist. Given this definition, we concluded that social science currently does not have theories.

However, we do have *conceptual models* that answer some of the questions we know to ask. Further, as the substantive knowledge from conceptual models accumulates, we come closer to

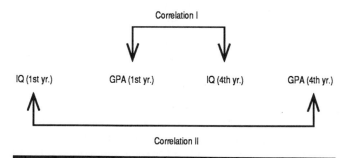

FIGURE 4.2   Illustration of the Data Base for a Determination of the Independent Variable and the Dependent Variable Using the Cross-Lagging Procedure

the development of theories by adding to the knowledge base.

When one begins a piece of research, it is profitable to begin with a conceptual model. This is essentially an interpretative network of concepts and constructs worked out into propositional form and formulated after completion of the review of relevant literature. These propositions will be transformed from the language of conceptualization into hypotheses and be tested. The hypotheses may be analytical wherein the relationship between the variables will be measured with a correlational or associational statistic and the results logically interpreted with the method of concomitant variation. Since this method does not permit identification of the independent and dependent variables, the researcher will need to cite some other criteria, such as the time priority considerations, in making this assessment.

Interestingly, the conceptual model can serve as an addendum to the time-priority considerations. That is, the model suggested by the established scientific literature may offer information germane to the identification of the independent and dependent variables. While the conceptual model is not likely to be a complete explanation of the phenomenon of interest, it may be of help in assessing causality. The social scientist must always be somewhat skeptical about the results of research. Therefore, we argue for amassing as much support as one can in reaching conclusions. If the method of concomitant variation and the time-priority consideration of observation can be reinforced by a conceptual model that argues a causal relationship, so much the better.

The Modes of Elaboration

Introduction. This final section is devoted to a discussion of the pioneering work of Patricia Kendall and Paul Lazarsfeld, who initiated an analytical strategy called the *modes of elaboration*.[12] Further, the work of Morris Rosenberg in *The Logic of Survey Analysis*[13] is equally insightful and is an extension of the basic analytical strategy developed by Kendall and Lazarsfeld.[*]

Test Factor. Prior to discussing the modes of elaboration, the notion of a test factor must be introduced. A test factor is similar to a controlled variable. From our discussion of Kish's categories of variables, you will recall that class I variables are the objects of the research. Further, while class II variables are not the objects of the research, they have been manipulated so their effects upon the class I variables have been either eliminated or relegated to a constant effect. As such, a class II variable is controlled. Now, while a test factor is a controlled variable, not all controlled variables are test factors. For a variable to be a *test factor*, the researcher must hold this variable constant and couple this control with one of the analytical strategies identified as the modes of elaboration. Thus, while some equate test factors with controlled variables, we do not. We reserve the concept of a test factor, then, for those controlled variables that are part of a research strategy developed by Kendall and Lazarsfeld and later expanded by Rosenberg.

With this distinction in mind and some understanding of Pearson's r, let us begin our discussion of the modes of elaboration. Kendall and Lazarsfeld identified three modes of elaboration—interpretation, explanation, and specification. All three *usually* assume that one has some correlation between two variables. It is often a correlation that we did not expect or one which is in the opposite direction than predicted. Indeed, we usually begin to think about the modes of elaboration because something appears to be wrong or unusual about the correlational value obtained between two class I variables. It is through the

---

[*]For those students interested in a more in-depth examination of the empirical demonstration of causality and, more generally, in examples of superior research in the social sciences, we recommend additional reading of the basic notions contributed by these three social scientists.

introduction of a third variable as a test factor that one hopes to understand more clearly the nature of the association between the two class I variables.

Parenthetically, Figures 4.3, 4.4, and 4.5, which are used to illustrate points about the modes of elaboration, contain symbols such as t_1 and t_2. These symbols represent comparatively the points in time when the designated variables occur. For example, a t_1 variable would occur before a t_2 variable. Again, these designations place the variables in a time sequence.

Mode of Elaboration of Interpretation.   The first mode of elaboration is that of *interpretation*. In this mode one selects (as a test factor) a third variable that, in the time sequence, occurs between the supposed independent variable and supposed dependent variable. The test factor, then, is an intervening variable in the mode of elaboration of interpretation. Further, the test factor must be a variable that is correlated with both the supposed independent and dependent original class I variables. See Figure 4.3.

For example, suppose we measured a sample of college students for degree of success while in college. We will operationally define success in college as one's grade point average at the end of the sophomore year. Further, suppose that we measured type of high school attended by dichotomizing this variable between public and private schooling. If we correlated the two variables of

success in college and type of high school attended, what would we expect to find? A logical conceptual model would hold that those students from good preparatory backgrounds will do better in college than those from poorer preparatory backgrounds. Since private schools are usually smaller in size, able to select which students they will enroll, have smaller classroom sizes that provide more individualized time, and are able to recruit from among the wealthier families, and, thus, have some of the best technological and mechanical aids supportive of a superior educational environment, one would expect those students who attended private high schools to achieve a greater measure of success in college than those who attended public high schools.

Our conceptual model argues, then, that students from private secondary schools will have a higher GPA in undergraduate school than public high school students. The formal hypothesis is: Quality of high school attended varies positively with collegiate success. Since high school attendance occurs prior to entrance into college, quality of high school is perceived as the independent variable and success in college as the dependent variable. Using Mill's strategy of concomitant variation, assume we found a fairly strong negative correlation value of -0.721 between these two variables, representing the opposite of that which our conceptual model suggested. That is, public high school graduates seem to perform better academically than private high school graduates in their first two years of undergraduate study. This would be a clear opportunity for the use of some sort of mode of elaboration. There must be an additional factor or series of factors responsible for this seeming contradiction.

Using the mode of elaboration of interpretation, we can pick a third variable, control on it, and redo the correlation between the two original variables. If the new correlation value drops significantly upon controlling on the test factor, we would argue that the test factor is important and must be included in interpreting the relationship between the original two class I variables. On the other hand, if the correlation value stays about the

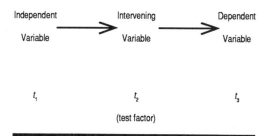

FIGURE 4.3   Time Sequence* for the Mode of Elaboration of Interpretation

*The designations (t_1, t_2, and t_3) refer to different time periods as this figure shows the sequence of these variables in time.

same after controlling on the test factor, one would argue that the test factor is a class IV, irrelevant, variable.

Suppose we pick the intervening variable of academic achievement in high school. It may be that most colleges and universities do recognize the superior quality of a private high school education over that of public school systems and, therefore, require applicants from public high schools to have substantially higher high school grade point averages to be accepted into their collegiate program. With this possibility in mind, let us redo the correlation between type of high school attended and success in college—while holding constant the test factor of high school achievement by testing only those students with high school grade point averages between 3.0 and 3.5. We now find the correlation between type of high school attended and success in college has dropped to –0.123. Does this result mean the conceptual model is wrong? Well, yes and no. It is true that private high school students generally do better in college than those from public high schools, but not for the reasons cited earlier. In fact, college admissions personnel know this and have introduced an intervening variable that accounts for the seeming contradiction. By accepting only those public high school students with superior academic achievement in high school, they deflect the logical relationship suggested in our first conceptual model. However, empirically, because of the intervening variable, there appears to be a strong negative correlation between quality of high school attended and success in one's collegiate program.

To summarize, the mode of elaboration of interpretation offers an intervening variable as a test factor, which helps make sense of the relationship between the originally independent and dependent variables.

Mode of Elaboration of Explanation. The second mode of elaboration is that of *explanation*. Here, the research strategy is similar to that of interpretation with two exceptions. First, the test factor is an antecedent variable, which occurs prior

to both the supposed independent and dependent variables. Second, the analytical strategy is different. Here, we are trying to determine if the original correlation is a true or spurious relationship. If one finds a *spurious correlation*, it will be because the antecedent test factor is really the cause of both the supposed independent and dependent variables. But if the relationship is a true one, the test factor will be shown to have little or no effect upon the original two variables. (See Figure 4.4.)

In every other way, the mode of elaboration of interpretation and explanation are the same. They both involve selecting a third variable that is to be controlled and turned into a test factor. In both modes, the correlation between the original two variables is redone, holding the test factor constant. Moreover, a substantial change in the original correlation value is taken as evidence of the appropriateness of the test factor in the analysis.

For example, let us return to the "study" of the degree of melting tar in the small Texas town and the polio rate for the continental United States. Suppose that the Pearson *r* correlation between the melting tar and the polio rate was +0.729. While this value indicates a strong, positive association in the data, what sense does it make? In what conceivable way can the tar in one small area in Texas be a causal factor of or be caused by the polio rate in the continental United States? We have obtained an empirical result that does not appear to make any logical or theoretical sense. Probing further the nature of this association

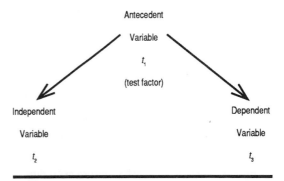

FIGURE 4.4 Time Sequence of the Mode of Elaboration of Explanation

through the mode of elaboration of explanation, we select degree of heat as an antecedent test factor. This variable comes prior to the melting of the tar and prior to the increase in the polio rate. Further, it is correlated with both the polio rate and the degree of melting tar.

If by holding the test factor constant and recalculating the correlation between the melting tar and polio rate the correlation value weakens significantly, we would conclude that the original result of +0.729 was spurious. That is, the reason for the original result of +0.729 was the correlation of the degree of heat, which was the real independent variable, with both the degree of melting tar and the change in the polio rate being dependent variables. The heat caused the tar to melt and heat caused the polio virus to be more virulent leading to an increase in the incidence of poliomyelitis.

The mode of elaboration of explanation, then, involves selecting a third variable that is antecedent to both of the correlated class I variables and that is correlated to each of them and treating this third variable as a test factor.* In the mode of elaboration of *both* interpretation and explanation, a reduction in the correlation value presents evidence supportive of the causal relationships suggested respectively in Figures 4.2 and 4.3. However, if the correlation values remain about the same, then one has evidence that the supposed original causal analysis is further strengthened. The researcher profits in either case. In the first case, the researcher uncovers a relevant causal factor. In the case of interpretation, one discovers a causal chain. In the case of explanation, one discovers a new independent variable and two dependent variables. However, if the second correlation value remains about the same as the first, one has uncovered a true class IV, irrelevant, variable. Information emerges no matter how the computations turn out.

Mode of Elaboration of Specification.   The final mode of elaboration is that of *specification*. In this mode, we are looking to specify or to indicate those conditions under which the original correlation will be strengthened or weakened.

In the modes of interpretation and explanation, the strategy was to see if the original correlation could be weakened in order to substitute a different causal model. In the mode of specification, one assumes the original correlation is an indicator of a causal relationship. Here specification functions to indicate the situations under which one may expect the original relationship to get stronger, somewhat weaker, or stay the same. Put another way, when using the analytical strategy of interpretation or explanation, the researcher selects but one category or attribute of the test factor to investigate. However, in the mode of elaboration of specification, at least two categories or attributes of the test factor must be employed. Here the strategy is to see how the original correlation is affected under two or more different categories of the test factor.

Let us take an example relevant to the contemporary social movement of gender equality between degree of formal education and the acceptance of job equality for women. Our study will deal with the nature of education on people's attitudes about employed women. Suppose that we have a sample of 200 people with half having graduated from high school and half from college during the past year. Thus, we operationally define education into high school and college graduates. Assume also that we have some way of measuring each person's degree of acceptance of job equality, resulting in relevant quantitative values. After correlating degree of education with degree of acceptance, assume that a value of +0.456 emerged. Such a value would be consistent with previous research that suggests that higher degrees of education were associated with greater

---

*The reader should be aware that this *supposed* newly discovered causal relationship *may* be in need of further elaboration. Thus, any *definitive* causal interpretation is not warranted.

degrees of liberalness. Thus, the correlation value of +0.456 tells us that there is a positive association between education and acceptance but, oddly, the correlation value is not particularly strong. Our conceptual model would argue, among other things, that greater education leads to a mental acuity better able to analyze complex situations. One would expect those with greater degrees of education to see more readily that discrimination against women in the employment arena on the basis of their sex is wasteful to society and as such does not permit a whole category of people from making the most out of the talents that they possess. But we are puzzled with our data. We did register a positive association between degree of education and degree of acceptance, but the strength of the correlation is not what we expected. Therefore, we might decide to use the mode of elaboration of specification.

Is there some other variable operating here to influence the relationship between education and degree of acceptance? Suppose we look at the sex of the respondent and divide the sample between the males and females. While education would still appear to affect positively a person's attitude toward equality, we would expect the effect on female respondents to be greater than the effect on the male respondents. In all likelihood, the female respondents were exposed to a traditional socialization of gender roles. That is, they were probably socialized to at least partially subscribe to an expressive set of roles. Such might include the anticipation of marriage and occupancy of a supportive role to a more instrumental husband. However, when exposed to a more liberal and expanded education, they may accurately perceive a wider range of life and career opportunities that could be beneficial to their self-interest. Conversely, our male respondents, with their increasing education, recognize the rationality of an increased scope of roles for women but see greater competition for career opportunities from an expanded pool of skilled persons. Despite this potential threat to their own self-interest and ability to achieve, we would expect—at least from an ideological per-

spective—a positive correlation between education and acceptance for both males and females. We would, however, expect a stronger correlation for females than for males.

After separating the males and females into their respective categories and recalculating the correlation between education and acceptance for each sex, we could well find that the correlation value for our males was +0.392 and the correlation value for the female respondents was +0.801. If we had obtained these results, we would have derived empirical evidence supportive of the strategy of the mode of elaboration of specification. We would have specified the conditions—male and female—on which the original value of +0.456 was strengthened (+0.801 for females) and weakened (+0.392 for males).

Clearly, we have taken a rather simple situation and coupled it, for the purposes of illustration, with a simple conceptual model. While our example has a specificational test factor that has only two possible subcategories, male and female, we could have selected one with many more. If we had chosen religion, for example, we could have specified at least three major categories—Catholic, Protestant, and Jewish. Or, if we had chosen social class, we could have selected out at least six categories—upper upper, lower upper, upper middle, lower middle, upper lower, and lower lower.

Second, it should be recognized that if we had chosen a specificational test factor with more categories, we could have gotten a more complicated and varied set of correlation values across each category involved. When comparing the correlation value under each specificational condition, we could have gotten an increase, no change, and a decrease. Or, multiple increases and one decrease. Or, one increase and multiple decreases.

Third, one specificational category may have a comparatively greater or lesser change from the combined figure when compared to the other. For example, X and Y may show a +0.678 correlation value, while category A may have a value between X and Y of +0.600 and category B a value between

X and *Y* of +0.868. In such a case, one subcategory goes down very little, while the other goes up considerably from a comparative point of view. This discrepancy may be due more to the difference in the number of cases that composed category *A* when compared to category *B* than to the substantive influence of the test factor. Caution is warranted in the analysis since such conditions may lead to erroneous conclusions.

Finally, one may use or identify more than one specificational test factor. For example, in the above situation we could have not only separated out the males from the females on the specificational variable of sex but also separated out those who are employed and those who are not employed on the dimension of employment status. The only restrictions imposed on such a strategy are the limitations of sample size. If the researcher ends up with too few cases in any of the subcategories, the credibility of the data may be threatened.

Concluding Comments on the Modes of Elaboration. First, the researcher is the one who must decide whether to pursue any of the various modes of elaboration strategies. How does one make that decision? Generally one would consider an elaboration model when the preliminary results of the data analysis indicate values that appear peculiar. Parenthetically, one should realize that there *are* almost always deviant cases in the social sciences and/or that one's conceptual model may be in error. Thus, one's results, while they may be different, are not necessarily in error if the results appear to be peculiar or are contradictory to the model. In the long run, however, if your results run contrary to the established body of literature, it may be because your situation is more complex or convoluted in some fashion. The modes of elaboration could be useful in sifting and sorting out this confusion.

Second, once the decision to use the modes of elaboration strategy is made, one must decide which variables to treat as test factors and in which elaboration strategy. The conceptual model will provide some assistance in response to these ques-

tions. As in many situations, it is the relevant literature coupled with the researcher's general knowledge and intellectual imagination that are the major sources of potentially relevant test factors.

Third, note that the elaboration strategy may be a multiple-step process. Suppose that an empirical situation was as described in Figure 4.5. Further, suppose that we began a research study by finding a fairly strong correlation between *Z* and *Y*. Several additional studies subsequently supported the correlation between *Z* and *Y*. Thus, we concluded that *Z*, which occurred at time (t_4), was the independent variable and *Y*, which occurred at time (t_5), was the dependent variable. Nevertheless, we were troubled because the relationship between *Z* and *Y* did not seem to be logical. Indeed, the relationship seems to be similar to the melting tar and the polio rate discussed earlier. As a result, we decided to pursue our research with the mode of elaboration of explanation by selecting *A* as an antecedent test factor under the presupposition

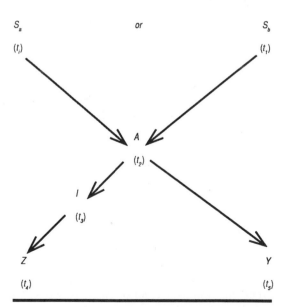

FIGURE 4.5 Hypothetical Relationship Among a Number of Variables for the Purpose of Illustrating Different Notions Relevant to the Modes of Elaboration

that the relationship between Z and Y was a spurious relationship. After controlling on A and recalculating the correlation between Z and Y, we noticed a significant decrease in the value of the association, concluding that the original correlation between Z and Y was spurious and that the new causal model should be the independent variable A that caused both dependent variables Z and Y. However, while the causal decision between A and Y seemed logically and empirically sound, the relationship between A and Z seemed much like that between superior college achievement and public high school attendance, as discussed earlier. We decided to further investigate by using the mode of elaboration of interpretation. We selected I as an intervening variable at time (t_3) between the independent variable A at time (t_2) and the dependent variable Z at time (t_4). Holding the intervening test factor constant, the new correlation value between A and Z decreased, suggesting that test factor I did function to interpret the relationship between A and Z. Finally, we investigated the specificational variable of S and found that for one category of S (S_b), the correlation between A and Y increased. However, for the other subcategory of S (S_a), A caused I which in turn caused Z. We conclude that social relationships are often complex, as we have indicated in Figure 4.5.

Finally, there is no guarantee the researcher will discover what is true. One may stumble into something that is pragmatic in the sense that it works—such as the tar in the Texas town and the polio rate in the continental United States. Such is the correlation between Z and Y in Figure 4.5; it works predictively but it is spurious, not causal. Similarly, the correlation between A and Z, while true, needed the mode of elaboration of interpretation to make sense of it. Our point is that one's first research effort is not guaranteed to generate a complete conceptual model as schematically presented in Figure 4.5. Rather, a model of this complexity may not emerge until several studies have been conducted. Remember that we could have selected one or more test factors that, when tested, resulted in no reduction of the original correlation value, indicating that the potential test factors were, in truth, class IV, irrelevant, variables. Thus, the elaboration mechanism can and may have to be a multistep, on-going research strategy as the researcher goes about the hard work of more fully understanding the nature of complex relationships.

SUMMARY

Chapter 4 functions essentially to present a critical discussion of the general notion and criteria for the demonstration of a causal relationship. We began with a simple example through which we illustrated some of the properties of and one of the reasons for the necessity of the probability model. We discussed the seeming contradiction between the idea of the probability model and the idea of causation—a contradiction that may be explained satisfactorily if one introduces the concept of chance. Thus, causation is the idea that one factor or set of factors is responsible for the emergence of another factor or set of factors. Because of probable inadequacies in the conceptual model and the methodological procedures, we are willing to settle for a probabilistic interpretation of causation retaining the concept of chance to account for the remaining unrecognized causal factors (or those that are disregarded, as in the case of a nomothetic explanation). After this overview of causation, chance, and probability, we moved to some specific criteria on which causal relationships could be argued. First, we presented the notion of necessary and sufficient conditions. If reality were such that only one independent variable is the sole cause of only one dependent variable, these criteria would hold, both of which identify properties of the *independent* variable. A necessary condition is something that must happen for the dependent variable to occur. And a sufficient condition is such that it will always be followed by the dependent variable. We concluded that while these criteria for causality were impeccable, they assume an empirical relationship that rarely characterizes social science data, i.e., that one variable is the single cause of another variable.

Mill's canons of evidence for causality provide four criteria for establishing causality: (1) method of agreement; (2) method of difference; (3) method of residues; and (4) method of concomitant variation. Both the method of agreement and the method of difference assume the simple causal circumstances of one independent variable and one dependent variable, which is not a realistic assumption for the social sciences. While the method of residues is a multivariate technique, it assumes more information about causal situations than the social scientist is prepared currently to deliver. Thus, we are left with the method of concomitant variation, which suggests that if a change in one or more factors is accompanied by a change in one or more other factors, the two sets of factors are in a causal relationship. In truth, one should say that because of the conceptual differences between the idea of causation, on the one hand, and association or correlation, on the other hand, the method of concomitant variation presents *a* piece of evidence for causality. That is, while Mill's three other canons give one conclusive evidence, the method of concomitant variation does not. In defense of the concomitant variation canon, one may say that it can be applied to a wide range of empirical situations. The essence of the argument is to understand that a causal relationship *must show* an association or correlation, but an associational relationship *does not guarantee* a causal one. For this and for other reasons presented in this chapter, the social scientist finds the method of concomitant variation more suited to relevant research needs than the other three canons.

Given a preference for the method of concomitant variation, the social scientist is encouraged toward a causal interpretation of essentially associational measures if the correlations obtained have strong magnitudes and if they are consistently attained when calculated under a variety of testing conditions.

Since one of the major difficulties with the method of concomitant variation is its inability to distinguish the independent variable or variables from the dependent variable or variables, we moved to various time-priority notions through which this problem could be solved. Three techniques were offered: (1) logic; (2) observation; and (3) cross-lagging. A logical determination of the appropriate sequence involved the use of the researcher's reasoning capacity or common-sense powers. An observational determination suggests that the researcher can actually "see" the time sequence occurring in the empirical world. Finally, cross-lagging could be used where observation could not be done and when common sense suggested two equally plausible time sequences. Cross-lagging involves an empirical, correlational determination over time on the same sample of cases, wherein one could interpret which variable or variables occurred first by actually measuring the degree of association under differing assumptions.

Next, we argued briefly that while scientists recognize their conceptual models are not theories, nor are these conceptual models without merit. Thus, one's conceptual model may suggest support for a cause-and-effect relationship and suggest which variables are independent and dependent.

We concluded with an introduction to the modes of elaboration. We defined a test factor as a controlled variable *and* as a variable that had been selected intentionally because a mode of elaboration strategy was being pursued. The mode of elaboration strategies involve selecting some number of variables other than the class I variables and treating these extraneous variables as class II, controlled, or held constant, test factors.

First, the mode of elaboration of interpretation involves holding constant a third variable that is intervening in time between the supposed independent and the supposed dependent class I explanatory variables. If the strength of the association between the original class I variables is substantially reduced upon controlling for the intervening variable, one would argue the independent variable worked through the intervening variable on its way to influencing the dependent variable. If not, the intervening variable is really a class IV variable.

Second, the mode of elaboration of explanation involves holding constant a third variable that is antecedent to the supposed independent variable and dependent variable. If the recomputed association between the originally supposed class I variables is significantly reduced, one would argue that the antecedent test factor should be considered as the independent variable and that both of the originally correlated class I variables should be considered as dependent variables. Further, the original correlation is usually referred to as a spurious correlation. However, (as in the mode of elaboration of interpretation) if the recomputed association remains about the same, the test factor should be considered as a class IV, irrelevant, variable.

Finally, we discussed the mode of elaboration of specification. In specification, we anticipate changes in the original association so that for some subcategories of the test factor the association would be decreased while for others the association would be increased. It is not just a reduction in the association that is anticipated, but a fluctuation in the associational value as one ranges over various subcategories of the test factor.

Lastly, we noted that the use of one or more of the modes of elaboration would be more characteristic of a maturing science in the pursuit of more complex, causal models. We urged the reader to again examine the relevance of the conceptual model, as it is this model to which one turns in search of possible test factors.

KEY TERMS

Causation
Chance
Conceptual model
Correlational consistency
Correlational magnitude
Cross-lagging
Explanation
Interpretation
Longitudinal study
Method of agreement

Method of concomitant variation
Method of difference
Method of residues
Modes of elaboration
Negative canon of agreement
Necessary condition
Pearson's r
Population
Population parameter

Positive canon of agreement
Post hoc fallacy
Probability
Sample
Sample mortality
Specification
Spurious correlation
Sufficient condition
Test factor

REVIEW QUESTIONS

1. Define causation, chance, and probability, and discuss the relationships among these three ideas.

2. How is a theory related to causation, and how are probability and chance related to an empirical model?

3. If it is true that one factor (X) and only this one factor causes one other factor (Y) and only that factor, which criteria for the demonstration of this causal relationship would apply here?

4. Of Mill's four canons of evidence for the demonstration of causality, which one does the social scientist usually use? Cite any one reason why this canon is the one of choice.

5. Discuss how correlational magnitude and consistency function to strengthen a causal interpretation between two factors.

6. Under what conditions must one use the cross-lagging procedure to determine which factor is independent and which is dependent?

7. How is one's conceptual model relevant to Kendall and Lazarsfeld's modes of elaboration?

8. What are the similarities and differences among the modes of elaboration of interpretation, explanation, and specification?

9. How does a test factor differ from a class II, controlled, variable?

CHAPTER 5

THE CONCEPTUAL MODEL

INTRODUCTION

We have made considerable mention of the conceptual model in earlier chapters. Within this chapter we focus upon the specific nature of this important component of science and relate it to our previous discussions.

Your authors have discovered, through the teaching of research methodology to sociology, psychology, and health-science students for two decades, that dividing the scientific method into two separate, but related, components is appropriate. We have labeled these dimensions the conceptual model and research design, respectively.

The subsections, or dimensions, that make up these components do not differ significantly from those most students have learned in high school or college science courses as the scientific method. The organization that they provide, however, will enable you to more easily grasp the tasks that confront the researcher.

You will remember from our earlier discussion that a conceptual model is a working paradigm in which there may be acceptable answers to some of the relevant questions about our phenomenon. Within the conceptual model we attempt to generate a cluster of concepts and/or constructs and their relationships that will permit us to examine a subject of interest. We do not expect this cluster of concepts and/or constructs to be complete, but we will, if we have done a thorough job, have confidence, after working through the model, that those selected are relevant. The determination of whether they are relevant will be made by testing the ideas from collected data.

We have elected to use the term *conceptual model* to encompass the first four components of the research effort: (1) the research topic; (2) the relevant literature to the topic area; (3) the presentation of the proposition or propositions to be investigated; and (4) the identification of the independent and dependent factors and the clarification of any ambiguous terms present in the proposition or propositions with theoretical definitions. None of these considerations require any usage of quantitative procedures. Indeed, each of these components will only require a manipulation and understanding of concepts and/or constructs. Therein is the reasoning behind the label, the conceptual model.

The discussion for the remainder of this chapter will focus on these four areas. We will examine the meaning and purpose of each, how the researcher approaches the tasks of each, and how the conceptual model will lead to an empirical examination of the proposed explanation of the problem of interest. We conclude with a discussion of two issues: (1) significant generalization versus radical empiricism and (2) statistical versus substantive significance.

THE RESEARCH TOPIC

We noted in our discussion of science that the researcher, in formulating a problem to investigate, asks two types of questions: (1) problematics that are an outgrowth of one's natural curiosity to know and to understand, and (2) problems that are perceived as difficulties one is motivated to attempt to eliminate. All research, then, of whatever kind, is set in motion by the existence of a situation defined by someone as either a problematic or a problem.

Generally, the researcher interested in the first situation is involved in doing *basic research*. That is, the interest in the area proposed for investigation is motivated by just that—pure interest. Students of problems of the second order are involved in doing *applied research*. The results of such studies can be immediately applied to an area of concern for the society or some part thereof. The conclusions reached, for example, may have immediate impact through the implementation, cancellation, or alteration of some social policy.

DIFFICULTIES IN SELECTING A RESEARCH TOPIC

So Many Topics

The selection of a problematic or problem area to investigate is often seen as the most difficult step a researcher must take. This is particularly true in the social sciences where the potential questions to be asked are so numerous.

An Original Topic

A second difficulty rests upon the desire by many students to formulate a problem and study an area that has not been examined previously. This is a concern that is particularly, but not exclusively, difficult for researchers with little or no experience at formulating a research project. While the interest in exploring virgin areas is a goal worthy of admiration, it virtually insures frustration, especially for the student being initiated into the procedures of research. Without more research experience, the student is likely to have difficulty in arriving at a manageable segment of the problem area to investigate.

The desire to formulate such a project is often based upon the false notion that all research that is judged worthy must be unique and original. Many students have heard of the importance of original research from their professors in the physical, chemical, and biological sciences. These academic disciplines deal with data and measuring instru-

ments that are much more precise than those of the social sciences. While there is a lesser need for replication than is true in the behavioral and social sciences, it makes a valuable contribution to all sciences. In the social and behavioral disciplines, the presence of change is so constant that replication is necessary. Such a situation reinforces our commitment to maintain a healthy attitude of skepticism by insisting upon this critical orientation that requires us to test and test again.

Too Big a Topic

A third major difficulty in the selection of a topic for investigation is the selection of one that is too large to manage effectively. Although this is a difficulty also faced by experienced researchers, it is exaggerated for the beginning student, who often wants to investigate and recommend a solution for an entire social pathology in the first research venture. Alcoholism, drug abuse, adolescent parenthood, or juvenile delinquency are illustrative of social problem areas for which such grandiose proposals and solutions have been offered.

It is not likely that anyone, regardless of the size of available staff or budget, could successfully examine such a large or ill-defined area. It should be clear, however, that what we do undertake as a research effort will be influenced by whether: (1) we are working alone or have a research staff at our disposal; (2) we are paying for our research effort, or we are the beneficiary of a research grant or contract; and (3) we are under any time constraints to bring the project to closure.

In short, there is nothing inherently good or bad with large or small efforts, or those which are new or replicative efforts.

An Example of Topic Selection

Let us illustrate the selection of a problem by focusing on the notion of social status. Historically, social analysts have endeavored to examine social stratification on the basis of a general status hierarchy. That is, individuals have been perceived as being occupants of a general status rank equal to, above, or below that of other persons. This has usually been stated as occupying the upper, middle, working, or lower classes, or some derivative of this theme. However, many scholars who are critical of this orientation, particularly with regard to urbanized-industrialized societies, have suggested that individuals are ranked simultaneously on a variety of status hierarchies.

This shift of attention by many students, from the unidimensional to multidimensional analysis, has followed the lead work of Gerhard Lenski.[1] In so doing, the majority of such researchers have concerned themselves with the implications of stress for status-inconsistent individuals. The most frequent dependent variable examined, i.e., the consequence of status inconsistency, is that of political behavior or preference. Again, to refer to the pioneering efforts of Lenski, it has been suggested that persons who are not characterized by consistent status patterns in their status ranks (e.g., education, occupation, income, racial-ethnic status, sex, age, and so forth) tend to support a politics of change.[2] Thus, political parties or programs that advocate change of the current system, whatever it may be, are more likely to find favorable endorsements among status-inconsistent individuals than from those persons more consistent in their status profiles. Such favorable attitudes are seen as being derived from the rationale that change will contribute to a reduction in disparity being experienced by the individual. Such disparity, ambiguity, or marginality of an inconsistency in terms of role definition may well generate a feeling of stress or social discomfort. The potential elimination of such stress or discomfort, then, might stimulate the endorsement of opposite positions.

It should be noted that although liberal orientations are traditionally associated with a politics of change, and therefore with political responses of status-inconsistent individuals, Rightist political positions are also variously associated with programs of change. Therefore, the basic notion presented here is that status inconsistency leads to stress, which in turn gives rise to favorable attitudes toward policies of change to the political Right or Left.

What we have done in this example is to take our interest in the concept of social status and reduce the potential myriad of dimensions to a manageable level. The urbanized-industrialized culture of the United States is so complex that the potential number of strata is quite large. To gain a firm grasp of these virtually unlimited potentialities would be extremely difficult, if not impossible. However, by examining the general overall profiles as evidenced by a few status characteristics, e.g., occupation, education, income, race, and ethnicity, of our sample, we maximize the opportunity to answer some of the relevant questions about the phenomenon of status. Further, we are interested in the implications of status occupancy. Again, the potential for investigation is virtually limitless. However, almost every aspect of our lives is in some way influenced by the political order. By selecting the dimension of political preference we increase the number of answers we might obtain, or inferences we might make, and do so from a limited perspective that can be managed.

In sum, the first section of the conceptual model involves not only the selection of a topic area but also its reduction to a manageable and practical level.

REVIEW OF THE LITERATURE

You will remember that the review of the literature in any research project functions, *in part*, to sensitize the reader to those concepts and constructs that have already been recognized as important and to the relationships among these factors for which there is some support from previous research. We emphasize the qualification *in part*. If the topic is unique or of a contemporary nature, there may be little, if any, literature of an empirical nature to review. If that is the case, the researcher will have to be imaginative in terms of what literature may be applicable and one may have to rely more heavily upon the nonprofessional publications that are relevant to the topic area.

As the available literature is reviewed, one must keep in mind that a conceptual position is being constructed from which to launch the research project. The references included in this review should encompass both theoretically oriented writings and research reports of data presentations.

While a variety of conceptual models may be available through the review of the literature, the task is not to inventory this variety but to summarize the relevant literature selected. One might find that such items as reference-group theory, conflict theory, and socialization theory could apply to the project. However, a more specific subcomponent of the wider theoretical orientation could better suit the investigator's purpose. For example, if socialization theory has been selected as the principal perspective, one may wish to concentrate on the subtheme of symbolic interaction. In addition to noting that which has been suggested by previous researchers, the investigator should approach this review with a critical perspective. That is, note should be taken of any methodological assumptions which were made, or any gaps seen in the work being referenced. For example, was the sample that was studied selected from the listings in a telephone directory? If it was, the sample is, by definition, biased toward the more affluent. Is the sample in question from a local area as opposed to a national one? If so, regional and local bias have been built into the study. If a study is reported as a part of the literature review, without criticism, readers will assume the writer is in total agreement and does not question the methodology, interpretation of results, or any other aspects of the research.

The section on the review of the literature will provide a rationale for the concepts and/or constructs included in the propositions to be investigated and their particular status (i.e., independent, dependent, or controlled). The publications included in the review should deal with the concepts and constructs, the relationship between these concepts and constructs, or some aspects or attributes of the dimensions suggested by these concepts and constructs.

In reviewing the literature the investigator should also examine the results of other studies for consistency. One will want to evaluate the consistency of other studies in terms of congruence of results, research design, and methods of research.

The researcher will want to assess the validity of the studies reviewed, i.e., the degree to which the conclusions can be inferred to a larger population segment or to the population as a whole. While we will discuss the distinction between logical and mathematical or statistical inference at a later point, the reader will learn to gain a feel for studies that have been well designed and well executed.

In sum, what the review of the literature section should contain is a grounding for the study in some type of conceptual model that will justify the proposition or propositions and facilitate interpretation of the data that are ultimately collected.

HOW TO BEGIN THE LITERATURE SEARCH

First Considerations

Students often initiate their literature review by going to the card catalog of the college or university library. They have an idea of the factors they wish to study, and they search for book titles that suggest that other researchers have previously combined these particular variables in the same manner they desire. Generally, such a venture to the library terminates in frustration. However, sometimes valuable reference material is attained, particularly if the student is looking for work by a specific writer or if the variables in question are separated in terms of their attributes and one then looks for material accordingly.

We recommend that the review of the literature begin with an examination of the appropriate abstracts. A list of excellent review sources would include the *Historical Abstracts*, the *Guide to Periodical Literature*, and the *Social Sciences and Humanities Index*. Those with which we most strongly encourage our students to begin are the *Sociological Abstracts*, *Psychological Abstracts*, and/or the *Dissertation Abstracts.** In the case of the sociological and psychological abstracts, several issues per year are published. The current year's issues will usually be found in loose form in the reference room. Issues from previous years will be bound in annual volumes. The *Dissertation Abstracts* are published annually in two volumes. The volume in which we are most likely to be interested includes abstracts for those doctoral dissertations accepted in the social and behavioral sciences and in the humanities. The remaining volume will carry abstracts of dissertations done in such fields as mathematics, chemistry, physics, and biology.

The abstracts provide a table of contents of subject areas covered in that particular edition, listed according to numbers, from which the researcher can then select those applicable to the general topic area. The abstracts represent a summary of the works that have been completed and are usually a paragraph or two in length. Those studies that appear promising can, then, be examined directly in the referenced original source.

The *Dissertation Abstracts* are approximately 350 words. The greater length is important because the dissertations themselves are not usually directly available. The exception are those that are published in book form or were completed at your own university.

If it is decided that a particular dissertation is needed, a copy may be obtained in two ways.** One may borrow it from the university where it was written through the Interlibrary Loan System. Your college or university library is a member of this system, and you can order such through its offices. The order will generally be sent to the university that conferred the doctorate degree upon the author of the dissertation. A copy of the dissertation will then be sent to your library, and you will be notified of its arrival. You should be cautioned that this process can take up to several weeks. If you are under any type of deadline pres-

sure, you are advised to make the decision to borrow any dissertation you are interested in early in the time frame budgeted for your project.

The second way to obtain a copy of the dissertation is to purchase it. This can be done by ordering a copy from University Microfilms, housed at the University of Michigan in Ann Arbor, Michigan. A paper bound copy of the dissertation will be sent directly to you. The major concern with this approach for most students is the price. They are expensive.

Other sources one may be interested in, but which are absent from your home library, can be attained via the Interlibrary Loan System. Further, you should not feel limited to the resources available in one facility. If you live in or close to a major metropolitan area, there are any number of libraries that are available to you. In all probability there are other colleges and universities in your area that usually grant privileges to students from neighboring schools. Some may not permit removal of the resource material, but they will allow use on the premises as a visitor. If you need some resource material and the library personnel will not permit its removal, you can always order it through the Interlibrary Loan System. In other words, there is always a way of obtaining needed material. An excuse that will not be accepted is that the library did not have such and such. The serious student is expected to be more resourceful and committed to scholarship than to limit a search for materials to one library.

How Much Is Enough?

A legitimate question students often ask is, how far back into the abstracts or other reviewer sources should one go? There is no single answer. The most common response is to review that which is appropriate, although we recognize that does not equip you with the answer you would like. We remind you that the purpose of the review of the

---

*For a more complete listing and description of review sources available, see Pauline Bart and Linda Frankel, *The Student Sociologist's Handbook*, Fourth Edition, (New York, New York: Random House, 1986.)

**A third choice, which is available only to those students fortunate enough to be attending a college or university in or around the Washington, D.C., area, is the Library of Congress. Every dissertation is put on microfiche and stored in the nation's library.

literature is to provide a rationale for the concepts and constructs you ultimately include in your proposition or propositions. The articles and studies reviewed should deal with these factors and the relationships between them. Remember the task is not to inventory everything ever written. Indeed, this would be virtually impossible in some problem areas, e.g., juvenile delinquency, where the studies and theoretical publications are voluminous.

Obviously a partial answer to the question revolves around other questions. For example, what is the purpose of the study? Is it basic or applied in nature? If applied, who is it for? Is it possible that major policy decisions will be made on the basis of your results? Studies being done under the auspices of large grants and those with far-reaching consequences may dictate a more in depth examination than small budget, local exploration, or descriptive efforts allow.

In general, the guideline we offer is to continue to review the literature until you are consistently reading the same results. This does not mean that you are encountering accounts of the same study, but that whoever did the research and wherever they did it are finding much the same thing that others have found elsewhere, or that the discrepancies in the reported results are being consistently presented by the researchers whose work you have consulted.

What If Little Relevant Literature Is Found?

Some topic areas present the opposite difficulty—an absence of studies in the area or what studies that have been done are few in number and/or there is very little in the way of conceptual models available. The enigma confronting the researcher in this situation is not a matter of reducing an enormous volume of references to a manageable level but rather of providing a theoretical rationale for the constellation of concepts and constructs considered for study.

There are at least two directions we can recommend, the preferred approach being a combination of the two. On the one hand, there may be a collection of sparse but well-organized scientific and scholarly literature. On the other hand, the literature may be more popular and more journalistic in nature. Perhaps we could illustrate this difficulty and an approach to addressing it by using the early stages of the contemporary women's movement as an example. While we recognize this is a huge subject with untold complex issues, let us assume a unidimensional approach in the sense that little empirical research had been done on any aspect of it in the early stages.

The absence of solid research data and analysis, however, did not reduce the intensity of interest that was clearly manifest by the population in general or by the lay media in response to that interest. This, then, represents one source of literature to review in order to facilitate selection of a manageable segment of the topic area and to arrive at a constellation of variables we believe are relevant to that segment.

One might, for example, on a daily or weekly basis, survey relevant articles printed in newspapers or news magazines, or items presented by the news departments of radio and television. This procedure is called content analysis, and although it is a principal method of historians, it has also served social and behavioral scientists well in the past.* It should be noted that the *Reader's Guide to Periodical Literature* would be particularly helpful to the student for a survey of this nature.

In addition to the more traditional press, special-interest publications often evolve. With regard to the women's liberation movement, the publication of *Ms* magazine filled a major void, along with the changing nature of articles carried by *Ladies Home Journal, Woman's Day*, and the like.

Currently, those interested in the women's liberation movement can gain access to an up-to-date bibliography by obtaining the periodical *Women's Liberation: A PM Bibliography*. How-

---

*An in-depth discussion of content analysis is presented in Chapter 12, "Content Analysis and Secondary Analysis."

ever, earlier students of this subject did not have this source available.

Beyond the lay press or a special purpose bibliography that may or may not be available, the student of a topic area with limited literature available may have to interpolate from other literature sources although such may be only indirectly relevant or suggestive. In our exploration of the women's movement, we might argue that women have traditionally constituted a minority group within the American culture. We are aware that the census of 1940 was the last to report a numerical superiority of males, but in sociological terms females have remained a minority in terms of political power. Consequently, we might investigate available literature on other minority segments of the population (e.g., the civil rights movement by African Americans) and suggest that much of the same phenomenon may be occurring in terms of the women's movement.

In summary, it is emphasized that the review-of-the literature phase of the research project is one of critical importance. It provides the conceptual foundation from which to launch the empirical analysis on the chosen topic. The recognition of this critical import underlines the necessity of the interplay between the qualitative and quantitative aspects of the scientific method—that is, the marriage between conceptualization and methodology. This is an unavoidable conclusion, and work that fails to embrace both components is unnecessarily limited in its value. We, therefore, strongly encourage the student to invest considerable effort in the development of a conceptual model.

PROPOSITION OR PROPOSITIONS TO BE INVESTIGATED

Propositions should flow *logically* from the formulation of the topic and review of the pertinent literature. Indeed, the student might be assisted by perceiving the conceptual model as similar to the function of a logical syllogism. That is, each study

or theoretical source consulted should serve as a premise with the proposition or propositions serving as the logical conclusion or conclusions. Thus, the conceptual model is really an argument employing the rules of deductive logic. We begin with the large overview of a topic; survey any number of previous efforts within the area, theoretical and/or empirical; and deduce a specific set of propositions.

We mean something quite specific by the term *proposition.* You will recall that we defined a proposition as a statement that describes some characteristic or which posits a relationship between two or *more* concepts or constructs that we hope to investigate.

The wording of this definition is as important for what it fails to say as for what it does say. We emphasize the term *more* in the phrase *two or more concepts or constructs.* As we have argued, current knowledge of social phenomena, while far from total, is beyond the stage where we can justify serious analysis of a two-concept proposition. We do not know of a single phenomenon of interest to social thinkers that has been satisfactorily explained by one independent factor. Although it is possible, theoretically at least, for one factor to be *the* cause of a phenomenon, it is unlikely in social research. Therefore, almost all research in the social behavioral realm must involve consideration of more than one independent factor.

To illustrate, let us recall the earlier example of status consistency versus status inconsistency with regard to political preference. We have no hesitancy in accepting the notion that one's status profile contributes to one's political preference, but we would not consider the idea that such was the *only* factor contributing to that preference. We are aware, for example, that it is important to know not only the extent of one's educational achievement, but also where one achieved that education, what one's major field of study was, and other such questions. We know one's area of residency (e.g., rural versus urban, or South versus North) and the type of residency (e.g., apartment versus home) are important in shaping a person's political orientation; we know the respondent's significant others will influence one's political thinking (e.g., spouse, friends, fellow workers, or students).

In short, we are arguing that social science research has moved beyond the simple statement of a relationship between one X factor and one Y factor. By the same token we have not progressed to the point where all of the factors that are relevant to the subject matter being studied are known and can be taken into account.

We have discussed two general types of propositions. You will recall they were labeled descriptive and analytical propositions. The category of descriptive propositions references a particular class of phenomena. It focuses on a specific unit of analysis in terms of a characteristic or series of characteristics. Descriptive propositions contain only one concept or construct and are not generally specified by researchers. Analytical propositions, on the other hand, posit relationships between two or more concepts and/or constructs. The researcher, then, is much more likely to focus on an analytical than a descriptive proposition. This is not to argue that descriptive propositions are not important, but that their value is of a different nature. For example, descriptive propositions are often included in the summary and conclusion sections of a research report and may lead to additional research. In this case the descriptive proposition has served to stimulate *heuristic research*; that is, it has encouraged additional inquiry.

The primary focus of this discussion, then, will be on the analytical type of proposition. It offers a reference point and leads to an empirical test, when translated into a hypothesis in the language of hypothesis testing.

DIFFICULTIES IN PROPOSITION FORMULATION

The construction of a clear proposition for investigation is not a simple task. We offer a discussion of some of the difficulties.

Paucity or Plethora of the Literature

To a great extent the formulation of an area of investigation will be simplified or made more difficult as a function of the review of the literature. The review should suggest the factors that one will ultimately include as explanatory or class I factors. However, when the literature is sparse, it is more difficult to tease out the relevant factors that should be or appropriately could be included for study.

Similarly, when the literature reviewed is voluminous, it may be frustrating to narrow one's choice of factors to include. The researcher must apply creative and logical skills to this selection process. You will recall our earlier mention of selecting the conceptual perspective that best fits the topic area and of using that perspective as a guide to the literature review. In order for that suggestion to be effective, however, one must understand and be somewhat knowledgeable about the particular perspective selected. If conflict theory is to be the vehicle, the basic premises of that paradigm must be understood. If you do not feel comfortable with your current knowledge, an examination of the conflict paradigm is encouraged. Indeed, a review of this nature is a good idea to incorporate into each research procedure. This will permit one to always approach the literature review with a fresh exposure to the theoretical perspective to be used.

Conceptual and Methodological Linkages

A second major area of difficulty of proposition formulation for many beginning researchers is the inability to utilize an existent framework logically, i.e., to bridge the gap between theoretical knowledge and the utilization of that knowledge in a research effort. This problem stems from one of the primary criticisms we hold of the contemporary educational system. We refer to this as the pigeonholing of information or knowledge.

In general, the undergraduate student is asked by the college or university to satisfactorily complete approximately 40 courses of study in a semester-based program, or 60 classes in a quarter-oriented school. Successful completion brings the conferral of a bachelor's degree. It has been our observation, however, that only a limited number of institutions request their students to integrate the knowledge gained in these academic efforts in any meaningful way.

When a suggestion to require such an effort is introduced, students invariably offer a vigorous protest. This is understandable, and we recognize the inevitable anxiety that would accompany such a requirement. Nevertheless, it is unfortunate that an expectation of this type is not more widespread because most students will continue to have 40 or 60 isolated pockets of knowledge without an overview or understanding of how these pieces of information fit together to form a more panoramic view.

Most students are not exposed to comprehensive exams and the experience of writing a thesis until they reach graduate school. Anxiety and fear are not absent from the graduate student and may be exaggerated because the stakes are so high. Nevertheless, most students overcome these hurdles and begin to understand how their academic discipline fits together. For the first time they are beginning to see the big picture. Invariably, the rewards outweigh the price.

We mention these comprehensive ideas because a research project represents such an effort at integration. It requires linkages between relevant conceptual models and the methods to be used. The conceptual model requires reexamination of some of the ideas from criminology, the family, or medical sociology, for example. A research project requires an integration of those ideas into a specific conceptual perspective, and it requires that one deduce a limited number of explanatory factors into a propositional format to submit for operationalization into a hypothesis. These areas must be connected for a research project to have merit.

In sum, we would argue that knowledge of a theoretical perspective is a necessary condition for generating a solid proposition for investigation, but it is not a sufficient condition. The student must also see the applicability of the perspective to the topic area in question and how that perspective will facilitate the investigation of the proposition or propositions.

Methodological Omissions

The final major difficulty in proposition formulation is not being acquainted with available research techniques. This is an understandable void for the student taking the first course in research methodology. The major purpose of this course is to fill, or at least minimize, that void.

You will become familiar with the current state of knowledge from the material provided by your professor and from the discussion of this textbook. As your understanding grows, so will your awareness of what can or cannot be done in social research.

SOME COMMENTS ABOUT FUNDING, TIME, AND THE FINISHED RESEARCH PRODUCT

Social research is a more complex issue than whether one can gather a body of data with which to examine the validity of a proposition. A number of considerations should be discussed. These will deal with money, disposition of completed manuscripts, demands registered by the funding agency, time constraints, and ethical considerations.

Money

One must consider the cost of a proposed project in conjunction with the financial abilities one brings to the project. Does the researcher plan to pay the costs of the research out of personal moneys, or is it anticipated that a research grant or contract will be obtained? How extensive will be the moneys required? If moneys are to be provided from an outside source, public or private, will they be sufficient? Many researchers have to reduce their original intentions because of inadequate funds. This is often due to the researcher's failure to accurately anticipate the costs of the project. If the researcher is housed in an institution, such as a university or research hospital, and most of us are, what percentage of a grant or contract must be paid to the institution for providing the researcher with an office, secretarial assistance, supplies, computer time, and similar expenses? These costs range from 10 percent to 50 percent of the overall allowance of the grant or contract. Will you have a research staff, and if so, how large? In addition to the size of the staff, you must recognize the level of expertise each member brings to the project. Everyone must be paid, and paid according to that person's role within the overall effort. Will you require a statistical consultant? Will you offer incentives to your respondents to participate in the study?

These and many other issues arise during the planning and conducting of a research project. Clearly, doing research can be expensive, but it is not necessarily so. The guide word is *anticipate*.

There is a great deal of financial assistance available to researchers, particularly for applied research. Much of it, however, is never applied for because researchers are unaware of its existence. Instead, most researchers apply for funds from the major recognized sources, e.g., government agencies and major private foundations.

When money is provided, the researcher should examine what the expectations of the granting agency are. While most agencies will fund projects that are exploratory, they will do so at the lower cost levels. Larger grants and contracts are generally reserved for work that has a sound theoretical basis and that is not at the beginning level. It must be clear from the start whether the request for funding is to study what the researcher wants or what someone else wants.

Disposition of the Manuscript

Second, the researcher will want to know what is to be done with the completed manuscript once the study has been brought to closure. If such is dependent upon the nature of the results, the researcher wants to know that as well. A conditional orientation is likely to place a great deal of subtle pressure upon the researcher to find what the fund-

ing agency wants found. It is one thing for a researcher to elect to be a shill, but to be manipulated into being one is quite another.

Demands of the Funding Agency

Third, the researcher must consider the type of feedback the funding agency expects during the life of the grant or contract. Annual written reports or on-site visits are standard, and the researcher would be expected to comply. One of the major reasons for the annual report has been the failure of some researchers to complete a project after accepting moneys for the effort. That is why we continue to add the term *contract* to *grant* in our discussion. That is, many funding agencies now agree to fund a project for a certain period of time, and the researcher agrees to complete a certain portion of the project within that time frame. If the researcher has done so, a second period of time will be funded, and so on until the project is completed. If the researcher fails to make satisfactory progress, the contract can be cancelled by the funding agency.

Similarly, some granting agencies expect a great deal of personal service as well as completion of the project. One of your authors was once a recipient of a relatively small grant from a private agency. The grant ran for a period of two years. Virtually every week the agency wanted a public lecture to a gathering in some city. Although expenses were covered, the travel took so much time that the project was not getting done. An understanding was finally worked out, and the project was completed, but a proposal for funding was never sent to that agency again.

The message here is that funded research is a cooperative venture among all parties concerned. A researcher has the right to ask the type of questions cited above. Similarly, the funding agency has the right to a well done and completed study. Beyond that, agreements must be worked out as to what can be done with the results, speaking engagements, and the like.

Because of the complexity and competitiveness of gaining access to private and public agency moneys, many researchers are electing to fund their own research, thereby obligating themselves to no one. The major drawback is that most of us do not have sufficient funds for the research we would like to conduct, therefore somewhat limiting our projects. Nevertheless, this is the avenue most often pursued by beginning researchers. We suggest, therefore, a realistic assessment of what can be accomplished within such limitations.

Time Constraints

The fourth consideration of this dimension that will affect the scope of a research project is time. Most students, working on their first research effort, are under the restriction of a quarter or a semester time frame. In some circumstances this is extended to an academic year, but even then the student may find the time constraints to be severe.

One must remember that a considerable expenditure of time is made during the selection of the topic and the review of the literature. A major period of time will also be required for the data-collection phase, assuming one collects one's own data.* Therefore, one must give careful thought to available methods, the financial resources from which one can draw, and the time requirements as the selection of the explanatory variables of the proposition or propositions to be examined is made.

Ethical Considerations

The fifth complexity that enters into the consideration of methods and procedures is that of ethical considerations. Technical capabilities may be known and available to study a particular issue, but to employ them, without question, could be a serious error.

In the most straightforward of projects the researcher is obligated to obtain the permission of the potential respondent. If the respondent is a child or young enough to be considered a minor

by law, permission must be obtained from the potential participant's parents, guardians, or others assigned legal responsibility for the care and well-being of the child.

One of your authors has done research in the area of adolescent parenthood. One phase of the research was to examine the long-range outcomes and consequences of such births. In light of this aim, it was determined that educational records would be an important part of the assessment. Permission had to be obtained from each set of parents as well as the district school superintendent, even though the data were to be treated as group data; i.e., they would not, or could not, be traced back to any individual within the study population.

On another occasion a local television station wanted to do a film essay of the interaction between adolescent mothers and their children during a clinic visit. Permission had to be gained for filming the infants from their mothers, and to film the adolescent mothers from their mothers or the grandmothers of the infants.

Although this may seem a bit excessive, the principle behind obtaining permission is a sound one. None of us wants to be guilty of invading anyone's privacy without benefit of an invitation. For example, a great deal of insight into the behavioral patterns of persons who are terminally ill might be gained if cameras and sound-recording devices were strategically placed, i.e., hidden, to record every move and sound made by such patients. In the interest of accumulating knowledge it is tempting to agree to this type of data-collection procedure. How would you feel, however, if the data were being collected on you or on a significant other such as a spouse or parent?

In summary, then, the physical existence of a method, procedure, or technique does not assure its availability for usage. Determining which capabilities to use is dependent on a number of other considerations, with only the most apparent hav-

---

*See Chapter 12, "Content Analysis and Secondary Analysis," for a discussion of alternative sources of data.

ing been discussed here. We have more to say on the issue of ethical research in Chapter 16.

CLASSES OF PROPOSITIONS

We have stated that two types of propositions may be formed following the review of the literature: descriptive and analytical. We have also noted that the analytical type of proposition is that which a researcher is most likely to formulate for investigation. We can further distinguish propositions that are eligible for investigation by examining a number of subtypes.

Commonsense Propositions

The first of these can be labeled simply as commonsense propositions, or those which can be seen as stemming from folk wisdom. After all, folk knowledge of social relationships is plentiful. Unfortunately much of what is believed to be true is often a confused mixture of clichés and moral judgment. Examples of what has been felt to be self-evident by many, but which is patently false are: bad children are born that way, African Americans make up the majority of welfare lists, or exposure to pornography makes people more likely to commit sex crimes.

A *commonsense proposition* is a statement of a relationship that the general public believes to exist as an empirical uniformity. Thus, commonsense propositions are ones which flow out of the widely shared public beliefs that characterize any society. Social and behavioral scientists have inherited the task of testing and translating this type of idea into useful knowledge. Although it is clear that sociology is much more than common sense, these commonsense ideas are fruitful for study. Indeed, Peter Berger, in his classic *Invitation to Sociology: A Humanistic Perspective*, has argued that debunking folk wisdom is a major function of sociology.[3] One cautionary note is in order. Propositions, whatever their nature, must have empirical referents. That is, to be testable the proposition must be translated into the language of hypothesis testing wherein the concepts and constructs have been transformed into variables that are operationally defined. If such is not possible, the proposition has little utility in any scientific sense. Further, a statement of absolute moral certitude can not be evaluated through the scientific method. Thus, a moral or value judgment cannot serve as a testable hypothesis. For example, we could not test the proposition that criminals are no worse than businesspeople, or that sex criminals should be publicly whipped or worse under the assumption that the results would lead to absolute, irrefutable certitude. It is possible, however, to test whether people *feel* that criminals are worse than businesspeople, or that sex criminals should be publicly whipped. But to investigate such a notion as a potential dictum for inclusion in the data bank of absolute knowledge is not possible through the scientific epistemology. The temptation to exercise such personal beliefs is, of course, particularly strong when selecting a problem area and formulating propositions for testing relevant to folk wisdom and common sense.

Propositions of the Middle Range

While not mutually exclusive from common sense or folk wisdom, a second class of propositions, and perhaps those that are most frequently examined by sociologists, are those that are concerned with relationships that Robert Merton has labeled, *"theories of the middle range."*[4] In contrast to and as a critique of the work of Talcott Parsons' effort to build an all encompassing "total system of sociological theory,"[5] Merton advocated a lesser effort that would be more modest in scope. He felt the grandiose approach was premature, given the current state of knowledge. While recognizing we were not prepared for the all-embracing theory, he noted that we were more advanced than examining minor or simple day-to-day routines. Thus, he felt the necessity of examining relationships that fell between these two extremes.

By examining propositions of this type, the knowledge base would be expanded and the opportunity to examine a systemwide conceptual model would be closer. Merton followed this stratcgy and contributed to the growth of sociological knowledge when he offered significant adjustments and modifications to the approach of functional analysis, which is employed by the pioneering anthropologists, most notably Bronislaw Malinowski and A. R. Radcliffe-Brown.

A type of middle-range proposition that has been profitable to social and behavioral scientists is that of ideal types. The purpose of this type of proposition is to examine the existence of logically derived relationships between empirical uniformities. For example, if we were students of the transportation industry and elected to study the automobile, we might examine the relevant relationships of a particular type of car using this approach. That is, we might wish to examine such issues as gear ratios, horsepower to fuel consumption, ability to withstand impacts at various speeds at the front and rear ends of the car, or other such issues. We could then address the question of how well the examined car measured up against projected standards.

Similarly, and more relevant to our subject matter, the concentric zone "theory" developed by Ernest Burgess can serve as an illustration.[6] The city studied was Chicago during the 1920s. The conceptual model was based on such factors as land use and the relationship between social status and distance from the center of the city. In addition to location vis-à-vis the center of the city, a portion of one's status was seen to be related to majority/minority group membership and the association between minority group status and marginality. All of the ideas examined were predicated on the notion that city growth is in the form of concentric circles.

A surface glance at other cities will quickly indicate that all cities do not reflect a concentric growth pattern,* nor do all minority group members qualify as marginal persons. The failure of growth patterns or residence descriptions to meet the criteria advanced by Burgess, however, does

not mean that we should toss this conceptual model out as being invalid or useless. It has functioned, and will continue to function, heuristically. That is, it serves as a stimulant to additional research efforts with regard to urban development, residential patterns, and diverse land usage—subjects of enormous contemporary interest. It also continues to serve as a barometer against which other research efforts can be compared or as a complement to the knowledge gained through additional efforts. Such is the purpose of propositions derived from ideal typical conceptual models.

Explanatory Propositions

The final class of propositions are those that are explanatory in nature. It is within an *explanatory proposition* that we approach the more grandiose, all encompassing type of theoretical effort epitomized in the work of Talcott Parsons.

Permit us to continue with the transportation example already mentioned to illustrate theories of the middle range. As our knowledge of individual models of cars grows, we would want to expand our examination to include all types of automobiles sold in our country. In addition, we would want to control for specific extraneous variables. For example, we would want to control for the more severe emissions controls required in the state of California; the rather special fuel-system adjustments required to accommodate the high altitude of Colorado; and the special viscosity requirements of engine oils required to prevent freezing in the arctic temperatures in Alaska.

As we accumulate more information, we will be in a better position to understand and intelligently purchase an automobile. The important dimensions that go into making such a decision have been explained more adequately.

Similarly, if we continue our interest in urban growth and land use, we would serve ourselves well by examining other ideal, typical conceptual

---

*Indeed, Chicago is one of the few metropolitan areas that exhibit this pattern of land use. While the work of urban sociologists at the University of Chicago was brilliant in many ways, one of their enduring faults was to devote almost all of their field time to empirically examining aspects of Chicago—which is rather atypical in land use patterns for American cities.

models of urban development, most specifically Homer Hoyt's sector hypothesis[7] and Chauncy Harris and Edward Ullman's multiple nuclei theory.[8] By combining the observations of all three efforts and by deriving testable propositions from them, one will be much closer to being able to explain the wide variety of phenomena relevant to urban development.

Note that we said *closer*. We will not be able to totally explain these phenomena. Total explanation of any phenomenon has escaped the capabilities of the social sciences to date. However, explanation remains the objective for social and behavioral scientists, just as it is for scientists from any academic discipline.

The researcher is now equipped with a number of tools to formulate a proposition that can be translated into operational terms for empirical examination. These propositions will be of a type (descriptive or analytical) and class (folk wisdom or commonsense, middle range, or explanatory) and they will reflect a relationship that is posited as being associational or causal.

THE FORMAT OF THE PROPOSITION

Introduction

In this section we discuss a format for the presentation of one's research propositions. Attention is given to the placement of the class I factors; the nature of the relationship among the explanatory factors presented; the identification of the class II, controlled, factors; and related issues. As an example, let us pose the following proposition: A working male's self-image varies positively with his amount of formal education, holding constant marital status, age, and wife's employment status.

Substantively, we want to sample some number of married, employed males between the ages of 24 and 35, some of whom have wives who are employed, and some with unemployed spouses. These men will be measured on the variables of their self-image and the amount of formal education that they have attained. After separating those

males with employed wives from those with unemployed wives, a measure of association will be done on the two variables of self-image and amount of formal education.

Placement of the Class I, Explanatory, Factors

Since we are thinking in terms of a hypothesis, the variables of amount of formal education and self-image are the objects of the research. They should be the first variables the reader encounters in the proposition.

Nature of the Relationship Between the Class I Factors

The nature of the relationship between these two class I variables should be clearly indicated. We argued earlier that there are two possible relationships among factors—a causal relationship and an associational or correlational relationship. While such are the possibilities, we also argued that any formal statistical assessment of causality was, strictly speaking, impossible. Rather, the statistical techniques available to the researcher were all associational measures. Finally, of the four canons of evidence for causality suggested by Mill, only the method of concomitant variation seemed to be currently appropriate to social and behavioral scientists. Therefore, while we may want to interpret an associational statistical evaluation as a cause-and-effect relationship, such would be an act of faith and judgment on the part of the researcher and not warranted by the statistical procedure. While we do not want to stifle this inductive leap of faith, we do feel the formal statement of the proposition or propositions to be investigated should be consistent with the data-analysis procedures used to evaluate it and with the underlying logic of the appropriate canon of causality being invoked.

In sum, there are no statistical formulas that measure causality. We prefer the formal statement of the proposition to indicate an associational relationship among selected class I factors because such is consistent with the nature of the statistical evaluation and with the basic logic of the method of concomitant variation. Finally, when suggesting an associational relationship among the class I factors, the researcher only has two possibilities from which to choose: (1) a positive association or (2) a negative association.

Identification of the Class II Factors

As you will recall from our discussion of Kish's variables, any analytical hypothesis must have at least two class I explanatory objects of the research and may have some number of class II, extraneous but controlled, variables. Further, while the troublesome class III, extraneous, uncontrolled, and confounding, variables are very much in evidence, and the class IV, extraneous, uncontrolled, and assumed-to-be-irrelevant, variables abound, neither class III nor class IV variables will ever appear *in* the hypothesis. Therefore, any formally given statement must have class I factors and may have some number of class II factors.

To separate the class I factors from the class II factors, we suggested the use of the phrase *holding constant*. This phrase clearly identifies that which follows it to be class II, controlled factors. Therefore, the remaining identified factors must be class I factors or the objects of the research. Setting off the controlled factors serves as a clear and efficient way to apprise the reader of the nature of all noted factors.

DEFINITION OF TERMS

The next task of the researcher who is constructing the conceptual model is to present theoretical definitions for all of the concepts or constructs contained within the proposition or propositions that are confusing or ambiguous. The experienced researcher will have learned that this refers to virtually every term contained within the statement or statements.

We have defined a theoretical definition of a concept or construct as a definition using other concepts or constructs. Further, the researcher is not promising the reader that the definitions provided are true or false, only that they are simply stated in the manner in which the terms will be employed for that particular project.

By defining the terms in as precise a manner as possible, the researcher accomplishes three objectives. First, the reader is informed of the manner in which a concept or construct is perceived by the researcher, thus indicating how it will be used in the current project. Second, if the reader of the study wants to compare the results attained in the current work with those of other studies on the same subject, consistent or inconsistent usage of terms becomes immediately apparent. Third, if the reader elects to conduct a study in the same area, the current definitions can be preserved or altered, depending upon preference instead of chance.

The emphasis in this phase of the conceptual model is on precision. While the need to define terms is often recognized, there may be an accompanying presumption of clarity for many terms that is not warranted.

This problem manifests itself in three ways. First, many terms that should be clarified are defined with the assumption that everyone knows what they mean. Indeed, the terms in question may be a part of most person's working vocabularies. However, when the necessity of precision is introduced, the confidence with which the terms have been used in the past dissipates. On occasion we have asked our students to take out a sheet of paper in class and define some commonly used concepts or constructs in order to illustrate this immediate decline in assurance.

The concept of juvenile delinquency can serve as an example, or more accurately, two examples. What constitutes being a juvenile? The legal parameters simply pose an upper age limit. However, a researcher may not feel comfortable in treating twelve year olds in the same manner as sixteen year olds. Similarly, the delinquent act of breaking into a gum ball machine is quite divergent from a brutal assault or murder. To treat dissimilar age groupings or offense categories in a uniform manner invites an absence of reliable results. This type of imprecision only invites murky pronouncements upon completion of the study and would not facilitate understanding of the phenomenon in question. The lesson is to not overlook terms to be defined, regardless of how widespread their usage.

Second, the definition for one ambiguous term is written with another or a series of other ambiguous terms. Juvenile delinquency will serve again as an example. The type of theoretical definition provided for this term is often something such as "the violation of a legal statute by someone 17 years of age or younger." This type of definition is useless to the readers of a research report in which juvenile delinquency is an explanatory variable. The proliferation of laws and the wide spectrum of ages renders the determination of a focal point virtually impossible. We are relatively confident that a researcher interested in the phenomenon of juvenile delinquency would not attempt to investigate such a broad scope of the issue. Further, at what point within the judicial process is one labeled a delinquent? We know, for example, that the number of juveniles apprehended represents only a small percentage of the criminal acts perpetrated by juveniles; the number bound over for trial a smaller percentage; the number convicted smaller still; and the number incarcerated the smallest percentage yet.

The reader will recall our earlier discussion of practical decisions. The widest population that could be sampled realistically would be those arrested, but even here the question of gaining access to interview these juveniles or to review their files would be difficult.

The researcher, then, would be well advised to formulate a theoretical definition that would reflect consideration of practical issues as well. Perhaps our hypothetical investigator would prefer to examine juveniles who fall between the ages of 14 and 15 and who have been convicted of a felony. This is still a fairly broad definition, but the researcher has clearly communicated the parameters of the variable to the readers. This will assist them in their review of the current study and in any decision they might wish to make with regard to replication.

Third, some students employ definitions that owe their origin to a "private world." Every segment of our culture has a number of terms that have meaning only to that segment of the population. Since a researcher always writes for a heterogeneous, professional audience, these terms of limited applicability should be avoided. A few of these concepts have managed to evolve into a more widespread acceptance and usage, e.g., chutzpah from the Jewish subculture. However, avoidance is still the rule or guideline we would recommend.

We would similarly discourage the use of slang terms, either as concepts within the proposition or propositions or as definitions or parts of definitions for those concepts included. While slang terms are not generally limited to specific segments of the population, they have a tendency to be short-lived in much the same way that a fad lasts only a short period of time. By the time a study is published, any slang terms employed might be out of use.

In short, the purpose of providing theoretical definitions is to introduce precision and clarity. To accomplish this aim, the researcher must define every term within the proposition or propositions that is remotely ambiguous or confusing and do so with a careful, reasoned assessment of what the term means vis-à-vis the research project in question. In almost all cases this means the avoidance of language that is reflective of and limited to a subsection of the population or that is slang.

SPECIFYING THE INDEPENDENT AND THE DEPENDENT FACTORS

The final task for the researcher constructing a conceptual model is to specify which class I factors are independent factors and which are dependent factors. The classification of the class I factors as independent or dependent is often a matter of choice for the researcher and largely depends on the purpose of the research.

Causal Purposes

If the researcher is searching for a causal interpretation of the association, an attempt must be made to determine the time order of the factors. We have already spoken at length in Chapter 4 concerning various strategies for determining the time order of factors, and we direct your attention to a review of that chapter.

Predictive Purposes

Sometimes the researcher is less interested in the causal nature of the relationship and more concerned with predicting a specific outcome. Should this be the researcher's interest, the independent factor or factors must be those whose values will function as an aid in predicting the missing values of the dependent factor or factors. Strange as it may seem, in the case of prediction it may be wise to consider a factor to be independent that is really caused by another factor posited in the proposition. It also may be wise to consider the independent factor to be dependent. In other words, the time-priority considerations may point to variable X as the cause of variable Y, wherein X would be the independent variable and Y the dependent variable. However, the researcher may wish to reverse this observable and logically arrived at causal sequence *for the purposes of prediction* because it may be easier to measure the dependent than the independent variable. If such is the case, the researcher is well advised to treat the caused dependent variable as being independent. Finally, since one will assess the effectiveness of the prediction with a correlational measure, it is clearly acceptable to use either set of factors in order to predict the other.

A discussion of the selection of the proper statistical procedure is beyond the scope of this chapter. We have more to say about these matters in later chapters. We mention them here because a proper statistical procedure cannot be chosen without knowing which factors are independent and which are the dependent. The researcher's responsibility for identifying the independent and dependent factors, however, falls within the purview of the conceptual model.

THE CONCEPTUAL MODEL AND THE RESEARCH DESIGN

We have divided the scientific method into two components: the conceptual model and the research design. This was *not* done, however, to suggest that these admittedly separate and distinct entities are unrelated. Indeed, we have argued for the necessity of their integration throughout these pages. Rather, we elected to do this in order to facilitate the student's examination of the phases of a research project and to increase the understanding of the interfacing of these parts. We have noted our concern with the tendency for pigeonholing information gleaned from a variety of sources. One simply cannot prepare good, solid research from such a perspective. The student must recognize the inevitable integration of the dimensions from both the conceptual and research-design components.

The lack of recognition of the complementary nature of the conceptual model and the research design has led to two misguided emphases, which have been perpetuated by some social scientists: (1) the debate between the significant generalizer and the radical empiricist and (2) the confusion of statistical and substantive significance.

SIGNIFICANT GENERALIZATION VERSUS RADICAL EMPIRICISM

Unfortunately, the different functions we suggest between the conceptual model and the research design have found expression in the nature of the commitments that have been made by some social scientists in the past. The conceptual model has sometimes been seen as the province of the theorists, who have focused upon qualitative issues. Conversely, the research design has found support from quantitatively oriented scholars, who have most often been statisticians and research methodologists.

While both positions have been populated by dedicated and concerned thinkers, they have often indicated a schism within their respective academic disciplines, which has been difficult to bridge. In some cases the respective advocates have resembled two armed camps, hurling verbal assaults at one another. The quantitatively oriented have been called "positivistic purists," "mechanics," "radical empiricists," and worse. They have been summarily dismissed by conclusions such as "they don't know whether what they say is important or not, but they know that it is true."

On the other hand, those who have concentrated their attention on largely qualitative concerns have been disparagingly labeled "theoreticians" and "significant generalizers" and described by the statement: "they don't know whether what they say is true or not, but they think that it is significant." The problem has been exaggerated by generations of students having been taught from these vested positions of their professors. That is, they have been exposed to the conflict, elected a side, and formulated an orientation which is, in turn, presented to their students, and so forth.

In sum, the *significant generalizer* is one whose propositions are at such a high level of abstraction that their translation into the language of hypothesis testing is virtually impossible. Since the factors that are of importance to the significant generalizers cannot be operationalized, empirical data cannot be gathered to test these ideas. But the significant generalizers sweep away these objections with the claim that their ideas are very important because of their wide ranging applicability.

On the other hand, the *radical empiricist* seems almost consumed with the need to test and deal with operational definitions of variables. While not a disadvantage in itself, such rank empiricism often prevents the radical empiricist from selecting any factor that cannot be easily operationalized.

In other words, the radical empiricist is overly concerned with measurement and testing to the exclusion of the general importance of the work in theoretical terms.

The end product of this unfortunate debate has been a quagmire. On the one hand, we have been treated to mundane, somewhat useless data analysis that is reflective of methodological beauty. On the other, we have seen broad encyclopedic interests presented that cannot be empirically verified. We believe the appropriate response of the contemporary researcher lies with the insistence of a marriage between the orientations that both these positions represent. Until such is practiced by social scientists as a whole, the advancement of our knowledge base will proceed at a much slower pace than is necessary.

To emphasize this point, we suggest that the scientific method resembles an hourglass, being broad at the respective ends and narrowing in the middle. The top half represents the conceptual model, while the bottom half symbolizes the research design. The conceptual model, which utilizes deductive logic, begins with the broad base of a topic area and gradually narrows the focus until an investigative proposition is derived. Within the research design, more parallel to inductive logic, the researcher usually selects a sample from a larger population base in order to test the propositions presented. The results, whatever they may be, are inferred to the larger or broader population base. Thus, we move from the specific sample to the general population from which it was selected.* Further, the study conclusions become the basis for substantive revisions of the conceptual model with which the researcher began. At this point, one "turns the hour glass over" and moves onto a subsequent study, and so it goes. Good research involves an integrated and complementary marriage between the conceptual model and the research design.

We could do no better in summarizing the importance of the integration between theory and methods than to cite the conclusions offered by

---

*We recognize we are taking a few liberties of interpretation with the rules of deductive and inductive logic, but we have found this analogy to be quite helpful.

Merton in his essays of "The Bearing of Sociological Theory on Empirical Research," and "The Bearing of Empirical Research on Sociological Theory."[9] He has suggested that there should be a working relationship between a conceptual model, which is empirically testable, and empirical studies, which are theoretically oriented.

It is further noted that researchers most often begin their research efforts by formulating a conceptual posture and conclude their efforts through empirical examination. Quite frequently, however, observations are made that were not anticipated, or those that were anticipated are made more clear. New and different propositions for investigation, then, can easily evolve from the research-design component of the scientific method. Recognizing this likelihood, Merton noted that "an explicitly formulated theory does not invariably precede empirical inquiry, that as a matter of plain fact the theorist is not inevitably the lamp lighting the way to new observations."[10]

We are hopeful this will be remembered as you examine the quantitative techniques and methods in the subsequent chapters. As you assemble the various discussions of a research design, you will find that continuous referral to the conceptual model will be indispensable, just as one could not move on to the next phase in the conceptual model without benefit of the previous one.

STATISTICAL VERSUS SUBSTANTIVE SIGNIFICANCE

A conflict that has often evolved into an argument centers on the relative merits of statistical significance versus those of substantive significance.[11] The proponents of their respective positions have not arrived at them without reason. This has been particularly the case for those who advocate statistical significance.

Statistical significance refers to a result which has a high probability of not happening through the fluctuations of pure chance; that is, after the researcher has selected the degree of tolerable error, a statistically significant result is not something that could have occurred solely because of sampling error. Reinforcement for this position

has been gained, perhaps inadvertently, by what appears to be an insistence upon results that are statistically significant by editorial boards of professional journals. This unfortunate conclusion is supported by the work of Theodore Sterling, who surveyed the psychological journals for a 10-year period. He found only one article that reported results that failed to reach statistical significance at the 0.05 level or better.[12] Because research and publication are the lifeline for scientists, it is not surprising this editorial-board emphasis has become a guideline for many researchers.

Perhaps more importantly, the insistence upon statistical significance has resulted in the selection of research topics that are less than substantively important. That is, the researcher's concern to obtain statistically significant results has often diverted attention away from substantive significance. *Substantive significance* refers to results that are meaningful to one's conceptual model or to the decision-making apparatus that accompanies applied research. For example, consider two sections (A and B) of introductory students whose mean midterm scores were 72.5 percent and 74.8 percent, respectively. If section A had been exposed to a traditional course and section B to an innovative, new instructional method, the researcher might want to know if the new instructional procedure was worth implementing more broadly. Therefore, one might do a test of significance to determine if the difference between the two mean descriptive statistics was a true difference or an aberration of sampling design. That is, is the difference due to random error or is it truly due to a difference in instructional procedure?

After doing a test of statistical significance, it might be found that these two means are highly statistically significant. That is, one could not have gotten this much difference in the scores by pure random sampling error. One would conclude that the results are statistically significant—that this difference is *not* the result of sampling error. But are they substantively significant? We do not think so. When one looks at the *descriptive statistics*, there is but a 2.3 percent average difference between the two sections. In other words, both sections are still averaging a C grade.

Therefore, while the results are highly statistically significantly different (probably because of the large number of students in both sections), the actual descriptive statistics on exam performance are virtually identical. To choose to report only statistically significant research results implies that statistical significance is more important than substantive significance. However, we doubt that one would recommend revamping the instructional curriculum (especially if substantial costs are involved in doing so) if one is to gain a mere 2.3 percent increase in the substantive scores of each section.

In our example, the emphasis on attaining statistically significant results has diverted attention from that which is substantively important. Such is an inversion of interpretive priorities and is not warranted in scientific work. In sum, inferential statistical procedures measure an important, but limited, characteristic of one's research. The scientist must not forget the substantive importance of the research.

SUMMARY

In this chapter we have focused upon the components and some issues germane to one's conceptual model.

First, we focused on identifying the topic area and registering a statement of the basic problem or applied problematic. To narrow an area of interest to a manageable level is often thought to be the most difficult task of the entire research process.

Second, we discussed the review of the relevant literature. By reviewing previous research efforts within the topic area, the researcher looks for variables identified as important, local or regional biases of earlier investigators, inadequacies of the current literature, and methodological errors committed by other researchers. The review will provide information with which to orchestrate a rationale for inclusion of the concepts and/or constructs to be incorporated into the proposition or propositions to be investigated.

We discussed a number of reference sources to facilitate the researcher's review of the relevant literature, the most significant being the *Sociological Abstracts*, *Psychological Abstracts*, and *Dissertation Abstracts*. General guidelines for approaching the review of areas with plentiful resources and strategies in areas with relatively little available material were offered.

Third, we discussed the statement of the proposition or propositions to be investigated. We emphasized the likelihood and importance of considering multiple concepts and/or constructs as potential causes of a phenomenon in social research. In this regard, we addressed several difficulties encountered in the formulation of propositions, which included limited literature resources, the absence of a conceptual model, difficulties in bridging conceptual and methodological issues, and an absence of familiarity with available methodological tools.

We also noted some practical concerns when formulating propositions. One of these is the cost of doing the study and the source of funding. If the project is funded by a public or private agency, the investigator will want to know about the disposition of the final manuscript, what the funding agency will demand, any time constraints under which the research is being conducted, and the relevant ethical considerations.

Also germane to proposition formulation is the class of proposition or propositions to be examined. We discussed those recognized as commonsense propositions, propositions of the middle range, and explanatory propositions, noting those of the middle range were the most frequently presented by social scientists.

Additionally, we included a discussion of the format of the proposition or propositions to be tested. Here we were concerned with the identification and placement of class I and class II factors, in conjunction with the nature of the relationship posited among the explanatory factors.

Further, we addressed the theoretical definition of terms, i.e., all concepts and constructs that might be confusing. Within the conceptual model the focus is on offering precise definitions, which inform the reader of how terms are used in the research effort and provide a basis for comparison or replication for other investigators. We noted the researcher must be careful to avoid defining an ambiguous term with another confusing term, to consider practical issues in forming the definitions, and to avoid private or slang concepts.

Lastly, the researcher constructing a conceptual model must specify which class I factors are independent and which are dependent. This specification will be influenced by whether the investigator is entertaining a causal or predictive function.

We concluded with a discussion of the interrelationship between the conceptual model and research design as the two major components of research. Within this discussion we identified those who have emphasized the conceptual model over the research design as being significant generalizers, while those with the reverse preference being radical empiricists. We concluded that neither orientation alone was fruitful for the progression of scientific knowledge. Further, we suggested that reporting statistically significant research results without evaluating the substantive significance of these same results was an inversion of the priority system that science intended.

KEY TERMS

Applied research	Heuristic research	Research design
Basic research	Proposition of the middle-range	Research topic
Commonsense proposition	Proposition to be investigated	Significant generalizer
Conceptual model	Radical empiricist	Statistical significance
Explanatory proposition	Relevant literature	Substantive significance

REVIEW QUESTIONS

1. Compare and contrast applied research with basic research. How do these concepts relate to problems and problematics discussed in Chapter 1?

2. List and discuss the functions of the component parts of the conceptual model.

3. What considerations are there when one is reviewing the literature on a topic about which much is written and about which little is written?

4. Write an analytical hypothesis containing at least three variables, treating two variables as explanatory and the remaining variable or variables as controlled.

5. What are the three classes of propositions, and how do they differ?

6. What is meant by *significant generalizer* and *radical empiricist*? Why are the positions held by these advocates considered less than useful by your authors?

7. Define *statistical significance* and *substantive significance*, and illustrate the difference with a hypothetical example.

8. In what ways might one consider a radical empiricist to be concerned with statistical significance and a significant generalizer to be concerned with substantive significance?

SAMPLING DESIGN, OPERATIONALIZATION, AND SCHEDULE TESTING

In Part I, we presented a series of general ideas about the nature of science and scientific methodology, which was followed by a final chapter entitled "The Conceptual Model." In doing so, we have established a pattern whereby we discuss the general conceptual aspects of each major section before moving to the more specific issues and their resolution.

Part II presents the issues of sampling, operationalization, and the formal testing of one's measuring instrument. We have combined these important functions because under most research circumstances they must be accomplished prior to going into the field to gather one's data.

Before we discuss the specific choices of sampling procedures, with their advantages and disadvantages, we introduce the basic philosophy and major orientations. We do this in order to provide some understanding of and justification for the myriad of details that must accompany the more pedestrian nuts-and-bolts considerations that are associated with the actual selection of the elements one will investigate.

We have argued that there is an intimate connection among the conceptual model, the methodological procedures, and the statistical techniques in any well-conceived research study. Nowhere in the research process is this interaction more obvious and crucial than in the issue of sampling.

We believe the ultimate source for any question on sampling design is Leslie Kish's book, Survey Sampling.[1] *We first mentioned Kish in connection with a classification of different types of variables. While Kish's book is excellent, it is not written for those students who are beginning their studies of research methodology.*

Therefore, we present, in a more simplified manner, the important notions he offers regarding sampling theory. We seek the middle ground between the once-over-lightly treatment that characterizes many sampling treatments and the full explication provided by Kish. We do this because we feel that some of the contradictions and different positions taken within the literature on sampling can only be satisfactorily addressed after some background is presented in the general theory and logic of sampling. For example, some writers argue one may draw a simple random sampling without replacement, others argue one must have replacement, and still others argue it depends. In most cases, authors take one of the three positions suggested above, while failing to mention the other two possibilities. We do not believe a definitive response to this issue is available at this time. Therefore, it may be that any one of the three choices may be appropriate depending upon the particular research circumstances. We feel you need to know there is a difference of opinion

101

concerning the procedure through which one draws a simple random sample. Further, we feel you need to have some acquaintance with the general theory and logic of sampling before you can begin to deal with the more practical question of how to rectify this, as well as other issues, in this context.

Chapter 6 is devoted to a discussion of many of the issues that are relevant to a background in the theory and logic of sampling and with which one must be at least somewhat familiar in order to make an informed choice of sampling design. Therefore, we speak at some length about such issues as the nature and differences between sampling error and nonsampling error, the reasons for and functions of sampling, and how statistical and probability theory are related to the various sampling designs available to the researcher.

Finally, we combine theoretical, methodological, and statistical concepts and issues. We have incorporated most of the statistical matters into Chapter 6, so that your instructor will be able to adjust your reading material more easily toward the course objectives. In Chapter 7, we present a nuts-and-bolts discussion of four basic probability and several nonprobability sampling designs. The advantages and disadvantages of these sampling procedures as well as some of their applications are presented.

The issues related to operationalization comprise the subject matter of Chapters 8 and 9. In Chapter 8 we concentrate on several general issues relative to schedule design and then focus on a descriptive as well as a comparative analysis of the formal testing procedures relative to reliability and validity.

In Chapter 9 we return to the hypothesis with which we were working in the sampling design in Chapter 7. In the final chapter of Part II, we will apply much of the earlier discussion in Chapter 8

to an example involving the construction of a schedule designed to measure one's self-image. Finally, attention is given to additional details relevant to schedule construction.

Thus, in Part I we looked essentially at the broad general theory of methodology. We wanted to prepare you for the details to follow by introducing you to the basic assumptions and premises that make the strengths and the weaknesses of the scientific method more understandable. We concluded Part I with the conceptual model in which we discussed the conceptual or theoretical dimensions germane to any well-conceived social, scientific research study.

Certain assumptions are warranted at this stage in the research process. First, we assume that one has determined the nature of the research topic. There may be some minor subsequent revisions, but we assume the researcher has settled on some specific area of research. Second, we assume that the researcher has done a reasonably thorough review of the literature. In so doing, the researcher has been looking for help in identifying those concepts and/or constructs that previous scientific research has indicated as important. Also, the researcher has looked for various potential relationships and for whatever methodological and statistical procedures have been useful. Third, we assume the researcher has formulated a conceptual model that will function to organize and to give substantive meaning to the remainder of the study. Finally, we assume the researcher has formally presented some number of propositions to be investigated and that these propositions flow logically out of and concisely summarize the conceptual model. Therefore, it is the nature of the units of analysis and the operationalization and testing of one's measuring instrument with which the researcher must next grapple.

CHAPTER 6

THE THEORY AND LOGIC OF SAMPLING

INTRODUCTION

This and the next chapter are about the units of analysis that the scientist investigates. We shall come to see many interrelationships, but before the pieces can be put together, we will have to discuss a number of seemingly disparate items that are germane to sampling.

Units of Analysis

Consider that you are interested in the relationship between a patient's income level and that patient's attitude about the nature of the health care being received. While the two variables are attitude and income level, these two variables do not exist, in reality, by themselves. Rather, they come "attached" to people, for example, Jones' income and Smith's attitude about the health-care delivery system. While one is concerned with these two variables, one must also be concerned about the units of analysis within the study. In this case, some group of people must be chosen, and the scientist will measure *their* incomes and *their* attitudes.

The reader will readily understand that in a majority of cases within the social and the behavioral sciences the unit of analysis is some number of people. Thus, the psychologist may set up an experimental data-gathering design in which sophomores in Psychology 101 are asked to participate. Perhaps a market analyst may solicit a number of shoppers who have Sears, Roebuck credit cards for a study of customer behavior. A sociologist may mail a questionnaire to a number of attorneys to determine their reactions to a recently passed Supreme Court ruling.

However, such is not always the case. The units of analysis may be elements other than people. In a demographic study concerning population shifts, the unit of analysis could be several geographic regions of the country. In content analysis, the units of analysis could be popular songs, books, or letters. Therefore, it is important to realize, first, that social scientists must select a unit of analysis before any variables can be measured and, second, that these units of analysis may or may not be people.

A note of caution is appropriate. If one's unit of analysis is the American corporation, one can not interview IBM. Rather, one must interview some number of persons who work for or are knowledgeable about IBM. If one is interested in the family structure of the United States, one can not interview families. One must talk to persons who are in families. Therefore, one must be cautious in interpreting data that emerge from such studies. For example, if Mr. Burnett said his income was $35,000, it may be erroneous to assume that the Burnett family income was $35,000. It could be that Mrs. Burnett is pursuing a career path that generates an additional $42,000 of yearly income, making this couple's family income a very comfortable $77,000. In short, it is important for the researcher to be aware of what the unit of analysis really is and ensure that appropriate data are being gathered on that unit.

Ecological Fallacy

One major problem concerning units of analysis is the possibility of an error called the ecological fallacy. An *ecological fallacy* is the attribution of some value that is descriptive of one unit of analysis to the value of some other unit of analysis. For example, assume one discovers that one particular census tract in an urban area had a median income of $52,000. This particular measure would be descriptive of the values of family income for the entire census tract from those families who responded to the survey. To assume that the Burnett family, who lives in that census tract, had an income of $52,000 would be an ecological fallacy. The $52,000 statistic is descriptive of the group of families who compose the census tract, but it does not necessarily reflect the financial condition of any particular family within that census tract any more than Mr. Burnett's own *individual* salary had to reflect the Burnett *family's* income.

The Example

The following example will facilitate our discussion of the issues surrounding sampling design. Consider that the president of the university is contemplating whether to institute a tuition increase for next year. The president wants to know if the student body can reasonably be expected to defray some of the increasing expenses brought by inflation. Further, since the topic is appropriate to your research methods course, the president has decided to turn the project over to your class. In fact, the president is in need of only one piece of information: each student's annual income. From this figure, a tuition task force will determine how much of the increase in the expenses to pass along to the students. Since some expenses will be incurred in doing this project, a $525 research grant has been arranged from the university's institutional-development fund. Assume further that there are 20 students enrolled in your methods course. In this and the next chapter, we will intermittently return to this example to illustrate selected sampling issues. At this point, we must address the notions of a population and a sample and of population parameters and sample statistics.

ISSUE 1: THE NEED FOR SAMPLING

Population Versus Sample

To begin, we need to clarify the concepts *population* and *sample* in order to discuss why sampling is a necessary component to social and behavioral research. A *population* is defined as the total number of elements that exist at the time of the study and that possess some characteristic of interest to the researcher. If one is interested in studying juvenile delinquents, the population of juvenile delinquents would be all those persons who fit the theoretical definition offered. In our example, the population of the university is every currently registered student—a total of 15,000 students.

A *sample* is some part or portion of the population. It is a smaller number of elements that have been selected for study from the total number of elements contained in the population. Finally, *sampling* is defined as the process through which one selects the elements from the population for inclusion in the sample. It is the set of procedures followed and the decisions made as the researcher goes about the task of selecting the units of analysis for the study.

Reasons for Sampling

While social and behavioral scientists are usually interested in the characteristics and relationships among the characteristics within some defined population, they will almost always study those items by selecting a sample. There are several reasons for dealing with samples rather than populations.

Large Size of Population.   First, some populations, if not infinite in number (such as the number of times one *could* toss a coin in the air), are large enough to make drawing a sample a necessity. For example, while one may have the money and the inclination to conduct face-to-face interviews with everyone in the United States population, such a study would not be feasible because of the large size of this population. Even if such were physically possible, by the time the researcher collected the data on the second half of the population, the data collected on the first half would be hopelessly out of date. The researcher, then, is forced to select a sample simply because of the largeness of the population.

Time Limitations.　Second, while the researcher's spirit may be strong in wishing to study all of the population elements, there may not be time to do so. In the practical world, the amount of time that a study requires is one of the factors that determine whether a sample is drawn. Think about your last term paper. You had to meet a deadline for the paper's submission and honor other academic and nonacademic commitments at the same time. Similar time constraints apply to the researcher.

Financial Limitations.　Third, as in most human endeavors, one's activity costs money. Should you be interested in a major study, it may be necessary to hire a staff to assist you in its design, execution, and data analysis. Again, while you might wish to investigate the population, you may not have sufficient funds to do so.

Unknown Population.　Fourth, while the researcher may have the time and money to study a small number of cases in some population, a complete listing of the population elements may be impossible. For example, we know a sociological researcher who was interested recently in studying the incidence and type of drug addiction in the United States. While the federal government was quite interested in treatment programs for drug addicts, accurate information on the nature, degree, or location of drug users was not available. Nor could the scientist study the population, even if the interest, money, and time were available, because there is no accurate listing of those who are addicts. This doesn't mean that there aren't lists, but such lists cannot be assumed to be com-

prehensive or representative. To be known as a drug user courts arrest and ostracism from many segments of the public at large. Those persons inclined to use drugs are not likely to be open about their behavior. Thus, lists of drug addicts are likely to contain only those persons who have received treatment or have been arrested for drug use or some other type of drug involvement.

Destructiveness of the Evaluation Procedure. Finally, samples are often mandatory because of the nature of the research done on the study elements. Consider the manufacturer of fireworks who wants to investigate the degree of care taken in the preparation of his products. If every firework were ignited, one would have an accurate count of the proportion that malfunctioned, but the manufacturer would have no product left to sell. Similarly, the physician cannot test all of the patient's blood. Thus, in any type of quality control research, a sample is drawn so that a majority of the product will be left for sales distribution if it is found acceptable.

To summarize, samples are drawn because the population is too large, there is not adequate time to investigate the population, the researcher doesn't have sufficient funds, the full population may not be available or known to the researcher, and the study may be destructive or alter the object of interest in some way. All these reasons are negative because they focus on why populations can't be studied. We have been working under the assumption that the researcher would want to study the population if it was feasible. However, this may not be the case. To see why, let us return to the study on the feasibility of a tuition increase.

Back to the Example

Remember there are 20 students in your class, your research grant is for $525, and the president wants to know each student's annual income. Your professor could be egalitarian and equally distribute the grant moneys among all the participants in the class. If so, each person, including your instructor, would receive $25 for participating in the study. Further, all would share equally in gathering data from the population. With 20 students gathering data from a population of 15,000 students, each class member would be responsible for contacting 750 students. That works out to be a little over three cents ($0.03) per person in the population. While we have all done unpaid, volunteer work, consider how much time would be required to contact 750 students by telephone. Further, the president wants the results of the study within two weeks. Thus, your class does not have the time or financial support for a complete enumeration of the population. The class decision is to draw a sample of 100 students.* In sum, because of the time constraints and limited budget, the scientist could not and would not want to study the population but would select a modest, but adequate, sample.

Given that a sample of 100 persons is to be contacted and questioned about income, each student assistant would be responsible for five people, which is not an unreasonable task for the time frame or the monetary compensation. The data-gathering phase is concluded when each student has secured five incomes from five different sampled persons with the class having a total of 100 values for student income. You will recall that in Chapter 4 we had some difficulty making sense out of 20 midterm grades. We doubt the 100 values of income would be any more comprehensible as an aggregate of raw data, which then leads us to a consideration of population parameters and sample statistics.

ISSUE 2: SUMMARIZING DATA

Population Parameters

A *population parameter* is a descriptive mathematical value that condenses and summarizes empirical data contained in the universe. As such,

it functions as a summary measure relevant to some characteristic of the population. Such parameters are identified by Greek letters to distinguish them from sample statistics which are mathematical values derived from samples. There are a great number of types of such summary measures ranging from measures of central tendency and variation to measures of association.

Descriptive Statistics

A *descriptive statistic* is a mathematical value that summarizes empirical data contained within a sample. This function is the same as that performed by a population parameter. Indeed, the two formulas may well be the same with the exception that Greek letters symbolize parameters and Arabic letters symbolize sample statistics. It is not our purpose to inventory or even suggest the dimensions of such an inventory of the large number of formulas found in any statistics book. But we do want to illustrate the conceptual and methodological points that are raised in one's sampling design. Therefore, although we need to deal with a few statistical formulas, we will simplify this task by only focusing on *one variable*. There are two possible dimensions of a single variable that might be relevant for a descriptive statistical analysis: (1) the dimension of central tendency and (2) the dimension of variation.

Central Tendency.   *Central tendency* refers to a single value of some variable that purports to be a typical value of a whole set of such values. Thus, the various measures of central tendency tend to have values that fall somewhere toward the middle of the range of values that compose the entire set.[1] We have selected the mean or arithmetic average as our measure of central tendency here. The *statistical mean* is the sum of all the individual scores or values divided by the total number of values. Thus, the formula is:†

---

*While we will discuss the nature of the sampling procedure and the appropriate sample size later, assume here that 100 persons are adequate and that the sample was properly drawn.

†The formula for a sample mean would substitute n—the sample size—for N—the population or sampling frame size, and x_i for X_i.

$$\mu \text{ (for population data)}$$
or
$$\overline{X} \text{ (for sample size)} = \dfrac{\sum\limits_{i=1}^{N} X_i}{N}$$

You will recall we used this formula earlier in Chapter 4.

Variation. *Variation* is the degree to which the values of some variable differ from one another among the elements being measured. Variation focuses on the spread or the dispersion in a set of measurements. Indeed, it is because of variation that sampling is such a problem to the social and the behavioral scientist. If *any one* element in the population was truly a mirror image of any other element in the population, one would only have to draw a sample of one element. But such is rarely the case. Thus, John's salary is different from Fred's salary, and the mean salary between John and Fred may or may not accurately reflect the total mean population parameter of all those people in the population from which John and Fred were drawn. Of course, variation amongst variables is what scientists focus upon. Therefore, scientists want the sample to accurately reflect variation within the population.

To illustrate, we will discuss one measure of variation—the standard deviation. "The *standard deviation* is the square root of the arithmetic average of the sum of the squared deviations around the mean in a distribution."[2] For population data, the formula is*:

$$\delta \text{ (population data)} = \sqrt{\dfrac{\sum\limits_{i=1}^{N} (X_i - \mu)^2}{N}}$$

where

δ = the standard deviation of the *population*
μ = the population mean or average of some variable

TABLE 6.1 Computational Table for the Standard Deviation of the Population of 20 Methodology Midterm Scores Listed in Table 4.1

CASE	SCORE (X_i)	($X_i - \mu$)	($X_i - \mu$)²
1	84	7.35	54.0225
2	78	1.35	1.8225
3	62	−14.65	214.6225
4	72	−4.65	21.6225
5	70	−6.65	44.2225
6	90	13.35	178.2225
7	66	−10.65	113.4225
8	92	15.35	235.6225
9	70	−6.65	44.2225
10	83	6.35	40.3225
11	69	−7.65	58.5225
12	83	6.35	40.3225
13	80	3.35	11.2225
14	90	13.35	178.2225
15	63	−13.65	186.3225
16	72	−4.65	21.6225
17	76	−0.65	0.4225
18	85	8.35	69.7225
19	68	−8.65	74.8225
20	80	3.35	11.2225

Sum	1533	0.0	1600.55
Mean = 76.65		Standard Deviation = 8.945	

X_i = the value of the variable for the ith element
N = the total number of elements in the population

However, if one is using data derived from a sample to *estimate* the population standard deviation, then a slight revision in the above formula must be made.[3] This revised formula is:

$$s \text{ (sample data)} = \sqrt{\dfrac{\sum\limits_{i=1}^{n} (x_i - \overline{X})^2}{n-1}}$$

---

*Gene Lutz argues that this definition is purely mathematical in nature and, therefore, cannot and should not be subjected to a verbal description.

TABLE 6.2 Computational Table for the Standard Deviations for the Four Simple Random Samples of Five Student Methodology Midterm Grades Listed in Table 4.2

SAMPLE/CASE	SCORE (x_i)	($x_i - \overline{X}$)	($x_i - \overline{X}$)²
SAMPLE I *CASE*	*MEAN ($\overline{X}$) = 69.0*	*DESCRIPTIVE* *STANDARD DEVIATION (s) = 7.211*	
1	63	−6.0	36.0
2	62	−7.0	49.0
3	70	1.0	1.0
4	80	11.0	121.0
5	70	1.0	1.0
Sum	345	0.0	208.0
SAMPLE II *CASE*	*MEAN ($\overline{X}$) = 74.6*	*DESCRIPTIVE* *STANDARD DEVIATION (s) = 6.914*	
1	85	10.4	108.16
2	78	3.4	11.56
3	72	−2.6	6.76
4	68	−6.6	43.56
5	70	−4.6	21.16
Sum	373	0.0	191.20
SAMPLE III *CASE*	*MEAN ($\overline{X}$) = 77.2*	*DESCRIPTIVE* *STANDARD DEVIATION (s) = 11.819*	
1	72	−5.2	27.04
2	90	12.8	163.84
3	72	−5.2	27.04
4	63	−14.2	201.64
5	89	11.8	139.24
Sum	386	0.0	558.80
SAMPLE IV *CASE*	*MEAN ($\overline{X}$) = 72.6*	*DESCRIPTIVE* *STANDARD DEVIATION (s) = 11.194*	
1	84	11.4	129.96
2	85	12.4	153.76
3	63	−9.6	92.16
4	69	−3.6	12.96
5	62	−10.6	112.36
Sum	363	0.0	501.20

where

s = the standard deviation of the *sample*
$\overline{X}$ = the sample mean of some variable
x_i = the value of the variable for the ith element
n = the total number of elements in the sample

In this case, $n-1$ rather than n is used, because sample data provides "an underestimate of its [the population's] standard deviation."[4] The use of $n-1$ is particularly important if the sample size is *small*. Therefore, we have used the first formula for the computations in Table 6.1 and the second formula for Table 6.2.

Quite simply, one subtracts the mean of some characteristic from each element's value on that characteristic, squares all the differences, adds the squares together, divides by the total number of elements, and takes the square root of the quotient. Thus, the standard deviation is a mathematical measure of the average dispersion or variation of a particular characteristic around the adjusted mean. A large value indicates great spread, while a small value indicates little spread.

In Tables 4.1 and 4.2 we presented a population of 20 midterm grades and drew four simple random samples of five scores each. Tables 6.1 and 6.2 indicate the necessary computations and the results for determining the mean population parameter (μ = mu), the four sample means ($\overline{X}$ = X bar), and the standard deviation of the population (δ = sigma) and the four sample standard deviations (s).

While these data are too few for the statistical analysis and interpretations which are given, we have kept them simple here because they are hypothetical and we want you to do the calculations with us. They are relatively simple, and Tables 6.1 and 6.2 should help you cross-check your reading of the formulas.* Again, the emphasis is on the logic and interpretation of these statistical items.

The Example

Continuing with our example of the feasibility study for a university tuition increase, assume that after all 100 values of income are summed and divided by 100, the resulting mean is $2,211. The value of $2,211 is a descriptive statistic in that it summarizes the empirical evidence of all 100 reported incomes of the students sampled.

Your class will then prepare a report to the president, in which the objective and methodology of the study are explained. In the results section the class will report that the mean value of income for the 100 students sampled is $2,211. The report is mailed and beats the two week deadline by three days. You are confident an adequate and responsible survey has been done.

Two days later, however, your professor receives a telephone call from the president's office. Apparently, she is unhappy with the study. The president would like to know the mean of the university *population*. She's upset that the class would send her a report in which only 100 students were sampled, when she wants to know what the figure is for all of the 15,000 students. The difficulty here was your class did not have the time or money to study the entire population. While researchers are compelled to use samples for practical reasons, they are interested in parameters. In other words, what one has is a descriptive statistic relevant to a sample, and what one wants is a population parameter that is descriptive of the totality. This brings us to the issue of inference.

ISSUE 3: MAKING INFERENCES FROM THE SAMPLE TO THE POPULATION

Introduction

To understand the process of making inferences, one needs to understand the differences and impli-

---

*By doing these calculations, we hope you will develop a greater appreciation for and understanding of the nature of statistical analysis. It is important to gain this understanding in light of the usage of computers today. This knowledge will permit correct programming and accurate calculations of very complex formulas for incredible numbers of data in very little time.

cations between sampling and nonsampling error; what inferential or inductive statistics are; the nature of the population, sample, and sampling distributions; the standard normal distribution; probability theory; the degree of sampling error one is willing to tolerate in any specific study; and the nature of the sampling procedure or design (along with a few relatively simple statistical formulas used to illustrate this interrelated cadre of notions).

Sampling and Nonsampling Error

Whenever samples are used, it is for reasons of efficiency, and the researcher's desire is to have the sample reflect some characteristic or series of characteristics within the population.*

Sampling Error.   *Sampling error* refers to the difference between the value of the descriptive statistic for the sample and the value of the true population parameter, which is due *solely* to the sample's not being representative of the population. Earlier, when we drew four simple, random samples of five midterm grades from a population of 20 midterm grades, we calculated the mean grade for each sample and discovered that each mean value differed from the population mean by differing amounts. (See Tables 6.1 and 6.2.) These differences were due solely to sampling error. There is likely to be some unrepresentativeness in a sample, simply because it is a sample and not an entire population. This variation is said to be caused by chance. Chance, you will recall, is the total fluctuation from the truth due to factors that are unknown to the researcher and that are lumped together under the rubric chance. We know, then, that sample descriptive statistics will not precisely reflect the population parameters, *in part,* simply because of sampling error. But sampling error is not an insurmountable difficulty. While we know that sample descriptive statistics are subject to sampling error, we also know that these errors follow certain patterns for *specific statistics* and for *specific sampling designs*. The likelihood of these errors being of certain magnitudes can be determined by the use of inferential statistics in conjunction with the sampling distribution of the specific descriptive statistic.

Inferential Statistics.   Along with descriptive statistics, there are inferential or inductive statistics. An *inferential statistic* functions to measure the likelihood that some descriptive statistic determined on sample data is also a correct estimate of the population parameter. In other words, an inferential statistic is a measure of the probability that what has been found to be true of the sample is also true of the population from which the sample was drawn. Thus, while sampling errors occur, inferential statistics can be used to determine their magnitudes within desired limits of accuracy. In sum, while forced for practical reasons to calculate descriptive statistics on samples as estimates of the desired population parameters and knowing that such leads to sampling errors, inferential statistics help the researcher to assess these errors by giving the researcher some notion of the sampling errors' patterns of occurrence and their likelihoods.

Nonsampling Error.   *Nonsampling error* refers to the difference between the value of the descriptive statistic and the value of the population parameter which is due to reasons *other than* sampling error. If one studied the entire population, the mean income of the population would, in all likelihood, not be an accurate measure of the population parameter since its determination would be subject to additional errors despite sampling error's being reduced to zero.[5]

---

*We discuss the criteria for representativeness later in Chapter 7. But, here, we would like to continue the discussion of the reasons for sampling by giving our final reason, which is related to the notion of error in samples. Therefore, we will *assume* that those criteria to be mentioned subsequently on the selection procedures for a proper sample have been applied.

Examples of Nonsampling Errors

Nonsampling errors are quite diverse in nature. Some of the more typical ones are the following.

Nonresponse.   First, *nonresponse errors* occur when a person chosen to participate in the study refuses to do so. Nonresponse can occur in two ways. On the one hand, a respondent may simply refuse to participate by refusing to talk to the interviewer or by throwing the schedule into the trash can, resulting in what is called *total nonresponse*. Those who have been sampled but cannot be located also fall into this category. There is little the researcher can do in situations such as these with the exception of following the guidelines suggested in the chapter on surveys (see Chapter 10). Such total nonresponses may be a function of the nature of those who have been sampled and the nature of the study itself. Such should be considered in the planning stage in order to select a data-gathering technique that is likely to minimize its occurrence.

On the other hand, *selective nonresponse* errors may occur when the respondent participates in the study but refuses to answer one or more, but not all, of the items in the survey. For example, when interviewing middle-class people, one of your authors found considerable reluctance on the part of the respondents to a question concerning the person's income level. Middle-class people don't really like to talk about their salaries, fees, or investment income to strangers. While such problems do occur, many can be minimized through pretesting of the measuring instrument and subsequent revision of the troublesome items (See Chapter 9).

Nonresponse, be it total or selective, is a concern because the respondent chosen to represent the population will not be represented. Of course, this refusal to participate will be known to the researcher—unless the study guarantees respondent anonymity. What isn't known, however, is the nature of the missing responses. In other words, we know error is introduced into the study, but the nature of the error is difficult to determine. This is not a sampling problem per se, since the respondent was sampled. Rather, in one way or another the nonrespondent's failure to participate introduces error into the representativeness of the values of the descriptive statistics that are generated from those who did participate.

Item Misinterpretation.   A second source of nonsampling error is the misinterpretation of items. An *item misinterpretation* occurs when the respondent reads the item in a way other than the way in which the researcher intended, resulting in a response that is inappropriate to the researcher's objective. For example, in a mailed questionnaire the researcher may want to assess the respondent's educational level and present the following fill-in-the-blank question: "What was your last year in school?" The researcher anticipates responses such as "two years of high school" or "tenth grade" or "48 credit hours in college." While most of those sampled would respond in terms such as these, some proportion of the sample will respond with answers such as "1944" and "1967" or "I'm still in school." Again, an adequate pretest (see Chapter 8) should rectify most instances of item misinterpretation.

Falsified Answer.   Third, nonsampling error may be introduced in the form of a *falsified answer.* Although the respondent provides an answer to an item, it may not be a truthful answer. For example, the homeowner may falsify information when speaking to the property assessor who is inquiring about the number of bathrooms in the homeowner's residence or whether the basement is finished. Respondents may inflate their income if they think such may elevate their stature in the eyes of the interviewer. Here, the truth is "adjusted" to serve the respondents' own perceived purposes.

Inaccurate Answer.   Fourth, one often incurs inaccurate answers. An *inaccurate answer* occurs when the respondent genuinely forgets to report a relevant piece of requested information. For example, when asked how many children are in the family, parents frequently mention all their children by name—all, that is, except the newborn infant. When asked about the family's income the husband may report his wife's and his income, but inadvertently neglect to mention their recently graduated daughter's income.

Coding Error.   Fifth, in preparing data for analysis, there may be coding errors as the raw data are assembled for computer processing. A *coding error* results when the numerical designation for some particular attribute is used for a different attribute. For example, one may be coding the item on the respondent's sex by assigning the number *1* to the male response; the number *2* to the female response; and the number *3* to the respondent's failure to answer this item or to the interviewer's failure to record such information. It may happen, particularly as fatigue sets in, that the coder unintentionally codes a male with a *2* and/or a female with a *1*.

Summary of These Examples.   These are a few of the many examples of nonsampling errors that are encountered in the social and behavioral sciences. Note that many of these difficulties are specific to studies dealing with people.

Types of Nonsampling Errors

While there are many examples of nonsampling errors, they may be categorized into one of two general attributes on the dimension of their effect upon descriptive statistics.[6]

Bias.   The first attribute is bias. *Bias* is the type of error that tends not to cancel another out and that, therefore, tends to accumulate. For example, because youth, beauty, and vivaciousness are valued in American culture, some respondents may report their ages to be a few years lower than their true ages. Thus, biases are distortions that occur in the same direction. Although social scientists know about many of the variables that elicit biased responses and the direction in which the bias is likely to be expressed, they do not know the degree to which the true value has been changed. Thus, the problem is that while we know that some people generally reduce their reported ages, we don't know by how many years.

Random Error.   The second attribute is random error. A *random error* is one that tends to cancel another out.[7] Recognizing that random errors are mistakes, some argue that when one adds the random errors on a single variable, they tend to cancel each other out so that one ends up where one would have been if the random errors had not been made in the first place. The clear implication is that random errors, while mistakes, are not mistakes that should trouble the researcher because they are, in a curious way, self-correcting. We don't agree. Consider the data in Table 6.3, which deals with a sample of persons measured on sex and salary. As we noted, coding errors are often cited as examples of random error. If the researcher wanted to prepare the data for machine processing by changing the *raw data* (that is, the data as they

TABLE 6.3   Data Gathered from a Sample of 10 People by Sex and by Annual Salary

CASE	NAME	SEX	SALARY	CASE	NAME	SEX	SALARY
1	Susan	Female	$ 2,000	6	Carl	Male	$25,000
2	Sandy	Female	6,000	7	Dean	Male	32,000
3	Marion	Female	11,000	8	Joe	Male	22,000
4	Cathy	Female	7,000	9	David	Male	29,000
5	Greta	Female	1,500	10	Tom	Male	57,000
	Mean = $5,500				Mean = $33,000		

have been collected) into some sort of numerical codes, males could be coded with a *1*, females coded with a *2*, and no answer coded with a *3*. A coding mistake would be made when a female, say Marion in Table 6.3, is coded with a *1* instead of a *2* or when a male, say Joe, is coded with a *2* instead of a *1*. As we said, such mistakes tend to cancel out; that is, for every time a male is miscoded as a female, a female will be miscoded as a male. Thus, if Joe were designated as a female and Marion were designated as a male, although two mistakes would have been made, the result would still be five females and five males in the sample. The implication is that such mistakes do not matter because one ends up with the same result one would have had if the two errors had not been made. But do we really?

We believe that the self-correcting property of random errors is misleading. The tendency for such errors to cancel out is true only for certain measures— such as the proportion of males and females—and only if one is considering a characteristic of a single variable and not combinations of variables. Thus, it is true that the percentage of females in Table 6.3 is 50 percent and if the cited random coding errors are made, it will still work out to 50 percent. However, what if one was interested in the mean salary of the males and females in one's sample. Assume that each person's salary was as shown in Table 6.3. The mean value of the five females' salaries is $5,500, while the mean value of the five males' salaries is $33,000. Given that these two mean income values are valid, consider a miscoding error on the sex of *both* Marion and Joe. That is, let's put Marion with her $11,000 salary with the males and Joe with his $22,000 salary with the females. If one recalculates the mean value of salary for those *now classified* female and male, the values will be, respectively, $7,700 and $30,800. The recalculated mean value of the females' income is not the same as the original figure, nor is it for the males. We conclude that random error only cancels out on the variable on which the error occurs and then only for *selected* descriptive measures, such as the proportion or percentage of the sexes studied.*

In all fairness, however, we should note that we could have miscoded Sandy and experienced no change whatsoever in the salary *range* of the females. Clearly, one must be careful to evaluate the nature of the statistic and its sensitivity to random error. Nevertheless, in essence, we believe the term *random error* to be a highly suggestive concept that can be, in a majority of analytical situations, misleading in its interpretation.

Relationship between Sampling Error and Nonsampling Error

Sampling error results because one must use some sort of sample, while nonsampling errors are a consequence of other factors and can occur if one is studying a sample or a population. We now consider the *relationship* among sampling error, nonsampling error, and total error as well as the implications of these relationships.

Both Blalock and Lazerwitz have argued that the relationship between sampling and nonsampling error can be conceptualized as indicated in Figure 6.1.[8] The relationship among sampling error, nonsampling error, and total error is described by the Pythagorean theorem. Quite simply, the *total error* is equal to the square root of the sum of the squares of the sampling and the nonsampling error:

$$\text{Total error} = \sqrt{\left[\frac{\text{sampling}}{\text{error}}\right]^2 + \left[\frac{\text{nonsampling}}{\text{error}}\right]^2}$$

It is important to realize that any measurable decrease in one leg of the triangle without a corresponding decrease in the other leg will lead to a less than dramatic reduction in the total error within the study (see exhibit *B* in Figure 6.1). That is,

---

*Note that the range of values—a descriptive measure of the dispersion within the data—may not cancel out. The five correctly coded females have salaries that range from $1,500 to $11,000. However, miscoding Marion and Joe, as we did above, changes the female range to $1,500 to $22,000. The range of incomes for the males would similarly be altered by coding error.

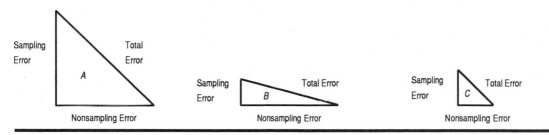

FIGURE 6.1   The Relationship among Sampling Error, Nonsampling Error, and Total Error

unless one substantially reduces both sampling and nonsampling error (see exhibit *C* in Figure 6.1), one's total error will remain significant.

A final comment is germane to nonsampling error. There are no statistical formulas that measure the degree to which there is nonsampling error. At this point in the development of the art of statistical analysis, one cannot measure the incidence or degree of nonsampling error. We know it occurs, but we do not know to what degree it occurs in any one study.

Assessing Sampling Error

Introduction.   By necessity, this section must be one of the more statistical and mathematical. We argued earlier that the topic of sampling brings together conceptual, methodological, and statistical matters. The theory of probability and numerous statistical issues converge when measuring sampling error. We have tried to keep the formulas and calculations presented at the minimum number possible.* In this subsection, we focus attention on the notions of data distributions, the standard normal distribution, confidence levels, the descriptive standard deviation, and a brief word about meeting assumptions.

Types of Distributions.   There are three types of data distributions: (1) the population distribution; (2) the sample distribution; and (3) the sampling

distribution.[9] There is also a fourth, nondata, theoretical distribution called "standard normal distribution."

Population Distribution.   The *population distribution* refers to the relative frequency with which the values of the population fall into a value or a category of values from all of the theoretically possible values on some measurement. Recall the example of midterm grades for the methods course. The examination had a possible range of values from 0 percent to 100 percent. The population distribution is the number of times that a particular score characteristic of some number of persons in the universe actually occurred from among all the possible scores. In our example, if we plotted the frequency of occurrence of the 20 scores in the total population, the data would be as indicated in column one of Table 6.4. For example, note that no one in the population received a perfect score of 100 and no one received a grade below 62.

Sample Distribution.   The *sample distribution* is the frequency with which scores from those sampled persons fell into certain values or categories of values among all values possible. For example, columns two through five of Table 6.4 indicate the sample distributions of the four simple random samples of five cases each. Note in Table 6.4 that while no one sample distribution can be a perfect reflection of the population distribution

---

*Further, the data that we will use may not be from a sample of sufficient size. Again, we have chosen to somewhat oversimplify our examples to encourage you to do the calculation with us. In this way, we hope the example will be more meaningful. As we've repeatedly maintained, our concern is with the conceptualization and understanding of these matters.

TABLE 6.4 Frequency Distribution of Actual Midterm Scores for a Hypothetical Population of 20 Students and Four Simple Random Samples of 5 Students from That Population

POSSIBLE SCORE	POPULATION FREQUENCY	SAMPLE I FREQUENCY	SAMPLE II FREQUENCY	SAMPLE III FREQUENCY	SAMPLE IV FREQUENCY
100					
.					
.					
92	1				
91					
90	1			1	
89	1			1	
88					
87					
86					
85	1		1		1
84	1				1
83	2				
82					
81					
80	2	1			
79					
78	1		1		
77					
76	1				
75					
74					
73					
72	2		1	2	
71					
70	2	2	1		
69	1				1
68	1		1		
67					
66	1				
65					
64					
63	1	1		1	1
62	1	1			1
.					
00					
Mean	76.65	69.0	74.6	77.2	72.6

because the sample must have fewer numbers of elements than the population, each sample also contains a distribution of scores *different from* any other sample distribution, *even though* the sampling procedure was the same for all four samples. Note as well from Table 6.5 that the mean scores, ranges, and standard deviations among the four samples all vary. Thus, each sample distribution is

TABLE 6.5   Values of Selected Measures for the Population and the Four Samples Posited in Tables 6.1 and 6.2

UNIT OF ANALYSIS / STATISTICAL MEASURE	NUMBER OF ELEMENTS	MEAN	ACTUAL RANGE	STANDARD DEVIATION
Population	20	76.65	62–92	8.945
Sample I	5	69.0	62–80	7.211
Sample II	5	74.6	68–85	6.914
Sample III	5	77.2	63–90	11.819
Sample IV	5	72.6	62–85	11.194

likely to be different from any other sample distribution on any number of possible descriptive statistics.

Sampling Distribution.   The *sampling distribution* is a theoretical distribution of all of the possible combinations of values of a particular descriptive statistic for a sample of some specified size that could have occurred by pure chance. This is a deceptively simple definition. First, the specific sampling distribution will depend upon the size of the sample. Second, it will depend upon the specific descriptive statistic that is being used in that different statistics *may* have different sampling distributions. Third, it will depend on the type of sampling procedure used to draw the sample. Finally, it will depend on what could happen only by random chance factors. Thus, if one changes sample size, sampling procedure, or the selected descriptive statistic to be calculated on all the samples, the nature of the sampling distribution may also change.

In sum, there are three distributions. The population distribution is observed when each element in the population is measured. The sample distribution is achieved by measuring each element of the sample with the same measure. The sampling distribution is registered by pure chance for a particular statistic that was used to summarize all the possible specific measures of each element.

After drawing a sample, the investigator will have one sample distribution of values that will need to be summarized by some descriptive statis-

tic. Further, if one wants to know the likelihood that what was found to be true of the sample is true of the population, an inferential statistic will have to be calculated. It is here that the sampling distribution becomes important. Certain descriptive statistics have known sampling distributions. For example, if the researcher were to draw an infinite number of simple random samples from the *same* population of elements and calculate the mean statistic for some dimension within that sample, the sampling distribution for that statistic would be a normal curve. One should be aware that there are several possible normal curves that could be recorded. Some are narrow and peaked, while others are broad and flat. Figure 6.2 offers an example of three possible normal curves.

The Standard Normal Distribution.   The final distribution to be discussed is of the greatest importance to the scientist. The *standard normal distribution* is the one normal curve the researcher would get *if* the mean were zero and if the standard deviation were one. As Lutz argues, the standard normal distribution has characteristics and properties that are useful if one's data, which may be normally distributed in a number of ways, can be adjusted or transformed into this standardized form.[10] By so doing, the researcher can compare the data against a theoretical distribution and against any other study using the standardized normal curve. Therefore, the major advantages of using the standard normal distribution are: first, the probabilities of certain things happening have

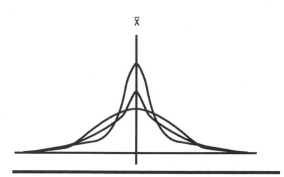

FIGURE 6.2 Three Different Normal Curves That All Possess the Same Mean

already been worked out (see the appendices of any statistics book), and, second, the researcher's probabilities can be compared to those of other research efforts.

If the sample mean for some characteristic is 187.7 in study A and 221.1 in study B, these respective descriptive values are important in *describing* that characteristic in both these studies. It may be, however, that the sample distributions in studies A and B differ as indicated by the different normal curve distributions in Figure 6.2. Therefore, comparisons would be difficult, and what could have happened by pure chance through sampling error would have to be determined for the normal curve descriptive of study A and for a different normal curve descriptive of study B.

However, by transforming one's data to standard scores and using the *one* normal distribution called the standard normal distribution, such comparisons are possible. Further, comparisons between *any* study and the table of probabilities that describe the standard normal distribution can be made. A final advantage to using the standard normal distribution is that there is only one distribution for a number of different statistics if determined on *a* simple random sample of any moderate size. Given the right conditions, the probabilities of certain values occurring from a great number of

statistical procedures, from simple random samples containing a wide range of elements, can be assessed using *one* theoretical distribution—the standard normal distribution.*

Our desire is to use the characteristics of the standard normal distribution because it is impervious to differing sample sizes and the nature of the variable being measured. This is true as long as the researcher uses a simple random sampling procedure and only certain descriptive statistics. Thus, this particular normal distribution has known probabilities that facilitate decisions concerning the values and worth of descriptive statistics. Hence, some notion of the degree to which the descriptive sample statistic is expected to differ from the population parameter because of sampling error is provided.

Properties of Standard Normal Distribution. Figure 6.3 depicts the standard normal curve with some of its properties. The standard normal distribution has all the characteristics of any normal distribution. First, it is unimodal and has a symmetrical bell shape. Second, the mean (average score), median (the middle-most score), and modal category (the most frequently occurring value) are the same value, which is indicated by the peak of the curve. Third, the vertical axis, called the *ordinate* (or *Y* axis), represents the number of elements that possess some degree of the characteristic being measured, which, in turn, is represented by the horizontal axis called the *abscissa* (or the *X* axis). Where the two axes lines or coordinates meet is called the *origin,* and this point represents zero elements on the *Y* axis and a zero degree of the characteristic on the *X* axis. Fourth, most descriptive statistics of a majority of the simple random samples fall closer to the mean rather than away from it. As one moves away from that point on the abscissa that represents the mean, median, and mode, in either direction, the number of elements possessing that value de-

---

*The results of *all* statistical formulae are not normally distributed; but most are. We direct your attention to a statistics text for information on which techniques are and which are not. While there are other theoretical distributions, the basic logic and procedure for their uses are the same as for the standard normal distribution.

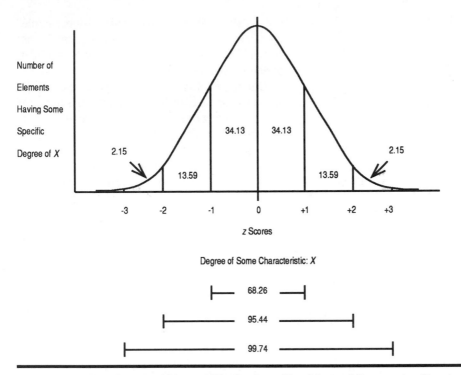

Number of

Elements

Having Some

Specific

Degree of *X*

FIGURE 6.3   The Standard Normal Distribution with a Mean of Zero and a Standard Deviation of One in Which the Individual Scores Have Been Transformed into *z* Scores and Showing the Percentage of Scores That Fall into Various Sections of the Distribution

creases. For example, note that few elements possess a value of *X* less than three standard deviations away from the mean in *either* direction. The fact that most of the elements in the sample tend to cluster closer to the mean rather than the extremes is due to a mathematical law called the *central limit theorem*. This theorem states that the sampling distribution from repeated samples of a large size will be nearly normal in shape *even if the characteristic being studied is not normally distributed in the population.*[11] Fifth, different areas under the curve represent different proportions of the number of possible elements. That is, the area between one standard deviation above and below the mean contains 68.26 percent of all the possible values of an infinite number of simple random samples. Similarly, the area under the curve between two standard deviations above and below

the mean contains 95.44 percent of all the cases. Finally, the area of three standard deviations above and below the mean contains 99.74 percent of all the cases. The only way the standard normal distribution differs from other normal distributions is that the data have been transformed into *z* scores with a mean of 0 and a standard deviation of 1.

In sum, the *most important point* is that this is the variation that occurs when one measures and plots the distribution for the same descriptive statistic from an infinite number of simple random samples selected from the same population. If one strictly adhered to the criteria already cited, this is the distribution one *would observe solely because of sampling error.*

Returning to our example involving midterm grades, we calculated the mean population parameter (μ) of all 20 scores and found it to be 76.65

percent. We also calculated the standard deviation of this population and found it to be 8.945 (see Table 6.1). If we had a large number of population scores, we would have had to draw a sample of them, as we did with the 100 students from the university population of 15,000. Therefore, let us *assume* that we drew one simple random sample (in this case, Sample I as shown in Table 6.2) and that the population parameters of the mean (μ) and the standard deviation (δ) are *not known* to us. Instead, we found the Sample I mean to be 69.0 percent and the standard deviation (s) to be 7.211. We would like to know what the population parameters are, but we only have information from our sample.

We know the mean from repeated samples will be distributed as a normal distribution. Careful study of the normal distribution shows that the actual mean of the *population*, as indicated by the mean of this distribution, is the most likely score. That is, our value of 69.0 percent is more likely to be the population parameter than any other single score. Therefore, we will treat our mean value from the sample (69.0 percent) as an *estimate* of the population value. We do know that our sample value of 69.0 percent could be different from the population parameter just because of sampling error or the fact that our sample was not totally representative of the population. Further, the standard normal distribution will allow us to guess the likelihood that our sample descriptive statistic of 69.0 percent is an accurate estimate of the population parameter. Permit us to examine how that is done.

The standard normal distribution allows construction of a *confidence interval* around the estimate of the population parameter. That is, if the mean of the sample is the best possible estimate of the population parameter, or (μ), we can use the standard normal distribution to create a range of values around this estimate within which we will be confident, to a predetermined degree, that the population parameter falls. First, one has to decide what degree of accuracy is desired. If the traditional level of 95 percent is selected, we would want to be correct 95 out of a 100 times that the

true mean of the population will fall somewhere within the range of values that can be established statistically. The general definitional formula for establishing confidence intervals is the following:

$$\text{Confidence interval} = \begin{bmatrix} \text{the value of an} \\ \text{observed descriptive} \\ \text{statistic} \end{bmatrix}$$

$$\pm \begin{bmatrix} \text{a selected} \\ \text{tabular} \\ \text{standard score} \end{bmatrix} \begin{bmatrix} \text{the standard} \\ \text{error of the} \\ \text{statistic} \end{bmatrix}$$

In this case, the specific formula would be:

$$CI = \overline{X} \pm (1.96)\frac{(s)}{\sqrt{n}}$$

where

CI = the confidence interval
$\overline{X}$ = the mean of the sample
1.96 = the standard score that represents 95 percent of the cases from a standard normal distribution
s = the *inferential* standard deviation
n = the total number of elements in the sample

Recall that one standard score above or below the mean of a standard normal distribution contains 68.26 percent of all the possible cases and two standard scores above or below the mean contains 95.44 percent of all the cases (see Figure 6.3). The appropriate statistical table will show that the value of 1.96 will encompass exactly 95 percent of all the cases that could have occurred through sampling error for any statistic that is normally distributed. A different level of confidence would dictate selection of a different standard score from the table.

Earlier we discussed the descriptive sample statistic of standard deviation (s). This (s), however, is different. It is not the *descriptive* standard deviation; it is the *inferential* standard deviation. As we have illustrated, some descriptive sample statistics, such as the mean, can be used as estimates of the population parameter. Other descriptive statistics do not make good estimates because they are biased. The descriptive standard deviation is one of these. However, statisticians have made an adjustment in the formula, if one wants to use it inferentially. This adjusted formula is:

$$s = \sqrt{\frac{\Sigma (x - \overline{X})^2}{n - 1}}$$

The terms in this formula are identical to those in the formula for the descriptive standard deviation with the exception of *1* being subtracted from *n*. By substituting the data for Sample I (see Table 6.2), the inferential standard deviation can be calculated as:

$$s = \sqrt{\frac{208}{4}}$$

$$= \sqrt{52}$$

$$= 7.211$$

The value of the inferential standard deviation (*s*) is needed to determine the standard error in the confidence interval formula. By making the appropriate mathematical substitutions, we have:

$$CI = \overline{X} \pm (1.96) \left(\frac{s}{\sqrt{n}}\right)$$
$$= 69.0 \pm (1.96) \left(\frac{7.211}{\sqrt{5}}\right)$$
$$= 69.0 \pm (1.96)\ (3.22)$$
$$= 69.0 \pm 6.31$$
$$= (69.0 - 6.31) \longleftrightarrow (69.0 + 6.31)$$
$$= 62.69 \longleftrightarrow 75.31$$

Thus, we would have 95 percent confidence that the population mean (μ) falls somewhere within the range of 62.69 percent to 75.31 percent. This assumes that the only source of sampling fluctuation was random chance. Notice that we used the sample mean (69.0 percent) as the midpoint for this range.

You will note the discrepancy between the upper limit of our range (75.31) and the population parameter of 76.65 reported in Table 6.1. We

made a conscious error so you could see the logic of one statistical procedure without having to do extensive mathematical calculations. While we hope this objective was accomplished, our example was too simple. In order to properly use the standard normal distribution, one must have a sufficient sample size. We also *assumed* the population's standard deviation (δ) was unknown, which usually would be the case. As we have seen, if the sample size is too small and if the population standard deviation must be estimated by the inferential standard deviation formula, the standard normal distribution cannot be used appropriately.

We can address this problem by recalculating the confidence interval with a t distribution. The *t distribution* is a different type of theoretical probability distribution and should be used when one has a small sample and an unknown population standard deviation. Again, working at the 95 percent level of confidence, we would substitute a different value taken from a different standard statistical table (in this case, 2.776) for the value of 1.96.* Using this value to recalculate the confidence interval results in:

$$CI = 69.0 \pm (2.776)\ (3.22)$$
$$= 69.0 \pm 8.94$$
$$= (69.0 - 8.94) \longleftrightarrow (69.0 + 8.94)$$
$$= 60.06 \longleftrightarrow 77.94$$

Clearly, this range contains the population parameter (μ = 76.65 percent) as indicated in Table 6.1. We hope it is apparent that if one fails to abide by the assumptions that underlie the proper use of statistical tools, one runs a high probability of significant misinterpretation.

A GLOSSARY OF SAMPLING TERMS

Various juxtaposed sampling terms illustrate different sampling levels and many of the assump-

---

*Parenthetically, we are not fully explaining these statistical decisions and formulas because we don't want this to become a statistics text. However, we do recommend a careful reading of any number of excellent books on statistics: see Blalock, Jr., 1972; Lutz, 1983; Hays, 1963; Mueller, Schuessler, and Costner, 1977; and Walker and Lev, 1953.

tions that the scientist makes when drawing samples. Because we were partially concerned with statistical inference earlier in this chapter, we were more interested in meeting the requirements for a proper statistical analysis. In this section, we are more concerned with numerical adequacy and degree of representativeness.

Universe

The *universe* contains all of the possible cases subsumed under some general conceptual heading. For example, when one uses the *theoretical* term *college students,* one is really referring to every person who ever attended college, is currently attending, or will attend in the future. Thus, the universe is a theoretical notion that can never be totally operationalized. This is similar to the difficulty we discussed regarding the difference between scientific proof and scientific verification. That is, because future cases of something have not yet occurred, they cannot be studied. Hence, we cannot be sure that what is correct at the time of the study will hold for the future. While scientists use these conceptual terms in the language of communication, they are never in a position to operationalize and test their empirical equivalents. Such generalization is an act of faith on the part of the scientist.

Population

You will remember that the *population* is all of the cases that exist at the time of the study. For example, if we wanted to study college students, the existing population would be everyone currently enrolled in college. As Kish puts it, "the population must be defined in terms of (1) content, (2) units, (3) extent, and (4) time."[12] In this way the universe is translated into a more limited, but existing, entity.

Study Population

The *study population* refers to all those elements that exist and from which the sample will be drawn.

For example, the study population could be everyone enrolled at your school. While we are getting closer to something that is manageable, it is always difficult to list all of the elements in a study population. A few first year students may have already departed from the campus without officially withdrawing, or the names of some students who registered late may not appear on the list you are using. In essence, you should realize that a complete list of a study population is difficult to constitute.

Sampling Frame

The *sampling frame* is the compiled list of elements from which the sample will be drawn. While it is the hope of the scientist that the sampling frame is identical to the study population, this is not likely to be the case. The objective is to achieve as much congruity between the sampling frame and the study population as possible. Kish is instructive in suggesting ways in which lists of elements can be "cleaned."[13] All the researcher can do is anticipate some difficulties and make some accommodations.

Practically, the researcher is not likely to have a complete listing of the existing population. Therefore, it is important to select a study population that is believed to be typical of the existing population. If the researcher is interested in studying college students, for example, an educational institution with students who are perceived to be somewhat typical of those currently enrolled at the collegiate level should be selected. In sum, since the realities of social and behavioral research will impose limitations on one's optimum sampling design, careful judgment must be exercised in the selection of an appropriate study population. This is especially important because when you generalize your study results to the population in the conclusion of your study, you are stepping beyond what your data will permit. While you must do this if you adhere to the scientific tenet of generalizability, you must do so cautiously.

Sampling Element

The *sampling elements* are the cases to be studied. For example, if 100 students were selected from a sampling frame, each selected student would be an element. The sampling elements are the entities from which data will be extracted.

Summary

These are the most important terms in the sampling vocabulary. It should be clear that scientists make a series of decisions that are not immediately obvious when they draw a sample. We will, subsequently, speak only of the sample and the population, but you should understand that the sample is what the scientist ends up drawing. The population is a more hypothetical unit that the scientist hopes to tap into and to which conceptual conclusions will be addressed. This is not done, however, without conscientiously attempting to pick a typical study population and without seriously attempting to purge inappropriate elements from and add appropriate missing elements to the sampling frame. With this introduction to some of the more subtle difficulties in creating a sampling design, we turn to the criteria that make for a good sample.

CRITERIA FOR A GOOD SAMPLE

There are essentially two criteria for a good sample: (1) efficiency or practicality and (2) representativeness.

Efficiency

Assuming that the researcher will study a sample rather than the population, one should seek a sample that is the most efficient. The more elements one selects, the longer the study will take and the greater the cost in time, effort, and expense. While one must have a minimum number of elements to legitimately interpret the data, studying more elements than necessary is wasteful. In the case of sampling, more is not necessarily bet-ter. We address the question of how large a sample must be in the next chapter.

Representativeness

Second, the sample should represent the characteristics contained in the population. *Representativeness* refers to the degree to which the sample is similar to the population on those characteristics of interest to the researcher.

Heterogeneity Versus Homogeneity

Homogeneity suggests that a population or sample of elements is very similar on one or more of the dimensions in which the researcher is interested. For example, all of the students enrolled in your school have in common the educational institution that they attend. Similarly, the women who try out for the field hockey team are homogeneous on the dimension of sex. Whatever attributes are shared within the population or the sample generate the characteristic of homogeneity.

Conversely, *heterogeneity* refers to a population or sample that is dissimilar on one or more of the characteristics in which the researcher is interested. For example, while your fellow students are homogeneous with regard to educational institution, they are probably heterogeneous on the dimensions of income, major field of study, and anticipated graduation date. Indeed, these dimensions may separate subclasses of elements that are homogeneous within the subclass but heterogeneous between subclasses.

The more heterogeneous the population, the larger the sample must be to achieve representativeness. In fact, if every element in the population were identical, one need only draw a sample of one, while a heterogeneous population requires greater numbers to achieve representation.

SUMMARY

Our primary objective in this chapter has been to help you see the interrelationship between conceptual concerns, methodological concerns, and statistical matters. We cannot overemphasize the differences among these areas and the significance of each as an integral component of the well-conceived study. Recognize, as well, that each statistical procedure must be treated as a separate operation. What is true for one technique may not be true for another. For example, the sample mean could be used as an unbiased indicator of the population mean, but the descriptive standard deviation could not be similarly inferred. This necessitated the use of a slightly different formula. Further, the proper use of any of these formulas required meeting certain mathematical assumptions.

We began with attention to the units of analysis and the potential for the ecological fallacy. Next, several issues related to sampling were presented: (1) why one needs to sample; (2) summarizing data with attention to the statistical elements of population parameters and sample statistics—both descriptive and inferential with specific reference to the mean as a measure of central tendency and standard deviation as a measure of variation; (3) making statistical inferences from the sample to the population with attention to sampling and nonsampling errors, inferential statistics, some examples of nonsampling errors, types of nonsampling errors, and the relationship between sampling and nonsampling error; (4) measuring sampling error with a focus on three kinds of data distributions—population, sample, and sampling—and the standard normal distribution, which is of key importance in assessing sampling error and the construction of a confidence interval about some descriptive statistic; (5) a comparison of various terms in the sampling vocabulary with attention to the concepts of universe, population, study population, sampling frame, and sampling element; and (6) the criteria for an appropriate sample focusing on efficiency and representativeness as well as the implications of homogeneity and heterogeneity within the population from which the sample is to be taken.

A clear and simple hypothetical example was interspersed throughout the chapter to illustrate the various issues, concepts, and relationships that were theoretically presented.

KEY TERMS

Abscissa	Nonresponse error	Sampling distribution
Bias	Nonsampling error	Sampling elements
Central limit theorem	Ordinate	Sampling error
Central tendency	Origin	Sampling frame
Coding error	Population	Selective nonresponse
Confidence interval	Population distribution	Standard deviation
Descriptive statistic	Population parameter	Standard normal distribution
Ecological fallacy	Random error	Statistical mean
Falsified answer	Raw data	Study population
Heterogeneity	Representativeness	Total error
Homogeneity	Sample	Total nonresponse
Inaccurate answer	Sample distribution	Universe
Inferential statistics	Sample statistic	Variation
Item misinterpretation	Sampling	

REVIEW QUESTIONS

1. What is the *ecological fallacy* and how does it relate to sampling?
2. What are the reasons for sampling?

3. What is the difference between the concepts of a population parameter and a sample statistic?

4. Distinguish between sampling and nonsampling error, and their relationship to total error.

5. What is the difference between descriptive and inferential statistics?

6. What are the types of nonsampling errors, and cite various examples.

7. Distinguish among a population distribution, a sample distribution, and a sampling distribution.

8. What is the standard normal distribution, its relationship to simple random sampling, and its relationship to inferential statistics?

9. Construct an integrated sample (in the same context) illustrating the concepts of universe, population, study population, sampling frame, and sampling elements.

10. What criteria are relevant to drawing a representative sample?

CHAPTER 7

THE CHARACTERISTICS AND TECHNIQUES OF DRAWING PROBABILITY AND NONPROBABILITY SAMPLES

INTRODUCTION

In the preceding chapter we addressed several issues that are related to sampling design. In this chapter we discuss the essential nuts and bolts of various sampling strategies with their advantages and disadvantages.

Occasionally, we refer to material from the last chapter, with which additional notions are developed. The bulk of this chapter, however, is devoted to probability and nonprobability sampling designs. We conclude with an example of how to use a list in order to select an appropriate sample.

COMPARISON OF PROBABILITY AND NONPROBABILITY SAMPLING

Probability Sampling

A *probability sample* is one in which the likelihood of selecting any one element from the sampling frame is known. That is, every element in the population *must* have a known likelihood of being included in the sample. Many of our colleagues refer to such samples as *random samples,* a practice that, we feel, is confusing. To use the term *random* to denote probability sampling creates confusion with the subtype of simple random sampling. We will always use *random* with the adjective *simple* to denote a specific type of probability sample. In sum, a sample is a probability sample if the researcher can determine the likelihood of inclusion of any element.

Nonprobability Sampling

Conversely, a *nonprobability sample* is one in which the likelihood of selecting any element from the sampling frame is *not* known. While nonprobability samples do not permit a statistically valid estimate of sampling error, they are not without their important uses in social research.

Our discussion will include several types of basic probability sampling designs: (1) simple random samples; (2) systematic samples; (3) proportional and disproportional stratified samples; and (4) single-stage and multi-stage cluster samples. We will also discuss several forms of nonprobability sampling techniques.

To assist a better understanding of this material, consider the data presented in Table 7.1. This table lists, by the nature of the academic program and by the class in school, a hypothetical categorization of 15,000 students attending a major university.

TYPES OF PROBABILITY SAMPLES

Simple Random Sampling

Preconditions. Two preconditions must be met before a simple random sample can be selected. First, one must generate an accurate listing of the sampling frame. A list is accurate when each element in the study population is listed once and

TABLE 7.1   Number and Percentage of University Students Currently Enrolled in a Hypothetical School by Class in School and by Nature of the Educational Program in Which the Student Is Registered

PROGRAM/CLASS	FRESHMEN	SOPHOMORES	JUNIORS	SENIORS	GRADUATE	TOTAL
DAY	2,000 (13.3)	1,700 (11.3)	1,650 (11.0)	1,750 (11.7)	350 (2.3)	7,450 (49.7)*
EVENING	1,600 (10.7)	1,300 (8.7)	1,050 (7.0)	650 (4.3)	250 (1.7)	4,850 (32.3)*
SUMMER	900 (6.0)	600 (4.0)	300 (2.0)	600 (4.0)	300 (2.0)	2,700 (18.0)
TOTAL	4,500 (30.0)	3,600 (24.0)	3,000 (20.0)	3,000 (20.0)	900 (6.0)	15,000 (100.0)

*The cell percentages added across the rows total a slightly different value than the row subtotal percentage due to the rounding of these values.

only once. While this may appear to be a simple task, in practice it is quite difficult. However, assume we have a reasonably accurate alphabetic listing of the students who have been cross-classified as shown in Table 7.1. The second precondition is that of numerical adequacy. The researcher must decide in advance how many elements are desired in the sample.

To draw a *simple random sample,* the researcher is expected to adhere to two criteria. First, each element in the sampling frame must have an equal probability of being selected. Second, each selection must be made independently of every other selection.

Equal Probability of Selection.   To understand *equal probability of selection,* consider drawing a simple random sample of 5 marbles from a jar containing a population of 10 different colored marbles. If the 10 marbles are thoroughly mixed, when one makes the first selection, the probability of any 1 marble of the 10 being picked is 1/10 or 0.100. Let us assume the first marble chosen is put aside in a saucer. The remaining marbles will have a 1/9 or 0.111 chance of being selected with the second choice. If we continue in this fashion, the

remaining marbles will have a 1/8 or 0.125 chance of being selected on the third draw, and so on. If we proceeded as indicated, we would have violated the criterion of each element in the population having an equal probability or chance of being selected. In order to meet this criterion, one must sample with replacement.

Sampling with replacement means each selection is returned to those elements remaining before the next choice is made. Thus, if we chose the red marble in our first draw, we would note the red marble as our first sample choice and return it to the jar prior to making our next choice. In so doing, when one chooses for the second time, the probability of selecting any one marble in the jar will still be 1/10 or 0.100. If we chose the green marble second, we would note this and return it to the jar before making the third choice. Thus, by sampling with replacement, one maintains the same probability for every sample selection throughout the sampling process.

Issue: Sampling with or without Replacement.   The investigator is not usually confronted with such a simple situation as drawing a simple random sample of 5 marbles from a population of 10.

Let us return to our study of student incomes that the president of the university requested. Recall that we needed a simple random sample of 100 students from the population of 15,000. The probability of the first selection of any element in the population being selected would be 1/15,000 or 0.0000667. Without replacement of each selection, a slight increase in the probability of selection would occur for the remaining students. Thus, the probability for the selection of the 100th student would be increased to 1/14,901 or 0.0000671. This represents a total probability change of +0.0000004. Clearly, unless one is selecting a relatively large proportion of the population *and* if the population itself is comparatively small, sampling without replacement does not significantly alter the probability of subsequent selections. For example, if we drew four 50 percent simple random samples without replacement from population sizes of 15,000, 500, 100, and 20, the probabilities would vary as indicated in Table 7.2. These probabilities only change significantly when the total number of elements in the population from which one is sampling is very small. For this reason, many argue that one may sample without replacement if the number of elements in the population is large.[1] Conversely, some social scientists argue more strongly for simple random sampling with replacement.[2] This debate concerning the necessity of replacement in the simple random sampling design is ongoing.

Our position is to not violate the assumption. With the large number of ways in which errors can enter a study, we see no reason to allow those that can be easily avoided, for example, by using a table of random numbers.

Independence of Choice. *Independence of choice* is maintained when the selection of any one element from the sampling frame has no impact on the selection of any subsequent element from that frame. Each choice, then, is made as a separate decision.

Again, consider the simple example of selecting 5 marbles from 10 different ones. Assume we are sampling with replacement and have made the first four selections: the red, green, blue, and white marbles. After returning the fourth selection, we choose the red marble, again. What do we do now? If we return the red marble and make a sixth choice and if we pick next the black marble, we have violated the assumption of independence of choice. That is, the only reason we picked the black marble is because we picked the red marble twice. The selection of the black marble was not made independently of all other selections.

Issue: The Multiple Selection of the Same Element. As with the issue of simple random sampling with or without replacement, statisticians and methodologists have taken various positions on the issue of the multiple selection of the

TABLE 7.2 Probability Changes for a 50 Percent Sample under the Conditions of the Simple Random Sampling Design without Element Replacement by Selected Choices and by Population Size and Sample Size

SELECTION CHOICE FOR A SAMPLE SIZE OF 0.5 (N) / POPULATION AND SAMPLE SIZE	N = 15,000 SAMPLE = 7,500	N = 500 SAMPLE = 250	N = 100 SAMPLE = 50	N = 20 SAMPLE = 10
First choice	0.0000667	0.00200	0.0100	0.0500
Middle choice	0.0000889	0.00267	0.0133	0.0667
Last choice	0.0001333	0.00398	0.0196	0.0909

same element. Some argue that multiple selection is foolish; after all, one cannot reliably interview, submit a questionnaire to, or do the same experiment on the same person twice.[3] Others argue that, when sampling with replacement, if the same element reappears, one merely disregards it and continues the sampling procedure until the desired sample size is achieved with each element different from any other sample element.[4] On the other side of this issue are those who feel strongly that one must strictly adhere to the independence of choice criterion.[5]

We agree with those who meet the assumption of independence of choice. The essential rationale is not, strictly speaking, a sampling reason. Rather, it is a statistical, data-analysis reason. That is, the majority of the descriptive and inferential statistical procedures assume the sample has been attained through strict adherence to the criteria of equal probability *and* independent selection. Kish writes:

> Why, then, does srs (simple random sampling) loom so large in sampling theory? First, because of its simple mathematical properties, most statistical theories and techniques assume simple random selection of elements, though usually from an infinite population and with unrestricted selection. Second, all probability selections may be viewed as restrictions on simple random selection . . . , which suppress some combinations of population elements, whereas srs permits all possible combinations. Third, the relatively simple srs computations are often used on data obtained by more complex selections. This procedure leads to good approximation in situations where the distribution of the variable in the population is effectively random. But this assumption of random distribution is often wrong and leads to gross mistakes.[6]

In his statistics book, Blalock writes, "when we sample without replacement, we violate the assumption of independence and that, strictly speaking, we therefore must modify our (statistical) formulas to take this fact into consideration."[7]

Many of the statistical formulas available to the social scientist were designed to function *in-ferentially* under the strict assumption that a simple random sample has been drawn. If one does not meet these sampling assumptions, various correction factors have to be introduced because of biases that influence the values resulting from these calculations.

Unfortunately, some practitioners either do not make the corrections or don't know that one has to make them. Indeed, such adjustments under a variety of different sampling conditions appear to be a major focus of Kish's classic work.[8] Further, these corrections are complicated adjustments and would require a sampling expert with a strong background in mathematical statistics.

Therefore, we take the position that one must meet assumptions that underlie the sampling procedures and all methodological and statistical procedures. Many of the misuses of simple random sampling, however, can be minimized by using a table of random numbers.

Using a Table of Random Numbers.   A table of random numbers is a listing of integers that has no discernible mathematical pattern. While other procedures have been attempted to generate a simple random sample, a table of random numbers is the preferred technique. See Table 7.3 for an excerpt of such a table.

To use a table of random numbers, the researcher must determine a starting point within the table. Should one start at the first row and the first column on the first page, or should one start at the eighth row and the ninth column on the second page? Actually, it does not matter, as long as the starting point is randomly selected. Since this section is being written on the 26th day of the month, let us arbitrarily start with the second row and the sixth column of Table 7.3; that is, with the first 0 in row two. If we wish to select 100 persons from a list of 15,000 names (as we did for the university president's study), we must construct a series of numbers with the same number of digits as the total number of elements in the sampling frame. In this example, we need five-digit numbers and will create such numbers by reading across row two beginning with column six and including the next four columns. Thus, our first random number of five digits would be 04805, which is shown in Table 7.3 as the boxed number in the upper left-hand corner.

At the same time, we would have an alphabetic listing of all 15,000 students at the university, which we would number serially starting with 1

and concluding with 15,000. For example, if Michael Aaron was the first person on the list, he would receive the number 00001, and if Sally Zymbalist was the last person on the list, she would receive the number 15,000. Each element in the sampling frame is assigned a different five-digit number ranging from 1 to 15,000. Since the

TABLE 7.3   An Excerpt from a Table of Random Numbers

```
1 0 0 9 7 3 2 5 3 3 7 6 5 2 0 1 3 5 8 6 3 4 6 7 3 5 4 8 7 6 . . .
3 7 5 4 2 [0 4 8 0 5] 6 4 8 9 4 7 4 2 9 6 2 4 8 0 5 2 4 0 3 7 . . .
0 8 4 2 2 6 8 9 5 3 1 9 6 4 5 0 9 3 0 3 2 3 2 0 9 0 2 5 6 0 . .
9 9 0 1 9 [0 2 5 2 9] 0 9 3 7 6 7 0 7 1 5 3 8 3 1 1 3 1 1 6 5 . . .
1 2 8 0 7 9 9 9 7 0 8 0 1 5 7 3 6 1 4 7 6 4 0 3 2 3 6 6 5 3 . . .
6 6 0 6 5 7 4 7 1 7 3 4 0 7 2 7 6 8 5 0 3 6 6 9 7 3 6 1 7 0 . . .
3 1 0 6 0 [1 0 8 0 5] 4 5 5 7 1 8 2 4 0 6 3 5 3 0 3 4 2 6 1 4 . . .
8 5 2 6 9 7 7 6 0 2 0 2 0 5 1 6 5 6 9 2 6 8 6 6 5 7 4 8 1 8 . . .
6 3 5 7 3 3 2 1 3 5 0 5 3 2 5 4 7 0 4 8 9 0 5 5 3 5 7 5 4 8 . . .
7 3 7 9 6 4 5 7 5 3 0 3 5 2 9 6 4 7 7 8 3 5 8 0 8 3 4 2 8 2 . . .
9 8 5 2 0 1 7 7 6 7 1 4 9 0 5 6 8 6 0 7 2 2 1 0 9 4 0 5 5 8 . . .
1 1 8 0 5 [0 5 4 3 1] 4 9 8 0 8 2 7 7 3 2 5 0 6 2 5 6 7 2 4 7 . . .
8 3 4 5 2 9 9 9 6 3 4 0 6 2 8 8 9 8 0 8 3 1 3 7 4 6 7 0 0 7 8 . . .
8 8 6 8 5 4 [0 2 0 0 8] 6 5 0 7 5 8 4 0 1 3 6 7 6 7 6 7 9 5 1 . . .
9 9 5 9 4 6 7 3 4 8 8 7 5 1 7 6 4 9 6 9 9 1 8 2 6 0 8 9 2 8 . . .
6 5 4 8 1 1 7 6 7 4 4 6 8 5 0 8 5 0 5 8 0 4 7 7 6 9 7 4 7 3 . . .
8 0 1 2 4 3 5 6 3 5 1 7 7 2 7 0 8 0 1 5 4 5 3 1 8 2 2 3 7 4 . . .
7 4 3 5 0 9 9 8 1 7 7 7 4 0 2 7 7 2 1 4 4 3 2 3 6 0 0 2 0 1 . . .
6 9 9 1 6 2 0 3 6 6 2 5 2 2 9 1 4 8 3 6 9 3 6 8 7 2 0 3 7 6 . . .
0 9 8 9 3 2 0 5 0 5 1 4 2 2 5 6 8 5 1 4 4 6 4 2 7 5 6 7 8 8 . . .
9 1 4 9 9 [1 4 5 2 3] 6 8 4 7 9 2 7 6 8 6 4 6 1 6 2 8 3 5 5 4 . . .
. . . . . . . . . . . . . . . . . . . . . . . . . .
. . . . . . . . . . . . . . . . . . . . . . . . . .
```

Taken from Hubert M. Blalock, Jr., *Social Statistics,* New York, New York: McGraw-Hill Book Company, Inc., 1960, p. 437, which was originally published by the RAND Corporation in 1955.

first five-digit random number generated from our table of random numbers after a random start was 04805, we would go down our sampling frame to that student who had been numbered 04805 and that student would be the first element in the sample.

If we desire a sample of 100 and if the student with the number 04805 is our first selection, we need to move through the table of random numbers in some way to generate 99 more students. It does not matter what direction we follow as we move through this table. We could drop down to row three for the next number right underneath our first number—in this case, 68953. Alternatively, we could move over row two to the next available five-digit number by moving one digit at a time—in this case, 48056. We could even move across the rows in groups of five digits—in this case, 64894. Again, it does not matter *how* one generates the second random number. What *is* crucial is that one *must continue the same pattern* throughout all the selections. To illustrate, let us drop down to the five digit number directly below our first choice. The second random number generated would be 68953. Since our list only goes to 15,000, we disregard this number and continue moving down the five columns underneath our original selection. The third random number is 02529, which is also boxed in Table 7.3. The student who is numbered 02529 then becomes the second sample choice. Continuing this pattern, the next two numbers—99970 and 74717—are disregarded since there are no students in the sampling frame with these numbers. The next usable number is 10805, which identifies the third student in our sample. Similarly, we select student 05431 and student 14523 for our fourth and fifth sample elements, respectively.

After selecting 14523 on the last row, we go back to the top of the page and generate a second set of five digits. We could move to the right one digit and thereby start with the five digits in row one in columns seven, eight, nine, ten, and eleven. If we did this, the first random number would be 25337, the second would be 48056, and the third

would be 89531. Indeed, if we did this, we'd have to go down to row seven before we would get our sixth sample person—in this case, 08054. Our seventh sample person would be 02008, and so forth. When one comes to the bottom of the page for the second time, a third column of five digits must be created *using the same* procedure we used to create the second column. In this case, we would move a single digit to the right and reject 53376. The most crucial criterion in using a table of random numbers is to always generate one's digits through the same pattern. The pattern does not matter, but it must be the same throughout the sampling procedure.

By using a table of random numbers, the effect is also to accomplish sampling with replacement. Further, one avoids the laborious and unnecessary task of placing each element on a separate piece of identical paper and thoroughly mixing them. When properly used, a table of random numbers guarantees equal probability of selection and independence of choice.

Since each selected element is replaced, it could be that an element would be selected again. But what of Lutz's concern mentioned earlier? How would one handle the multiple selection of the same person in an interview study? Would this person be interviewed twice? Of course not. The researcher would contact the person, set up the interview, and proceed through the data collection with this person in exactly the same way one would handle any person who had been selected once. However, this person's data would be duplicated and treated as if there were two people in the data-analysis stage.

In sum, using a table of random numbers simplifies the mechanics of drawing a simple random sample while maximizing adherence to both criteria of equal probability of selection and independence of choice.

Advantages of Simple Random Sampling.   There are two major advantages to simple random sampling. First, the design does not require the researcher to have much knowledge of the study population. One only needs an accurate list. Second, a simple random sample allows the researcher to use inferential statistical procedures. Earlier we noted that data from any type of probability sample could be treated inferentially, *theoretically speaking*. However, data from simple random samples can be subjected to inferential analysis, *practically speaking*. As we illustrated in the previous chapter, the standard normal distribution is one of several theoretical distributions that could have happened by pure chance. It is this type of theoretical distribution whose values appear in tables in the back of statistics books.

You should be aware that the tabular statistics for given levels of significance *are always the same* for *any* sample size above some minimum number for the *simple random sampling design*. For example, the 95 percent level of significance has a 1.96 tabular score for a simple random sample of 100, 200, or 1,252 people. This is one of the great strengths of the standard normal distribution. Other sampling designs generate theoretical sampling distributions that change shape every time one varies the sample size, thereby necessitating a new set of tabular statistics.

To conclude, most statistics texts emphasize the need for simple random sampling as a cornerstone to the legitimate use of many of the formulas that are presented therein. William Hays writes:

The model of simple random sampling is the basis of almost all the discussion to follow. The classical procedures of statistical inference rest upon the sampling scheme in which each and every population element sampled is independent of every other, and is equally likely to be included in any sample.[9]

Hays continues:

Unless this assumption (simple random sampling) is at least reasonable, the results of inferential methods mean very little, and these methods might as well be omitted. Data that are not the product of random sampling may yield extremely valuable conclusions in their own right, but there is usually little to be gained

from the application of inferential methods to such data.[10]

Disadvantages of Simple Random Sampling.

All other things being equal, simple random sampling designs are more practical for most statistical evaluations than are other probability sampling designs.

The caveat, however, is that all other things are not equal. Ultimately one must realize that the objective is to *conclude* a study with a simple random sample. That is, one may select an accurate simple random sample but not secure relevant data from everyone. Apart from the nonsampling error, which is inevitably introduced, the simple random sample could be very unrepresentative of the sampling frame from which it was taken *if every selected element does not participate in the study*. Every element within the sampling frame is given an equal probability of being selected, which ensures a better representation of the total frame. However, if people refuse to be interviewed or to return a completed schedule in a mailed questionnaire study, the sample will not, by definition, be representative. If nonresponse results, the logical and statistical principles will not operate as they were conceptualized because the equal probability of selection criterion has been violated. The fact that the violation is a product of the nonparticipant's own action does not alter the absence of information from the data base. It would be suspect, then, to proceed with one's proposed analysis using inferential statistics.

If this is the case, why do statistics courses emphasize procedures based upon assumptions that are rarely, if ever, met in the social and behavioral sciences? Briefly, there are three reasons. First, statistical reasoning is not solely for the use of the social scientist. Second, formulas that are presented are usually the simplest possible. Thus, one of the major advantages of simple random sampling—the ability to use inferential statistics—is generally inappropriate because of idiosyncrasies of the social researcher's normal units of analysis. Third, there is the issue of robustness.

The characteristic of robustness permits somewhat of a retreat from the position just presented. *Robustness* is the idea that some statistical formulas are reasonably impervious to violations of some of the assumptions that underlie their proper use. That is, some statistics are sufficiently robust to lead to correct interpretations despite violations. For example, Lutz writes, "the t statistic will often result in correct decisions about null hypotheses even when its assumptions are not well met. Statisticians call such a test *robust.*"[11]

He also adds, "Student's t-ratio is referred to as a *robust test,* meaning that statistical inferences are likely to be valid even where there are fairly large departures from normality [one assumption] in the population distribution."[12] The degree of robustness, then, makes the violation of assumptions less critical for some statistical measures than for others.

A second disadvantage of simple random sampling is the chance that one could draw an unrepresentative sample despite adhering to both criteria. Look again at Figure 6.3. By pure chance, about 5 percent of the time, a simple random sample whose mean descriptive statistic is two standard deviations above or below the population parameter will be drawn. While we seek a *representative* sample of the university population, we could draw a simple random sample containing 100 *first-year* students. While that is not likely, it could happen.

Summary.   Even with the cited disadvantages, we believe simple random sampling is more negative than suggested by the positive accolades it generally receives. It is, therefore, reasonable to explore alternative sampling designs.

Systematic Sampling

A *systematic sample* is generated when an investigator selects every nth element from a sampling frame after a random start within the first sampling interval.

Preconditions.   Before one can draw a systematic sample, the same two preconditions that held for simple random sampling must be met. That is, the researcher must have an accurate listing of the study population and decide prior to beginning the selection process how many sampling elements are necessary.

The Procedure.   The first step in drawing a systematic sample is to divide the desired sample size into the total number of elements in the sampling frame, thereby establishing the *sampling interval.* If we wished to generate a sample of 500 students from the university sampling frame of 15,000, we would divide 500 into 15,000 resulting in a sampling interval of 30. This determines that we will sample one element from each interval of 30 elements.

$$\text{Systematic sampling interval} = \frac{\text{total number of elements in the sampling frame}}{\text{desired sample size}} = \frac{15,000}{500} = 30$$

The second step is to divide the list into intervals of 30 elements each. While this is understood, one usually does not do this, since the sampling interval, once determined, can be added to each preceding selection to determine the next sample element.

Third, we turn to the table of random numbers and select the first element in the same manner as we did in the case of simple random sampling. Since we are writing this section on the 28th of the month, let us enter Table 7.3 on the second row and the eighth column. Since we need to generate a two-digit number between 01 and 30, we will use columns eight and nine and proceed down these columns until we find an appropriate number. Since our starting point is 80, which is not within the 01 to 30 range, we ignore this number and proceed until we find a number that does fall within the desired range. This doesn't happen until we reach the ninth row, which contains the number *13.* Element 13, then, would be the first element selected and would be designated as our *random start,* or where we begin.

Fourth, we select the remaining sample elements in one of two ways. We can select from each remaining interval that element which falls in the 13th position, or we can add the interval size to the number of the random start to determine the second choice. This latter process is continued until one generates a number that exceeds the total number of sampling frame elements. In our university example, rather than marking off a list of 15,000 students into intervals of 30 and counting down 13 spaces, it would be easier to add the sampling interval value to the value of the preceding choice. In this example, we would sample element 13, add 30 and sample element 43, add 30 and sample 73, add 30 and sample 103, and so forth until we'd gone through the entire sampling frame.

This procedure would be, clearly, more appropriate if the sampling frame was already sequentially numbered. Such might be the case for invoice numbers in a business firm or for patients admitted to a hospital. Most lists, however, do not have any type of sequential numbering system. The university list of students is more typical and is likely to be alphabetically organized. Some lists, e.g., a metropolitan telephone directory, are too large and change too quickly to make sequential numbering possible. Here, one would be better advised to use the first procedure of selecting each subsequent element in the same position as the initial random start. One might feel, for example, that one person from each of the white pages of a telephone directory would generate an adequate sample size. Therefore, one might systematically sample every 10th person from the second column of entries on every page of the directory.

Advantages of Systematic Sampling.   There are two basic advantages to a systematic sampling design. First, the procedure is quick and easy to do. Of all the probability designs we will discuss, this one takes the least amount of time and effort.

Second, most sampling experts argue that *if* the list is randomly organized, a systematic sample will result in a reasonable *approximation* of a simple random sample.[13] Blalock writes, "If the ordering used in compiling the list can be considered to be essentially random with respect to the variables being measured, a systematic sample will be equivalent to a simple random sample."[14]

Blalock is not saying the sampling frame must be ordered randomly. Indeed, most lists are ordered in some manner. Rather, he is suggesting that if the order reflects a dimension that is irrelevant to the objects of the research, the order doesn't matter. In fact, some writers argue that systematic sampling is better than simple random sampling because the choices of the sampling elements are spread over the entire sampling frame.[15] Richard Scheaffer, William Mendenhall, and Lyman Ott write, "A systematic sample is *frequently* spread more uniformly over the entire population and thus can provide more information about the population than an equivalent amount of data contained in a simple random sample."[16]

In sum, the presence or absence of an initial ordering of the list seems to be perceived as an advantage by some and a disadvantage by others. Whether an ordered list will have positive or negative consequences will largely depend on the interval size and the random start, as well as the nature of the order. As in all matters concerning sampling, specific conditions and their consequences are not easily determined through the application of a simple rule. Finally, while a systematic sample may be considered an approximation of a simple random sample, it cannot be strictly considered such because it violates both simple random criteria. First, there is not an equal probability of selection. In our example, all the elements in the first interval had a 1/30 chance of being selected. After we selected the random start at the 13th element, element 43 had a 100 percent chance of being selected and element 42 had a 0 percent chance of being selected. Second, the independence of choice criterion was violated as well. We picked elements 43 and 73 because we picked element 13. Further, once we selected the element within a given interval, all the remaining elements within that interval had no chance of being selected as we moved on to the next interval.

Disadvantages of Systematic Sampling.   There are two major disadvantages to systematic sampling. First, since the criteria for a simple random sample have been violated, one is precluded from using inferential statistics."*

Second, the nature of the order of the list may create biases. Three situations may contribute to such bias: (1) a trend, (2) a periodic, or cyclical, characteristic, and (3) some type of clustering effect.

First, there may be a *trend* on the list. Some lists are ordered by the prestige or importance of office, salary levels, seniority, or some other characteristic that may be of relevance to the study. For example, some union lists are organized by seniority, while a list of professional baseball players may be ordered by batting average. If one were to select a systematic sample from such lists, different random starts may produce rather different systematic samples, especially if the sampling interval is a large one. To illustrate, if one starts toward the top of a large interval of baseball players, a systematic sample would result in those players whose batting averages were higher than the others in their respective intervals; or if the random start were toward the bottom of the interval, each selected element would be lower than most other persons within that interval. In the first case, the systematic sample would overestimate the batting average, while in the second an underestimate would result. The key here is the size of the sampling interval or the proportion of the sampling frame included in the sample. The smaller the sampling interval, the more likely the effect of a trend will be minimized. Conversely, if a trend *is* relevant and *if* the sampling interval is small, a systematic sample may be best because it guarantees that all degrees of the trend will be represented.

A second source of bias may come from a *periodic*, or *cyclical*, characteristic. That is, there may be a repeating pattern. Consider an urban research project in which the researcher wishes to sample housing units within a group-home neighborhood. See Figure 7.1, which illustrates the pattern of housing in part of the neighborhood. As one moves down Maple Avenue, there is a pattern

to the housing units, with the exception of the first and the last address. That is, as one walks down the north side of Maple Avenue from Oak Street to Elm Street, crosses over to the south side of Maple Avenue, and walks back toward Oak Street, one walks by three inside houses (102, 104, and 106), two outside houses (108 and 110), three inside houses (112, 114, and 116), two outside houses (118 and 119), three inside houses (117, 115, and 113), and so forth. *If* one's sampling interval were to coincide with the cyclical pattern, two different random starts may produce rather different samples. For example, if the sampling interval is equal to five, a random start of one would generate all outside houses: 100, 110, 119, and 109, while a random start of three would result in all inside houses: 104, 114, 115, and 105. When one considers that end or corner homes are slightly wider with more ground around them than inside homes and, therefore, tend to cost more, a sample of all outside or end homes may represent those families that are slightly more wealthy than those families represented by a systematic sample of inside homes. As this hypothetical neighborhood is designed, it contains 40 percent end homes and 60 percent inside homes. One should obtain these proportions in the sample in order to maximize representativeness.

The third source of bias concerns those lists that tend to *cluster* elements having similar characteristics. Recognize, for example, that most lists of people are arranged alphabetically by surname. Some surnames are typical of ethnic groups and tend to cluster together. For example, the following names were found sequentially in our metropolitan area telephone directory:

Korcheski	Kordish
Korcynski	Kordiszewski
Kordecki	Kordonski
Kordek	Kordula
Kordick	Kordusky

Here, we would suggest that those of Polish heritage are heavily represented. Further, we found

---

*Inductive *reasoning,* however, plays an important role here, even though the use of inferential *statistics* is questionable.

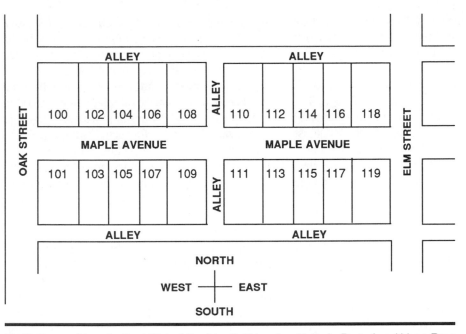

FIGURE 7.1 Hypothetical Plat of Residential Housing Units in Part of an Urban Row House Neighborhood

approximately 31 pages of listings from McAbee to McWilliams—in all likelihood a concentration of those with English and Irish heritage. If one's sampling interval was substantial, one might completely skip over these cases and not represent them in the systematic sample. In the telephone directory we were using, there are 1903 pages, four columns to each page, and approximately 105 entries per column, which works out to be some 799,260 phone numbers. If we sampled every 100th page, after a random start we might well skip over the 31 pages containing names beginning with Mc and, thereby, not represent about 13,020 elements. Consider another example in which university students are classified according to their major. A systematic sample from a list of those clustered by academic discipline might leave unrepresented or underrepresented students in the smaller departments. Similarly, student lists are often organized by social security number, which is closely related to the student's region of residence. This could result in an unrepresentative sample of students based on geographic areas.

Summary. Systematic sampling is quick and easy and presents a reasonable approximation to a simple random sample, if the order of the list, sampling interval, and random start don't conspire to produce a biased sample. However, recognizing a trend, a cyclical pattern, or several clusters on a list does not preclude one from drawing a systematic sample. Rather, one must carefully study the nature of the list and the consequences of varying sampling intervals and random starts. Systematic sampling, as in all sampling designs, requires the researcher's active and intelligent participation.

Stratified Sampling

Stratified sampling involves separating the sampling frame into some number of relevant subcategories that are relatively homogeneous and then sampling within these subcategories using a probability process. Before the researcher selects one element, all of the elements in the sampling frame are sorted into some number of categories in which the researcher is interested. Sampling is then done to achieve either of two types of stratified samples: (1) proportional or (2) disproportional.

Preconditions.   There are three preconditions for either subtype of stratified sampling design. The first two are shared with simple random sampling and with systematic sampling. First, one must possess an accurate list of the sampling frame. Second, one must decide upon one's sample size. Third, one must have accurate information on the stratification factor or factors. For example, if one wanted to sample some number of males and females, an accurate listing of the study population would be needed as well as accurate data on each person's sex.

Proportional Stratified Sampling.   A *proportional stratified sample* results when one achieves the same proportion of various attributes of some dimension or number of dimensions within the sample as appear in the sampling frame. For example, if we sample the university population indicated in Table 7.4 so that the respective proportions of freshmen, sophomores, juniors, seniors, and graduate students are equal for the sample and the sampling frame, we would have created a proportional stratified sample. This objective is accomplished by dividing the university sampling frame into the five school classification

strata and sampling *each stratum using the same sampling fraction.* The *sampling fraction* is the proportion of elements one will select from each stratum. If we want a sample of 300 students, we divide the desired sample size of 300 into the total number of elements in the sampling frame (15,000). Since the result is 50, our sampling fraction would be one sample element for each 50 sampling frame elements or 1/50. Applying this sampling fraction to each stratum, we would sample 90 freshmen, 72 sophomores, 60 juniors, 60 seniors, and 18 graduate students. Table 7.4 compares the number and percentage of each class between the sampling frame and the proportional stratified sample. The data in the table indicate the same percentages of the strata that are maintained between the sampling frame and the proportional stratified sample.

How does one make the selections within each of the strata? There is some difference of opinion within the sampling literature. Some argue that the within strata, sampling procedure should be done through the simple random process.[17] The argument is that one will have achieved simple random samples for all the strata, which is, of course, true. However, this is not the same thing as saying that one has a simple random sample of the entire sampling frame. Consider a sample of 90 freshmen students that has been drawn by the simple random process from a frame of 4,500

TABLE 7.4   Number and Percentage of University Students Currently Enrolled in a Hypothetical University by Class in School and by the Nature of the Analytical Unit

CLASS IN SCHOOL/ ANALYTICAL UNIT	SAMPLING FRAME		PROPORTIONAL STRATIFIED SAMPLE	
	NUMBER	*PERCENT*	*NUMBER*	*PERCENT*
Graduate	900	6.0	18	6.0
Senior	3,000	20.0	60	20.0
Junior	3,000	20.0	60	20.0
Sophomore	3,600	24.0	72	24.0
Freshmen	4,500	30.0	90	30.0
Total	15,000	100.0	300	100.0

freshmen. Each freshman would have had a 1/ 4,500 chance of being selected. When one moves on to sample, in a simple random fashion, the 72 sophomores, each sophomore would have a 1/ 3,600 chance of being selected. These two probabilities are, obviously, not the same.

Further, we have violated the independence of choice criterion in that when we got our "quota" of 90 freshmen, we moved on to the sophomore stratum, leaving the remaining 4,410 (assuming no multiple selections) unselected freshmen with no further chance of inclusion.

In sum, if the researcher wants to treat each stratum sample separately, the simple random process of selection within each stratum would be necessary and appropriate. However, if one wants to consider the combination of all the strata samples into a single sample characteristic of the sampling frame, a simple random selection process within each stratum will not result in a single simple random sample.

Others argue that one may select the elements within each stratum by using any type of probability process.[18] Blalock writes, "[W]e take either a simple random sample or a systematic sample within each stratum."[19]

Since one will not have a simple random sample of the sampling frame after using the simple random selection process on each stratum, we recommend using the simpler and faster systematic process. Not only is this easier, but if there should be some sort of undetected trend on one's list, the systematic selection process would be more likely to tap into the nature of the trend because choices are guaranteed to be made throughout the list.

Advantages of Proportional Stratified Sampling. Proportional stratified sampling has three advantages. As we mentioned earlier, sampling decisions are affected by the degree of heterogeneity or homogeneity within the sampling frame. If a sampling frame is highly homogeneous, one will be able to draw fewer numbers of elements for representativeness than if the frame is highly heterogeneous. The first advantage of proportional stratified sampling, then, is that it increases the

representativeness of the sample because one is sampling from homogeneous strata. Again, we quote Blalock:

> *There may be sampling errors* within *each stratum, and there may be errors* between *strata with respect to the relative numbers selected. . . . In [proportional] stratified sampling we have eliminated this type of between-strata variation and are left only with the within variation.*[20]

Thus, proportional stratified sampling may generate a sample that is more representative of the sampling frame than one could attain through either the simple random or the systematic processes.[21]

However, three cautionary notes are necessary. First, if one creates strata on a dimension that is essentially irrelevant to the research, the above mentioned advantage is null and void. Again, note the importance of the conceptual model, which can provide insight into possible dimensions on which to create strata for sampling purposes.[22]

Second, when one creates strata on one dimension, there may be substantial heterogeneity within each stratum on one or more *other* dimensions. Consider again Table 7.4. Income levels of freshmen and sophomores, on the one hand, and juniors and seniors, on the other hand, could be measurably different. Perhaps there would be heterogeneity within each stratum because of differentials on another, unmeasured dimension, e.g., sex. Whatever the reason and whatever the consequence, there may be a substantial degree of heterogeneity within the strata because of differences on dimensions that were not considered. Such possibilities should occur to you, and the review of the literature stage may suggest their nature.

Third, the heterogeneity within strata on dimensions other than those on which the researcher has focused may be such that this additional heterogeneity is evident for only some of the strata. To stay with our example of university students, it may be that first- and second-year students have few skills of interest to employers when compared to juniors and seniors. However, it may be there is more heterogeneity within the junior and senior strata than within the freshman and sophomore strata. That is, while we are correct in surmising lower degrees of specialized skills among freshmen and sophomores, hence a high degree of homogeneity in these two strata, we may be conceptually attributing too much homogeneity to the junior and senior strata. It may be that *some* juniors and *some* seniors have chosen majors that are attractive to employers, e.g., accounting, market research, and computer science, while *other* juniors and *other* seniors have chosen majors such as history, English, or philosophy that are not as attractive. This latter group of juniors and seniors may be more similar to the freshmen and sophomores. Thus, in one stratum there may be a much greater degree of homogeneity on a recognized or an unrecognized dimension than exists in a different stratum.

Let's put this in perspective by recalling the discussion of homogeneity and heterogeneity and sample size. If we create a situation in which the strata reflect an irrelevant dimension, the sampling procedure will not make a positive contribution to the study. If the situation reflected an increased sample representativeness with strata on a relevant dimension but failed to recognize additional relevant dimensions, we will believe that the variation within strata has been eliminated and may be tempted to pick too small a sampling fraction, thereby generating too few elements to create a representative sample. Finally, if there is differential heterogeneity in the strata after creating them, the same sampling fraction will generate a more representative sample for the homogeneous strata than for the heterogeneous strata. It should be clear that to create an efficient and representative sampling design, one must think, and not simply follow, some predetermined series of steps.

In sum, there are three advantages of a proportional stratified sample. First, one will arrive at a sample that is more representative of the population than one may achieve with a simple random sample *of the same size*. The second advantage is a corollary of the first: because proportional strati-

fied samples tend to be more representative than simple random samples of comparable size, one can draw a *smaller* proportional stratified sample, which increases the efficiency of one's sampling design. Third, while a properly selected proportional stratified sample is more representative of the population, it also provides the researcher with information on each stratum and on the population as a whole.[23] Scheaffer, Mendenhall, and Ott write "[w]hen stratified sampling is used, separate estimates of population parameters can be obtained for each stratum without additional sampling."[24]

Disadvantages of Proportional Stratified Sampling.   There are three disadvantages to proportional stratified sampling. First, James Black and Dean Champion[25] argue that stratification generally reduces sampling error over a simple random sample of the same size. However, if one stratifies on a variable or series of variables that are irrelevant to the investigation, the result may increase the sampling error because of the bias caused by this inappropriate stratification. While we agree, we would add that the researcher is unlikely to stratify solely for the sake of stratification. That is, one is likely to want to stratify to guarantee representation on some number of dimensions that have been defined as important to the research. We mention this as a "disadvantage" because it is true, albeit unlikely. Rather, one generally elects to stratify because the conceptual model suggests it. It is more likely that one will fail to stratify on an indicated dimension.

Second, one must have accurate information on the stratification dimension or dimensions as well as an accurate listing of the study population elements. The stratification procedure, then, could increase the bias in one's sample because of inaccurate information. For example, it is likely that juniors and seniors have greater incomes than freshmen and sophomores. Therefore, we would want to accurately represent the proportions of both categories. However, the lists of enrolled students' designated class in school is one of the least accurate available pieces of information in most colleges and universities. Thus, one has the problem of inadvertently introducing bias because of inaccurate information on the stratification dimensions.

Third, one cannot legitimately use inferential statistics. As we argued earlier, the standard normal distribution statistics *for proportional stratified sampling* do not exist.

Disproportional Stratified Sampling. *Disproportional stratified sampling* is accomplished when different sampling fractions are used to select the elements after the strata have been established. Because different sampling fractions are used, the proportions of the strata in the sample are different from those proportions in the sampling frame. For example, assume that we are interested in comparing freshman students with graduate students. If we drew a simple random sample, we could end up with too few students drawn from the graduate student stratum. Indeed, a proportional stratified sample of 300 total students using a sampling fraction of 1/50 would generate only 18 graduate students. (Again, see Table 7.4.) We would, in all likelihood, not feel confident with data from only 18, since graduate student populations can be quite heterogeneous. Therefore, the researcher should choose a larger number of students from this stratum. Perhaps 90 students using a 1/10 sampling fraction would be suitable. However, while the problem of an insufficient number of elements from the graduate student stratum may have been solved, a different problem will arise through use of a *proportional* stratified process. Using a 1/10 sampling fraction, one would have 450 freshmen, 360 sophomores, 300 juniors, and 300 seniors, for a total proportional stratified sampling of 1,500. By using a larger sampling fraction, one can obtain a sufficient number of elements from small strata, but one gains too many elements from the larger strata.

This points strongly, then, to drawing a disproportional stratified sample. From those small strata, one would use a larger sampling fraction than one would use on the larger strata.

Assume that we would like to have 100 students from each of the five strata. Again, referring to Table 7.4, we would use a sampling fraction of 1/45 for the freshman stratum, 1/36 for the sophomore stratum, 1/30 each for both the junior and senior strata, and 1/9 for the graduate student stratum. As with proportional stratified sampling, one may use a simple random or a systematic process of selection within each stratum. Again, we recommend the systematic process because it is easier. While these sampling fractions result in 100 students being selected from each stratum, it is not necessary that one construct sampling fractions to generate equal numbers of elements from each stratum for a proper disproportional stratified sample. We did it here to simplify some of the calculations and for the reader's ease in understanding this material (see Table 7.5). Indeed, it may make more sense to select a *different* number of elements from each stratum. Consider that the purpose of this sampling procedure is to better represent the study population by ensuring representation from already predetermined critical strata. If one stratum is known to be more heterogeneous than another, it will require more elements than the more homogeneous stratum for adequate representation. The sampling specialist *almost always* seeks a balance between the greatest degree of representativeness and the most efficient sample design.

Let us continue our search for the average student income by surveying each of the 500 students sampled. After asking each person's income, we would have 500 values of income or 100 values for each of the five strata. Assume that the mean for each *stratum* was as shown in Table 7.5. If we add the mean incomes for all the five strata and divide by 5, we get $3,340.

$$\frac{\$3,000 + \$5,000 + \$4,500 + \$2,200 + \$2,000}{5}$$
$$= \frac{\$16,700}{5} = \$3,340$$

However, this figure is inaccurate. By calculating the $3,340 figure as we did, we assumed that each stratum represented 20 percent of the study population. While each stratum represented 20 percent

TABLE 7.5   Values for a Disproportional Stratified Sample of the University Students Shown in Table 7.1 by Class in School and by Selected Descriptive Statistics

CLASS / STATISTIC	NUMBER IN THE POPULATION	PROPORTION IN THE POPULATION	SAMPLING FRACTION	NUMBER IN THE SAMPLE	PROPORTION IN THE SAMPLE	MEAN INCOME
Graduate	900	0.06	1/9	100	0.20	$3,000
Senior	3,000	0.20	1/30	100	0.20	5,000
Junior	3,000	0.20	1/30	100	0.20	4,500
Sophomore	3,600	0.24	1/36	100	0.20	2,200
Freshman	4,500	0.30	1/45	100	0.20	2,000
Total	15,000	1.00	—	500	1.00	—

in the disproportional stratified sample, it did not represent 20 percent of the study population. Therefore, the mean income value for each of the strata must be adjusted to reflect that stratum's contribution to the total population.

Weighting a Disproportional Stratified Sample. Weighting a disproportional stratified sample refers to the adjustment of each stratum's values to reflect the population's proportion on that stratum. That is, the value of any one stratum will be adjusted so that its contribution to the study population's total value is in proportion to the stratum's representation in that population. This can be accomplished by assigning a coefficient to each stratum's descriptive statistic that is equal to the proportion of the study population that is contained within that stratum.[26] Therefore, we can calculate a more representative estimate of the population mean using the following formula:

$$\text{Estimated mu } (\mu) = \sum_{i=1}^{S} W_i \, (\overline{X}_i)$$

where

$W_i =$ the weight of the ith stratum
$\overline{X}_i =$ the mean of the ith stratum
$S \ =$ the total number of strata

Therefore, we would multiply each stratum's mean value of income by its proportion in the study population and add the results. Thus, let W_1 equal the weight for the first-year students and $\overline{X}_1$ equal the sample mean income of the freshman stratum; let W_2 equal the weight for the sophomores and $\overline{X}_2$ equal the sample mean income of the sophomore stratum . . . and W_5 the weight for the graduate stratum and $\overline{X}_5$ the income mean for the graduate students.

$$
\begin{aligned}
\text{Estimated mu } (\mu) &= W_1(\overline{X}_1) + W_2(\overline{X}_2) \\
&\quad + W_3(\overline{X}_3) + W_4(\overline{X}_4) \\
&\quad + W_5(\overline{X}_5) \\
&= 0.30 \,(\$2,000) + 0.24 \\
&\quad (\$2,200) + 0.20 \,(\$4,500) \\
&\quad + 0.20 \,(\$5,000) + 0.06 \\
&\quad (\$3,000) \\
&= \$600 + \$528 + \$900 \\
&\quad + \$1,000 + \$180 \\
&= \$3,208
\end{aligned}
$$

This value may also be attained by multiplying each stratum mean by the inverse of the sampling fraction for that stratum *and* its sample size, adding all the results, and dividing the resulting sum by the total number of elements in the study population. Here, that would be:

Estimated mu (μ)   =   45 (100) ($2,000)
                       + 36 (100) ($2,200)
                       + 30 (100) ($4,500)
                       + 30 (100) ($5,000)
                       + 9 (100) ($3,000) /
                       15,000
                     = $3,208

Advantages of Disproportional Stratified Sampling. There are four advantages of disproportional stratified sampling. First, it is beneficial in assessing differences among the strata. Here, the weighting problems and procedures are irrelevant because the objective is *not* to evaluate an aspect of the study population but to compare the subcategories within that population. Disproportional stratified sampling can guarantee sufficient numbers of elements in those categories of interest to do this comparative analysis. For example, if one would wish to compare freshmen with seniors, one would divide the sampling frame into strata on class in school. Since the researcher is only interested in freshmen and seniors, those who fall into the sophomore, junior, and graduate-student strata can be discarded from the sampling frame.

Second, of all the probability sampling designs that are available, disproportional stratified sampling is the best for efficiently representing those strata that have radically different numbers of elements. Because different sampling fractions are used, disproportional stratified sampling can guarantee that those strata which contain fewer elements will be adequately represented. Conversely, by using a smaller sampling fraction, one can avoid oversampling strata that contain comparatively large numbers of elements.

Third, disproportional stratified sampling permits usage of a smaller sampling fraction on those strata that are known to be more homogeneous, while it permits usage of a larger sampling fraction on those known to be more heterogeneous. In this way, one's sampling efficiency—a major goal of the entire process—can be more easily achieved. Further, the weighting procedure allows adjustment of the strata information to minimize the effects of disproportionality and to reflect more accurately the parameters of the study population.

Fourth, the researcher may want to do further analyses on some but not all the strata.[27] One might want to focus more intensively, say, on the graduate-student stratum because of its supposed greater heterogeneity. If this is the case, disproportional stratified sampling will guarantee a sufficient number of cases in this stratum so that subdivisions, not planned for the other strata, can be effectively examined.

Disadvantages of Disproportional Stratified Sampling. There are three disadvantages of disproportional stratified sampling. First, for the same reasons cited for an incomplete simple random sample, a systematic sample, or a proportional stratified sample, one cannot use inferential statistics.

Second, Blalock writes that disproportional stratified sampling "tends to complicate problems of analysis and should therefore not be used unless it is clearly to one's advantage to do so."[28] Similarly, Sheldon Olson writes that "[t]he implications of this weighting in terms of later statistically based inferences are rather complex."[29] Of course, if one has chosen the disproportional stratified sampling design to probe for differences among strata, this objection is irrelevant. It only becomes central when one feels the need for this sampling design because of the large differences in numbers of elements within the strata *and* because of the subsequent desire to inductively extrapolate sample data to the sampling frame.

Third, as with proportional stratified sampling, accurate information on the stratification dimensions is necessary for the correct formation of the strata prior to sampling. Similarly, this information is required for any subsequent weighting of these strata, which may be appropriate prior to their use as an estimate of a population parameter.

Summary. Because of the complexity of the issues surrounding both proportional and disproportional stratified sampling, it is not easy to offer advice on whether to employ such a sampling design. We refer the interested student to Kish.[30] However, one should remember that many of the difficulties cited become mute if the researcher is doing a comparative study among strata and has little interest in representing the entire study population. In this situation each stratum can be considered a sample from a different study population.

Cluster Sampling

Cluster sampling differs from the previously mentioned probability designs in that individual elements are not the initial object of the researcher's attention. Rather, *cluster sampling* involves the selection of *groups* of elements. By selecting naturally occurring groups of elements, one is likely to maximize the homogeneity within the selected groups and the heterogeneity among the groups. Additionally, cluster sampling does not require an accurate listing of all the study population's elements. Two forms of cluster sampling are available: (1) single-stage or (2) multistage.

Preconditions.   An accurate list of the study population's elements is not required because cluster sampling assumes an accurate list of the groups of elements. In fact, a major advantage of cluster sampling is that one can draw a probability sample when such element listings are unavailable.

For example, if one wanted to draw a sample of people who live in a major city, no list exists that would accurately reflect the names of all residents within the metropolitan area. The telephone directory is inadequate because poorer people (who do not have telephones) and the wealthy (many of whom have unlisted telephone numbers) are underrepresented in it and middle-income persons (who are most often in the directory along with a few additional listings for their children) are overrepresented. Additionally, it would require extensive data "cleaning" to purge the numbers of business, commercial, and professional organizations and associations. Real estate tax roles would

only contain those persons who own property, thereby excluding all those who rent or lease property and including those who are absentee landlords. Even if these conditions did not prevail, the mobility patterns of persons moving in and out of the community are such that a printed list is out-of-date before it is published. Therefore, the use of any urban list *of people* is likely to be unrepresentative.

Nevertheless, while the local government's assessment office records may not accurately reflect all of the current property owners, it has a reasonably accurate listing of street addresses, which have been organized into blocks, districts, and counties. It is from these and similar lists that one may use cluster sampling to generate a relevant list of people.

Single-Stage Cluster Sampling.   *Single-stage cluster sampling* involves the initial random selection of some number of clusters and the subsequent measurement of all those elements within the selected clusters. If a single-stage cluster sample of college students was drawn, one could list every section of every course and then randomly select a designated number of sections. The researcher would then investigate each student in every section selected.

Multistage Cluster Sampling.   Users of cluster sampling are more likely to elect the multistage variety. Here, one begins with an accurate listing of groups of elements and randomly samples some number of clusters as described above. The initially selected clusters are called *primary sampling units,* which are generally subdivided into smaller clusters called *secondary sampling units.*[31] For example, we could sample college students by selecting a number of *courses* from those offered. Assuming we select 10 courses (the primary sampling units), we still could have a large number of students were we to stop with a single-stage cluster sample. Instead, we might list all the sections offered for the 10 courses and select 2 sections (the secondary sampling units) from each of the

10 courses, thereby generating 20 sections of students. In essence, then, *multistage cluster sampling* involves the successive creation and sampling of ever smaller clusters of desired elements until a reasonable number and distribution of elements has been created.

Multistage cluster sampling is virtually inevitable when surveying from an urban sampling frame. The researcher will normally begin with geographic areas defined by census tracts as the primary sampling units, with blocks within the tracts serving as the secondary sampling units. The sampled blocks could be further divided into street addresses as the *tertiary sampling units,* and those addresses selected divided into apartments as the *quaternary sampling units.* Finally, some way of randomly selecting from those persons who live in the selected apartments would conclude the final stage.

Advantages of Cluster Sampling.   There are two major advantages to cluster sampling. First, it is a probability process that does not require a difficult-to-achieve accurate total listing of the potential sampling elements. Second, it can have economic advantages. Since clustering is often geographically based, survey costs can be reduced when interviewing is used because travel time between sample elements will be reduced.

Disadvantages of Cluster Sampling.   Geographic proximity to the sample elements, however, has negative consequences. Scheaffer and his coauthors write:

> *Elements within a cluster are often physically close together and hence tend to have similar characteristics. Stated another way the measurement on one element in a cluster may be highly correlated with the measurement on another.*[32]

One of the goals of sampling is to accurately reflect the variety that exists within the population. The problem is that those factors that cause people to cluster together are likely to reflect mini-mum variance. For example, persons living in an urban neighborhood are likely to share identity on dimensions such as race, educational attainment, ethnicity, life style, and socioeconomic position. Thus, the economic advantage of clustering may be counterbalanced by the minimal variance within the sample. To avoid this difficulty, one can select a large number of clusters containing relatively few elements. That approach would maximize the chances of tapping the variation of different geographic groupings.

Second, as Blalock notes, a cluster sample is less efficient because it generates a larger sampling error than a simple random sample of the same size.[33] This is also the case when contrasted to a proportional stratified sample of the same size. However, one sacrifices a major advantage of proportional stratified sampling when using a cluster design because of the duplication of elements from within homogeneous strata or clusters. For this reason, cluster sampling demands more elements than the simple random design, which, in turn, requires more than the proportional stratified design for comparable analyses.

Third, successive sampling of ever smaller clusters, and ultimately, of some number of elements within these clusters violates the general criteria of independence of choice and of equiprobability of choice, which are so important to the assessment of random chance fluctuation. Finally, Blalock warns us that the introductory-level statistical formulas normally found in most statistical textbooks "cannot be used with cluster sampling."[34]

Summary.   Because of their rather radical departures from the principles underlying probability sampling, single-stage and multistage cluster sampling designs should be undertaken with extreme care.

TYPES OF NONPROBABILITY SAMPLES

Nonprobability sampling occurs when the probability of inclusion of any element from the sampling frame cannot be determined. Statistical determination of chance fluctuation in the data derived from such samples is impossible. While this loss is important, nonprobability sampling is not without virtues. One of the major advantages of almost all nonprobability sampling designs is that they are, generally, more economical in terms of effort, time, and money than probability sampling designs. In this section, we discuss briefly some of the ways to draw and use nonprobability samples.

Accidental Samples

An *accidental sample* is also called a haphazard, availability, and convenience sample. Here, the researcher selects elements for study that are convenient and accessible, while attempting to select "typical" cases. Despite this effort, representativeness is always a concern when using any nonprobability sampling design.

One of the worst abuses of representativeness— along with the "call-in" to register one's opinion —in accidental sampling is the man-in-the-street interview. The television news teams solicit frequently a 10- to 15-second comment from one to three people for inclusion in the evening's news broadcast. The comments are then often followed by the television personality's suggesting that these comments reflect the attitude of the city's citizens. This is obviously absurd.

However, some research would not be done were it not for the accidental sample. Perhaps the best-known examples of accidental samples are those in Alfred Kinsey's classic survey of sexual behavior and, more recently, those in William Masters and Virginia Johnson's study of the physiological effects of sexual behavior. Many medical research efforts are of this voluntary nature. The testing of the effects of a new drug therapy must rest upon those who volunteer to contract the disease and who realize that the therapy is far from an accepted and fully understood vehicle of treatment. Accidental samples, then, are sometimes not the best way to investigate some problems; but they may be the only way.

Quota Samples

In *quota sampling,* the researcher selects known proportions of elements in specified categories. The purpose is to achieve within the sample known percentages of certain theoretically determined important categories of typical elements from within the population. This is the same objective of a proportional stratified sample. In quota sampling, the selection of elements is not accomplished through a probability process, since the researcher decides whether the element that fits into the desired category is representative. As with proportional stratified sampling, one must know what the proportions on the categories of the key variables are prior to the sample selection, although without a probability basis there is no need for an accurate total listing from which to sample.

Sometimes the researcher will have information on the distribution of various attributes of a variable or series of variables but not have an accurate (and convenient) listing of elements on these variables. For example, census reports indicate the proportions of persons from various ethnic backgrounds within a metropolitan community. These proportions can be used in a quota sampling design without a list of who is classified in which categories. Thus, while not possessing the rigor of random selection from within categories of known size as in proportional stratified sampling, quota sampling would be appropriate where the proportions in the sampling frame are known and where one's conceptual model indicates the relevance of this information.

Judgmental, or Purposive, Samples

The *judgmental,* or *purposive, sample* is a nonprobability sample in which the researcher is free to select any element that the researcher deems appropriate. One selects elements that are perceived to be typical through the exercise of one's knowledge about the population to be studied.

While many point to the potential for unrepresentativeness because the sole criterion for selection is that the element "looks good" to the researcher, wc would argue for the positive aspects of judgmental sampling. Consider the social scientist who has spent 30 years of serious study and research into the nature of juvenile delinquency. This researcher ought to be able to decide whether Frank or John or Bill are "typical" juvenile delinquents. Judgmental, or purposive, sampling calls upon the social scientist's expertise. When circumstances prevent the use of more stringent probability methods, we do not believe this knowledge should be discounted.

Referral, or Snowball, Samples

The last nonprobability sampling technique discussed here is the *referral*, or *snowball*, *sample*. In this case, a person selected for study assists the researcher by identifying other relevant people and, sometimes, establishing the initial meeting between the researcher and the referred person. Referral samples are often the only way to do certain types of social research, particularly in an area of social deviance.

For example, suppose one was interested in an exploratory study of drug addicts to assess the nature of thc drug subculture. Since drug usage is frowned upon and is illegal, those persons who participate in the drug subculture are likely to be covertly involved or discovered and undergoing punishment or receiving treatment. If one wanted a representative sample of drug addicts, a list of known offenders, if available, would not be representative because the persons on this list would only be those detected, labeled, and subjected to some type of rehabilitation or punishment. Clearly, those participants who have yet to be arrested and/or convicted would not be on anyone's formal list and, therefore, would not be available for selection. Hence, the referral, or snowball, sample would be most appropriate. The researcher would make contact, usually, with a person who is also known by the researcher to be involved with the drug subculture. The nature of the study would be explained, and participation in the study would be requested. Hopefully, the drug user would recognize the researcher's seriousness and not fear the request as a ruse of entrapment. At the conclusion of the interview, the researcher would ask the respondent to identify other persons in the drug subculture. In this way each element in the sample is asked to help refer the researcher to others who have experiences or characteristics germane to the study. This process is identical to a family physician's referring a patient to a specialist, who is not known to the patient, for additional treatment. This referral mechanism paves the way for the researcher by helping to identify appropriate persons for study and by helping to establish the researcher's credibility to the potential respondent or respondents.

The researcher who elects to use a referral sample must reflect some concern with ethics. The researcher also runs some risk from legal authorities for maintaining the confidentiality of those studied. These are matters for discussion elsewhere in this text, but we point to their relevance in doing research in an area of social deviance with a referral sample. Of course, referral sampling is not restricted to studies of deviance, but such a sampling design is especially useful in those areas of study in which the normative aspects of the larger culture have little moment.

Summary

Nonprobability sampling designs rest strongly on the researcher's knowledge of the research situation and ability to select typical elements for study. The major difficulty is with one's inability to use established inferential statistics in a conventional manner. For the reasons offered earlier in this and the preceding chapter, this difficulty should not be considered a major one. The researcher's expertise—which has been gathered through a lifetime of study—should not be discounted. Such knowledge conscientiously applied can result in highly representative samples from which logically inductive extrapolations to sampling frames can be made. As we have suggested earlier, difficulties with the prerequisites necessary for a simple random sample are of greatest concern when people are the units of analysis.

SELECTING AN APPROPRIATE SAMPLE SIZE

We have postponed discussion of sample size until now because it is an issue that cannot be adequately discussed without knowledge of different probability sampling designs, the nature of probability theory, one's conceptual model, and how these components interact with one's anticipated statistical analysis.

There are two bromides that suggest a simple answer to the question: how big a sample should the researcher select? The first is the 1/10th rule, which suggests that one-tenth (or 10 percent) of the sampling frame should be included in the sample.[35] This rule is not especially helpful because, among other things, the appropriate sample size will depend on the size of the sampling frame. For very small sampling frames, a sample of 10 percent may be too small; for large sampling frames, one-tenth would be wasteful of effort and financial resources. For example, a 10 percent sample of the United States would result in the selection of millions of persons. As we said in Chapter 6, while sampling error decreases as the proportion of the sampling frame included in the sample increases, the total error will remain significant unless there is a corresponding decrease in nonsampling error, which, of course, is not likely in view of the larger number of cases whose data must be processed. Black and Champion write:

> [S]tatisticians can easily illustrate that when a probability sample reaches a certain size, such as 1,000, its efficiency for estimating population parameters is not much different compared with probability samples of 10,000 or even 1,000,000.[36]

The second bromide—the bigger the sample, the better—does not have much methodological credence either. "Some researchers fall prey to what we shall refer to here as 'the fetish of the large sample.' This is the urge to obtain a sample so large that few will question its significance."[37]

Criteria to Consider in Determining Sample Size

There are several criteria to consider when determining one's sample size. The first is the degree of heterogeneity within the sampling frame concerning those variables of interest to the researcher. For example, suppose we are interested in drawing a sample of typical college students. First-year students have a wider range of intellectual ability than do seniors. That is, we recognize that among first-year students will be some high achievers who will move on to successful completion of their studies, but there will also be some low achievers who will not complete their undergraduate studies and who will withdraw before their senior year. Hence, with respect to heterogeneity of educational ability, one would recognize more heterogeneity among first-year students than among seniors. Should a representative sample of first-year students be desired for comparison with a representative sample of senior-level students, the researcher will obviously need to generate a greater number of freshmen than seniors. Thus, one's sample size must be larger if the sampling frame has greater variation on one or more dimensions in which the researcher is interested.

Second, the researcher must consider the degree of sampling error to be tolerated in the data. We know sampling error produces values of the sample statistics that differ from the values of the true population parameters. We also know the larger one's sample size, the smaller will be the sampling error, assuming an absence of a corresponding increase in nonsampling error. Therefore, the researcher must also determine the degree to which error is acceptable due to having a sample that is not representative of the sampling frame from which the sample was taken.

Third, one must consider the sampling procedure to be employed. If the researcher knows that certain categories are important contributory factors to the dependent variable or variables, such information would argue strongly for a proportional stratified sample if one wanted the most representative design possible. As we noted earlier, the only source of variation on the stratified variables would be between the strata. Thus, a smaller number of elements could be sampled than if one were to use a different probability design. If stratification is not possible and if a simple random design were chosen, a larger sample would be necessary to maintain a constant sampling error. Finally, if a cluster design was selected, the sample size would have to be greater than that for a simple random sample.*

Fourth, one must consider the research objectives as these impinge on the data analysis one anticipates after the raw data have been collected. To remain with our working example, it may be that one wants a reasonably accurate descriptive statistic for the sample as a whole, e.g., the mean income of undergraduate students. Further, the researcher may want to break out the subcategory of first-year students for closer analysis so that their particular retention rate can be estimated. If the first measurement objective necessitated selecting 100 students, the second measurement objective might also require 100 first-year students. Therefore, because of these multiple objectives, the researcher may be required to sample a larger number of elements than would be required to meet adequately any one single objective.

Fifth, we must always be sensitive to *sample mortality*. As we have discussed, it is one thing to select a sample, but quite another to conclude the data-gathering phase with adequate, relevant information from all of those selected. People have a way of disappearing from the sample through the course of a study. Some refuse to participate ("My husband told me not to answer any of these questions"), some participate but give some responses that cannot be used because of their irrelevance ("Yeah, but let me tell you about . . ."),

some can't be contacted ("He's not here now, but you could try . . ."), some are found to be irrelevant ("Gosh, I haven't worked there for over 20 years now"), some change addresses or move out of town in the middle of a longitudinal study, or some may have actually died. The reasons for sample mortality are legion. "In sampling human populations, it is wise to anticipate a loss of 10 to 20 percent of the cases in the original sample (and sometimes more!) and to plan the initial sample size accordingly."[38]

Sample mortality is an unfortunate fact of life in social research, and the researcher should consider the extent to which it is likely to occur in the study and sample in excess in order to compensate for its anticipated effect.

Finally, while most of our discussion has focused on that which is methodologically required for analysis, one must not lose sight of the primary reason one is drawing a sample: that is to maximize one's time and cost investments in gathering data. A sample must, of course, be big enough to permit a legitimate interpretation, but it should not be so big that it is wasteful of funds or time.

These six criteria, then, are general factors to consider in the selection of an appropriate sample size. Depending on the nature of one's study, greater or lesser numbers of elements may be necessary.

Some Suggestions on Actual Numbers

We offer three general rules of thumb. First, many standard formulas for statistical analyses are based on the law of large numbers, the central limit theorem, and the normal distribution. Hays writes:

In general, the larger the sample size, the more probable it is that the sample mean comes arbitrarily close to the population mean. *This fact is often called* the law of large numbers, *and is*

---

*One would be well advised to select a few cases from a large number of clusters rather than a large number of cases from a small number of clusters because of the anticipated homogeneity within clusters. For example, if we chose all physics majors, we would select students who are generally more mathematically inclined, while art majors would excel in the more creative areas. Therefore, we could better tap into the existing heterogeneity by selecting a few cases from a large number of clusters.

closely allied both to Bernoulli's theorem and the Tchebycheff inequality. . . .

. . . [T]he central limit theorem . . . is an extremely general principle letting us know the approximate form of the sampling distribution . . . provided that the sample size is relatively large[,] . . . the sampling distribution of the mean approaches a unimodal, symmetric form known as the normal distribution.[39]

These principles are important factors in probability theory and in the legitimate interpretation of many statistical values. What this all boils down to is that most statisticians are agreed that 30 elements would be the minimum required for a legitimate interpretation without going to other procedures specially designed for smaller numbers and based upon different theoretical distributions, e.g., the binomial distribution.[40] Kenneth Bailey continues, "However, many researchers regard 100 cases as the minimum. One reason is that there are often several subpopulations the researcher wishes to study separately or several variables to be controlled for."[41]

Bernard Lazerwitz concurs and extends the minimum of 100 cases to each stratum in a stratified sampling design.[42] Indeed, we would agree with the minimum criterion of 100 elements for an additional reason. Quite often the researcher is interested in calculating the proportions or percentages of those cases that fall into two or more categories on the dependent variable for each category on the independent variable. To calculate these descriptive statistics on too small a base or total number of cases will clearly distort the interpretation of these statistics.

Second, Olson offers a variation on this rule of thumb for contingency tables when he argues that one's total size should be an average of 20 cases per cell of the table.[43] Thus, if one's table had three categories on the independent variable and four categories on the dependent variable (assuming a two variable hypothesis), this 3 x 4 table would contain 12 cells necessitating 240 cases. While one accomplishes essentially the same objective, we would argue that 100 cases per category for the *independent* variable (or a total of

300 cases) not only generates sufficient numbers but also guarantees enough cases in all the categories of the independent variable. We agree with Bailey and with Lazerwitz; the 100 minimum results in sufficient numbers and even allows for a modest, if not radical, sample mortality.

Finally, several statistics and sampling texts suggest a mathematical formula for determining sample size. Again, we refer to Black and Champion[44] for the following formula:

$$\text{Desired sample size} = \overline{X} \pm Z \, \frac{\hat{\delta}}{\sqrt{n}}$$

where $\overline{X}$ refers to the desired descriptive statistic, Z refers to the standard score appropriate to one's chosen level of significance, $\hat{\delta}$ refers to an *estimate* of the *population* standard deviation, and n refers to the sample size. This formula assumes a descriptive statistic whose values from repeated simple random sampling designs would be normally distributed. Black and Champion argue that since our objective is an estimate of an appropriate sample size or n, we need the desired degree of accuracy in place of $\overline{X}$. For example, suppose that one was interested in estimating the average number of years of seniority of persons who belong to a labor union and that one is willing to have the estimate be accurate to plus or minus one-half year. Further, if the researcher is willing to work at the 0.05 level of significance, the value of Z would be 1.96, i.e., the Z score that corresponds to this level of significance in the standardized normal distribution. With both of these values available, the answer should be reasonably easy for the researcher to determine. The third factor is the standard deviation within the population, which, of course, the researcher does not know. Therefore, this value must be estimated, which means one must determine its value *prior to* securing any information from the specific sample to be studied. The researcher is in a catch-22 situation: the researcher can't get an accurate estimate of the population's standard deviation without actual data from an appropriate sample and can't determine how many cases is an appropriate sample without an accurate estimate of the population standard deviation. All is not lost, however. It may be that one can determine a reasonable value of the population standard deviation after a review of the literature *from* a previous study whose sample is similar to the sample one is about to draw. Suppose such an estimate is 3.82; the formula can be manipulated thus:

$$\overline{X} = Z \frac{\hat{\delta}}{\sqrt{n}}$$

$$\sqrt{n}\ \overline{X} = Z\ \hat{\delta}$$

$$\sqrt{n} = \frac{Z\ \hat{\delta}}{\overline{X}}$$

$$n = \left[\frac{Z\ \hat{\delta}}{\overline{X}} \right]^2$$

$$= \left[\frac{(1.96)\ (3.82)}{0.5} \right]^2$$

$$= 225 \text{ persons}$$

Given the decisions made, 225 persons would be reasonable for our union study. Note from the formula that the need for increased accuracy, a higher level of significance, plus an increasing estimated standard deviation all conspire to increase the need for a greater sample size.

AN ILLUSTRATION

In this final section, we would like to think through a hypothetical sampling problem with you. Suppose that we want to test the hypothesis that a working male's self-image varies positively with his degree of education, holding constant race, marital status, age, and wife's employment status. This hypothesis could easily be derived from the sex role and social change literature. Assume that the operational definitions not specifically mentioned have been adequately provided. The class I variables are self-image (the dependent variable)

and degree of education (the independent variable); the class II variables are the remaining variables specified in the proposition: respondent's occupational status (employed), sex (male), race (white), marital status (married), age (25–35 years of age), and wife's employment status (a specificational variable dichotomized into employed wife and unemployed wife). All the class II variables are to be controlled by sampling only those persons believed to be in the one-category indicated with the exception of wife's employment status, which will be reported for the two categories indicated. Finally, all the controlled variables would have been shown in the previous literature as having some impact on either or both of the class I objects of the research; hence, they have been one-category controlled or treated in terms of the specificational mode of elaboration.

Thinking ahead to the data presentation, assume that two tables will be sufficient and that each table will be a two by two (2 x 2) celled one where education is dichotomized into those with low education who have graduated from high school or have less formal education and those with high education who have an undergraduate college degree or more formal education. Similarly, self-image will be subdivided into those with a high self-image score and those with a low self-image score.

As a final preliminary, we need to make some reasonable guess about how many persons to select. Since our independent variable is education, we want to generate enough cases within the different subcategories of *education* and the specificational variable of *wife's employment status* to do a meaningful analysis. Suppose that we will need 200 males with employed wives: 100 husbands with high education and 100 husbands with low education. Also, we will choose 300 males with unemployed wives: 150 husbands who have high education and 150 husbands who have low education. We chose these numbers because of the anticipated data analysis, sample mortality, and similar problems that will reduce the number from whom these data can truly be used. Note that we intend to sample more men with unemployed wives than men with employed wives. More married women are entering the labor force, and we have every reason to believe that our operational definition of a unemployed wife *during the sampling phase* of the research may be somewhat in error. If so, this will necessitate drawing more persons from this category. With these preliminary decisions made, we turn to a step-by-step procedure for selecting the sample.

The initial step is to determine where one would find the working men. Should we go to a street corner and grab whomever will participate? No. Should we put an advertisement in the newspaper? Of course not. For several reasons, we would recommend selecting persons from a large corporation. First, since most persons find employment in a bureaucratic structure, we would be selecting a sampling frame that is characteristic of a large number of American workers. Second, by dealing with a single firm, the researcher fortuitously controls a large number of unmentioned, yet potentially important, variables. For example, every worker would be covered by the same company health plan, work under the same sick leave and vacation policy, be within the same salary structure, be governed by the same retrenchment policy, and so forth. In short, many of the occupational, education, political, and geographic or regional variables would be held constant in this fashion. Third, a large firm presents a great number of persons from whom to select. Since we have determined that we need 500 people with some very definite characteristics, this is an important consideration. Finally, selecting persons from a large corporation will provide us an opportunity to illustrate how one would use an established list of people for one's own research study. With these ideas in mind, and because the authors live in the Baltimore metropolitan area, we will prevail upon the Social Security Administration (SSA) whose

headquarters are located in the region. The SSA would be appropriate because they employ a large work force with diverse educational backgrounds. The SSA may also be sympathetic to our study because it could provide information that the SSA could use for its own purposes.

One must next secure the organization's permission to use their data. Telephone calls will have to be made; appointments set up to explain the nature of the study to those who have the authority to grant access to the files, intra-SSA consultations done about the possible ramifications of the researcher's study, and so forth. These preliminaries are crucial before permission can be granted. From the agency's point of view, they will want to know if the researcher is a competent professional, if the study meets professional and agency ethical standards, if the study will cause embarrassment or any costs to the agency, and if there is any agency benefit to participation in the study. We will assume that there are no difficulties with these and similar questions and that the SSA grants us permission to use their employee files.

The file list will contain the names of thousands of employees, many of whom will not be appropriate for our study. Therefore, the next step is to purge these elements. One should begin with the easiest variables with which to deal and move toward those which are more difficult. This is done so that after each successive wave of eliminations, the determination of the subsequent, more difficult variables can be done on fewer remaining elements. Since we are interested in surveying working men, we can first eliminate all females from the list. Next we eliminate all those whose race is other than white or Caucasian.* Next, we will eliminate all those whose marital status is other than married. Since the current divorce rate is substantial, there is no reason to suppose that

---

*There may be a problem here since federal antidiscriminatory legislation prohibits the mandatory inclusion of such information on race. However, each agency must have some way of determining racial and ethnic background since reports must be periodically filed to demonstrate compliance with federal law. We assume this information is available through one channel or another.

while any male worker might have been married when he made application to the SSA, he is still married at the time of the study. Consider additionally that employees rarely update their original employment application information without considerable prodding from the agency or a personal reason such as not having one's estranged wife continue as a beneficiary. We would expect some sample mortality here, although most divorced persons remarry and we are only concerned that the person is married. Next, we eliminate all those who are over 35 years of age and under 25 years of age. This can be done by subtracting 25 and 35 from the current year and retaining only those persons whose year of birth falls into the indicated range. Some minimal errors will be made here. For example, some persons will be selected who are 24 because the current year is the one in which they will be 25, but at a date subsequent to drawing the sample. Such errors should be inconsequential since we are trying to generate an age cohort of males who, if they went to school, were subjected to similar information about sex roles and political social movements. Finally, we will eliminate all those persons who report an education or achievement level greater than high school but less than a baccalaureate degree. At this point we will have eliminated all of the unneeded categories in terms of the class I and class II variables. Conversely, we have remaining in our sampling frame working males between the ages of 25 and 35, who are white, were married at the time of their initial employment with the SSA, and have either of the two desired educational backgrounds.

From this point on we will be creating categories or strata with those persons who remain. Next, we separate into two categories those who are high school graduates or less and those who have a college degree or more. Again, some errors will be made because some of those who started at the SSA with a high school diploma will have continued their education. If someone went back to school to work on a college degree after joining the agency but dropped out of college after three semesters, this person would necessarily be a casualty to

sample mortality. However, if he finished college he would not be lost but switched from the low to the high category (but not until the data-gathering phase had been completed).

Having created the necessary educational strata within our sampling frame, we turn to the specificational variable of the employment status of wives. This variable will be difficult to operationalize accurately, but we should be able to do somewhat better than pure random chance. All employment applications contain items about the applicant's current residential telephone number and a request for a name and telephone number of the person to contact in case of emergency. One may assume that if the person's last name and telephone number given for the emergency response is the same as the applicant's, the applicant has put his wife in the blank for the person to be contacted and she is unemployed because the number is the same as the applicant's home phone. To make these assumptions will create the greatest degree of inaccuracy of all the assumptions we've made so far. Indeed, it is quite possible for one to be gainfully employed, but to work out of one's home. Further, with increasing occupational opportunities for women and with the rise of inflation eating away at the purchasing power of the family, many families will have become two wage-earner ones following employment of the male by SSA. It is for these reasons that we must sample more men with "nonworking" wives than we think we need.

At this point we have created four strata and will need to select 100 men from each of the two employed-wives categories and 150 men from each of the two unemployed-wives categories. Obviously, we are developing a disproportionate stratified sample, because it is impossible for the anticipated proportions on these variables in the sample to mirror the proportions of these variables in the sampling frame.

Finally, we need to select the sampled persons through a probability process, and we would recommend the systematic procedure because it is the simplest and most efficient. Thus, after establishing the appropriate sampling fraction for each stratum and making our selections, we will conclude the sampling phase with a disproportional stratified sample drawn by a systematic process.

Perhaps, two points should be noted. First, since some of the assumptions made during the sampling phase may not be accurate, the researcher will need to cross-check the values assumed for the class I and class II variables during the actual data-gathering phase. Second, much of the preliminary operationalization of variables, as well as the controlling of extraneous variables, can be done through the development and execution of a carefully considered sampling design. The design of one's sample is a crucial phase in the execution of a research study.

SUMMARY

In this chapter, we have discussed the major types of probability sampling designs with their respective advantages and disadvantages. Also, brief mention was given to several examples of nonprobability sampling designs. Finally, the issue of an appropriate sample size was presented, and an extended example was given assuming the existence of a formal list, which could be treated as a sampling frame. In this concluding section, several major points need to be highlighted.

First, our discussion has only tapped the surface of a complicated, but fascinating, methodological subspecialty of sampling design.

Second, one must understand that an appropriate research design will frequently necessitate a mixed sampling design—that is, some sort of blending of a probability procedure with a nonprobability procedure, or the blending of two or more probability procedures. We have not illustrated that here; nor do we feel it is appropriate. We simply remind the reader that one should not and cannot be an unthinking automaton to any element of methodology. Rather, different prob-

lematics and problems will require the construction of different sampling designs—designs that need not slavishly replicate a narrow, restrictive adherence to a strict set of rules. However, as appropriate as these alterations may be, adjustments in statistical formulas and other data-interpretation modifications may also be necessary.

Third, we emphasize that sampling may be correctly considered a branch or subspecialty of applied mathematics and statistics. Therefore, one should not hesitate to consult a sampling expert. Help with how alterations in the pure sampling designs discussed earlier will bias the interpretation of statistical analyses or how to improve one's available lists to begin to approach the condition where every element is listed once and only once, for example, are among the many other germane topics with which the sampling specialist can assist the researcher.[*]

Finally, recall that the relatively simple statistical formulas and the intended interpretations that one finds in the first course in statistical analysis usually assume that one has extracted these raw data from a sample derived by the simple random probability process. It is for this reason that the simple random procedure is so frequently touted in the social and behavioral sciences. As we argued earlier, drawing a simple random sample is infinitely easier than ending the data-gathering phase of the research with such a sample intact. Hence, many of the assumptions that underlie most introductory statistics presentations are not very realistic when it comes to social science research. Compromises and alterations may have to be made and one's statistical analyses may require adjustment and interpretative caution. However, even with these difficulties, we believe that almost any problem raised in this text is amenable to a scientifically and methodologically sound adjustment.

---

[*]Indeed, one should note that consulting opportunities for sociologists as methodological experts are a growing and lucrative career option.

KEY TERMS

Accidental sample
Cluster sampling
Disproportional stratified sample
Equal probability of selection
Independence of choice
Judgmental sample
Multistage cluster sampling
Nonprobability sampling
Primary sampling units
Probability sample

Proportional stratified sample
Purposive sample
Quaternary sampling units
Quota sampling
Random sample
Random start
Referral sample
Robustness
Sample mortality
Sampling fraction

Sampling interval
Sampling with replacement
Secondary sampling units
Simple random sample
Single-stage cluster sampling
Snowball sample
Stratified sampling
Systematic sample
Tertiary sampling units
Weighting

REVIEW QUESTIONS

1. What are the preconditions and the criteria for a simple random sample?

2. Why is it so important to conduct a simple random sample with replacement? What does the standard normal distribution discussed in Chapter 6 have to do with simple random sampling? How does robustness figure into all of this?

3. What are the types of probability sampling designs? What are their respective advantages and disadvantages?

4. Which sampling designs maximize representativeness? Which are appropriate for probing differences among groups?

5. Cite several reasons why nonprobability sampling designs are useful.

6. Discuss the criteria to consider when determining one's sample size.

7. What are the ethical ramifications of using a referral sample in research into deviance?

8. What are the different functions provided by proportional and disproportional stratified samples?

9. How would you go about constructing a multistage cluster sampling design of your college or university?

CHAPTER 8

THE CONSTRUCTION OF SCHEDULES AND GUIDES

INTRODUCTION

In this chapter and the next, we will be concerned with the design and testing of one's measuring instrument. In the present chapter we focus on issues that pertain to the construction of the measuring instrument. While we recognize a variety of other data-gathering procedures (which are discussed in Part III), we restrict our thoughts here to the schedule necessitated by the interview and questionnaire, because they subsume the maximum number of issues surrounding the construction of a measuring instrument.

Before we get into the design of particular items, we need a substantive proposition on which to focus. Assume that the researcher is interested in testing the hypothesis which we presented in Chapter 7: the self-image of working males varies positively with degree of education, holding constant race, marital status, age, and wife's employment status. To refresh one's memory, we are holding constant race, marital status, and age with a one-category control. That is, all those working men whom we will investigate will be of the same race (white), the same marital status (married), and the same age category (25–35 years of age). Further, while we will control on wife's employment status, we shall do so with a block variable control wherein some men have employed wives and some men do not. With these objectives in mind, let us turn to the preliminary decisions.

SOME PRELIMINARY DECISIONS

In measuring the eight variables in this hypothesis, we should use different types of measures because they are of different levels of complexity. Since each subject is male, employed, has a specific level of education, and shares a common race, marital status, and age category, the first six variables can be adequately measured with a single item. Further, the working status of the subjects' spouses can also be determined with a single item. The self-image of the males, however, is a complex variable that will necessitate the construction of an index. An *index* contains multiple items all thought to measure a single variable.

If we continue with the theoretical definition of self-image offered earlier, you will recall that self-image was an attitude. Therefore, we must construct statements rather than questions to evaluate this variable. Further, an index seems more appropriate than a scale, for we are interested in the respondent's degree of positive self-image rather than determining some specific point at which that person's self-image seems to break down.* Finally, we must decide how many items to include in the index. Let us suggest 48 items, as this number will certainly be sufficient to measure the person's degree of positive or negative self-image and will provide sufficient items to perform the desired reliability test discussed in Chapter 9.

---

*The notions of a single item, index, scale, and composite measure are largely the subject matter of the next chapter and are dealt with there in some detail.

One must also decide (1) between the questionnaire or interview data-gathering strategies, (2) between a measuring instrument which is a schedule or a guide, (3) between a general or a specific schedule item format, and (4) on the nature of the response categories. We turn to a brief discussion of each of these.

Data-Gathering Strategy

First, we make a firm distinction between a questionnaire and an interview. A *data-gathering* strategy includes questionnaires and interviews, which are often confused, in our opinion, with structured schedules and unstructured guides, respectively. A *questionnaire* is a self-administered data-gathering procedure in which the respondent is asked to read and reply to the items presented. An interview is usually a face-to-face conversation (although telephone interviews are increasingly being done) between an interviewer and a respondent for the purpose of eliciting information. In short, when a questionnaire is used, the respondent must do the work of reading and responding to the measuring instrument. When an interview is used, an interviewer assists the respondent in the data-gathering process.

Nature of the Measuring Instrument

Second, a *schedule* is a carefully prepared set of specific items to which the researcher wishes the respondent to reply. A *guide* is a general list of topics that the researcher wants to cover. The schedule is ordered with specific items, and the respondent or interviewer is obliged to follow this order without entertaining additional items, even if specific circumstances may seem to encourage this. The guide is more general in terms of the actual items, and the respondent or the interviewer is not bound to the particular order or even to those items listed. When using a guide, the interviewer is encouraged to branch off into any additional line of questioning that seems fruitful. In short, *schedule* and *guide* refer to the nature of the measuring instrument being used, while *questionnaire* and *interview* refer to the nature of the setting through which the data will be obtained.

Format of the Schedule Items

Third, the items that compose a schedule or guide can be specific or general. If a question or statement is written in a broad, global fashion, it is referred to as a *general* item. For example, if one asked "Well, how's it going?", this would obviously be a general question, since it opens the door for the respondent to talk about anything. "Things seem to be going rather well lately" would be an example of a general item in statement format. However, if a question or statement is written in specific language and directed to a narrow, well-defined context, we call it a *specific* item. For example, if one asked "Well, how do you feel about the President's latest policy statement on the nature of national defense?", this would be a specific item, since it directs the respondent's attention into a very definite and limited context. Similarly, "I like my new job" would be an example of a more specific item in statement format.

Usually, one constructs general items when doing exploratory research or probing for information about whose nature the researcher is unsure. In short, if the scientist does not know what to ask about the subject matter, general items allow the respondent to mention those things about which the respondent would like to talk and which, hopefully, are the things that are important to the situation the researcher hopes to understand. On the other hand, if the researcher is hypothesis testing, specific items should be used. In hypothesis testing, the researcher begins with well-defined hypotheses. The investigator knows what information is needed and writes specific items to obtain relevant information.

Nature of the Response Categories

Finally, one's response categories may be structured or unstructured. A *response category* is the way in which the researcher would like the respondent to reply. If an *unstructured response category* is chosen, the respondent uses the respondent's own words to reply to the items presented to the respondent. When a *structured response category* is used, the researcher presents already-thought-out response options from which the respondent must choose. Some examples are the *Likert response categories* (strongly agree (SA), agree (A), don't know (DK), disagree (D), strongly disagree (SD)); yes, maybe, no; and never, sometimes, frequently, all the time.

The major advantage of unstructured responses is, of course, that the researcher is able to capture the respondent's feelings and behaviors as they are presented. The disadvantage of unstructured responses is that they are difficult to compare from one respondent to another. The same words have different meanings to different people, for example, and it is very difficult—if not to catch, then certainly to record—inflections and changes in tone as the respondent speaks with the interviewer. The obvious advantage of structured response categories is that they are always comparable from one respondent to another, thereby facilitating comparisons among different individuals. The disadvantage of structured response categories is that they are tantamount to putting words into the respondent's mouth. There are tradeoffs to either selection, so that neither is clearly superior in all circumstances to the other. In sum, unstructured response categories rely on the respondent's own words, while structured response categories force the respondent to choose from the options that are presented.

Thus, when constructing a measuring instrument, the researcher must make four general decisions: (1) to use a questionnaire or an interview, (2) to use a schedule or guide format, (3) to construct specific or general items in the schedule or guide, and (4) to use structured or unstructured response categories.

CRITERIA FOR SELECTING APPROPRIATE ITEMS

Introduction

Following are several general criteria that must be considered in the selection of appropriate items for a measuring instrument. We assume that one will be framing an index, which is a series of different items designed to measure a single variable since single items usually pose fewer difficulties than indices. Finally, most of the considerations relevant to index construction are also relevant to the construction of other types of measures, which are discussed in detail in Chapter 9. Five criteria are presented: (1) the conceptual definition of the variable to be measured; (2) face validity; (3) unidimensionality; (4) response variation; and (5) item format.

The Conceptual Definition

Before appropriate items can be selected for an index, one must have a clear theoretical definition of the construct or concept to be measured.

Face Validity

Face validity refers to the selection of items that the researcher feels are logically related to the variable to be assessed. The researcher constructing the index is responsible for determining the item's appropriateness, i.e., whether it will appear to measure the variable on the face of it.

Parenthetically, the use of face validity does not constitute a sufficient assessment of instrument validity. The array of formal validation procedures compose, in part, a major section of the next chapter. However, face validation is a useful *preliminary* technique appropriate only in the *construction* of the measuring instrument. As such, face validity guards against gross inadequacies in one's items.

Unidimensionality

An index should measure only one dimension; it should have *unidimensionality*. If the concept is multidimensional, an indicator will be necessary. Nevertheless, whether an index or an indicator is required, one must be sure that the items selected measure only one dimension at a time. For example, as sociologists found in various research studies, people may select different responses when different dimensions are being assessed. If one is interested in multiple dimensions, the multiple sets of items should not be interchanged. After all, one wouldn't give a student credit for biological information if the student excelled on a mathematics test.

Response Variation

Each item should generate a range of responses; this is referred to as *response variation*. Essentially, the essence of scientific measurement is to identify and separate differences in units of analysis. For example, one would not ask a sample of people if they like cherry pie. Since almost everyone likes cherry pie, this item would not separate one person from another. More seriously, an objective test item that everyone answers correctly or incorrectly does not separate the better from the poorer students. In sum, one must choose items that differentiate individuals in your sample from one another on those variables that are of interest. After all, scientific information is generated on the basis of these class I and class II variables, their distribution, and the reasons for their distribution.

Item Format

In designing an item, one must choose between two format styles: (1) the statement and (2) the question. A *statement* is quite simply a declarative sentence. For example, "The President of the United States needs to take more decisive action in foreign policy matters" would be a statement. In essence, one is encouraging the respondent to answer how he feels about the statement that is offered. A *question,* on the other hand, asks the respondent for a more specific, or direct, response.

"How many children are in your family?" would be an example.

We're not really sure why, but the results seem to be easier to understand and interpret when one tries to measure *attitudes using statements* and *behavior or action using questions.* Thus, if one wants to know how the respondent feels, the researcher will offer a number of statements to which the respondent will react. However, if the researcher wants to know what the respondent has been doing (what his actions were), then a direct question is asked.

Summary

Before getting into the details of proper item formation, the researcher needs to be sure about what to measure, consciously asking whether the item logically relates to the variable of interest, being careful not to let extraneous dimensions enter into the measure, being attentive to those items that will generate different responses, and being sure to choose the proper format for the item—either a statement or a question.

CONSTRUCTING AN INDEX

Introduction

Parenthetically, while we said we needed 48 items in this measure, we will write only 10 examples here as representative of the 48. To begin the more difficult task of constructing the index to measure self-image, we consider the issues of the wording of the statements, the order in which the items are presented, the nature of the response categories, how these response categories are coded, how the codes will be handled, what format the entire index will take, whether any of the items should be weighted, and the nature of the directions one should include. While there are many factors to consider, we strongly recommend that one deal with one dimension at a time, since it is easy to get confused by the large number of these factors. In short, it is best to be systematic to the point of being methodical in this stage of the research design.

Selecting and Writing Items

The first step involves the writing of a large number of items for possible inclusion in the index. Initially, one should not be concerned with the grammar or wording of each item. It is best to get the idea of the particular item down on paper and then return to review it in terms of grammar, style, and other considerations.

Once the substance of the items has been determined, the researcher must scrutinize carefully each item to make sure that it is written properly. There are a myriad of rules and suggestions in the literature suggesting various standards to employ in revising one's items. Figure 8.1 paraphrases a few.*

Some comments are needed concerning the suggestions in Figure 8.1. First, criterion 2 focuses on the inclusion of items that are irrelevant to the variable being operationalized. Face validation will help the researcher to avoid this difficulty. Criterion 3 reinforces the notion that any item that the sample will answer in the same way results in the lack of response variation and, therefore, should not be asked in the first place. Criterion 5 demands that appropriate language be used for your sample.

Criterion 6 attempts to avoid the complex issue. A *complex issue* is one in which the respondent is asked to respond to two or more issues in the same item. For example, suppose we asked the following question: "Should the president raise taxes to pay for additional Defense Department projects?" The respondent could feel any number of ways about this question: (1) the president should not raise taxes and should not increase the Defense Department budget; (2) the president should not raise taxes, but the Defense Department's budget should be increased by reducing some other federal unit's budget; (3) the president should raise taxes, but these increased taxes should not be used by the Defense Department; (4) taxes should be raised, and the Defense Department should have its budget increased; but the president shouldn't do this, it should be the Congress that initiates the changes, and so it goes. Clearly, the above question is really three questions in one: (1) should the Defense Department's budget be increased; (2) should taxes be raised to pay for this increase; and (3) should the president be the one to initiate these changes? By combining all three issues into one question, frustration is likely to develop in finding an answer for the respondent who agrees with some of the suggestions and disagrees with others. This does not mean that one cannot ask about complex issues. Rather, it means that the complex issue must be broken down into its component parts, and each part should be asked individually in separate items.

Criterion 8 precludes the use of double negatives. For example, consider the following: "The boss should not refuse to honor an employee's request for sick leave." The reason for avoiding a double negative is that the respondent can so easily misread the item by only reading one of the negative terms, thereby "understanding" the exact opposite of what the researcher intended to present.

---

*Parenthetically, one of the most highly researched methodological topics revolves around the nature of a proper item in the operationalization of any variable. We suggest several sources as particularly good—some old and some more recent: William J. Goode and Paul K. Hatt, *Methods in Social Research* (New York, New York: McGraw-Hill Book Company, 1952); A. L. Edwards, *Techniques of Attitude Scale Construction* (New York, New York: Appleton-Century-Crofts, 1957); Stanley L. Payne, *The Art of Asking Questions* (Princeton, New Jersey: Princeton University Press, 1951); Paul B. Sheatsley, "Questionnaire Construction and Item Writing," *Handbook of Survey Research,* Peter H. Rossi, James D. Wright, and Andy B. Anderson, ed. (New York, New York: Academic Press, Inc., 1983), pp. 195–230; Norman L. Bradburn et al., *Improving Interview Method and Questionnaire Design* (San Francisco, California: Jossey-Bass, 1979); and Raymond L. Gorden, *Interviewing: Strategy, Techniques, and Tactics,* Fourth Edition (Homewood, Illinois: The Dorsey Press, 1987), especially pp. 292–300. Again, these are but a few of the large number of excellent bibliographic sources that contain suggestions on the proper way to construct good items.

1. Avoid items that can be interpreted in more than one way.
2. Avoid items that do not refer to the variable being studied (i.e., face validity should fulfill this requirement).
3. Avoid items that are likely to be endorsed or rejected by everyone (lack of response variation).
4. Select items that cover the whole range of the variable you are trying to measure; this means that one should write items that are both positive and negative.
5. Include language that is appropriate to the nature of the sample one expects to study; e.g., items presented to college graduates and items presented to third graders should not be worded the same.
6. Focus on only one complete idea in each item. To do otherwise is to construct a complex item, which cannot result in accurate responses.
7. Avoid the use of words such as *always, all, none,* and *never,* since these words introduce confusion and ambiguity.
8. Avoid the use of double negatives.
9. Avoid the use of all negative words such as *not* or *never;* if one wants to write a negative (as opposed to a positive) item, use a negative idea rather than negative words to negate a positive idea.
10. Avoid ambiguous items such as "What is your income?", which can be interpreted by the respondent in a number of different ways; make use of words such as *hourly, weekly, biweekly,* or *yearly,* for example.
11. Avoid asking about the respondent's intentions to do something, e.g., "Would you go to the baseball game if someone gave you a ticket?" People generally do not predict their own future behavior very accurately because of changing circumstances and situations.

FIGURE 8.1   Some Criteria That the Researcher Should Invoke When Revising Items for Possible Inclusion in an Operational Definition of Any Particular Variable

Further, the phrasing is awkward to read and comprehend.

But what about criterion 4, which suggests that positive and negative items should appear in an index in order to measure the entire range of feelings or behaviors? Criteria 4 and 8 are not really contradictory. We urge you to avoid using negative words such as no, not, and never (because they are easily misread), but not to avoid the use of negative as well as positive ideas. See Figure 8.2 for an example. Choice I uses the negative word not in item 2, while the first item contains no negative words. Here, if the respondent fails to correctly read item 2 by leaving the not out, the respondent will reply as the respondent would for item one, and an error will occur. But this kind of error is greatly reduced in Choice II. Here, the same ideas appear; item 3 is certainly positive and item 4 is certainly negative, but we have done this without using negative words at any time. While the researcher should avoid negative terms, one must write negative items to ensure the whole range of feelings or behaviors are assessed.

In sum, these are but a few of the useful notions to keep in mind when constructing a measuring instrument. Perhaps, our best advice is to be somewhat skeptical about one's own choices and, therefore, to be very careful. However, that is why item analysis and validity testing are relevant (see Chapter 9).

Some Specific Examples of Items for an Index on Self-Image

In this section we will suggest several possible items for inclusion in the index. Figure 8.3 contains 10 items pertaining to the measurement of one's self-image. The items are written in both positive and negative fashion in order to suggest positions along the whole self-image range. You will note that we have presented a roughly equal number of positive and negative items in an at-

Choice I

1. The boss likes me.
2. The boss does not like me.

Choice II

3. The boss likes me.
4. The boss hates me.

FIGURE 8.2 Two Examples of Ways to Write a Positive and a Negative Item to Assess an Employee's Perception of How the Employer Feels about the Employee

1. I feel good about myself.
2. People generally like me.
3. I really feel lonely.
4. People try to avoid me.
5. I feel that I can do anything that I really put my mind to.
6. Sometimes I feel that life is a waste of time.
7. I get along well with other people.
8. I can adapt well to new situations.
9. I'm discouraged with how things have turned out for me.
10. Almost everything I try turns out badly.

FIGURE 8.3 Examples of Items That Could Be Used in an Index to Measure the Variable of Self-Image

tempt to discourage the emergence of the response set that is sometimes called the *acquiescence tendency*. The *response set* is the tendency of some respondents to reply negatively or positively to the presented items. Therefore, a good schedule design requires positive and negative items and a random mix of their placement. This will help maintain the respondent's interest, although it will not guarantee the absence of the response set. However, if the response set does occur, the random arrangement of both positive and negative items will illustrate that it has occurred. For example, Figure 8.4, contains a hypothetical example of a response set. The Xs under the heading A indicate that the respondent has chosen to agree with all of the statements offered. A close look at the nature of these statements will indicate that such a response pattern is contradictory. For example, to agree with statement 1 is to register a positive response about oneself, but to agree to statement 4 is to register a negative response. Most people are not totally consistent in their responses, but this respondent seems to be waffling between the positive and the negative statements by answering the same way to each item. While the random mixing of positive and negative items did not seem to encourage interest and attention from this particular respondent, the occurrence of the response set is clearly evident because of the contradictory pattern of responses.

The Order of the Items

While the order of the items is important in determining the occurrence of a response set, it should also be considered in terms of the possibility of a response to one item biasing a response to a subsequent item. For example, in assessing the general health of a sample using several questions that ask about specific diseases, the order of the questions may elicit different responses. If one started with the question, "Did you experience a serious illness last year, such as a heart attack or treatment for cancer?", in all likelihood the answer to this question would bias a subsequent question if one asked "Were you sick last year?" This more general item would probably get a greater number of "no" responses if asked after the first question cited above than if one asked this more general question before the more specific one. After all, most of us would not complain about the 24-hour flu when the researcher seemed interested in heart disease and cancer. Therefore, if one is interested in all illnesses, it would be better to start the measuring instrument with the more general items before entertaining questions about specific diseases. Also, one is advised to move from the less serious to the more serious situations, to minimize the respondent's failure to mention appropriate data.

	SA	A	DK	D	SD
1. I feel good about myself.	[ ]	[X]	[ ]	[ ]	[ ]
2. People generally like me.	[ ]	[X]	[ ]	[ ]	[ ]
3. I really feel lonely.	[ ]	[X]	[ ]	[ ]	[ ]
4. People try to avoid me.	[ ]	[X]	[ ]	[ ]	[ ]
5. I feel that I can do anything that I really put my mind to.	[ ]	[X]	[ ]	[ ]	[ ]
6. Sometimes I feel that life is a waste of time.	[ ]	[X]	[ ]	[ ]	[ ]
7. I get along well with other people.	[ ]	[X]	[ ]	[ ]	[ ]
8. I can adapt well to new situations.	[ ]	[X]	[ ]	[ ]	[ ]
9. I'm discouraged with how things turned out for me.	[ ]	[X]	[ ]	[ ]	[ ]
10. Almost everything I try turns out badly.	[ ]	[X]	[ ]	[ ]	[ ]

FIGURE 8.4 An Illustration of Responses to a 10-Statement Index on Self-Image That Evidence a Response Set

The Sieve, or Filter, Item

It is here that the sieve question may be very useful. A *sieve question* (which is sometimes called a *filter question*) is one that separates those who should answer a series of questions from those for whom these questions would be irrelevant. Suppose the researcher wanted to measure the knowledge that a sample of students retained from their research methods course. If some students had never been exposed to this subject matter, it would be pointless to ask them what they knew about research methodology. Here the sieve question ("Have you ever taken a research methodology course?") will sift those students who have taken the course from those who have not. Figure 8.5 illustrates the format using an example that pertains to the sample's participation in intercollegiate sports. The initial question is the sieve

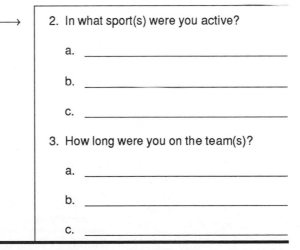

1. Have you ever participated in the intercollegiate sports program while you were an undergraduate student?

[ ] Yes ⟶ 2. In what sport(s) were you active?

[ ] No (Go to item 4.)

    a. _____

    b. _____

    c. _____

3. How long were you on the team(s)?

    a. _____

    b. _____

    c. _____

FIGURE 8.5 An Illustration of the Format and Use of a Sieve Question on the Variable of Student Participation in Intercollegiate Sports

question that separates those who have played such sports from those who have not.

Lastly, consider the case where one wishes to obtain information about the respondent's distant past. Consider taking an oral history from a group of senior citizens who are all in their 80s and 90s. If you wanted to know what their annual incomes were in 1920, we would guess that many could not immediately recall accurately the figure. One can, however, ask questions that will help the respondent recall this information. For example, one could ask how old they were in 1920. This question could be followed with one about the city or town in which they were living as well as with whom and in what kind of residence they were living. In this way one jogs the memory so the respondent can frame a more distinct mental picture of the past before the important question is asked. (The format of the question may be important as well. For example, rather than ask what one's annual income was—a fact that could be subject to considerable error—it would be better to ask what the hourly wage was. Many people cannot remember how much they made, but do remember their hourly wage.) In this context of recalling the past, the order of the questions may play a crucial part in obtaining more accurate data to important questions.

In sum, the order of the items is important to consider. First, if one believes that all the items are equally important and that no one item will bias the response to any subsequent item, the order of the items should be determined randomly using a table of random numbers. However, if one believes that different orders will produce different responses from the same people, we suggest ordering the items from general to specific and from not so serious to serious. Indeed, the researcher can pretest several different orders to see which one best accomplishes the research objectives. Second, sieve questions save the respondent and the researcher valuable time as well as minimize the respondent's frustration at being asked questions that the respondent cannot answer. Finally, when one wishes information from a sample about "historical" or past events, one is best advised to create the context for the respondent prior to asking for the desired information.

Nature of the Response Categories

After framing good items and establishing a proper order for them, the next step is to select response categories. We argued earlier that while unstructured responses are very useful in exploratory research or research in the context of discovery,[1] in all likelihood structured response categories are more appropriate when one is hypothesis testing. Figure 8.6 contains some of the choices that have been used frequently in social research.

Use of the Likert response categories has been quite successful in the assessment of attitudinal variables. They continue to be strongly recommended for such research. First, the various Likert response categories denote different points over the entire range of possible feelings. Second, they are clear in their meaning to almost all respondents, researchers, and consumers of research.

In determining the specific category to employ, common sense and the previous experiences of researchers are invaluable aids to decisionmaking.

---

1. Likert response categories: strongly agree, agree, don't know, disagree, and strongly disagree.
2. Yes, maybe, no.
3. Never, rarely, occasionally, fairly often, frequently, all the time.
4. Always, often, occasionally, seldom, never.
5. Dislike very much, dislike, indifferent, like, like very much.
6. Excellent, good, fair, poor.
7. Definitely true, more true than false, more false than true, definitely false.
8. Never, less than half the time, about half the time, more than half the time, always.
9. Never, once, 2 or 3 times, 4 or 5 times, 6 or more times.

FIGURE 8.6   Some Possible Structured Response Categories That Can Be Used in Social Science Surveys

This would be particularly true of category 9 in Figure 8.6.

Figure 8.7 illustrates the format for both the statements suggested in Figure 8.3 and the Likert response categories selected. Note the positions of the statements and the response categories. This format—with the statements to the left and the response categories to the right—makes for the efficient use of schedule space. If the format that follows were used, each item would consume more space than it needs to, thus raising the costs of printing and mailing (if it is used) the measuring instrument and causing consternation for the respondent because of its apparent "huge" size.

1. I feel good about myself.
    [ ] Strongly agree
    [ ] Agree
    [ ] Don't know
    [ ] Disagree
    [ ] Strongly disagree

The format suggested in Figure 8.7 is, therefore, more economical and professional. Note that the response categories are headed by the designations "SA," "A," "DK," "D," and "SD," which must be explained to the respondent. Further, all the response categories should be lined up vertically underneath their respective headings. When this is done, as suggested in Figure 8.7, it is called a *matrix format*. Not only is it an efficient use of space, but this format will reduce the measurement errors of miscoding and unintended marking.

Format of Structured Response Categories

A number of possible formats have been used to present structured response categories, several of which are illustrated in Figure 8.8. Format 1 can lead to sloppy responses because the desired check mark may be put in with more flourish than desired, thereby making it more difficult to determine which choice was made. Format 2 and format 3 suggest an enclosed space into which the re-

---

We want you to read a number of sentences, and we want to know how you feel about them. To help you, we would like you to answer by picking the response that comes closest to how you feel about the sentence. There are five choices: strongly agree (SA); agree (A); disagree (D); strongly disagree (SD); and don't know (DK).

Remember, we want to know how you *feel* about these statements. There are no right or wrong answers; only how you feel.

Please put an "X" within the bracket which best fits how you feel about each statement.

	SA	A	D	SD	DK
1. I feel good about myself.	[ ]	[ ]	[ ]	[ ]	[ ]
2. People generally like me.	[ ]	[ ]	[ ]	[ ]	[ ]
3. I really feel lonely.	[ ]	[ ]	[ ]	[ ]	[ ]
4. People try to avoid me.	[ ]	[ ]	[ ]	[ ]	[ ]
5. I feel that I can do anything that I really put my mind to.	[ ]	[ ]	[ ]	[ ]	[ ]
6. Sometimes I feel that life is a waste of time.	[ ]	[ ]	[ ]	[ ]	[ ]
7. I get along well with other people.	[ ]	[ ]	[ ]	[ ]	[ ]
8. I can adapt well to new situations.	[ ]	[ ]	[ ]	[ ]	[ ]
9. I'm discouraged with how things turned out for me.	[ ]	[ ]	[ ]	[ ]	[ ]
10. Almost everything I try turns out badly.	[ ]	[ ]	[ ]	[ ]	[ ]

FIGURE 8.7 An illustration of a 10 Statement Index on Self-Image with the Accompanying Likert Response Categories

FORMAT 1	FORMAT 2	FORMAT 3
_____ Yes	( ) Yes	[ ] Yes
_____ No	( ) No	[ ] No
_____ Don't Know	( ) Don't Know	[ ] Don't Know

FIGURE 8.8 Different Formats for the Presentation of Structured Response Categories on the Schedule

spondent is encouraged to place a mark. These latter two formats are more desirable, because they will lead to less measurement error through miscoding. Brackets are probably the best, although parentheses are acceptable. The researcher must also supply an appropriate direction to place an *X* rather than a check mark in the designated space.

Coding the Response Categories

How does one move from all those check marks on the schedule to the data so nicely presented in the tables of the report? The first step is to code the response categories.* *Coding* is the assignment of numerical values to one's response categories. Continuing to use the Likert response categories for illustrative purposes, there are a number of coding possibilities, which are illustrated in Figure 8.9.

In considering these five options, we will focus on only the first item suggested in Figure 8.3: "I feel good about myself." If this item was coded as in option four, a "strongly agree" response would receive a code of zero (0) and a "strongly disagree" response would be assigned a code of four (4). In answer to this item, a "strongly agree" response would be interpreted as a positive response, indicating a good self-image. Conversely, a "strongly disagree" response would be inter-

preted as negative and indicative of a poor self-image. To code the responses as indicated in option four is to assign a number close to zero for a highly desirable quality and a large number to a highly undesirable quality. This coding process would be similar to a golf score in which the lowest score is the best score. Because we are generally oriented to think that a larger number is better, we reject option 4 as flying in the face of what most people would call common sense.

Option three is mathematically the most logical. The plus signs indicate positive values and the minus signs indicate negative values. Further, associating numbers with the signs indicates different degrees of positive and negative orientations. Therefore, to "strongly agree" with this item is to have a highly positive self-image and would be indicated by a plus two (+2), while a "strongly disagree" response would be assigned a minus two (−2) and is indicative of a negative orientation. While logical and easier to understand than option four, option three has one major disadvantage. Those who will be translating the responses on the schedule onto data cards, coding sheets, or directly into the computer must make two determinations rather than one. That is, they must choose a plus (+) or minus (−) sign *and* a one (1) or a two (2). This two-step process will generate more measurement error than the more simple one-step operation in option four. Therefore, for the reason of

---

*How the codes are handled and eventually entered into the tables of the report (if that is the researcher's intention) are subjects for discussion in a subsequent chapter. At this point, we address only how one codes the response categories that appear on the schedule.

OPTION/RESPONSE	SA	A	DK	D	SD
One	[4]	[3]	[2]	[1]	[0]
Two	[5]	[4]	[3]	[2]	[1]
Three	[+2]	[+1]	[0]	[−1]	[−2]
Four	[0]	[1]	[2]	[3]	[4]
Five	[1]	[2]	[3]	[4]	[5]

FIGURE 8.9   Possibilities for Coding Likert Response Categories

the increase in measurement error, we reject option three.

Option two gives every response category a single number that is progressively in order, with the most positive orientation receiving the highest number (5) and the response category with the lowest orientation receiving the smallest number (1). This meets the objection of option four, since the higher numbers indicate more positive self-images, and the objection of option three, in that it does not entail the use of a plus or minus sign. The lowest possible response, however, will seem to have some degree of positive self-image because it received a one (1)—an implication that may not be warranted.

Since option five combines the disadvantages of option two and option four, it is similarly rejected.

Lastly, option one addresses all of the difficulties that are associated with the other four coding schemes. The poorest self-image one could obtain comes from responding with a "strongly disagree" and would be coded with a zero (0). To most people when one has zero of anything, one has nothing of it. Zero logically implies none of the particular quality that is being measured. Therefore, the first option is the soundest, in our opinion, because it eliminates the two-step problem of coding both a sign and a number, it eliminates the mental gymnastics of option four where the low number is the best and the high number is the worst, and it gives a clear implication to the notion of a zero point in this index. However, you should realize that starting the coding scheme at zero does not make this index a ratio level of measure-

ment. Any of the options listed in Figure 8.9 are mathematically correct. We favor option one because it is the easiest to explain to a consumer of research who may not be a professional statistician or research methodologist.

Coding Positive and Negative Items

Let us return to Figure 8.3 for items 1 and 6. Item 1 reads "I feel good about myself," while item 6 reads "Sometimes I feel that life is a waste of time." Clearly, the first item is a positive one and the second is a negative one. That is, if one strongly agrees with item 1, that person would be expected to have a positive self-image and, therefore, we would code this response category with a four (4). Conversely, if the respondent strongly agrees with item 6, one would be expected to have a strong negative self-image and we would code this response category with a zero (0). In both cases the respondent selected the same response category, "strongly agree," but the coding process is different because of the substantive nature of the items. See that one switches the coding sequence from that illustrated in option one in Figure 8.9 when the response is given to a negatively written item.

To look at this another way, consider a "strongly agree" response to item 1 and a "strongly disagree" response to item 6. If the respondent selects strongly agrees to item 1, it is indicative of a positive self-image and should be coded with a large number. Similarly, if the respondent strongly disagrees that life is a waste of time, a positive self-image has been indicated and should be coded with a high number.

As we have argued, mixing positive and negative items in one's index is desirable, because it allows for a wider range of possible feelings and permits the researcher to check for a response set. When one switches to a negative item, however, the codes for the Likert response categories must also change to account for the switch in the tone or direction of the item itself. Thus, the researcher should be careful in coding the items in the index to note the direction (i.e., either positive or negative) of the item.

The "Don't Know" Response in the Likert Response Categories

Special attention is necessary when dealing with the "don't know" or "no opinion" response. The coding scheme in Figure 8.9 suggests that the "don't know" response carries an intermediate value of two in option one between the strongly agree value of four and the strongly disagree value of zero. Indeed, if one has properly constructed an index with positive and negative items, the "don't know" response should carry a value that is in between what one would interpret as positive and negative regardless of the direction of the item. Because many people do not wish to take a stand when confronted and asked for an opinion, the "don't know" response can be a fortuitous choice through which the respondent may gracefully be excused from what is perceived to be a troublesome issue or a painful process of making a decision. Therefore, the researcher should try to discourage the use of the "don't know" response.

Some methodologists would argue that one should never use the "don't know" response. That is, if one is interested in the Likert response categories, only four should be used, omitting the "don't know" category and thereby forcing the respondent to make a choice from among the other four. While this would eliminate the difficulties mentioned above, we argue against this. After all, the "don't know" response is a legitimate response in that there are times when the respondent may feel that a choice between a positive and a negative orientation cannot be made. For this reason, the researcher should make this option available to the respondent. That does not mean that the researcher should encourage the respondent's use of this option just because the respondent is uncomfortable making any type of positive or negative choice. Therefore, the researcher should vary the *position* of the "don't know" response to discourage its use.

Remember that we are focusing here on the survey and that surveys may have the interview or questionnaire format. For questionnaires, the researcher should organize the Likert response categories so that the "don't know" response category comes last. Therefore, the sequence from left to right for a questionnaire schedule (see Figure 8.7) would be: strongly agree (SA), agree (A), disagree (D), strongly disagree (SD), and then don't know (DK). The rationale for this format is twofold. First, it will discourage the use of the "don't know" response, because the respondent must go to the last category to find it. Second, it will obviate the appearance of being the middle or average re-

NATURE OF THE ITEM/CODE VALUE	SA	A	D	SD	DK
Positive schedule item	[4]	[3]	[1]	[0]	[2]
Negative schedule item	[0]	[1]	[3]	[4]	[2]

FIGURE 8.10   An Illustration of the Position of the "Don't Know" Response Category When the Likert Response Categories are Used in a Questionnaire Study Involving a Schedule and the Subsequent Coding Strategies for These Categories

sponse. This change will, obviously, force an adjustment in the coding sequence. A positively written item would be coded 4, 3, 1, 0, and 2, and a negatively written item coded 0, 1, 3, 4, and 2. Figure 8.10 summarizes these decisions.

For an interview, the placement of the categories can remain as indicated in Figure 8.9. If so, the coding remains as in option one. Thus, the interviewer is the only person who will see the schedule, as the respondent will be presented with the items verbally and will reply verbally. However, when one is using an index during an interview, one of the most boring things that can happen is for the interviewer to continuously repeat the structured response categories. To avoid this problem, one can provide the respondent with a three-by-five inch index card with the response categories listed, which will make the interview go more smoothly. The response categories should be listed on the card starting with *strongly agree* and ending with *don't know*. Such a card may look like the following:

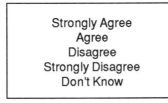

Weighting Items in the Index

We have discussed the concept of weighting in the context of sampling and specifically when we looked to make a disproportional stratified sample representative of the sampling frame from which it was taken. We again use the concept of weighting, but this time its meaning is considerably different.

Weighting an item in an index means giving that item some differential amount of influence when compared to the other items. That is, if one weighted the fifth item, then the fifth item would have a value that is different from the values of the other items that compose the index. The tendency is to consider any one item in an index as equally

able to tap the variable that is being measured. Therefore, in most cases, the issue of weighting does not arise. Occasionally, however, one will write an item that must be weighted because it relates to the underlying variable being measured in a significantly different way than the other items. For example, consider the brief list of items suggested in Figure 8.11, which are designed to measure marital discontent. Note that the items are in the form of questions, since we are measuring a behavior or action. In questions 1 through 4, the intent is to measure the ordinary or less serious kinds of marital difficulties, but item 5 is quite different.

Beating one's spouse is an indication not only that marital discord exists but also that it is extremely severe. If the researcher were coding a "no" response to any of the first four questions with a zero (0) and a "yes" response with a one (1) (assuming the high number indicated greater degrees of marital discontent), surely it would be necessary to give a "yes" response to question 5 a greater value than one (1). To only give such a response a one (1) is to equate beating one's spouse with having an ordinary argument—an equation that is not reasonable. Even though question 5 is of a different magnitude than the remaining questions, it is a telling indication of marital discord. It is, therefore, a legitimate question and could find a meaningful place in the index if it is fairly weighted. It would have to be given more impact

---

1. Do you argue with your spouse?
2. Do you ever leave the house and go for a walk when you are having a disagreement with your spouse?
3. Do you try to get back at your spouse when you are angry?
4. Do you express dissatisfaction with the little things that your spouse fails to do "correctly" for you?
5. Do you ever beat your spouse?

FIGURE 8.11 Items for Inclusion in an Index to Measure Marital Discontent

in the composite measure than the other items. Thus, the code for the "yes" response should be multiplied by some coefficient so that this particular item will be felt more or have more impact on the total score of the composite measure.

What that coefficient should be we will not say. The weighting of items in an index is a very tricky business. It is something that is best left to an advanced course in research methodology. We raise the issue here because you should be wary of items in your index that stand out from the rest. However, one should not be overly concerned about the nuances of one's items in an index. As Earl Babbie has said:

> Basically you must decide whether to give each item an equal weight in the index or to give them different weights. Although there are no firm rules, I suggest—and practice tends to support this method—that items be weighted equally unless there are compelling reasons for differential weighting. That is, the burden of proof should be on differential weighting; equal weighting should be the norm.[2]

In sum, weighting is a very difficult business, and the general feeling of most researchers (including us) is: When in doubt, don't.

Directions for Completing the Index

The last point in our discussion of an index is a reminder to include specific directions for the completion of the section of the schedule containing the index. The index is likely to be one section of a multisection schedule. Since the index is not likely to start the survey, the respondent will need help in registering appropriate responses when moving from one type of item to another. It is a common mistake of many beginning researchers to rush into the items on the schedule without properly preparing the respondent for what the respondent is asked to do. Appropriate directions are important in acquiring accurate data efficiently while minimizing frustration for the researcher and respondent.

Directions should, first, help the respondent make the transition from one kind of task to an-

other. If the respondent has been answering a series of questions about personal background through a series of essentially single-item questions and an index suddenly appears with a corresponding change in the nature of the questioning, assistance is needed. If the composite measure is an index in matrix format with structured response categories, the respondent will encounter a number of questions or statements and be asked to choose responses from among a limited number of preselected categories. One needs to make this known to the respondent; to identify the structured response categories; and to explain what these categories mean, if the respondent seems puzzled by them (see Figure 8.7).

Further, in preparing the respondent to work through an attitudinal index, the researcher must impress upon the respondent that there are no correct or incorrect answers to any of the items. In an attitudinal study, since the researcher seeks the feelings of those sampled, the respondent must understand that there are no preconceived notions of what the respondent is supposed to say. Some topics are such that those sampled may reply with the *socially desirable response*—the response that all good, nice, moral people would make. For example, it has long been surmised that middle-class whites admit to less racial prejudice than actually exists. In another instance, the sexual prowess proudly and loudly proclaimed in the men's locker room is likely to exceed reality. Hard-working parents are likely to exaggerate the amount of quality time they devote to their children. Finally, academic types are likely to depreciate the number of hours logged before the television set.

Conversely, it has been our experience that certain people are quite cooperative and willing to participate in a study. They are so cooperative that they try to give you the answers that they think will please you. Some elderly people, for example, who live alone are so anxious for company that they will try desperately to keep the interviewer sitting there to steal a couple of additional moments in order to converse with another person. So, one must impress upon the respondent that there are no right or wrong answers, only answers that reflect their feelings about the items presented.

The following is an example of a set of directions to be read by an interviewer to the respondent. Notice that it helps to make the transition, clarifies what is going to happen, explains the nature of the response categories, and encourages honest, truthful replies:

> *We've asked you a number of questions about yourself up to this point, and now we want to do something different. We want to read a number of sentences to you, and we want to know how you feel about them. To help you, we would like you to answer by picking the response that comes closest to how you feel about the sentence. There are five choices: strongly agree (SA), agree (A), disagree (D), strongly disagree (SD), and don't know (DK).*

[Hand the card with the responses to the respondent.]

> *Remember now, we want to know how* you *feel about these statements. There are no right or wrong answers; only how you feel. Do you have any questions?*

[Pause to let the respondent have a chance to ask something.]

> *If not, then let's try a couple of examples to make sure that you understand this.*

[Give the practice items to the respondent, clarify, explain, and then proceed with the index. BE SURE TO CAREFULLY PUT Xs INSIDE THE BRACKETS. DO NOT USE CHECK MARKS.]

The bracketed and italicized material is instructions for the interviewer. If the data-gathering technique had been a self-administered questionnaire, the instructions about the response categories would have been a little more elaborate, since there is no interviewer to answer the respondent's questions. In a questionnaire survey, it should be emphasized that the respondent place an "X" within the brackets rather than a check mark on the schedule. As we indicated earlier, check marks can often run over into the spaces designated for other

responses causing either a miscoding of the respondent's reply or greater coder fatigue, both of which can lead to substantial measurement error.

SINGLE ITEM CONSTRUCTION

Introduction

In this section, we concentrate on the construction of single items. Of course, much of that which was discussed under the rubric of the index applies here. A number of factors are presented that are, for the most part, distinct and separate from one another. We should also note that all of these considerations will not apply in all cases when one is operationalizing concepts and constructs.

The Probe Question

Understanding that interviews are examples of social interaction as well as mechanisms for gathering information, one must realize that all the problems of normal social interaction will be relevant to interviewing. Thus, when certain items are asked, the respondent may well reply with the usual, stereotypical answer that often characterizes normal conversation. For example, if one asked the respondent the question, "How are you doing?", one might get a reasonably stereotyped answer from the respondent, "Fine." How many times have you responded "Fine" to such a question when you were not doing fine? When such responses are given, a *probe question* will be necessary to elicit further information and to break through the stereotypical response. In this example, the probe question might take the form "How's that?", which encourages the respondent to elaborate by communicating that the interviewer really is interested in the respondent.

Some typical probes are the following: (1) would you like to expand on that, (2) could you explain that again, (3) I don't understand, so could you say that again, (4) please elaborate, and (5) that's interesting, tell me more. The important thing about probes is that they should not suggest the nature of the response to be given; for this reason, probes are often qualified with the term *neutral.*

The Antagonistic Question

A variation on the theme of the probe question is the antagonistic question. The *antagonistic question* is usually an abrasive question, which is likely to aggravate the respondent. Further, it is usually about a subject matter that will almost guarantee that the response will be stereotypical or what was called the socially desirable response earlier.

For example, if you were studying marital discord and asked "How many times last month did you beat your spouse?", the respondent is likely to vehemently deny ever beating anyone and evidence a high level of indignation that the interviewer would ask such a question. Perhaps the researcher has knowledge that the respondent is a spouse beater. That is, the sample may have been drawn from a list of persons who are known to have had marital difficulties and who have been seeking professional help for such extreme responses as beating their spouses. Here, the researcher might choose to use an antagonistic question and say, "Now, almost everyone has marital problems occasionally and sometimes things get pretty bad. When was the last time you beat your spouse?" To phrase the question this way and to preface it with the sentence given says to the respondent that, first, the interviewer will not be shocked by a truthful response, since this behavior is more common than the respondent might think. Second, it suggests to the respondent that the interviewer has heard all this before and is not going to be shocked by any new revelations that the respondent might reveal. Finally, the antagonistic question says to the respondent that the interviewer already knows that the respondent is a spouse beater (strongly suspects such, or wouldn't be surprised if such was the case) and that, therefore, there is no need to "tiptoe around" this issue with feigned indignation and a socially desirable response.

There is one final caution in the use of antagonistic questions. Such questions do offend people, scare some, and violate the norms of the society. Therefore, they should be used sparingly and only when it is necessary to the research. Indeed, under the impetus of federal legislation and a growing attention among professional social scientists to the ethical implications of research, the antagonistic question may be a strategy whose time has passed. The human subjects protection review boards, which are proliferating on university campuses today, are not likely to approve such an item. Should it be necessary to use this type of question, however, its schedule position should be near the end, since the interviewer will need to have developed as much rapport as possible with the respondent prior to asking the antagonistic question.

RESPONSE CATEGORIES TO A SINGLE ITEM

Introduction

Earlier we dealt essentially with an attitudinal variable and utilized the Likert type of structured response categories in our illustrations. Here we want to expand on the notion of structured response categories by suggesting some other possibilities and formats. Before we do, however, two general principles of constructing response categories need to be emphasized: inclusivity and mutual exclusiveness.

Inclusivity

Inclusivity refers to a situation in which all of the possibilities included in one's data can be categorized into one or another of the categories presented. For example, consider a question that asks the respondents to check their religious preferences. If the response categories were Protestant, Catholic, and Jewish, we would not have enough categories for all of the data one would normally expect from a sample of Americans. While we

Place an *X* next to the response that best characterizes your religious preference:

[ ] Catholic
[ ] Protestant
[ ] Jewish
[ ] No preference
[ ] Other: _____

(Please specify here.)

FIGURE 8.12   Illustration of the Proper Format and Designation of Structured Response Categories for a Single Item Dealing with the Respondent's Religious Preference

could categorize a vast majority of Americans, we would not be able to place those who were Buddhists, Moslems, or had no preference. Therefore, the best way to present structured response categories to the item asking for one's religious preference is to offer as choices the most frequently appearing categories (which can be determined through a pilot study), a response that allows the person to reply "no preference," and an "other" category with the request to specify one's preference in the blank provided. See Figure 8.12 for an example.

Mutual Exclusiveness

The second criterion for the proper use of structured response categories is to guarantee that all the responses obtained can be classified into only one category that has been listed. Again, let us return to the religious preference variable. Suppose that the categories were: Methodist, Presbyterian, Episcopal, Lutheran, Protestant, Catholic, Jewish, no religious preference, and other. Any person who selected any of the first four choices could also select the fifth choice of Protestant. Therefore, such a person could be counted twice in the study while everyone else would be tallied only once. *Mutual exclusiveness* refers to a property of the structured response categories and signifies that a person who is correctly placed into one category cannot be correctly put into any other category from among those offered. When

one is creating structured response categories, it is important that *all* of the responses can be classified and that the classification is into only one category.

As with most principles and suggestions in methodology, there are exceptions. If one would like to know how many of a whole series of choices the respondent favors, multiple responses to the structured response categories would certainly be appropriate. For example, if one was studying the degree to which senior citizens are isolated from contacts with others, one might ask a question as it appears in Figure 8.13. You'll notice in this illustration that the respondent can mark more than one response to indicate all of the behaviors that characterize that person's activities during the stated period.

SCHEDULE FORMAT

In this section, attention is given to guidelines for the general format or appearance of a schedule.

Cover Sheet

It is always wise to include a cover sheet. The *cover sheet* should contain the following: (1) the title or name of the study of which the schedule is a part; (2) the organization or agency that is sponsoring the research; (3) if an interview, the interviewer's name, address, and telephone number; (4) the date on which the schedule was done

Check all of the activities in which you participated during the last two months. (Place an "X" next to each one that applies.)

[ ] Wrote a letter to a friend	[ ] Went shopping by yourself
[ ] Went to lunch or dinner by yourself	[ ] Went to lunch or dinner with a friend
[ ] Talked to friends on the telephone	[ ] Received a letter from a friend
[ ] Had a friend come visit for part of a day	[ ] Had a friend stay overnight
[ ] Went to a movie, play, or concert	[ ] Went on an overnight trip
[ ] Had a day trip to some place of interest	[ ] Went shopping with a friend(s)
[ ] Went to a senior citizen center for one or more activities	[ ] Went out for personal business, such as banking or other financial arrangements

[ ] Other:_____

(Please specify.)

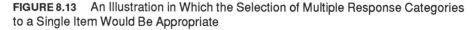

FIGURE 8.13   An Illustration in Which the Selection of Multiple Response Categories to a Single Item Would Be Appropriate

(if an interview) or the date on which the schedule was received (if a questionnaire); (5) a statement of anonymity or confidentiality (if such is appropriate); (6) any further information that is appropriate and unique to the particular study; and (7) directions or important things to remember (if any).

The title or name of the study is important if one happens to be doing multiple studies at the same time. Quite often this is the case when one is involved with a contract research firm. If the schedule gets misfiled, the title will assist in more efficiently placing it where it belongs. Obviously, listing the sponsoring agency is a courtesy and a professional touch that will help to develop greater rapport with the respondent. If one is doing an interview, the interviewer information is helpful if there are questions about the data that the interviewer placed on the schedule. This information helps the researcher who may need to contact the interviewer concerning these data if they were not recorded in the manner in which they should have been done.

The date is important, especially if the study is one that extends over a relatively long period of time. Consider a study on residents' attitudes about an impending urban housing project. Interviewing a large sample may extend over an entire summer. If the local newspaper reports a story about a corrupt or incompetent staff person's working for the local housing agency, this information may bias the responses of the sample gathered after the article appears. It would be very important to separate those schedules that were completed before and after the news story to assess how this particular event may have affected the sample's responses. We discuss (see Chapter 10) the mail-back bias when we talk about mailed questionnaires where the date is important in assessing the direction of missing data from nonrespondents.

Further, it may be that one is looking for persons whose replies seem particularly insightful in order to contact them for additional study. In this case a designation of "restudy" or "no restudy," along with the respondent's name, address, and telephone number could be included on the cover sheet. Such information allows the researcher to easily separate those whom the researcher wishes to study further.

Finally, important directions or guidelines for the interviewers to remember (if an interview survey), or which the investigator would like the respondent to see and remember (if a questionnaire survey), should be placed on the cover sheet.

Position of the Spaces to Be Checked

If one is using structured response categories, the spaces into which the Xs are to be placed should appear in some uniform format. That is, for single items, the response categories should all be to the left or to the right of the specific responses given. The researcher should not switch their positions throughout the schedule, because the respondent or interviewer may miss more items. Again, when an index or scale is being used, we strongly recommend the matrix format because of its consistency and efficient use of space.

Spacing for Open-Ended Responses

When one wants the respondent to reply in the respondent's own words, adequate space should be given for such replies. It has been our experience that when such replies are expected, one is usually presented with a modest one or two blank lines (sometimes even with single spacing between the lines). Such will certainly discourage the respondent from giving any kind of response, but if one can be solicited, it is likely to be a polite, stereotyped one. It is important to give the respondent a generous amount of space for comments if such are desired. Accordingly, we would argue against the provision of lines since they appear to encourage a response of predetermined length. Indeed, we suggest using the back of the page if more space is needed.

Coding Space

It is useful to make space on the schedule for codes that will eventually be keypunched onto cards or entered directly into a computer from a keyboard or terminal. One can accomplish this by placing a vertical line down the right-hand margin of the schedule. To the right of the vertical line, place a horizontal line of five spaces or so and a number underneath the line which corresponds to the column number or number that the code will

occupy on the data card, data file, or spreadsheet. Finally, one should place at the top of each page in this right hand margin the words *Do not write in this space*. This will discourage the use of this space until the coders translate the check marks into their appropriate numerical codes. The provision of a column for codes will greatly decrease the possibility of omitting one or more items from the coding sequence and significantly reduce transposition errors.

Neatness

Neatness is particularly important when developing a schedule for a questionnaire and is strongly advised for an interview. The general neatness of a schedule is important in gaining accurate information and in increasing one's response rate. The more professional the schedule looks to the respondent, the more seriously it will be taken. Neatness is positively correlated with a higher response rate and with greater accuracy of data transposition and analysis.

Commercial Printing

One should consider having the schedule commercially printed. Commercial printers can use smaller and neater type than can be obtained from most computers or typewriters. They can use different size type for different purposes, and the overall look of the schedule can look quite professional, which is always a plus when administering one's measuring instrument. It may be that the costs will not be that much more since the commercial printer may use fewer sheets of paper, thus saving additional postage costs as well.

Summary

One should try to improve the overall appearance of one's measuring instrument wherever possible. A good appearance will always improve the response rate; cut down on response, coding, and data-analysis errors; make the schedule easier to administer; and lead to less respondent, interviewer, and analyst fatigue. As Erving Goffman argued in his discussion of impression management, if one wants the subjects of one's study to take the study seriously, it must appear that the researcher took the study seriously by showing attention to these and similar details.[3]

AN EXAMPLE

Introduction

We conclude this chapter by presenting an abbreviated example of a social science study and its accompanying schedule. We have focused on material that pertains to operationalization and on issues discussed earlier. This section will function as an extended working summary. One must, again, be impressed by the fact that research methodology is a series of integrated decisions that involve methodological choices, conceptual issues, and statistical choices. We have purposely introduced a number of errors. You are encouraged to locate them and to suggest solutions. To assist you, we have placed a number next to each error, and we will discuss each one and what corrective adjustment should be made. In addition, try to find any errors that are not noted. Before criticizing the specific schedule, one must have some knowledge about the overall study, which is offered in Figure 8.14.

Point 1 questions the use of a questionnaire data-gathering design. Since the sample involves workers on the assembly line in a routine manufacturing situation, one might have reason to suspect that the level of education of most of these workers is not very high, probably no more than a high school graduate. If this is true (and the pilot study or a quick check of the workers' application forms in the personnel records will answer this question), one can anticipate a large nonresponse rate. Therefore, it would be much better to use the interview data-gathering technique.

Point 2 suggests that one class I variable in the study is the degree of prestige that each occupational slot possesses. If the sample contains 100 assembly line workers, all these employees would share roughly the same attribute of being essen-tially semiskilled, assembly line workers. Thus, the sample is inadequate because it does not contain sufficient degrees of occupational prestige. However, it may be that one is interested in the different degrees of status that automotive industry workers bestow upon themselves. One such study found that the workers who put the electrical systems into automobiles had the highest prestige of all the different job slots on the major assembly line because the electrical workers were the only persons who had to go to school to learn their particular jobs. Although they had school for only a few days, it was sufficient to distinguish them from their fellow workers. If the latter is the case, the researcher has made no provision for determining what each respondent's specific job classification is. This could be easily done by asking this question and providing a blank with a "Please specify" designation. Either way—and the conceptual model should suggest which way the researcher intends to conceptualize the variable of occupational prestige—the measuring instrument is deficient in its present form.

Point 3 notes that 100 persons will be selected. We doubt that this number of workers will be sufficient to do the kind of statistical analysis that the researcher will want to do at a later time, but this information is not given so a definitive critique is not possible.

Point 4 indicates that the study was done in the fall of 1984, a time when the automotive industry was experiencing heavy competition from foreign imports. Layoffs and cutbacks in production were common in some plants, and the researcher should have checked to see if such a slump happened in Dearborn, Michigan. If so, the timing for an attitude study would be unfortunate because the workers could have been anxious due to this contextual variable. A study at this time was tapping into an atypical period in the life of the workers at the Ford Motor Company.

Point 5 indicates that the study contains a "guide." The study is a hypothesis testing one in which the researcher begins the study with a firm proposition that can be, and presumably has been, substantiated through the review of the literature

Assume that the researcher wants to assess the variable of the degree of the feeling of alienation experienced by a representative sample of assembly line workers doing a routine job for a major corporation. The data are to be gathered using a structured questionnaire (1) containing, among other items, the index that appears below. The hypothesis being tested is that worker's attitude toward work varies positively with their degree (2) of occupational prestige. The researcher plans to submit this index to 100 (3) assembly line workers employed at the Ford Motor Company assembly plant in Dearborn, Michigan. The year is 1984 and the study is being done in the late fall (4).

Guide (5)

1. How many times have you been absent (6) recently? (7)
   Once (8) (9)
   Twice
   3 or more (10)

2. If any employee was performing his social role (11) inadequately (12), his superior should: (13)
   _____ fire him (14)
   _____ ignore the inadequacy (15)

	(16)	(17)	(18)		SA	A	?	D	SD
3. I feel good about my work.			(19)		[0]	[1]	[2]	[3]	[4]
4. I like my family. (20)					[0]	[1]	[2]	[3]	[4]
5. I get along well with my superiors. (21)					[0]	[1]	[2]	[3]	[4]
6. My boss does not dislike me. (22) (23)					[0]	[1]	[2]	[3]	[4]
7. I'm making good progress on my job. (24)					[0]	[1]	[2]	[3]	[4]
8. Anyone who takes more sick leave than the company gives should be fired. (25) (26)					[0]	[1]	[2]	[3]	[4]

FIGURE 8.14   An Illustration of Part of a Hypothetical Study

and by the presentation of a conceptual model. A general guide is not what is needed. Rather what is needed is a specific schedule that will generate appropriate information for the assessment of already known and stated variables.

Point 6 will probably generate some confusion among the respondents. Certainly, the respondent will know the number of absences. However, there may be instances of absence because of legitimate illness or worker disability on the one hand, and absences due to alienation, too much weekend, alcoholism, and a variety of other reasons on the other. This first question fails to differentiate between absences that are legitimate and those that are not. The researcher should make such a dis-

tinction because the illegitimate absences are pieces of behavior that could indicate worker alienation. Further, you might argue that the researcher wants to measure the workers' feelings and not their behaviors, and you would be correct. However, behavior can be taken as a cross-check against the attitudinal items that follow later in the schedule.

Point 7 focuses on the word *recently,* which is vague and, therefore, should be eliminated. The researcher should specify some specific time frame. For example, the question could be asked using "the last two weeks" or "the last month" as the time designation. Whatever specific time frame is used, it should be clear and not so long a period of time that the respondent is unlikely to recall accurately the information that is asked. Also, one must guard against the socially desirable response according to which the respondent would understate absences.

Point 8 identifies the fact that there is no space for the respondent to mark an answer or directions about how to proceed. In this case brackets should be used, and the respondent told to place an "X" within the brackets that are next to the most appropriate answer.

Point 9 refers to the fact that the given structured response categories are poor. First, they do not include all possibilities. What would one reply if the respondent had not been absent at all? Second, the range of responses is not very insightful. The last category lumps together the respondent who suffered from the three-day flu with the person who was chronically absent for, perhaps, a large part of the time period specified.

Point 10 is somewhat trivial, but attention to detail is never wasted effort. The first two response category choices are written out and the last is numerically specified. It would be better to be consistent, although neither way is preferable.

Point 11 identifies a concept *social role* which, while meaningful to the sociologist, is quite likely to be unknown to those in the sample. The use of technical terminology should be avoided unless one is dealing with a sample of people who would know and use such terminology.

Point 12 is a variation on the same theme as point 11. The word *inadequately* may not be a technical term, but it may be one that is beyond the vocabulary of some of the persons in the sample. Again, the pretest of the measuring instrument should indicate that *social role* certainly and *inadequately* possibly should be eliminated in favor of wording that is more familiar to those being studied.

Point 13 refers to the fact that this item (item 2) is likely to be irrelevant to the objectives of the study and should, therefore, be eliminated. However, if a case can be made for this item, points 14 and 15 become relevant.

Point 14 suggests that the space for the respondent's mark should be a set of brackets as indicated in the Likert response categories of items 3 through 8. Again, the use of lines encourages a more sprawling check mark that may be hard to interpret as mentioned earlier in Format 1 of Figure 8.8.

Point 15 reflects the fact that the two response categories given for this item reflect the extremes of possible responses on the part of the superior. Indeed, neither response seems appropriate given the nature of the item.

Point 16 refers to the fact that all previous schedule inclusions asked for responses to single items. Now, the schedule is shifting to a matrix format and a series of attitudinal statements. Proper instructions should be given to facilitate the transition to a different type of item format.

Point 17 recognizes the absence of an explanation of the meaning of the abbreviations "SA," "A," "?," "D," and "SD." While the social researcher is familiar with these designations, there is no reason to suppose the respondent is. Remember, again, that the researcher said that the data-gathering procedure was to be a questionnaire, which is self-administered and must, therefore, be carefully explained to the respondent. Further, since the respondent's attitudinal feelings are sought, he should be informed in the directions that there are no correct or incorrect answers to these statements in order to reduce the reporting of the socially desirable answer or one that the respondent thinks will help out the researcher.

Point 18 focuses on the position of the "?" or "don't know" response category. In an interview, its position should be as indicated here. In a questionnaire, on the other hand, it should be placed to the extreme right of the sequence of responses to discourage its use.

Point 19 focuses on the coding scheme that has been selected for the Likert response categories. Since item 3 is a positive item, if *strongly agree* is selected, the respondent would receive a score of zero (0). If the respondent strongly disagreed with item 3 the respondent would have a negative attitude and would receive a score of four (4). Therefore, high numbers would indicate alienation—a correct interpretation. However, we would suggest that, while the coding scheme and its interpretation are correct, it would be better to have the low numbers indicate negative feelings and high numbers indicate positive feelings. This could be done by reversing the direction of the existing coding *if and only if* the researcher also changed the variable in the hypothesis from degree of alienation to something such as degree of worker satisfaction.

Point 20 indicates an item that has no relevance to the work place and measures a dimension of happiness other than occupational. Therefore, it should be eliminated from the index.

Point 21 focuses on a tricky problem. Most of those who work in positions of intermediate occupational status will have more than one superior. It could be that many employees get along well with one superior and not with another. The researcher must recognize that and compensate for it through the use of a sieve question.

Point 22 focuses on the use of a negative word in an item. As we have noted, negative *ideas* are appropriate, but negative *words* should not be used.

Point 23 focuses on the juxtaposition of the negative word *not* and the negative word *dislike* (a double negative), which is a cumbersome way of writing a positive item. This would be much simpler and clearer if it read, "My boss likes me." As it stands, the item is hard to understand, as the pretest and an item analysis would most likely demonstrate.

Point 24 focuses on an item that has the potential to cause difficulty. Progress on the job is not an attitudinal variable, but a behavioral one. Therefore, it is irrelevant to the index on worker satisfaction (or alienation). However, one could make a case that one's objective position within the corporation is one of several important factors in determining one's attitude of satisfaction. While this item may be informative, it should not be included in the index itself.

Point 25 identifies an item that is irrelevant. The item does not focus on the worker's attitude about work but, rather, on the worker's feelings about company policy.

Point 26 denotes that the substance of this item does not recognize the difference between legitimate and illegitimate absences. Further, it is written in such a way that it does not permit recognition of any extenuating circumstances.

There are several other points of criticism that should be made. These points are not directed to any particular thing that appeared earlier but to the proposal itself. Point 27 refers to the index itself. If one elects to eliminate items 4 and 8 as irrelevant, the index as stated has too few items to adequately measure the major variable of the study. The shortage of items will also prevent the use of the split-half reliability test that we argue for in Chapter 9. Indeed, even with these two items, the size of the index is inadequate. Clearly, more items are needed. Finally, point 28 recognizes that all the items in the index are written in the same direction. That is, they are all positive, which will prevent the researcher from determining if a response set has occurred. Again, one cannot prevent the occurrence of the response set, but one can recognize its existence if the items are half positive, half negative, and randomly ordered.

SUMMARY

We began this chapter with a discussion of operationalization, which is the process of developing objective measures of one's variables. The focus was primarily on many of the nuts-and-bolts issues that accompany the selection and refinement of any measuring instrument. We chose to focus on the survey, because surveys require the social scientist to make a greater number and variety of decisions than are necessary for the other data-gathering techniques in the behavioral sciences. Thus, we were able to address more issues and concerns.

After some preliminary context setting, we discussed five criteria for selecting items: (1) one's conceptual definition; (2) face validity; (3) unidimensionality; (4) response variation; and (5) item format.

Next, an index to measure self-image was used principally to illustrate the writing and selection of items; the importance of item ordering; the type of response categories used, their placement and order, coding, and the use of positive and negative items; the weighting of items; and directions to help the respondent produce accurate and relevant responses.

Additionally, in addressing the construction of single items, we introduced the probe question, the antagonistic question, the need for response categories to be inclusive of all the empirical possibilities as well as mutually exclusive of each other, and the actual format of the schedule with attention to the cover sheet, the positioning of the response category spaces, the use of open-ended responses, the column for coding purposes, neatness, and commercial printing.

Finally, we presented a partial research design, sampling design, and measuring instrument that served to illustrate the interrelationships among these three components of any research study. The example contained numerous errors, the nature of which was discussed in conjunction with their corrective adjustments.

KEY TERMS

Acquiescence tendency	Index	Response variation
Antagonistic question	Interview	Schedule
Coding	Likert response categories	Sieve question
Complex issue	Matrix format	Socially desirable response
Cover sheet	Mutual exclusiveness	Specific item
Data-gathering strategy	Probe question	Statement
Face validity	Question	Structured response category
Filter question	Questionnaire	Unidimensionality
General item	Response category	Unstructured response category
Guide	Response set	Weighting
Inclusivity		

REVIEW QUESTIONS

1. Distinguish between a questionnaire and an interview, a schedule and a guide, general and specific items, and structured and unstructured response categories. What dimensions are presumed by each of these attributes?

2. Discuss the criteria for selecting appropriate items for a measuring instrument.

3. Discuss any 10 concepts or choices involved in constructing appropriate items for inclusion in a schedule.

4. What is the difference between a probe question and an antagonistic question? Under what conditions would each be used?

5. What do *inclusivity* and *mutual exclusiveness* mean to the selection of appropriate response categories?

6. Discuss the dimensions relevant to the format or appearance of a schedule to be used in a questionnaire data-gathering study.

CHAPTER 9

ISSUES IN MEASUREMENT AND OPERATIONALIZATION

INTRODUCTION

At this point, let us reconnoiter. The researcher has selected a research topic, reviewed the literature for an appropriate conceptual model through which to organize and interpret the data gathered, determined specific propositions to be investigated, and selected the specific sample to study. Finally, assume the researcher is interested in a survey—either a questionnaire or an interview.

In this chapter we turn to the design and testing of the measuring instrument. We assume that an adequate measuring tool for those variables in which one is interested does not exist so that the fullest treatment of the issues of measurement and operationalization can be presented within the practical limits of space.*

Many authors of research methods books place this subject matter before the discussion of sampling. However, we argue that one needs a clear idea of the sample (at least in general, if not the specific list of those to contact) before one can design an appropriate measuring instrument. As a simple illustration, the language and vocabulary used would, obviously, have to vary if one interviewed a sample of college professors or students in an elementary school class. Therefore, the nature of the sample must be understood before the measuring instrument can be constructed.

LEVELS OF MEASUREMENT

Introduction

All scientific numbers cannot be interpreted in the same way, because they have not been arrived at through the use of identical measurement procedures. Statisticians generally recognize four *levels of measurement:* nominal, ordinal, interval, and ratio.[1] Each of these levels represents a different set of mathematical principles, thereby permitting different types of interpretations. The levels-of-measurement assumptions have, too often in our opinion, received insufficient emphasis. The violation of these levels-of-measurement assumptions can lead to misinterpretation and distortion, as we shall illustrate.

Nominal Level

The *nominal level* of measurement is the simplest of the four levels. On this level one is either sorting the units of analysis into categories or identifying each unit with a number. For example, if we sorted a class of students into those who are female and those who are male, we would have measured the class at the nominal level. Whenever one categorizes or classifies the data and these categories *cannot* be thought of as ordered along an underlying continuum, the nominal level of measurement has been used. If one found 15 females and 10 males in your methods class, this means that there are 15 persons in one category and 10 persons in the other. At the nominal level, one attribute is not interpreted as better or worse than another attribute on the underlying dimension. Each attribute would just be different. Among the variables in the social sciences that are *measured* at the nominal level are sex, race, ethnicity, region of the country, and religion.

---

*Other data-gathering techniques may not require the full complement of issues and procedures outlined here.

There are several points to remember when establishing categories at the nominal level. First, each category should be mutually exclusive with all of the other categories; that is, if a case is classified in one category, it should be impossible to categorize the same case in another category on the same dimension. The following categories on religion—Catholic, Protestant, Jewish, and Methodist—will serve to illustrate this notion. These religious labels are not mutually exclusive, since a Methodist would, obviously, be counted in the Methodist category *and* in the Protestant category, resulting in a double enumeration of one case.

Second, the categories taken together should include all the cases studied. In the example offered, a Buddhist would not fit into any of the categories listed. Therefore, the list is inadequate for the task that it claims to handle. However, no matter how hard one tries to anticipate the variation in some variables, the researcher cannot guarantee to anticipate everything and indeed doesn't need to. In response to the question of religious affiliation, one should, when conducting research in the American culture, list the three major religious affiliations—Catholic, Protestant, and Jewish—and a fourth category entitled "other" with a blank marked "Please specify" for those few respondents who have religious persuasions other than the three listed (see Figure 8.12). The "other" category allows the researcher to study the filled-in responses to determine if there are significant numbers of unanticipated categories that should be incorporated into the study. A second reason for the "other" category is that it gives the respondent a place to offer a different response than the researcher has considered. This could be important for the poorly educated respondent who may not understand what the other categories really are or how the respondent's particular orientation relates to the categories that have been presented. For example, a respondent may claim to be of a particular religious orientation but not understand that this is considered one of the Protestant denominations. Finally, in an effort to record accurately what a respondent *is,* one must offer an opportunity for the respondent to say what he or she *is not.* While the response categories of "Catholic," "Protestant," "Jewish," and "other" cover all *religious* bases, one should also include a category labeled "none" or "no affiliation" for those persons who do not identify with any organized religion.

A second way cases are measured at the nominal level is by labeling them with numbers. When this is done, the number identifies the case but has no quantitative meaning. Most colleges and universities use the student's social security number as the primary identifier. Think about these numbers mathematically. While the social security number 220-89-9998 is greater than 203-76-6543, this does not denote numerical superiority or inferiority. The first number simply *identifies,* say, Mr. Smith and the second *identifies* Ms. Jones.

One final point about the nominal level of measurement remains. It may be that the researcher measures a variable at the nominal level because the scientific community has not developed a more sophisticated way of assessing the variable. For example, think again about the dimension of sex and its male and female attributes. Conceptually or theoretically and through one's observations, we have every reason to believe that maleness and femaleness are variables with values that can be observed to fall on a continuum rather than into distinct and disparate categories. Think of those males you have observed who appear to be male chauvinist pigs and those males who are more effeminate in their demeanor. Consider those females who appear incapable of little but directing the servants and pouring tea, as opposed to those who are more aggressive and capable in business and the professions. While theoretically there is reason to perceive these attributes in a continuous fashion and observations support this conceptual orientation, we continue to measure sex as a dichotomous variable at the nominal level. We do this because we do not know how to operationalize sex in any other way. In this case, our theoretical notions are clearly more sophisticated than our operational capacities.

Ordinal Level

The *ordinal level* of measurement permits ranking relative to the degree of some common characteristic that the items possess. Here one assigns the number *1* to the case that possesses the most amount of the variable being measured, the number *2* to that element that possesses the second highest amount, and so forth, until one has ordered all of the elements from the one with the most to the one with the least amount. If two or more elements share the same amount, their respective ranks in the ordering must be summed and the mean assigned to each. Consider that one was ranking persons by age and found that Frank and Joe were both 38 years of age. If the next two ranks to be assigned were 10 and 11, one would determine the mean of these two ranks, i.e., 10.5, and assign the rank of 10.5 to both Frank and Joe. Similarly, if three people were tied for ranks 7, 8, and 9, all three would be assigned the rank of 8 (i.e., $7 + 8 + 9 / 3 = 24 / 3 = 8$). What results is an ordered list wherein any one element's position has been determined by that element's comparison to all of the other elements.

When variables are measured at the ordinal level, one has information that is unavailable at the nominal level. At the ordinal level, the researcher can compare any two elements and their respective ranks to determine whether the first element is greater than, equal to, or less than the second element. The ordinal level allows one to measure differences in what is conceptually supposed as a continuous rather than a discrete dimension. Consider Figure 9.1. If you knew that item *A* ranked first, *B* ranked second, and *C* ranked

third, you could be assured that *B* fell somewhere *between* points *A* and *C* in Figure 9.1, although you could not tell where in that area. An alternative perspective suggests that numerical ranks have little quantitative meaning but are numbers whose meaning is derived from the element's *comparison* to other elements. For example, if told that Frank, Joe, and Bill ranked first, second, and third, respectively, on age, you would know that Joe was older than Bill and younger than Frank, but you wouldn't know anything about their absolute ages. They could be 82, 78, and 76. They could be 82, 40, and 16. They could be 16, 13, and 12. The only information one would know is their *order* on the variable of age.

Interval Level

The *interval level* of measurement has two characteristics. First, there is some agreed upon, constant, standardized unit of measure. For example, this could be an inch, foot, yard, meter, mile, ounce, pound, gram, or Celsius degree. Second, there is an *arbitrary zero point*. That is, there is a point that the scientific community has agreed to call zero. A good example of the interval level of measurement would be the Celsius thermometer. Zero degrees Celsius is that point at which water freezes at sea level and 100 degrees Celsius is the point at which water boils. We mark off 100 equal intervals between the zero point and the 100 degree point and in this way construct a Celsius thermometer.

Because there is a constant unit of measure, one not only can say that element A, which measures 30 degrees Celsius, is colder than element B, which measures 50 degrees Celsius (as one could have said had the ordinal level been used), but also one can now say how much colder item *A* is than item *B*. In this case, we know that *A* is 20 Celsius degrees colder than *B*, because we used a constant unit of measure. Thus, a constant unit of measure allows the researcher to say how much more or less something else is, which is a piece of information not available at the ordinal measure-

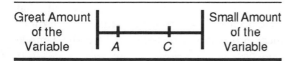

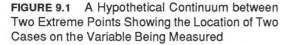

FIGURE 9.1   A Hypothetical Continuum between Two Extreme Points Showing the Location of Two Cases on the Variable Being Measured

ment level. However, the arbitrary zero point is not a true, or absolute, zero point. That is, when one records a zero value at the interval level of measurement, it does *not* mean one has found the least possible amount of the variable. Therefore, one can obtain negative values at the interval level of measurement. Thus, while zero degrees Celsius is cold, it is not the coldest it can get.

It is not easy to find good examples of interval-level measurements in the social and behavior sciences, but we can suggest one that meets the arithmetic requirements. If one were to measure a person's wealth, such would be recorded at the interval level. Since the value of wealth would be measured in dollars, we have a constant unit of measurement. While one can't receive a salary check for less than zero dollars, one could have a sizable debt on the home mortgage. Thus, when both income and debt are combined, one might owe more money than one is currently worth; hence, one's wealth (meaning total financial position) would be measured in negative dollars. For the most part, however, few variables are measured at the interval level of measurement in the social sciences.

Ratio Level

The final level of measurement is the ratio level, which has two characteristics. First, like the interval level, the *ratio level* of measurement has a constant unit of measure. Second, the ratio level has a *nonarbitrary,* or *absolute, zero point.* Thus, when a value of zero is recorded at the ratio level, this is the least amount possible of the variable being measured. In other words, one cannot have negative values on the ratio level of measurement. For example, if height is measured at the ratio level of measurement, there is a constant unit of measure, say feet, and a nonarbitrary zero point. It is impossible to be shorter than zero inches tall. There are many social measurements that arith-

metically are at the ratio level: age, salary, amount of formal education, to mention but a few.

When the ratio level of measurement is used, one has all the interpretive information that one had with the nominal, ordinal, and interval levels plus the notion that one can determine, because of the nonarbitrary zero point, how many more times one case possesses the variable being measured when compared to other cases. For example, if one found that John was 60 years old and Bill was 20 years old, we would know that John had more age than Bill (an ordinal interpretation), that John was 40 years older than Bill (an interval interpretation), and that because zero years of age is the least amount possible,* John is three times as old as Bill.

Importance of the Levels of Measurement

These various levels of measurement are important because they comprise one dimension in the series of assumptions that underlie the legitimate use of the data-analysis procedures available in statistics. Statistical formulas are mathematical formulas that require mathematical operations such as addition, subtraction, multiplication, division, squaring, and square roots. Because of these mathematical operations, one must consider the level of measurement in one's operational definitions. Any statistical procedure requires that the data fed into the formula conform to a minimum level of measurement. For example, the Pearson product-moment correlation technique requires that the two variables being correlated be measured at the interval or ratio level of measurement.[2] If one puts ordinal or nominal data into this formula, the resulting value will not be the same as that obtained when the criterion for the levels of measurement is met. Other statistical procedures use data that have been created through less rigorous measurement procedures; for example, see the lambda statistics.[3]

---

*One might argue that the developing fetus is, say, three months from being born (hence, a person is minus three months of age), thereby accounting for the prenatal state with the result that age would be an interval-level variable. While this is fine for the biologist, we would argue that social scientists, particularly sociologists, do not recognize the prenatal state as social. Therefore, age starts at birth.

Please note two interconnected points here. First, the nature of the statistical analysis one does will require a specific level of measurement on which the statistic depends and from which the statistician has developed certain acceptable interpretations. Therefore, the researcher must keep this prerequisite in mind when operationalizing class I and class II variables.

The reader should not have to be overly concerned here for two reasons. First, as discussed earlier, some statistical procedures are more robust concerning violations of measurement assumptions. Second, there are many statistics that measure a common property but that are designed to accommodate data at different levels of measurement. Of course, there may be a specific statistic one would like to use because of its strong interpretation. This being the case, one must design an operational measure that meets the requirements and presuppositions of the data-analysis procedure.

We would like to register two concerns for your consideration. The first is with the implications of using a statistic that assumes a higher level of measurement than one has. Despite statistical robustness, it is our position that researchers who do this are making unwarranted additions to the strength of their interpretations. This type of addition could have significant implications for policy implementation or change, program development, or a myriad of other applied decisions made on the basis of the statistical analysis of data.

The second concern is with a consideration of the substantive interpretation of variables as well as the arithmetic characteristics. That is, while some social variables can be said to be interval or ratio mathematically, we would question whether such can be paralleled substantively. We said salary could be treated as an interval-level variable, and it *can* in terms of *measurement*. However, ask yourself if an increase in annual income from $200,000 to $205,000 would mean the same thing to the recipient as a change from $5,000 to $10,000. The interval is the same, but we would argue that the interpretation and the life-style implications would be quite different. Similar illustrations can be made for age, education, and many other important social variables.

Putting these two issues together gives rise to the question of whether social scientists are registering exaggerated claims through their statistical interpretations.

Summary of the Levels of Measurement

Figure 9.2 summarizes the four levels of measurement. As one moves from the top of Figure 9.2 to the bottom, each subsequent level of measurement subsumes all the information contained in the previous levels and provides additional information. Thus, while nothing is lost from the preceding levels, the new level adds additional interpretations. Since the function of measurement is to assess differences among elements, the farther down the list of levels one goes, the more sophisticated will be one's knowledge. Thus, all other things being equal, it is wise to seek the most rigorous level of measurement possible since this level will provide the most information about the variable. All other things are rarely equal, however; thus, while it may be possible, it may not be necessary to use the most sophisticated measurement procedure. Remember that the entire research process is an effort to seek a balance among a large number of disparate, yet related, factors.

LEVEL	SELECTED CHARACTERISTICS
Nominal	Categorization and labeling
Ordinal	Ranking or ordering
Interval	Constant unit of measure; arbitrary zero point
Ratio	Constant unit of measure; nonarbitrary, or absolute, zero point

FIGURE 9.2 Four Levels of Measurement and Selected Characteristics

Changing Levels of Measurement

Sometimes the researcher will want to change the level of measurement. For example, it may be that the researcher designed a measure to generate ratio data because of the desire to use a statistic that assumes a ratio level of measurement. Upon completing the analysis, the results may indicate a possible relationship or characteristic that was not originally anticipated. The researcher may now want to do a different analysis using a different statistic. If the additional procedure requires that the variable be measured at the ordinal level, the researcher must transform the data from the ratio level to the ordinal level. Thus, some conditions may arise in which the level of measurement of the data may have to be altered.

It is permissible to transform one's data from a more rigorous level of measurement to a less rigorous level. In the example cited above, it would be legitimate to change ratio-level scores into ranks at the ordinal level. Of course, information is lost, but no distortion of the data would result. However, there is no legitimate way to transform data from a less rigorous level to a more rigorous level. A quick example will illustrate which transformations are legitimate and which are not. Table 9.1 contains one variable measured on both the ordinal level and the ratio level. Starting with the ratio level, it is easy to see how these data could be transformed without distortion into the ranks shown. One simply takes the person with the great-est age and assigns that person the rank of 1 and so forth. But consider the reverse. Assume that one started with the ordinal data in column two of Table 9.1 and did not have the ratio values. Could you guess any of the ratio figures? No. If you were told that George was 65 and Irwin was 48, then the only thing you could say for sure was that Jack's age was somewhere in the range between 49 and 64.

Further, we said that all statistical procedures demand, among other requirements, that certain levels of measurement be achieved for their legitimate use. Of the several measures of central tendency, the mean requires that interval or ratio data be used. If we added all five ages at the ratio level and divided by 5, the resulting value would be 44.4 years. Now, if we put the ordinal rankings into the same formula, the result would be 3. It should be clear that the researcher runs a grave risk of distortion and misinterpretation when the assumptions of the levels of measurement are violated.

In sum, one may start at any point in Figure 9.2 and transform the data without distortion to any level that precedes the starting level. However, there is no way to transform data to a subsequent level.

The Relationship between One's Conceptual Model and the Appropriate Level of Measurement

One's achieved level of measurement may change with a change in the conceptual dimension *even though the measurement units and techniques remain the same.* Suppose one wanted to measure family income, which was defined conceptually as the amount of money a family has at its disposal. The operational definition might measure the number of dollars that accrue to the family during some time period. If one then set out to measure all the take-home salaries, interest payments on back accounts, dividends on investments, gambling profits from the Friday-night billiards sessions, and all other sources of cash, one would come up with a certain dollar figure that could be

TABLE 9.1 Hypothetical Data on the Variable of Age Measured for Five Persons on Both the Ordinal and Ratio Levels of Measurement

PERSON/LEVEL	RATIO	ORDINAL
George	65	1
Jack	50	2
Irwin	48	3
Abe	32	4
Michael	27	5
Mean ($\overline{X}$) =	44.4	—

considered a ratio level of measurement. That is, one can't get paid negative dollars; paychecks can't be any lower than zero dollars.

However, what if the family's wealth was measured? When the dimension of wealth is considered, we are conceptually thinking about the family's total financial picture. Thus, while the operational definition must include everything mentioned in the preceding paragraph, one must now include the dollar values of those items of debt that the family has amassed. If there is a substantial mortgage on the house, for example, it may be that the family owes more money than it makes during the measurement period. Hence, the family's wealth falls into the negative part of the monetary continuum, which would transform this variable to one measured at the interval level. Here, the arbitrary zero point is simply that point where the family's incomes and debt obligations balance.

Let's change the dimension again. This time let's measure the family's social class position, theoretically defined as the degree of prestige accorded to the family because of its location in the society. Assume that one uses income as an operational measure of class and finds that the Smith, Jones, Groskovitch, and Williams families have annual incomes of $560,000, $550,000, $20,000, and $10,000, respectively. The income difference between the Groskovitch and Williams families is $10,000, and this differential is sufficient to put the Groskovitch family in a higher status position than the Williams family. There is a $10,000 income differential, as well, between the Smith and Jones families, but one would argue that both these families fall in the same social class position. While the difference between the Groskovitch and Williams families was sufficient to grant the Groskovitches more prestige, this same difference was insignificant as a discriminator between the Smith and Jones families. Here, income would have to be considered ordinal in nature since there is no constant unit of measure. This also serves as

an illustration of the difference between the mathematical or statistical and the substantive dimensions of the same variable.

In sum, all three variables of income, wealth, and social class position were measured using the same units—dollars. Yet, these measurements had to be interpreted differently because of the nature of the underlying dimensions being measured. Again, all numbers cannot necessarily be interpreted the same way in all circumstances.

TYPES OF MEASURING INSTRUMENTS

A cursory look at the literature on social science measurements indicates a vast array of measurement procedures, which can be categorized into a limited number of types: (1) item; (2) index; (3) scale; or (4) indicator.

Item

An *item* is a single question or statement. For example, "What is your sex?" is an item. In this case, there are two logical response categories: "male" and "female." However, if one asked, "When were you born?" the researcher could expect the answer to be any one of 366 different days over a period of many decades. We are not concerned with the number or variety of replies offered in response to a statement or question but rather *how many* of these statements or questions are used to measure a variable. Obviously, many of the simpler variables can be adequately measured using a single item. Additional examples of a single item are sex, age, place of residence, telephone number, amount of education, car ownership, United States citizenship, race, marital status, and employment status.

Composite Measure

A *composite measure*[4] contains two or more items designed to assess a single variable.* There are

---

*We basically subscribe to the distinctions which Earl R. Babbie makes among composite measure, index, and scale, and we have borrowed from his discussion.

three reasons for using a composite measure. First, a single item may not adequately assess the variable being measured. Therefore, a composite measure—or multiple items—must be used. For example, consider an objective midterm in your research methods course where the obvious objective is to measure the degree to which the student has mastered the relevant material. If your professor gave you *one* statement to which you were to reply true or false, would you feel that this single item was an adequate measure of your knowledge? Of course not. There are some variables that cannot be adequately assessed using a single item; therefore, a composite measure is necessary. In sum, rarely are complex matters amenable to a single item.

Second, while a single item may be adequate to measure some variables, the researcher may need a composite measure for others. For example, if one wanted to measure political orientation, a single item such as, "In what political party are you registered, or which one would you select if you were to register?" could be used. The researcher could classify those who selected the Republican party as conservative and those who selected the Democratic party as liberal. However, students of political behavior would be quick to point out a wide range of political orientation within either of these political parties. There are a number of conservative Democrats and liberal Republicans. Therefore, to measure the political dimension of conservatism-liberalism with a single item leads not only to errors of classification but also to the equation of all those who offer a common response. If a classification into extreme categories with some degree of error is all that is needed, then a single item may be satisfactory. However, if one needs a more refined measure to separate various degrees of the variable, a composite measure is needed.

Finally, a composite measure is an effective data-reduction device. That is, the responses to a composite measure can be reduced to a single value of the variable measured. But this sounds contradictory. If the researcher desires a single value, why not use a single item—thereby resulting in one response value? If the variable being measured is a complex one—requiring a composite measure, the resulting multiple responses can be reduced to a single value. Consider again the research methods exam. Since one item will not be sufficient or valid, the instructor asked many items to adequately test your knowledge of the material. However, the instructor does not put into the grade book how each student did on every item that comprised the test. Rather, the instructor translates each student's total responses into a single score for all the items on the test. Thus, the complexity of the situation forces the researcher into using a composite measure, but a composite measure subsequently permits the reduction of a great number of individual responses into a single value.

Index.   A composite measure may be structured in two ways: (1) an index or (2) a scale. An *index* is a composite measure whose responses are summed to generate a score. Most objective college examinations are of this type. For example, if 100 questions were asked and each correct answer is worth one point and each incorrect answer is worth zero points, the student's score is calculated by summing the zeroes and ones that are attached to the response categories. Thus, a score of 85 means the student picked 85 correct and 15 incorrect responses.

Further, the series of items that compose an index do not have to be arranged in any specific order. In our example, as the student moves from one question to the next, each item carries an equal weight in its contribution to the total score.[*] Thus, missing question 37 on an objective examination will result in the same penalty as missing question 42 or 53 or 65. Furthermore, missing question 37 does not suggest an increased likelihood of missing question 38 or any subsequent question.

---

[*]There are exceptions to this general statement. Recall, for example, the discussion of weighting in the preceding chapter.

An index, then, is a composite measure wherein each item is thought to measure the underlying variable equally with every other item.

Scale. A *scale* is a composite measure that has an *internal intensity order*. That is, items are arranged in a definitive order that is reflective of different degrees of the variable. For example, if one wanted to measure a sample's degree of political involvement, there is a wide range of possible behaviors from the politically apathetic person who never votes to the person who has a full-time career in politics. To measure where a person falls on the continuum between these two extremes, one should construct a scale. Figure 9.3 lists items that could be used in a political involvement scale.

In Figure 9.3 all seven items are different and are directed toward the variable of political involvement. What makes the items in Figure 9.3 a scale rather than an index is that there is a definite intensity order to these seven items. As you read down the list of questions, notice that each subsequent question asks about behavior that is believed to demand a greater degree of political commitment than the preceding items. Thus, in a scale the items are ordered from high to low amounts or from low to high amounts of the variable being measured. Whether there is an increase or decrease in the amount of each subsequent item is not of concern; rather, it is important only that some order exists.

If the respondent is given two response categories from which to choose (for example, "yes" or "no"), the point at which the respondent switches from one reply to another indicates the degree to which the variable is possessed by the respondent. For example, the items that appear in Figure 9.3 are ordered so that it is unlikely that a person who does not have sufficient political interest to vote (item 2) will go to a precinct headquarters and stuff envelopes (item 5).

Consider another example. If one wished to measure a student's mathematical ability and made up a mathematical test containing six problems: (1) an addition problem; (2) a subtraction problem; (3) a multiplication problem; (4) a long division problem; (5) an algebra problem; and (6) a problem in differential calculus, these problems form a scale. If a student could not accurately do the addition and subtraction problems (items 1 and 2), it is unlikely that this person could accurately complete items 3 through 6, since the first two items focus in part on skills that are necessary for the successful completion of the latter problems. Thus, each of the mathematical problems requires a different level of mathematical skill, and the problems are ordered from that which requires the least number to that which requires the greatest number of skills.

Comparison of Indices and Scales. Indices and scales share two characteristics. First, they are composite measures. Second, they provide a measure of the degree to which the subject being tested possesses the measured variable. What differentiates indices from scales is that the items in the scale are ordered and the items in an index have no discernible order. Again, we emphasize it

---

1. Are you a registered voter?
2. Did you vote in the last primary or general election?
3. Do you follow political events in the media in newspapers, on radio, or on television?
4. Have you ever made what you consider a substantial monetary or financial contribution to someone's political campaign or some social issue?
5. Have you ever stuffed envelopes or done other clerical jobs for a political candidate or in support of a social issue?
6. Have you ever worked part-time calling voters on the telephone or going door-to-door in a neighborhood on behalf of someone running for office or for some social issue, such as the environment?
7. Have you ever run for office or worked full-time as an organizer for someone else's political campaign?

FIGURE 9.3 An Ordered List of Items Selected to Measure the Behavior of Political Involvement

is the *items* that must be ordered, not the response categories, for a composite measure to be a scale.

Finally, which type of composite measure is better? First, scales have the advantage of indicating more precisely the point at which the respondent possesses the measured variable. In the illustration of the scale of mathematical skills, to unsuccessfully work the long division problem while successfully completing the multiplication problem tells the researcher exactly which mathematical skills are possessed and which are missing. Second, if a scale is used in the interview data-gathering context, the interviewer theoretically may stop asking items at the point when the respondent switches from one response category to the next. For example, if the respondent is not a registered voter (item 1 in Figure 9.3), there is little reason to ask if that person has worked in a clerical job or door-to-door or actually run for political office (items 5, 6, and 7 in Figure 9.3).*

Indices, however, do not indicate which skills are present or absent, because any item is presumed to measure the variable to the same degree as any other item. Rather, indices result in an overall score of degree that can be used to establish an ordinal comparison with other respondents' scores. Thus, an 85 percent correct test score indicates a student who did better than one with 65 percent correct, although one cannot tell the particular items either student missed. However, some composite measures must be in index form, because the variable being measured does not lend itself to any internal order. For example, in an introductory sociology test, several items may pertain to the substantive areas of the family and other items may be designed to tap student knowledge in the area of collective behavior. These two sets of items do not suggest different levels of difficulty in knowledge of sociology. Rather, they test different substantive contexts. There is *no possible order* of items here, as was possible on the math test suggested earlier.

Second, because there is no order, the interviewer *must* present *all* of the items to each respondent in the interview data-gathering process. Thus, scales are more efficient than indices in interviews because they save time and, therefore, interviewer costs. On the other hand, the moneys saved in interviewing costs may be spent during the operationalization and instrument-testing phases of the study. To construct an index one must select items that are different from one another but that measure the same variable. For a scale, one must meet not only this criterion but also two additional criteria. First, any item *must* measure the variable to a different *degree* than all of the other items, *and* second, one must demonstrate that these items are in the *proper order*. Meeting these additional criteria is not an easy task. It is our opinion that indices provide information which is almost as good as that provided by scales and that unless one's sample tends to be very large, the cost savings during the data-gathering phase will not offset the added time that a scale demands in the operationalization phase. Parenthetically, recall from the discussion of sample size in Chapter 7 that bigger is not necessarily better. All things considered, indices provide quite adequate information and are easier to construct than scales. Indeed, the measurement literature will show that almost all composite measures are indices rather than scales.

We join others in distinguishing between the use of the terms *index* and *scale*. We make this distinction for the reasons cited above, and we believe it to be warranted and useful. However, many social scientists do use these two concepts synonymously.

Indicator

An *indicator* is a multi-dimensional measure that includes two or more indices or scales. An indicator measures a variable that is not only complex

---

*This discussion assumes an acceptable coefficient of reproducibility, whose nature is addressed later in this chapter when the Guttman scale is presented.

and, therefore, not usually amenable to a single item, but also is thought to incorporate more than one dimension. For example, the variable of intelligence is one that psychologists agree is quite complex. That is, intelligence refers to a number of different analytical abilities, such as reading and mathematical comprehension, and conceptualization and reasoning.

In another context, sociologists at one time defined conservatism as an attitude that resisted change and liberalism as an attitude that was supportive of change.* These definitions worked well in explaining all sorts of different behaviors until political sociologists noticed that African Americans in Alabama (who were hypothesized to be liberal) seemed sympathetic to Governor George Wallace (who was running in the 1968 national presidential primary within the Democratic party and whose campaign was, to most political observers, one that could be categorized as racially conservative).† This empirical evidence made no theoretical sense in terms of the traditional definitions of these concepts until subsequent research indicated that there were several different dimensions reflected in the public perception of these terms. Thus, African Americans, who were correctly perceived as politically liberal, did sympathize with Wallace who was politically conservative, not because of his racial and political postures, but because Wallace was an *economic* liberal and had opened up many formerly closed state jobs to African Americans. Thus, African Americans felt positively toward him for his economic liberalism, not for his political and racial conservatism. This research led to what seems with hindsight a rather simple idea—that the concepts of liberalism and conservatism must be considered anew when used in different contexts. Thus, a person could be liberal educationally and politically yet be conservative religiously. If the researcher was interested in the respondent's political posture, an index or scale would suffice. However, if one was concerned with the respondent's overall stance toward conservatism or liberalism, an indicator with several composite measures would be needed. Of course, all the difficulties that accompany the use of a composite measure apply to an indicator. The use of an indicator is further complicated by the need to discover some way to combine the scores from several composite measures into a single score that is representative of one's overall orientation.

Summary

There are three basic types of measures: (1) an item that is a single statement or question, (2) a composite measure that takes the form of an index or a scale and that is more than one item but addressed to a single variable, and (3) an indicator that is multidimensional.

SELECTED POPULAR COMPOSITE MEASURES

Introduction

All of the details of writing, selecting, and refining single items apply to the construction of composite measures. In this section, we focus on a few of the more well-known measures: the Likert scale, the Thurstone equal-appearing interval scale, the Guttman scale, and the semantic differential. We will briefly describe the process of constructing each of these measures, central characteristics of each, and conclude with a comparison of the four.

The Likert Scale

The *Likert scale* is a composite measure that has the characteristics of an index. The Likert scale

---

*We admit to a certain degree of oversimplification in these two theoretical definitions, but the purpose of this definition is as an illustration. Hence, this is not a discourse on political sociology, and therefore, we request indulgence from the reader.

†While Wallace received very few votes from the African-American population in Alabama, attitudinal measures focusing on African Americans' perception of Wallace indicated positive feelings toward him from within the African-American community.

must be distinguished from the "Likert look-alike." In their final form, the scale and the look-alike are on the surface identical; but a true Likert scale is one that not only uses the Likert response categories but also has been constructed using a specific procedure. Therefore, we will refer to the Likert scale as an index that has been designed in the manner that Rensis Likert suggested; it is described briefly below. However, even when these procedures are used, the Likert "scale" is not a scale in the sense that this term is developed here, because the Likert "scale" does not possess an internal intensity order.

Construction Procedure.   One begins by writing a very large number of single items reflecting the variable being measured using the face-validation procedure to determine each item's initial appropriateness. The researcher then submits the pool of items to a sample of persons who possess the same general demographic characteristics as those whom the researcher ultimately wishes to measure. The response categories are coded as discussed in Chapter 8, and the sum of the codes to all the items is obtained. This sum functions as a total score on all the items and is believed to reflect the respondent's position on the variable being measured.

Next, the researcher does an *item analysis* on the results. That is, one correlates the value of the coded response to *each item* with the summed total to *all* the items being evaluated. For example, one uses the code to the response category for item one as one variable and the summed total for person one as the second variable. These two variables are correlated for the whole sample, using the Pearson product-moment correlation formula discussed in Chapter 6. If one obtains a strong, positive correlation, the item is retained for the scale. If the correlation is close to zero or negative, the item is rejected. Those items that are selected for the scale are finally checked to see that they generate a *range* of values from the sample, since a lack of response variation would indicate an item that is not useful to the researcher.

When these steps have been accomplished, the researcher selects the number of items that are desired for the Likert scale.

Characteristics.   There are a number of features of the Likert scale that need to be noted. First, there is no internal intensity order. Each item is thought to measure the underlying variable about as well as any other item, although on rare occasions some items are weighted (as discussed in Chapter 8). Because of this, one can only determine the degree to which the respondent possesses the underlying variable by summing the individual response codes and comparing the response scores. Thus, an ordinal level of measurement evolves, which is similar to the performance on a university examination. In such an examination, the professor sums the number of correct answers to obtain scores, such as 82 or 67. The student with the 82, then, is seen as having tested better than the one receiving the 67.

Second, a Likert scale is designed on the basis of evidence obtained from a sample of persons who possess similar characteristics to those for whom the measure is intended. For this reason, some argue that it should not be used on a sample that is greatly different from the one used to construct the measure. Harry Upshaw writes:

> *We have argued that the functional unity of a Likert scale is specific to a population of respondents, and we have argued that the statements which fare best under the item analysis selection criterion tend to be those expressing extreme affect toward an attitude object.*[5]

Third, as indicated in the second half of the above quotation, the items that are likely to be selected for inclusion in the scale are usually the extreme items. As such, a more moderate posture is not reflected in the items themselves. However, one could argue that the five-point response pattern (from strongly agree to strongly disagree), which is usually used, allows the respondent some possibility for moderation even if the content of the items does not.

Application. Once framed, the Likert scale is given to the sample to be measured, and the total score of any one person reflects the degree of intensity which that person possesses on the underlying variable being assessed.

Evaluation. The major advantage of the Likert scale is that it is the easiest to construct of all of the measures discussed in this section, because it is less time-consuming than the others. The major disadvantage, however, is that the sum has a potentially confusing interpretation. That is, it is possible for respondents to obtain identical scores yet arrive at them in different ways. Therefore, one drawback to the Likert scale is that it does not possess a clear pattern (or internal intensity order) that would merge a particular score with a specific pattern of responses. This difficulty becomes mute (or at least minor) if the researcher is only interested in the rank order of different persons on the variable being assessed. If one is simply looking for an ordinal interpretation of degree, the Likert scale is sufficient. Indeed, of the four types mentioned, the Likert scale is the most frequently used.*

Thurstone Equal-Appearing Interval Scale

E. L. Thurstone tried to alleviate one of the difficulties encountered in Likert scales by seeking to construct items that differ in reflecting the degree of the variable being measured. Thus, while Likert items tend to indicate the extremes of the variable, items on the *Thurstone equal-appearing interval scale* were supposed to reflect a continuum of degree from one extreme to its opposite.

Construction Procedure. To build a Thurstone equal-appearing interval scale, the researcher begins by gathering a very large number of items

thought to be germane to the variable to be assessed. Similarly, a large number of judges who are knowledgeable about the variable to be assessed are asked individually to sort these items into, usually, 11 piles, which are identified by the letters *A* through *K*. The judges are told that *A* represents the most favorable position, *F* represents a neutral position, and *K* represents the most unfavorable position. Thus, each pile is supposed to represent 1 point in an 11-point measure of degree from 1, representing the highest or most of the variable being assessed, to 11, the lowest or least of that variable. The value of each item is determined by the median† of all the ratings given to a particular item. For purposes of illustration and simplicity, consider that there are only three judges and that items one and two were given the following scores, respectively: 3, 4, and 6; and 2, 8, and 11. Item one would carry the value 4 and item two the value 8 in this procedure. If any of the items are assigned a wide range of values (as was the second in our hypothetical example), it would be eliminated from consideration for inclusion in the final scale, because the judges could not develop a rough consensus on it. Further, those items that the judges placed at *both* extremes would also be discarded. Once those items that cannot be placed in roughly the same pile are eliminated, the researcher then chooses the desired number of items from *each* of the piles. The selected items are, then, randomly placed in a matrix format with the response categories "endorsed" and "not endorsed" to frame the final Thurstone scale.

Characteristics. This composite measure contains items that, in and of themselves, reflect different degrees of the variable being assessed. Those items from pile 1 are those that the judges feel tap the underlying variable to the greatest degree, while those from pile 11 reflect the least degree. Thus,

---

*This conclusion must be tempered with the knowledge that there are many Likert look-alikes, which have not been constructed through the use of item analysis using the Pearson correlation statistic from a sample similar to the one that will be tested formally. Only under these conditions would we call the measure a Likert scale.

†The median is the middlemost score, or that score above which 50 percent of the cases fall and below which 50 percent fall.

unlike the Likert scale, whose items tend to reflect only the extremes, the Thurstone scale has moderate positions represented by the items selected from the mid-range piles (e.g., 5, 6, and 7).

Application.   The items selected for inclusion in the Thurstone scale are randomly ordered without any indication of their median-scale values. The sample is, then, asked to select only those items that they endorse. Each person's score on the Thurstone measure is determined by selecting the *mean* value among all those items that the respondent endorsed. For example, if the respondent endorsed five items whose values were 1, 2, 6, 9, and 11, then this respondent would have a score of 5.8 on the Thurstone measure.

Evaluation.   First, as with the Likert scale, one can arrive at the same score on the Thurstone scale in a number of ways. For example, assume that the first respondent agreed with three items that had individual scores of 5, 6, and 7, while a second person agreed with three items having scores of 2, 6, and 10. Both persons would have a median score of 6, although they would have agreed to different items. Second, this characteristic, which is shared with the Likert scale, makes the interpretation of the scale values difficult. It is for this reason that the Thurstone scale, while it has *items* that reflect differing degrees of the underlying variable, is not a true scale because it possesses no internal intensity order. Third, while the median values assigned to each item in the scale reflect the collective perception of the judges, they may not reflect that of the respondents who are actually being measured. Thus, one must assume that the judges think and feel in an identical manner as the subjects being measured, which is an assumption some methodologists are unwilling to make. Fourth, one of the principal characteristics that Thurstone hoped to achieve was an interval level of measurement using this scale. He wished to have the items put in pile four to be pretty much equi-distant between the items in piles three and five. While he suggested the use of a large number of judges to try to develop an unbiased measure,

most would agree that he was unable to demonstrate convincingly a constant unit of measure through this scale process—a crucial component to an interval level of measurement. Upshaw comments that: "the category-scale which Thurstone described for measuring the pro-anti implications of statements probably does not provide an interval scale [level of measurement]."[6]

Finally, the Thurstone procedure, if done properly, is cumbersome and time-consuming. One should amass a couple of hundred items initially and use 50 to 100 judges to effectively accomplish the construction of the Thurstone equal-appearing interval scale.

Because of the procedure required and the doubt that many have concerning the interval level of measurement of the Thurstone scale, it is a scaling mechanism that is rarely used.

Guttman Scale

We have noted that the Likert scale does not have an internal intensity order and that the Thurstone scale, while it has items that reflect different intensities, lacks an overall order to all the items. The *Guttman scale* is the only scale we will discuss that attempts to create an actual intensity order among all the items.

Construction Procedure.   The researcher begins by selecting a large number of items that presumably reflect the entire range of feelings from strongly negative to strongly positive. These items are then submitted to a large sample of persons who are believed to possess characteristics similar to those persons ultimately to be measured. This sample is asked to agree or to disagree with each item. The score of each item is obtained by assigning a one to each agree response and a zero to each response of disagreement. The rank order of the items is next determined. That is, the items with the highest score would be those items that had the largest number of agreed responses. Those with the lowest scores are those items with which fewer respondents agreed. These scores, then, become the basis for the researcher's selection, usually, of a limited number of items reflecting the range of values obtained. The selected items are, then, put in order ranging, usually, from the milder statements with which great numbers of the sample agree to stronger ones with which only the most extreme persons in the sample agree. That is, as one descends the Guttman scale, fewer people would agree with the subsequent items.

Characteristics. If constructed properly, a Guttman scale will not only indicate the intensity of the person's feelings about the underlying variable but also reflect exactly the pattern of these feelings. That is, if a respondent agrees with item five, agreement should also be registered for items one through four. Similarly, if this same person disagrees with item six, disagreement would be expected for all the subsequent items starting with item seven. Thus, a proper Guttman scale reflects intensity *and* the specific pattern of feelings. Therefore, a score of five on a Guttman scale should only be attainable through a single pattern of responses to the scale items.

Application. One distributes the measuring instrument to the sample, and any one person's score is the point at which that person switches from an "agree" response to a "disagree" response.

If the items are ordered from least intense to most intense, an early point of response change indicates low intensity, while a late point of response indicates high intensity. Conversely, if the items are ordered from most intense to least intense, an early switching point would indicate a high intensity and a later switching point a low intensity. See Figure 9.4, which illustrates the response patterns of two people, Susan and Kari.

The "High to Low Item Intensity" portion of the illustration orders the punishment possibilities from strong to mild. Thus, when asked their feelings about capital punishment (item 1), both Susan and Kari were opposed to this option. However, when asked about long-term imprisonment, Susan replied that she favored this option, while Kari remained in opposition. For Susan, item 2 was the response-category switching point and she would receive a score of two. Kari continues to oppose punishment options until item 4, at which point she agrees with the suggested sanction. She receives a score of four on this measuring instrument. Notice also that because of the internal intensity order, both Susan and Kari continue to respond favorably to the remaining items after they have picked their respective switching points. Thus, when a Guttman scale is ordered from high to low intensity, a low score (Susan's two) indi-

HIGH TO LOW ITEM INTENSITY			LOW TO HIGH ITEM INTENSITY		
RESPONSE GIVEN:	AG†	DIS	RESPONSE GIVEN:	AG	DIS
1. Capital punishment		S,K*	1. Give second chance	S,K	
2. Long imprisonment	S	K	2. Probation	S,K	
3. Substantial fine	S	K	3. Small fine	S,K	
4. Small fine	S,K		4. Substantial fine	S	K
5. Probation	S,K		5. Long imprisonment	S	K
6. Second chance	S,K		6. Capital punishment		S,K

FIGURE 9.4 Illustration of Different Directions of Guttman Scale Items, Different Response Patterns,† and Differing Interpretations of These Response Patterns to the Question: What Punishments Should Courts Consider When Dealing with Felons?

†AG = Agree and DIS = Disagree.

*S = a respondent named Susan, and K = another respondent named Kari.

cates a greater intensity than a high score (Kari's four). That is, the score is negatively correlated with feeling intensity.

The "Low to High Item Intensity" portion of Figure 9.4 orders the punishment possibilities from mild to strong. In this case, both Susan and Kari agree that item 1 (giving the offender a second chance) is a favored punishment option. Indeed, they both agree with all the options until item 4, where Kari switches to disagreeing with a substantial fine and receives a score of four. Susan, however, agrees with all the punishment options except the last and receives a score of six. Thus, when the items are ordered from low to high intensity, there is a positive correlation between the Guttman scale value and the intensity of feeling. Note also that when Kari switches, she continues to disagree on the remainder of the items.

Clearly, one may order a Guttman scale in either direction. While most researchers use the initial items to indicate little of the variable being measured and the final items to indicate heavy amounts of the variable, it is not a rule to do so. Which direction you choose will be largely a function of how the items read to the respondent.

The Coefficient of Reproducibility.   The *coefficient of reproducibility* is a measure of the scalability of the Guttman measure.[7]

$$CR = 1 - \left[\frac{number\ of\ errors}{total\ responses} \right]$$

Staying with our example of punishment options in Figure 9.4, if our Guttman scale was perfectly arranged, the pattern illustrated in Figure 9.5 would follow. As you can see, if a person agreed with the highest-intensity punishment, then that person would also find the lower-intensity punishments acceptable. Case 1 in Figure 9.5 illustrates this pattern. Case 7 illustrates a person who would reject all the listed punishment options. Case 3 characterizes a person who rejects the first two punishment options but accepts the remaining four. So each case in Figure 9.5 illustrates an ordered pattern of acceptance or rejection of punishment options, which fall in a logical order of severity (see Figure 9.4). In sum, if all empirical measurements fell perfectly into the pattern, a pattern of three rejections and three acceptances could only be attained in the way shown in case 4.

CASE NO.	ITEM NO.					
	ITEM 1	*ITEM 2*	*ITEM 3*	*ITEM 4*	*ITEM 5*	*ITEM 6*
1	+	+	+	+	+	+
2	−	+	+	+	+	+
3	−	−	+	+	+	+
4	−	−	−	+	+	+
5	−	−	−	−	+	+
6	−	−	−	−	−	+
7	−	−	−	−	−	−

FIGURE 9.5   The Response Pattern to a Perfect Guttman Scale Reflecting Agreement with the Punishment Choices Suggested in Figure 9.4*

*A + means the respondent thinks the punishment is appropriate, and a − means the respondent thinks the punishment is inappropriate. Further, the choices are ordered from high to low intensity.

However, there may be some respondents who do not fit into any of the seven case patterns shown in Figure 9.5. For example, rather than follow the pattern in case 2 (i.e., −, +, +, +, +, +), a respondent might reply in a different pattern (i.e., +, −, +, +, +, +). While the empirical pattern does not seem logical—that is, the person accepts capital punishment but rejects long-term imprisonment—it was obtained empirically and would be classified as an error in the Guttman procedure.

Returning to the coefficient of reproducibility (*CR*) formula, we have six punishment options with two possible response choices for each option. Making the necessary substitutions in the formula, we have

$$CR = 1 - \frac{1}{(6)\,(2)}$$
$$= 1 - \frac{1}{12}$$
$$= 1 - 0.083$$
$$= 0.917$$

Any value for the coefficient of reproducibility (*CR*) that is equal to or greater than 0.90 is generally considered strong enough to assume that the data meet the scalability criterion. Hence, in this case with these data, one would argue that the measure, while not perfect, is close enough to be used and interpreted as a Guttman scale.

Evaluation.   One of the major advantages of a Guttman scale is that the respondent's score indicates exactly (if the coefficient of reproducibility is 1.0) which statements the respondent accepts and rejects. If the researcher's results generate a coefficient of reproducibility that is 0.90 or higher, we would still argue that the Guttman scalability property is present. Thus, when doing a survey, the Guttman technique allows the researcher to determine a reasonably accurate list of activities or procedures that reflect the sample's attitudinal posture. However, while this interpretation might be crucial in the area of policy setting or attitudinal analysis, it is less significant if the researcher is only interested in the degree to which a particular attitude is held and not in the specific feelings involved.

A second advantage of the Guttman scale is that it provides a clear way to demonstrate a scale's unidimensionality. This second advantage can also be seen as a disadvantage, since researchers are coming increasingly to the conclusion that attitudes are invariably multidimensional. Consider our earlier example of the seeming contradiction in the high level of acceptance of Governor Wallace in Alabama and his racist political policy. Alternatively, consider the recent research on intelligence, which suggests that there are different dimensions of what we used to call "IQ." Given this trend and the unidimensional nature of Guttman scales, they will either be used less extensively or probably be combined with other techniques—most specifically Likert scales.

A second disadvantage with Guttman scales is that they seem to be strongly dependent for their scaling property on the population or sample being measured. That is, given a different population, the Guttman scale may have a lower coefficient of reproducibility than it has with the population on which the Guttman scale was originally framed. Further, this scaling property is likely to change through time within the population being observed, since people's attitudes do undergo change. Thus, changes between and within the populations examined are likely to invalidate the position of some items in the internal intensity order and render other items irrelevant.

A third disadvantage is that the procedure for constructing a Guttman scale, as with the one involved in the design of Thurstone equal-appearing interval scales, is complex and time-consuming.

The Semantic Differential

Charles Osgood's *semantic differential* differs from those measures already discussed, because the underlying assumption is that the attitude one is trying to measure is multidimensional. Here the researcher requests the respondent's reaction to a number of dimensions assumed to characterize the variable being tested.

Construction Procedure.   After determining the situation on which to focus, the researcher must select some number of dimensions on which to direct the respondent's attention. For example, consider that one is seeking to evaluate a sample's feelings about abortion. First, the researcher would need to select a number of dimensions about which information is sought. Suppose that we selected the following: (1) morality or correctness of abortion; (2) monetary cost; (3) the stigma attached to obtaining an abortion; and (4) ease of accomplishment.

Second, the researcher must select polar-opposite terms for each extreme on each of the dimensions included. For example, monetary cost could be characterized by the pair *cheap* and *expensive,* and the ease of accomplishment might use the pair—*easy* and *hard.* Generally, these paired polar opposites are separated by a seven-point "scale," and the semantic differential takes the format shown in Figure 9.6.[8] The seven spaces between the polar opposites can be coded from one to seven or in whatever way makes sense. The higher numbers can be used to indicate favorableness,

while the lower ones, unfavorableness. If one fears the emergence of a response set, the researcher can alternate the position of these adjectives by putting the positive adjective on the left-hand side of the dimension and by putting the positive adjective on the right-hand side of the next dimension.

Application.   In administering a semantic differential, the researcher asks the persons to be measured to mark an "X" at the point between the two adjectives that best characterizes how they feel. The respondent should be reminded that only one X is to be used on any one line and that an X should appear on every line. The nature of the dimensions, as well as the code values, should not appear on the measuring instrument. If the coding is done as indicated, then the sum of all the codes should indicate the respondent's general attitude on all the dimensions to the item being evaluated. Of course, such a simple sum assumes that all the dimensions are of equal importance to the respondent, which, in reality, would probably not be the case. Alternatively, the researcher could interpret each of the dimensions independently, saying that the individual was highly favorable on one dimension but not very receptive on a different dimen-

Directions: Place an X in the space that most closely represents your feelings about abortion. Remember that there is no right or wrong answer here; only how you really feel. Put an X on each line and only one X per line.

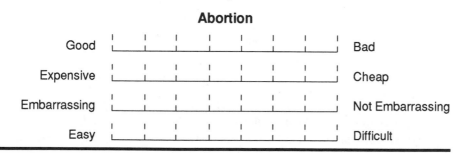

Abortion

Good		Bad
Expensive		Cheap
Embarrassing		Not Embarrassing
Easy		Difficult

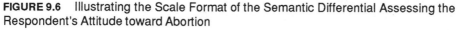

FIGURE 9.6   Illustrating the Scale Format of the Semantic Differential Assessing the Respondent's Attitude toward Abortion

sion. Depending on the assumptions that the researcher is willing to make, the semantic differential contains a number of interpretation options.

Evaluation. The major advantage of the semantic differential is the recognition that attitudes are often multidimensional. This forces the researcher to think consciously about these dimensions and incorporate them into the measure. Further, while the polar-opposite adjectives used to anchor the ends of the seven-point continua are suggestive of the dimension being assessed, they are subject to enough interpretation so that the respondent may think about the object in slightly different ways yet still feel comfortable with a response. If this happens, the specific response will not embrace the same meaning as the researcher might have supposed when the semantic differential was constructed, but it still records an overall degree of favorableness or unfavorableness on the part of the respondent.

The major difficulty is that one is not able to predict an attitudinal pattern as one can with the Guttman technique.

Summary

Table 9.2 presents a comparison of the major characteristics of the five types of measures we have discussed. First, note that the single item and Likert-scale measures are, comparatively, used more frequently than the Thurstone or Guttman types. This appears to be for several reasons: (1) the practical reason that the Guttman and Thurstone techniques take too long to construct and test; (2) the Guttman and Thurstone techniques assume unidimensionality, which is increasingly felt to be unwarranted, and attitude research shows much greater complexity than was originally supposed; and (3) the Thurstone measure tried to generate interval-level data but largely failed, although this does not appear to be troublesome to some researchers.

TABLE 9.2   Comparison of Selected Dimensions of Various Types of Measures

MEASURE/ DIMENSION	NUMBER OF ITEMS	MULTI- DIMEN- SIONAL	ITEM DEGREE	EVALU- ATOR(S)	EASE OF CON- STRUCTION	GENERAL USE	INTERNAL ORDER
Single item	1	No	N/a	Researcher	1	Heavy	N/a
Likert index	2 or more	No	No	Respondent	3	Moderate*	No
Thurstone scale	2 or more	No	Yes	Judges	4	Light	No
Guttman scale	2 or more	No	Yes	Respondent	5	Light	Yes
Semantic differential	2 or more	Yes	No	Researcher	2	Light	No

*Many researchers construct Likert-scale "look-alikes" to the extent that there are multiple items and the Likert response categories are used. To qualify as a legitimate Likert index, one must construct a large number of possible items, administer all the items to a sample of respondents, perform an item analysis on all these items, and select only those that show small ranges in their codes and that correlate highly and positively with the total Likert index score.

The debate is not so much over the matter of whether or not the measures are really interval or not, but rather over the advantages or shortcomings of assuming an interval level even if the data may only be ordinal.

. . . one may assume that the techniques produce ordinal level measurements that are routinely treated in the social sciences as if they were interval level measures.[9]

For these reasons, Guttman and Thurstone equal-appearing interval scales are being supplanted by the Likert scale in contemporary social research. They are discussed because they are part of the history of the development of measurement in the social sciences, and they clearly illustrate the problems of item selection and dimensionality, which are so much a part of operationalization.

ACCURACY OF THE MEASURING INSTRUMENT

Any scientist must be concerned with the accuracy of the operational definitions used. This general characteristic of accuracy has three basic dimensions: (1) reliability; (2) validity; and (3) precision.

The Pretest

An important first step in testing the measuring instrument is called the pretest. The *pretest* is a full dress rehearsal of one's anticipated research design to see if there are any bugs in the design.[10] Among a whole list of considerations, the pretest functions to identify difficulties such as misinterpretation of items by the respondent, items that are too confusing to elicit a reply, directions that are unclear, and other similar problems with the measuring instrument and the general design of the study.

For example, a colleague once designed a measuring instrument in which he wanted to measure educational level. To do so, he asked the question: "What was your last year in school?" Most respondents interpreted the question in the way the researcher had hoped; i.e., answering with replies such as "two years of college" or "seventh grade" or "an A.A. degree." However, a small percentage of those pretested gave an answer such as "1944" or "right after the Second World War." Obviously, this latter group had read the question differently than it had been intended by the researcher. The pretest functions to identify this type of error in a research design.

How does one draw a pretest sample? You'll recall in Chapter 7 we suggested that after drawing a probability sample, there was every likelihood that additional cases would remain. From these remaining cases, a small number of persons (say, fifty) can be selected to participate in the pretest. It is not necessary to select this sample through a probability process because it is not being used inductively to represent anyone. For this reason the pretest sample can be selected by whatever procedure is deemed to be most efficient. The two important factors are that (1) the pretest sample must be representative of the persons in the main sample and (2) the pretest sample should have little possibility of interacting with those who have been selected for the main study.

In sum, the pretest is important because it is based on the important premise that no amount of thinking can substitute for empirical knowledge. William Goode and Paul Hatt write:

In short, the pretest accepts the fact which has been documented thousands of times in scientific research—that no amount of intuition, native talent, or systematic thought will substitute for the careful recording, tabulating, and analysis of the research facts.[11]

Further, the results of the pretest will furnish needed data on which to base the reliability and validity tests, to which we now turn.

Reliability

Reliability Defined.   Reliability refers to the degree of consistency that a measurement procedure has. A *reliable measure* is one that will produce the same results when applied repeatedly to the same sample, assuming the sample is reasonably stable. There are three reliability tests[12] available to the social scientist: (1) the test-retest procedure, (2) the multiple-forms procedure, and (3) the split-half reliability test.

Test-Retest Procedure. The *test-retest reliability* procedure is a variant on the classical experimental design in that one generates data from one experimental group and one control group (see Figure 9.7). First, one creates two groups of respondents who are reasonably matched, using the strategies we have discussed for controlling on variables with particular emphasis on randomization. One group is designated the experimental group and the other the control group. The experimental group is exposed to the measuring instrument at two different times (the test and the retest times), and the results of both these measurements are noted, respectively, as S_{et} (score for the experimental group at the test time) and S_{er} (score for the experimental group at the retest time). The measuring instrument is administered to the control group only during the retest period and this score is noted as S_{cr} (score of the control group at the retest time). The three obtained scores are then compared, using the following equation:

$$\text{Unreliability} = S_{er} - S_{et} > S_{cr} - S_{et}$$

That is, if the difference between the scores obtained from both the test and retest periods of the experimental group is greater than the difference between the test-period score for the experimental group and the actually obtained retest score for the control group, then the measure is unreliable.

The basic premise behind this equation is that the researcher can legitimately expect the initial submission of a measure to create a change that will be reflected in the score of a second. Therefore, in the test-retest procedure one does not allow the control group to become biased because this group is only exposed to the measure once at the retest period. Since both groups have been randomly determined, the assumption is that they are initially comparable and, therefore, the control group would have gotten the same score as the experimental group (i.e., S_{et}) if it had also been measured during the test period. Finally, if the difference between the actual test and retest scores for the experimental group is greater than the difference between the test score for the experimental group (which is an estimate of the control group's test score) and the actual retest score for the control group, the measure will be deemed unreliable.

Multiple-Form Procedure. The *multiple-forms reliability* test involves the construction of two different forms of the same measuring instrument (see Figure 9.8). Each subject is given both forms, and the individual scores on each form are correlated; that is, any individual's score on form 1 is correlated with that individual's score on form 2. This procedure is followed for all of the individuals in the reliability sample. Usually, the Pearson product-moment correlation technique is used.[13] It is the researcher's responsibility to select the minimum correlation value that is acceptable. We do not offer a suggested magnitude except for the general guideline that it be positive and strong. If

---

Given: The researcher selects an appropriate number of persons for the test-retest reliability procedure and *randomly* divides the persons into the experimental and control groups.

GROUP/ SCORE	TEST (TIME 1)	RETEST (TIME 2)
Experimental	Yes S_{et}	Yes S_{er}
Control	No no S	Yes S_{cr}

FIGURE 9.7 A Schematic Illustrating the Test-Retest Reliability Procedure

Given: A measuring instrument containing 50 items numbered 1 through 50 is devised. The researcher gives a sample of 100 persons the measuring instrument twice: (1) on form 1 the items are arranged from 1 to 50 and (2) on form 2 the items are arranged from 50 to 1. The scores from both forms are correlated using the Pearson product-moment correlation. A strong positive correlation value is evidence of reliability.

INDIVIDUAL	SCORES TO FORM 1	SCORES TO FORM 2
1	X_1	Y_1
2	X_2	Y_2
3	X_3	Y_3
.	.	.
.	.	.
.	.	.
99	X_{99}	Y_{99}
100	X_{100}	Y_{100}

FIGURE 9.8   A Schematic Illustrating the Multiple-Forms Reliability Procedure

the correlation value is larger than the preset minimum, reliability has been determined.

Critique of the Test-Retest and Multiple-Forms Procedures.   Both the test-retest and multiple-forms procedures have decided disadvantages as reliability tests. Consider a multiple forms test of a midterm wherein form 1 listed 100 objective items from 1 to 100 and form 2 listed these same 100 items from 100 to 1. There is every reason to suppose that the reliability sample would recognize the similarity of items and that this recognition would bias the administration of form 2. To avoid such bias, some researchers argue one should create two entirely different forms or versions of the measure. In this case, one would write 200 different test items. To do this creates the problem, as we see it, that one would essentially be contrasting the results of two measuring instruments—the first 100 items with the results of the second 100 items. As a simple correlation between two different measures, it would represent a deviation from the definition of reliability.

The bias of the first administration of the measure, if any, can be determined by the test-retest procedure through the use of a control group. But while the main disadvantage of the multiple-forms procedure is rectified, the test-retest procedure creates a different problem. You'll recall that the test-period measure for the *control* group had to be estimated from the performance of the experimental group under the assumption that the control and experimental groups were equivalent. We questioned this assumption of equivalency in the discussion of randomization in Chapter 3. In essence, we argued that one cannot determine whether the experimental and control groups would have scored the same without testing both, but to do so eliminates the possibility of determining the presence of bias from the first test in the second administration score.

In sum, the researcher is caught between the proverbial rock and the hard place. The test-retest procedure evaluates the possibility of a bias but not the equivalence of the two groups. The multiple-forms approach makes the equivalence of the two groups irrelevant but does not assess the first test administration's potential bias on the second administration of the measure. Neither of these difficulties are present in the split-half procedure.

Split-Half Procedure.   In the split-half reliability test, the problem of the equivalence of the experimental and the control groups in the test-retest procedure is eliminated because the researcher uses *only one group.* The problem of bias created by multiple administrations of the measure is eliminated because the reliability sample is *given the measure only once.* Thus, in the *split-half reliability* procedure, after the measure is given to the reliability sample once, the items of the measure are themselves randomly divided into halves. If the order of the items was determined randomly when the measure was constructed, the two halves can be created simply by aggregating the scores from all the odd-numbered items and all the even-numbered items. For example, if one wanted to do a split-half procedure on the 100-item objective midterm mentioned earlier, each

Given: The measuring instrument of 50 items is given to a sample of 100 persons *once,* and then the items are divided into halves by placing the odd-numbered items into the first half and the even-numbered items into the second half. The total scores to the first half (*X*) and to the second half (*Y*) are determined. These two sets of scores are correlated for all the 100 persons, and the result is adjusted by the Spearman-Brown prophecy formula. A strong positive correlation is evidence for reliability.

INDIVIDUAL	SCORE FROM FIRST HALF	SCORE FROM SECOND HALF
1	X_1	Y_1
2	X_2	Y_2
3	X_3	Y_3
.	.	.
.	.	.
.	.	.
99	X_{99}	Y_{99}
100	X_{100}	Y_{100}

FIGURE 9.9 A Schematic Illustrating the Split-Half Reliability Procedure

student's total number of correct answers to the 50-even numbered questions and the total number of correct answers to 50-odd numbered questions would be correlated using the Pearson product-moment measure of association. Again, the researcher must determine the minimum positive value required for the demonstration of reliability. Before the obtained correlation is evaluated, it should be adjusted with the *Spearman-Brown prophecy formula,*[14] where r_n equals the adjusted value and r_1 equals the actual value obtained.

$$r_n = \frac{n\, r_1}{1 + (n - 1)r_1}$$

This adjustment compensates for the fact that one's correlation value is affected by differing numbers of items. That is, this formula compensates for the mathematical aberration that two correlation values will be somewhat different simply because of the *number* of values that were entered into the formula. Since the split-half procedure in this example correlates 50 items from one half with 50 items from the remaining half, the correlation value is different than it would have been if there were two sets of 100 items to correlate, even if the values of these items were the same.

Finally, the split-half technique requires a certain minimum number of items before it can be used. Goode and Hatt[15] recommend 16 to 20 items, so that each half would contain a minimum of 8 to 10 items. Since it is better to err on the side of too many than too few, we feel that the minimum should be 24 items or some even number greater than this. To create a few additional items for safety's sake should not be difficult, given the basic reason for using a composite measure in the first place. You'll recall that multiple items are necessary to assess adequately complex situations and/or to generate a range of responses on which to distinguish persons from one another.

Summary. We feel that the split-half reliability test is the best of the three reliability tests discussed because of the elimination of the two design disadvantages which are endemic to the test-retest and multiple-forms procedures. However, the multiple-forms and split-half techniques *cannot be used* to demonstrate the reliability of a *scale.* Scales can only be assessed with the test-retest procedure. Further, the split-half technique is appropriate only when one's index contains the minimum number of items.*

*The reliability procedures discussed above are appropriate when formally testing composite measures that take the form of schedules. Should one choose a data-gathering procedure other than a survey, different procedures will have to be devised. For example, if a research design required participant observation, the researcher would want to know if several observers could reach a consensus about the variables to be observed. If one was measuring aggressive behaviors in children in a controlled setting and had trained a number of observers as to what to note, observer reliability could be checked by showing each observer a video tape containing some predetermined number of aggressive behaviors. If one's observers were to record consistently the same number and types of aggression, reliability would be demonstrated. Obviously, the reliability procedure must be adjusted to the research setting.

Validity

Validity Defined. *Validity* refers to a measuring instrument's ability to accurately measure what it claims to measure. For example, if you emptied your pockets and counted your money and repeated this procedure 15 minutes later, you would have a reliable, but not valid, measure of your annual income. Validity is concerned with obtaining operationally what one has defined theoretically in the conceptual model. In this section we discuss and compare five basic procedures for measuring validity: (1) face validity, (2) jury opinion, (3) known groups, (4) criterion validity (both predictive and concurrent), and (5) construct validity.

Face Validity. Earlier we defined *face validity* as "the selection of items that the researcher determines are logically related to the variable to be assessed." We argued that this procedure was an important criterion in the *construction* of a measuring instrument. As a formal test of validity, face validation contains a major problem in that the researcher who designed the measure may have difficulty evaluating, in an unbiased and dispassionate way, the results of his or her own work.

Jury Opinion. *Jury-opinion validity*[16] involves the selection of experts in the area relevant to the measuring instrument. One then submits the instrument to these experts for their assessment of its validity. For example, if one designed an index to measure the adequacy of residential housing, one would select a panel of experts—persons who are knowledgeable about residential construction, such as architects, construction engineers, various people in the crafts (carpenters, plumbers, and the like), and housing inspectors—to form the jury. The experts would examine the measuring instrument and decide whether it was valid. The researcher must determine the size of the jury, the specific individuals who comprise the jury, and the degree of consensus that must be achieved. We suggest a jury of at least seven persons, who

have different approaches to the variable to be measured, and recommend the researcher ask for and carefully consider any negative comments from any of those on the jury. If three or more persons object to a particular item, it should probably be eliminated or substantially revised.

This is a better validation procedure than face validity because first, there is more than one person doing the evaluation; second, the persons evaluating the measure are persons who are experts in the area to which the measure applies; and third, they do not have vested interests as the creators of the instrument. The disadvantages of jury opinion are that even experts are sometimes in error. You will recall, for example, that at one period in the history of science, all scientists believed that the earth was flat.

Known Groups. In the *known-groups validity* test, two groups are given the measuring instrument.[17] Each group is known to reflect opposite ends of the continuum on the variable to be assessed. For example, if one constructed an index to measure acceptance of abortion, the known-groups technique could be used to evaluate validity by selecting a pro-choice group of persons and a pro-life group. It is already known that the pro-life or right-to-life group will oppose abortion and would be expected to score low, while the pro-choice group would be expected to register a high score on the measuring instrument. After submitting the index to both groups, the researcher must decide if the data are strong enough in the predicted directions to justify concluding that validity has been determined. As with the multiple-forms and the split-half reliability procedures, one must determine the minimum cutoff values for validity through the known-groups process.

One of the principle difficulties in using the known-groups technique is that one is able to frequently determine one group of people at one end of the continuum on the variable in question, but it is difficult, if not impossible, to constitute a group at the other end. For example, if the researcher was interested in measuring positive self-image, one might draw a sample of persons with a poor self-image by sampling carefully among those who seek counseling or therapy. Where would a comparable group with a positive self-image be located? Also consider the variable of religiosity. One group would certainly contain those who have made religion a profession, but location of a group of nonbelievers would be much more difficult.

Criterion Validity. *Criterion validity*[18] involves the use of some well-accepted standard against which the results of the to-be-validated measure will be compared. That is, one takes the measure for which validation is sought and compares its results against the results of a well-accepted standard. Criterion validity can be accomplished in two ways: (1) predictive criterion validity and (2) concurrent criterion validity.

Predictive criterion validity is the demonstration of how well forecasts from the to-be-validated measure compare to the empirical data gathered at some subsequent time. For example, on the presidential election-night telecasts, the major networks use their respective voter-profile analysis to make predictions of the outcome of selected political races. Thus, one candidate will be declared the winner by a given percentage of the popular vote. This estimate can be predictive validated by comparing the closeness of the prediction, which the measure affords, with the actual vote.

Of all the procedures for testing validity, we believe that this is the most sound. The researcher uses the measuring instrument to make the prediction and then compares the actual results to check its accuracy. Assuming no major errors in securing the actual results, one has conclusive evidence for the validity of the measure.

While this argues strongly for the use of predictive criterion validity, this procedure may not be practical or ethical in many instances. The occurrence of the actual event against which one will compare the prediction may be too far into the future to be of practical use. Second, if the predicted event is one that has detrimental consequences, one will not want to wait to validate the measure. Rather, the measure's principal function is to indicate a problem in its formative stages so that remedial or corrective action can be taken. For example, a measure that accurately predicts urban riots would hopefully indicate the precursors of riots so that some attempt to head off such a consequence could be made. Conversely, the predictive measure that points to the likelihood of a student's failure to navigate successfully an undergraduate college career is of little use to the student if one must wait for that student's failure before it can be used. Therefore, while predictive validity provides the best data on validity which we know, it is data which is available after the fact and, therefore, is of limited practical, remedial value.

Concurrent criterion validity compares the results from the measure to be validated with the results of a well-accepted measure. For example, if one designed a measure of intelligence and sought to validate it against the Stanford-Binet IQ test, one would be doing a concurrent criterion validity test. Here, one sample of people are given both the to-be-validated test and the well-accepted standard. Next, the scores from both these tests are correlated, and a positive value stronger than the predetermined minimum would demonstrate concurrent criterion validity.

If there is well-accepted standard, why would one want to construct another measure and validate it? It may be that the accepted standard creates scores at one level of measurement and the researcher is seeking data at a higher level of measurement. It may also be that the well-accepted standard is a comparatively much longer composite measure. To save time and reduce the expense of administering the accepted standard, one is seeking a more streamlined and efficient measure.

Construct Validity. The final test is called construct validity.[19] Construct validity is the most elusive of the validation procedures because of the nature of the thing one is trying to validate. A construct is a general abstraction about a series of things that are also thought to be abstractions. For example, the attitude of political conservatism is a theoretical construct which cannot relate *directly* to anything concrete, because it is an attitude. Hence, we have a curious problem. When one tries to operationalize a construct, one is essentially trying to find *concrete* items that reflect an *abstract, nonconcrete* entity. In other words, one is trying to operationalize something which is not believed to be concrete—and this is a contradiction. Thus, validation of a construct is a complicated and multifaceted process.

Construct validity differs from the two criterion validation procedures in three ways. First, since the construct is not directly observable, one attempts to find measurable characteristics that would be theoretically consistent with the presence of the construct. For example, assume we are interested in measuring political conservatism-liberalism. The construct of conservatism is an attitude that cannot be directly measured. If it is present—even though it can't be measured objectively—it would be expected that this attitude would affect one's political behavior, which, of course, can be measured. Therefore, on the basis of a theoretical understanding of the nature of conservatism, one would expect to find some correlation to people's measurable behaviors. The emphasis is on the word *some*. Since an attitude and a behavior are not the same, the researcher can not expect the correlation between attitude and behavior to be as strong as in concurrent criterion validity, where one is correlating the results of two objective, concrete measures. Nonetheless, the researcher would expect *some* correlation between the construct and a piece of behavior that is theoretically consistent with that construct. Therefore, one characteristic of construct validity is the selection of a behavioral response that is thought to be theoretically consistent with the presence of the construct. In our example, we would expect political conservatives to register in the Republican party, because the Republicans have the reputation of being more conservative than the Democrats. Similarly, one would expect liberals to register in the Democratic party. The correlation, however, may not be perfect or even very strong. The social scientist knows that there

are a minority of registered Democrats who are conservative and registered Republicans who are liberal, but party choice should be associated with the political attitude of conservatism-liberalism for many.

Second, with criterion validation one compares a single empirical standard with the measure to be validated. Because of the indirectness of the process in construct validity, more than one item must be used. In our example, because one did not expect a strong correlation between political conservatism and party choice, the researcher must generate additional items that, while indirect measures, would be theoretically consistent with the presence of the construct. Again, one would expect moderate rather than strong associations, but one would also expect all of these correlations to point in the hypothesized direction. Thus, theoretically, one would have expected political conservatives to have voted for Republican George Bush in 1988 and, similarly, political liberals to have favored Michael Dukakis. So, one could add presidential preference to party preference as a second logical behavioral response consistent with this political construct. As a third item, one might suggest the voter's position on a local fluoridation bond issue or referendum vote. To fluoridate the community's water supply is to take political action in the public interest, which, by imposing an action on the entire community, represents a certain amount of governmental interference in one's personal life. Therefore, a person who favors fluoridating the water supply is more likely to be politically liberal than one who does not. Thus, in an attempt to validate the construct of the political attitude of conservatism, we have picked three behavioral, empirical items that theoretically should correlate with this construct: (1) political party choice; (2) preferred presidential candidate; and (3) position on a fluoridation issue. Many other empirical items that should correlate with the construct could be selected. However, for simplicity's sake, we have held this illustration to these three.

Before discussing the third difference, let us see how the first two points operate in the example of political attitude we have introduced. Assume that we constructed a 50-item index to measure this construct of political attitude, that we think a high score is indicative of a conservative posture, and that we think a low score is indicative of a liberal posture. If we gave the index to a number of people, we could separate those with high scores (the conservatives) from those with low scores (the liberals). If the measure is valid, our conceptual model suggests that a person who scores high on the index is probably registered in the Republican party, favored George Bush as the presidential choice, and voted against the fluoridation issue. Similarly, a person who scores low on the index would most likely be registered in the Democratic party, favor Dukakis for president, and vote in favor of fluoridation. Assume that when the respondents replied to the index on political conservatism, they also responded to the single items of party preference, presidential choice, and fluoridation position and that these data became the basis for Tables 9.3 through 9.7. Rather than treat any particular variable as the independent variable, the percentages in these tables are based on the grand total, thereby indicating a simple descriptive percentage for each cell on the bivariate distribution of the variables being analyzed. The *C* and the *L* designations in the row and column headings identify the category as either logically or theoretically conservative or liberal, respectively.

Table 9.3 indicates hypothetical data from a sample of 550 voters on their party preference and their choice of presidential candidate. The number included within the parenthesis in each cell indicates the percentage, while the remaining number represents the cell frequency. If the conceptual model we constructed is correct, we would expect the two cells containing the number of persons who reported their choices as Bush and Republican and as Dukakis and Democratic would contain the larger percentages and over 50 percent of the total number of persons studied. These cells contain 45.4 percent and 26.4 percent, respectively, and their combined total—71.8 percent, is a clear majority of those studied. While not a perfect correlation, the conservative party and candidate choice (45.4 percent) and liberal party and candidate choice (26.4 percent) occur more frequently than a liberal party choice with a conservative candidate choice (10.0 percent) or a conservative party choice and a liberal-candidate choice (18.2 percent).

Table 9.4 shows the distribution of this same sample of voters on the variables of party choice and their position on the fluoridation issue. Again, the majority of those studied selected a party preference and a fluoridation position—be it conservative (40.0 percent) or liberal (22.7 per cent)—that was consistent with our conceptual model. Thus, a total of 62.7 percent of the sample followed the predictions made from the conceptual model, while

TABLE 9.3 Number and Percentage of Voters Sampled by Choice of Presidential Candidate and by Party Preference

CANDIDATE/PARTY	REPUBLICAN (C)	DEMOCRATIC (L)	TOTAL
BUSH (C)	250 (45.4)	55 (10.0)	305
DUKAKIS (L)	100 (18.2)	145 (26.4)	245
TOTAL	350	200	550

TABLE 9.4   Number and Percentage of Voters Sampled by Position on the Fluoridation
Issue and by Party Preference*

POSITION/PARTY	REPUBLICAN (C)	DEMOCRATIC (L)	TOTAL
DISAGREE (C)	220 (40.0)	75 (13.6)	295
AGREE (L)	130 (23.6)	125 (22.7)	255
TOTAL	350	200	550

*The cell percentages may not add to exactly 100.0 percent due to slight distortions caused by rounding procedures.

only 37.2 percent did not. While the reader will see that the association in Table 9.4 is not perfect, note also that the predicted association is much weaker in Table 9.4 than it is in Table 9.3 (62.7 percent following the model compared to 71.9 percent). We shall have more to say about this after we look at Table 9.5.

Table 9.5 shows the relationship between the sample's position on the fluoridation issue and the choice of presidential candidate. This time there is a slight plurality who selected responses consistent with the conceptual model. The conservatives who chose Bush and disagreed with fluoridation accounted for 30.9 percent, which, when added to

the liberals (21.8 percent) who chose Dukakis and agreed with the fluoridation proposal, amounts to a small plurality of 52.7 percent.

In essence, we would argue that there is little association between position on fluoridation and candidate choice in Table 9.5, which brings us to the third point of difference between construct validity and the other validation procedures discussed earlier. In all the other procedures, if a strong positive correlation was not found, the measure was deemed invalid. Also, if one's prediction was not confirmed by the future empirical evidence, the predictive criterion test indicated a lack of validity. Further, if the experts on the jury

TABLE 9.5   Number and Percentage of Voters Sampled by Position on the Fluoridation
Issue and by Choice of Presidential Candidate*

POSITION/PARTY	BUSH (C)	DUKAKIS (L)	TOTAL
DISAGREE (C)	170 (30.9)	125 (22.7)	295
AGREE (L)	135 (24.5)	120 (21.8)	255
TOTAL	305	245	550

*The cell percentages may not add to exactly 100.0 percent due to slight distortions caused by rounding procedures.

denied the measure, if the obtained scores from known groups were other than hypothesized, or if the correlation obtained from the concurrent criterion procedure was not strong and positive, one had conclusive evidence for rejecting a claim for validity. Such is not the case with construct validity. Because a construct can not be *directly* measured, one must make do with objective items that the general conceptual model suggests *may* be associated with the construct. When one fails to obtain the anticipated association, it could be for any one of three reasons. First, it could be that the measure is invalid. Second, it could be that the measure is valid, but the empirical item believed to be associated with the construct is not correlated because the conceptual model is inaccurate. Third, it could be both of the above. That is, the conceptual model may be so weak as to suggest an oversimplified theoretical definition of the construct leading to the selection of improper items in the attempt to measure it, *and* the conceptual model may suggest logical empirical connections to the construct that a more enlightened understanding of the study phenomenon would reject. In sum, the failure to achieve empirical evidence for one's predictions in construct validity casts as much doubt on the conceptual model as it does on the operationalization of the instrument offered to measure the construct.

Let us return to our example. Table 9.3 showed the strongest association of all three tables. Studying Tables 9.4 and 9.5 would suggest, perhaps, that the researcher should rethink the item of position on the fluoridation issue, because this variable is the common factor in both sets of data, and the other two variables—party and candidate choice—seemed to show a stronger association. While it may be that opposition to fluoridation is consistent with a politically conservative attitude, *it may also be* that, in contrast to our conceptual model, acceptance of the fluoridation issue may not be consistent with a liberal attitudinal posture. It would also seem reasonable to interpret fluoridation of the community's water supply as consistent with another construct—one's attitude about health care and preventive medicine. It could be

that the persons sampled who agreed with fluoridation may have done so because they wanted healthier families while those who disagreed are more worried about the increased taxes necessary to implement the project rather than its political implications for self-governance and self-determination. In sum, the measure of the construct might be fine, but the objective item sought in the validation process may be faulty. Assuming then that the fluoridation item taps into a health issue more than a political one, the researcher would revise the conceptual model accordingly and eliminate the fluoridation position as a behavioral consequence of political conservatism. That leaves us, theoretically, with the two behavioral outcomes of political conservatism—party choice and presidential candidate choice.

Consider the 50-item measure of political conservatism mentioned earlier. Assume that this measure can be scored so that there is a theoretical range of values from 0 to 100. A score close to 0 would indicate a liberal, and a score close to 100 would indicate a conservative. After we have purged the items theoretically thought to relate to this attitude but which did not withstand empirical scrutiny (such as the fluoridation item), the researcher can work with the remaining items and the construct scores themselves.

Let us assume that the political conservatism scores fell into three distinct categories: (1) high scores; (2) moderate scores; and (3) low scores. Table 9.6 shows the distribution of the sample by political conservatism score and by political party. Logically, one would argue that if a politically conservative attitude is associated with the party and presidential candidate choices, any person who picked both the Republican party and Bush should be more conservative than a person who picked either. Finally, a person who picked neither the Republicans nor Bush should logically have the smallest political conservatism score.

If we focus only on the 260 persons who scored high on the index of political conservatism and plot their distribution on the variables of party and choice of presidential candidate, Table 9.7 would result. The statistical values reported in Table 9.7

TABLE 9.6   Number of Persons Sampled by Choice of Political Party and by Score on the Political Conservatism Index

PARTY/SCORE	HIGH	MODERATE	LOW	TOTAL
REPUBLICAN	240	95	15	350
DEMOCRATIC	20	40	140	200
TOTAL	260	135	155	550

require some comment. First, the table only focuses on the 260 persons who had in common high political conservative scores by their distribution on party and candidate choice. Thus, the cell in the upper left-hand corner of the table (i.e., Bush and Republican choice) indicates that of the 250 persons who both voted for Bush and were registered in the Republican party, 210 of them scored high on political conservatism. Finally, the 80.8 per cent means that 80.8 percent of the 260 high scorers on the index of political conservatism fell into this cell.

Table 9.7 shows a distribution among the high scorers on political conservatism that is consistent with our conceptual model. That is, the highest percentage (80.8 percent) of the high scorers on the index were also registered Republicans and supporters of Bush. Only 1.5 percent of those

deemed highly politically conservative selected Dukakis and were in the Democratic party. Finally, those cells which contained "mixed" conservative items (e.g., Democratic party choice but voted for Bush or Republican party choice but voted for Dukakis) had comparatively moderate percentages of those who were highly politically conservative, 6.2 percent and 11.5 per cent, respectively.

Finally, the construct validity procedure should work for the cases that fit theoretically and those which do not. That is, if those who score high on political conservatism are expected to fall mainly in the conservative categories on party choice and candidate selection, then those who score low on political conservatism should also be expected to not be represented in the Republican party and the Bush camp. In other words, if an index value that

TABLE 9.7   Number and Percentage of Voters Sampled Who Had High Scores on the Index of Political Conservatism by Party Choice and by Selection of Presidential Candidate

CANDIDATE/PARTY	REPUBLICAN (C)	DEMOCRATIC (L)	TOTAL
BUSH (C)	210 of 250 (80.0)	16 of 55 (6.2)	305
DUKAKIS (L)	30 of 100 (11.5)	4 of 145 (1.5)	245
TOTAL	240 of 350	20 of 200	550

TABLE 9.8   Number and Percentage of Voters Sampled Who Had Low Scores on the Index of Political Conservatism by Party Choice and by Selection of Presidential Candidate*

CANDIDATE/PARTY	REPUBLICAN (C)	DEMOCRATIC (L)	TOTAL
BUSH (C)	3 of 250 (1.9)	38 of 55 (24.5)	305
DUKAKIS (L)	12 of 100 (7.7)	102 of 145 (65.8)	245
TOTAL	15 of 350	140 of 200	550

*The cell percentages may not add to exactly 100.0 percent due to slight distortions caused by rounding procedures.

falls at one extreme of the continuum of the construct correlates with a certain constellation of behavioral variables, then an index value at the other end of the construct continuum should not correlate with the same constellation of behavioral variables. Table 9.8 represents those 155 persons who scored very low on the political conservatism index in terms of their distribution on the variables of party and candidate choice. The cell values should be interpreted in the same manner as the preceding table. These data clearly support empirically and logically the predictions we have offered in this example. Thus, of the 155 persons who scored very low on political conservatism, 102 of them (65.8 percent) voted for the liberal candidate (Dukakis) and were registered in the liberal political party (Democratic). Similarly, only three persons who scored low on political conservatism (1.9 percent) voted for the conservative candidate and were Republicans. Finally, moderate figures are reported for those who were conservative in their choice of candidate but liberal on party choice and for those who were liberal on candidate choice but conservative on party choice. Thirty-eight persons who scored very low

on the political-conservatism index (24.5 percent) and were registered Democrats picked the conservative Bush. Twelve persons who had low political-conservatism scores were found to vote for the liberal candidate (Dukakis) but had registered in the conservative Republican party. In sum, of those who had the lowest political-conservatism scores, 65.8 percent picked the liberal party and candidate choice; 32.2 percent showed a conservatively mixed party and candidate choice; and only 1.9 percent picked both a conservative response to party and candidate choice. Table 9.8, then, shows data that empirically and conceptually support the notion of the validity of the political-conservatism index.

In construct validity, one is empirically and logically testing the index to be validated and the conceptual model. Therein is the frustration of construct validity. That is, when the predictions are not verified, it is difficult to determine if it is because of the invalidity of the measuring instrument or the inadequacy or inaccuracy of the conceptual model. Inadequacy of the conceptual model may have been the reason the fluoridation position did not correlate well with political conservatism.*

---

*Parenthetically, notice that we earlier made a distinction between a theory, which is a total explanation of some phenomenon, and a conceptual model, which is believed to be a partial explanation. The usefulness of this distinction should be apparent now that we have discussed the topic of construct validation. It is very difficult to develop and validate an accurate measure of a variable if one's conceptual ideas about the construct are not complete. Indeed, it may be impossible.

Summary. We presented five general ways to test the validity of one's measuring instrument: face validity, jury opinion, known groups, criterion validity (predictive and concurrent), and construct validity. The face-validity technique is useful in the construction of the measuring instrument, and for that reason face validity should never be used in the formal testing for validity. While jury opinion is a significant improvement because it involves experts, we recognized that experts can be wrong. The known-groups technique represents an improvement because of the quantitative results that it generates. The difficulty, however, comes in being able to identify two groups known to be at the extremes of a continuum on the dimension one wishes to measure.

The criterion-validation procedures provide a mixed outcome. Predictive criterion validity offers conclusive evidence and is, therefore, the best validation technique we know. In this technique, predictions from the to-be-validated measure are compared with the empirical data obtained at some future time. The problem is that one must wait for the predicted event to occur before the validity technique can be assessed. Finally, construct validity is the most nebulous of the procedures mentioned, because of the interrelatedness of the measure's validity and the theoretical accuracy of the conceptual model.

Thus, the only procedure that generated substantial confidence is predictive criterion validation. Despite the possibility of painful consequences and the time required for them to manifest themselves, this evidence allows the researcher to determine conclusively if the measure is valid. We again urge you to recognize in the context of validity the difficulty that is imposed upon the scientist because of the two languages which science uses (see Chapters 2 and 3). Finally, when contrasting reliability *and* validity testing, reliability can be assessed on an absolute empirical basis, while validity can be tested only in a relative sense since one must use criteria external to the measure itself.

Precision

Precision refers to the closeness of the measured value to the value of the variable being measured. Thus, in measuring a table that was 40 inches long, if a metal tape measure registered the table's length as 39.8 inches and if a cloth tape measure indicated 35.9 inches, we would say that the metal tape measure was more precise than the cloth tape.

Precision is an issue that is not frequently discussed in the social sciences. Indeed, most social scientists believe that the more precise a measure is, the better is the measure. Although such *may* suggest greater accuracy, we would argue with this interpretation, because precision comes at a cost usually of time and considerable effort. Our colleagues in psychology quite often report in their laboratory studies a rather precise description of the environment in which the experiment was carried out. Sometimes the measurements of the room in which the studies were conducted are given down to the hundredth of a meter. While such a measurement is surely precise, it seems to us to be superficial. That is, if the subject of the experiment is incapable of discriminating between relatively small changes in the nature of the environment, such precision does not seem to be necessary.

In sum, highly precise measurements are often not necessary and in some cases rather difficult to interpret. Consider a student who got an 83 percent on the midterm and another student who received an 84 percent on the same examination. Is there a marked difference between these two students? We think not. Rather, both students have achieved to almost the same degree and will, in all likelihood, be assigned a B grade by the instructor. Sometimes, the more precise figures that arise from one's measurements give the researcher a false sense of accuracy. As with the example of midterm scores, minute percentage differences cannot be meaningfully interpreted as significant differences. (Recall our earlier discussion of sociological significance and statistical significance.) Thus, extreme precision often causes the researcher to make distinctions that are not meaningful and that are likely to cost the researcher time and effort in the construction of the measuring instrument.

SUMMARY

In this chapter we began with a discussion of the various levels of measurement and their relevance to data interpretation and statistical analysis, as well as their relationship to the implications of one's conceptual model. Next, we compared and contrasted the characteristics of an item and three forms of composite measures: (1) index, (2) scale, and (3) indicator. Attention was also given to item analysis as an important statistical technique in the decision to include specific items within a composite measure.

Then, we looked at a few specific composite measures: the Likert scale, the Thurstone equal-appearing interval scale, the Guttman scale, and the Osgood semantic differential. Attention was given to the procedures used to construct these measures, some of their general characteristics, how they are administered, interpretation of results, and a brief look at the advantages and disadvantages of their use. In general, we noted that the Thurstone and Guttman procedures are largely of historical interest, that the Likert scale is currently increasing in use, and that the semantic differential shows potential for future usage since more modern conceptualizations of attitude research indicate complex, multidimensional orientations. This section did illustrate the questions asked and the struggles of the social scientist in the task of operationalizing ideas.

Next, assuming completion of the construction phase of operationalization, we looked at three tests that the researcher should do: the pretest, reliability test, and validity test. Three reliability tests particularly appropriate to the testing of schedules were presented: test-retest, multiple-forms, and the split-half reliability test. It was decided that the split-half technique is generally the best and easiest to do, although one must use the test-retest procedure if testing the reliability of a scale.

Six different validity tests were discussed: face validity, jury opinion, known groups, criterion validation (both predictive criterion validity and concurrent criterion validity), and construct validity. We concluded that face validity should only be used in the formation and design of the measuring instrument. Jury-opinion and concurrent criterion validity have their problems and should be avoided if alternative procedures are available. Construct validity is difficult because one is trying to measure something that does not exist concretely or objectively. Therefore, a multivarious attack is made here, which tests the conceptual model underlying the construct as much as the actual measuring instrument itself. While we have confidence in the known-groups technique, we pointed out the difficulties of finding known groups from both extremes in order to do the known-groups assessment. Finally, the predictive criterion validity technique was felt to be the best procedure, although certain practical difficulties were noted. It was concluded that the formal testing of validity requires additional development and that the current problems are largely the result of the way in which the scientist has put the scientific method together.

Lastly, the precision of one's measuring instruments was discussed with the caution that an overly precise measure is often misleading and unnecessary.

KEY TERMS

Indicator	Multiple-forms reliability	Reliable measure
Internal intensity order	Nominal level	Scale
Interval level	Nonarbitrary zero point	Semantic differential
Item	Ordinal level	Spearman-Brown prophecy formula
Item analysis	Precision	Split-half reliability
Jury-opinion validity	Predictive criterion validity	Test-retest reliability
Known-groups validity	Pretest	Thurstone equal-appearing interval scale
Levels of measurement	Ratio level	Validity
Likert scale		

REVIEW QUESTIONS

1. Compare and contrast the four levels of measurement. Which transformations from one level to another are permitted? Which are not?

2. What are the four general types of measures used to operationalize variables, and what are their advantages and disadvantages?

3. Cite the reasons why a researcher may wish to use a composite measure rather than a single item.

4. How do Likert scales, Thurstone equal-appearing interval scales, and Guttman scales differ? What mechanisms are used to construct them?

5. How does the semantic differential differ from the other composite measures cited? Why is this measure important?

6. What is the difference between a Likert scale and a Likert "look-alike"?

7. Discuss the three tests of reliability. What advantages does the split-half procedure have over the test-retest and multiple-forms procedures? Which technique must be used if one has a Guttman scale?

8. List in order from the worst to the best the various validity tests discussed. Justify your choices.

9. Why is construct validity so difficult? What does one's conceptual model have to do with this validation procedure?

PART III

DATA-GATHERING:
PROCEDURES AND DISCUSSION

In this section, we address the ways social scientists collect data.

Our discussion begins with the survey techniques that are probably the most popular and frequently used because we concluded Part II with a discussion of the design and testing of the measuring instruments most likely to be used in surveys.

Chapter 11 is devoted to experimental and quasi-experimental research designs. The experimental designs are the most sophisticated for developing evidence of causal relationships.

Content and secondary analysis are discussed in Chapter 12. These techniques involve the use of inanimate sources of information, such as census reports, biomedical data reports, public health information, published and unpublished manuscripts and books, letters, and the like. What sets content analysis and secondary analysis apart is

that whatever the researcher does with these data will not affect the subject matter; i.e., they are not reactive.

We conclude Part III with a chapter on observation, unobtrusive measures, and exploratory research. The general thrust of this chapter is that the researcher needs to be a skilled observer. In the context of exploratory research, observation plays a key role in uncovering important variables and their relationships. Unobtrusive measures or nonreactive measures are important because they allow the researcher to gather data without disturbing the subject matter. Observation is a tricky business because of the degree of interaction that the researcher has with the subject matter. We discuss this last because we believe exploratory research is one of the more difficult strategies to pursue, requiring virtually all of the researcher's skills.

CHAPTER 10

SURVEYS: INTERVIEWS AND QUESTIONNAIRES

INTRODUCTION

The use of the survey design is the predominant data-gathering procedure in the social sciences today. Surveys are heavily used in political science, health science, economics, sociology, and social geography, as well as applied areas such as marketing in business, counseling, and public-opinion polling. There is a veritable mountain of materials that has been written on these data-gathering designs and the conditions for their appropriate use. Therefore, although it would be foolish to suggest that this chapter is a complete review, we do address the major issues that surround the use of interviews or questionnaires.

Organization of This Chapter

The material in this chapter is ordered on two levels: first, by the type of survey design: questionnaire, face-to-face interview, or telephone interview; and second, a rough chronological sequence, in which the various sections are presented in the order in which they are normally conceptualized, considered, and executed in a research project that utilizes the survey design.

There are some points where this sequence must be abandoned, however. For example, the decision concerning the appropriateness of the questionnaire or interview design for the research objectives requires descriptive information that is discussed early in this chapter. Also, we present some additional issues that are germane to the formation of the questionnaire schedule or interview guide apart from those already discussed in Chapter 8. It is to those additional issues that we now turn.

Some Preliminary Considerations

We have previously discussed our concern for a clear use of technical terminology. The use of survey terminology is considerably varied. For example, many researchers use the term *questionnaire* to refer to the process through which the data are collected, while others use it to refer to the nature of the measuring instrument itself. Therefore, in this first section we will offer a clarification of the dimensions of the survey process.

A *survey* is a data-gathering procedure, which usually involves contacting a sample of persons and soliciting their cooperation in providing responses to items of interest to the researcher. There are two broad types of surveys: interviews and questionnaires. An *interview* involves social interaction between a *respondent*, the person who replies to the interviewer's queries, and an *interviewer*, who is charged with seeking accurate responses to various questions and recording the respondent's responses. As such, interviews can be, and usually have been, face-to-face situations of social interaction between the interviewer and the respondent. However, with the aid of *random-digit dialing* (RDD), which is discussed later in this chapter, and *computer-assisted telephone interviewing* (CATI), the telephone interview has become more popular recently. Thus, whether the interviewer is sitting in front of the respondent or talking on the telephone, the interview data-gathering technique requires a minimum of two persons—one asking questions or presenting statements and the other responding to them.

Questionnaires generally function in the same way that interviews do in terms of the items presented and the purposes for which they were designed. However, questionnaires differ from interviews in that they are self-administered. The self-administered questionnaire charges the respondent with the tasks of reading the items and making appropriate responses in the allocated spaces. Questionnaires can be of two basic types: (1) the *mailed questionnaire,* for which the schedule is sent to the respondent who is asked to respond and mail it back to the researcher or (2) the *nonmailed questionnaire,* for which the researcher hand delivers the measuring instrument that is read and completed by the respondent and then immediately collected by the researcher. An in-class examination is analogous to a nonmailed questionnaire. Of course, these two standard designs are subject to variations. For example, the researcher might hand deliver the measuring instrument but ask the respondents to mail the completed schedule back—an appropriate tactic when respondent anonymity is desirable.

Further, it is important to identify different types of survey measuring instruments. If the measuring instrument is a *schedule,* it usually contains *structured items,* which means that the items presented are, for the most part, specific ones designed to elicit specific information, usually in *close-ended response categories* that the researcher has predetermined to be of interest to hypothesis testing. Conversely, an *interview guide* is generally composed of *unstructured items,* which means that the items asked are more general, allowing the respondent an *open-ended response,* or the maximum latitude, to answer the items in whatever manner the respondent wishes—the format most appropriate in the exploratory research context.

In sum, there are several dimensions to be considered in planning a survey: (1) the nature of the data-gathering setting: questionnaire or interview; (2) the nature of the measuring instrument: schedule or guide; (3) the nature of the items to be asked: structured, unstructured, or some combination; and (4) the nature of the response categories: open-ended, close-ended, or some combination. Without reiterating the material discussed earlier

on operationalization, remember also the decisions that must be made on the use of composite measures or single items.

THE QUESTIONNAIRE

Definition and Function

As we have just explained, *questionnaire* data-gathering design involves a measuring instrument that is self-administered in that the respondent is responsible for reading and responding to the items presented. Questionnaire designs are most appropriate when the researcher has a firm idea of the objectives of the research study.

While it is possible to design a questionnaire with unstructured items, which allows the respondent to respond in his or her own words, such a design is rarely used. The chief problem with an unstructured schedule and open-ended responses is that the respondent must be highly motivated to complete the schedule, a characteristic that is rarely observed. Therefore, the majority of questionnaire designs utilize structured items and close-ended response categories. However, occasional use of fill-in-the-blank items (e.g., the response to the question: "If you are presently working, what is the nature of your occupation?") and completely open-ended responses (e.g., the response to the question: "Now that we've asked you a number of items in which we are very interested, is there anything which you would like to mention?") are frequently used in structured measuring instruments. In light of the limited use of the unstructured schedule format, the remainder of this section is devoted to the questionnaire containing a schedule of structured items.

Designing the Schedule

There is little to add that has not been covered in Chapters 8 and 9, in which we discussed construction of the measuring instrument as well as its pretest, reliability, and validity tests. However, to briefly reiterate, the pretest is vital to the success of the questionnaire because the schedule must be clear to the respondent. Because this is a questionnaire design, the directions for completion must be clear and the schedule should not contain items or contingency questions that are too complex to complete. Remember that an interviewer will not be present to assist the respondent. Careful preplanning of the schedule is, therefore, important, because once the data-gathering phase has begun, the securing of data is completely dependent upon the respondent's reaction.

The Cover Letter

The schedule sent to the respondent should always be accompanied by a cover letter. The *cover letter* is the researcher's first contact with those sampled and is important in conveying several aspects of the study. While somewhat dated, William Goode and Paul Hatt's book[1] is, in our opinion, a classic on certain aspects of research design. Don Dillman's book[2] also offers excellent suggestions on the content and order of the items contained in the cover letter. Included should be (1) the initial sentence; (2) sponsorship of the study; (3) why the respondent was selected; (4) a discussion of anonymity or confidentiality, if relevant; (5) the rationale for the study; and (6) a few miscellaneous items. We will briefly address each of these components.

The Initial Sentence.   The first point to be made in the cover letter is an appeal for the respondent's cooperation. It is the researcher's "sales pitch" in which one hopes to interest the respondent in participating in the study. One should create interest in the research with the first sentence, and this effect should be looked for in the pretest of the questionnaire design. However, one should not be so specific about the substantive concerns of the research that the respondent is influenced toward one position or another. Nor should the cover letter create a threat to the ego of the respondent. Thus, if doing an attitudinal study, one may not have to mention the specific attitude of interest. Dillman writes that "[t]he appeal of the TDM [Total Design Method] is based on convincing people first that a problem exists that is of impor-

tance to a group with which they identify, and second, that their help is needed to find a solution."[3]

Thus, one does not appeal for help for the researcher but asks the respondent to serve as an intermediary whose opinions and knowledge can affect the outcomes of problems and concerns.

Sponsorship of the Study.   Ample evidence exists to indicate that a potential respondent is more motivated to participate if the respondent thinks a major organization is sponsoring the research. Therefore, while one should not be dishonest about the nature of the research, one should try to present a sponsoring agent so that a maximum degree of prestige is communicated. Caution, however, is needed here. For example, if people's attitudes toward abortion are being examined, an announcement that a pro-choice group is a sponsor would create a bias in the sample. Those who favor the pro-choice policies would be most likely to want to participate and those who favor a pro-life posture would be likely to decline. Further, those who do not want to be involved in either position on this issue may be frightened by the mention of either organization. If one secures the support of a major research university, the National Institute of Health, or the National Science Foundation, one is in a much better position to maximize participation. In sum, organizational sponsorship is helpful in soliciting the respondent's participation if the organization does not create a negative image in the respondent's mind. It does not matter whether this image is correct; it will be the one upon which the respondent acts in making the decision of participation.

Respondent Selection and Participation.   It is important to explain to the respondent why the respondent has been selected. In the rationale portion of the letter, the researcher should justify the importance of the study and attempt to convince the respondent that his or her replies are essential to the study. Under the premise that flattery will get you everywhere, one way to encourage participation would be for the researcher to remark that the respondent is one of a number of persons sampled whose replies will represent the information and opinions of a great number of persons.

Second, increased participation may be encouraged through a number of possible monetary appeals. Respondents can be offered money in exchange for their participation. However, if this appeal is used, a minimal amount is suggested, because the total cost to the researcher could be considerable if the sample is large. Further, a larger sum may be perceived as payment for services rendered and, in view of what the researcher can realistically pay, would not be likely to be seen as adequate compensation. Offering to compensate the respondent with, say, a dollar represents token or symbolic appreciation for one's cooperation. Some researchers have been successful with a gambit such as, "We'd like to have your two cents worth on the subject of . . . ," wherein the researcher includes two pennies, or "We'll give you a penny for your thoughts," for which the researcher encloses a penny. Such minimal amounts can gain the respondent's attention without suggesting an insulting level of payment.

The third approach, which perhaps is more preferable, is an appeal to the respondent's sense of altruism. The researcher notes a higher goal and compliments the respondent by suggesting the requested responses are significant in reflecting the feelings and knowledge of the group being studied. Indeed, when one is sampling *key respondents,* those with specialized knowledge, they frequently can be appealed to on this basis.

Finally, if at all true, the researcher can say that the respondent has been sampled by a "scientific selection process." This is a set of buzzwords which, for many, denote importance and suggest science at work. Since science is viewed favorably by most persons, an appeal based on the notion that the study is scientific and that the respondent has been scientifically selected to represent an important group of persons constitutes a maximum approach in many cases.

Anonymity. *Anonymity* means that the respondent's responses will be handled in such a way that no one will be able to establish the respondent's identity. On the other hand, *confidentiality* means that although the respondent's identity will be known to the researcher, the researcher agrees never to divulge it to anyone else (see Chapter 16). A guarantee of *anonymity* or *confidentiality* should be presented in the cover letter. It should be noted, however, that anonymity cannot be guaranteed if there is a need for callbacks, if a panel sampling design is being used, or if validation checks will be conducted. Ethically, the researcher must be scrupulously honest in making claims about anonymity or confidentiality. Indeed, because of the follow-up procedures, Don Dillman argues that anonymity cannot be given, because the maintenance of the personal theme, which the total design method attempts to create, requires the researcher to know who has replied and when.

Rationale. The *rationale* for the study seeks to justify to the respondent why the study should be done. One can always mention that the study will lead to the expansion of scientific knowledge. As Raymond Gorden[4] has noted, the respondent is often flattered by the opportunity of being a part of an activity that transcends his or her self-interest. Further, if the topic is one that could lead to applied or practical knowledge, it may motivate the respondent to participate because it may be perceived to be needed and important.

The Results. One should always offer to send the interested respondent a *summary* of the study results. It may not always be possible because of the time and cost, but, where possible, it is a courtesy that should be extended to the respondent. If such a request is received, it must be honored. Never use this as a ruse for a motivational appeal.

The Researcher's Address and Telephone Number. The researcher should include his or her address and telephone number so that the respondent can contact the researcher with any questions or concerns about the study. In an era when so many business appeals are made through telemarketing under the guise of a survey, respondents have ample justification for skepticism concerning the seriousness of the researcher's study. For those potential respondents who would like to verify the information that is contained in the cover letter or who have questions about one or more of the items contained within the schedule, an easy means of contacting the director of the project is desirable.

The Researcher's Appreciation.   Finally, the letter should close with a statement of thanks, giving the researcher's name and formal title. Keep in mind that the respondent is giving up time for the benefit of the researcher, although one hopes the data gathered will ultimately be of some benefit to the respondent.

The Appearance of the Cover Letter.   Up to this point, our attention has been on the content of the cover letter. In the present subsection, a few suggestions are given concerning the appearance of the cover letter. (Indeed, some of these suggestions carry over into the appearance of the schedule and any other printed items that the respondent will see.) The cover letter should appear on quality paper containing the sponsoring organization's letterhead, if such is available. The letter should be personally prepared. Salutations such as "Dear Resident" or "To Whom It May Concern" are not helpful in generating a cooperative attitude. The use of a quality word processing computer software package makes the personalization of each letter easier, and quality high-speed printers have eliminated the drudgery of typing each letter. Given today's technology, there is no reason why a high-quality personal cover letter cannot be sent to each respondent. While time consuming, each letter should be personally signed using the pressed-blue-ballpoint-pen technology,[5] which involves using a soft blotter-type pad underneath the letter and signing with a ballpoint pen to ensure that the respondent can feel the indentations made from the pen. This will reassure the respondent that the letter was not mass produced and signed by a machine. It is also acceptable if one uses a fountain pen, so that the ink will smudge when dampened, indicating that each letter was hand signed.

It should be noted that one does not have to personally sign thousands of cover letters, but that such can be done with the aid of a signing machine. With such a tool, the signature of the researcher is actually signed into a computer, which transfers the signature in ink to whatever documents are fed into the machine. Some research indicates that a personal, handwritten sentence or two in addition to the typed text improves the response rate, since it leaves the impression of a more personalized cover letter. Perhaps the thank-you part of the letter can be so appended. Lastly, research reveals that the color of the paper on which the cover letter and the schedule are printed does not seem to influence the response rate, although one must be careful to choose paper that is light in color to make reading the text easier. One can always be confident in the selection of white paper.

Summary.   The initial contact with the respondent should convey the image that the research is serious, the topic is important, and the researcher is politely asking for the respondent's assistance. If the schedule has been professionally printed and the cover letter prepared as suggested, one will maximize the likelihood of creating a favorable impression on the respondent.

The cover letter is the researcher's first attempt to impress upon the respondent the need to participate in the study. In a mailed questionnaire design, particularly, there is no interviewer to try to convince the respondent. Everything must be accomplished through the cover letter. Careful attention to detail is important to the probability of success.

The TDM [Total Design Method] for mail surveys relies heavily on personalization throughout the implementation process. It is the major vehicle for conveying to the respondent the critical messages that the study is important and that the respondent's participation is important to its success. Personalization involves much more than putting a respondent's name and a real signature on the cover letter, the simplistic way in which it is often viewed. The test of whether personalization is achieved rests not with individual techniques, but with the overall effect that is produced, that is, whether respondents feel that they are accorded individual attention.[6]

Mailing the Schedule

A number of considerations are connected with the mailing of the measuring instrument, cover letter, and return envelope. In this section, we look at some mailing options, the materials that should be sent, and the timing of the mailings.

Mailing Options. The mailing options can be divided into two subcategories: outgoing and return. The *outgoing mailing* can be sent to the respondent by first class or bulk rate. It is generally thought that the first class option, while more expensive, creates a better impression on the respondent. Significantly, a first-class mailing will distinguish the researcher's work and does not associate this work with advertising, which tends to use bulk rates. The *return mailing* also has two options: the stamped envelope and the business-reply envelope. Even though the cost per envelope is slightly higher, the business-reply envelope is generally cheaper because one only pays for those that are returned. Thus, if one anticipates a smaller response rate, substantial savings can be achieved through the use of the business-reply envelope. However, there is some consensus that the use of the stamped envelope will elicit a larger response rate. We could offer many other nuances here, but the key is to create the impression that the respondent is special and that the researcher is making it as easy as possible for the respondent to participate.

What to Mail. The *initial mailing* should include the cover letter, schedule, return envelope, and possibly a return postcard. The postcard is suggested if the researcher wants to maintain the anonymity of the respondents. The respondent should be informed of this promise in the cover letter and, again, on the actual schedule. However,

while guaranteeing anonymity, the researcher will want to minimize postage costs of subsequent mailings by not sending follow-up materials to persons who have already responded. To accomplish this, the researcher can include a separate postcard with the respondent's name and address on it. The respondent is instructed to return it *separately* when the schedule has been completed and returned. In this way, the researcher will not be able to identify who completed any given schedule but will know to cross the respondent off the follow-up list when the postcard is received. This strategy reduces mailing costs and minimizes aggravation to the respondent who would otherwise keep receiving communications from the researcher.

A single mailing always results in a lower response rate than a study using a number of follow-up mailings. The *first follow-up mailing* should contain another, but shorter, cover letter, another copy of the schedule (because the respondent may have lost or misplaced the first one), and another stamped return envelope. The cover letter should again encourage the respondent to participate by stressing the importance of the study and the respondent's participation. One should also thank the respondent for participating in the event that the respondent has mailed a completed instrument, which has crossed in the mail with the first follow-up request. Some researchers have argued that the first follow-up mailing should only be a letter of encouragement or reminder. The argument is that sending an entire additional package of materials to the respondent will be interpreted as a lack of confidence in the respondent's integrity. The additional mailing will certainly make the study more expensive. We see merit to both positions, and a more definitive answer will have to wait for additional research.

The *second follow-up mailing* should contain a third letter, the schedule, and the stamped return envelope. This mailing assumes that the respondent has been very busy and has somehow misplaced all the relevant materials.

Finally, the *third follow-up mailing* should contain a fourth letter, the schedule, and the stamped return envelope and should be sent by *certified* mail. Any further follow-up mailings are generally thought to be of marginal value. The respondent is unlikely to respond to a fifth solicitation and will probably consider additional requests as harassment on the part of the researcher.

Monitoring the Returns.   An important component in the mailed questionnaire survey is the monitoring of returns. Two graphs should be kept. The first should show the number of schedules returned per day. The second should show the cumulative proportion of schedules returned through the course of the survey. By monitoring the results of the survey in this way, the researcher can determine when to post the follow-up mailings. That is, when one sees that the returns are falling off, one can proceed with the next mailing.

Dillman argues that the first follow-up mailing should be done precisely one week after the initial one. It may take the form of a postcard, which thanks those who have already responded or reminds those who have not yet responded to do so. One should be sure to type each person's address, easily done with a computer and a good word processing package, and sign it with the pressed-ballpoint-pen technique. The second follow-up procedure should be done as described above, with the third follow up done precisely seven weeks after the initial mailing. Dillman argues that one of the most effective procedures to convey that the respondent is a necessary component to the research study is to write in one or more of the follow ups that "as of today we have not yet received your questionnaire [sic]."[7]

When to Mail.   We will begin with a negative and say that one should never mail or *do* a survey in the month of December. One should always consider the nature of the sample in choosing a mailing date. For example, university professors, institutional staff, or college students should not be contacted at the conclusion of the academic term. To ask the general public to respond to a research study during the income tax season is unwise, and attorneys should not be contacted during the month of August, which is when most

judicial systems virtually close down while the justice system goes on vacation. In essence, the researcher must think about the nature of the sample in order to avoid a mailing period when the sample is likely to be thinking about other considerations. Two other timing considerations are that the cover letter should be dated to correspond to the date on which the mailing is to be done, and the materials should be mailed on a Monday or a Tuesday to maximize the probability that the respondents will receive the package in the same week that it was posted.

Obviously, some of the follow-up materials must be prepared prior to the initial mailing to avoid overburdening the research staff. Arguing that timing is crucial, Dillman urges meeting these deadlines and in the way that has been described.

Checking the Actual Returns

Degree of Completeness.   When the researcher begins to receive the returned schedules, they should be checked for completeness. If a postcard is received indicating a schedule is on the way, that respondent's mailing labels for the follow-up procedures or the respondent's name and address in the mail-merge word processing file should be eliminated. If respondent anonymity has not been guaranteed and if the researcher has asked for and received the telephone number of the respondent, a telephone call should be placed to the respondent to inquire about any items that have been omitted, any responses that seem unintelligible, or any responses that appear particularly interesting about which the researcher would like to probe further.

Identification Number.   Whether anonymity has been granted or not, the researcher should immediately put an identification number on the schedule in order to be able to reference it. For example, it may be that the respondent gave a particularly insightful open-ended response to an item on the schedule and the researcher would like to quote this respondent, anonymously. The identification number functions to identify which schedule is the one that contains such a quotation.

The Date Received. Finally, it is important to note the date on which the schedule was received. Such information may be significant in interpreting the responses obtained. For example, if one were assessing the sample's attitudes toward political credibility, there may be a sharp change in the nature of the responses after a television announcement about sexual indiscretions of a member of Congress, or an announcement about massive overcharges by defense contractors. It may be that an incident will occur in the middle of one's survey that will have or could have a decided effect on the sample's responses. The date of receipt will help the researcher to determine the degree to which such events have an effect on the sample's responses.

The date is also important for making an estimation of the characteristics of those respondents sampled who never return the schedule. By carefully checking the responses to key variables through the course of the study, the researcher is often able to make reasonably accurate estimates of the characteristics of those who failed to participate in the study. If, for example, the early returners are the most highly educated of those who return completed schedules and if the educational attainment of the remainder of the returners decreases in a progressive manner throughout the return period, one may speculate that those who failed to return the schedule at all would be persons with the lowest educational attainment. If the early respondents have had great exposure to the situation on which the study focuses and the later returners have had only moderate exposure, one might consider that the nonreturners had little or no exposure to the substance of the study. In sum, the date can function in more than one important way.

Acceptable Response Rate to Mailed Questionnaires

While a simple random sample may be selected to begin a study, it is unlikely such a sample will be maintained at the conclusion of the questionnaire data-gathering phase. Nevertheless, we should note "that the body of inferential statistics used in connection with survey analysis assumes that *all* members of the initial sample complete and return their questionnaires [sic]."[8]

Thus, the *response rate* is of considerable concern in a survey. Respondent failure to participate may lead to serious biases in the results, because those persons who fail to participate are likely to be different from those who do.

Therefore, the issue of an acceptable proportion of responses in the mailed questionnaire is an important question. Unfortunately, there is little agreement concerning the answer. Babbie[9] has argued that a response rate of 50 percent is adequate for the analysis of the responses, but that a rate of 60 percent is good and 70 percent is very good, implying that one is not likely to do much better. His argument is that the quality of the data is much more important than the nature of the response rate. In reality, however, quality and quantity often go hand in hand. While Babbie is more liberal with the issue of an acceptable response rate, Kenneth Bailey[10] argues for about a 75 percent response rate, a belief shared by David Nachmias and Chava Nachmias.[11] These writers suggest it is possible to attain higher rates with attention to the details of the research design. Further, Dillman has carefully monitored response rates in 48 studies and claims that the Total Design Method has resulted in an average response rate of 77 percent where this method has been used to its fullest and an average rate of 71 percent where the TDM has been partially used.[12] Indeed, with certain specialized populations the TDM has resulted in response rates in the 90th percentile. However, Dillman cautions that the TDM has not been tested in some sampling situations that are less forgiving, such as large metropolitan communities.[13]

There are other considerations that affect the response rate. If the researcher delivers or picks up the schedule, the response rate is higher than for one that is mailed. Lower response rates are to be expected when the sample to be surveyed is heterogeneous. Response rates tend to drop when respondents are less educated or not interested in the subject matter of the study, when the items are highly personal or embarrassing, when the items are difficult to understand, and when sample members are likely to have physical difficulties, such as arthritis or poor eyesight.

Another issue that has been previously thought to be an important component affecting response rate is the length of the schedule. More current research seems to suggest that length does not matter, as long as the length is reasonable. Thus, if one has a schedule that is interesting to the respondent, a good return can be expected regardless of the length. Despite this optimistic projection, some caution is warranted. If the schedule appears to be too large, the respondent may be frightened off without discovering how interesting it is. If the researcher has included a multi-item assessment of a variable and followed the advice of many to put one item on a page, the schedule may appear larger than it is. To illustrate by exaggeration, if the researcher can honestly say that the 100-page schedule can be completed in 22 minutes, that information should be put in the cover letter. In this way, a seemingly intimidating length will hopefully be minimized in the eyes of the respondent.

A couple of reminders are in order here. In terms of the appearance of the schedule, remember to spread the items out rather than jumble everything together for the sake of a few additional pages. Second, keep in mind that a lengthy schedule will necessitate additional postage costs, which can be sizable if the sample is large and if there are multiple follow-up mailings.

A Final Thought

We close this section on the mailed questionnaire with a notion from Dillman. Dillman has done considerable empirical research into the effects of various questionnaire design components and applied a social science conceptual model to organize his thinking about this data-gathering technique. From this experience, he argues that surveys are a special form of social interaction. Thus, the social exchange model which was developed initially by George C. Homans, who brought it from economics to sociology, has been applied to Dillman's thinking. The social exchange model suggests that people engage in social interaction to the degree that they will receive rewards from the interaction and be able to minimize the costs of such interaction. In other words, a simple cost-benefit analysis is applied to the respondent's position in a survey situation. A review of the notions discussed earlier, and many of those to be subsequently presented in this chapter, will reveal that the procedures and strategies suggested are in one way or another designed to reduce the costs and increase the rewards of the respondent's participation. This is what is particularly interesting about Dillman's work: not only is it an excellent discussion of the survey data-gathering design, but it is also guided and informed by credible social scientific, theoretical conceptualization.

THE FACE-TO-FACE INTERVIEW

Introduction

The researcher generally has much more flexibility in planning different kinds of interview data-gathering strategies. You will recall we argued that intellectually there is no reason why the questionnaire procedure could not contain an unstructured series of items with open-ended responses requested. Practically, this would not be wise because it would demand a maximum amount of motivation on the part of the respondent, i.e., more than one should reasonably expect. However, the interview procedure has greater flexibility because the interviewer does the recording and directs the interview session.

Types of Face-to-Face Interviews

There are several types of *face-to-face interview* data-gathering designs: (1) those using a structured schedule, (2) those using an interview guide, (3) those with some combination of a schedule and guide, and (4) those that are totally unstructured. Although we discuss the first two alternatives, it is not necessary to present the combination variety because it simply combines elements of the first two. The need, however, for a combination technique will be clear after we have dealt with the first two. Discussion of the totally unstructured alternative is more appropriate to exploratory research and is discussed when that subject is raised in Chapter 13.

The *structured schedule interview* is one in which the researcher has predetermined what items to ask and what response categories to make available to the respondent for selection. As such, the measuring instrument for this type of interview is the same as that used for the structured mailed schedule discussed earlier. Little further needs to be said here except that the structured schedule interview is one that is likely to be the survey design of choice when one is hypothesis testing and when the sample is likely to produce a high nonresponse rate.

The *interview guide interview* is one in which the researcher has provided general statements and question areas for the interviewer to present to the respondent. The interviewer is given a wide range of discretion in probing and framing questions concerning these areas. Thus, this type of interview design is more spontaneous and free flowing than the structured schedule interview is. Finally, if the interviewer is using an interview guide, one is likely to be doing an exploratory study rather than hypothesis testing.*

Designing the Interview Schedule

Most of the relevant issues of questionnaire schedule design have been discussed earlier in this chapter and in Chapter 8. While one does not have to be quite as careful in the schedule format for an interview, attention to proper format will help the interviewer to record the respondent's answers more easily. This will also significantly reduce coding errors in the data-preparation phases of the study. Therefore, the format and content of the interview schedule must generally be under the same set of constraints that we discussed earlier in the context of the design of the measuring instrument.

Once the schedule has been formulated, pretested, reliability tested, and validity tested, the researcher is ready to train the interview staff.

Training the Interviewers

While there are a number of steps in the training process of interviewers, the basic premise is that a well-informed and well-trained interviewer will be able to accomplish the research objectives more efficiently. Therefore, the researcher is advised to not economize on the interviewer training period. Careful attention to detail at this point will pay dividends in generating more reliable and valid data.

The Overview. The first step is for the project director to provide an overall view of the study. In general, the conceptual model, specific hypotheses to be tested, nature of the sample, anticipated preparation of the data, and analysis of the results of the study should be discussed with the interviewers. A broad perspective rather than copious details is the proper tact to take.

The Schedule. The second step involves an item-by-item and section-by-section review of the schedule. The project director should explain each item; what is being sought; what the directions for each section mean; how to use the probes, if such are included; how to record the responses; what nonverbal cues to look for; what informal observational tasks the interviewer is to do; and so forth. That is, *every* detail pertinent to ensuring that each item is handled the way that the researcher desires should be discussed.

---

*There are a number of more specialized types of interviews, for example, the focused interview, the police-interrogation interview, the counseling interview, and others that have been derived essentially for specific situations and purposes. Here, we are only concerned with the two major types that are used generally in a research rather than an applied context.

Additionally, attention should be given to factors such as the importance of asking the items in the order in which they have been written. This is particularly important if one is seeking responses to an attitudinal assessment and if one is hypothesis testing with a structured schedule and structured response categories. One should also stress the need to be neutral in the presentation of potentially controversial items, what to do if the respondent balks at responding to one or more items, and how to handle interruptions while the interview is going on. The researcher should handle each item by itself, asking for any questions from the interviewers *before* going on to a subsequent item. Taking it slowly and carefully is the approach advised in this stage of the training session.

The Practice Interviews.   The third step involves the study director's going through the interview as it is to be done. Any comments that the study director would like to interject by way of explanation as the interview unfolds should be held until the entire interview is completed. Then, comments about various facets of the interview that emerged during the interview would be appropriate to mention and discuss.

The fourth step involves pairing the interviewers and doing a couple of practice interviews. One person of each pair should assume the role of interviewer, and the other person the role of respondent. After the first practice interview has been completed, the pair should switch roles and do the interview another time. The project director and the staff should circulate and listen to the interviews so that positive and negative comments can be introduced for the group's benefit in the next stage.

Group Discussion.   The fifth step involves a group discussion of the feelings of the interviewers, any potential problems with which they would like help, any pertinent remarks that the director and the staff would like to make, and so forth. What is crucial here is that one is creating a situation in which the interviewers are becoming familiar with the measuring instrument and the interview format, and learning whether the interviewers possess the desire and skills to do the task that they are being asked to do. For example, the researcher may be called upon to help with an applied scientific study for a nonacademic or nonresearch group. One of your authors was asked to design, organize, sample, train, and execute a study for a regional church group. To cut costs of collecting the data, the church wanted to utilize volunteers as interviewers, who had never done interviewing and needed to be trained. The training session was important for the skills that these laypersons accumulated and for the personal insights revealed. I will never forget one senior citizen who pulled me aside toward the end of a rather long day of training and said, "Guy, I can't do this!" It is better to find out during the training session that an interviewer does not feel comfortable with the task than to find a high degree of interviewer bias in the middle of one's study. In sum, the interviewer training session is helpful to the interviewer and the project director.

Accessibility during the Field Stage.   The last step occurs during the actual interview phase. The project director should be accessible to the interviewers, who may develop additional questions about aspects of the study that did not emerge during the training sessions. As we argued earlier when we discussed the pretest, no amount of training will substitute for actually doing several interviews. Indeed, a trained interviewer or the project director often will accompany an interviewer trainee on the latter's early interviewing experiences. This field experience, coupled with a supportive and knowledgeable expert, permits instant feedback.

The need to maintain contact with the interviewing staff during the interview phase is important for a second reason. If the interview staff is dispersed over a large geographic area, the lone interviewer may develop a sense of estrangement or abandonment in the field. Contact with one's staff to not only ensure the validity of the data but also provide support and understanding for the staff is an important component in maintaining the high quality of the study.

Making Contact with the Sample

Introduction.   A key step is making proper contact with the community in general and with the person sampled specifically. Making contact is really a two-step process: (1) the introduction of the research study to the community (if it is a locally based study) and (2) making contact with the specific persons sampled.

Informing the Community.   If the study design calls for sending interviewers into a particular area, it will facilitate the ultimate success of the investigation to inform the community that a study is under way. This will provide preliminary evidence of cooperation or resistance to the execution of the study. For example, it was found that after the annual University of Michigan Detroit Area Study had been under way for several years, the poor people of Detroit eventually became weary of "those students poking around our neighborhood all the time." It is important for the researcher to know if there are endemic factors that might interfere with the smooth flow of the interview process.

The project director should write a letter to the local chief of police or sheriff announcing that a study will be under way in the near future and soliciting this person's cooperation. The actual dates of the study should be given in so far as these are available, and the sponsorship and nature of the study should be explained. In this manner, if any of those sampled feel the need to check with the "local authorities" concerning the new people who are tramping around the neighborhood, the authorities can vouch for the authenticity of the research staff. Press releases to the local newspapers and television stations may help legitimate the study in the eyes of the community.

Contacting the Sample.   After having made every effort to inform the community that a study is in progress, one may proceed to make contact with the specific persons sampled for the study. Since the concept of the cover letter has been discussed in the context of the mailed questionnaire data-gathering design, we would simply suggest here that a similar letter be prepared which, in this case, will be called the *letter of introduction.* The letter of introduction should be mailed about a week prior to the arrival of the interview team and should contain the same information which a cover letter contains. This introduction paves the way for the first face-to-face contact between the interviewer and the respondent. The persons sampled are informed of their selection and that they will be contacted soon. It has been argued by some researchers that the letter of introduction is unnecessary.[14] However, we believe it prevents the respondent from being hit straight out of the blue with a choice for which there is little time to consider.

Additionally, the interviewer should carry another letter of introduction and an identification (ID) card with a picture of the interviewer on it to facilitate verification that the interviewer is indeed the person to whom the letter of introduction refers. If obtaining such an ID card is difficult, most local police stations will supply these cards at cost for interviewers. Police departments willingly provide this service, because it makes validation of the interviewers easier. The letters of introduction—the one mailed prior to the beginning of the study and the one the interviewer carries—should contain a telephone number for the respondent to contact if the respondent wishes to verify further that the person so named is legitimate and if the respondent has any questions about the nature of the study. Any such fears on the part of the respondent should be dealt with seriously, as it is crucial that they be dispelled before any rapport, which is so important to a successful interview, can begin to be established. Indeed, one might seriously consider establishing a local "field office," to which the respondent may feel free to make a local telephone call or visit. Such will also facilitate the project director's supervision of the interviewing staff.

Once the interviewer has made actual contact, the interviewer must put the respondent at ease and build rapport. If the respondent seems uncomfortable, the interviewer may take some moments to talk about some reasonably noncontroversial subject. One might pick the weather, for example, a topic about which almost everyone will have something to say and which is not likely to cause tension between the interviewer and the respondent. When the respondent appears to be at ease, Dillman argues that the first question should be one that will evoke the respondent's interest. Indeed, it may be a question that has little or nothing to do with the subject in which the researcher is primarily interested. The function of the first question is to get the respondent interested and to begin building a commitment on the part of the respondent to become a part of the interview process.

Characteristics of the Interviewer

A comment or two is in order concerning the personal characteristics of the interviewer. As Dillman points out, the interview situation is interpreted by the respondent, not so much as a situation in which scientific research is going on, but, more likely, one where the respondent and the interviewer are socially interacting. If the respondent perceives the interview situation as social interaction, all the usual impediments to honest and comfortable human social interaction will be applicable.

Thus, the characteristics of the interviewer should be as similar to the characteristics of those sampled as possible. It is recommended that the respondent and interviewer share the same sex, race, social class position (within reason), general age range, and manner of dress. A couple of caveats should be mentioned here. First, in a general way the respondent is expecting an *interviewer* to show up at the door, not the next-door neighbor. That is, the interviewer is indeed functioning in a system of social interaction, but it is a system in which the respondent is expecting someone who has assumed the role of interviewer. The inter-

viewer should always maintain an appropriate role within the interview situation. Second, and more specifically, the interviewer can not take on the pose of a working or lower class person. Interviewers are not, by definition, working- or lower-class people, and such an appearance would probably be noted as a phony affectation and would jeopardize rapport and the seriousness of the study. William F. Whyte, in his classic study *Street Corner Society,*[15] explains that he became a participant observer in a working-class neighborhood and studied the Norton Street gang in the Italian section of Boston. Within this gang, profanity was often used in the normal conversation of the gang members. Whyte noted that after a year or so he felt accepted into the gang and remarks that one day he uttered a stream of profanity about something. The other members of the gang did a double take and one of them replied, "Bill, you're not supposed to talk like that!" Not only was it obvious that Whyte had not totally blended into the group, it was also clear that this working-class group did not expect a college graduate to speak in the same manner that they did.

Additionally, the interviewer's manner of dress should be similar to the respondent's except that the interviewer is not expected to be in tatters or dirty clothing. In this case, it is better to err on the side of cleanliness. The essence of the interviewer image is to convey that one is in the proper role, to have an appearance that does not bring attention to the interviewer and that does not inhibit the respondent from replying in a truthful way.

Further, the interviewer should be as neutral as possible in the way that items are presented to the respondent. *Neutral* does not mean *boring*. If the respondent's interest is minimal, the interview is likely to be a painful experience for the respondent and interviewer. However, when the items are presented to the respondent, there should be no hint as to what the "right answer" should be.

The Interview Setting

While it is important to consider the characteristics of the interviewer, it is also important to structure the environment in which the interview is to be done in order to achieve maximum efficiency, accuracy, and rapport. In this section, attention is given to the setting of the interview. The relevant issues generally fall into two basic categories: (1) the physical setting in which the interview is to be done and (2) the specific role and posture of the interviewer.

The Physical Setting.   If the interview is to generate accurate information, the setting must be one in which the respondent and the interviewer feel comfortable and in which neither person is distracted from the task at hand. For example, if the study centered around worker attitudes and feelings about the work situation, interviewing the respondents on the job is likely to make them uncomfortable. Since the interviewer would have to get permission from management to conduct the study, management would know that some employees are being contacted for this study. Further, if sampled workers were seen talking to the interviewer and if negative features of the work situation were reported later, workers might be hesitant to participate in the study for fear of retribution, or, if the respondents participate, they may be less than candid in the answers given.

Consider another research objective, one which leads the researcher to study the degree of marital happiness among husbands. If this study were done in the respondent's home, the possibility of the man's wife being present at the time of the interview would most likely stimulate the husband to censor his responses. In such a case, it would be a good design decision to send a team of two interviewers who would interview the husband and wife at the same time but in separate rooms. This would minimize the likelihood of one spouse's overhearing or volunteering information for the other. Indeed, if the researcher was interested in marital happiness, it might be wise to examine both the husband and the wife.

In the above examples, the interview setting involved a "people problem" in the sense that the respondent may feel uncomfortable if the respondent's comments were overheard or if it

was known that the respondent was included in the study.

There are other setting problems that do not involve a concern with what other people think or believe. It may be that the environment is distracting and interferes with eliciting valid data. In many cases, the interviewer will have little choice of the physical setting, since most interviews are done in the respondent's home. While the home affords a maximum level of privacy, it can also be a major source of distraction. For example, if one was interviewing a young mother, the probability of frequent interruptions from the children may cause the mother to give the interviewer less than her undivided attention. In addition, the father's comment that he will be "along in a minute" to a young child starts to turn into an eternity for that child if the interview takes any appreciable amount of time. So even though the reluctance-to-participate factor is low, the setting may provide too many distractions for the respondent's comments to be of maximum validity.

Consider, as well, the distractions imposed on the interviewer. One of your authors was interviewing a young mother in a proposed urban renewal area. The mother was eager to participate and invited the interviewer to sit in the only chair in evidence in the living room. After sitting down, the mother's two children proceeded to climb into the interviewer's lap while he tried to juggle and organize a reasonably bulky schedule. While such circumstances are distracting for the most skilled interviewers, consider what the feelings of a novice might have been.

One final example will suffice to introduce other aspects of the setting: noise, heat, or cold, for example. It may be that one has difficulty conducting the interview because the respondent's home is adjacent to a major thoroughfare and the traffic generates a great amount of noise. The lack of air-conditioning in the home of a poor inner-city resident during the summer may also create an uncomfortable setting.

There are ways to combat almost all of these difficulties, but the problems generally must be anticipated before they occur. One cannot announce immediately after being admitted to the respondent's home that it is too noisy to do the interview and reschedule it. Remember that the respondent is likely to be a busy person whose time is important, and to waste it is not what the interviewer would want to do. Again, checking the nature of the neighborhood prior to sending one's interviewers out and similar preinterview activities may go a long way toward avoiding some of the problems with the setting in which the interview is to be done.

The Role of the Interviewer in the Interview Setting.   Earlier we presented a lengthy discussion about the steps to be taken in the preparation of the interviewer. At this point, we want to concentrate on a few additional thoughts that are relevant to the way in which the role of the interviewer should be enacted within the interview setting.

First, and of primary importance, one must remember the respondent is participating in the research study as a volunteer. The information that is communicated to the interviewer is given under the assumption that the information will be used for research purposes. Therefore, the information is confidential, if not anonymous, and should not be discussed with anyone other than the study director.

Second, one should not anticipate a response by helping the respondent complete a statement or formulate an idea. Rather, the interviewer should wait patiently for the respondent to frame the thoughts the respondent wants to communicate. Indeed, one of the most effective probes is that of silence; silence, while not putting words in the respondent's mouth, communicates that the interviewer is waiting for additional information.

Third, the interviewer should not summarize or rephrase the respondent's open-ended responses. Where such responses are called for, the interviewer must strive to record the respondent's reply as accurately as possible. The reason for this is twofold. First, the meaning conveyed by the respondent with one set of words may be different from the meaning conveyed by the interviewer's

substitution of different words. Second, sometimes the data analysts will want to have an exact recording of the respondent's comments because the items to which they pertain will have to be coded. While many items are precoded, sometimes the coding and interpretation of the respondent's comments must be delayed until such comments have been rendered. To put this another way, sometimes the researcher is interested in what the respondent would want to add to the interview. Accurately recording the respondent's comments is mandatory if the conceptualization of the responses has to be done after the data are collected.

Fourth, the final issue involves whether the interviewer should read the items exactly as they are written. There is a difference of opinion regarding this issue. Most researchers argue that the item should be read by the interviewer *exactly* as it is written. The argument is that subtle changes in the wording are likely to produce different responses from one respondent to another, and sometimes even from the same respondent. Generally, we tend to agree, but a caveat is warranted. If the item is designed to measure an *attitude,* it should be read exactly as it has been written. It is true that subtle shifts in wording of attitudinal items can produce different responses. Thus, if the respondent seems to be confused or does not understand what the item means, the interviewer must simply reread the item slowly, but exactly, as it is written and then pause to let the respondent think about it. Finally, when attitudinal items are being presented, they should be presented in the same order for all the respondents.

However, we would argue that the same position is unnecessarily rigid when applied to *behavioral* items. If one is interested in a more concrete piece of behavior, a rephrase of the question may be useful in gaining more valid data. We draw an example from the personal experience of one of the authors who was working on an urban renewal project. The survey was supposedly a family survey, but, in truth, it was an in-depth probe of the family's financial condition. Such information was necessary, because the local planning agency needed to know how much each urban renewal family could be expected to reasonably pay for redevelopment housing. The housing was to cost a certain amount to build, and the local planning agency had to arrange for the degree of subsidization that would be necessary. Thus, the family's financial condition had to be measured. One of the items on the schedule was a question which read: "What is your income?" This question was to be asked of everyone within the household. The most frequent reaction to this question was a long period of silence before the respondent would answer. Since your author represented local government, it was my distinct feeling that each person was quietly thinking, "What should I tell this person? Should I say the truth? If I give them a figure which is low, will I get more benefits? Or, if it's too high, will the Internal Revenue Service be after me?" While I can't be sure what the respondent was thinking, I was sure that the respondent was thinking something and that the answers that I received to this question were probably made on the basis of some consideration other than the truth. As a result, I changed the question asking, "Could you give me a rough estimate of your income; just a rough estimate?" This restatement of the question was taken by every subsequent respondent (except one who didn't want to talk to me about anything) as a nonthreatening question. The replies were surprisingly detailed and accurate. More than one respondent dug around in the desk in the living room looking for the last paycheck stub, which was then handed to me so that I could copy the gross and the net figures down to the last penny. Clearly, the first version of the question was viewed as threatening in some way and did not elicit valid data. The second version did. Such a problem should have been discovered during the pretest, but it wasn't (largely because there was no pretest in this applied study). While it is difficult to misinterpret an item that is designed to generate information on a person's behavior, attitudes are harder variables to measure, and subtle changes in wording can result in different replies. Questions about behavior, however, are much less subject to subtle

distinctions and can withstand changes in wording that are offered in the name of greater clarity.

Using Probes

Some attention must be given to the use of probes. In truth, if one is hypothesis testing with a structured schedule and structured response categories, the use of any type of probes is likely to be limited. If one is doing an exploratory study, however, or if one is interested in the respondent's feelings after the necessary information has been gathered, the probe may be helpful in eliciting further responses. *Probes* are verbal and nonverbal reactions on the part of the interviewer, which are designed to elicit additional information, expand an idea already offered by the respondent, redirect the respondent's attention, or clarify the respondent's position. As such, probes should not be of such a nature that they communicate to the respondent how that respondent should answer. In other words, probes should be neutral. Let us look at a few examples.

Eliciting Additional Information. If the respondent said something that seems appropriate for the study and the interviewer would like to know more about it, the interviewer might say, "Is there anything else you could tell me about this?" This kind of question is helpful in encouraging the respondent to talk further about the area that has just been discussed.

Expanding an Idea. If the interviewer would like the respondent to give more details about something, the researcher could use a probe such as, "What you've been talking about is very interesting. Could you tell me more about that?"

Clarifying a Comment. If the respondent says something that is interesting but the interviewer is not sure exactly what the respondent said, a probe is called for. Appropriate probes would be "How's that?" or "What do you mean by that?" Both of these questions encourage the respondent to think further about what the respondent has just said and to offer the respondent the opportunity to say something more about the subject.

Redirecting of the Respondent's Attention. Sometimes, in the course of an interview, the respondent will say something that is of particular interest to the interviewer. However, at the time the respondent may be too involved and excited to elaborate for the interviewer. If the interviewer were to interrupt with a probe at that moment, the respondent might think the interviewer really doesn't want to hear what he or she would like to say. In this circumstance, the interviewer should make a brief note of the statement of interest and when the respondent seems to have finished speaking, the interviewer may ask, "Earlier you mentioned your experiences in the military. Would you like to tell me more about that?" In this way, the interviewer maintains a greater degree of rapport but is able to get the respondent to return to a specific point of interest.

Silence. We again note the use of the silent probe. When two people are talking and a degree of rapport has been established, silence is one way a conversationalist can stimulate the other to continue. If the speaker stops talking and the listener does not say anything, there is that awkward moment when someone is supposed to be saying something. Silence can be a very effective stimulant to continued conversation. So can the occasional use of such short phrases as "Uh, Huh" or "I see." These phrases communicate that the interviewer is listening and expects the respondent to continue. The interviewer, while not wanting to influence the nature of the respondent's answers, certainly wants to convey interest in what the respondent has to say.

Let us close this section on probes with an experience of one of your authors. My wife and I had occasion to attend a dinner party at which another couple attending were not known to either of us. I was seated next to the wife of the newly introduced couple, and I must report that I found her conversation to be rather dull. Further, I was really tired and didn't make much of an effort to maintain my end of the conversation. When we were returning home, my wife remarked that I was not my usual "jolly" self. I replied that I was just tired. Later, when my wife called the hostess to thank her for the evening, the hostess said that the new couple's wife had really enjoyed her conversation with me. In truth, I had said little, but, as is often the case, one can build a positive reputation as a conversationalist if one keeps quiet and lets the other people do the talking. See the power of the silent probe!

THE TELEPHONE INTERVIEW

Introduction

Much of what we have said about face-to-face interviewing is germane to the *telephone interview*. Some considerations are not. For example, the interviewer does not need to share characteristics such as race, sex, or age with the respondent or to dress in a particular manner. While the carryover from our discussion of the face-to-face interview should be reasonably clear, a number of issues in successfully executing a telephone interview should be mentioned.

Previous Problems with Telephone Interviewing

One of the most pervasive objections to telephone interviewing in the past has been that telephone interviewing almost always produced a biased sample. First, those persons who tended to be poor were less likely to have telephones and, therefore, had no chance to be included. Second, there was a limited number of persons who had unlisted telephone numbers so that sampling from the telephone book assured omission of these persons as well.

Today, both of these problems have been substantially reduced. Recent research has indicated that the proportion of persons having telephones has grown from 72.5 percent in 1958 to 92.8 percent in 1976.[16] It can be safely argued that almost everyone—particularly those in urban areas—currently have telephone service. While the number of families with telephones has steadily risen, the number of persons with unlisted numbers has also risen. Although this trend has increased the potential for bias, this second objection to telephone interviewing can be compensated for by a newly conceived sampling technique called random digit dialing.

Random Digit Dialing

Random digit dialing (RDD) is a telephone sampling process wherein a computer program randomly selects any number of four-digit numerical sequences for previously selected telephone exchanges. The researcher supplies the first three numbers—which correspond to the local telephone exchange—of the seven-digit local number, and the computer generates on a random basis the remaining four numbers. Random digit dialing overcomes the problem of the unlisted telephone number, because the computer will pick any sequence of numbers from 0000 to 9999, regardless of whether the number is listed or unlisted. However, random digit dialing is not free of problems. First, some phone numbers are generated for commercial businesses that may be inappropriate for one's study. This type of problem is not crucial, however, since the researcher can apologize and offer an explanation that the RDD process is unable to separate business from residential numbers.

There is a more severe problem, however, that can be solved, but not easily. The telephone company has at its disposal 10,000 possible numbers for each exchange. For example, if the local exchange was 123, the telephone company could assign each telephone unit starting with 123-0000 through 123-9999, or 10,000 individual phone numbers. Often, however, every possible number has not been assigned. That is, the telephone company may have allocated only 123-0000 through 123-5698 at the time when the researcher uses the RDD procedure. Thus, numbers 123-5699 through 123-9999, while possible for future individual telephone lines, are currently not in use. Therefore,

when the RDD procedure generates, say, 123-7896, the number may ring but there will be no one to answer. A prerecorded message from the telephone company will intercept the call with a message like "This number is not in service."[17] This message may mean any number of things from "the number is not assigned," "the person who had it really exists but has asked for a new number," or "the person who had it really exists but has had the telephone service discontinued for some reason." The only way to eliminate this confusion is to contact the telephone company and ask for a list of the numbers that have been allocated for each relevant exchange. Unfortunately, some telephone companies are reluctant to provide such information. Further, while a relatively minor problem, the telephone customer does have the right to request a specific final four digit number if that number is not currently being used. Thus, while the telephone company may have sequentially used numbers 123-0000 through 123-5698, this does not mean that someone cannot have number 123-7500 or 123-9000 by individual request. This latter problem is likely to create only a minimal error in the RDD procedure.

In sum, we would argue that RDD is an important breakthrough in sampling procedure for the telephone interview, because it reduces the chances of omitting those with unlisted numbers. There remains, however, the minor difficulty with unused numbers' being miscounted as "unable to contact" persons.

Computer-assisted Telephone Interviewing

A more recent development is the emergence of computer-assisted telephone interviewing. *Computer-assisted telephone interviewing (CATI)* involves an interactive computer program with which the researcher preprograms the questions to be asked along with appropriate prompts and probes, if any, as well as the proper sequence and the coding process to be used for entering the respondent's responses. By so doing, the interviewer is able to follow the schedule items on a computer monitor while the interviewer talks with the respondent. When the respondent replies, the interviewer immediately enters the respondent's replies into the computer using the keyboard. The responses are automatically coded and entered into a data file that has been predefined and organized for the preliminary data analysis.

In essence, CATI eliminates the face-to-face interviewing steps of hand recording the responses, subsequent coding of these responses, and entering the coded responses into a computer data file. Because CATI anticipates these three steps, they are preprogrammed, combined, and executed automatically when the interviewer records the responses. Further, a stricter control over the question order is possible, since the interviewer must follow the sequence of items as they appear on the computer monitor. Therefore, this process is more efficient in that it substantially reduces the time necessary to prepare the respondent's responses for analysis and it eliminates the potential for a great amount of measurement error, such as the inaccurate transposition of coded material.

Persuading the Person Called to Participate

Telephone interviewing is a recommended format of interviewing because of the obvious economy of time and money when compared to face-to-face interviewing. While it is possible for the randomly digit-dialed person to refuse to participate by simply hanging up the telephone, experience indicates that hanging up is behavior that most people find difficult to do. That is, telephone etiquette seems to dictate politeness on the part of the person who answers the telephone. So, while it may appear to be easy to hang up on a strange voice, most people do not or cannot do so. This reluctance is to the advantage of the researcher as it has led to reasonably high response rates to the telephone interview design.

However, a word of caution is appropriate. One of the fastest growing sales strategies is in the telemarketing industry, where callers contact potential clients in an attempt to sell various products and services. The telemarketing people often claim that they are doing a "survey," which quickly turns into a sales pitch. Such marketing strategies

may sour the general public on participation in scientifically based nonsales-oriented research surveys. We suspect that everyone who is reading this paragraph has been called away at some time from the dinner table, for example, by someone who is inquiring about putting aluminum siding on your brick home or by someone who would like to sell you a new hot-air furnace when you have radiators filled with hot water. Such marketing efforts are numerous for the same reason that telephone interviewing is desirable—the cost and the time to do them are considerably less than sending salespeople into the field.

For the reasons suggested above, it is necessary for the telephone interviewer to generate almost instant rapport with the respondent. If one is using the random digit dialing procedure, it is not possible to contact the respondent prior to the phone call to attempt to persuade the respondent to participate. The researcher has much the same difficulty that exists with the mailed questionnaire. If the cover letter in a mailed questionnaire design does not create interest, the respondent is not likely to participate. Similarly, if the first few comments made by the caller in a telephone interview survey do not immediately peak the respondent's interest, one may have lost such a person as a participant. However, if one has a list of persons with their phone numbers and addresses from which the calls will be made, the researcher could write potential respondents a letter similar to the cover letter before the call is made. This may allow the respondent to think somewhat about the request, hence reducing the respondent's need to make an immediate and unconsidered judgment concerning participation.

Is the Telephone Answerer the Right Person?

While the caller may reach the desired telephone number, the person reached may not be the desired respondent. Therefore, the telephone interviewer must be prepared to react to children, who may be home when the parents are not, or the baby-sitter. It may be that one is interested in sampling any adult person who is living at the address. If the researcher has a choice of respondents, the researcher has to decide if the first person who answers the phone is appropriate or whether some further sampling strategy is to be pursued, such as alternating male and female respondents.

Summary

Telephone interviewing is a comparatively new survey design. With the assistance of random digit dialing and computer-assisted telephone interviewing, the telephone survey has the potential to greatly reduce the costs of the interviewing process and the problem of unlisted phone numbers. However, the possibility of respondent irritation due to the heavy volume of telemarketing may create reluctance to participate in this form of interviewing. It is a little early to tell, but research on these sampling and data-gathering strategies will be done, and the results will be interesting. Currently, it looks as if RDD and CATI will prove to be valuable research techniques for the social scientist in the future.

COMPARISON OF THE QUESTIONNAIRE AND THE INTERVIEW DESIGNS

Introduction

We have delayed comparison of the mailed questionnaire, face-to-face interview, and telephone interview until now, because we wanted you to have some familiarity with the characteristics of each procedure.

Before we look at the differences, let us mention some of the advantages and disadvantages of all three, which generally fall under the rubric of the survey design.

Advantages and Disadvantages of Surveys

Advantages.   One of the key advantages of the survey design is that it is particularly appropriate for assessing characteristics of a large number of people. Second, the survey design is the only really viable avenue through which one can measure people's attitudes. One can observe other

people's behavior (or the documents and artifacts that they produce), but the only way to measure a feeling or attitude is to ask the person what that person is feeling. Third, the survey design can be used in exploratory research and hypothesis testing, as the unstructured interview using an interview guide and the structured questionnaire or interview using a schedule, respectively, illustrate. Fourth, even though there are differences, each technique is an efficient data-gathering device. Fifth, surveys can be used in the investigation of a large range of topics. Sixth, surveys are particularly good if the researcher is interested in collecting data that are to be analyzed comparatively from one respondent to another.

Disadvantages.   The survey is not without some difficulties. First, though behavior can be measured with a survey design, it is not being directly measured as could be done in an observational design. Rather, behavior is measured indirectly as it is reported to the researcher. Thus, such reports may be erroneous due to respondent errors, such as deliberate lying to preserve one's self-respect, misinterpretation or misreading of schedule items, misinformation due to memory failure, and the face-saving socially desirable response, to cite but a few. (However, it is possible to construct items in ways that are likely to minimize these problems.)

Second, surveys—especially those using a structured schedule—are not flexible. To maintain comparability between respondents, the same items should be presented in the same order. Should an insight emerge during the data-gathering phase, adjustments in the focus of the measuring instrument will be difficult, if not impossible. (However, one might compensate for the inflexibility of the schedule by adding additional items *at the end* of the schedule to handle the circumstances that were unanticipated in the construction and pretesting phases of the research design.)

Summary.   These characteristics reflect advantages and disadvantages of any type of survey design, although any point may be more pronounced for one type as opposed to the others. We now turn to a comparison of the three basic survey designs with attention directed to specific dimensions.

Comparisons

Introduction. There are a number of concerns when considering a survey design. Among those to be discussed are the nature of the study, the cost in money and time, the nature of the sample to be investigated, the response rate, difficult schedule items, interviewer contributions, contextual factors, and supervision of the interviewers.

Nature of the Study. Any type of questionnaire design presumes that the researcher has a pretty firm notion of what is needed to attain the objective of the study. However, if the objective is in the context of discovery or if the study is exploratory, the interview design is strongly recommended. Further, if one is searching for interesting but as yet unknown aspects of the research object, the formation of a general list of questions (an interview guide) in response to which the respondent is encouraged to talk at length in the respondent's own words is well advised. Use of a guide allows the interviewer some degree of flexibility in terms of the topics on which to probe and on which to change the basic focus of the interview when previous respondents have indicated dimensions of seeming importance that have not been anticipated in the planning phase of the study.

Use of the questionnaire is advisable when the researcher has a clear notion of the objectives of the measuring instrument, while use of the interview guide and interview design would appear crucial to the discovery of information. Thus, structured questionnaires would seem desirable if one were hypothesis testing, while unstructured interviews would be best if one were doing exploratory research.

Costs. By far the most expensive survey design is the face-to-face interview. Since the interviewer will be in the field for substantial periods of time, the interview training period must be greater. Fur-

ther, any telephone contact with the "home office" for the purpose of discussing field problems will be substantial, especially if the sample extends beyond the confines of a single metropolitan community or geographical area. If interviewers must spend nights in the field, the costs of travel, lodging, and meals must be added to the research budget, as well as the interviewer's salary. Finally, it is not uncommon for an interviewer to only complete two or three interviews per day. Even this virtually maximum effort must be tempered by frustrated efforts to contact respondents who forgot the appointment or who were unwilling to talk at the moment that the interviewer arrived. For these specific reasons and others, face-to-face interviews are very expensive as compared to questionnaire designs and telephone interviewing.

Telephone interviewing involves contacting those sampled and administering the measuring instrument over the telephone. Obviously, certain costs are substantially reduced: field expenses (no lodging, travel, or meals), interviewer salaries (less actual interviewing time because of easier call-back procedures), training costs (because training can continue through the actual interviewing with the aid of the study supervisor), and general expenses (because all the interviewers can be headquartered in the same place).

The mailed questionnaire design is the least expensive survey design, with the major cost being postage. In this design, the costs of human labor are reduced to a minimum.

Costs can also be measured on the basis of the time spent executing the study. From this viewpoint, mailing the schedule consumes the least amount of time in that the schedule is moving through the mails to everyone in the sample at the same time. The telephone interview is the next most time-consuming, because a staff of interviewers must sit at the telephones and call each person in the sample. Face-to-face interviewing is most time-consuming, since the interviewer must not only make contact with the respondent (as in the telephone interview) but also go to the respondent. This travel is much more time-consuming than the mailed questionnaire or the telephone interview techniques.

When one's sample is geographically dispersed, the questionnaire design is quite useful, because it eliminates the travel, lodging, and meal costs that the interview design would incur. Further, a mailed questionnaire design gets the measuring instrument to everyone in the sample at approximately the same time.

Nature of the Sample to be Investigated. The most desirable data-gathering design to use may be indicated by the nature of the persons whom the researcher wishes to contact. If the sample is composed of persons who are likely to be interested in the subject matter of the survey and if they are reasonably well educated, the mailed questionnaire has a high probability of being successful. For example, if one wanted to assess the feelings of the members of the National Rifle Association about the antigun legislation that has passed recently in the state of Maryland, this group would be very anxious to make its feelings known and would willingly participate in the survey. Similarly, members of the American Medical Association are likely to be interested in any study of health care. Alternatively, ask any professor what should be done about general university requirements, and one would be in for a longer discussion than the questioner might want to endure. Since the mailed questionnaire puts the burden of completion on the respondent, interest will result in a higher response rate.

However, if the sample is likely to have little or no interest in the research, the interview technique would seem to be more appropriate. The central reason for utilizing the interview data-gathering technique is that respondents often find it difficult to deny the interviewer. After all, the interviewer is making a major effort in time and energy to contact the respondent at the respondent's convenience. So, if one can make face-to-face contact with the person sampled, it is usually difficult for the respondent to reject the interview, especially if the interviewer follows the proper role requirements discussed earlier. Conversely, if the recipi-

ent of the mailed questionnaire schedule is not interested in the research subject, it is easy to toss the instrument into the trash can. In sum, one has to exert substantial effort to thwart a well-trained interviewer who is standing on the respondent's front porch.

One should also consider the mental and physical abilities of the sample. For example, if the sample has low educational attainment, the mailed questionnaire will likely generate a high nonresponse rate of persons who cannot complete the instrument. With a less literate sample, the face-to-face interview will generate a higher rate of response and a better completion of the items on the schedule itself. Further, the mailed questionnaire may be difficult to complete, even for the willing person, if the respondent is a senior citizen. Infirmities such as arthritis may make writing the responses difficult, or the size of the print may be difficult to read. In these cases, the face-to-face interview is recommended.

Response Rate. While the mailed questionnaire is likely to have the largest nonresponse rate of the three types of surveys, it will vary significantly. Again, if the research subject interests the respondent, the response rate will be higher than if the subject does not. There is little question, however, that if one's interviewers have been properly trained, the face-to-face interview will generate very high response rates. With the likelihood of persons hanging up, the telephone interview probably results in an intermediate response rate.

Difficult Schedule Items. It may be that the researcher has included a series of contingency or filter items on the schedule. These items may be difficult or impossible for most respondents to follow on their own, so the mailed questionnaire should be avoided in favor of the interview techniques—either face-to-face or telephone. The interview designs are likely to reduce significantly the "don't know" or "no answer" choices that the respondent is more likely to make on the mailed questionnaire. Finally, if the researcher has a limited number of embarrassing items, the mailed questionnaire, which is (or could be) anonymous, should encourage the respondent to reply, since the respondent will not have to risk sacrificing self-esteem in the presence of the interviewer. Parenthetically, it is possible to combine the interview with the questionnaire design to cover embarrassing or highly personal items. That is, the interviewer can proceed with the part of the schedule that is not embarrassing in the interview mode. When the embarrassing part must be done, the interviewer can give the respondent a paper with the embarrassing items and ask the respondent to fill in the answers. This technique saves the respondent from having to talk about the items. The disadvantage is that the interviewer will have to make a notation on the respondent's questionnaire portion of the schedule so that the questionnaire and interview parts can be combined during the data analysis. Such a notation would interfere with the implied anonymity of the respondent's participation on the questionnaire portion of the interview—a question of ethics with which the researcher will have to wrestle.

Interviewer Contributions.   A primary advantage to the face-to-face interview is what the interviewer can do in addition to presenting the schedule items. First, the interviewer can observe those items that appear to be upsetting to the respondent. Second, the interviewer can note inflections or voice changes indicating a higher level of excitement or agitation on the part of the respondent. Third, the interviewer can note the surroundings in which the interview takes place. Often, such observational data can provide important clues about the respondent—data about which the interviewer does not have to and, maybe, would not want to ask. For example, the interviewer may note from the type of magazines or books that are lying about the living room additional information about the interviewee, using the long heralded Chapin Living Room Scale to assess the socioeconomic status of the household.

The interviewer can also better control the nature of the setting for collecting the information. For example, the interviewer may be able to reduce the number of distractions from other members of the household by asking the respondent if there is a quiet place where they can talk. Further, the interviewer can note the precise time during which the interview was done. (We know time of day, week, month, and year may function as class III variables. Noting the time and date provide data indicating the direction and intensity of their impact.) If the order of the schedule items is largely unimportant, the interviewer has some degree of flexibility in going through the interview, thereby permitting the use of probes as they may seem appropriate. Additionally, if a part of the research objective can be better served through the use of visual aids—pictures, graphs, or similar items, the face-to-face interview design is helpful. Indeed, if one has a matrix of Likert response category items, the interviewer can explain the meanings of the responses and hand the respondent a card with the responses already printed on it. This will reduce the boredom of their repetition after each item is read. Finally, the interviewer can control who responds to the survey. None of these considerations are possible when the respondent is dealing with a mailed questionnaire.

Of course, the interview situation has its drawbacks. It bears repeating that the face-to-face interview will be expensive compared to the telephone interview or the mailed questionnaire. One risks some degree of interviewer bias, although the proper training of one's interviewers should significantly reduce this difficulty. Finally, the face-to-face interview precludes any pretense toward anonymity on the part of the respondent.

Contextual Factors.   One should consider the neighborhood or community in which the data are to be gathered. If one is working in a large metropolitan community (particularly in areas with high crime), the respondent and interviewer are likely to feel some degree of uneasiness. In such cases, the telephone interview may be a better strategy to pursue.

Supervision of the Interviewers.   The project director will want to occasionally check on the work that the interviewers are doing. If the training has been good and the interviewers are paid a fair wage, falsifying the data and similar difficulties with interviewers are likely to be minimal. Nevertheless, one should check on the progress of the interviewing staff. This process is quite difficult if the interviewers are conducting face-to-face interviews but more easily achieved if the staff is in the "bull pen" at the project director's laboratory or office. In a central location, the director can work simultaneously with the entire interviewing staff.

A CONCLUDING COMMENT

We cannot condense this chapter into a few statements. Rather, let us take this opportunity to say that there are a great number of legitimate variations on the central themes that we have presented. Probably no where in social research is it more obvious than in survey data-gathering designs that the researcher cannot operate by the numbers. Knowledge of the nature of one's sample, the complexities of the measuring instrument, practical limitations connected with the funding and scope of the proposed research, and other important dimensions all conspire to make certain data-gathering approaches more desirable than others. Clearly, for every time we say "Do this," there will be a situation in which the suggested strategy is not the most desirable. Again, knowledge of the details presented in this chapter is no substitute for thinking about one's research study.

Finally, we end the way we began by urging you to check the bibliographic citations. There are a number of excellent treatises that provide much more information and insight into the nature of the survey designs than we can incorporate into a single chapter. We particularly recommend Dillman (1978) and Gorden (1987), both of whom have devoted considerable time and effort to the study and testing of various approaches to the survey designs.

KEY TERMS

Anonymity	Interview guide	Random-digit dialing (RDD)
Close-ended response categories	Interview schedule	Rationale
Computer-assisted telephone interviewing (CATI)	Interviewer	Respondent
	Key respondents	Response rate
Confidentiality	Letter of introduction	Schedule
Cover letter	Mailed questionnaire	Structured items
Face-to-face interview	Nonmailed questionnaire	Structured schedule interview
Follow-up mailings	Open-ended response	Survey
Initial mailing	Probe	Telephone interviewing
Interview	Questionnaire	Unstructured items

REVIEW QUESTIONS

1. Let's assume that one wanted to study nursing home patients' attitudes about the quality of health care they are receiving. Choose the more appropriate research-design posture among each pair of choices given.

   a. Interview or questionnaire
   b. Schedule or guide
   c. Structured or unstructured measuring instrument
   d. Open-ended or close-ended response categories

2. Why does computer-assisted telephone interviewing (CATI) seem such a promising survey data-gathering technique? What advantages does it have over the face-to-face interview and the mailed questionnaire?

3. In a mailed questionnaire design, why is the cover letter so important? What does *monitoring the returns* mean, and why is this significant?

4. What are the steps in the interview training procedure, and what is one trying to accomplish here?

5. What are probes? Identify the different functions that probes have.

6. Why is random digit dialing (RDD) important to computer-assisted telephone interviewing (CATI)?

7. List the advantages and disadvantages of the face-to-face interview and the mailed questionnaire data-gathering designs.

8. Under what conditions is one's response rate to a mailed questionnaire likely to be acceptable?

CHAPTER 11

EXPERIMENTAL AND QUASI-EXPERIMENTAL STUDY DESIGNS

INTRODUCTION

Upon completion of the conceptual model, the investigator has reached that point in the research project where a number of methodologically relevant decisions must be considered. Is the research *exploratory* in nature, whereby some preliminary insight is the objective? Is *description* of some particular social activity or segment of the society the focus? Is the investigator proposing to *explain* some phenomenon? Indeed, most research efforts will be reflective of all of these questions, but the emphasis of one will influence the eventual selection of a specific research design.

Further, if the researcher adopted a practical view in the initial thinking or idea stage, some attention has already been afforded considerations of financial resources in support of the project, the availability of potential respondents, time constraints, the need for a research staff, and so forth. To be candid, response to these questions will have inevitably influenced the nature and extent of the original statement of the problem and, ultimately, the hypothesis or hypotheses to be tested.

The interaction of these thoughts and constraints points to the inextricable intertwining of the conceptual model and the research design, a point we have emphasized throughout this text. That is, although a research effort requires consideration of a number of steps, all of the procedures go together to form a singular, overall effort. Not only do the parts comprise a whole, but also, as we have noted, decisions rendered for one step also affect the decisions in other areas. Nowhere is the importance of this interaction more evident than in the investigator's selection of a study design, particularly an experimental or quasi-experimental design.

DISTINCTION OF ALTERNATIVE DESIGNS

The purpose of generating a hypothesis is to present a statement of a relationship between variables that can be tested empirically. In the chapters of this unit our focus is directed toward selecting a design and a method of data collection that will permit that examination and, ultimately, will lead to the decision of whether to reject or fail to reject hypotheses.

In making a data-gathering decision, the researcher may select from experimental, quasi-experimental, and non-experimental designs and methods. Although each of these categories of methods has been used profitably in the testing of hypotheses, they should not be viewed as being equal. Each has capabilities that recommend usage in some circumstances and not in others.

If all things were equal, the scientist would employ an experimental design. However, the investigator must always address three feasibility questions: (1) is it physically possible to conduct the proposed study; (2) are financial resources available to support the study; and (3) does the study violate any ethical considerations?

In the real world all things are rarely equal, and one or more of the feasibility questions often result in a negative response or one of inadequacy relative to the selection of an experimental design. In this light, and consistent with our earlier discussions of many methodological considerations, which method the researcher elects to pursue will depend upon the problem to be investigated, why the study is being conducted, the resources available, and other relevant issues. In responding to these issues, we encourage flexibility and urge the researcher to refrain from forcing a stronger method or technique when it does not fit.

Ultimately the researcher is interested in establishing causality, or lending evidence of such, for the independent variables in their relationship to the dependent variable. To do this, one must construct a blueprint. This can be accomplished by answering the questions of what is to be examined, why the particular phenomenon is to be studied, and how it will be studied. In a nutshell, the what, why, and how questions summarize the purpose of research design.

Although the experimental and quasi-experimental approaches differ, it is our contention that the general logic of testing hypotheses experimentally remains the same. Because of this similarity, we have elected to include them in one chapter and to address the non-experimental alternatives in the other chapters of Part III.

BASIC CONSIDERATIONS

The investigator conducting an *experiment* is in a position to control the introduction of the independent variable or variables. That is, the experiment requires the purposeful manipulation or alteration of one or more independent variables. The researcher can determine not only which members of a sample are exposed to the stimulus but also the intensity of such exposure. By virtue of this control, the researcher is in a position to examine the effect or effects of the independent variable or variables as directly as possible. This ability to observe the causality of the independent variable or variables represents the most important advantage of the experiment.

If an experiment is to maximize an effective hypothesis test, however, the control of the independent variable or variables must be accompanied by control of all other variables (i.e., changing Kish's class III and class IV variables into class II

variables), which might influence the phenomenon being studied. While this level of control is more likely to be maximized in a laboratory setting, most questions of interest to the social scientist simply do not lend themselves to laboratory investigation. Even in those that do, one must be careful in projecting the results from the artificial environment of the laboratory to the real world.

A second condition that applies generally to experimental designs is that the persons who compose the groups that will be exposed or denied exposure to the test stimulus must be selected randomly. If this condition is satisfied, the researcher has additional, although not complete, confidence that any observed differences between the groups can be attributed to exposure to the stimulus in question. Again, while this procedure can be accomplished somewhat easily within the confines of a laboratory, the circumstances of the real world can often frustrate this effort. Indeed, the ideal situation calls for what is termed a *double-blind experiment* in which neither the members of the study population nor those conducting the experiment are aware of who is exposed to the test stimulus and who is not. This requires the administration of a placebo to the control group. A *placebo* has the appearance of the test stimulus, but it is a facade. For example, sugar pills are often used as placebos in medical and pharmacological research.

Indeed, in testing the effects of a new medication, the placebo and double-blind components can be used profitably. The examining physicians are not told which patients are receiving the test drug, and the patients in the control group are given the sugar pill (placebo) which does little but dissolve. In this manner those doing the observing are not as likely to note change when no change has occurred or to fail to observe that which has occurred. We will discuss the double-blind approach in greater detail when we introduce the classical experimental design. At this point, however, the logic of experimentation serves to illustrate the importance of randomization in determining causality.

There are other advantages and disadvantages to experiments. For example, experiments are:

Example **241**

(1) convenient in that the researcher determines when they will be conducted; (2) they are usually, although not always, cheaper to conduct; and (3) they are easier to repeat. Indeed, *replication* has always been recognized as a most helpful way of increasing the confidence in one's results.

On the other hand, the impossibility of experimenting with some real world conditions and the lack of reality of the laboratory environment argue against use of the experiment.*

All of us have conducted individual experimentation throughout our lives. We have, for example, determined which suntan lotion aids us in achieving the best tan, or, at least, reduces the likelihood of a bad burn, by testing a variety of them over a number of summers. Also, we have learned a set of study habits that aid us in determining how much effort we must invest to learn a given volume of material. However, the conditional requirements, especially with regard to control, for conducting an experiment on a larger population base are often inappropriate for the use of experimental designs for the investigation of many social science research questions.

UNITS OF ANALYSIS

The concept of units of analysis was introduced in Chapter 6. You will recall that testing a hypothesis requires the selection of units of analysis that will permit specific examination of the variables presented in that hypothesis. Since we are interested in social science propositions, the most obvious units of analysis for our ideas are people. However, tapping individuals will not always result in the most efficient or accurate assessment of our propositions. We often are better served by examining a collection of individuals who are bound together in some distinctive set of social relationships, which may be a social group. You'll recall

the example of income for the Burnett family presented in Chapter 6. We will obtain a much more accurate understanding of the financial well being of the Burnett family by looking at family income than if income of a single member of the unit were examined. Similarly, sociologists study social groups such as fraternities and sororities, neighborhoods within a community, and athletic teams as units of analysis. The sociologist's interest in groups also extends to more formal collections or organizations such as corporations, branches of government, or church structures. Finally, social researchers may find an excellent source for units of analysis among social artifacts, which we discuss in Chapter 12. That discussion reflects the importance of personal and public documents, such as newspapers, books, films, television programming, letters, and diaries, as materials suitable for content analysis. Titles, chapters, and specific articles might serve as units of analysis from these sources.

Serious thought about the most appropriate units of analysis is important because of the potential for committing an *ecological fallacy,* i.e., attributing some value that is descriptive of one unit of analysis to the value of some other unit. The researcher must examine the hypothesis to be tested carefully and select the proper unit. To fail to do so invites the likelihood of committing an ecological fallacy and, quite possibly, registering an erroneous decision regarding the overall hypothesis.

EXAMPLE

Let us say that we share the concern expressed by the former Secretary of Health, Education, and Welfare Joseph Califano when he suggested that adolescent pregnancy represents the number one health problem confronting teenagers in America

---

*College students, for example, are often used as subjects in laboratory experiments. We would argue that it is not reasonable to believe they can assume the roles of political figures, civic leaders, major figures in the business world, or any other role that they have not experienced. Nevertheless, results of laboratory studies that have dealt with manipulation of power, economic decisions, social programs, and other important social dimensions have been presented as strong evidence for one set of actions or another. While this is an often-found difficulty, it is important to understand that it is a problem of sampling rather than one of the data-gathering design.

today. There are currently approximately one million pregnancies per year among adolescents. Of these, approximately 650,000 result in full-term deliveries. After a review of the relevant literature of this large-scale social problem, we believe that a full social- and medical-intervention program would facilitate an increase in healthy deliveries for those adolescents who are pregnant, reduce the number of subsequent pregnancies during the adolescent period of these mothers, increase the number who return to school following delivery, ultimately contribute to more productive workers in the economic marketplace, and reduce the number of persons receiving economic assistance from local, state, and federal governments.

To generate confidence for the hypothesis, we wish to gather empirical evidence. Clearly, our preference would be to select an experimental design that called for a minimum of two groups. One group, the *experimental group,* would be exposed to the proposed intervention effort, while the other group, the *control group,* would not.* Overall selection and assignment to the respective groups would be done by a statistically random selection process. Further, we would control the content of the intervention effort, as well as the frequency, duration, and intensity of exposure of the subjects to the stimulus.

The first question, of course, is whether we can bring this ideal experiment to fruition. To answer, we must address the three feasibility questions noted earlier. The first problem we face is the physical possibility of establishing such a program. We would require the cooperation of an obstetrics-gynecology staff and administrators of a conveniently located hospital. We would also require a staff of health educators, social workers, and counselors to provide the educational component of the intervention effort. Some hospitals have such persons on their permanent staff, and to locate such an institution would be an enormous

help. Although not likely, let us assume that we do manage to discover such a hospital.

In order to conduct our experiment, the Department of Obstetrics and Gynecology would have to agree to provide all medical services that might be required from the time the pregnancy is confirmed, throughout the prenatal period, and concluding with the postpartum visit. Not only do we seek traditional obstetrical care, but we are interested in these particular adolescent patients who are being seen every two weeks during pregnancy. Although this is a more frequent visit schedule than that maintained by more mature pregnant women, we feel this recommendation is reasonable in light of the greater risks faced by adolescents. That is, we are seeking medical attention for prospective mothers who are not yet mature, biologically or socially. Consequently, they are nurturing the growth and development of a fetus and their own growth.

We also want the prospective mothers to be exposed to a component of the intervention educational program every two weeks. We are planning seminar presentations on relevant subjects such as nutrition, human sexuality, family planning, infant care, maternal expectations, and the importance of continuing their formal educational efforts. Similarly, the counselors and social workers will provide an opportunity for the prospective mothers to discuss their fears, hopes, anxieties, and other concerns on a one-to-one basis.

It is obvious that the provision and coordination of all of these medical and social services at these frequent intervals will require a cooperative spirit among all staff members—medical and educational.

For the purpose of continuing our discussion, let us assume that in the face of the national and local incidence of adolescent pregnancy and parenthood, a local hospital, with medical and educational staff, has agreed to provide the requested

---

*The control group would, however, receive traditional medical attention during the pregnancy and delivery, which would make it, strictly speaking, a *comparison group*. For humanitarian and ethical reasons, the researcher would not want to deny the normal medical procedures to these patients as they would have to be denied to a "control" group.

services and at the frequent intervals for which the study design calls. Perhaps they will insist upon some maximum number of patients or length of time the program will be continued. These are likely to be reasonable limits, however, within which we can live. Therefore, the first feasibility question of physical possibility has been answered in the affirmative, and our hypothetical example of a pure experimental research design is still a realistic possibility.

The second question is whether the study is financially feasible. In reality, we could not address the question of physical possibility without substantial input from the financial dimension. We will, therefore, take our proposed study to a number of grant-giving agencies. Since this is a hypothetical illustration, we will argue that adequate funding is obtained.*

The third question focuses upon whether the proposed study can be conducted ethically. In our opinion, this question could be responded to in an affirmative or negative manner. Which of these answers is given will be dependent upon some of the decisions we make regarding the parameters of the study. It is certainly ethical to provide the medical care, educational exposure, and counseling opportunities that we have proposed.

The ethical difficulty arises with the assignment of pregnant adolescents to either the experimental or control group. In our opinion, one cannot ethically assign persons on a random basis to a treatment or nontreatment group. If a prospective mother knows of our program and wishes to participate, we believe she must be permitted to do so. Conversely, if she does not wish to participate, we do not believe she can or should be forced into the program. Indeed, this question of inclusion and exclusion interferes with most efforts in medicine to conduct pure experiments in order to assess the efficacy of different treatment modalities. It should be emphasized that self-selection into

either of the groups would have an impact upon the interpretation of any social or social psychological data to be analyzed.

Our study could be further compromised by the interaction between the medical and nonmedical components of the staff. Although cooperation has been promised, it is quite possible—indeed probable—that physicians would question the legitimacy of nonmedical personnel's being privy to the medical records of the prospective mothers. Parenthetically, this overlap between the physical and ethical dimensions should suggest that feasibility and ethical issues are not mutually exclusive.

The ethical considerations in this study clearly obviate the potential for a pure experiment. We emphasize, however, that this does not suggest we terminate the study. Rather, it recommends the use of a quasi-experimental design. In all candor, most social science research efforts, and particularly those conducted outside of the laboratory, represent some form of compromise with the ideal experiment. Negative responses to one or more of the feasibility questions lead the researcher to the quasi-experimental alternatives.

EXPERIMENTAL DESIGNS

Introduction

The basic designs of proof were introduced by John Stuart Mill over a century ago. Despite a century that witnessed an incredible explosion in scientific interest, practitioners, and accomplishments, his canons of evidence for causality, with but minor modifications, remain the basis of experimental pursuit. The reason is that simple logic does not change. One modification for which we strongly argue is the substitution of the term "evidence" for "proof." As we have previously noted, "proof" denotes a finality that we do not believe

---

*One must be careful from whom funds are requested. The expectations of some funding agencies sometimes exceed that which is reasonable. One of your authors once received a relatively small grant and was then expected to travel to a different city each week to speak about the study. There was so much travel and preparation for the presentations that there was very little time to conduct the study. One should avoid this type of circumstance.

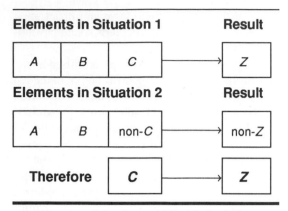

Elements in Situation 1   **Result**

| A | B | C | → | Z |

Elements in Situation 2   **Result**

| A | B | non-C | → | non-Z |

Therefore | C | → | Z |

FIGURE 11.1   John Stuart Mill's Method of Difference

can be justified in any arena of science, but especially not in the social sciences. However, rather than offer another detailed discussion of Mill's designs, we encourage your review of our presentation in Chapter 4.

The Classical Experimental Design

Introduction.   The first experimental design is the *classical experimental design,* illustrated in Figure 11.2. It is reflective of the canon of the *method of difference* (Figure 11.1), explained by Mill. His objective here was to address the weaknesses of the positive and negative canons of agreement. Although there are still weaknesses, this design does represent a substantial improvement. It can be stated as follows: "If there are two cases which have all factors in common except that in one case there is a factor and a phenomenon while in the other case there is no factor or phenomenon, then there is a causal relationship between the factor and the phenomenon."[1]

We invite you to examine the similarity between Mill's conceptualization and the classical experimental design used by the contemporary researcher, which is presented in Figure 11.2.

Although the two diagrams presented in Figures 11.1 and 11.2 may appear to be quite different, they are in fact virtually identical.* You will observe that Mill's method of difference has two situations. This is mirrored by the classical design where one must also have a minimum of two groups. Looking more closely at the two diagrams, we find additional parallels. The method of difference suggests that Situation 1 and Situation 2 contain the element labeled *A*. The classical design is similar in that an observation (measurement)—B_e and B_c—is recorded for both groups prior to administering the test stimulus. Similarly, both of Mill's situations contain the element *B*, while both groups in the classical design are measured (A_e and A_c) after the test stimulus has been administered to the experimental group (E_1). The exposure of the experimental group (E_1) to the test stimulus within the classical design reflects the presence of element *C* within Situation 1 of the method of difference. By the same token, element *non-C* in Situation 2 is equal to the denial of exposure to the test stimulus by the control group (C_1). It is important to note that in the method of difference a very specific absence is referred to by the element *non-C*. Clearly, elements *A* and *B* are not *C,* but they do not constitute the specific element *non-C*. Similarly, the label *non-Z* refers to a specific absence of the effect in which the researcher is interested.

The presence of *Z* or *non-Z* in the classical design is assessed in terms of differences between the two sets of measurements for the respective study groups. If the hypothesis being tested is

---

*In Figure 11.2 and all the remaining figures in this chapter, we have tried to be consistent in our use of symbolization. Thus, *B* (uppercase *B*) refers to a *measurement* taken at time one (t_1), or a before measure, and *A* (uppercase *A*) refers to a *measurement* done at time three (t_3), or an after measure. The stimulus will intervene between the before (*B*) and after (*A*) measures at time two (t_2), if appropriate. Additionally, the *e* (subscript lowercase *e*) refers to an experimental group measure, while *c* (subscript lowercase *c*) refers to a control group measure. If there is *more than* one experimental or control group, the numerical subscript will identify which group is indicated. Finally, the *E* or *C* (uppercase *E* and *C*) refers to the particular *group* that is otherwise identified within the figure.

GROUP	BEFORE (t_1)	STIMULUS (t_2)	AFTER (t_3)	
Experimental (E_1)	B_e	Yes	A_e	Difference 1 = $A_e - B_e$
Control (C_1)	B_c	No	A_c	Difference 2 = $A_c - B_c$

[Overall Difference 3] = [Difference 1] − [Difference 2]

FIGURE 11.2 The Classical Experimental Design

accurate, Difference 1 ($A_e - B_e$) will be larger than Difference 2 ($A_c - B_c$). The logic of the two designs, then, is identical. Again, Mill argued that meeting these conditions constituted proof that the factor and the phenomenon were causally related. Indeed, if one adheres strictly to logic, the variable relationship would have been proven. However, in concert with our previous discussions, we prefer to use the phrase *providing evidence for or against.* We encourage this more cautious approach because it is recognized that other factors could contribute to the observation of a difference besides exposure to the experimental stimulus (the supposed independent variable). Simply from a logical perspective, the observed results may be the product of a variable or configuration of variables (Kish's class III and IV variables) not controlled by the researcher.

There are other considerations that could easily lead the researcher to an erroneous conclusion that we discuss later in a section noting the disadvantages of experiments.

An Example of the Classical Design.   To illustrate the classical design, we might test the hypothesis that exposure to a documentary film will reduce prejudice of college students toward the elderly. Ageism is a topic of increasing importance in our culture as the proportion of the population classified as senior citizens continues to

increase. Indeed, by definition, we all have a personal stake in how the elderly are treated and will be treated in the future.

The first two steps in conducting any experiment are to select the units of analysis and the experimental environment. With that in mind we have elected to test our hypothesis by selecting a sample of students from the sampling frame of students enrolled this semester in the social problems course at our university. A simple random sample will be drawn and subsequently assigned on a random basis to either E_1, the experimental group (the group to be exposed to the test stimulus of a documentary film), or C_1, the control group (the group to be denied exposure to the film).

The selected students will be notified of their inclusion and asked to report to the "laboratory" (classroom or auditorium) at a specified time. The students will be informed that they have been asked to participate in an important social survey, but they will not be told the specific nature of the inquiry. Everyone selected will then be asked to respond to a schedule containing items that will provide an empirical indication of the incidence of prejudicial attitudes held by these students toward the elderly. The scores obtained from the respondents in the two groups should be approximately equal if we have properly randomized the assignments. These scores will be reported in the cells identified as B_e and B_c in Figure 11.2, and they will serve as the baseline data, the results of the first measurement.

The experimental group (E_1) will then be invited to view the film. This viewing can be immediate or postponed to a more convenient time. The researcher will control the time of exposure as well as the times of measurement. If the film is shown immediately, the researcher may wish to ask the members of the control group (C_1) to relax but not to leave. This would minimize the influence that uncontrolled intervening variables might have upon subsequent measurements.

The second measurement can occur anytime after the film has been viewed by the experimental group. Again, it can be immediate or delayed, with advantages and disadvantages for either approach. Whenever the measurements are taken, they will be examined in terms of the prestimulus assessments. These scores will be reported in the cells identified as A_e and A_c in Figure 11.2.

Respondent Sensitivity.   If the hypothesis is supported, the greater difference will be recorded for E_1 (the experimental group) or $(A_e - B_e)$, but, in all likelihood, a difference also will be recorded for the control group (C_1). Even in a laboratory setting, the social scientist does not have the luxury of a totally controlled environment. People are going to register events and activities that take place, and that includes having already been exposed to the measuring instrument. Earlier exposure, as well as other uncontrolled-for experiences, often influence subsequent responses. It is reasonable, then, to expect some variation in response by members of the control group, despite their having been denied exposure to the independent variable. Consequently, it is important for social scientists to look at a third difference, which is the difference between Difference 1 and Difference 2. Although generally smaller than Difference 1, it is this third difference that is the more likely effect

attributable to the causal or independent variable (in this case, the stimulus).

The problem of *respondent sensitivity* can be partially addressed by extending the time interval between the first and second measurement. By partially solving one problem by such an extension, however, the researcher opens the gate to the possibility of others. The most important of these is the possibility of occurrence of an intervening event that is relevant to the topic being investigated. Federal legislative action affecting Social Security benefits would almost certainly have some influence upon the attitudinal perspective of the subjects in our example. If not a widely reported event, persons may be dramatically affected by a personal event, e.g., a grandparent who might be discriminated against for a job or denied an apartment to rent.

Recently, some thinkers have argued that the measurement taken prior to exposing the experimental group to the test stimulus is not necessary if the membership of the respective groups has been determined by a simple random assignment. However, this procedure is felt to guarantee the groups are equal and properly matched.* To deny the groups initial exposure to the measuring device would avoid sensitizing the respondents for the "after" (t_3) measurement.[2] Donald Campbell and Julian Stanley acknowledge, however, and we agree, that it is difficult to forfeit the comfort of knowing that the two groups are equal after an initial assessment. If it can be accommodated, then, we encourage the preservation of the first measurement period (t_1).

To return to our example of prejudice toward the elderly, we can note that we have controlled for who is studied, how they are studied, and when they are studied. This control and the fact that the design is the best for establishing causality should lend considerable confidence to the results attained. While these are clearly the two major ad-

---

*The reader is referred to Chapter 3 where this assumption about randomization was discussed. We will not reproduce that argument here.

vantages of the experimental design—i.e., control and causality—we must be aware of some of the disadvantages of conducting experiments in the social sciences.

Disadvantages. Beyond respondent sensitivity, the idea of placing people in a laboratory can be problematic because of its artificial nature. In our study we would communicate something to the respondents by asking them to come to a central location that mailing them a schedule to complete would not, although to elect to mail the measuring instrument would result in a much smaller percentage of return. However, electing to examine the hypothesis from respondents located in a more natural setting would present so many uncontrollable variables that the results would be questionable. The central dilemma the researcher must address, then, is whether to introduce the artificiality of a laboratory setting thereby maximizing control or to forfeit some control for the sake of working in a more natural environment.

Reactive Effect. In a laboratory setting, we must be concerned with both the researcher's and subject's effects upon the results, which are known as the *reactive effect*. A researcher obviously has expectations of the way in which the study will result. Indeed, the elements of financial commitment, time expenditure, and considerable effort constitute strong vested interests in the results. Because of such investments, the experimenter may give off unconscious suggestions to the respondent. Herein lies an irony to the attainment of accurate results. If rapport has been established, subjects will often register the responses they believe the researcher wants.

Another reactive effect is called the *Hawthorne effect,* a term that came from the study of the Hawthorne plant of the Western Electric Company in Chicago.[3] In that study the researchers were examining the effect on the productivity of female workers assembling telephone relays after varying a number of factors such as rest periods, different quitting times, and the provision of refreshments or noon meals. As expected, they found that productivity increased when workers were provided with rest periods, earlier quitting times, and meals. What was not expected, however, was the higher productivity within the control group for whom the original work conditions remained unchanged. Ultimately the researchers partially explained this higher productivity in terms of higher morale generated by the attention that was being paid workers by the research staff. Thus, the workers may positively respond when they know they are a part of a research project.

Double-Blind Experiment. The best method to counteract the reactive problem is to conduct the research using a double-blind experimental design. To do this, someone other than the investigator must assign subjects to the experimental and control groups. Ideally, in a double-blind study some form of intervention is registered for both groups. The experimental group receives the *genuine test stimulus* while the control group is provided some form of placebo treatment. In this manner neither the researcher nor the subjects are aware of who is in either group. If it is not feasible to provide a placebo to the control group, the double-blind procedure can still be used to eliminate the researcher's knowledge of which group is which. We recommend that the double-blind design be followed whenever it is possible to do so, particularly if part or all of the measurement procedure involves the researcher's observational skills.

Solomon's Three-Group Design

Clearly, a number of problems exist for the researcher, even with the use of the classical experimental design. One improvement in the classical design that specifically addresses the problems of respondent sensitivity and reactivity is the extension of the classical design from one control group to two.[4] This improved design permits the researcher to assess and to eliminate the degree to which respondent sensitivity has influenced the results observed in the second measurement period.

Solomon's three-group design is presented in Figure 11.3. Note that the design is the classical experimental design with the addition of a second control group.

You will recall that the classical design requires measurement of the experimental (E_1) and control (C_1) groups prior to and after the introduction of the test stimulus to the experimental group. We have discussed the problem that any difference noted in the scores for the experimental group between the two testing periods can be a product of the test stimulus *and* the first measurement, as well as other outside factors. Any change noted for the control group (C_1) can be attributed to the first measurement and these outside factors.

With the addition of a second control group (C_2), we are able to isolate the effect of the test stimulus. This is accomplished by exposing the second control group (C_2) to the test stimulus but only measuring these respondents in the second measuring period, i.e., at time three (t_3), thus providing no opportunity to become sensitive to the measuring device prior to receiving the test stimulus.

The researcher can now work with these differences. The experimental group (E_1) reflects the effects of the first measurement *and* the test stimulus; the first control group (C_1) offers the effect of the first measurement only; while the second control group (C_2) gives the effect of only the test stimulus. Thus, the total effect in the experimental group (E_1) is assessed by subtracting the second measurement from the first (Difference 1 = $A_e - B_e$). Total effect among the control groups (C_1 and C_2) is obtained by adding the pretest effect of C_1—(Difference 2 = $A_{c1} - B_{c1}$) to the test stimulus effect of C_2—(Difference 3 = $A_{c2} - B_{c2}$).

The problem we obviously encounter is that there is no measurement for the second control group (C_2) in the first measurement period, time one (t_1). This problem is addressed by using the mean of the two scores registered for the experimental (E_1) and first control (C_1) groups. This average figure has been judged to be acceptable to researchers because the three groups are more or less equal. This presumed equality, of course, is dependent upon the three groups having been selected by the simple random procedure.

The differences we now have will permit us to separate the causal effect of exposure to the measuring instrument at time one (t_1) and that attributed to the test stimulus—or will they?

GROUP	BEFORE (t_1)	STIMULUS (t_2)	AFTER (t_3)	
Experimental (E_1)	B_e	Yes	A_e	Difference 1 = $A_e - B_e$
Control-1 (C_1)	B_{c1}	No	A_{c1}	Difference 2 = $A_{c1} - B_{c1}$
Control-2 (C_2)	No B_{c2}*	Yes	A_{c2}	Difference 3 = $A_{c2} - B_{c2}$

$$*B_{c2} = \frac{B_e + B_{c1}}{2}$$

FIGURE 11.3   Solomon's Three-Group Experimental Design

Interaction.   In social science investigations, the researcher must be aware of what is known as an *interaction effect*. We noted earlier that people are affected by activities and events of which they are aware. Continuing with our example of university students and ageism, we have stated that one way to reduce sensitivity to the measuring instrument is to delay the second administration for some time after the test stimulus, or delay administering the test stimulus for some time after taking the first measurement. We have also addressed some of the problems inherent in that approach. For the purpose of this discussion, let us say that after all things were considered, we elected to take the second measurement immediately after exposure to the test stimulus. Even those students who were not able to determine that the study was designed to assess ageism from the first administration of the questionnaire would probably reach this conclusion from exposure to the measuring instrument and the film. Since most people do not wish to be seen as prejudiced, it is reasonable to suppose that the respondents who have guessed what the experiment is about would alter their response patterns—the *social desirability response*—to avoid this label. If this occurs (and there is a strong likelihood it will), the researcher must be concerned with the effects of the first measurement, test stimulus, and the insight gained by some respondents by exposure to both. It is this combined information that constitutes the interaction effect. Fortunately, the Solomon three-group design permits the assessment of this additional effect. The formula is:

$$I = [A_e - B_e] - ([A_{c1} - B_{c1}] + [A_{c2} - B_{c2}])$$

where

I = the interaction

A_e = second measurement (t_3) of the experimental group (E_1)

B_e = first measurement (t_1) of the experimental group (E_1)

A_{c1} = second measurement (t_3) of the first control group (C_1)

B_{c1} = first measurement (t_1) of the first control group (C_1)

A_{c2} = second measurement (t_3) of the second control group (C_2)

B_{c2} = the first measurement—which is the mean of the two actual measurements made—i.e., $[(B_e) + (B_{c1})] / 2$

To assess the incidence of prejudice against the elderly by the students, assume that we have put together an index of 200 statements. The larger the total index score, the more prejudiced that respondent is likely to be. Although the two groups tested in the first measurement period would not be likely to register identical scores, we will argue they did in order to keep the numbers simple. In our hypothetical example, the respondents recorded an average achieved score of 75. The antiprejudice documentary film is then presented to the experimental group (E_1) and to the second control group (C_2). Following a brief respite for comfort and refreshment, all three groups return for the second administration of the same set of statements.

In the second measurement period we observe a reduction in the average prejudice score to 45 for members of the experimental group (E_1), and an average score of 65 for the first control group (C_1). Clearly, by being denied exposure, the 10-point reduction registered by the control group (C_1) cannot be said to be caused by the test stimulus, nor can it be explained by the interaction effect since that would require exposure to the first measurement and the test stimulus. The difference must be accounted for by exposure to the first measurement and other uncontrolled variables (class III and, possibly, class IV). This would only leave a 20-point reduction to be accounted for by exposure to the test stimulus, but some of this difference may be attributed to the interaction effect.

To assess this possibility, we examine the average score recorded for the second control group (C_2) during the second measurement period. Assume this score to be 60. You will recall that this score is in turn subtracted from the average score attained by the experimental and first control groups for the first measurement or, in this case, an average of 75. Thus, the test stimulus effect for these data is 15. Substituting the values attained, we can estimate this interaction effect as:

$$I = [45 - 75] - ([65 - 75] + [60 - 75])$$
$$= 30 - ([-10] + [-15])$$
$$= -30 - (-25)$$
$$= -30 + 25$$
$$= -5$$

Thus, the total difference observed for the experimental group can be identified and attributed to the effect of the test stimulus (15), exposure to the first measurement (10), and the interaction of the two (5).

Solomon's Four-Group Design

Despite the complicated nature of the three-group design, we cannot identify the effect of uncontrolled variables (class III and IV) unless we add a fourth randomly selected group to the experimental design.[5] The diagram for this experimental design, *Solomon's four-group design,* is presented in Figure 11.4.

The additional group is not measured during the first testing period, nor is it exposed to the test stimulus. The only measurement for this group (C_3) occurs in the second measurement period (t_3). The same assumption made for the score recorded for the second control group (C_2) in the first measurement period is made for the third control group (C_3). That is, both C_2 and C_3 are assigned the average of the scores registered for E_1 and C_1 in time period one (t_1).

In our example, we would expect a score of 75 to be registered for the first measurement if such a measurement were taken. If any score other than 75 is observed in the second measurement period for control group three (C_3), the difference would be seen as an effect of uncontrolled variables. Obviously, such differences cannot be attributed to the first measurement, exposure to the test stimulus, or an interaction effect between the two. With

GROUP	BEFORE (t_1)	STIMULUS (t_2)	AFTER (t_3)	
Experimental (E_1)	B_e	Yes	A_e	Difference 1 = $A_e - B_e$
Control-1 (C_1)	B_{c1}	No	A_{c1}	Difference 2 = $A_{c1} - B_{c1}$
Control-2 (C_2)	No B_{c2} *	Yes	A_{c2}	Difference 3 = $A_{c2} - B_{c2}$
Control-3 (C_3)	No B_{c3} *	No	A_{c3}	Difference 4 = $A_{c3} - B_{c3}$

* B_{c2} and $B_{c3} = \dfrac{B_e + B_{c1}}{2}$

FIGURE 11.4   Solomon's Four-Group Experimental Design

the addition of a fourth group, then, a more refined assessment is possible.

Assume we obtain an observed score of 73, or a change of 2 points for the third control group (C_3) in the second measurement period for our hypothetical experiment. This two-point discrepancy is seen as the effect of the uncontrolled variables and is subtracted from the interaction effect.* Thus, for this example we are able to refine our assessment of the interaction effect to a more precise level of three. What is of greatest importance to the researcher is that the assessment of interaction effects permits the expansion of understanding of the effect of the independent variable upon the dependent variable.

Factorial Design

The experimental designs that have been presented only permit the researcher to examine the causal effects of one independent variable. However, social scientists are often confronted with questions that require the systematic manipulation of *two or more* independent variables. Gaining additional insight into a phenomenon by studying two or more variables simultaneously is a great advantage of the *factorial design.* As you have learned, however, one does not receive without giving, because, in this instance, the researcher must increase the number of experimental groups. If we take the simplest situation possible, i.e., two independent variables with dichotomous values, a minimum of four experimental groups is required because all possible variations must be represented.

We can easily extend the ageism study to the factorial design with the addition of a seminar presentation by a panel of experts on the issue of prejudice and discrimination against the elderly. As was true of the documentary film, some of the students selected to participate in the study would attend the seminar, and some would not. The resulting four groups are represented by Figure 11.5.

SEMINAR PRESENTATION/ DOCUMENTARY FILM	YES	NO
Yes	E_1	E_2
No	E_3	C_1

FIGURE 11.5 Combinations of Stimuli to Experimental Groups for Ageism Experiment for a Dichotomous Two-Independent Variable Factorial Design

They are (1) E_1 = subjects are exposed to the seminar *and* the film; (2) E_2 = subjects are exposed to the seminar, but not to the film; (3) E_3 = subjects are exposed to the film, but not the seminar; and (4) C_1 = subjects are denied exposure to both stimuli.

Note, for this illustration, the fourth group (C_1) is, in fact, a control group. However, this is not what generally occurs in that the dichotomy usually results in a high-low division rather than presence-absence as reflected in this example. When this is the case, respondents with a low assessment on both variables have still been exposed to both stimuli. Therefore, it would be necessary to select a fifth group to serve as the control group in order to gain a more complete analysis of the effects of the two independent variables. Figure 11.6 presents the more typical minimal factorial design where X and Y represent the two independent variables, and H and L, written as subscripts, represent the high and low assessments, respectively.

A simple illustration of a division of values based upon intensity could be an examination of the combined effects of exercise and consumption of cholesterol on health level. One independent variable (X) is the amount of exercise one performs while the other independent variable (Y) is the level of cholesterol one consumes in one's

---

*Solomon's design assumes that the interaction and other confounding components discussed above possess the property of additivity, i.e., that they are all separate entities in their effect and add to the total observed score.

GROUP	BEFORE (t_1)	STIMULUS (t_2)	AFTER (t_3)	
Experimental-1 (E_1)	B_{e1}	$X_H Y_H$	A_{e1}	Difference 1 = $A_{e1} - B_{e1}$
Experimental-2 (E_2)	B_{e2}	$X_H Y_L$	A_{e2}	Difference 2 = $A_{e2} - B_{e2}$
Experimental-3 (E_3)	B_{e3}	$X_L Y_H$	A_{e3}	Difference 3 = $A_{e3} - B_{e3}$
Experimental-4 (E_4)	B_{e4}	$X_L Y_L$	A_{e4}	Difference 4 = $A_{e4} - B_{e4}$
Control-1 (C_1)	B_c	No	A_c	Difference 5 = $A_c - B_c$

FIGURE 11.6   Factorial Design Assessing Two Dichotomous Independent Variables

diet. Both variables can easily be divided between high and low values, with the investigator controlling the quantity of both for each respondent in all four experimental groups.

As was true for the Solomon three- and four-group designs, the researcher can test for interaction when employing the factorial design. By including an assessment for interaction and an examination of the effect for uncontrolled variables, this design furthers understanding of the effects of the respective independent variables.

Some Additional Thoughts

The four experimental designs we have presented are the most complete alternatives social scientists have available to test hypotheses and propositions. They are not perfect because variables that we do not or cannot control, or of which we are unaware, will always be present. All such class III and IV variables can affect the data analysis and are, therefore, external threats to the validity of social science studies.

We have mentioned the difficulties of respondent sensitivity, time lapse between measurement periods, and reactivity for both the researcher and respondent. These difficulties and others are substantially increased when the researcher attempts to take the investigation out of the laboratory.

The most important loss the investigator experiences when research efforts move to natural settings is that of control. It is more difficult to control the membership of the experimental and control groups, what stimuli they are or are not exposed to, and the nature and intensity of the independent variable or variables. It is sometimes difficult, if not impossible, to randomly assign participants to the experimental and control groups.

Indeed, there are many circumstances that prevent a measurement prior to the sample's exposure to the test stimulus.

One general example will be sufficient to illustrate our concerns. Focusing on the substantial interest of attitudinal research, many investigations have been directed toward prejudicial attitudes as they relate to a variety of demographic characteristics such as age, race, sex, ethnicity, and geographic location. We return to the question of whether exposure to a documentary film will have any effect upon reducing the expressed degree of prejudice by a sample of respondents. Clearly, we can control who is shown this film and who is not. Just as clearly, however, we cannot control many other relevant factors. For example, we will have had no influence on previous exposure to prejudicial attitudes (what our respondents have seen on television, read in newspapers, or heard in lectures) or discussed with others between measurement periods. That is, it may be beyond one's capacity to control for many of the class III variables that exist in this context. This fact should not prevent examination of the question, but it does mean an alternative method must be adopted. In all likelihood that method will be one of the quasi-experimental designs. It is to these designs that we now briefly turn.

QUASI-EXPERIMENTAL DESIGNS

Introduction

The modifier *quasi* is used to suggest that the researcher is using one of those designs that do not have all of the control expected in a purely experimental design. Indeed, some thinkers hold that if the researcher cannot meet all of the control expectations, an experiment cannot be performed. Although we are somewhat sympathetic with the purist's perspective on other issues, we feel that this posture is too strict in this context.

The credibility and information that can be obtained from quasi-experimental designs has been greatly enhanced over the last 20 years by the publication of Campbell and Stanley's *Experimental and Quasi-Experimental Designs for Research*[6] and Cook and Campbell's *Quasi-Experimentation: Design and Analysis Issues for Field Settings*.[7] Both of these efforts are excellent, in-depth discussions that examine a wide variety of relevant designs to assess cause-and-effect relationships. Although a thorough review of all these designs is beyond the scope of this effort, we will look at a few of those that are most frequently used.

As with the experimental designs, the basis for the quasi-experimental designs is the classical design, or Mill's method of difference, and the logic-of-testing hypotheses remains the same. The difficulty is that none of the *quasi-experimental* designs have the full complement of at least two randomly assigned groups, a minimum of two measurements each, and only one group exposed to the test stimulus. With the obvious weaknesses that such absences imply, we would always seek to employ one of the experimental designs, even in natural environments where we might have to conduct the research with less control of subjects and stimulus.

However, the experimental designs are not always possible. When they are not, the usage of one of the quasi-experimental designs is recommended. Purists argue that one is better off not doing the study than using one of these alternatives. We strenuously disagree and stress the importance of permitting a study to flow naturally, rather than force the use of stronger methods, designs, or statistics that do not fit the parameters of the project.

Let us look at some of these basic alternative approaches that do not meet the requirements of the classical design, but which are often employed by contemporary investigators.

Succession (Before-and-After) Design

The *succession (before-and-after) design* is so named because it calls for, in succession, the measurement of one group prior to exposure to the test

GROUP	BEFORE (t_1)	STIMULUS (t_2)	AFTER (t_3)
Experimental (E_1)	B_e	Yes	A_e

Difference 1 = $A_e - B_e$

FIGURE 11.7   The Succession (Panel) or (Before-and-After) Quasi-Experimental Design

stimulus, exposure to the stimulus, and a subsequent measurement. This design is sometimes also labeled the *panel design* because the investigator selects a single panel of respondents to assess. A diagrammatic representation of this design appears in Figure 11.7. The dotted lines denote observations that are not present.

Thus, the succession design is parallel to the classical design in terms of the experimental group, but it reflects the obvious weakness of not having a control group. Any difference that is recorded, i.e., $A_e - B_e$, must be attributed to exposure to the test stimulus, although this may not be the case. However, some insight into the phenomenon of interest will be gained, and the results may stimulate additional research. At a minimum, we know that a change has occurred and the direction of that change, even though we are not able to specify the causal factors responsible for the change with any certainty.

As the example that follows illustrates, it may be extremely difficult for practical and ethical reasons to structure an experimental design. Therefore, one may seek preliminary evidence for causality through the succession design. That is, before one tries a more difficult experimental design to isolate the causal factor or factors, it would be wise and economical to see if the stimulus (and other factors) resulted in any change, even though the causes of that change (if such is found) are not "nailed down" using the succession design.

An Example.   We illustrated the experimental designs with a hypothetical study to assess the reduction of university students' prejudicial attitudes toward the elderly following exposure to a film. For the sake of simplicity, let us remain with this general topic. Let us assume that a sample of students from the sections of social problems offered this semester was selected. Those selected were asked to respond to a number of statements relevant to this issue during the first week of the semester. These selected students will be asked to respond to the same items during the final week of the semester. The test stimulus in this example, however, is not a documentary film or a seminar presentation but exposure to the course on social problems. It is apparent that a great deal of control is forfeited, because we can not regulate, with any precision, the stimuli affecting any selected student. Some students will read the assigned readings; others will read those in addition to optional recommended sources; while still others will read only part or none of those readings assigned. Uncontrolled variation of exposure will also occur with some students' participating in relevant discussions in and out of the classroom, while others will avoid such; class attendance will vary among the participants; and the topics addressed by the different professors teaching the course will not be identical, nor will those that are the same be managed, emphasized, or presented in the same manner.

Nevertheless, differences observed at the end of the semester will be viewed as representing some evidence for the impact of the course on social problems. It may be that these changes would have occurred anyway. They may be reflective of an event which occurred during the semester, other courses in which the students were enrolled, dormitory or Greek-house discussions, and the like. The point is that without a control group we do not know if any, or all, of these factors contributed. To tap these would require, at the very least, a matched control group of students not enrolled in a section of the course on social problems.

It should be recognized that this design could be used to test the impact of any exposure. From the perspective of undergraduate education, for example, exposure to a single lecture or to attending four years of college could be assessed using this design. The key point is that the investigator has substantially less control than with the experimental designs. A general rule of thumb, however, is that the shorter the delay between the first and second measurements, the lesser the need for a control group.

Time-Series Design (an Extension of Succession Design)

The strength of the succession (before-and-after) design is the presence of multiple measurements for a single group. Indeed, the investigator can continue to take measurements of this group or, for that matter, to measure several times prior to

and following exposure to the test stimulus as is illustrated in Figure 11.8. The number of before-and-after measurements should be equal as should the time intervals between the before-and-after-test assessments, unless one's conceptual model indicates otherwise.

Although the *time-series-design* presents the investigator with additional data and, thereby, may strengthen the researcher's confidence in the results, it does not address the primary weakness of the succession design, which is the absence of a control group. However, assuming that the experimental stimulus is at least in part responsible for the change in the after measurements, one is able to offer some preliminary estimates of the short-, medium-, and long-range effects of the stimulus by looking at the changes in the dependent variable after the stimulus is introduced (e.g., refer to A_{e1} at t_5, A_{e2} at t_6, and A_{e3} at t_7 in Figure 11.8).

Cross-Sectional Design

A quasi-experimental design that meets the objection of an absent comparison or control group is the cross-sectional design. The weakness of this design, however, is the strength of the succession design. That is, the *cross-sectional design* calls for only one measurement to be taken for each group included in the study. The cross-sectional, quasi-experimental design is diagrammed in Figure 11.9, with the missing cells denoted by dotted lines.

This design requires a cross-sectional sample selection in which the respondents of the two or

GROUP	BEFORE MEASUREMENTS			STIMULUS	AFTER MEASUREMENTS		
[Time]	t_1	t_2	t_3	t_4	t_5	t_6	t_7
Experimental (E_1)	B_{e1}	B_{e2}	B_{e3}	Yes	A_{e1}	A_{e2}	A_{e3}

FIGURE 11.8 The Time-Series Design

GROUP	BEFORE (t_1)	STIMULUS (t_2)	AFTER (t_3)
Control-1 (C_1)	B_{c1}		/
Experimental-1 (E_1)		Yes	A_{e1}

Difference 1 = $A_{e1} - B_{c1}$

FIGURE 11.9   The Cross-Sectional, Quasi-Experimental Design

more groups are as closely matched on the salient dimensions as possible. Change or difference is determined by comparing B_{c1} with A_{e1}, i.e., the difference = $A_{e1} - B_{c1}$. Since each group will be measured only one time, we can never be sure the two or more groups are really similar. The irony of the cross-sectional design is that we are attempting to assess change that occurs over time by taking measurements for each group at one point in time, albeit for the control group at t_1 and the experimental group at t_3.

An Example.   To illustrate this design, let us assume we are interested in any change in political orientation that occurs among college students during their four years of undergraduate study. Assume also that we do not have the opportunity to use a succession design, which would tap a selected sample of first-semester freshmen and then wait until they are second-semester seniors to remeasure their political attitudes. The cross-sectional design offers a possible solution to such time constraints. We can select a sample of freshmen *and* a sample of seniors *currently* enrolled. We would, of course, take care to match the two groups for age at the time of first enrollment, sex, major field of study, College Board scores, private versus public secondary school education, and other clearly relevant demographic characteristics. If we observe a difference in political attitudinal orientation for these two groups, we have obtained some evidence to suggest that exposure

to a four-year university experience has an effect on this dimension.

If we wished to expand upon this design, we could select a sample of currently enrolled sophomores and juniors. From data collected from all four classes, we might gain some idea of the impact on political attitudes each of the four years of college exposure might have. That is, does the greatest change seem to occur after the freshman, sophomore, junior, or senior year?

Despite enlargement, however, the researcher is left with only one measurement per group. Herein lies an important issue. The cross-sectional design requires the assumption that the group or groups, having been exposed to the test stimulus or some part thereof, were, prior to the exposure, equal to the group that has not yet been exposed and that the group that has not yet been exposed will be equal to the exposed group after receiving the test stimulus. When the time required for exposure is substantial, as would be for the four-year period required in our example, this assumption is more difficult to embrace. This is because of the many events beyond the researcher's control that may occur and that could influence such attitudes. Imagine that we had attempted to conduct this study during the Watergate period. Clearly, the resignation of the president and vice president of the United States, with at least some degree of disgrace, could alter one's political attitudes. To assume seniors having just witnessed this phenomenon were like freshmen who had also just witnessed the same when they were freshmen would be foolish. When the seniors were freshmen, this type of political scenario might well have been seen as the bizarre side of one's imagination.

It is interesting to note that what constitutes the strength of the succession design represents the weakness of the panel design and vice versa. With either, it is clear the investigator forfeits substantial control. However, either may be the best available design for the circumstances with which the researcher must work. Further, we would argue that increasing the number of groups and reducing of the time lapse represented across the entire sample would help in lending more confidence in the results of the cross-sectional, quasi-experimental design approach.

After-Group Design

Social scientists are often confronted with a circumstance that is already present. That is, we may have the existence of two or more groups after the fact where only one of these groups has been exposed to a particular element. This type of situation suggests the usage of the *after-group design*, which is illustrated in Figure 11.10. Again, the missing cells are indicated by dotted lines.

Perhaps you will recognize this diagram as a partial reproduction of the Solomon four-group design. Indeed, the after-group design is an ap-

proximation of the randomly selected groups three and four of the four-group design. You will recall that they were added to permit the assessment of interaction (I) and the effect of uncontrolled variables.

Unfortunately, the observations in the after-group design do not allow for the more precise analysis available in the Solomon four-group design. This may be, however, all we have.

A further shortcoming in the comparison of these two designs is that the two groups in the after-group design do not represent statistically, randomly selected and assigned respondents. In addition to an absence of control over those who comprise the sample or over the administration of the test stimulus, the major difficulty with this design is that the researcher does not have any baseline data with which to compare the post-stimulus assessments. As with other quasi-experimental designs, then, we can never be sure of the extent of the influence that the experimental variable has exerted.

An Example. To illustrate the after-group design, let us assume an interest in urban studies. Students of urban ecology often find this design suitable and recommended for studying situations in which a jurisdictional or legislative ruling has arbitrarily divided a neighborhood or segment of a community. We have long recognized potential difficulties that arise between what urban scholars

GROUP	BEFORE (t_1)	STIMULUS (t_2)	AFTER (t_3)
Experimental-1 (E_1)		Yes	A_{e1}
Control-1 (C_1)			A_{c1}

FIGURE 11.10 The After-Group, Quasi-Experimental Design

label administrative areas and natural areas. Natural areas are formed by persons who share similar characteristics, and where the dominant factors may be economic, religious, or racial-ethnic identity. Natural areas are formed without any concern for constraints such as size or shape. Therefore, they may be large or small in territory and in number of persons who reside in them. Conversely, city planning agencies, city councils, or other governing bodies, in arranging areas to be served, such as school districts, voting districts, and health care clinics, would prefer to have each district reflective of approximately the same number of persons. As a result, the formation of administrative areas frequently fragments natural areas in terms of their cohesiveness as a political force or in forcing their children to attend different schools than their friends.

Imagine that we are specifically interested in the academic performance of children within a particular natural area that has been divided by administrative assignment into two districts. Let us further imagine that the elementary school of one of the administrative areas has been selected as a target school for computer instruction. Ultimately, we do observe a difference between children assigned to the two districts. Can we attribute these differences to exposure or nonexposure to computer instruction in these two schools? To examine this, we would select representatives from the two administrative areas in order to maximize

similarity on other relevant factors such as income level, size, and stability of family. If, after controlling for as many other relevant factors as possible, we are now able to observe differences between the academic performance levels of the children from the two schools, we have some confidence that exposure to different school computer curricula may explain the differences observed.

Clearly, in the absence of before measures for both groups, we will be denied the opportunity to assess any differences for which the experimental exposure actually accounted. However, many studies that begin as quasi-experimental efforts graduate into more sophisticated experiments after some preliminary evidence has been gathered to lend support to what is believed to be the causes of the phenomenon.

Single-Cell Design

Another quasi-experimental design that is particularly useful in a heuristic manner is the *single-cell design*. Although a researcher can never demonstrate cause and effect using the single-cell design, suggestive evidence can be gathered. From a scientific perspective, however, it simply represents a snapshot of what exists at the time of investigation.

Useful as it may be as a tool of suggestion, the single-cell design represents the antithesis of the

GROUP	BEFORE (t_1)	STIMULUS (t_2)	AFTER (t_3)
Experimental-1 (E_1)		Yes	A_{e1}

FIGURE 11.11   The Single-Cell, Quasi-Experimental Design

classic experimental design with which we began this chapter. There is a total absence of control in sample selection and manipulation of the test stimulus. Thus, we have come full circle from maximum control to minimum control. Figure 11.11 offers a diagram of this zero-control design.

The questions of when and why one would use this design are answered in terms of the interest of social scientists in studying phenomena that are more or less spontaneous. Although from an historical perspective the use of the single-cell design has not been limited to the spontaneous occurrence, we believe that justification of its employment is primarily centered in those circumstances.

An Example. We suspect you would be interested in understanding, as much as possible, the underlying causes of a riot if it were to occur on your campus. First, riots are not planned, as a rule, so that one does not have an opportunity to gather preriot measurements. Second, securing a matched control group of the participants would be virtually impossible. One is left, then, with the participants who can be observed from one's vantage point or points or those willing to come forward following the riot to respond to interview or questionnaire measuring instruments.

We urge considerable caution with interpretations made from data collected via this design. At least one comparison is required to suggest any scientific evidence. Nevertheless, the procedure offers a point of departure for more in-depth examinations.

A final note concerning single-cell analysis is that reports from this perspective are often more journalistic than scientific. Consider what we know about the sinking of the Titanic, or the reaction of many citizens to Orson Welles' Mercury Theatre program of the invasion of Martians. Yet, some insightful persons recorded their observations of these happenings, and we have used these suggestions to gain a much greater understanding of collective behavioral phenomena through more complete investigative strategies.

SUMMARY

This chapter has focused upon the experimental and quasi-experimental research designs most frequently employed by social scientists. We noted that prior to selection of a study design, the researcher must address the feasibility questions of physical possibility, financial resources, and ethical considerations.

The central experimental design discussed was the classical design. It is central in that all other designs are derived from this approach, which was originally introduced as the method of difference by John Stuart Mill over a century ago. Refinement to the classical design was introduced through the Solomon three- and four-group designs and the factorial design. The Solomon designs facilitate the researcher's dealing with respondent sensitivity, reactivity, and interaction effects. In addition, the Solomon four-group design permits an assessment of the effect of uncontrolled, class III and IV variables upon the outcome measure. Researchers wishing to examine the impact of more than one independent variable can turn to the factorial design.

We also discussed a number of quasi-experimental designs. While caution should be exercised, we argue the use of these partial representations of the classical design is recommended when the classical design parameters cannot be met.

The discussion included the succession and time series designs in which only one group is available and measurement is made at least one time before the occurrence of the test stimulus and one time after. Also discussed was the cross-sectional design in which two or more groups at different stages of a process relative to the test stimulus in question are measured at one point in time.

The chapter concluded with a description of the after-group design and the single-cell, or one-shot, study. While we noted these two approaches are quite weak, they may represent the only opportunity the researcher has available to examine a phenomenon of interest.

KEY TERMS

After-group design	Experimental group	Reactive effect
Before-and-after design	Factorial design	Replication
Classical experimental design	Genuine test stimulus	Respondent sensitivity
Comparison group	Hawthorne effect	Single-cell design
Control group	Interaction effect	Social desirability response
Cross-sectional design	Method of difference	Solomon's three-group design
Double-blind experiment	Panel design	Solomon's four-group design
Ecological fallacy	Placebo	Succession design
Experiment	Quasi-experiment	Time-series design

REVIEW QUESTIONS

1. How do quasi-experimental designs differ from experimental designs?

2. Pick any experimental and any quasi-experimental design, and compare each design's ability to control extraneous variables.

3. How do the use of a placebo and a double-blind experimental design improve the validity of one's data in an experimental design?

4. How does a comparison group differ from a control group?

5. Create an example of Solomon's four-group experimental design, and show why it is superior to the three-group and classical designs.

6. What is a factorial design? What is its major advantage over the other designs presented?

7. Illustrate one practical situation and one ethical dilemma that would prevent the use of an experimental design.

8. Identify any four quasi-experimental designs. Define what each one is. Explain what information (even if tentative) can be gained.

9. What advantage does a time-series design have that none of the other designs have?

10. Identify four different difficulties that relate to those who participate in quasi-experimental or experimental studies that present validity problems for the interpretation of the results.

11. If one were to eliminate the discussion of one research design in this chapter, why would one most likely select the single-cell, quasi-experimental design for exclusion?

12. Show how John Stuart Mill's canon of the method of difference is achieved in the classical experimental design. What assumption is made here that the study of people generally invalidates? [HINT: Consider Solomon's work.]

13. Review question: Compare experimental and survey data-gathering procedures *generally*. Under which conditions would the researcher be most likely to want to use either?

CHAPTER 12

CONTENT ANALYSIS
AND SECONDARY ANALYSIS

INTRODUCTION

In each of the data-gathering procedures we have discussed, the researcher has had to make a decision regarding the people to be studied and then to gather data directly by means of a questionnaire, interview, or experimental observation. In this chapter, we discuss two other rich and fertile sources of data that are nonreactive data-gathering strategies. Content analysis and secondary analysis both involve the extrapolation of data from already existent sources.

Many students, when first informed of these data-gathering procedures, conclude that they are so simple and straightforward that one would be foolish to examine their research ideas in any other manner. Quite the contrary, the processes of content and secondary analysis are complex and require substantial skill. Indeed, the researcher must initially confront the primary challenge of examining information that was not collected specifically for the purpose of the researcher.

In the past, many scholars have incorporated content analysis within the overall notion of secondary analysis. In that perspective, secondary analysis has been defined as the analysis of *data* collected for some purpose other than that of the researcher. The student will observe that the term *data* is printed in italic type. We have done so for the purpose of emphasis and for focusing attention on the fact that virtually any resource can be used to abstract meaningful information of a sociological nature. These data can take the form of (1) personal or public documents, e.g., letters, diaries, biographies, employment records, school records, health records, newspapers, magazines, books, and journals or (2) data in the more tradi-tional sense of the word, e.g., census data, data from previous survey research efforts, or data from data banks.

It is this dichotomy of the nature of the data that distinguishes content analysis and secondary analysis. *Content analysis* is generally invoked when we are interested in studying an issue that can be examined via communication sources. Conversely, *secondary analysis* is more likely to be employed when a quantitative inventory of existing data is used.

Our discussion reflects this distinction, and we begin with content analysis.

CONTENT ANALYSIS

Content analysis has long been a popular method of research among historians. Indeed, preserved documents of past events are often the only data sources available to the interested student.

Sociologists, however, with the notable exceptions of Karl Marx, Max Weber, Emile Durkheim, and Pitirim Sorokin, all of whom employed historical data for some of their respective analyses, have not used this procedure as frequently as one would expect. Indeed, many of those social scientists who have used the procedure have done so to examine trivial or mundane issues—studies that have done little to recommend content analysis as a desirable procedure. More recently, content analysis has enjoyed growing acceptance and usage. We believe it to be a valuable asset to the researcher's available alternatives.

Content analysis has been defined in several ways, but we can do no better in summarizing the nature of it than to offer the definition provided by Bernard Berelson. He said that "content analysis is a research technique for the objective, systematic, and quantitative description of the manifest content of communication."[1] As we did in Chapter 1 in our discussion of the definition of science, let us examine more closely the components of this definition.

Objectivity

In using the word *objectivity*, we do not refer to nor expect researchers to maintain a value-free existence. As we have noted elsewhere, that would be impossible and foolish. *Objectivity*, an important consideration in any scientific inquiry, refers here to articulating clearly the parameters employed in the classification of the content in any communication used for analysis. For example, one might wish to determine the general orientation of newspapers published within the regional area. That is, are they more likely to focus upon local issues of interest or do they tend to direct their attention to national or international events? In order to introduce objectivity into an inquiry, the researcher would select specific criteria on which to make this judgment. Examination of the headlines of each edition for a specified period of time or of the content of the editorials carried by the respective papers might be used. The point here is that any criterion may be used, but one must be precise in the parameters employed for classifying the content of any form of communication used for the analysis. This procedure is analogous to that of operational definitions discussed in Chapter 3. You will recall that one of the primary reasons for insisting on a clear statement of the operations or procedures to be used in measurement is to facilitate replication. The same point is applicable here. Without an explicit statement of the rules used, it would be virtually impossible for the study to be repeated.

Systematic

As we have previously noted, science is not a random or haphazard activity. The scientist selects a problem and the methods for examining the problem in a *systematic* manner. Similarly, the application of the method selected is systematic. To continue with our newspaper illustration, assume that one has available five daily and Sunday newspapers—the *Times, Ledger, Post, Sentinel,* and *Sun.* It would be inappropriate to decide to examine the content of the headlines of the *Times,* the editorials of the *Ledger,* the sports section of the *Post,* the political content of the comics in the *Sentinel,* and the society page of the *Sun.* Any of these areas would constitute a legitimate basis for content analysis, but not in a mixed format. Whatever basis one selects must be applied *systematically* to *all* of the communications included in the analysis. That is, if one chooses the editorial content of the *Ledger,* one must restrict the analysis to the editorial content of the *Times, Post, Sentinel,* and *Sun.* Science requires systematic selection of the problem area, the methods, and the application of those methods throughout the research effort.

Quantitative

Most social scientists face the challenge of assigning numbers to qualitative dimensions at some point in their research projects. In content analysis the *quantitative* effort begins by simply counting. The general procedure is for the scientist to select some word or words, theme or themes, or other symbol or symbols to represent the phenomenon in question and then to count the number of appearances of the chosen unit of analysis.

For example, to tap local interest, one might select references to the issue of whether the municipality will finance the renovation of a park and recreation area, editorials dealing with a proposed increment to the local sales tax, the attention paid to how well graduates of the local high school are doing in the colleges and universities they are attending, or the military service into which they elected to go. Similarly, headlines pointing to national unemployment rates, the prospect of war or peace, or the national incidence of illegal drug usage or criminal activity could signal a more national orientation.

If one is attempting to gather information for an issue of contrast, such as the question of local versus national orientation of newspapers, caution in the selection of the indicator symbols must be exercised. Perhaps you decided to conduct such a study during a presidential election year. Presidential elections are always accompanied by local and state elections as well as local referendum issues on which the voters are asked to register a preference. All of these political contests, local and national, as well as the referendum issues are provided newspaper attention prior to election day. Consequently, you would not be able to effectively use words of a political nature, e.g., election or campaign, as indicators of a local or national orientation. That is, these words are likely to appear in articles or editorials written about both the local and national elections and related concerns.

A further general point of caution should be registered concerning the selection of fragments of a communication document, such as words or phrases. The main thrust of a communication or a series of communications may be missed if the researcher is satisfied with a summary of these partial indicators. In order to ensure a more comprehensive understanding of the phenomenon under investigation, then, we suggest that these types of data be used in conjunction with other data collection procedures and forms of analysis. For example, one might use a primary document written by someone who witnessed or participated in the process being studied.

Manifest and Latent Content

The final point of Berelson's definition of content analysis is for the researcher to examine the *manifest content*. This calls for the investigator to focus on that which is explicitly presented within the communication. For example, in reviewing a newspaper account regarding defense spending, one might count the number of times words denoting weapons were used to determine a prowar (hawkish) or antiwar (dovish) orientation. While this procedure would certainly provide an easy coding criterion, it may lead to inaccurate conclusions. Therefore, some researchers have also examined the *latent content* or the underlying implication or meaning of a given communication. In our defense spending example, one would register a hawkish or dovish orientation of the author after reading the entire article. While the frequency of appearance of weapons terms may well influence this latent evaluation, it would be based upon additional considerations.

Latent content analysis clearly involves the risk of differential interpretation at different points in time by a researcher or approaching the material from different reference perspectives by multiple investigators. To further illustrate the risk of latent content analysis, consider a researcher who is tempted to suggest local implications from a nationally oriented article on unemployment, drug abuse, or crime. If the unemployment rate is reported to be high on a national basis, the researcher may conclude that it is high for the local area or soon will be. While it may very well be that the local unemployment rate is high, such cannot be concluded on the basis of an article that deals with a national point of reference.

While a training course would facilitate the establishment of interpretive standards, it is doubtful the problem of individual interpretations would be completely eliminated. Although many studies have been done using latent analysis, we encourage analysis of that which actually appears—the manifest content—and suggest foregoing a reading between the lines—the latent content. In sum, content analysis which is based upon these four considerations—objectivity, a systematic approach, quantitative enumeration, and a focus on manifest content—has been quite reliable.

Types of Data Used in Content Analysis

Introduction.   Content analysis can be, and probably has been, applied to virtually all forms of communication, including such obvious forms as written and spoken words, film, gestures, or body language. Of course, this broad statement of applicability presumes that the subject one is interested in investigating has been treated, directly or indirectly, in some available form of communication. Indeed, there are some areas of interest that can be better investigated by content analysis than any other procedure available to the researcher. This is most obviously the case when examining issues relevant to those who are deceased.

Primary and Secondary Sources. The researcher has a wide array of communication sources available for use in content analysis. These are generally seen to fall into two basic categories: (1) written documents and (2) filmed documents. Both of these categories are further divided between primary and secondary sources. *Primary sources* are those provided by persons who were present or actually experienced the event in question. Conversely, *secondary sources* are generated by persons who were not present for the event, but who were in receipt of sufficient information to construct a document. For example, the persons who were eyewitnesses (primary observers) could be surveyed, or primary sources that do exist could be examined. In addition to the dimensions of document form and closeness to the event (primary and secondary source), Bailey[2] has noted that one can distinguish between documents in terms of the purpose for which they were constructed and the degree of structure incorporated into the text.

In terms of purpose, written documents can be requested for a specific study. For example, we might ask pregnant teenagers to write accounts of the social circumstances of their pregnancies. A comparative study could then be done in terms of whether the prospective grandmothers had been adolescent parents, the number of siblings, birth order, socioeconomic conditions, educational attainment, and peer pressure.

The vast majority of documents examined by investigators, however, were created for some purpose other than that of the researcher. These can be of a personal nature, such as private correspondence or diaries, or impersonal communication, such as those associated with businesses or other formal organizations. Business letters, minutes of meetings, membership lists, and so forth are examples.

The purpose of the documents to be studied will provide insight into the dimension of structure. Personal documents (e.g., letters and diaries) tend to be less structured and informal; impersonal documents are usually much more structured and formal in nature. Any form of communication relevant to the functioning of an organization would fit into this latter category. Examples would include letters written to and from clients of a business or law firm, applications for employment or for research monies to public or private foundations, minutes of departmental or business meetings, memoranda sent to and from an office, or any other communication that would seem to be too important to rely simply upon memory. These types of primary communication would also constitute illustrations for a special subcategory of written data for content analysis—records.*

Written and Filmed Documents. The written word is the most plentiful source of material for the researcher considering content analysis. Our ability to communicate symbolically is what permits the continuity of any interpersonal or intergroup relationships. It is, after all, this ability that distinguishes us from other animal forms. In essence, our communication skills permit each generation to begin where the last one stopped.

The inventory for secondary written sources is virtually unlimited. The printed mass media, newspapers, magazines, transcripts of radio and television broadcasts, journals (academic and avocational), newsletters, and books of fiction and nonfiction could and have served researchers well. Parenthetically, it should be noted that any of these documents that were created as firsthand accounts by the writers, reporters, or authors would represent primary documents.

---

*We should point out that documents may convey ideas other than those intended or said by the writer. For example, a business letter regarding an application for employment might say: "All of our positions are filled at this time." In fact, the author may mean that the applicant would not be hired if he or she were the last person on earth.

A problem with many of the primary sources mentioned above is their availability. Private communication, whether it be personal or impersonal, is not easily obtained. Further, that which is obtained is likely to be limited. As a result, studies utilizing such material are often more similar to a case study than a survey research effort. This is generally not a problem with secondary sources. Virtually any library will have any number of these resources. The research projects one can conduct using such documents are limited only by one's imagination and creative efforts.

Records.   Within this discussion, further mention of the subcategory of records should be made. These documents constitute a unique category of written resources—official records. Some of these are primary and are in the form of the business communications we noted above. Others are more secondary in nature, e.g., governmental records, and are available in most university libraries in bound volumes or on microfilm. *The Congressional Record,* which is an edited record of the floor proceedings of Congress, of some speeches that were never made but were distributed, and of the delegates' voting records, is a case in point.

Additional sources of records are those that reflect public interests and concerns. Health, arrest, and conviction records are illustrative. While these may be of substantial interest to the researcher, they generally require agency permission for access.

Filmed Sources.   Film documents also suggest the dichotomy of primary and secondary sources. Primary film sources can range from private and personal snapshots or slides to home movies or videotapes that have been generated by the researcher, who was an eyewitness to the event. Secondary film sources include motion pictures, filmstrips of a documentary nature, television programing, or still photographs in magazines or newspapers, which a researcher might select as suitable data sources. We have labeled the commercial/professional film sources as secondary, although in a few instances, particularly in the filming of a documentary, the film maker may be generating a primary document in that the process of an actual event as it unfolds is being recorded.

In the past, film sources have not been extensively used in content analysis. Perhaps television programing has been the most frequently employed, particularly with regard to research in the area of violence. The failure of researchers to avail themselves of these data is unfortunate, since they provide a rich reference to themes, issues, and beliefs that are or have been endorsed by the culture or subcultures depicted. Further, as newspapers and magazines are examined to uncover the vested interests or political orientations of editors, so also can television news. For example, you, with stopwatch in hand, could select one of the major network news programs, find a comfortable chair, get a piece of paper and a pencil, and observe and chart three things. They are (1) the subjects or stories covered, (2) the amount of time afforded the coverage of each, and (3) the manner in which the story was covered. Evaluation of the last item has to do with whether the story was presented by the anchorperson, whether it was presented with moving-film footage, whether it was presented as a still photograph, or whether it was presented by a roving reporter positioned in front of a symbolic scene such as the Capitol building or the White House for visual background emphasis. After doing this for one network, switch to one of the others and repeat the procedure. At the conclusion of the exercise a variance in the manner in which news stories are evaluated and presented will in all likelihood be apparent. This information can then be used to respond to such questions as bias and special interest.

The major difficulty with the use of film documents is their availability. Clearly, primary personal sources are most difficult to gain access to, as is the case with personal primary written documents. However, secondary film sources are also difficult to obtain once the current showing has been completed, although the emergence of home-video services for commercial films may presage future changes. It is possible to gain access to the transcripts of some television programs by writing the network or networks on which they were shown. If such a request is honored, the researcher would have a written document of the dialogue, albeit without the visual film stimulus. Increasingly, however, there are film libraries from which such documents can be borrowed. Similarly, television stations often keep videotapes of some or all of their programming to which the student may gain access.

Steps in Coding Content Data

Throughout this text we have emphasized the importance of the interaction between the conceptual model and the research design. Decisions regarding data collection procedures and analysis cannot be of much value unless they are made with regard to the propositions articulated in the conceptual model.

The use of content analysis does not excuse the researcher from this emphasis. To fail to select the appropriate coding procedures to adequately tap the proposition or propositions put forth for examination would result in little more than wasted effort.

The analyst must make a number of decisions within the coding process. It is, in fact, a three-step effort that includes (1) selection of the categories, (2) selection of the unit or units of analysis, and (3) selection of the system of enumeration to be used. Each decision related to these three steps must be seen as interrelated.

Categories.   Perhaps the most important decision the researcher must make is to select the categories that will serve to guide the coding process. As noted by Ole Holsti, "categories should reflect the purposes of the research, be exhaustive, be mutually exclusive, independent, and be derived from a single classification principle."[3] As

we will observe, however, some of these criteria are more easily met than others.*

Relevant Categories.   The first requirement is for the categories selected to reflect the purpose of the research. This requires the analyst to examine the proposition or propositions of the research effort and the definition of terms provided in the conceptual model to ensure the categories selected will permit assessment of the stated variables. Determining the indicators of what will or will not result in inclusion of the respective categories is, in effect, operationally defining the variables.

To illustrate this notion, assume one is interested in studying the relationship between sex and discrimination in the labor force. The researcher elects to use the largest and most powerful newspaper in the area as the data source. Perhaps an article appears during the period of time established in the research parameters that cites average income differentials of men and women in the labor force. The salary statistics clearly indicate that women earn fewer dollars than men. Would these data be helpful in the decision you must make regarding your proposition? The answer is an emphatic, "No!" The information provided in the article would not allow you to distinguish if there was a differential between what women and men in the same job were earning, the number of years of seniority represented by the female and male labor force, the number of male and female workers engaged in part-time or full-time employment; or other such relevant questions. Clearly, many class III variables are present here. It is these types of indicators that are necessary, then, to determine which data fit into the response categories selected by the researcher in order to test adequately a hypothesis.

Exhaustive Categories.   Second, the categories selected must be exhaustive. This requirement

---

*We acknowledge a primary debt to Holsti, and secondarily, to Fred Kerlinger[4] and to Ken Bailey[5] as major sources of input to this discussion. Indeed, the work of Holsti has been of major importance to us throughout the preparation and writing of this chapter. While we do not attempt to present all of the points offered in his excellent book here, he has served as an impetus to our thinking.

holds that any relevant item within the sample data can be assigned to one or another existing category. This is a very difficult and can be a virtually impossible criterion to completely satisfy. Consider again the broad issue of sex and discrimination. The researcher attempting to count every word, combination of words, phrase, sentence, paragraph, or theme that might be relevant to this issue would be confronted with a very difficult task. It is suggested that the researcher select and define categories as carefully as possible. For example, the researcher might elect employment discrimination as a category, but distinguish among the subcategories of management, white-collar workers, blue-collar workers, and so forth. Additional categories should be established for coding articles that reflect discrimination in other areas, such as education, political events, and housing. Subcategories that are germane to these areas should also be identified. In sum, the better the definition, the closer will be the approximation to the criterion of exhaustiveness.

Mutually Exclusive Categories.   Third, the categories must be mutually exclusive. That is, the researcher should not be able to allocate any given piece of content data to more than one category. Using the previous illustration of local versus national interest, assume that an article has been published on recently introduced national legislation with specific local implications, e.g., on nuclear power plants where such a plant is located in the local community. An article of this nature could be placed in both categories (local and national), which would obviously violate the requirement of mutual exclusivity. This type of difficulty again argues for careful and unambiguous operational definitions.

Independent Categorization.   The fourth requirement of sampling categories is that of independence. This, as with the requirement for exhaustive categories, is often difficult to meet. The requirement for independence means that the allocation of one piece of content data to a category will have no effect upon the assignment of any other

data to that category or any other category within the classification schema. The difficulty of meeting this criterion is especially present when the researcher is working with a scale of some dimension. To illustrate, consider expanding the measure of earning-power discrimination between men and women discussed earlier to include intervals of intensity as well as direction. Let us assume five intervals, or increments, of intensity ranging from equal rewards for equal work for men and women to substantial differences in pay and perquisites for employees in the same job. Since the resulting scale, by definition, will be ordinal, the establishment of categories and assignment of items will be accomplished on the basis of relative comparisons. Therefore, the assignment of any item to any one of the categories along this scale will affect the assignment of every other item that follows. In order for a scale to be valuable, it must be relevant to the data available. Therefore, the points on the continuum that compose the scale will be adjusted or redefined in reference to the material being used. Once again, the more careful and precise the definitions are, the more likely one is to meet this requirement.

Unidimensionality.   The final requirement is that each category is to be derived from only one classification principle. This rule is reflective of the notion of *unidimensionality*. That is, a conceptual dimension can and should only translate into one empirical variable. Let us again refer to our illustration of discrimination against female workers. Suppose an article appeared in the newspaper that focused upon smaller economic rewards for nonwhite workers as contrasted with white workers. Presumably, the white and nonwhite categories of workers contain females and males. Indeed, let us assume the article notes that the nonwhite labor force contains more female than male workers, while the sexual balance is in the reverse direction for white workers. The researcher, newly introduced to content analysis, might be tempted to use this article as supportive evidence for the proposition that females are discriminated against in the labor market. However, it is apparent such an article could also be coded as relevant to racial discrimination. While sex and race represent two dimensions that have been shown to be related to discrimination, they cannot be evaluated as one dimension.

In summary of the criteria for category construction, we emphasize (1) careful selection of the categories to be used and (2) careful definition of those selected.

Units of Analysis—Recording Units.   Once the researcher has selected the categories, the task of choosing the units of analysis must be confronted. In general, researchers who have used written documents have used one of five *units of analysis,* or *recording units.*

Single Word, or Symbol.   The most simple and straightforward of these choices is the *single word,* or *symbol.* In our example of the local or national orientation of newspapers, one might simply count the number of times the name of the local community was employed as opposed to references to other major metropolitan areas such as Washington, D.C., or New York City. As long as the analyst restricts the time frame and the number of documents to be surveyed to reasonably small parameters, the use of the single-word unit has some advantages. The principal advantage is that the subjective aspect of coding is virtually eliminated. A related benefit is realized if the analyst has assistants who participate in the coding process, because the need for judgment is eliminated. Therefore, the reliability of the coding is likely to be quite high.

On the other hand, when a study requires surveying a large volume of printed matter, the single-word unit has rarely been used. For example, if the researcher wished to examine each editorial of a newspaper that has been publishing for 100 years, the magnitude of the task of examining single words is obvious. The advent of the computer, however, has brought some relief to this type of effort. When documents have been computer stored, the costs in time and money have been substantially reduced and tediousness of the loca-

tion of terms and concern with reliability have been virtually eliminated.

Despite the advantages of using words as the unit of analysis and improvements to the process by computer manipulation, some studies in which researchers are interested cannot be conducted using this unit. The inapplicability may be due to the nature of the materials to be analyzed, the variables to be measured, the hypotheses to be examined, or the conceptual model to be assessed.

Theme.   Second, if the researcher is unable to use words, the theme as a unit of analysis may be used. The *theme* refers to the overall purpose, aim, or goal of a document. According to Holsti, the theme "is the most useful unit of content analysis."[6] There are some areas of content analysis in which the theme is virtually the mandated unit of analysis. Researchers interested in value orientation or belief systems would find this to be the case. For example, one might be interested in themes such as nuclear energy and its potential for altering life or the effect of industrialization upon the environment.

However, the use of the theme as a unit of analysis is not without problems. It generally takes longer to identify and subsequently code themes. Unlike words (noted above) or sentences or paragraphs (discussed below), the theme does not have clear-cut boundaries. Words are separated by a space on either side, sentences begin with a capital letter and end with a period or other punctuation, and paragraphs are identified by indentation. The theme may be apparent from a few words, or it may require much more investigation, including multiple volumes. Reaching agreement among several coders in the absence of such clear indicators is difficult and may undermine reliability.

In essence, we are saying that use of the theme as a unit of analysis introduces subjectivity into the coding process. The researcher is not likely to be able to limit the analysis to the manifest content of the document or documents being studied. Therefore, while we do not disagree with Holsti's claim that the theme is perhaps the most useful unit of analysis, we would urge you to gain some experience with content analysis before attempting a project using it as the unit of analysis.

Sentence or Paragraph.   The third and fourth units of analysis are the *sentence* and the *paragraph*. Despite the easily recognized boundaries of each, they are rarely used as a researcher's choice of units of analysis. The reason for their lack of popularity is that they often contain more than one dimension and, therefore, are quite difficult to code. The following sentence will serve as an illustration: "Although a number of arguments of discrimination against women remain, women are currently enjoying higher educational achievement, larger salaries, and greater political power than ever before." In this case one unit of analysis, i.e., the sentence, contains words that could be assigned to five different categories—women, discrimination, education, salary, and power—but does not clearly fit into any single category. Despite the labor involved, the word or symbol would have been the preferred unit of analysis here.

The problem of subjectivity is also present with the sentence or paragraph. Indeed, this problem will always be present when more comprehensive units of analysis are employed. A well-defined coding schedule can be constructed for the word or symbol, but this is not easily accomplished with other units. Consequently, the related issue of reliability is a concern when using any unit other than the word or symbol.

Item.   The final unit of analysis sometimes used by researchers who have elected content analysis is the item.* The *item* refers to the entire document, whether it be a book, film, television program, or whatever. This unit, as with the sentence and paragraph, presents coding difficulties not in identifying the boundaries but in deciding upon the category of placement. If one read a book about war with a love story interwoven into the plot, in which category should it be placed—war or romance?

In addition to the item's being a unit that is too crude for most research purposes, it is really very similar to the theme. The only distinction seems to be that the item does refer to a total piece of communication, while the theme can refer to only parts of one document or multiple documents.

Another consideration confronting the researcher is that a recording unit may not lend itself to classification without some additional reference to the context in which it appears. A *context unit* is larger than the recording unit and affords the researcher the opportunity to assess more accurately the manner in which the recording unit is used. Let us use location of a nuclear power plant as an illustration and assume that the decision to locate a nuclear power plant in a specific community is currently under discussion. The researcher is interested in determining whether the editorial perspective of the local newspaper is a positive or negative one. Initially the analyst may have elected to use the words *nuclear power plant* as the unit of analysis. However, registering the number of times *nuclear power plant* appeared in editorials would not indicate whether the editorial direction was favorable or unfavorable. To obtain this information, our researcher would have to elect a context unit. That unit could be the sentence, paragraph, theme, or entire editorial in which the word appeared.

It should be recognized that every research effort does not require the election of a context unit. However, when a project does suggest such, the researcher should make a selection in terms of the hypothesis or hypotheses being examined and with some attention toward efficiency.

Systems of Enumeration.   Before we discuss the final step of the coding process, three general points need to be stated.

---

*Throughout this text, we have attempted to have each term or concept refer to one idea. While the term *item* was used in reference to an element within a measuring instrument, we have elected to remain consistent with Holsti's labeling and employ *item* here as a unit of analysis, or recording unit.[7]

First, as noted, all three steps of category selection, selection of the units of analysis, and the system of enumeration must be seen as interrelated. Initially, the analyst selects categories that will permit measurement of the variables and a testing of the hypothesis or hypotheses. With those categories firmly in mind, the researcher then elects the unit of analysis. It may be that classifying in terms of the categories elected does not result in a good fit. If this is the case, the researcher may consider altering the categories, selecting a different unit of analysis, or both. The third step of electing a system of enumeration is taken with recognition of the decisions made in the first two steps and with reference to the purpose of the study. Again, one is reminded of the importance of the integration of the conceptual model and research design.

Second, it may be necessary to distinguish between the unit of analysis and the *unit of enumeration,* or *scoring unit.* While many instances reflect no difference between the two, other situations do. To illustrate, let us return to the local versus national orientation of the five newspapers we hypothetically placed in your area of residence, i.e., the *Times, Ledger, Post, Sentinel,* and *Sun.* Thus, the unit of analysis is that of the individual newspapers. As we did earlier, let us also assume that one has decided to use the frequency of the appearance of the name of the community and the frequency of the appearance of the names of other major metropolitan areas each day in each newspaper as the indicators of direction or orientation to facilitate your decision. The unit of enumeration, or scoring unit, then will be the appearance of the name of your community and the names of others. Following the time frame one has selected, one could then rate the five newspapers (units of analysis) by counting the presence or frequency of the respective community references (units of enumeration). The key point to remember here is that the community references are the units of enumeration—not the units of analysis. The former are used to score the latter.

Third, we mention the importance of noting the overall number of units of analysis that are examined. In our example we would want to know the number of editions reviewed for each newspaper included in the analysis. Our purpose would be poorly served if we only knew that your local community was referred to 17 times but did not know the base number of opportunities for it to be mentioned. This final step of the coding process introduces the necessity to quantify the variables to be measured.

With these considerations in mind the analyst has four systems of enumeration from which to select: (1) presence or absence of the category within the document, (2) frequency of appearance of the category within the document, (3) the volume of space and/or time provided the category, and (4) the intensity of expression.

Presence or Absence. This system of enumeration is the simplest of those available, merely requiring the researcher to note whether the categories selected are represented by the selected units of analysis or enumeration within the documents being studied. To illustrate, recalling our five hypothetical newspapers and the issue of discrimination against women in the labor force, assume we have identified a number of mutually exclusive categories, e.g., lower incidence of promotion, lesser level of entry credentials, lower levels of pay, and fewer retirement benefits. Assume, as well, that we will review each edition of each of the five newspapers for a period of one year. Our task is to identify which, if any, of these papers holds an editorial policy that is discriminatory. While we have satisfied the nominal system of enumeration of presence or absence, we are not likely to be very confident about the conclusions reached from these results. For example, the *Times* may have had only one reference to one category for the entire year, but we would have to classify it as a discriminatory newspaper because of that one reference.

However, if one's research objective was to identify those newspapers that have addressed different societal issues (e.g., pollution, welfare rights, abortion issues, and so forth), then the presence or absence nominal classification would be appropriate.

Frequency. Returning to our issue of the newspaper's discriminatory posture, we would be more comfortable with the conclusions if we also assessed *how often* our categories are represented in each newspaper. We are likely to discover that while reference to one or more of the categories may appear in each of the selected newspapers, they will appear more frequently in some than in others. This, then, would allow establishment of an ordinal ranking in terms of incidence.

Obviously, knowing the number of times a category is represented offers stronger evidence than just knowing if the category is present. While the assessment of frequency of appearance is *employed more often* than any other system of enumeration, note that an underlying assumption with this measure is that each occurrence of the recording unit is equal. Regardless of the unit of analysis, the assumption of equal weight is not always warranted. When the analyst believes this assumption is inappropriate, still more informative systems of enumeration are available.

Space and Time. The frequency assessment can be improved if the researcher wishes to code the volume of space devoted to a category, e.g., two columns as opposed to one or one-half. The time measure is also helpful in examining film documents, e.g., the exercise of timing different stories on television news programs discussed earlier. An important consideration of using space as a measure is that it can be weighted in terms of where the content was located. That is, articles on the front page or editorial page may be seen as more important than those found inside and, therefore, be assigned a higher weight value.

If we elected to focus on the amount of space used as the system of enumeration in our discrimination example, we would record the length and width of each story relevant to the four categories carried by each of the five hypothetical newspapers. The most common frequency space assessment is the number of column inches afforded the category. Just as frequency assessment improved our confidence over presence and absence as a measure, use of the amount of space will increase confidence over the use of frequency alone, which will make our ordinal rankings of the five newspapers more likely to be accurate in terms of the direction of their editorial policy toward discrimination against women in the labor force.

There remain, however, two major difficulties that the space/time system does not address. First, the measurement of space/time allocation does not permit the researcher to distinguish the actual direction of the values or bias of the author of the article, program, or whatever. Similarly, since space measures are not designed to measure content, we cannot assess the strength of the statement or statements.

Intensity. These space/time problems are addressed in the final system of enumeration. Let us continue with the example of discrimination against women in the labor force. Assuming the following three statements have appeared in one or more of the five newspapers, consider the content of each:

1. Women are currently gaining entry into management-level positions with less education than that required for men for the same job.
2. Women are currently gaining entry into management-level positions with substantially fewer years of education than required for men for the same job.
3. Women are currently gaining entry into management-level positions with an apparent disregard of their education, while men are required to meet strict standards of educational attainment for employment in the same job.

The reader of any of them will, in all likelihood, conclude that the author of each is somewhat of a sexist and has a prejudiced attitude that might lead to discrimination against women within the labor market. Thus, the direction of the statements is clear. The reader might also discern some differences of degree or intensity between the statements. In order to code these differences, however, we must be able to assign numerical values.

The researcher accomplishes this by employing an available composite measure.* In this case we are interested in establishing a simple, ordinal scale. Although we would agree that the authors of the above statements are all sexist, we would not suggest they are equally prejudiced. Rather, as the statements are presented, they represent an order from least to most sexist. Therefore, we would expect someone who registered agreement to the third statement to also agree with the first and second statements. People who disagree with the third, but agree with the second would be expected to also agree with the first statement. Finally, people who disagree with the third and second may still agree with the first, or they may disagree with all three statements.

If we were using frequency as our system for coding and statement one appeared in the *Post* and statement three in the *Ledger,* we would be forced to evaluate both papers equally in terms of discrimination against women in the labor force. By examining these statements in terms of intensity, however, it is clear that the *Ledger* maintains a stronger sexist approach than does the *Post.*

In contrast to the other systems of enumeration, the assessment of intensity provides the researcher with the most accurate indication of the content of the document. However, it is also one of the more difficult aspects of coding in that the additional subjective judgment of intensity is required. This means that the researcher must be concerned with the elements of language to the extent that they may indicate varying degrees of intensity.

One procedure for coding intensity, which is discussed by Holsti[8] and developed by Thurstone, is the *paired comparison technique.*[9] This technique requires the researcher to register a comparison of every possible pair of stimuli to determine which receive the higher and which receive the lower ranks. In our example of statements concerning entry into the labor market, the following system of paired comparisons could have been used.

1 versus 2   2 versus 3   1 versus 3

The student should realize that in conducting an actual research effort, many more items would be included for comparisons. Nevertheless, you should be able to observe that if 1 is lower than 2 or 3, and 2 is lower than 3, a basis for an attitudinal scale would be in evidence.

Sampling

Sampling is the final methodological consideration of content analysis that we discuss. Although we have placed it last, we do not mean to imply that the researcher postpones sampling considerations until all other decisions are made. Indeed, as we have emphasized, methodological decisions cannot be made singularly, but rather must be considered in concert.

Since sampling has been discussed in considerable detail in Chapters 6 and 7, our discussion of sampling at this juncture is brief. With the voluminous nature of much of the material available to the analyst who has elected a content analysis data-gathering procedure, selection of a sampling procedure is a virtual necessity. Failure to sample the available number of newspapers, magazines, books, government documents, letters, and other written forms would present a task so formidable that such fertile data might be seen as discouraging rather than encouraging.

The first, and most important, step is to determine a sampling frame, or a listing of units from which the sample is to be selected. A portion of this task is met when the research problem is determined. Continuing with the problem of the editorial direction of five newspapers with regard to women in the labor force, we could further narrow the sampling frame by restricting the study to a time frame such as the last year, the last three months, or whatever.

By the same token, we will be limited in any inferences about editorial bias we can make. If our interest was broader and we wished to infer to an

---

*See Chapter 9 where composite measures are discussed in detail.

entire state, region, or the country, and for a much greater time frame (e.g., 20, 50, or 100 years), our task would have been much more complex. Indeed, every newspaper in the respective area selected that was published during part of or the entire time frame would have to be included.

Once the list has been constructed, the researcher can sample by any of the probability techniques we have discussed earlier—simple random, systematic, stratified, or cluster sampling. The analyst must first select which units will be used for the sample. In our example, that means which newspapers will be surveyed. This decision is followed by which editions of the newspapers selected will be used; whether the entire edition will be reviewed or whether attention will be limited to the front-page section, or editorial page, or book reviews, for example; and the election of the specific units of enumeration—entire articles, editorials, paragraphs, sentences, or words.

By judicious usage of the sampling techniques available, the researcher can reduce the volume of material to a manageable level and have confidence in the representativeness of that which is selected. Let us now turn to a more inclusive review of the advantages and disadvantages of using content analysis.[10]

Advantages and Disadvantages of Content Analysis

Advantages.   Perhaps that which most strongly recommends content analysis is its *economy*. While some documents may be difficult or expensive to obtain, in general content analysis represents a saving of time, money, and effort. The manifold problems the researcher may encounter in gathering one's own data are at least minimized. For example, one does not have to coordinate a schedule with that of those to be interviewed, or worry about unreturned schedules in questionnaire designs and whether they represent respondents who would not or could not cooperate. The analyst generally does not have to worry about a research

staff and having sufficient money to pay them. In essence, the only necessity is to have access to the material to be analyzed.

Secondly, content analysis may be the only procedure available for studying those who are deceased. The researcher may not be completely satisfied with the material available, but if it is the "only game in town," one will have to compromise. Any effort to examine *inaccessible* subjects, then, might result in a search for available documents to provide some degree of understanding.

A third important advantage of using content analysis is one that is shared by other *unobtrusive measures.** That is, it is a *nonreactive* method. The writers of the newspapers, magazines, books, and so forth, do not, in all likelihood, conceive of their work being used as data by a social scientist. However, nonreactive does not mean free from bias, which unfortunately suggests a disadvantage of content analysis. More specifically, the existence of a piece of written communication suggests a survival bias. Most documents are written on paper and, unless carefully preserved, will disintegrate or be discarded, as when file cabinets are purged to make room for more recent memoranda. Further, if a researcher is interested in examining an issue as it relates to a cross section of the population, the use of content analysis will probably bias the results in favor of the more highly educated. A distinct correlation exists between educational achievement and voluntary reading. Because newspapers, magazines, and similar forms are commercial enterprises, they are much more likely to represent the viewpoint of those who compose the target population for their sales and those of their advertisers. Therefore, the perspectives of the lesser educated are likely to be afforded little, if any, attention. Analysis of such documents, then, would clearly not represent a complete cross section of the population. Thus, the nonreactive characteristic of content analysis must be seen as an advantage *and* a disadvantage.

A fourth advantage of content analysis is that it can be used to study a phenomenon of interest

---

*We mention unobtrusive measures but briefly here. They will be dealt with in more detail in the next chapter.

over a long period of time, i.e., longitudinal analysis. If we were interested in examining the change in attitude toward women in the labor force since 1900, we could study that attitude change by examining newspapers published throughout this century. Although it would be possible to examine this issue by conducting survey research of persons living within this time span, it is likely that such research would result in a great deal of expense and error. The data would probably be biased in that (1) we would be dependent upon the accuracy of the respondent's memory, (2) the exposure that any given respondent would have to the culture as a whole would be limited, regardless of the degree of accuracy of his or her memory, (3) respondents may not wish to acknowledge the degree of sexism that once existed, and (4) the respondent may present recollections to maximize how he or she appears to the researcher.

A final advantage we should make note of is the *quality* of the communication. In general, documents are authored by trained writers, especially newspapers, magazines, journals, books, or speeches. The information presented is likely to be much more precise, organized, focused, and, therefore, more valuable to the researcher than would be written responses to a distributed questionnaire.

Disadvantages.   Despite these recommendations, there are costs that are somewhat unique to this procedure. Perhaps the most important difficulty is that the materials were not written or filmed for the purpose for which the researcher intends to use them. For example, political speeches often reflect campaign strategies designed to elicit votes rather than the speaker's true feelings about the subject matter. A bias, by definition, is introduced by the author's filtering of the information used to produce the document. If secondary sources were used, two filtering processes have already been introduced to the data. Students learn during their efforts for their first academic term paper that the encyclopedia is not an ideal source. The reason, of course, is that the material presented in such publications represents (1) the writer's interpretation of the subject matter and (2) an effort to condense

the original material into a much shorter or concise package. It is reasonable, then, to anticipate that some degree of bias has been permitted to enter and may, therefore, influence the accuracy of what is presented. This is likely to occur whether we are searching for information about a conceptual model, an event, a person's biography, or whatever.

Selective Document Survival.   We have noted the fragile nature of documents. Since they are most often recorded on paper, some effort must be made to preserve them if they are to survive. Obviously the same degree of concern is not registered for all those documents that social scientists might have an interest in examining. This *selective survival* is a problem with which the researcher must deal, and it can have several negative consequences.

First, it may be that some of the documents needed are missing. Selective survival, then, can contribute to the problem of *incompleteness,* which can also be noted when documents do not contain a total accounting of the situation being discussed. Without prior experience or knowledge of these occurrences, the researcher is at a distinct disadvantage.

Second, primary personal documents, such as letters and diaries, are often written with the presumption of knowledge on behalf of the reader. Consequently, a researcher electing to use sources of this nature is particularly vulnerable to this difficulty.

Third, an additional concern with incompleteness is evident when the document to be used does not contain information that would allow the researcher to tap the hypothesis or hypotheses directly. One must often interpret the content, which has the effect of reducing confidence in the final analysis. In essence this focuses on latent content analysis, the use of which must be done cautiously.

Finally, incompleteness has on occasion turned out to mean *lack of availability.* That is, there are areas of interest to researchers for which there are no documents. In some cases records were not kept, in others they have been destroyed, and in still others they may be unavailable because of confidentiality or for national-security reasons.

Sampling Bias.   Earlier we noted the likelihood of *sampling bias* against less-educated persons in our study using newspapers. This is a frequent difficulty of content analysis in that the data are almost always verbal. Persons with less education read and write less than their more highly educated counterparts. The written mass media is not directed toward them, nor are they likely to create their own documents. Consequently, they are often underrepresented, misrepresented, or not represented at all in a study using content analysis. The researcher must be aware of this and be cautious with any observations that are inferred.

Document Format.   Another weakness of content analysis is that many documents of interest *lack a standard format.* Although sources such as newspapers or magazines are regularly published in somewhat of a standardized presentation (e.g., front page, editorial page, and sports page), many others, especially personal communications, are not. If the source approaches standardization, comparison research is possible. However, in those cases where there is not a regular format, comparison efforts are, at best, difficult.

Time Dimension.   Even when comparability is possible, studies that call for longitudinal analysis must be adjusted for comparability over time. Despite the fact that the capacity for longitudinal analysis represents a strong advantage of content analysis, events occasionally occur that significantly alter the interpretative framework. Consider the cataclysmic political events of the resignation of Vice President Spiro Agnew, which was closely followed by the resignation of President Richard Nixon. A study of political attitudes across a time frame that contained these two events would have to register adjustments in order for comparability to be meaningful.

Coding.   Finally, we note coding difficulties as a disadvantage of content analysis. Since the focus is on documents, that are written in words, quan-

tification is difficult. When the additional problems of lack of standardization, variation in length and space, and contrasts in content and subject matter are included, coding becomes particularly problematic.

Summary

Despite these weaknesses, however, content analysis is a procedure that we feel justifies more usage than it has received in the past. It is a fertile procedure for investigating any problem or issue for which the content of communication can serve as a basis of inference. The analyst who elects it as a method, however, must adhere to the basic guidelines outlined in this chapter. As we said at the outset of this chapter, the absence of fieldwork does not excuse the researcher from selecting appropriate problems for investigation, being creative or imaginative, and, in general, performing the hard work that science demands.

SECONDARY ANALYSIS

Secondary analysis, as with content analysis, invites the researcher to examine materials that already exist. Because of this similarity, many of the comments we have made concerning content analysis are also applicable to secondary analysis. The basic difference between the two approaches is that secondary analysis is directed toward quantified data that already have been collected rather than words that have already been written or spoken. Both also share the characteristic that they have been initially produced for reasons other than those to which the researcher intends.

Simply stated, *secondary analysis* is "the extraction of knowledge on topics other than those which were the focus of the original surveys"[11] or other data-gathering processes. We might add to this the notion of reexamining data collected for the same problem area but with new or different techniques of analysis. Despite the apparent simplicity of this definition, we suggest that secondary analysis is deceptively complex. The absence of very many substantial pieces of research utilizing this procedure prior to the 1960s, as noted by

Herbert Hyman, probably speaks more to the absence of skill "in the principles and procedures of secondary analysis of survey data"[12] than to any other singular cause.

Certainly the feasibility of performing secondary analysis is much greater now than for previous generations of researchers, because there are many more data sources available. Hyman writes that "because of substantial support from public and private funds archives of data have multiplied in number and their holdings have greatly increased."[13]

Further, the wider availability and understanding of computer facilities now enable the researcher to examine large volumes of data that would have represented an impossible task for earlier analysts. With the increasing availability and facility for the components of analysis, secondary analysis has become a much more viable method for social science researchers.

Change of Order

The situation confronted by the secondary analyst is considerably different from that dealt with by the primary analyst. The biggest difference is that the data are already collected. This eliminates the difficult tasks of schedule construction, distribution, and collection of data. Conversely, it usually also means the data will not fit the purposes of the investigation as well as original data would have. This absence of fit often requires altering the order in which the researcher approaches the research project.

Scientists are taught to approach research by identifying the problem area to be investigated and then proceeding to the process of data collection. Similarly, we proceed from dimensions to variables and from propositions to hypotheses to testing. Adoption of secondary analysis may force a departure from, or even a reversal of, this normative pattern. The researcher might have to confront such questions as: what type of explanation will the available data permit, or which concepts or constructs will the available variables serve as operational assessments? It is only after becoming

familiar with the available data that one can begin to generate hypotheses for examination.

From a methodological perspective, the primary analyst is, in essence, responsible for planning the entire research effort. The decisions involved are made with an eye toward maximizing the fit between the research design and the conceptual model and minimizing problems of analysis and interpretation. While the secondary analyst is free from these constraints, the quality of the resulting project will depend upon the skill of the researcher in selecting the appropriate survey or surveys and in substantively extracting meaningful data from them. As noted by Hyman:

> *In primary analysis the design is achieved by* prearrangement *of parts of the survey. In secondary analysis it is achieved by* rearrangement *of a survey or the combination of several surveys rearranged as if they were components of a larger planned inquiry, and by the elimination of those portions of one or more of the original surveys that would frustrate or complicate the analysis.*[14]

This process is anything but simple. Recounting in a personal journal their difficulties with a secondary study of the effect of father absence on the development of children, Janet Hunt and Larry Hunt acknowledge the difficulty they experienced establishing a focus from a large volume of data to the specific questions they were interested in addressing.[15] This would suggest the problem of seeing the trees but not the forest. There is often so much data that the elimination of some, or rearrangement of other components, requires considerable insight and understanding. Although the computer is of great assistance to the secondary analyst, the researcher must register considerable thought before the data analysis is initiated. To immediately begin to manipulate the data would likely be a wheel-spinning procedure.

The Procedure

The techniques of analysis available to the secondary researcher are essentially the same as those used in the analysis of any other type of data. The big difference is that the secondary analyst must work with what is at hand. While excused from many constraints and considerations of the primary analyst, the primary analyst does have the major advantage of formulating the design to address the specific research question or questions. While the primary researcher may be forced to use a smaller sample, shorten the interview, or condense the observations, the focus of the study can be preserved. Since the secondary analyst cannot develop any aspect of the survey, the researcher's developmental skills must be reflected in other ways.

Location of a Data Source. The first step for the secondary analyst is to locate an available data source that will best suit the research objectives. We suggest a review of the data sources held in your university library. Most universities house data gathered by the federal government, your state government, or even the government of your locality. Indeed, your first reaction may well be one of surprise at the sheer volume of available information. Rather than attempting to review every source, we recommend that you begin your effort by selecting data relevant to your general area of interest.

For example, if you are interested in a demographic issue, census data would be a good place to start. The census, beginning in 1790 and published each decade thereafter, has a wealth of demographic data on the population of the United States reported for a variety of political jurisdictions.

Census data are divided into first- and second-order variables. The *first-order variables* are fertility, mortality, and migration. These three are canvassed, coded, and presented in a reasonably uniform manner for countries throughout the world. This provides the student with the opportunity to perform some longitudinal and/or international comparisons, if such are relevant areas of interest.

Second-order variables reflect all of the remaining information that census data contain. These variables are often of greater interest to

social scientists as they reflect such variables as educational achievement, occupational classification, sex, income, and age. However, comparability among the second-order variables with census enumerations of other cultures is not as easily attained.

Another major area of interest to many students is that of corrections, law enforcement, and criminology. A helpful secondary source in this area is the Federal Bureau of Investigation's (FBI's) quarterly publication, *The Uniform Crime Report.* This document is a standardized presentation of all criminal activity reported to and recorded by the police throughout America.

Beyond the large holdings of most college and university libraries are a growing number of data archives. The data resources contained in these archives, as in the governmental documents, are available to anyone who would like to use them. The procedure for attaining these data is to write the archive and request a copy of the specific data and codebook in which you are interested. One such facility is the Survey Research Center (SRC) located at the University of Michigan in Ann Arbor. While there is a charge for some of these data, it is minimal.

Study of the Data Bank. Once the researcher has a copy of the codebook, the task is to examine which attributes have variable measurements. Upon beginning this review, it is not uncommon for the analyst to become excited over the wealth of material available. Indeed, the quality of the data often surpasses what the researcher could have gathered personally, since these data are often collected on a national sample and there is usually more data than could possibly be used for the particular study the analyst has in mind. Recognizing the saving of time and money from gathering this body of information, the researcher's first reaction is often to see these circumstances as fortuitous and the task confronting the researcher as a straightforward one.

Data Reduction. After familiarizing oneself with the data set, the next task is to reduce the global perspective to a more narrow collection of available items. That is, the analyst must achieve a focus.

Ideally, completion of this task is represented by formulation of the research question or questions. Frequently, however, the effort to narrow the items to a more precise subset results in a proliferation of additional questions with which the researcher must deal. Some of these are substantive in nature, while others are procedural.

We will use our experience with the Survey Research Center data bank to illustrate the subsequent steps the secondary analyst must take. The general problem area of our research project centered on the effectiveness of socioeconomic status (SES) as a predictor variable for political preference. The research design called for this analysis to be done on a particular national political contest. Before deciding to utilize the Survey Research Center data base, a preliminary review of similar data collected for earlier national elections was undertaken. That is, codebooks of similar national studies conducted by the Survey Research Center had been examined prior to receipt of the codebook for the election in question. Therefore, it was felt that a great deal of the focusing work had been accomplished.

Operationalization.   In this study, it had been decided to construct an index for the predictor or independent variable of SES. It was further decided to employ the available measurements for the variables of occupation, education, and income. In each of the previous codebooks reviewed, each of these variables was assessed for both the respondent and the head of the household. Therefore, the analyst had a choice of whether to look at data for the respondent, the head of the household, or both in those cases where they greatly differed.

The data in question were consistent with previous assessments for two of these dimensions: education and occupation. Unfortunately, this edition of the Survey Research Center data only contained total family income for the final dimension.

Few would not argue that income is important to the assessment of SES. Indeed, it is difficult to conceptualize an adequate measurement of SES without some type of income input. How could that be accomplished? The other indicators were formulated for individual respondents and individual heads of households. We couldn't combine this input and obtain family occupation or family education. Even if such a measure could be constructed, it is likely that most households surveyed would have more than two members. Further, it is likely that some of these additional members, e.g., older offspring or grandparents, would have some level of income. If that assumption is valid, how much did they contribute to the total family income? It would be unreasonable to respond to this question with a standard percentage for every household surveyed.

In this case, it is clear that narrowing the global perspective introduced more questions. Confronted with the problem of not being able to examine income in conjunction with education and occupation for either the respondent or the head of the household, what should we do?

We had three basic alternatives from which to choose: (1) we could alter our general area of interest from SES and political preference to something else; (2) we could collect primary data from a much smaller sample with the size limited by the very important concerns of money and time; or (3) with the assumption of a high correlation among education, occupation, and income, we could reformulate our assessment index of SES to exclude the dimension of income and continue with the secondary analysis.

Following a great deal of thought and soul-searching, the final alternative was elected. It was felt that the richness of a national probability sample and the quality of data collected by well-trained interviewers could not be forfeited in light of a question of national interest and importance. While we could have designed a primary study that would have permitted a direct assessment, the costs in terms of time, money, and the loss of a national sample would have been substantial. This example should illustrate the importance of maintaining flexibility throughout the process of secondary analysis.

New Ideas for Old Data: Perceptual Acuity

In exercising flexibility, the secondary analyst is often challenged by the need for imagination and creativity. Can data or a configuration of data be isolated so that it will contribute to further understanding of a social question? Can suitable and acceptable measurements for dimensions be found where other researchers have largely failed?

The central ingredient necessary for effective secondary analysis, content analysis, or any other unobtrusive measure is *perceptual acuity*. A simple definition of *perception* is "stimulus plus past experience." Any element within one's culture can serve as a stimulant and, in terms of its physical dimensions, will be identical for anyone to observe. However, each of us has a unique background of previous experience. Interpretation of any given stimulus is likely to reflect these differences. To illustrate the importance of perception, we have occasionally asked our students to draw a house. The stimulus of the request is the same for every student, but when the drawings are submitted, we have noted divergent architectural designs. We will usually see facsimiles of homes that are of a ranch style; row house or town house style; colonial mansions; apartment buildings; log cabins; or mobile homes. All of these styles are reflective of the types of experiences students are most likely to have had or dreams of what they would like to achieve. Despite conducting this exercise over a number of years, we have never received a drawing of an igloo or thatched hut. Homes of this type were not within our student's previous experience or widespread exposure. On the other hand, if we were to conduct this exercise among Eskimo students or residents of New Guinea, the opposite results might well be obtained.

An additional point of importance regarding perception is provided in the work of Walter Lippmann. Lippmann suggested that one perceives a situation by defining it and then seeing what has been defined, rather than seeing it and defining what has been seen.[16] Despite the time lapse since this observation, we believe that Lippmann's suggestion is generally still the case. The secondary analyst must be cautious to avoid this type of error, since any data the secondary analyst seeks to examine will function as a stimulus and the researcher clearly brings past experience to the data examination. Much of that experience is quite useful, e.g., academic training and previous research experience. However, the researcher must approach the data with the widest of perceptual frameworks. Because the data were not created for research on the question area, artificially narrowing the potential of the data through one's limited experiential base would be unfortunate.

We encourage the student interested in using secondary analysis to be imaginative and creative. Reviewing a number of studies that have used secondary analysis will often open a floodgate of ideas. Familiarize yourself with the various types and forms of secondary data available. Free of many of the restraints confronted by the primary analyst, secondary analysis offers a ticket to an adventure in exploration.

Advantages of Secondary Analysis

Many of the advantages and disadvantages we cited for content analysis are applicable to secondary analysis. As with content analysis, the *economy* of time, money, and personnel is probably the biggest recommendation for the selection of secondary analysis.

Time and Cost. In many cases, data are available without cost. Much of the data of which we spoke is housed in libraries, but other sources are also available. Employment records, school records, and statistical health data are often easily accessed by requesting permission from appropriate officials.

Even when the data and codebook must be purchased, the charge is generally minimal. When one thinks of the costs of conducting primary research, even on a small scale, the costs of a secondary file pale by comparison. Postage alone, for even a small sample tapped by a mailed-questionnaire design, can present some big numbers, and wages for an interview staff could be, by comparison, astronomical. With a national sample and large data base inventories available, the use of secondary analysis can represent huge financial savings.

Quality of the Data.   A second advantage of secondary analysis is the richness in the quality of the data. Many of the files available have a wide-spread sample that may be national, or even international, in character. Further, these data are almost always collected on a sample selected on the basis of probability and reflect an extensive, in-depth level of inquiry. In short, most of us could not come close to duplicating the fertile nature of these data. As Hyman has succinctly said:

> *Secondary analysis benefits science in many ways, all stemming from one fundamental feature of the method. It expands the types and number of observations to cover more adequately a wider array of social conditions, measurement procedures, and variables than can usually be studied by primary surveys.*[17]

Hyman's words also suggest the two basic usages of secondary analysis. First, secondary data can be employed to verify the results of studies that used primary analysis. Second, secondary data can be used in conjunction with primary data to provide the researcher with a much more complete data package with which to test hypotheses.

In each of these applications, however, the effectiveness of the decision will be predicated on the perceptual acuity of the researcher.

Nonreactive Measurement.   The third advantage is that secondary analysis is a *nonreactive measure*. That is, no additional response, verbal or behavioral, is necessary on behalf of the study population. While the authors of documents may have had no idea that their work could or would serve as a data source, the architects of existing data sources may have been well aware of this potential. Indeed, some inventories are created specifically for this purpose. Nevertheless, subse-

quent analysis of data does not further impinge upon the persons who provided the responses to make up the data base.

This nonreactive quality of secondary data can be advantageous from two perspectives. The first is noted during periods of tension, e.g., an urban riot or a counterculture movement. The appearance of primary investigators on a scene of this nature could heighten or lessen the conditions contributing to the situation. That is, the intrusion could be viewed with hostility by the persons the researcher hopes to study or could be viewed by them as an opportunity for catharsis. Either way the researcher is the loser. In fact, the conditions contributing to the scene may have been the question on which the research was based. Rather than identifying them, the researcher may become one of them.[18]

The second perspective is concerned with respondent cooperation. Historically, social investigators have benefitted in that most persons tapped to be members of a sampling frame have been willing to participate. It would be unfortunate to see that base of cooperation begin to erode by unnecessary intrusion upon people's good graces.[19]

There is some evidence that this erosion has already begun. Catherine Hakin,[20] reporting on British respondents to social inquiry, has noted a decline in response rates beginning in the early 1970s. This factor alone would seem to serve as a strong recommendation to use secondary analysis, at least as an acceptable alternative.

Longitudinal Capability.   The fourth advantage is the capacity to examine a question longitudinally. Many data sources are collected at systematic intervals over time. Some governmental, statistical data banks are registered every three months, some every six months, and some on an annual basis. The full census, of course, is taken every 10 years. Private data banks are also often collected on a systematic basis or schedule.

Most of these sources make inquiry on the same topics in the same manner each time data are collected. Therefore, the date of origin of the particular source is the only limit to how far back the analyst can go.

Testing Innovative Methodological Techniques.   A fifth advantage is the opportunity secondary analysis offers to test new research or statistical tools. The researcher can be spared the large expenditures of primary data-gathering and obtain an accurate reading on the utility of newly evolved procedures in a much more expeditious manner.

Utility of Large Samples.   Finally, with secondary analysis, the use of a larger sample of units of analysis is made much easier than with most other data-gathering devices. In Chapter 7 we argued that a large sample size was not necessarily desirable because of the increase in measurement error that is likely to occur with a greater number of cases. In the case of secondary analysis, these data have already been collected and coded (usually by reasonably well-trained researchers), so that the chances of significant amounts of measurement error are minimized. By a careful recoding of existing data, further measurement error is virtually eliminated. This allows the researcher to handle significantly larger numbers of cases efficiently and soundly. Further, large numbers of cases allow the specification of conceptually meaningful subsets with sufficient numbers to permit reasonable analysis of a variety of emergent subissues.

Disadvantages of Secondary Analysis

As with virtually all methods, instruments, and analytic approaches, secondary analysis is not without drawbacks. The most often cited, and perhaps the most important disadvantage to consider, is that *the data to be analyzed were not collected for the purposes of the analyst.* In some cases, one or more of the variables of importance may not have been tapped. In others, the researcher may have to accept a compromise measurement, much as we described for the SES measurement with the SRC data. We have commented upon this difficulty

before and simply remind the reader that this provides an opportunity for the demonstration of imaginative and creative skills.

Second, the researcher may have minimal information concerning the manner in which the data were collected or how the sample was selected. The data base to be used, then, *may contain measurement or sampling error* of which the researcher is unaware. While the more well-established data bases, particularly those such as the ones mentioned earlier, are not likely to have large quantities of measurement or sampling errors, some caution is wise.

These two disadvantages give rise to concerns of *validity* and *reliability.* If the researcher is forced to accept a compromise measurement of a dimension or forgo assessing one or more dimensions, it is clear that the researcher may not be measuring what was intended, and the validity of the study would be suspect.

Reliability is also a special concern. Were the same topics in fact measured in the same way? We are not always able to answer this question, but we should be aware, for example, of the possibility that different interviewers may have asked the question in a different manner, with different emphasis, or with different subliminal cues. This possibility should cause the secondary analyst to exercise caution in the interpretation of any results, especially those obtained from longitudinal or cross-sectional data gathered by multiple interviewers.

Also relevant to reliability is the quality of the recording and record keeping. For example, we have recently noted a much more precise recording of medical histories in those health-service facilities that have computerized their medical records. The fact that they are much easier to read and categorize will also facilitate secondary analysis using these data in the future.

Finally, we simply repeat that the secondary analyst sometimes has difficulty achieving focus— that the researcher approaches the research from the perspective of rearrangement rather than prearrangement. This problem is exacerbated when the researcher is confronted with one or more large data files or when the scientist plans to work with aggregated data. With aggregated data the researcher must deal with broad groups, areas, or categories for which the characteristics of the individuals can no longer be identified. This can give rise to a difficulty, but one that can be resolved. If an aggregate data base has been selected from which to test a question of interest, obviously, the researcher must alter the unit of analysis from individuals to the aggregate categories. Upon completion of the analysis, researchers then often infer the results obtained to the individual respondents who comprise the aggregate. Whenever this type of inference is drawn, however, the researcher must keep in mind the potential for committing an ecological fallacy, which we discussed in Chapter 7. You will recall that this concerns the difficulty of concluding for one unit of analysis from analysis upon a different unit. Yet, such extrapolations can be fruitful if they are treated as *tentative* conclusions and subjected to further research where these "conclusions" are translated into hypotheses and tested on a more appropriate unit of analysis.

SUMMARY

This chapter has centered on the utilization of written or filmed materials and social data that were collected or generated for some purpose other than that of the social researcher. Attention was divided between content analysis, generally applied to the study of sources of communication, and secondary analysis, applied to quantitative data inventories.

Our focus on content analysis was aided by Berelson's definition, from which each concept—objectivity, systematic, quantitative, and manifest content—were examined. The general categories of written and filmed documents were discussed as potential sources of social data.

Our discussion included the variety of steps involved in coding content data and the criteria such coding procedures must meet. We noted the importance of distinguishing between the units of analysis—the word, or symbol; theme; sentence; paragraph; and item—and the unit of enumeration—its presence or absence, frequency of appearance, allocated space or time, and intensity. Sampling was briefly discussed, noting the similarities of sampling for content analysis with the general sampling considerations discussed in Chapters 6 and 7.

We completed the discussion of content analysis with a review of the advantages and disadvantages to its usage, concluding that it deserves more attention than has been previously registered.

In the discussion of secondary analysis, we noted that, while a fertile procedural resource, it is deceptively complex. While the growth in computer literacy will undoubtedly increase the number of investigators who employ secondary analysis, the history of substantial pieces of research using secondary analysis has been limited.

It first requires a change in the traditional order of doing research. Rather than defining the problem and then collecting data, one has to examine the available data and determine the nature of the questions that can be investigated. Our discussion of secondary analysis noted the central steps, which include the location of a data source, study of the data contained within the selected data bank, achievement of a focus or perspective through data reduction, and operationalization.

We argued that perceptual acuity, or the ability to see previously collected data from a different perspective, represented the most important skill needed by the researcher using secondary analysis. We further addressed the advantages that the approach represents, such as economy of time, effort, and money, a high quality of data, absence of reactivity, and, frequently, the possibility for longitudinal analyses and the use of large samples. There are disadvantages, however, the most significant being that the data were not collected for the purpose or purposes of the researcher. Further, the researcher is generally not in a position to evaluate the incidence of sampling error or measurement error, which, in turn, generate some concern with the validity and reliability of studies using these procedures.

Faced with a funding shortage or a limited research staff, however, content and secondary analyses represent excellent opportunities to investigate questions of interest that are limited only by one's imagination.

KEY TERMS

Content analysis
Context unit
First-order variables
Incompleteness
Item
Lack of availability
Latent content
Manifest content
Nonreactive measure
Objectivity
Paired comparison technique

Paragraph
Perceptual acuity
Primary sources
Quantitative
Recording units
Sampling bias
Scoring unit
Second-order variables
Secondary analysis
Secondary sources

Selective survival
Sentence
Single word
Symbol
Systematic
Theme
Unidimensionality
Units of analysis
Unit of enumeration
Unobtrusive measures

REVIEW QUESTIONS

1. How are content analysis and secondary analysis different from survey and experimental data-gathering designs?

2. What are the differences between content analysis and secondary analysis?

3. How does manifest content differ from latent content? Why is latent content more difficult to assess than manifest content?

4. Distinguish between primary and secondary sources and give examples.

5. What problems arise when one elects to use content analysis?

6. What are the steps involved in doing a content analysis?

7. Identify, define, and discuss the relevant considerations that pertain to the selection of categories in a content analysis.

8. What units of analysis, or recording units, are available to the researcher who uses written documents? Which is generally preferred? What is a context unit, and how is this relevant to content analysis?

9. Construct an example that illustrates the concepts of unit of analysis, context unit, scoring (or enumeration) unit, and recording unit.

10. What are the four systems of enumeration from which the researcher may select?

11. What are the advantages and disadvantages of a content analysis?

12. In what ways does a secondary analysis represent a significant departure from the normal chronology or progression of social scientific research?

13. What are the advantages and disadvantages of secondary analysis?

CHAPTER 13

OBSERVATION, UNOBTRUSIVE MEASURES, AND EXPLORATORY RESEARCH

In this final chapter in Part III, we have combined discussions of observation, unobtrusive measures,* and exploratory research, because all of these procedures rely heavily on the researcher's ability to observe—in the larger sense—significant social variables.

OBSERVATION

Introduction

Observation of others is a procedure in which we all engage every day of our lives. We may not always be aware of the observations we are processing, nor are we all equally proficient in discerning the subtleties of the patterns that we consciously examine. Nevertheless, a great deal of what we know and understand concerning the fears, aspirations, dreams, concerns, dislikes, and general attitudes of our friends, family members, supervisors, professors, and others is predicated upon our observational skill. Previous observation of them, or persons in similar social environmental circumstances, provides a knowledge base from which we select appropriate or inappropriate responses.

In other words, you have been functioning as an observer all of your life. In that sense, you have been developing as a social scientist as well. However, most of us fall victim to the temptation to believe what we have personally experienced is reflective of that which everyone undergoes. It is difficult to expand our perceptual awareness to include circumstances divergent from our own. Often, when we do observe persons who behave differently, we react by noting they are ignorant, crazy, or weird, or we offer some other patently ethnocentric response. Such a reaction, obviously, prevents an expansion of our knowledge base. When one stops to think of the dependency we have upon the observational perceptions of others, the significance of this difficulty becomes clearer.

To illustrate the extensiveness of this dependency, consider that most of us formulate our understanding of the world, or at least a large portion of it, from television news and printed news media. The journalists who provide us with verbal and pictorial information have selectively perceived the stories to report and how those reports should be presented. That is, the news we receive is dependent upon their observational skills. It is our hope that your reading and study of this chapter will equip you with improved observational skills and the ability to interpret the observations of others more critically.

While data collected by observation are often more qualitative than quantitative, this does not preclude hypothesis testing by observation. We further note that observation is sometimes referred to as field research. We have elected not to limit

---

*One reviewer suggested that we place the material on unobtrusive measures in the preceding chapter, since they are clearly nonreactive and, therefore, belong with content analysis and secondary analysis. While this is one way to look at the material, we prefer to leave it in the present chapter because, as with observation, the use of unobtrusive measurement hopefully catches the social situation in its most natural state. Conversely, the use of official statistics may contain bias,[1] and the use of official speeches, for example, may contain positions not truly held by the speakers.

our discussion to field investigation, however. While *field research,* or going where the action is, may dominate observational studies, excellent observational research has also been conducted in laboratory settings.

Sociological Observation

While you have observed an enormous volume of social circumstances involving your family, friends, organizations to which you belong, work environments, neighbors, and many others, it is probable you have not made such observations within a sociological context.

We introduce this thought after observing many of our undergraduate students who register for an internship or practicum experience during their junior or senior year. To accommodate this practical interest, the university has established a cooperative working relationship with some of the local hospitals, police departments, nursing homes, senior centers, and other relevant agencies. The student's responsibility within these environments is twofold: (1) to perform whatever tasks that are assigned by the agency and (2) to write a term paper in which the specific agency in which they served is discussed. The term paper description, however, is to be couched within a sociological frame of reference.

Few students do this well. Students serving their internship within a hospital may write of the number of terminally ill within a particular service but will not describe the nature of the roles enacted between physician and nurse or the change when the attending physician leaves the patient's room in the nurse's role performance from one of deference to one of authority. Students may note that informal discussions of a hospital staff focus upon nonmedical or nonhospital issues but fail to observe that these may be motivated as an avenue of escape from the constant stress and tension generated by the frustration of treating persons who are likely to die.

In short, we have found that students will record aspects of the physical environment but fail to note even the most basic social phenomena. There is no question we all make such observations. We all adjust our behavior when we interact with different persons. We don't say or do the same things when we are speaking to our boss as we do when we are with our friends having a good time. Indeed, our role performance is varied with different friends or even different members of our family.

Erving Goffman spoke to these differences when he observed that we divide our world into frontal and backward areas.[2] The frontal areas are more formal, while the backward areas are more relaxed. In building upon the classic work of W. I. Thomas[3] and his concept of the definition of the situation, Goffman argued that the manner in which we present ourselves to others is in accordance with how we define the social environment in which we are located. That is, we do what we feel will maximize positively the impression we create.

Think of specific occasions on which you have acted in a way to generate certain responses. Have you ever tried to push a door open when you should have pulled it open? What was your response? Did you appear to examine the door carefully in order to communicate that the direction to pull was poorly placed? Did you shake your head or utter a word of anger to communicate that you do not usually make such an error? If you adopted a response similar to these, you were suggesting a definition of the situation and a response that would put you in the best possible light. Most of us have had this type of experience.

Look around you. What are your fellow students wearing? Does their clothing reflect a managed impression? Are any wearing fraternity or sorority sweat shirts, pins, or other Greek-world indicators? If so, is there a hidden communication? Are members of fraternities or sororities communicating their social acceptance or their membership in a prestigious campus organization?

Becoming aware of the social phenomena that surround us and in which we participate is a major step toward increasing our sociological observation capacities. When we discuss these types of phenomena with our practicum and intern students, the improvement in their term papers is dramatic.

As these observational skills are brought into a sharper focus, we can begin to think of conducting observational research. One starts by making and registering observations from an appropriate vantage point. While observation rarely is the chosen procedure to determine cause-and-effect relationships, the data collected may well lead to such examination in subsequent research efforts.

If a researcher elects to utilize systematic observation as a data-collection method, a number of additional concerns must be addressed. The responses to these issues will determine what vantage point the observer will occupy. Our discussion now turns to the variety of research modalities included under the general method of observation.

Questions to Be Answered

Introduction.   The researcher electing to collect data by observation is immediately confronted by five additional questions. First, the researcher will have to decide whether to function as a nonparticipant or participant within the group that has been selected for study. Second, researchers must decide whether their presence as an observer will be known (overt) or unknown (covert). Third, there is the question of whether the observation will occur within a natural setting (field study) or a laboratory environment. Fourth is the question of the degree of control that the researcher has over the research setting. Fifth is the question of structure manifested in the observational categories. We briefly address each of these five dimensions of an observational study.

Degree of Involvement.   The first decision concerns whether the researcher will enact a participant or nonparticipant role. A *participant* is one who assumes a legitimate social position within the group being studied, thereby maximizing the ability to be in contact with and observe the structure and interaction of the group from an insider's vantage point. An example would be someone who joined a college sorority or fraternity in order to study it. A *nonparticipant* stance is one in which the researcher does not hold a social position within the group being studied.

One major advantage of the participant role is that it affords the researcher greater opportunity to be privy to more of the inner or behind-the-scenes functioning of the group. Again, membership in a sorority or fraternity would legitimately place the researcher within meetings, which could not happen if one was a nonparticipant. Conversely, a major disadvantage of the participant role is that the researcher may become integrated as a major figure in the group, thereby influencing the subject matter itself. For example, in an effort to study everyone's attitudes, the researcher may become popular, be reluctantly solicited for a sorority or fraternity office, and be elected into the decision-making apparatus.

Neither role is necessarily better than the other. The question should be answered with regard to who is being studied, why they are being studied, where the observation will occur, and the possible consequences of either stance. Beginning researchers often make this decision on the basis of whether they believe they are capable of merging with the study group. That is, can the researcher pursue a role that is identical or similar to those manifested by the group? To decide upon the participation question in this manner is unnecessarily limiting. One can occupy any number of roles that might be deemed relevant and that would provide an opportunity to conduct observation and gain insight into the group. For example, one of your authors has been recently observing a university football program. Given the age of your authors and their respective physical abilities, participating as a player was out of the question. However, functioning as a volunteer assistant coach provided a perfectly acceptable role and a vantage point from which significant interaction patterns could be recorded.

Another example might be a desire to study the daily workings of a hospital. Assuming the sociological researcher does not possess the entry credentials of a physician, nurse, physical therapist, or any other official hospital occupation, this problem could be surmounted by becoming a volunteer worker. One could donate time as a patient advocate or some other acceptable role that would permit observational access to the interaction patterns of interest.* We emphasize here not only gaining accessibility to the group of interest but also doing so in as natural a way as possible. Unless one is already a member of the group one wishes to study, one is—by definition—an outsider. Regardless of the role occupied, the status of newcomer may introduce the status of marginal man.† That is, new members often feel more like nonmembers or outsiders. As one acclimates oneself to the group, and as the group becomes accustomed to the newcomer's presence, the status of marginality will be reduced.

The issue of *marginality* in observational research has been addressed by Buford Junker, who has provided a fourfold classification to assess the degree of marginality the observational researcher (participant or nonparticipant) might experience at different stages of the research effort.[4] These stages are based upon the nature of the information available to the researcher and may be identified by the terms *public, confidential, secret,* and *private.*

The first stage of maximum marginality is likely to be experienced at the beginning of a project when the nature of the information the researcher has access to is *public.* Here one would not be privy to information that is not available to everyone. The second stage is *confidential.* Any observations of this nature that were to be reported would be offered without *identification of the source.* In the third stage, the information available to the researcher is *secret.* This is information that is available to members of the in-group, with effort exerted to prevent external distribution of such information. The final stage of the classification is *private.* Information of this type is of a personal nature to a member of the group. Observational opportunities that would provide insight into the latter two stages would clearly signal that one has minimized the status of marginality.

We note, however, that marginality is much like a double-edged sword; what is required of participation and that which is demanded of nonparticipation are in direct contradiction. Clearly, participation calls for the researcher to be involved, while nonparticipation dictates detachment from that which is being observed. This dilemma can create difficulties for the researcher as to what to report or in what manner that which is reported should be presented. If the researcher is able to maintain some degree of marginality, movement between and among the different components of the group will be more easily facilitated. On the other hand, nonparticipation may prevent the researcher from gaining access to the more hidden—and, presumably, more important and powerful—aspects of the study group.

Perhaps this dilemma can be illustrated with sociologists who are interested in medicine. Some are sociologists *of* medicine, while others are sociologists *in* medicine. Those *in* medicine are more likely to gain access to secret or private information, but they are also more likely to avoid reporting such information if it reflects negatively upon the hospital or professional individuals who have befriended the researcher. Furthermore, if they do report it, they are more likely to distort the presentation in a biased manner. Conversely, the sociologists of medicine make their observations from a more distant point, are not as likely to gain access to information of a secret or private nature, but are more likely to present an objective picture. Which is best? Which is more likely to result in policy change? The answer will differ from project to project, but these issues must be considered

---

*However, one disadvantage to the volunteer role is that the researcher may not be able to get within the inner circle to a sufficient degree to observe such behavior as power struggles and the interaction that leads to major policy decision.

†Although Robert E. Park originally introduced this term to refer to persons participating in the life of two or more different cultures (see *Race and Culture,* Glencoe, Illinois: The Free Press, 1950), it has subsequently been used to describe persons in virtually any circumstances in which dual, or even more, statuses might be assigned.

when addressing the question of whether to participate in the behavior to be observed.

Degree of Disclosure.   If the researcher assumes a *known,* or *overt, role,* he or she discloses a desire to study the group. Conversely, an *unknown,* or *covert, role* is one in which the researcher fails to inform the study group that they are objects of scientific inquiry.

With the second question, the researcher must elect either to be known as a researcher to those being studied or to decide against such knowledge. Once again, the nature of the group to be studied and the research environment will influence this choice. One issue the researcher must consider when deciding upon whether to be known or not is the *Hawthorne effect,* a phenomenon we have previously discussed. Fritz Roethlisberger and William Dickson discovered that workers at Western Electric were altering their production behavior in response to the knowledge that they were part of a study rather than their managerial input.[5] Modified behavior in response to observers has been evidenced in many research efforts since that time. While it is important to be aware of this potential, the Hawthorne effect should not dictate against the decision to be known if that would be a more natural decision.

Indeed, in conducting observational research, one often has a predetermined checklist of things for which to look. Making note of those items that are relevant to the checklist is facilitated if those being observed are aware such recordings are a part of the study. Being a known researcher may also aid in gaining supplemental information by interviewing the participants of the group. Being known as a research observer would, in all likelihood, legitimate the interview survey for those sampled.

A final concern for a researcher who elects to function in a covert manner is an ethical question. The unidentified researcher is, in effect, deceiving those being studied. The implication is that the participants will reveal information that they would not to someone they knew to be collecting data. The covert posture presents a dilemma which academic professional bodies have attempted to rec-

oncile, but, at this point in time, no consensus has been reached.

Nature of the Research Setting.   The third question the observational researcher must answer pertains to the research environment. The researcher can elect a *field research* utilizing a *natural setting* or conduct the research within the confines of a *laboratory setting.* Again, the purpose of the study and those to be observed will have substantial impact on this decision.

Perhaps the most important determinant of which study environment the researcher elects is the state of knowledge regarding the phenomenon. If the researcher is prepared to advance a hypothesis for testing and has a considered number of specific categories on which to observe behavior, a laboratory setting (if such can be constructed) is recommended. On the other hand, if an idea is in the exploratory stage, observation within a natural environment is preferred.

We are not arguing that one cannot examine an exploratory idea within a laboratory or test a hypothesis in a natural setting. Rather, we are simply noting that the state of knowledge will be a factor influencing the environmental decision. Indeed, election of a field study or laboratory examination may be largely influenced by the researcher's response to the fourth question.

Degree of Control.   The fourth question is the degree to which the researcher is able to control, hence manipulate, the research setting. While we discuss this dimension dichotomously, one must recognize that there can be degrees between the two extremes of minimum and maximum control.

Of course, the laboratory setting affords the researcher the maximum control over the research setting. As discussed in Chapter 11 on experimental designs, the researcher is able usually to determine, for example, who and how many persons are distributed into the desired number of experimental and control groups and when the before measure, the test stimulus, and the after measure are presented. Conversely, the natural setting is "natural" precisely because it can not be so manipulated.

Degree of Conceptual Structure.   The final question revolves around the degree to which there is a conceptual model capable of focusing the researcher's observational efforts in a meaningful way. For example, in Robert Bales's small-group interaction process analysis, 12 categories of interaction—6 positive and 6 negative—were identified.[6] With this conceptual scheme, he was able to classify the interaction within a small group in terms of who said what to whom in one of these 12 descriptive categories.

In essence, the conceptual model allowed Bales to focus his attention on relevant behavior and to organize these observations efficiently into meaningful categories.

Design Correlation.   A corollary notion to emphasize is that each of the five dimensions indicated by these questions are not necessarily independent of each other. That is, there may well be interaction in the sense that a particular choice on one dimension will dictate a correlated choice on another dimension.

For example, Bales was able to utilize his rather complicated observational scheme because he largely controlled the research setting by placing the research subjects in a single room equipped with one-way mirrors for unobtrusive observation—making him privy to the entire decision-making exercise. In a more natural field situation, this more structured observational research strategy is likely to be impossible because the researcher would not be able to hear all of the conversational give-and-take. Further, in the more natural but uncontrolled setting, the participants may not find themselves gathered together for the *entire* decisional process, thereby preventing the researcher from hearing parts of the communication process.

When designing an observational study, the researcher must always keep the goals of the study in mind. This may sound trite, but their importance warrants emphasis. Maintaining an awareness of the goals throughout the planning stages will facilitate determination of what is to be observed, and will help the delineation of whatever the categories of observation will be.

Research Modalities

Introduction.   Continuing the discussion of overlap or design correlation, if we combine the first two questions mentioned in the preceding section—the question of whether or not to participate in the group being studied and whether or not to be known as a researcher by those being studied, four possible observational modalities emerge. The researcher may function as a: (1) known participant, (2) unknown participant, (3) known nonparticipant, or (4) unknown nonparticipant.

No one of these modalities is inherently superior to the others. The answers to the two questions, as with the previous issues discussed, will most often be determined by the nature of the group to be researched and the environment in which the research is to take place. Indeed, classic research has been conducted employing each of the four possibilities.

Known Participant.   Most of the information concerning social behavior has been gained by the researcher's functioning as a known participant. This modality is descriptive of the manner in which we make observations in the groups to which we belong, as well as those we make of our surrounding social environment. These observations, however, are usually made without any type of research control or standardization.

Having reviewed the relevant literature, the researcher should decide what the aims of the research are. Based upon what one hopes to achieve from the project, the persons to be observed can be more judiciously selected. In many cases, the nature of those to be studied prohibits enacting a covert role within the group. The decision of how the researcher will observe the group is, then, virtually dictated; i.e., the researcher will assume a known or overt research role.

The researcher must initially establish rapport with the members of the group to be observed, which may be facilitated by having a friend within the group introduce the researcher to other group members. More generally, however, the group one wishes to study will be composed of strangers. In some cases, the researcher can legitimize his presence as a known researcher by presenting some credential, e.g., a university degree or a letter of introduction from a professional organization. This would be helpful, for example, if one wished to study students within a school environment, nursing home patients, or inmates within a prison. However, if one is interested in observing a less formal group, such as a street gang or a community of homeless persons, a confederate is needed.* Frequently, a confederate can be enlisted by simply asking someone to serve in that capacity or by finding someone who knows both the researcher and someone in the group to be studied. Whatever the specific circumstances, acceptance and a feeling of trust must be generated to ensure the researcher entrance to the group. Sometimes entrance to a group can be gained if the researcher is attacked or vilified by the research group's enemies.

Assuming rapport has been successfully established, the known participant can begin to focus on the categories of observation. Clearly, one cannot record everything that occurs. Since few controls are exerted upon the observer, it is necessary to employ consciously all those techniques for standardizing and categorizing data with which the researcher has been trained and is familiar.

The basic goals of the research effort will facilitate the formulation of the categories to be observed. Without question, many interesting occurrences and facts must be ignored or remain unrecorded. It is expected the researcher will maintain a log or diary of those observations that fit the observational categories. Notes should be taken immediately. This is one of the important advantages of being known to those being observed. Stopping to write in a logbook is not likely to stimulate apprehension because you are there to make such observations. Notes made during the day should be transcribed into a more thorough record at the completion of each day of the observation. One cannot put off the recording of obser-

vations until the closure of the study. No matter how interesting or fascinating the event, the researcher will not be able to reconstruct the entire occurrence after very much time has elapsed. It is unfortunate, but the human memory is not that retentive.

Assistance for consistent and accurate recording relative to any of the observational modalities can be achieved through the use of mechanical devices such as cameras (moving and still) or tape recorders. However, use of these tools can have negative consequences and introduce ethical considerations, which we discuss in a later section.

Further, the researcher is encouraged to register notes in the temporal sequence in which they happen, although appropriate category headings can be noted at the time of the first recording of the observations. It is likely that conscientious daily recordings, once categorized, will generate additional categories and cross referencing and will facilitate the search for causal relationships, intervening variables, and so forth, which the researcher could not anticipate at the outset of the investigation.

If one's study tends to be in the context of discovery or exploration, then the researcher must be more flexible about what to record. Here, one will not know for sure which observations are relevant, so recordings of as much as one is capable should be made. On the other hand, if one's study is more in the context of justification or hypothesis testing, the researcher is more justified in channeling observational energies to those variables suggested by the conceptual model. Perhaps, the operative rule of thumb would be: get as much information as possible, since one can always eliminate unnecessary observational data later and additional questions may arise during the course of the data collection that could not have been anticipated in the planning stages of the research.

---

*A distinction should be made between a friend and a confederate. A friend or acquaintance is just that. But a confederate is a person who plays an assigned part in the research process. For example, in Solomon Asch's classic work[7] on the group's influence on the responses of individuals, the person being studied did not know that the remaining people in the experiment had been told to respond in certain ways by the researcher, which is a clear example of the confederate role in social research.

These data-collection procedures do not have time limits. The project director may have suggested a specified period for observation, but a substantial extension may be required. Studies may be completed in days or weeks, but they may require months or years.

Once the observational stage has been brought to closure, the data are analyzed in much the same way data from any type of study are examined. While observational research is often employed to explore whether more focused research could be undertaken or more specific hypotheses could be formulated for examination, there is no reason the same quantitative tools of analysis cannot be used with these data. The only caution we offer here is a reminder that exploratory research is generally not conducted on a representative sample. This, of course, limits any inferences which can be made.

Unknown Participant. The degree of control that the researcher can exert when the researcher's presence is known (overt) is largely lost when the investigator elects to conduct the observation in a covert manner, thus functioning as an unknown participant. What is lost in control or structure, however, is counterbalanced by an absence of reactivity on the part of those being observed. In point of fact, the researcher will still want to have some type of structure to facilitate identification of what areas upon which to concentrate. Although one is not likely to be able to record observations during the period the group is being observed, focusing one's attention will enable a more complete set of notes to be registered at the completion of each observational session.

As was the case for the known participant, the investigator does not have to be involved in the same roles as those being observed. One reason for electing the modality of unknown participant, however, is to avoid a sense of awkwardness that might be experienced if the researcher did not enter the action at all. For example, as we noted earlier, one of your authors has been studying a university football team. While data for the first couple of years were recorded from the perspective of an assistant coach, more recent data has

been gathered by serving in the capacity of statistician for the team. The intensity of participation is not as great, but the presence is still justified by the researcher's group function. This has provided a greater opportunity for recording observations at the time they are made, while preserving the absence of reactivity.

Clearly, the role of unknown participant is particularly valuable for the earliest stages of exploratory research. The analysis of any data gathered can then be more systematically followed up in a more structured circumstance or in an experimental or survey approach.

Known Nonparticipant. Of the four modalities within which to conduct observational research, functioning as a known nonparticipant is the most difficult. Both the investigator and those being observed are likely to feel some sense of awkwardness or discomfort. It was the use of this modality that specifically gave rise to the Hawthorne effect. It is almost impossible to avoid contamination of data collected through reactivity. The problem is, of course, exacerbated by the absence of baseline data with which to compare the observations being made. The only solution is to continue the observation for a sufficient period of time so that those being observed fade back into their normal behavioral patterns.

It is probable that at various points in your life you have wished to impress some person or persons and behaved in a way that did not reflect your normal behavior. Perhaps you decided to put forth a more formal image, or you decided to elicit sympathy by demonstrating the characteristics of sadness. How long could you maintain the facade? Most of us have difficulty disguising ourselves for any sustained time. The researcher who adopts the known nonparticipant modality is hoping for the same difficulty among those persons selected for observation.

However, Whyte's[8] methodological discussion of a study that he did in a working-class Italian neighborhood in Boston indicates that long after Whyte felt he had been accepted into the Norton Street gang as a member, there was additional evidence that he was still considered somewhat of an outsider.

These problems, associated with a natural setting, can be somewhat abated if the researcher elects to conduct the research within a laboratory environment. Although the surroundings are not the natural ones found in field studies, all are aware of the purpose of their presence. They arrive at the laboratory with the understanding their behavior will be observed and recorded, thus requiring a minimal degree of interruption once the respondents have grown accustomed to the circumstances of the laboratory and the specific study.

Comfort within a laboratory setting is often facilitated by informal conversation between the observer and the subjects. This discussion may take the form of an informal interview and may be supplemented by an additional source or sources of data, e.g., photographic or audio recordings. The precise purpose of the study need not be conveyed to those being observed, but a general reason justifying the project is needed.

Research of this nature can be valuable. The influence others within a group might exert upon one's judgment, for example, has been investigated in a laboratory setting by Muzafer Sherif[9] and subsequently checked by Solomon Asch.[10] Both researchers were able to demonstrate a considerable degree of conformity in judgment. Sherif, using the autokinetic phenomenon—the idea that a stationary light, when viewed against a dark background, appears to move—had individual respondents judge the degree of movement until a reasonably consistent judgment was reached by each. Subjects were then placed in the research environment with two or three others and asked to make judgments aloud. The resulting judgments reflected clear evidence of the groups's influence upon the judgment from others. Asch subsequently examined this phenomenon by asking respondents to judge the more objective stimulus of presented line lengths. The respondents were shown three lines of differing lengths and asked which was the same length as a fourth. In a pretest virtually all of the respondents selected the appropriate line without error. Confederates of the experimenter were then grouped with a subject and instructed to give incorrect responses as to which of the three lines was identical in length. While the majority (two-thirds) of the study group provided accurate responses, the remaining one-third offered answers that were in conformity to the responses offered by the confederates.

Asch's use of confederates who were not known to the respondents does violate the parameters of the known nonparticipant modality. However, it is reflective of a combination approach, which can be used in observational research. We address a variety of combination efforts in a later section of this chapter.

Unknown Nonparticipant.   As can be deduced from the term *unknown nonparticipant,* the observer electing this modality is not integrated in any manner with those being observed. We suspect you have used this observational modality often in informal examinations of your social landscape. If you have ever participated in people watching by sitting on a bench in a park, shopping center, or beach and studying people as they passed, you have been an unknown nonparticipant.

This is a procedure, however, that is more frequently employed for research purposes within a laboratory environment. Perhaps the most well-known form of unknown nonparticipant in laboratory observation is the use of an observer, or team of observers, located behind a two-way mirror. For example, persons to be studied come into the laboratory and are assigned a task or provided a discussion topic. Observations of resulting discussions or behaviors are then recorded. While the respondents are aware they are being studied, they are unaware of who or how many persons are observing or in what way they are being observed.

This form of observation provides the researcher with a maximum degree of control over the research environment. The knowledge of what exercise in which the respondent will be participating permits the researcher to predetermine more easily a structure of observation. Indeed, if a team of observers is used, a predetermined division of labor of observation can be established. For example, one observer might be assigned the task of recording behavior that relates to tension reduction, another might record any incidence of anger, while a third could note any evidence of an evolving leadership pattern.

Clearly, when the investigator is in a position to establish this degree of control within the research environment, it is suitable for hypothesis testing as well as exploratory research. The structured laboratory permits the standardization necessary for such testing.

The nature of the interaction to be observed can be influenced by the type of task or behavior with which the respondent is confronted. Similarly, the environmental conditions can be dictated by the researcher. Clearly, control is exerted through the physical limits or parameters of the laboratory. Beyond the obvious, the researcher can control the length of the observational period; the time of the day, week, month, or year in which the observations take place; the size and membership of any group to be observed; and whether confederates will be employed. These salient issues, all of which have been found to influence behavior, can be held constant for any or all groups to be exposed to the laboratory. Parenthetically, the primary advantage of the laboratory environment is the ability to control the nature of the research situation, while the main advantage of the natural, or field, situation is its representativeness or normality. Rarely is the social scientist able to maximize both representativeness and research control.

Probably the best known of this type of observational study is Bales's interaction process analysis which we mentioned earlier.[11] Bales established 12 categories: shows solidarity, shows tension release, agrees, gives suggestions, gives opinion, gives orientation, asks for orientation, asks for opinion, asks for suggestions, disagrees, shows tension, and shows antagonism. These categories were then grouped into three more general units: social-emotional-positive; social-emotional-negative; and task neutral. The notion is that all behavior (verbal and nonverbal) can be perceived and allocated to one of these categories. If one is entering into exploratory research, Bales's classifi-

cation schema is quite helpful in providing some structure to assist in the identification of what to record.

An issue we have addressed previously deserves repetition here. Regardless of the degree of structure the investigator may provide within the laboratory setting and whether the researcher is known or unknown, the respondents are likely to alter their behavior in the beginning stages of the research project. You are reminded, however, that this altered behavior, or *masking,* is likely to be temporary. The solution to this problem, then, is to continue the observation over a sufficient time frame to afford the assessment of more candid behavior.

Additional Issues in Observation

Introduction.   Several brief comments need to be made concerning a few additional concerns when the data-gathering procedure is observation. Here we focus attention on the problems of singularity, which can be addressed through the use of the interview, and reactivity, which can be checked through the use of mechanical recording devices and unobtrusive measures.

Singularity.   One of the primary objections to social research is that the instruments are used singularly.[12] Countering this objection to singularity calls for the juxtaposition of data that have been collected via different procedures from the same group of respondents, which strengthens confidence in one's results. This is called *triangulation,* a process strongly endorsed by Webb et al. and your authors. Indeed, in a study conducted by one of your authors, a successful combination of interview data with two physiological measures (pulse rates and salivary measures of alkalinity and acidity) was achieved in assessing the direction of the subjects' expressed aggression, i.e., inward (self-blame or anxiety) or outward (anger).[13] While this study did not involve observation, it did demonstrate the efficacy of triangulation.

When the selected method of data collection is observation, the objection of singularity can be addressed through the use of the interview data-gathering procedure. Interviewing is frequently used in observational research, especially for projects conducted in natural settings. Since field research is almost always exploratory in nature, these interviews are most often of an unstructured or open nature.

Reactivity.   Also of significance in this chapter, and especially within the observational modalities in which the observer is known, is the importance of keeping the subject's *reactivity* in mind. The presence of the investigator alters, by definition, the research environment and may well cause an altering of the behavior being registered.

One way to compensate for reactivity, as well as singularity, is through the use of *mechanical recording devices.* These may be auditory or photographic in nature. The latter can be still or moving-film footage. The limitations of human beings to see, hear, or remember all of the stimuli to which they are exposed strongly recommend these supplements to the investigator employing observation. The ethics of research, however, virtually dictate gaining permission from those being recorded before such devices can be employed.

Summary.   Clearly, collection of verbal data from interviewing, recorded data from mechanical devices, and the researcher's recorded observations provide a solid base for triangulation. If all data sources were to provide evidence for a similar conclusion, the researcher would have additional confidence in pursuing research in this problem area on a more systematic basis.

A third response to the question of singularity of data sources and a second response to reactivity within social research is that of unobtrusive measures. It is to these significant data sources that we now turn.

UNOBTRUSIVE MEASURES

Introduction

Up to this point we have directed your attention to the problems of singularity and reactivity at several instances throughout this text. The manner in which the presence of a known investigator or the use of a particular measuring instrument might influence the behavior or attitudinal response of one being studied is a significant problem with which researchers must be aware and attempt to accommodate in some manner. This concern is clearly applicable to survey research in areas where the use of questionnaires or interviewers represent elements of possible change to the social circumstances that they are designed to assess. Alteration of the social environment that is the object of study is also a major concern in several of the observational modalities we have discussed.

Unobtrusive measures represent a significant response to this concern. We have elected to present our primary discussion of these measures in this chapter, because the principal mechanism for employing them is through observation. You will recall a few brief referrals to them, however, in Chapter 12, where we examined secondary and content analysis.

An *unobtrusive measure* of observation may be defined as "any method of observation that directly removes the observer from the set of interactions or events being studied."[14] Therefore, these measures are designed to mitigate reactivity that may have been generated from the intrusion of a survey instrument or the known physical presence of a researcher. Without question, consideration of some unobtrusive assessments can facilitate a more valid or accurate set of conclusions.* There are four basic types of unobtrusive measures: (1) physical traces, (2) archival analysis, (3) simple observation, and (4) contrived observation.[16] We examine and illustrate each of these with unobtrusive observations made from

---

*The most thorough and widely accepted presentation of thought regarding unobtrusive measures has been presented by Eugene Webb, et al. Consequently, we have relied heavily upon the presentation of these scholars.[15]

the study of the university football team mentioned earlier.

Physical Traces

A *physical trace* is a directly observable piece of evidence that enables the researcher to make relevant observations. There are two types of physical traces. The first of these is called an *erosion measure*. Assessments of erosion are focused upon the wear an object or environment might reflect. Reciprocally, the other type of physical-trace observation is that of an *accretion measure,* or evidence of deposits to objects or the environment over time.

Erosion Measures

If one spends very much time around a football team, it will become obvious that the player's helmet and shoes are the two parts of the uniform that communicate the player's degree of involvement in this sport. Every fall, each player is given a new pair of shoes and a new or refinished helmet. (The team in question throughout this discussion wears white helmets and white shoes.) The helmet is especially easy to read. When football players engage in contact with opposing players, the helmet is invariably a point of contact. The contact often results in scarring the paint, tearing the logo decal that is attached to the helmet, or gouging a groove or rut into the helmet. The more active a player is, i.e., the more important the role (starter versus bench warmer), the more likely the helmet will reflect these battle scars. The shoes present a similar picture.

Those players who see a lot of game action receive the greatest amount of attention during practice. Thus, one could easily triangulate this observational data with the more objective data of the statistics of the minutes or quarters played to determine one's relative status within the squad.

Accretion Measures

Accretion, or deposits, can similarly be observed by examining the helmets. Every week during the season, the coaching staff evaluates the performance of each player for the previous Saturday's game. Those players who "grade out" to 95 percent efficiency or better, or who contributed a "big play" receive a small decal to place on their helmets. A cursory look at the helmets of our team, then, would give the interested observer a good idea of who the stars of the team are.

Clearly, for these data to be valuable in the research process, those making the observations must be somewhat educated about this particular population. This is one of the major limitations of physical-trace data, but the use of the interview is helpful in providing such knowledge. Given that level of knowledge, these trace elements generate the possibility for categorizing members of the team. In this case, for example, we can compare those receiving more playing time with those who do not receive an opportunity to play or who play only in a substitute capacity. Similarly, we can compare these data for persons who perform at different positions within a football team. Do wide receivers evidence the same type of wear and tear of their headgear as, say, offensive linemen? The answer is no, and a quick look at the respective helmets would provide that type of insider information.

Archival Analysis

Archival analysis is the type of unobtrusive measure that utilizes public and private documents. Since we have discussed these data sources in considerable detail in the chapter on content and secondary analysis (Chapter 12), we will not repeat that discussion here, but mention should be made of the specific relevance of these documents to unobtrusive measurement.

While documents of public or private origin preserve the nonreactive nature of unobtrusive measurement, the researcher must realize that the architect of any of these sources may reflect a bias. If documents associated with a particular organization are being used as a source of data, this issue is made more complicated because the organization's agenda could introduce an additional biased perspective. Furthermore, as we have said elsewhere, the formal minutes of a committee meeting may bear little resemblance to the nature of the interaction that really transpired.

Both of these sources of bias are present within the documents available for unobtrusive study of our football team. The principal sources we would want to examine are: (1) the team's media guide, (2) the programs prepared for each game, and (3) newspaper and television coverage of the team throughout the season. The media guide and the game programs are prepared by the university's sports information director (SID) and his or her staff. In addition, these individuals prepare news releases for the local news media. Some of these are used word for word in articles that appear in the newspapers or are verbally related by sports announcers on radio and television. When they are altered, the flavor of what the SID suggested is not changed.

We can conclude, then, the SID and his or her staff have an enormous input in what is distributed in document form about the team. The SID at our university, as those at all schools, is interested in maximizing a positive image and story for the team. Similarly, he is interested in putting forth a positive image for the university. Therefore, we are not likely to read, see, or hear material of a negative nature. This does not mean the information distributed by the SID is not true. However, the bias will be reflected in some creative angles of presentation. At the beginning of each season, after reading documents prepared by the SID, we fully expect our team to win the national championship, have the starting player at each position make all-American, and our head coach selected as coach of the year. In point of fact, while the team has enjoyed national rankings, it has never won the national championship; while several of the players over the years have been named as All-Americans, they represent a small percentage of the number who have played; and while the head coach has been named regional Coach of the Year four times, he has never been afforded that honor at the national level.

Despite the directional bias noted in the narratives of these documents, they are valuable sources of information. Statistical data are not distorted, biographical information concerning players and coaches is not manufactured, and general information regarding the university is accurate. Information offered in these documents serves as an excellent validity check of responses offered in informal interviews. On occasion, for example, after checking some of the biographical data within these documents, I have found some players who offered exaggerated claims regarding their high school athletic achievements.

While it has not been a problem with the study of this football program, some researchers electing to use archival sources have had to be concerned with bias introduced by the selective survival of some sources.[17] This problem would be clearly manifest if one wished to study graffiti. If an outside location was the target of investigation, the researcher would have to be aware of erosion caused by the weather. Further, graffiti could be lost by being painted over by building maintenance personnel or scratched out by competitors or persons offended by the presentation.

Simple Observation

The third general category of unobtrusive measures identified by Webb and his associates are simple observations.[18] A *simple observation* includes those characteristics that can be discerned by merely looking at the subject matter; i.e., their discovery requires nothing more than the researcher's willingness to observe the research situation. These observations are further specified into five types.

The first subtype is that of *physical exterior signs*. These symbols may be consciously or unconsciously presented and may provide a great deal of information regarding the person or persons being studied. Webb et al. identify a number of external symbols that most of us use daily to help us form judgments of others. These include our form of dress; jewelry; hair length and style; and, for some, the presence, location, and type of tattoos.

Again, our football team provides any number of these external clues. One that is familiar to most football fans is the number of a player's jersey. Numbers are assigned to players in accordance with the position they play. Quarterbacks, often seen as the most important position on the team, generally wear numbers from 7 to 19. There are some notable exceptions to this rule. For example, Paul Horning wore number five when he won the Heisman trophy as Notre Dame's quarterback, and Daryle Lamonica, "The Mad Bomber," wore number three with the then Oakland Raiders. However, kicking specialists generally wear the very low numbers, one through six. On the other hand, offensive tackles wear numbers from 70 to 79, guards wear numbers from 60 to 69, linebackers generally wear numbers in the 50s, and so on. It is possible to get a good idea of position and, therefore, the relative status of a player from observing the jersey number.

Another important external clue on our football team is the color of the player's practice jersey. While everyone wears an identical uniform (except for the number) on game day, the color of a player's practice jerseys reflects a great deal. Defensive players on our squad wear blue jerseys, while offensive players wear white jerseys.* There are two exceptions to uniform color assignment. First, those players who are injured, and unable to participate in any contact drills, are identified by red, numberless jerseys. Second, the scout teams, that are generally composed of freshmen and that run the offensive plays and defensive schemes of the next opponent, wear yellow jerseys with the number of the player they are impersonating.

Thus, a great deal of information can be gleaned from simply examining this externally observable sign. The observer, for example, can determine when a player has been switched from offense to defense, or defense to offense; when a player has been promoted or demoted from or to the scout team, and so forth.

The second type of simple observation is called *expressive movement* or, more popularly, body language. As social actors, we communicate a great deal with our facial movements, hand gestures, the positioning of our bodies vis-à-vis something or someone else, or the general movement of our body. These communicated symbols offer the interested observer a basis for interpretation of the situation.

There are two forms that expressive movement can take. The first is *embodied posturing* and occurs when there is agreement between what one verbally communicates and the body language that accompanies what is said. Since football is a physical sport that requires a great deal of proper body positioning, there are many opportunities to observe this congruence, or the lack thereof, within a football environment. To take but one example, one of your authors coached the outside linebackers. One cannot effectively play the linebacker position while standing up straight. The position requires a posture which is called the "breakdown position." This involves bending at the knees, holding the shoulders back, and keeping the head up. If you try to assume this stance, we suspect you will find it uncomfortable. Nevertheless, it provides for maximum efficiency in terms of visually following the play and mobilizing oneself to determine the proper angle of interception with the ball carrier on running plays or to determine, if it is a passing play, whether to rush the passer or to drop back into pass coverage. When a coach corrects a player's posture, and the player says "yes, sir, I understand," and then makes every effort to adopt the correct stance, we have two observations that communicate the same thought.

Another example would be the body language displayed by a player who had just been removed from a game because of a poor performance. He may verbally indicate he understands and agrees with the coach's assessment of his performance, but he may physically communicate with his body something quite different than what he said to the

---

*Most of these jerseys have the same number the player wears during a game. Some of the freshmen, however, do not have numbers on their practice jerseys, which is an important status distinction.

coach. This is an illustration of data indicating the second form of expressive movement—*disembodied posturing*. This occurs when the message from the body is different or contradictory to that offered verbally.

A third form of simple observation is *physical location analysis*. Examining an individual or group's location within the study environment provides a rich nonreactive source of data. Two areas that can be clarified with such observation are, first, the relative status of an individual or group vis-à-vis the other actors and, second, the congruence between what someone says and the attitude they manifest in terms of their behavior.

Again, the football environment offers many opportunities to examine these types of issues. For example, every football team has an annual team photograph taken. On our team, senior members of the squad, both in terms of years spent on the squad and playing status, occupy the first row or two, while the back rows are staffed with freshmen and persons who do not receive much playing time in the games. A quick glance at the team picture for any given year would provide the observer with an idea of who the major contributors to the team's performance of that year were.

Another use of locational analysis is to assess congruence between verbal communication and attitude. For example, a couple of years ago we had a quarterback who was removed from a game because of a poor performance. When the player came to the sideline, he said he didn't know what was wrong with him, but he thought the head coach did the right thing by removing him. He then positioned himself as far as possible from the coaches and the remainder of the players. By his isolation and sulking, he was saying something quite different from his verbal pronouncements. The ultimate message he provided the coaching staff was one of anger and petulance over his removal.

Beyond these specific illustrations, one can observe who spends time with whom when the players are not on the football field. Locational observation of this nature provides a good idea of the degree of integration of the team at any point in time. That is, do the offensive players only spend time with other offensive players, or are defensive players included? Are the player's social groupings influenced by racial identity, class standing, major field of study, and so forth? These questions can be answered by having dinner with the team and observing who sits with whom, by sitting around the university union and seeing who comes in with whom, or by working in the library and observing who is studying together.

Language behavior represents a fourth form of simple observation. As noted by Webb and his colleagues, language study represents a huge continuum of potential data. They focused their attention on unobtrusive language,[19] and we will follow suit. Further, while we recognize the legitimacy of using space, time, and our bodies to communicate (which we illustrated above), we are limiting our attention here to spoken language. Unobtrusive observation of language has been done in a wide variety of circumstances and environments. We know, for example, persons speak differently and are more or less likely to be honest depending upon the degree of formality of a social circumstance. Language has been examined from the perspective of formal speeches, informal conversation, telephone conversations, and so forth. Similar to content analysis of documents, one can examine words, phrases, sentences, or complete conversations.

Language, and the manner in which it is delivered, is crucial within a football program. Language is one of the principal motivating tools available to a coaching staff and to players encouraging each other. A special vocabulary evolves that often has meaning only to members of that particular social group. Let us cite an example. We are not a major college football program. However, the phrase *"major college"* is a phrase that has long been employed to designate the football programs representing colleges and universities where emphasis is placed upon winning and economic success. Within our program, the term has been shortened to "major" and is used to describe anything that is evaluated positively; e.g., that was a major block, run, tackle, pass, or catch. The opposite end of the evaluation continuum is represented by the term "filthy." "That was a filthy effort" communicates to a player that his coach was dissatisfied with his attempt to execute properly. It is unlikely these descriptive terms would be interpreted accurately within other segments of the university population.

Our coaching staff always has plenty to say to the players at halftime of our games. The philosophy has always been to be more critical when we are ahead than when we are behind. However, on one occasion, when we were very far behind, our defensive coordinator presented a most critical appraisal of the team's performance in the first half. He yelled and screamed to a point where I thought he had lost control of himself. As we were walking back onto the field for the second half, he asked me: "How did I do, Doc?" His presentation had been an act to encourage a better second-half effort. It, or something, worked. While we played a better second half, we still lost the game.

I have had an opportunity to observe pregame motivational speeches, coaches' consoling players for making crucial errors, coaches' counseling players on personal issues, players' conversations on and off the field, and so forth. It has been an enormously enlightening experience and has convinced me of the great value of language observation.

The final form of simple observation is *time duration*. It is sometimes important to note the time any given observation is made, or the time expanse over which that observation is recorded. For example, we know that the diligence of work habits or study habits is not consistent across all time frames. One could make an important error of interpretation if only one time frame was employed for observation. By taking a cross section of times, a more accurate understanding of social events is possible.

This is clearly the case with football players. If one were to observe the manner in which players wear their helmets as they are going through their stretching and warm-up exercises, a somewhat informal approach could be determined. Chin straps are often unbuttoned, and air helmets are frequently deflated. When a contact drill is to be participated in, a chorus of snaps can be heard as the straps are put in place, and the equipment manager and his staff often have a very busy few moments as they pump up the air lining of the helmets.

The time of the week also suggests different levels of intensity. On Mondays, the team is generally relaxed and nursing bruises obtained from the contact in the game the previous Saturday. By Thursday, things are becoming pretty intense for the following Saturday contest. Although our team goes through the same basic practice schedule every day, these different levels of intensity in the course of the week for the same activities are easily observed.

A final example utilizing time duration is the comparison of different periods of the season. Behavior registered during the summer in the first few days of practice prior to the start of the season is quite different from that observed toward the completion of the year. In the beginning, everyone is happy to be back, playing football again, and seeing old friends and making new ones. As the season wears on, the attitude of the players and coaches becomes much more serious. Preparation for a football game is unbelievably complex. If the team is winning, one continues those efforts in order to continue to win. If the team is losing, players and coaches undertake that much more work in order to alter the course of the season.

Contrived Observation

Contrived observation is that which is made utilizing the mechanical devices of cameras and audio recorders of which we have spoken earlier. The human observer is not capable of including, or even noting all of the variables and circumstances within the environment in which observations are made. Some behavior or conversation may take place outside of the parameters in which the observer is working, some stimuli may be purposefully distorted, and the researcher may not be able to record all of the detail, remember that which has occurred previously, or any number of other possibilities that might interfere with the validity of the data.

Permanently recorded data can facilitate filling these observational voids. Such data also provide a reliability assessment on other recorded observations. Since it is a permanent record, these same data may function heuristically and stimulate further thought, formulation of hypotheses, and, ultimately, additional research. Indeed, to this end, we discussed the availability of radio, television, and film collections, which are a fertile source of data for content analysis.

The student must be aware that many research environments require the permission of those being recorded before such can be accomplished. Certainly, for example, if one is tape recording an interview, the respondent must offer permission to do so. Similarly, permission must be granted to film behavior of terminally ill patients in a hospital ward.

It is fortunate that the observation of the football program we have been discussing does not require such permission nor is the absence of such a violation of an ethical code. Football players are quite accustomed to having their playing performance recorded on film and subsequently evaluated by the coaching staff. All games are filmed for review by the players and the coaching staff. Indeed, game films of a previous contest with an upcoming opponent are studied repeatedly. In addition, all practice sessions are recorded on video cassettes by students from the mass media department. This photographic data is supplemented by an audio track so that verbal data is available as well. Although the assignment for the mass media students is limited to the filming and recording of the action of the practice, some peripheral activity, e.g., the players not engaged in a particular drill or the behavior registered between plays, is also recorded. The coaching staff has learned a great deal about players' attitudes and sense of commitment by viewing this type of evidence.

Finally, during game action, still photography is employed. Polaroid shots of the opposing team are used to determine what they are doing as a play starts and what changes they introduce in their alignment as the play unfolds. This affords the coaching staff information with which to make immediate adjustments in our defensive alignment or offensive-play selection. While still photography has not been used very often in research, the observational environment of a football program

does provide an ideal avenue. Within this research situation, one of the strongest features of these contrived observations is control by the researcher as to what will be recorded and the absence of reactivity from those being observed.

EXPLORATORY RESEARCH

Introduction

In previous chapters we have dealt with a number of methods of data collection that allow for the assessment of a hypothesis. That is, in focusing upon hypothesis testing, we have concentrated on procedures that were more quantitative in nature.

By contrast, in this chapter we have been more interested in those techniques that are more likely to be employed when the researcher is not likely to have a specific hypothesis to test. One may have a hunch or intuitive feeling but may not be prepared to submit it to a more rigorous examination.

Research of this nature, in which the investigator is exploring the possibilities of an idea or where little has been previously recorded, is referred to as *exploratory research*. The initial knowledge about a new topic begins with exploratory efforts. The broad knowledge base that we seek is reflected by the three basic questions under which exploratory research is conducted. The first question involves providing tentative answers to the questions that were motivated by the researcher's initial curiosity and searching for any variable relationships that appear to exist. Second, given the nature of the data collected initially, what more detailed and systematic investigation is warranted? Third, and assuming fruitful responses to the second question, what methods are most likely to generate profitable data?[20] We believe that exploratory research presents a most difficult problem for the social researcher.

Major Problems in Exploratory Research

The Lack of a Conceptual Model.   Consider the following metaphor. Exploratory research is like trying to find the needle in the haystack, except that the researcher does not know that he or she is looking for the needle. By definition, exploratory research is the initial probe into a topic about which one knows little or nothing. Thus, the review of the literature—through which one tries to construct a relevant conceptual model to guide one's research—is very hard. Because there is basically no literature to review, the researcher must try to suppose what the problem area is like and, then, read literature in a different area that the researcher's guesses might provide a relevant orientation. For example, if one knew nothing about the game of football, the researcher would have to start with some other type of sport that is believed to be somewhat like football. Or, if one didn't know anything about the drug subculture, one would have to search out the literature on, say, the juvenile delinquent subculture and try to image what possible parallels might hold for the unstudied drug subculture. In sum, the researcher would be in the middle of the haystack looking for something that is surely there but not knowing what that something would be.

The Researcher's Dilemma. Before the exploratory researcher can begin to frame what types of relationships exist, the researcher needs to amass a substantial amount of descriptive information about the problem area. This is difficult, however, because of a major dilemma.

The dilemma is that the researcher is essentially an outsider who wishes to gain access to the insiders' or subjects' views of the world. To put it another way, the main characteristics of the researcher's initial attempts to do exploratory research are those of marginality and unattachment. The researcher is not a part of the group that is being studied.

Marginality and unattachment are beneficial to the researcher in that these characteristics help bring an unbiased perspective to new subject matter. However, they make it difficult for the researcher to penetrate the social surface beyond the knowledge that is public. The researcher needs to be able to penetrate the subculture to be able to find the knowledge that is secret and private.

Indeed, this more buried secret and private knowledge is often considerably different from the perspective which the outsider has of the subjects. James Spradley[21] noted this in his classic piece of research on the homeless, jobless, urban nomad. Spradley found that the subjects' perceptions of themselves were not only different from various outsiders' views (police, medical personnel, and so forth) but also more detailed and complex than the outsiders' knowledge.

In sum, one of the first difficulties the exploratory researcher must address is to find a way to enter the subculture in order to tap the usually more rich and fruitful information.

However, entrance into the subculture is a two-edged sword. That is, if the researcher takes the position of an unknown participant (discussed earlier), it may be difficult to get to certain key informants or centers of power and influence. On the other hand, if the researcher elects to make the research objective known, the respondents and informants may be tempted to tell only that which they feel is good for the researcher to know. Thus, the social-desirability response and the managed impression become situations that may mislead the researcher from a true understanding of what is going on within the area of study.

Similarly, if the researcher decides to take a participant role, entrance may take longer to achieve but it will assuredly result in more accurate information. The problem here is the obvious ethical one of treating the research subjects as subjects without their knowledge. Additionally, the role of participant may be such that the researcher is unable to be divorced sufficiently from the subject matter in order to see the situation from an unbiased perspective. Rather, the ideologies of the subculture may intercede in the researcher's investigation. On the other hand, if the researcher chooses the nonparticipant role, certain key or "strategic research sites"—to use Merton's term—may be impossible to penetrate. For example, what actually goes on in the boardroom of a major corporation or during the discussions that prevail in the promotion and tenure proceedings of an academic department are not available to the nonparticipant researcher's *observation*. Other techniques of data-gathering must be used in these cases.

In sum, exploratory research is made difficult not only because there is little conceptual literature to assist the researcher but also because the researcher is usually an outsider who needs to get inside for the real story.

Data Collection Strategies.   The triangulation strategy discussed earlier is quite important in exploratory research. Any data-gathering technique has its own particular advantages and disadvantages. When one is trying to collect descriptive information in an attempt to identify the important social roles, social definitions, and social relationships of a situation that is largely unknown to the researcher, one must paint with a very large brush. That is, one must be willing and able to utilize many different data-collection procedures for which the distortions and disadvantages of any one of them can be compensated.

Many of the data-collection procedures that we have discussed can and have been used in exploratory research. These include interviews, questionnaires, content or secondary analysis, observation, and unobtrusive measurement. The most often-cited method of exploratory data collection, however, is observation. If we recognize that one of the most significant functions of research is to provide description of social interaction and environments, the utility of observation is immediately apparent. The researcher can simply begin by observing a social event or the social actors within a specific environment and by describing that which has been observed.

If the primary data-gathering strategy is observation, the interviewing of key informants is a close second. When certain patterns seem to be evident in the researcher's observation of the study group, these patterns can be cross-checked through the use of the interview—usually with the interview guide rather than the structured interview. General questions that allow the respondent to talk in his or her own words will often provide

confirmation for the researcher's initial observations and, sometimes, indicate that the researcher's initial classification scheme may have missed a critical point or two.

The key to gathering data in exploratory research is to be flexible. The researcher needs to look broadly in many different directions in the beginning, trying not to come to a premature closure on what one will concentrate. Along with this rather unstructured and general stance, the researcher must make complete field notes, because what appeared to be a minor point in the beginning of the observational period may turn out to be of crucial importance at the end of the study.* One needs to be able to resurrect accurate and detailed information from one's field notes when it becomes obvious that a particular interpretive schema is going to be used.

The Results of Exploratory Research.   Any data evolving from exploratory efforts are, by definition, tentative. Regardless of the method used to generate these data, it is unlikely a probability sample was selected. Therefore, the primary difficulty inherent in exploratory research, and that which renders data from exploratory efforts to be tentative, is an absence of representativeness. This does not mean that such research is useless and that the samples usually chosen for exploratory research are poor ones. Quite the contrary, the study persons may not be representative, but they may be key informants or persons who have had wide and long experience with the phenomenon under study. In asking questions of such persons, the exploratory researcher will be tapping into a valuable source of information through which important insights can be generated when exploring this new territory.

A Final Note.   Because of the vagueness and uncertainty that surrounds the execution of exploratory research, it is our opinion that the re-

---

*To this end, one's initial set of field notes should be composed daily and retained in chronological order. In the data-analysis stage, one makes *several copies* of the initial set in order to begin the "cut and paste" process on which the research focuses. The initial set should be retained as is, however.

searcher needs to be as well versed and competent as possible. This type of research is not recommended for the first research project for the student.

SUMMARY

This chapter has examined some procedures that are widely used by researchers engaged in exploratory research or in the initial phase of the search for knowledge concerning any phenomenon in which we might be interested. While these methods do not preclude hypothesis testing, they generally result in data that have been collected from a nonrepresentative sample and that, thereby, have limited inferential value.

Our discussion focused primarily upon observation. We noted the problems of objectivity, reactivity, and marginality. We also suggested five questions the researcher selecting observation as a data-collection method must answer. These are (1) whether to participate in some role capacity within the group being studied, (2) whether to be known as a researcher to the members of the study group, (3) whether to conduct the research within a laboratory or natural setting (field research), (4) the degree of control that the researcher will exercise over the research setting, and (5) the degree of conceptual structure present.

The responses registered for the first two of these questions determine which of the four observational modalities (known participant, unknown participant, known nonparticipant, or unknown nonparticipant) the investigator will use. Although each offers a differing degree of structure and control that may be exercised by the researcher, no single modality is inherently superior.

We presented the idea that the credibility of social research data can be enhanced through triangulation—the procedure of gathering data from multiple sources. Our discussion centered on unobtrusive measures, or removing the observer from the set of interactions or events that are being studied. The four basic types of unobtrusive measures—physical traces, archival analysis, simple observations, and contrived observation—which have been identified by Webb and his associates, guided the discussion.

Finally, we introduced the topic of exploratory research, which is done when the researcher begins to probe into a previously unknown topic area. The lack of conceptual help in the literature, the problems of being a marginal person who is unattached to the study group, and the need to use multiple data-gathering procedures all conspire to make the job of the exploratory researcher a most difficult one.

KEY TERMS

Accretion measure
Archival analysis
Confederate
Confidential
Contrived observation
Covert role
Disembodied posturing
Embodied posturing
Erosion measure
Exploratory research
Expressive movement
Field research
Hawthorne effect

Known nonparticipant
Known participant
Laboratory setting
Language behavior
Marginality
Masking
Natural setting
Nonparticipant
Overt role
Participant
Physical exterior signs
Physical location analysis

Physical trace
Private
Public
Reactivity
Secret
Simple observation
Singularity
Time duration
Triangulation
Unknown nonparticipant
Unknown participant
Unobtrusive measure

REVIEW QUESTIONS _____

1. What are the five questions which the researcher must answer when contemplating an observational data-gathering design?

2. Discuss the four degrees of marginality in observational research identified by Junker, and create an example of each stage in the same substantive topic area.

3. Using the first two research questions that deal with the researcher's degree of involvement and with the degree of disclosure, create a fourfold typology (participant versus nonparticipant and overt versus covert), giving an example of a research topic appropriate to each of the four categories.

4. What is triangulation, and how does it counterbalance singularity? Create an example showing how triangulation might be accomplished.

5. Four different difficulties that arise from the researcher's interaction with people threaten the validity of data. Identify, define, and illustrate these four types. Can you think of four additional difficulties that arise in other data-gathering procedures?

6. What is an unobtrusive, or nonreactive, measure? Give as many reasons as you can why such measures are important.

7. Identify and give an example of the four basic types of unobtrusive measures.

8. Define and illustrate embodied and disembodied posturing and an accretion and an erosion measure.

9. What is exploratory research, and why is it so difficult to do?

10. Review question: Compare and contrast exploratory research with hypothesis testing.

11. Review question: Observation plays a key role in the scientific enterprise. Discuss why the difficulty in making a relevant observation decreases as one moves from exploratory research to hypothesis testing.

PART IV

DATA PRESENTATION, DATA ANALYSIS, AND THE ETHICS OF SOCIAL RESEARCH

We assume that the researcher has by now picked a research topic; reviewed the relevant literature and formulated a conceptual model to direct the study; framed specific propositions to be investigated (defining those concepts and constructs that require theoretical definitions and identifying the independent and dependent factors); chosen the sample; constructed the measuring instrument along with its pretest, reliability test, and validity test; selected and executed a data-gathering design; and has the raw data partially coded, awaiting its presentation and analysis.

First, Chapter 14 focuses on data presentation; i.e., how one is to report the results of the study to the reader. Basically, one has two choices: (1) to present individual scores or (2) to group or collapse the data into a lesser number of more general categories. After a brief discussion on reporting individual scores, the majority of Chapter 14 is devoted to the discussion of the function, design, and operationalization of those dimensions that characterize tables.

Second, Chapter 15 brings together, in an extended example, as much of the material that has been presented in earlier chapters as is feasible. With the benefit of the example, one will see the formation of a conceptual model to direct the research, a return to the proposition used to illustrate the disproportional stratified sampling procedure, which concluded Chapter 7, and a structured schedule containing a Likert index used as the measuring instrument that was designed to be used in a survey using a face-to-face interview data-gathering design.

Chapter 15 also introduces several notions relevant to data preparation and presentation, such as the formation of a codebook, use of a computer code sheet, and the formation of a data base. Further, an actual SPSS[x] data processing program is presented to assist in the determination of some of the operational definitions required for the tabular presentation of the data, to reconstitute several variables on the basis of previously completed analyses, and to do a number of statistical calculations pertinent to evaluating the proposition mentioned in the sampling example at the end of Chapter 7, as well as several additional hypotheses that are suggested by and which emerge in the course of the data analysis.

In this way, Chapter 15 is both a discussion of data preparation, presentation, and analysis as well as a capstone review, which presents a concrete example of much of the material presented earlier.

Third, Chapter 16 discusses the important issue of ethics in social research. In this chapter we try to sensitize the reader to one of the basic human dilemmas of the role of a social researcher. That is, we focus on the tension between the social researcher as a human being and the social re-

searcher as a serious scientist. This essential tension is one that exists because the social scientist wishes to gather information that is unbiased, or not tainted with such considerations as the socially desirable response, and because the researcher wants to respect the rights and privacy of the respondent, who is usually quite willing to assist the researcher in his or her project.

Your authors have struggled with the placement of this chapter. Some reviewers argued that it should be placed in the very beginning of the book since it is so important to the execution of a professionally respectable, as well as methodologically sound, study. While we most certainly agree with the importance of ethics in social research, we decided to place it last—and for what we consider a very good reason. We strongly feel that the reader cannot truly appreciate the magnitude of the ethical situation in social research if one possesses little or no knowledge of what that method entails. How can one understand the nuances of informed consent or confidentiality or the invasion of privacy without knowing that an inter-

viewer may have been asked to observe the home surroundings *as well as ask the respondent the schedule items prepared for the interview? Does one not have to know that the researcher has a data-gathering option called the participant observer enacting a covert role to see the violation of certain ethical dimensions? In sum, we ask you this question: if you had no knowledge that a handgun could seriously harm or kill you, would you be frightened when approached by a would-be robber or would you simply be curious about that "funny-looking thing" in the robber's hand? We argue that the reader must have exposure to the principles of scientific methodology before a more complete understanding of the ethical component is possible.*

This position on ethics is, of course, in concert with our position all along in this book. Learning by the numbers is not as preferred as obtaining as full a background as possible before choices and issues have to be decided. We remain faithful to this principle in the placement of the chapter on ethics.

CHAPTER 14

DATA PRESENTATION:
INDIVIDUAL SCORES AND CROSS-TABULATIONS

INTRODUCTION

At this point we have discussed how to select a research topic; review the relevant literature; construct a conceptual model; identify propositions to be investigated; introduce the research design; choose the sample; operationalize all necessary variables; design the measuring instrument; test it for inadequacies, reliability, and validity; make any necessary adjustments; and gather and code the data. In this chapter we discuss how the results of a study are presented. Because reporting individual scores is reasonably simple and straightforward, the bulk of the present chapter is devoted to the construction of *cross-tabulations.*

Construction of tables and accompanying issues are subjects that are often neglected. Therefore, after a brief discussion of reporting individual scores, we focus upon on the major issues surrounding the construction of a useful table of research results.

REPORTING INDIVIDUAL SCORES

As one might suppose, the fewest number of decisions arises when one reports individual scores. For example, if your professor listed each score to the midterm taken by the 20 students in your class, the individual scores of the class would have been reported. Often, the presentation of individual scores is confusing to read, however, because of the large number of scores one must internalize. Therefore, the values for the variables often are combined in some way to facilitate their interpretation. This is one of the major functions of statis-

tical analysis, which is presented in the following chapter.

There is little to say about the presentation of individual scores with the exception of how one determines an individual's score when using a composite measure in index format. Assume we have measured a variable, which we have assessed with a composite measure in index format. The response categories were structured using Likert response categories. The hypothetical data from one person's schedule appears in Figure 14.1. The item numbers are provided as references to statements that correlate with the hypothetical variable of marital happiness. To the right of the vertical line in the last column is a series of underlined numbers. These numbers represent the codes of the responses that the sampled person gave to the interviewer. For example, the "4" to the right of the first item means that the respondent picked the "strongly agree" response, which was coded "4" because it was the category that logically evoked the greatest degree of marital happiness.

Further, notice that item 14 is coded "12." This is because the researcher decided to weight this item with a factor of 3, which appears in parentheses right before the space in which the coded score is to be placed. Thus, the 12 means that the respondent selected the "strongly agree" response and the value of 4 was multiplied by the weighting factor of 3 to result in a value for this item of 12.

Finally, notice that for item 10 and item 13, the respondent received a coded score of 1, which indicates a low level of marital satisfaction, while

ITEM/ RESPONSE	SA A DK D SD	CODE
1	([4]) [3] [2] [1] [0]	4
2	[0] [1] [2] ([3]) [4]	3
3	[0] [1] ([2]) [3] [4]	2
4	[4] ([3]) [2] [1] [0]	3
5	[4] ([3]) [2] [1] [0]	3
6	[0] [1] ([2]) [3] [4]	2
7	([4]) [3] [2] [1] [0]	4
8	[0] [1] [2] ([3]) [4]	3
9	[4] ([3]) [2] [1] [0]	3
10	[0] ([1]) [2] [3] [4]	1
11	([4]) [3] [2] [1] [0]	4
12	[0] [1] [2] ([3]) [4]	3
13	[0] ([1]) [2] [3] [4]	1
14	([4]) [3] [2] [1] [0]	(3) 12

FIGURE 14.1 Hypothetical Responses to an Attitudinal Index on Marital Happiness

Finally, note that the index suggested in Figure 14.1 has 14 items with a range of *possible* values of 0 (zero) to 64. That is, if the respondent picked all those responses coded "0" to each item, the resultant total would be 0. If, on the other hand, the respondent picked all the response categories coded "4," a score of 64 would have been attained, that is, 4 x 13 = 52 (for the first 13 items) + 12 for the weighted 14th item.

Note that while one might be tempted to treat these scores as interval-level data, the numbers do not possess a constant unit of measure necessary for the interval-level interpretation. Rather, these data should be thought of as ordinal. Thus, it can be argued that a respondent with a score of 64 has more marital satisfaction than another respondent who received a score of 32, but not twice as much.

In sum, when reporting individual scores, one notes the particular coded value to each item of interest. If the variable being measured happens to be a composite measure in index format, the researcher must add all the codes to all the items within the index to obtain one score that represents the respondent's answers. It is analogous to your instructor recording your midterm performance to represent your overall performance, rather than listing how you did on each item that comprised the examination.

CROSS-TABULATIONS

Introduction

The more difficult process is to present tabular information rather than individual scores. The most important suggestion we can make about the construction of tables is that the finished table should stand on its own. Tables in the literature are frequently deficient in one or more aspects. We suspect this is largely to decrease the printing costs. However, while some shortcuts save a few dollars, we argue that interpretations of tabular data are often made more difficult because of such shortcuts.

Therefore, the remainder of this chapter is devoted to a discussion of the design and interpreta-

all the other codes indicate a tendency toward a positive orientation to this variable. The respondent may not be totally consistent in his or her responses, as we have attempted to demonstrate.

In this way, the Xs that are marked on the schedule are translated into quantified values and entered in the right-hand margin of the schedule so that they will be easily seen by the data analyst. After all of the appropriate codes are entered, they are added with the resulting total representing the respondent's score on the index. If this procedure were followed for all 14 items, the respondent's score, in this example, would be 48.

tion of tables. Among the issues to be discussed are the parts of a table; the nature of a proper title; the stub of a table; the subcategories or subheadings and their location; criteria for determining meaningful subcategories; percentaging tables; the position of the cell frequency and the cell percentage values (if both are used); the placement of the independent, dependent, and controlled variables; how to handle nonresponses (either refusals or omitted cases); and other matters of appropriate style. Let us begin with the parts that compose any table.

Parts of a Table

Every table contains six basic subdivisions: (1) title, (2) stub, (3) subheadings, (4) body, (5) cells, and (6) marginals. Additionally, the table may have one or more explanatory footnotes. Figure 14.2 illustrates the basic subdivisions.

Any table should be, first, numbered for easy reference and given a *title* to identify what the table contains. The *stub* is located in the upper left-hand corner and identifies the major variables for which subheadings are given in the table. For example, if the designation *Social Class/Sex* appeared where the label *Stub* appears in Figure 14.2, then *Social Class* would refer to the subheadings that appear vertically *down* the left-hand

side of the table, in this case, subheadings 1 through 3. The designation *Sex* would refer to the subheadings *across* the top of the table, or, in this case, subheadings A and B. Note that the words *Social Class* and *Sex* identify the major variables that are to be in the table and that these two variables are separated by a diagonal (/). Again, the designation to the left of the diagonal identifies the variable whose subheadings identify the rows in the table, and the designation to the right of the diagonal identifies the variable whose subheadings identify the columns in the table. Should the titles of the variables that appear in the stub have names that are long, they can be abbreviated. For example, *employment status* could be truncated to *status*, since any ambiguity would be clarified by the title.

A *subheading* is a subcategory that identifies the columns at the top and the rows on the side of the table. These subheadings must be clearly specified, although one is permitted to use abbreviated forms. Notice that the title of the table is separated from the stub and subheadings of the columns by a single line and that the stub and column subcategories are separated from the body of the table by a double line. The last row of cells is similarly separated from the "Total" designation by a double line. Finally, the subheadings for the row variable are separated from the cells by a double line, as is

Table No.	Number and Percentage of Cases Sampled by Numbered Subheadings and by Lettered Subheadings.		
STUB	**SUBHEADING A**	**SUBHEADING B**	**TOTAL**
SUBHEADING 1	Cell 1	Cell 2	Marginal 1
SUBHEADING 2	Cell 3	Cell 4	Marginal 2
SUBHEADING 3	Cell 5	Cell 6	Marginal 3
TOTAL	Marginal 4	Marginal 5	Grand Total

FIGURE 14.2 The Major Subdivisions in Any Table

the last column of cell values and the "Total" column.

The *cell* refers to any of the six divisions (in this example) contained under the row and column subheadings. Thus, cell 1 refers to the information that is contained in the upper left-hand cell, which is characterized as falling into subheading A and subheading 1. Similarly, cell 6 refers to the information that is found in the bottom right-hand cell that contains information characterized by subheadings B and 3. Taken together, all the cells of the table—no matter how many there may be—are called the *body*. Further, the subtotals—that is, the *marginals*—are the totals of each row and each column. Finally, the "Grand Total" is, obviously, the total number of cases or frequencies that appear in all the cells or the body of the table.

The Title of a Table

An important aspect of any table is a proper title. We frequently see table titles with labels such as "Table 17.8.2," which, of course, says nothing about the nature of the information contained within the table, only that it follows Table 17.8.1 and precedes Table 17.8.3 (if such exists). As we have emphasized, tables should be able to stand on their own; that is, they should be able to be understood without any further reference to other sources of information. One of the principal ways to accomplish this objective is through the formation of a good title.

A good title should provide several pieces of information. First, it should identify the explanatory variables or the objects of the research. Second, it should indicate the nature of the controlled variables contained within the table. Finally, it should identify the nature of the values within the cells of the table, that is, whether they are frequencies, percentages, or both. Let us propose a formal style, which accomplishes all of these objectives, and let us use as an example the proposition concerning working males that we developed at the end of Chapter 7 on sampling design. You will recall that the proposition was that a working male's self-image varies positively with his de-

gree of education, holding constant race (whites only), marital status (married), age (25–35 years of age), and wife's employment status (dichotomized into those with wives who were employed and those with wives who were not employed). Note the following:

Table 1. Number and Percentage of White, Married, Working Males, 25–35 Years of Age, Sampled with Employed Wives by Degree of Positive Self-Image and by Amount of Education

First, all tables should be identified with the word *Table* and given some sort of numerical value, so that the particular table represented can be easily distinguished from other tables or figures. Second, notice that the words *number* and *percentage* are the first two pieces of information given in the title. These words refer to the nature of the information that is to be found *within* each cell of the table. In this case, both the frequency (the number of elements that are characterized by the subheadings identifying each cell) as well as a percentage value are to be reported. The middle part of the title—that is, "White, Married, Working Males, 25–35 Years of Age, Sampled with Employed Wives"—identifies all the class II, controlled, variables in the study, which tells the reader about the nature of the people who were studied. Finally, the title identifies the major variables— the class I variables (the objects of the research). We suggest that one highlight the class I variables through the use of the word *by*. When we say "*by* positive self-image and *by* amount of education," we are suggesting to the reader that these are the two central variables that are subdivided into strata or categories within the table.

In sum, while the title of the table is only 26 words, a great deal of information has been given. The reader knows that the table contains both numbers and percentages; the nature of the controlled variables and their particular values as well; and the major analytical variables, the class I variables in the study.

A parenthetical comment is in order. Note that the title indicates that the persons in the table all had employed wives, while the proposition to be tested suggested a sample of men with employed wives and a sample of men with unemployed wives. You may ask what happened to those men whose wives were unemployed. Quite simply, for the sake of a clearer presentation of the data, they would be contained in a *second* table. Hence, this particular class II, controlled, variable would be handled by placing those men with employed wives and those whose wives are not employed in two separate tables. Finally, note that most of the class II variables have been controlled through the sampling design with the remainder controlled through the data-presentation design.

Subcategories or Subheadings

As we have stated, any table must have clear subheadings across the top and down the left-hand side of the table. Two further points require comment concerning these subheadings.

First, the subheadings should be mutually exclusive and inclusive of all (or all but very selective) cases. *Mutual exclusivity* means that there should not be any overlap among the categories. Thus, if a particular case falls in subheading 2, it should not be able to appear in any other subheading that is offered for that particular variable. Categories should be *inclusive* so that all cases find an appropriate place in one of the subheadings. The one exception for excluding one or more cases is if these cases did not produce data on the desired categories of the variables contained in the table. For example, suppose that an interviewer was to ask several items on an index to measure the social-class variable posited earlier and that one of the respondents, Mr. Smith, refused to respond to these items. In this case, the researcher would have data on Mr. Smith for each of the other variables in the study but no information that could be used to determine Mr. Smith's social-class position. In this case, Mr. Smith should most properly be excluded from the table, but it should be noted that this respondent refused to answer those items pertaining to the social-class index in a footnote to the table.

Second, the subheadings *must be arranged in a specific order* if the variable being represented is an ordinal or stronger-level variable. The subheadings for the columns and the rows must be organized in an ordinal manner from high to low. For example, social-class categories would be properly used if ordered "Upper," "Middle," and "Lower." Or, social status could be given as "High," "Medium," and "Low." Age could be cited as "Senior Citizen," "Middle Age," "Young Adult," "Teenager," "Child," and "Infant." In each example the categories are ordered from a great amount of the variable being assessed to a small amount of it. An invalid organization would be "High," "Low," and "Medium." This invalidates a logical progression and would make the statistical analysis of relationships within the table impossible.

In sum, one should be careful about excluding elements and *always* making sure that subheadings are ordered. Of course, one is excused from the responsibility of ordering when the variable is at the nominal level of measurement.

Position and Format of Cell Values

We argue strongly for indicating both frequencies and percentages within the cells. *Frequency* refers to the actual number of elements that are characterized by the specified row and column subheadings, while *percentage* refers to the proportions (multiplied by the constant of 100). The frequency gives the reader valuable information about the magnitude within the cell, and the percentage gives the reader important information about the cell being studied when compared to the other cells. Thus, we feel both pieces of information are necessary to maximize interpretation of the data. Some researchers argue that one needs only the percentage figure if the frequencies are presented in the marginal totals or the grand total.* They argue that one can readily calculate what the frequency is,

---

*Whether one uses the marginal totals or the grand total for the base on which to calculate the percentage is an issue we address later in this chapter.

PROPER FORMAT FOR REPORTING CELL FREQUENCIES AND PERCENTAGES	IMPROPER FORMATS FOR REPORTING CELL FREQUENCIES AND PERCENTAGES	
152 (76.8)	152 (76.8)	152 (76.8)

FIGURE 14.3   One Proper and Two Improper Formats for Reporting Cell Frequencies and Cell Percentages

but our position is that the reader must have both values readily available to facilitate interpretation.

Since cell frequencies and percentages are to appear within the cells of any table, one should separate these two values so the reader does not confuse one with the other. The table should be designed so that the cell frequency appears in the upper left portion of the cell and the cell percentage appears in the lower right portion. See Figure 14.3 for an indication of the proper and two improper formats. In the two improper examples, the cell frequency and the percentage figures are presented vertically and horizontally, respectively. Both formats are inappropriate, because the reader may have difficulty when scanning down the column or across the row. The proper format separates the cell frequency from the cell percentage if one is scanning across the row or down the column. Note we have carried the percentage calculation to one decimal place, which is the generally

accepted standard. In so doing, there can be no mistaking which value is the frequency and which is the percentage.

Further, one should vertically and horizontally align all the frequencies and percentages in all the cells. That is, if the ones integer falls on position 15 in the first cell, then the ones integer should fall on position 15 in the cells that come directly below the first cell. If the frequency in the first cell is on row 34, then the cell frequencies in the columns across the page should also be on row 34. See Figure 14.4 below. Note that the cell frequencies are aligned across the rows and down the columns; the cell percentages are similarly aligned, and the percentage values have been carried out to one decimal place.

In sum, the format for reporting cell frequencies and percentages should clearly designate which values are frequencies and which are percentages.

VARIABLE 1/VARIABLE 2	SUBHEADING A	SUBHEADING B	TOTAL
SUBHEADING 1	152 (81.7)	34 (18.3)	186 (100.0)
SUBHEADING 2	53 (29.9)	124 (70.1)	177 (100.0)
TOTAL	205	158	363

FIGURE 14.4   The Proper Format for Reporting Both Cell Frequencies and Cell Percentages

Placement of the Independent and the Dependent Variables

There does not seem to be a consistently used convention concerning the placement of the independent variable or variables and dependent variable. Some authors suggest that they always put the independent variable on the top of the table. Others make no such suggestions. Nor shall we. The only consideration the scientist should have when constructing a cross-tabulation is to place the subheadings of the major variables to maximize the clarity of their presentation.

Consider that normally one has an 8 1/2-by-11-inch sheet of paper with which to work. If the dependent variable has five subheadings and the independent variable has three, it would be logical to put the dependent variable on the 11-inch dimension and the independent variable on the 8 1/2-inch dimension. That is, one should use the longer side of the paper for the variable that contains the greater number of subheadings. By so doing, one will be able to spread out the cross-tabulation to maximize its readability. This should be the only consideration in the researcher's decision to put the independent variable on the side or across the top of the paper. Remember, as well, that the sheet of paper can always be turned 90 degrees, in order to have the long side on the top of the paper.

In sum, we argue that the placement of the independent and dependent variables does not matter, unless placement would cause the data to be too cramped. As we shall discuss, percentaging the table will indicate clearly which variable is independent and which is dependent.

To inject one note of caution, researchers are increasingly utilizing computer equipment in the preparation of documents. The software (the programs that direct the computer) used may have idiosyncrasies that will determine placement of the dependent and independent variables. For example, it may be that the particular word processing program that the writer is using can only calculate percentages vertically. If such were the case, one would be required to put the independent variable on top of the table (that is, over the columns). Even this restriction is minimal, since one can always turn the paper 90 degrees to make a table more readable. Unfortunately, many journals poorly present tabular data, perhaps because of the added expenses of typesetting tables.

One final note is necessary. If one is including *more than two* variables in a table, one must be very careful. If there are two independent variables or if there is one independent and one class II, controlled, variable, they should *both* be placed on the same axis. To put it another way, the axis containing the dependent variables should *never* be contaminated with any additional *independent or controlled variables*. Multiple independent variables can be together and more than one combination of independent and controlled variables can be together, but the dependent variables should be alone on a separate axis. The logic is that the independent (and the controlled variables) have been determined and the researcher is interested in seeing how the dependent variable varies over these specified categories.

Percentaging Tables

Percentaging a table can be done in three ways: (1) down on the base of the column margin; (2) across on the base of the row marginal; or (3) on the base of the grand total. If one selects the first way and percentages down the column, then all the cell percentages in any column should add to 100.0 percent. That is, the percentages in all the cells under the subheading A will total 100.0 (subject to very small fluctuations due to the rounding of the resulting numbers). If one selects the second way and percentages across the row, then all the cell percentages in any row should add to 100.0 percent, given the same caveat concerning rounding. Finally, if one selects the third way and percentages on the grand total, then *all the percentages in all of the cells* would total 100.0 percent, subject to rounding variations. Note Table 14.1 as an example of a table that has been percentaged across.

TABLE 14.1   Number and Percentage of College Students Sampled Who Study by IQ and by Success

IQ/SUCCESS	HIGH	LOW	TOTAL
HIGH	82 (88.2)	11 (11.8)	93 (100.0)
LOW	21 (21.4)	77 (78.6)	98 (100.0)
TOTAL	103	88	191

In the first row, the first cell percentage of 88.2, when added to the second cell percentage of 11.8 in the first row, totals 100.0 percent. In row two, the 21.4 added to the 78.6 equals 100.0 percent. This is because these data have been percentaged across the rows by using each row marginal as the base on which to figure the cell percentage. Thus, $.82 / 93 = 88.2$ and $11 / 93 = 11.8$ (for the first row). Note, as well, that if one adds the two cell percentages in the first column—that is, the 88.2 and the 21.4—the total is not 100.0 percent and the cell percentages do not reflect the cell proportion using the marginal of 103 as the base. Clearly, percentaging across the rows and percentaging down the columns will result in unequal cell percentages. Let us return to Table 14.1, and recalculate the percentages on the same data, but this time, do so vertically. The results appear in Table 14.2.

As you can see, the cell percentages in Tables 14.1 and 14.2 are not equal, even though the cell frequencies, marginals, and grand total are identical. These percentages must be interpreted differently, depending on the direction in which they are calculated. The proper interpretation of the percentages in Table 14.1 assumes that IQ is the independent variable, while for Table 14.2 it is assumed that success is the independent variable. The point to note when comparing Tables 14.1 and 14.2 is that the direction in which they are percentaged is important and depends upon the location of the *independent* variable. Thus, in most cases, the researcher will have to identify the inde-

TABLE 14.2   Number and Percentage of College Students Sampled Who Study by IQ and by Success

IQ/SUCCESS	HIGH	LOW	TOTAL
HIGH	82 (79.6)	11 (12.5)	93
LOW	21 (20.4)	77 (87.5)	98
TOTAL	103 (100.0)	88 (100.0)	191

pendent variable, because this will influence the way the tables are percentaged. When we discussed the development of the conceptual model and the propositions to be investigated, we suggested that it was important to designate the independent and dependent variables. As you can now see, such a designation is important in the presentation of one's tabular data and, subsequently, to one's statistical analysis.

In sum, if the independent variable is on the side of the table, one percentages across the rows, using each row marginal as the base for the percentage calculations for the cells in that row. If the independent variable is on the top of the table, one must percentage down the columns, using each column marginal as the base for the percentage calculations for the cells in that column. Therefore, in a table that has been percentaged properly, the reader will immediately know which variable or series of variables are being interpreted as the independent factor or factors by noting the direction of the percentages.

What about the third way? When does one percentage on the basis of the grand total? This will be done when one wants to present a *strictly descriptive analysis of the distribution of the data.* If the researcher does not wish to present a causal or predictive interpretation of these data, percentaging on the grand total would be appropriate. The reader will find that this option is rarely used in social science, although it is found more frequently in exploratory studies than in explanatory studies.

In sum, one should always percentage in the direction of the independent variable (if one is posited). If one adheres strictly to this rule, one's interpretation of the data in any table can never be incorrectly done.

OPERATIONALIZING THE SUBHEADINGS IN TABLES

Introduction

In this final section, we will discuss the ways in which the subheadings in a table are operationalized. Indeed, this discussion applies to the more

general problem of operationalizing any type of categorization, whether it deals with a discrete or continuous variable. Rather than discuss this topic with measurement and operationalization, we postponed it until this point because of its relevance to the presentation for tabular data.

There are a number of criteria that have been proposed as relevant to this task: (1) the arbitrary collapse of data, (2) distribution based on statistical requirements, (3) statistical distribution, (4) observational differentiation, (5) theoretical or conceptual differentiation, and (6) empirical determination. All of these criteria are not created equal, a problem to which we now turn.

Arbitrary Collapse of Data

The least desirable mechanism for grouping data is the *arbitrary collapse of data.* Here, the researcher reduces the data by grouping the elements into categories chosen through the researcher's discretion. A good example of an arbitrary collapse of data is the procedure used by the U.S. Bureau of the Census in reporting the variable of age. In many census tables, age is broken down into five-year increments, e.g., 0–5 years of age, 6–10 years of age, 11–15 years of age, and so forth. The data, when reported in this fashion, have been collapsed into arbitrary categories of five-year increments.

The central problem with the arbitrary collapse of data is that the groupings are not based on any type of meaningful conceptualization. Consider the age category 16–20. The sociological and psychological literature would demonstrate that the persons so grouped would be quite different from one another. Sixteen-year-olds have just become eligible to drive (in most states) and, therefore, have a measurable increase in their social status among their peers. The 18-year-old has passed by the excitement of the 16-year-old's newly found freedom and is now a senior in high school, who is either planning to go to college or actively anticipating entering the armed services or the world of full-time employment. The 19-year-old is either adjusting to the difficulties of full-time employment, a military life-style, or a first-year student in undergraduate school. It is clear that this particular five-year age span contains persons who are involved in very different social worlds. Further, the maturity levels as one moves through this five-year period change considerably. To consolidate these persons into a single category is to suggest similarities among them that are not justified by the empirical evidence, hence, the term *arbitrary*. In this case, the divisions are without any supporting rationale other than a single person's view of what they should be.*

In sum, the arbitrary procedure of collapsing data has no virtue except for the reduced cost of presentation. While sometimes advocated, we argue that in social research there is never an instance when the arbitrary collapse of data is warranted.

Distribution Based on Statistical Requirements

Some statisticians have advocated grouping data to ensure sufficient numbers of cases for statistical analysis, that is, *distribution based on statistical requirements*. Without going into too many details, there are some statistical procedures that require a certain minimum number of elements for the legitimate use of the mathematical procedure. Therefore, it is sometimes argued that if one has too few elements or frequencies in a particular cell, these elements should be combined with the elements of an adjacent category in order to have the minimum number of cases for a legitimate analysis.

The problem here is that while the numbers may be sufficient, the researcher may have combined elements that are dissimilar, thereby thwarting the reason for categorizing the data in the first place. Let us return to the age example cited earlier. If one had too few numbers in both the 11–15 and the 16–20 age categories and if one decided to rectify this by combining these two categories, one would be treating 11- and 20-year-old respon-

dents in the same manner. Such a combination would not make sense in view of the differences that can be observed empirically.

In sum, the collapse of data to achieve the requirements of a desired statistical procedure must be done with caution, because one may destroy the substantive or theoretical meaning that the original separation represented. Further, with the emergence of more statistical procedures, such artificial manipulation of data is not necessary. If one cannot meet the assumptions for the legitimate use of any particular statistical procedure, one should search the statistical literature for another measure that assesses the dimension in which the researcher is interested and that would be more appropriate to the nature of one's data. Diligence will surely be its own reward, for no matter what the circumstances, one can usually find an appropriate mathematical device without distorting one's data. Finally, if the researcher wants to include two categories on a particular variable, the disproportional stratified sampling design discussed earlier will rectify the problem of too few cases. Thus, there is little need to consider the collapse of categories to achieve sufficient numbers.

Statistical Distribution Determination

One should be careful to not confuse *statistical distribution determination* with the one just cited. Collapsing categories to achieve sufficient numbers for analysis and doing a statistical distribution determination are not the same thing.

As we have argued, one of the central reasons for doing research is to see if different degrees of a particular independent variable will manifest any differences on a dependent variable. Therefore, it is necessary to separate elements with different categories or different degrees of the independent variable. It may be that this separation can be achieved through some type of statistical analysis. For example, suppose that one wishes to create several different categories of people on a variable

---

*While it is certain the Census Bureau realized in determining the five-year interval for reporting age that such was an arbitrary categorization, there probably is no categorization that would please all the users of census data. Further, the reporting of each individual age category, while highly desirable in that each census user could then collapse them into more meaningful categories, would be likely to incur considerable added expense of reporting these data to the Census Bureau.

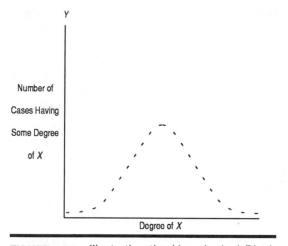

FIGURE 14.5 Illustrating the Hypothetical Distribution of Data on a Single Variable Identified as X

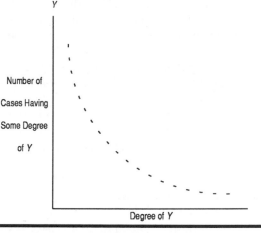

FIGURE 14.6 Illustrating the Hypothetical Distribution of a Single Variable Indicated as Y

and that the descriptive standard variation indicated there was a significant spread in the values of this variable.* If there appears to be variation in the independent variable and one wanted to devise several categories for further analysis, one might calculate the mean or the average of these elements and then determine the points of one standard deviation above and below the mean. In so doing, one would have separated the elements on this one independent variable into four categories: (1) more than one standard deviation below the mean, (2) one standard deviation or less below the mean, (3) one standard deviation or less above the mean, and (4) more than one standard deviation above the mean. *If these data are normally distributed,* the cases would have been divided into categories containing approximately 15 percent, 34 percent, 34 percent, and 15 percent, respectively, of the total number of cases analyzed.† In this way, one has statistically determined four different categories that are guaranteed to contain elements that differ from one another on the independent variable. Not only has one determined different categories, but one has guaranteed that

certain proportions of cases have been grouped together, thereby insuring sufficient numbers of elements in each category. Further, in the absence of any other procedure for determining cutoff points for categorization, the researcher will at least have the confidence that the group limits do circumscribe elements that differ from one another.

However, one note of caution is necessary. One should check to make sure that the total number of cases that are to be analyzed are normally distributed. While the procedure to construct such a distribution is rather time-consuming, it is worth the effort, as it will offer a strong indication of the descriptive nature of the distribution. Figure 14.5 shows how one may illustrate the actual distribution of data on one variable. The dots represent the total number of cases in the sample for that particular degree of the independent variable. The data in Figure 14.5 conform roughly to the notion of a normal curve and can be analyzed as suggested above to determine the cutoff points for each of the four categories. However, look at the data as reported in Figure 14.6. These data do not

---

*Again, recall that we are not interested in a complete demonstration of statistical procedures and, therefore, will keep discussion of them to a minimum. Suffice it to say that the descriptive standard deviation is one of several measures of spread or variation in the data.

†See Figure 6.3 in Chapter 6 for the precise percentages associated with the standard normal distribution.

begin to approach a normal distribution. Therefore, the use of the standard normal curve and its
accompanying z scores (as described in Chapter
6) would clearly distort the nature of the data. In
sum, it is important to determine the actual distribution of the data, despite the time-consuming
nature of the procedure.

Statistical determination of categories is a permissible procedure, but it should be used only
when the researcher has no other alternative and
only after plotting the actual distribution of the
cases on the variable on which the statistical determination has been done. Put another way, statistical determination should be used only when
all of the following three procedures have been
found to be unacceptable.

Observational Differentiation

Knowledge that the scientist has amassed in a
career of studying the subject matter should not be
disregarded. It may be that the researcher can use
his or her knowledge to make meaningful divisions among the data. Thus, the researcher may be
able to locate meaningfully natural divisions—
observational differentiation—in a particular variable.

Let us return to our example concerning age.
After one has studied teenagers for some time, one
should be able to posit some meaningful divisions
on the basis of observational knowledge. Would it
not make sense to argue that there are a number of
meaningful subcategories among teenagers when
one considers the patterns of social interaction?
For example, it would seem logical to argue that
13- and 14-year-olds generally group together,
because they are still in the middle school population rather than in the high school group. Further,
15-year-olds have the difficult combination of being new to the high school environment and unable to drive, which sets them apart from the rest
of the high school population. Most 16-year-olds
have access to a car, hence status, while 17- and
18-year-olds have had the opportunity to develop
more maturity and attain positions of importance
within the high school environment. Nineteen-
year-olds are either working or on to college as

first-year students, which effectively separates
them from all the other teenagers. Thus, it would
be reasonable to conclude that there are as many
as five age groupings among teenagers, and at
least three distinct social groupings. All of these
decisions were made on the basis of the researcher's
prior knowledge gained through observation and
study of the teenage population over time.

Permit us to carry this a bit further. While we
made rather fine distinctions between teenagers
(sometimes based on only a one-year differential),
consider those who have attained middle age.
While not wishing to engage in a debate concerning where this population begins and ends, let us
assume it is the age cohort between 35 and 60. We
have, then, a 26-year span, which probably contains two socially distinct groups. First, there is
the younger group, which is probably settled into
a career path and energetically pursuing the upper
strata of the hierarchy within that career. Here,
people are setting goals and trying to achieve
them. Second, there are those who are older for
whom the achievement of career goals has either
been achieved or found to have been unattainable.
This latter group may be pursuing a career which,
while not as lofty as previously hoped, is satisfying. The person is now "serving out his time"
without the constant pressure of achievement. If
that seems reasonable to you, given the inevitable
exceptions, such as Colonel Sanders, who started
his fried-chicken business in his 60s, then this 26-
year age span can be broken down into but two
categories: (1) striving for success and (2) settling
in and accepting that which one has been able to
achieve.

A couple of comments will crystallize the obvious. Observation or common sense indicates
that not all categories for any particular variable
must have the same range of values. For example,
a meaningful age category may be arrived at with
but a one- or two-year span, as in the case of
teenagers, or may encompass many years, as in
the case of those who have reached the middle
years. This serves to point out the absurdity of the
arbitrary classification.

Finally, let us briefly pursue one further variable. In dividing college students, one might ob-

serve different life-styles or different orientations to the educational environment. We would expect to find those who are academically inclined, constantly studying and driven by the realization that their anticipated goals are open but to a few; athletes, some of whom are primarily concerned with achieving a high level of performance in their sport in anticipation of a chance at a future professional contract in sports; the "collegiate student," for whom a reasonable balance of the academic and the non-academic has been achieved; and the "commuter" students, who travel daily to and from home. There are other categories, but the point is clear.

In sum, it may be possible for the researcher to establish cutoff points when categorizing the data, because the researcher has had the experience and knowledge gained through observation that separates the study population into meaningfully different subclasses. Quantification is fine and certainly a part of the process of doing scientific research, but observation is also a key to important insight and information.

Theoretical, or Conceptual, Differentiation

Often, the review of the literature may suggest meaningful subcategories that other researchers have found useful in previous research. Again, we suggest the interplay between the conceptual and empirical dimensions of research.

Utilization of subcategories which other researchers have formulated—*theoretical, or conceptual, differentiation*—is mandated when one wishes to compare the results of the current study with those of earlier studies. Indeed, if one is doing comparative research or if one is interested in the variable of change, the replication of previous subcategories may be necessary to accomplish these objectives.

Empirical Determination

The final procedure for operationalizing tabular subheadings is a combination of the statistical and observational determinations. In observational differentiation, we used observation alone as the means to determine category cutoffs. With the statistical distribution determination, we used mathematical procedures alone to determine cutoffs, as long as the general distribution of the cases was consistent with the particular mathematical technique being used. The *empirical determination* involves the use of a data-analysis procedure and the researcher's observational discretion to determine subcategories in the data.

For example, consider a situation in which the researcher has devised a new index to measure an attitude. Assume that there are 50 items in the index and that the coded structured response categories range from zero to four. Assuming that each item in the index is equally weighted, the researcher must first determine the *theoretical range* of values to the index. The theoretical range is determined by the maximum and minimum values possible. In this example, the researcher could not obtain a score below 0 nor one greater than 200 (that is, 50 times 4).

But how should one divide these possible values into meaningful categories? There is little reason to go to the existing literature, because the researcher is the creator of the measuring instrument and no previous guidelines will exist. Further, one cannot use observation to determine logical or commonsense divisions, because one can't see an attitude. This is the perfect spot for the empirical determination.

The researcher should plot the actual distribution of scores obtained on a continuum, so that the researcher can visually examine them in a comparative way. A *continuum* is a line on which the occurrence of various values of some variable may be represented.[*] For every position on the line that corresponds to the value of a case, a mark is made indicating that one case. In this way, the researcher can plot the distribution of the sampled cases. For example, consider the hypothetical data presented in Figure 14.7, where the data are all compacted into the right-hand half of the continuum. While the theoretically minimum value

---

[*]A continuum may be considered similar to an ordinate in the Cartesian system of graphic presentation.

Minimum Value = 0	Maximum Value = 200

FIGURE 14.7 Hypothetical Distribution of Cases on a Single Variable Where the Minimum Possible Value Is Zero and the Maximum Possible Value Is Two Hundred

Minimum Value = 95	95 108 143 162	Maximum Value = 162

FIGURE 14.8 Hypothetical Distribution of Cases on a Single Variable Where the Minimum Actual Value Obtained Was 95 and the Maximum Value Obtained Was 162

was zero, no respondents fell toward the minimum end of the continuum. Indeed, it is rare that anyone's attitude will be so extreme as to occupy either theoretical extreme. Therefore, the researcher should determine the *actual range* of values and let these values determine the minimum and maximum values for the continuum. If the actual range of values is between 95 and 162 on the 50-item index and if we let the continuum range from, say, 90 to 165, we can get a better look at the spread of the values than we could have in Figure 14.7. Look now at Figure 14.8, which illustrates these data. After the values to be categorized have been plotted, one studies the resulting distribution to see if there are any natural, empirical divisions in the data itself. That is, do the cases themselves separate into clusters, or groupings, that are distinct from one another? As one can see from Figure 14.8, the values of those sampled distribute themselves along this continuum into two basic clusters, or groupings. While most of the cases fall between 95 to 108 and between 143 to 162, there are some cases which fall between 109 and 142. However, these cases are minimal in number, and the bulk of those sampled fall into the two above-mentioned categories. Again, suppose that the researcher wants to treat this variable as independent and wishes to create a table containing some number of categories. Clearly, the data distribution in Figure 14.8 suggests a two-category table for the independent variable, which could be labeled "High" and "Low" and operationalized as all those cases having values between 143 and 162 and between 95 and 108, respectively. The few cases which fall into the middle would, in all likelihood,

be disregarded in the data analysis for this particular table.

However, suppose that we encountered a different situation. Consider the data presented in Figure 14.9. Here, three clusters of cases appeared on the continuum: (1) a low cluster of values between 60 and 75, (2) a medium cluster of values between 85 and 100, and (3) a high cluster of values between 110 and 125. Assume further that the number of cases between 76 and 84 and those between 101 and 109 were minimal. Note that the researcher can never definitively tell prior to using the empirical distribution procedure what the results will be. Thus, the researcher may have hoped for and proposed a table format that contained two subcategories on the independent variable. Subsequent analysis of the empirical distribution may indicate the need for additional subcategories, as in this hypothetical illustration.

Here, we must return to our previous discussion of sample size to append another consideration onto those noted in Chapter 7. We omitted this point earlier because the background necessary for understanding this consideration had to wait for the presentation of the notion of the empirical distribution. As we argued in Chapter 7, if the researcher wants to compare selected categories of the independent variable against various categories of the dependent variable, a disproportional stratified sample would be recommended, because it will guarantee sufficient numbers of cases on each of the desired categories on the independent variable. However, if the independent variable is an attitudinal one, which can't be observed, and if the researcher had to devise an

Minimum Value = V(min)		Maximum Value = V(max)
	.... ○ .... • •	
	60 75 85 100 110 125	

FIGURE 14.9 Hypothetical Distribution of Cases on a Single Variable Where Three Clusters of Cases Appear

Minimum Value = V(min)		Maximum Value = V(max)
	.... • •	
	40 60 80 87 89 93	

FIGURE 14.10 Hypothetical Distribution of Cases on a Single Variable Where Three Clusters of Cases Appear

index to measure it, then there is no way for the researcher to know prior to the data analysis how the scores to this index will be distributed. The researcher may plan to have two subcategories, but the empirical evidence may dictate that more than two subcategories would better represent the actual distribution. Therefore, when one is using this particular procedure to decide how many categories to have and what the cutoff points are to be, some allowance must be made for the unanticipated emergence of more than the initially desired number of subcategories. Thus, we would argue that the researcher should draw a somewhat larger sample than would seem necessary because of the possibility that these data may indicate more analytical categories on the independent variable than the researcher originally thought. In sum, the number of categories can always be reduced; if they have to be expanded, however, the researcher will need a sufficient number of cases to be able to do so.

The possible saving grace here is the pretest sample. Earlier we argued that the pretest was important, in part because it could be used to generate data for the reliability and validity tests, as well as an empirical check on the clarity and meaning of the items that appeared on the schedule. Here we would add that once the pretest illustrates the soundness of the measuring instrument, the data that comes from it should be analyzed as one intends to analyze the data from the study sample. One should put the data into the proposed tables and do the proposed statistical analyses to see if something has been left out and needs to be appended to the schedule. It is here that the pretest data may give the researcher some inclination of how the data will be distributed in the study sample.

Therefore, the pretest sample—if it mirrors the study sample (and we argued that it should)—may give one data that will indicate the possible distribution of the independent variable and allow the researcher to adjust the desired sample size prior to the data-collection phase.

Let us look at another empirical distribution illustrated by Figure 14.10. There are three clusters again, or are there? There is a cluster of cases with scores ranging from 40 to 60, a cluster of cases between 80 and 87, and a final cluster between 89 and 93. In this case, the researcher would be ill-advised to divide the data into three subcategories. While the clustering is indeed evident, we would argue that the differences between the two clusters toward the maximum end of the continuum is so slight that these two categories should be collapsed together and treated as one cluster.

This leads to another major point, which is to look at not only what the observational capacity of the researcher can determine but also what the quantified data can tell you. Here, the eye says that there should be three subcategories, but the quantified values do not. While the range of values between the high and the low cases for the lowest cluster is 20, the range of values between the lowest case and the highest case for *both* of the upper clusters is only 13. We would argue that this difference is insufficient for a meaningful difference between the two supposed upper clusters.

Finally, consider an attitudinal index of 40 items using the Likert response categories coded from zero to four where none of the items is weighted. The theoretical range of values is 0 to 160. Assume that Mr. Smith got a score of 102 and Mr. Jones registered a score of 107. Is there a significant difference between these two scores? We doubt it. It could be that Smith and Jones responded to 35 of the 40 items identically. On the remaining five items (assuming that the remaining items were all positive), Jones could have picked "strongly agree" while Smith could have picked "agree." Even though there is a five-point differential in the Smith and Jones scores, we would argue they are virtually identical in their attitudinal responses. Therefore, one must examine not only the values themselves but also the range of possible values and what the value of a single point really means.

It was this type of thought that brought us to the conclusion that the two clusters toward the maximum end of the continuum in Figure 14.10 were not that different.

SUMMARY

In this chapter we have concentrated attention primarily on the construction and interpretation of tabular presentations. After a few brief comments on reporting individual data, in which attention was given to the determination of scores to a composite measure in index format, we looked at the issues of the format of any table, stressing the need to include sufficient information within the table so that it could be read and understood without any accompanying text. More specifically, we focused on the nature of the title; placement of the cell frequencies and percentages; delineation of the body of the table from the marginal values, subheadings, and stub; the order that the subheadings should reflect (if the data were not measured at the nominal level of measurement); placement of the independent, dependent, and controlled variables; and the important issue of proper percentaging of the cells.

The final part of this chapter dealt with the critical issue of operationalizing the subheadings within any table. Several strategies were presented: (1) the arbitrary collapse of the data; (2) distribution based on statistical requirements; (3) statistical distribution criteria; (4) observational differentiation; (5) theoretical, or conceptual, differentiation; and (6) empirical determination. It was argued that the first two strategies were poor choices for the social scientist and that the third choice was dependent upon the sometimes unwarranted belief that one's data fit the distributional assumptions of the statistical process.

The fourth strategy involved making an observational differentiation based on the researcher's accumulated knowledge concerning the research situation. The fifth focused on the researcher's ability to find a conceptual model that provided meaningful input into this decision. The sixth strategy could be used when both the conceptual model and the researcher's knowledge were limited due to a lack of work done on the variable, as the case would be in an exploratory study or when a newly developed measuring instrument was used.

Thus, the final three strategies, it was argued, offered the soundest procedures for determining meaningful cutoff points for operationalizing tabular subheadings. Which of the last three are used would depend, of course, on the specific circumstances surrounding the research.

KEY TERMS

Arbitrary collapse of data	Frequency	Statistical distribution
Body	Inclusive	determination
Cell	Marginal	Stub
Continuum	Mutual exclusivity	Subheading
Cross-tabulations	Observational differentiation	Theoretical, or conceptual,
Distribution based on	Percentage	differentiation
statistical requirements	Percentaging tables	Title
Empirical determination		

REVIEW QUESTIONS _____

1. If one constructed an index containing 10 items using Likert response categories coded from zero to four, if one item was weighted with a factor of two, and if a second item with a factor of four, what is the theoretical range of values for this measure?

2. Define and illustrate the various parts of a correctly formulated table.

3. Why do the authors feel that (a) the arbitrary collapse of data, (b) the distribution based on statistical requirements, and (c) the statistical distribution determination are inadequate ways of creating categories on a variable?

4. Compare and contrast (a) the observational differentiation strategy, (b) the theoretical, or conceptual, differentiation criterion, and (c) the empirical determination strategy for creating categories on a variable.

5. Under what conditions is the researcher likely to select each of the three strategies mentioned in the preceding study question?

6. Create an example of the empirical determination strategy for operationalizing categories on a variable that would result in three categories. Label the three categories, and show their maximum and minimum values on the continuum.

7. Under what conditions would one percentage a table on the basis of (a) the column marginals, (b) the row marginals, and (c) the grand total?

CHAPTER 15

COMPUTERS, STATISTICS, SPSSˣ, AND A SUMMARY EXAMPLE

INTRODUCTION

In this chapter, we address several broad objectives: (1) an introduction to some additional statistical issues and techniques, (2) a brief discussion of computer technology, (3) an illustration of the SPSSˣ data analysis computer package, and (4) a discussion of how to accomplish these objectives through the use of a reasonably sophisticated example.

First, we want to introduce some basic notions and a few specifics that are involved in statistical analysis. While we cannot present sufficient information to provide the reader with statistical expertise, we will discuss some statistical issues and techniques and generate some illustrations.

Second, this chapter introduces the topic of computer technology. As with statistics, we cannot within the space limitations present a full explanation of computer technology in the social sciences, but we will discuss and illustrate some of the basics.

Third, we concentrate upon a brief illustration of the SPSSˣ software program. SPSSˣ (Statistical Package for the Social Sciences, Version x) is a well known and frequently used canned program, which social scientists have found useful in performing a variety of statistical procedures.

Finally, we will integrate these objectives through an illustration. It is our objective to develop a reasonably sophisticated picture through which much of our earlier discussions will come to life.

In sum, we feel strongly that one's conceptual model, research design, and statistical analysis— while different aspects of the research process— are not items to consider in isolation. After introducing these components separately, we deal with their interrelationships within the obvious limitations of space in this chapter.

THE RESEARCH PROBLEM

If you have spoken with adults at any length, you have probably heard many persons say that they hate their jobs, that they feel they are not appreciated, that they are not happy, or that they are looking for something new. Many people seem to express, sometimes in vague ways, a general malaise.

At the same time, ever larger numbers of people in our society are achieving greater educational skills. More people, from a wider range of social strata, are attempting to earn college degrees in the hope that education will lead to a happier, more productive, and rewarding life. Indeed, many of our fellow faculty proclaim that the liberal arts education is "education for living." It is education that will increase one's opportunity to enjoy civilized society, thereby enriching one's existence and ostensibly leading to greater happiness. Less articulate versions of this perception underlie statements such as, "You can't get anywhere without an education in today's society." Therefore, popular wisdom suggests a correlation between feeling good about one's self and the amount of education that the person has attained.

If we accept this general discussion as a starting point for a research project, it is reasonable to suggest that educational attainment ought to be positively associated with a person's positive self-image and that education and self-image could be considered class I objects of the research. While additional propositions could be entertained, let us concentrate on a single one involving educational attainment and self-image.

THE CONCEPTUAL MODEL

Introduction

In Chapter 5, we argued that a review of the literature helps the researcher to frame a conceptual model and that, once constructed, the conceptual model functions to identify meaningful propositions for investigation. Further, we argued in Chapter 3 that if there were conceptual weaknesses in the researcher's study, they were likely to be the result of the class III, uncontrolled and confounding, extraneous variables. Therefore, the literature should provide help in identifying such factors and in gaining insight into various methodological ways to execute the study. The following conceptual considerations could emerge as class III, confounding, factors in that they are likely to influence a person's self-image or educational attainment.

The Family's Financial Condition

Popular magazines, television programs devoted to looking at the condition of the American family, letters to the Ann Landers and the Abby Van Burens, and so forth often suggest that financial concerns are persistent causes of dissatisfaction among adults. This dissatisfaction stems from specific concerns such as future expenses (e.g., college tuitions or age-related hospital costs), debt retirement (e.g., paying off the home mortgage), and insufficient funds for current living (e.g., dining-out expenses, vacations for family members, or credit card payments). One way such financial

worries may be minimized is through the dual-wage-earner family in which both spouses are working.

Therefore, it would seem logical to move this class III factor into either the class II, extraneous but controlled category, or into the class I, explanatory-objects-of-the-research, category. If we select the former option, the revised proposition would be that educational attainment varies positively with positive self-image, holding constant a spouse's employment status. A fourth factor has inadvertently slipped into the proposition—that of marital status—in that we have assumed that the sample will contain respondents who are married. Let us conceptually consider marital status for a moment.

Marital Status

Emile Durkheim, in his classic sociological work, *Suicide: A Study in Sociology,*[1] argued that structural changes in society brought on social currents, which, in turn, created changes in behavior. These currents, however, could not be seen directly or assessed empirically. Instead, one had to investigate observable items, such as the suicide rate, and consider them as reflective of these social currents.

In looking at group suicide rates, Durkheim argued that the degree of group involvement tended to be associated negatively with the group's suicide rate. For example, he found that the suicide rate for single persons was higher than for married people. Further, he found that the suicide rate for married people was higher than for people who were married with children. Thus, when one looks at different levels of involvement in the family, those groups with lesser involvement (or responsibility) have higher suicide rates than those groups with higher involvement.

Given this, marital status is a class III, confounding, factor that influences self-image and, therefore, should be controlled. At this point, then, the proposition has expanded to the following: Educational attainment varies positively with positive self-image, holding constant spouse's employment status and the marital status of the study subject.

Race

While strides have been made since the 1950s in reducing racial discrimination (largely through the efforts of civil rights activists in the 1960s), prejudice and discrimination against the African-American population in America remain.*

Therefore, for many reasons, racial status is still a factor that must be considered as a class II factor, or controlled variable, in this study. Thus, the revised proposition would now appear as: Educational attainment varies positively with positive self-image, holding constant spouse's employment status, marital status of the subject, and the subject's race.

Subject's Employment Status

Thinking further about possible class III factors, the subject's employment status comes to mind. Max Weber in *The Protestant Ethic and the Spirit of Capitalism*[2] was one of the first to recognize the important relationship between the Protestant religions and the work ethic. Briefly, Calvin (one of the Protestant reformers from the sixteenth century) argued that success in one's work *may* be an important indicator that the person is one of the elect, has God's favor, and is predestined to eternal salvation. This idea, which, in varying degrees, is a ubiquitous one in many Protestant religions, has evolved into the notion that work is

noble, worthy, moral, and certainly important in how one is treated in the society.

For example, the Social Security Administration (SSA) maintains two separate payment programs. The first is for the beneficiary, or the person who is entitled to Social Security benefits because that person has been employed and has had salary deductions taken for the support of the Social Security program. The second is the Supplemental Security Income (SSI) recipient, the person who has not had salary deductions made specifically for the program from which the SSI recipient is benefitting. That is, the SSI recipient is participating in a federally sponsored welfare program for which tax dollars have been appropriated and which is administered through the SSA. Thus, the SSI recipients are persons who qualify because they are disabled, have disabled children, or are aged and not receiving sufficient support from other sources. It has been observed that when the payment recipients come to the Social Security offices to inquire about some aspect of the programs, two lines form: one made up essentially of the beneficiaries and one made up mainly of SSI recipients.† The point is that the SSA makes a distinction through the nature of its programs between those recipients who have *earned* their payments and those who are the recipients of payments through the general *welfare* of the society. Moreover, the recipients *themselves* seem to honor this distinction by generally gravitating to the line that contains similarly qualified persons.‡

For our purposes, note the importance of work which the American culture places on each adult. Work and its meaning have been and, apparently,

---

*Because of space limitations, we cannot entertain a full discussion, but it is our general observation that the level of discrimination that existed before the 1960s has been substantially reduced, although not eliminated.

†From personal communication with Professor Donald Frank, Department of Sociology and Anthropology, Towson State University.

‡We are not interested here in the many other moral, ethical, political, and economic ways in which the distribution of these funds can be perceived. Rather, this is one important way in which the SSA perceives the distribution of benefits and reflects this perception in the organization through which Social Security recipients are served by the SSA—a perception that is generally reflected by the recipients themselves.

continue to be important determinants to the self-image of most adult Americans.

Gender Roles

Strongly associated with the meaning of work in American culture is the perception of one's proper gender role or roles. Recent changes in American society have created greater opportunity in the labor force for women to pursue careers that are equal with men. Thus, women today have a choice between following the traditional wife-mother-homemaker social role, which was prevalent prior to the 1970s, and a role in the economic marketplace. The expected social role of men has stayed reasonably constant. While there has been some discussion about the role of house husband, such a role has been assumed by only a minuscule proportion of the male population. Rather, there currently seems to be some movement toward a more egalitarian sharing of family responsibilities between men and women.

Thus, sex of the study subject may be an important factor in the formation of positive self-image because of the changing gender role expectations of women and the adjustments made necessary within the family unit. These changes may create problems for males. For this reason, we should include the subject's sex as a class II factor, with the resulting proposition as follows: Educational attainment varies positively with positive self-image, holding constant spouse's employment status, and the subject's marital status, race, and sex.

Some Methodological Decisions Concerning the Proposition

At this point, we have reviewed the literature, decided what literature is important, and, on the basis of the content of that literature, framed a proposition that is consistent with the conceptual model. We have said essentially that we are interested in looking at the association, if any, between educational attainment and self-image. The con-

ceptual model also suggests that marital status, spouse's employment status (if the subject is married), and the subject's race and sex are class III, confounding, factors, which we have decided to hold constant—in one way or another—as class II factors. Note that the proposition functions as a summary of the conceptual model and is stated in the clear, straightforward way that we suggested in Chapter 5.

However, even further decisions have to be made. While the researchers have elected to control on the class II factors, no decision has been made on how these factors are to be controlled. Reviewing briefly, recall that block variable controls generally require much larger samples than would one-category controls, although the results of block variable controls are more widely applicable in inferring to the population. Further, consider that we want a range of values on the class I variable of educational attainment. Additionally, since we are interested in self-image—a variable that cannot be observed—we must use a survey, and an interview would seem also appropriate because of the low educational level of a portion of the sample. Thus, in view of the anticipated high costs of interviewing, it would be wise to reduce the size of the sample by controlling on the class II variables through the one-category control design.

To that end, let us decide to study only males since they are likely to have a greater degree of self-image problems because of recent changes in the gender role expectations in American culture. Further, these self-image problems are likely to be exacerbated for those males who are married, since they will have to contend with the wife's activities within the context of the family and other women's competition within the economic arena. Also, we will one-category control on race by sampling only white males because of the high unemployment rate and low educational attainment among a larger proportion of African-American males. Finally, we will control on the male's employment status with a one-category control as well, focusing on only those males who are working full-time. Thus, our proposition will finally read as follows:

> *Educational attainment varies positively with positive self-image, holding constant the respondent's sex, marital status, race, employment status, and spouse's employment status.*

THE METHODOLOGY

The Sample

Assume that the sampling design is as it was described at the conclusion of Chapter 7. That is, we will draw a disproportional stratified sample using a systematic process of white, employed, married males. Some of those sampled will have wives who are employed, while some will have wives who are not employed. Finally, some of the sampled males will have educational attainments that have been predetermined to fall into two categories: (1) a high school diploma or less education and (2) a college degree or more education. To somewhat simplify our illustration at this point, assume that we will *not* control on age. Finally, after having completed the sampling design, the anticipated numbers of persons in the categories suggested in Chapter 7 could not be achieved because of sample mortality and other reasons, but the sampling procedure did result in the numbers given in the data file, which is presented later.

Data-Gathering Design

Because of the high probability that the sample will not be interested in our study and given that a substantial portion of the sample (about half) will be of low educational attainment, we have concluded that a face-to-face interview would be appropriate. Further, the interviewers will be encouraged to set up appointments in the respondent's home in order to maximize the factors of comfortable surroundings and privacy for the respondent. This location should also expiate any anxiety feelings that the study is tied into the Social Security Administration. This will also prevent the use of the SSA personnel records from

becoming an issue. Finally, assume that we have designed a companion study through which to interview the respondent's spouse on a variant of this topic. While we will not go into the nature of the companion study, assume that it will be concurrent with our study and that its purpose is twofold: (1) to gather important comparative information from the spouse's perspective and (2) to occupy both the wife and the husband, who are the units of analysis, so that each may feel free to reply candidly. We anticipate that both spouses will be interviewed separately but at the same time by two interviewers. (Again, because of space limitations, we focus only on the portion of the study that focuses on the husband.)

Further, while interview data-gathering designs are expensive, this cost should be minimized since the respondents all reside in the same local metropolitan area, making overnight lodging and some meals for the interviewers unnecessary. Since we are using the Social Security Administration personnel records, we will have the respondent's home address and telephone number. The home address will allow us to inform both respondents through a letter of introduction that they have been selected for a scientific study and to follow-up this letter with a telephone call to establish a time for the interviews, which will be convenient for the respondent and the respondent's wife. Thus, because the study is a local one and because of the letter of introduction and phoning for an interview appointment, the call-back rate should be substantially reduced, saving interviewer time over what one would normally expect.

Operationalization

The variables will be measured using an interview schedule that contains largely structured items—questions to measure the respondent's behavior and social characteristics and statements to assess the attitudinal variable of self-image. The response categories will be close-ended, representing the response categories that have been preselected by the researchers in order to maintain the comparability of the responses given by the respondents and to satisfy the practical reason that such would significantly reduce the data preparation and coding time needed later.

Finally, the variable of self-image will be measured using an index in matrix format and Likert response categories. We assume that the schedule presented as illustrative has been pretested, tested for both reliability and validity, and is as it appears below (see Figure 15.1 on pages 331–337).*

As we begin the discussion of computers and computer technology, this is an appropriate time to interject that references are made to a specific computer program and the resulting tables. We have tried to be faithful to the formatting requirements demanded by the SPSS^x program which we are using. However, the printing requirements of the manuscript may, upon occasion, deviate slightly from the required formatting style required by SPSS^x. Therefore, the reader is cautioned always to refer to Appendix E, which contains the SPSS^x program as it would appear on one's computer monitor.

COMPUTERS AND HARDWARE COMPONENTS

Introduction

In this section we present a brief nontechnical and generic overview of computer hardware. Thus, there will be no discussions of the relative merits of particular microchips, or baud rates, and so forth. However, we will introduce you to the nature and function of the basic computer components. There are four hardware components in any computer system: (1) central processing unit (CPU), (2) keyboard, (3) monitor (CRT), and (4) printer.

Central Processing Unit (CPU)

The *central processing unit (CPU)* is the component where the computer system receives input from the keyboard, analyzes it according to specific programming instructions, and stores the re-

sults. It is here where everything seems to happen mysteriously. While the CPU can be broken down into subcomponents, which function in different ways, it is only necessary at this point for you to understand one of these subfunctions—storage.

There are two kinds of files that may be placed within a computer: (1) data files and (2) program files. A *data file* contains the information that is processed by the computer. A *programming file* contains statements that describe the location and nature of the data that appear in the data file, instructions pertaining to how the data files are to be manipulated, and, after such manipulation is done, instructions concerning how the results are to be reported.

The storage unit of the CPU can take a variety of forms. First, a *hard disk* is a permanently installed, internal structure where the data and program files are stored. Second, a *floppy disk* is a portable storage medium used to store data and program files. A *disk drive* is a structure that enables the CPU to take data off (*read*) or put data on (*write*) a floppy or a hard disk. The CPU can be made up of a variety of these components: a hard disk alone, a hard disk with one floppy disk drive, or a hard disk and two floppy disk drives. In sum, the disks are components that act as the storage cabinets of the computer system.

Keyboard

The *keyboard* is a typewriterlike structure with some additional function keys. The keyboard allows the researcher to input information into the central processing unit. The letter and number keys translate the respective letter or number into language that the computer can process. The *function keys* perform different operations that have been built into the software systems contained within the computer. The *software system* is a combination of programming instructions, which tell the CPU to do various operations, e.g., various mathematical operations. The information itself is translated into a *binary code,* which is a series of

---

*Note that for space and other considerations, some of the sections of the schedule are somewhat truncated and, therefore, are to be interpreted as illustrative rather than comprehensive.

zeroes and ones. Information as you and we know it—that is, letters of the alphabet and numbers in the base ten number system—is translated into strings of zeroes and ones, which is called the *machine language*. Computers can only process information if it is in this binary form, because the processing that is done in the central processing unit is done electronically.

Monitor (CRT)

The *monitor* is a structure that looks like a television screen. Indeed, it puts images on the monitor in the same way that images are put on a television screen, which is why it is sometimes called a *cathode-ray tube (CRT)*. Obviously, the monitor functions to present a visual image of what has been typed on the keyboard so that the researcher can follow along with what is being or has been entered into the CPU.

Printer

When programmed to print, the CPU sends electronic signals to the *printer*, which then translates these signals into the letters and numbers with which we are all accustomed. The printing function can occur on the monitor (CRT) so that the researcher can see it on the screen or it can occur on *hard copy*, which—to the rest of us—is paper.

Some Further Considerations

A *microcomputer* is a computing unit that can accommodate only one user at a time. If you have a computer at home, which is self-contained, you have a microcomputer. A *mainframe computer* is a larger-capacity computer, which has a number of dummy terminals connected to it. A *dummy terminal* is a keyboard and a monitor which is connected to the CPU. A dummy terminal is called a "dummy" because it can only input information from the keyboard to the CPU and receive output

from the CPU. The dummy unit itself—that is, the monitor and the keyboard—cannot do computations. However, because of the tremendous speeds with which mainframe computers work, the mainframe can accommodate many dummy terminals where multiple users are working on different projects with different software programs on different data files at the same time.

These dummy terminals are connected to the mainframe, where the actual data manipulations will occur, in one of two ways: (1) they are hard-wired or (2) they use a modem. When a dummy terminal is *hard-wired* to the mainframe, it means that immediately after the user turns the monitor on, the dummy terminal is in communication with the mainframe CPU. The *modem* is a peripheral device that connects the dummy terminal to the mainframe CPU through telephone wires. Here, one must dial the number of the computer center, which contains the mainframe, and if there is an open line (no busy signal), the dummy terminal is hooked into the mainframe CPU in the same way that you are connected when you telephone someone.

Summary

These, then, are the main hardware components of any computer system. If these are confusing for you, consider that all this business is much like your stereo system. The stereo system has different components: turntable, receiver, amplifier, tape deck, compact disc, and speakers. All of these components perform different functions. For example, the receiver converts AM and FM signals from broadcast towers into another electric form that the speaker ultimately converts into sound. However, as with a computer, the stereo will not play any great music unless one puts a record on the turntable, a tape in the tape deck, a disc in the compact disc player, or tunes in a commercial station. Similarly, one can hook all the components of a computer hardware system together and nothing will happen until you load some sort of software program into the CPU. So it is to the software that we briefly turn.

INTERVIEW SCHEDULE FOR A STUDY ENTITLED
"OPINION RESEARCH STUDY: SPRING 1990"

Time interview was started: _____   ID Number: _____

[Coder: Complete this.]

Date on which this schedule was completed: _____

Name of the interviewer: _____

INTERVIEWER PLEASE NOTE

THAT WHICH FOLLOWS AND WHICH IS WRITTEN IN CAPITAL LETTERS IS *NOT* TO BE READ TO THE RESPONDENT. THESE STATEMENTS ARE FOR THE INTERVIEWER ALONE AND ARE USUALLY INSTRUCTIONS THAT ARE TO BE FOLLOWED. THE MATERIAL THAT APPEARS IN LOWERCASE LETTERS IS TO BE READ TO THE RESPONDENT. IT IS *EXTREMELY IMPORTANT* THAT THE ATTITUDINAL MATERIAL IN PART I BE READ EXACTLY AS IT IS WRITTEN WITHOUT ANY INDICATION TO THE RESPONDENT AS TO WHAT AN APPROPRIATE ANSWER WOULD BE. IF THE RESPONDENT APPEARS TO BE CONFUSED BY ANY ITEM IN PART I, THE INTERVIEWER MUST SIMPLY REPEAT IT SLOWLY SO THAT THE RESPONDENT MAY HEAR THE ITEM A SECOND TIME. NO SUBSTITUTION OF WORDS OR PHRASES OR DEFINITIONS OF THE WORDS IN THE ITEMS SHOULD BE GIVEN. IT IS POSSIBLE FOR YOU TO REPHRASE ANY OF THE REMAINING MATERIALS IN THE OTHER PARTS OF THE SCHEDULE.

IF YOU OBSERVE SOMETHING THAT YOU THINK IS IMPORTANT BEFORE OR DURING OR AFTER THE INTERVIEW, YOU SHOULD NOTE WHAT IT IS BUT PUT YOUR OBSERVATIONS IN BRACKETS ([ ]). IF THE RESPONDENT OFFERS ADDITIONAL COMMENTS TO THE CLOSE–ENDED RESPONSE CATEGORIES, NOTE THESE COMMENTS—ALSO IN BRACKETS—AT THE POINT IN THE INTERVIEW WHERE THEY OCCURRED. PUT ANY SUCH COMMENTS IN THE LEFT-HAND MARGIN, AS THE RIGHT-HAND MARGIN WILL BE USED FOR CODING.

IF YOU HAVE ANY QUESTIONS OR IF ANY FIELD SITUATIONS OCCUR ABOUT WHICH YOU WOULD LIKE ADVICE, CALL THE SURVEY OFFICE AT 726-5000 FOR ASSISTANCE.

This study is a survey that has been designed to measure how you feel about certain things. We would also like to ask you a couple of questions about your social characteristics so that we can compare your answers to the answers of other people who are similar to you. Please understand that all the information that is collected will be put together with everyone else's answers so that it will be impossible to attach your answers to you. Finally, you have been selected by a scientific sampling process to be one of several hundred people whose ideas will represent thousands of people who are similar to you in the country. Do you have any questions I could help you with? . . . [PAUSE] . . . If not, let's begin.

READ THE FOLLOWING INFORMATION AND DIRECTIONS TO THE RESPONDENT. TAKE YOUR TIME, AND MAKE SURE THAT THE RESPONDENT UNDERSTANDS THE INSTRUCTIONS. WHILE YOU EXPLAIN WHAT THE LIKERT RESPONSE CATEGORIES ARE, HAND THE RESPONDENT THE THREE-BY-FIVE-INCH CARD THAT HAS THE RESPONSES ON IT.

In this first section of the interview, we would like to know how you feel about a number of statements. Please remember that there are no *right or wrong* answers. We just want to know how *you truly feel.*

EXPLAIN THE RESPONSE CATEGORIES IN YOUR OWN WORDS.

Do you have any questions? If not, let us begin. Remember that there are no right or wrong answers here, just how you really feel.

INTERVIEWER: *CIRCLE* THE CODE THAT CORRESPONDS TO THE RESPONDENT'S REPLY.

	[SA]	[A]	[NO]	[D]	[SD]	DO NOT WRITE HERE
1. I have the ability to get along with just about anybody.	(4)	(3)	(2)	(1)	(0)	_____ (1)
2. There is not much to laugh about these days.	(0)	(1)	(2)	(3)	(4)	_____ (2)
3. No matter what it is, I always seem to have bad luck.	(0)	(1)	(2)	(3)	(4)	_____ (3)
4. I feel good about myself.	(4)	(3)	(2)	(1)	(0)	_____ (4)
5. I'm happy with my work.	(4)	(3)	(2)	(1)	(0)	_____ (5)
6. I often have doubts about whether I'm doing the right thing.	(0)	(1)	(2)	(3)	(4)	_____ (6)
7. I'm a pretty level-headed person.	(4)	(3)	(2)	(1)	(0)	_____ (7)
8. No one pays serious attention to what I have to say.	(0)	(1)	(2)	(3)	(4)	_____ (8)
9. I always seem to make the wrong choice.	(0)	(1)	(2)	(3)	(4)	_____ (9)
10. I can hardly wait to get up in the morning.	(4)	(3)	(2)	(1)	(0)	_____ (10)

INTERVIEWER: LEAVE THIS LINE BLANK; CODER: ENTER TOTAL INDEX SCORE   _____
(11)

PART II

In this section of the interview, we would like to know something about who you are. I will ask you some easy questions and give you some short answers. Please pick the answers that are closest to your situation. These answers will help us to better understand the people who you represent in this study. Do you have any questions?

[IF THE RESPONDENT HAS QUESTIONS OR CONCERNS, DEAL WITH THEM SERIOUSLY AND FULLY.] THEN, PROCEED WITH THE QUESTIONS BELOW AND *CIRCLE* THE RESPONSE CODE THAT CORRESPONDS TO THE ANSWER THAT THE RESPONDENT GIVES.

12. OBSERVE, BUT DON'T ASK: Sex: (1) Male   (2) Female   _____
(12)

13. In what year were you born? _____   _____
[Fill in the year.]   (13)

14. When you first started working for your present employer, what was the last grade in school that you had completed?

   (8) Less than high school   (4) AA degree

   (7) Some high school   (3) Some college

   (6) High school graduate   (2) College graduate   _____
(14)
   (5) Technical/trade school   (1) More than college

          (9) No answer or can't remember

15. Are you presently employed?

   (1) Yes ─────────────────────→   16. How many hours of work do you
                                          average per week?   _____
(15)
   (2) No [GO TO 20.]
                                          _____   _____
(16)
   (9) No answer

                                      17. For what firm or company do you
                                          work?   _____
                                          _____   (17)

                                      18. How many years have you worked
                                          for your present employer?   _____
                                          _____ Years   _____ Months   (18)

                                      19. What do you do? [PROBE FOR
                                          SPECIFICS.]   _____
                                          _____   (19)

(continued)

FIGURE 15.1   **continued**

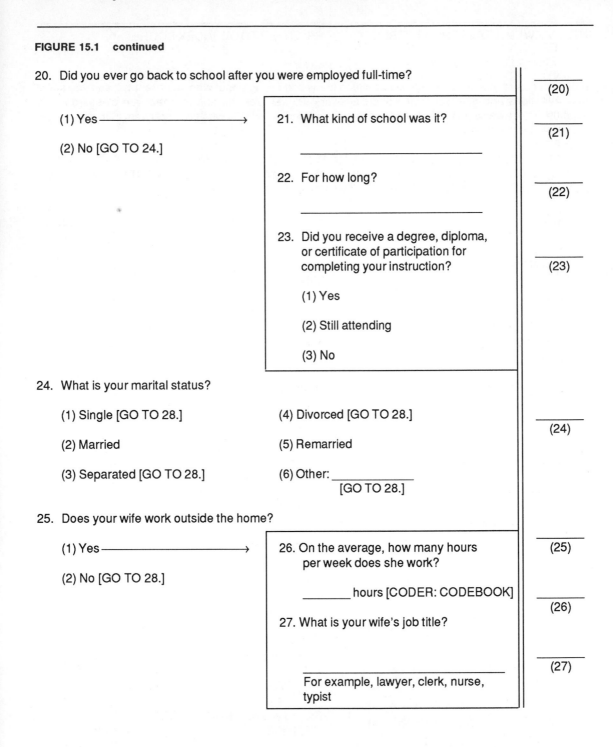

20. Did you ever go back to school after you were employed full-time?

      (1) Yes ⟶

      (2) No [GO TO 24.]

              21. What kind of school was it?

              _____

              22. For how long?

              _____

              23. Did you receive a degree, diploma, or certificate of participation for completing your instruction?

                  (1) Yes

                  (2) Still attending

                  (3) No

24. What is your marital status?

      (1) Single [GO TO 28.]   (4) Divorced [GO TO 28.]

      (2) Married   (5) Remarried

      (3) Separated [GO TO 28.]   (6) Other: _____
                                             [GO TO 28.]

25. Does your wife work outside the home?

      (1) Yes ⟶

      (2) No [GO TO 28.]

              26. On the average, how many hours per week does she work?

                  _____ hours [CODER: CODEBOOK]

              27. What is your wife's job title?

                  _____
                  For example, lawyer, clerk, nurse, typist

_____ (20)

_____ (21)

_____ (22)

_____ (23)

_____ (24)

_____ (25)

_____ (26)

_____ (27)

FOR PERSONS WHOSE MARITAL STATUS IS SINGLE, DIVORCED, SEPARATED, AND DESERTED, READ ITEM 28 *OMITTING* THE WORDS *WITHIN* THE PARENTHESES.

28. Could you give us a rough estimate of the amount of (family) debt which you (and your wife) are currently responsible for? That is, about how much do you still owe, exclusive of your mortgage, if any, for the car loan, the credit cards, and the major loans—such as a home improvement loan or a college tuition loan— which you have outstanding?

(1) Less than $10,000   (5) $25,001–$30,000
(2) $10,000–$15,000   (6) $30,001–$50,000
(3) $15,001–$20,000   (7) More than $50,000
(4) $20,001–$25,000   (8) No real idea at all

29. Do you have any children?

    (1) Yes ⟶

    (2) No [GO TO 38.]

> 30. How many children do you have?
>
>   _____ Children
>
> 31. Could you tell me what their ages are, approximately?
>
> _____   _____   _____
>   31   32   33
>
> _____   _____   _____
>   34   35   36
>
> 37. How many of your children are still living at home with you?
>
>   _____ Children are at home

38. INTERVIEWER: *CIRCLE* THE RESPONDENT'S RACE, BUT DO NOT ASK UNLESS IT IS IMPOSSIBLE TO OBSERVE.

    (1) African American   (4) Oriental
    (2) Hispanic   (5) White
    (3) Native American   (6) Other:_____
                                 [SPECIFY]

39. Could you give me a rough estimate of *your* annual income?

    _____

[INTERVIEWER: FILL IN THE AMOUNT GIVEN; BE PATIENT.]

INTERVIEWER: WRITE "N/A" IN ITEM 40 IF THE RESPONDENT'S MARITAL STATUS IS ANYTHING *OTHER THAN MARRIED OR REMARRIED.*

40. Could you give me a rough estimate of *your wife's* annual income?

    _____

[INTERVIEWER: FILL-IN THE AMOUNT GIVEN; BE PATIENT.]

_____ (28)

_____ (29)

_____ (30)

_____ (31)

_____ (32)

_____ (33)

_____ (34)

_____ (35)

_____ (36)

_____ (37)

_____ (38)

_____ (39)

_____ (40)

(continued)

FIGURE 15.1   continued

PART III

We've asked you a number of questions that will help us with the scientific research that we are doing, and we appreciate very much the time and effort that you have put into this interview. You've done a splendid job, and this is going to be very helpful for my research director.

Now is there anything which *you* would like to say to us? Is there anything at all which comes to mind when you think back on the interview questions that we have asked you?

[INTERVIEWER: PUT ANY COMMENTS VERBATIM ON THIS PAGE.]

IF THE RESPONDENT HAS NOTHING FURTHER TO SAY, AGAIN THANK HIM FOR HIS ASSISTANCE. IF HE DOES HAVE SOMETHING TO SAY, COPY IT DOWN AND THEN THANK HIM WHEN HE HAS COMPLETED HIS REMARKS.

_____

_____

_____

_____

_____

_____

_____

_____

_____

_____

_____

_____

_____

_____

_____

_____

[YOU MAY CONTINUE THE RESPONDENT'S REMARKS ON THE BACK OF ANY PAGE OF THE SCHEDULE, BUT BE SURE TO MARK AT THE TOP THAT THE COMMENTS ORIGINATED WITH THE RESPONDENT.]

INTERVIEWER: AFTER YOU HAVE COMPLETED THE INTERVIEW AND *LEFT THE RESPONDENT'S HOME,* IS THERE ANYTHING THAT YOU HAVE OBSERVED DURING THE COURSE OF THE INTERVIEW THAT YOU THINK WOULD BE OF INTEREST TO THIS STUDY. PLEASE WRITE YOUR COMMENTS, IF ANY, BELOW.

_____

_____

_____

_____

_____

_____

_____

_____

_____

_____

_____

_____

_____

_____

_____

_____

_____

_____

_____

[*INTERVIEWER: AGAIN, YOU MAY CONTINUE YOUR COMMENTS ON ANY PAGE OF THE SCHEDULE BUT IDENTIFY THEM AS YOURS AND PUT THEM ON A DIFFERENT PAGE THAN THE ONES USED FOR THE RESPONDENT'S COMMENTS.*]

FIGURE 15.1   Interview Schedule for a Hypothetical Study

COMPUTER SOFTWARE AND OPERATING SYSTEMS

Introduction

Without computer software and an operating system, the computer hardware is just a collection of very expensive transistors, wires, chips, and tubes. Once one has put the hardware together, one needs to tell that hardware how to work.

In this section, we will present a brief overview of the nature of computer software in general and a particular software package called SPSS^x. Both of your authors are users of this technology, not designers, so we will defer when it comes to the engineering aspects of computer technology.

Operating System

The *operating system* is the internal system of instructions that tells one hardware component what to do in relation to another hardware unit. It also tells any one component how to manage program and data files; i.e., how to store files, retrieve files when needed, label or name files, print files, and similar operations. While each computer manufacturer could design an idiosyncratic operating system, thankfully, this has not happened. Many manufacturers design their hardware components to share a common operating system. One popular example would be DOS—the Disk Operating System. Little more needs to be said here about operating systems, saving the idea that if many manufacturers use the same operating system, software producers will know that their products will work on a variety of different machines—a fact which encourages software producers to put the time and effort into different software applications.

Software

The term *software* refers to the programming instructions that are not intrinsically a part of the hardware and that are designed to perform various functions with information. Thus, a version of Ashton Tate's dBASE software is designed to help one manage a data base, while a version of

SSI Software's WordPerfect is designed for word processing functions. In other words, the different software packages are tantamount to putting different records on the turntable or different compact discs in the disc player.

If one has a hard disk, the software "records" may be stored on the hard disk, ready to be called up (loaded) into the CPU when one turns on the computer. If one does not have a hard disk, the software is stored on floppy disks, which are so-called because they are flexible (don't take this statement too literally). When one turns on the computer, one slides the desired software disk into the disk drive and tells the CPU in the disk operating system language through the keyboard to read the software programming instructions into the CPU and get ready to do some work. When one is finished, the user tells the CPU to take the data file from the CPU and store (save) it on the hard disk or another floppy disk until such time as the user will want to see or work on it again.

In sum, it is all relatively simple for those who are interested in *using* a computer; however, the design and formation of software programs is a bit more involved.

SPSS^x

Introduction. *SPSS^x*—the Statistical Package for the Social Sciences, Version x—is a canned, or already prepared, series of programming instructions that contains many of the data organization and data processing procedures that social and behavioral scientists use in the preparation and analysis of their data. There is a high probability that the mainframe computer center on your campus has this statistical package within it, as well as a number of other programming packages such as BASIC, COBOL, FORTRAN, PASCAL, and LISP to name but a few. While SPSS^x is also designed for microcomputers or stand-alone systems, we will focus on using a mainframe computer because of its greater speed and ability to handle many users simultaneously.

In using the mainframe computer (or any computer for that matter), the user will have to perform a series of operations: (1) the creation of a codebook, which functions to tell the coder how to code the responses that have been given on the measuring instrument; (2) the creation of a program for the data file, which defines what variables are contained in the data file, what the variables' labels are when they are to be printed out in the data output, where these variables are located in the data file, how much space each one occupies, and what the codes that are entered into the data variables themselves mean; and (3) the creation of a program file to process the coded information in the data file in the ways desired by the researcher. We will look into each of these three operations, creating illustrations that are consistent with the interview schedule presented in Figure 15.1 and that are consistent with the requirements for the usage of SPSS[x].

Creating a Codebook. The *codebook* functions in a number of important ways. First, it informs the coder how to translate the responses given on the schedule into numerical codes in the data file. Second, it tells the keyboard operator how to input the data into the computer. Finally, it explains where the coded information is found in the data file. In this way the codebook is very important in preparing the data for computer analysis. In this subsection we discuss and illustrate several aspects of the codebook.

The Coding Form. Before one can fully understand how to design a codebook, it is necessary to know something about the coding form. The *coding form* is a sheet of paper on which the actual numerical codes are placed prior to their entry into the computer. Figure 15.2 is an example of an IBM FORTRAN form on which the data for one individual respondent appears. Each page of the form contains 24 rows and 80 columns. The researcher may use any or all of the columns in any one row and any number of rows to represent data. Usually, but not always, the data are represented by numerical figures, which represent actual or real numbers—e.g., *45* could represent a person who is 45 years of age—or numbers that could represent something else—e.g., a *1* could be used to represent a male respondent and a *2* could be

used to represent a female respondent. Figure 15.2 illustrates the codes representing the responses of one person to the schedule which appears in Figure 15.1. To help the reader understand these codes, we added two additional pieces of information to Figure 15.2, which would normally not appear on the code form: (1) the name of the variable represented by the code and (2) the variable label that is to appear on the computer printout when the variable is reported.

Variable Name. For example, note that we have called the variable in the first row in column 26 "V1." The designation *V1* is the formal name that this variable will have in the SPSS[x] program, and it corresponds to the first attitudinal item, which is identified as item *1* on the schedule. Indeed, all the variables have been identified by the letter *V* and the number of the item on the schedule. This is done to facilitate the correspondence between code on the code form and the particular item on the schedule which that code represents.

Variable Label. Second, there is a short word description of the variable, which is the *variable label* or the identifier that we will ask the SPSS[x] program to give to the variable whenever it appears on the computer printout. Thus, *V1* not only represents the name for the first schedule item, but also is to be labeled on the printout as "Get Along."

In setting up a codebook, we recommend that each variable be ordered serially starting with the name *V1* and ending with *VN*. In so doing, the researcher can easily guarantee that no variables have been inadvertently omitted from either the codebook or the actual code form. Further, this sequence guarantees that each variable has a *different* designation, which is crucial to the operation of the SPSS[x] software program. For example, if one mistakenly gave two variables the same name, say, *TYPE,* the SPSS[x] program would not know which variable to select when the researcher asked the computer to do some kind of data manipulation on the variable *TYPE.* Additionally, this recommended identification of the variables allows an efficient way to represent each variable with a limited number of characters. A *character* in computer parlance is a single letter, number, or a mark—such as a dollar sign ($). SPSS[x] allows

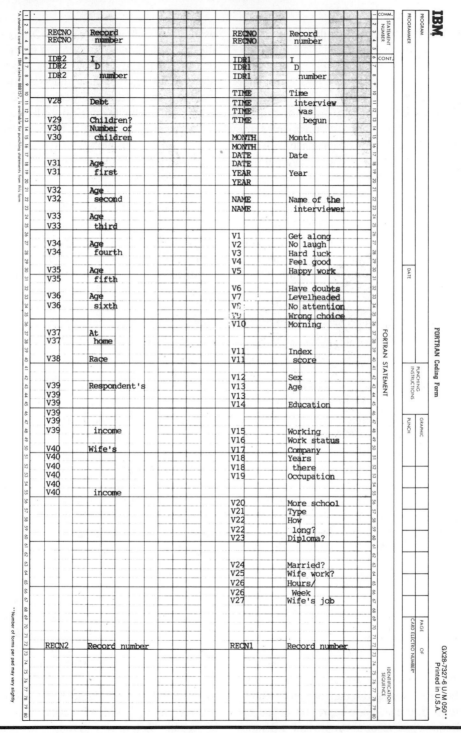

FIGURE 15.2   Annotated Code Sheet Showing the Codes for the First Respondent in Data Base 15.5

Reprinted by permission from IBM FORTRAN Coding Form, GX28-7327-6 U/M 050, copyright © by IBM.

the researcher to use a maximum of eight characters in the creation of a variable name. As one can see, this variable-name format permits the researcher to label almost 10 million different variables! Finally, the numerical designation also easily identifies the schedule item to which the variable is attached. Since the designation *V13* communicates little information about the nature of this variable to the reader, SPSS˟ allows us to give *V13* a more descriptive label, which in this case would be "Age" (see column 43 of record 1 in Figure 15.2).

Finally, notice that we have given the designation *Vi* only to the actual variables that pertain to or that were asked of the respondent. There are additional variables and variable labels that appear on the code form, but these are either pieces of information of methodological interest to the researcher (such as the time at which the interview was begun) or housekeeping details necessary to the successful execution of the SPSS˟ software program (such as "RECNO," which is the name given to the record number). The *record number* refers to a particular row of data. While the record number is optional, if each case has a single row of codes, a record number is absolutely necessary if the data for each unit of analysis require more than one row of entries. The record number *1* tells the computer to go to the column space or spaces designated in that row and not the column space or spaces designated in a different row. For example, column 60 in the first row (record 1) of Figure 15.2 contains a code representing whether or not the respondent attained some sort of degree for having gone back to school after he or she started work, while the code in column 40 in the second row reflects the respondent's classification on the variable of race (V38). The record number tells the computer in which row to find the desired information.

Additional Variable Names. Notice that we have given variable names to this additional information in order to use it if we wish. For example, *IDR1* and *IDR2* are the names given to a three-column variable in records 1 and 2, respectively, which we have labeled "ID Number." This variable allows us to single out any respondent from our data file. The identification number appears in columns 6 through 8 of both of the records for any respondent. Further, note that the variable name *TIME* is a four-column code in record 1 in columns 10 through 13 and reflects the time the interview was begun. Similarly, we have included in the data file such housekeeping variables as the month, date, and year on which the interview was done and a code for the name of the interviewer. These are important pieces of information to include. The date of the interview may be important if something happens in the course of the data-gathering phase that could influence the respondents' opinions about one or more items on the schedule. Or, if one was using a mailed questionnaire data-gathering design, the date may be useful in determining estimates of some of the characteristics of those who did not participate in the study. The interviewer's name is important if the study director wishes to talk to the interviewer about the interviewer's comments or something which appears unusual or interesting that the respondent said during the interview.

Blanks. An important point to make is that blanks can be useful in quickly detecting mispunches or errors that have crept into the data file through the data-entry process. Consider that one is entering 80 columns of data and that some portions of the data may be rather repetitive. For example, one may be entering a series of 10, *9s* and inadvertently punch 11, *9s* instead. After the 80th punch for a record has been entered, one will notice that one additional entry exists, which shouldn't be; i.e., the last entry is supposed to be in column 80 and column 80 has already been used. In a case such as this, it is obvious that a mistake has been made. If the entire 80 columns have been used, one must proofread carefully to find the error. On the other hand, if one's data looked as that illustrated in Figure 15.2, the problem would be more easily rectified. Notice in Figure 15.2 that a certain number of blank spaces have been inserted into the data file. That is, columns 1, 2, 5, 9, 14, 21, 24, 25, and so forth have been left blank. The use of blanks in this way helps to partition the data file into smaller segments, which are easier to read and check.

The second reason for using blanks is to save some space for subsequent additions to the data file. For example, in Figure 15.2 we entered the specific coded response for each of the first 10 attitudinal items in columns 26 through 36 (with column 31 left blank) of record 1 and which we identified as variables *V1* through *V10,* respectively. Let us assume further that in coding the schedule material, we forgot to sum the individual scores to obtain the "Index Score," which appears in columns 39 and 40 as variable *V11.* If we have left a few blanks throughout the data file, it becomes a relatively simple matter to redefine some of these blanks as locations for additional variables and to insert the codes for these additional variables into the blanks. Such omissions are not monumental, however, since SPSS^x does allow one to use the RECODE command to recode the data or to add additional variables and values of these variables through the programming process itself—an example of which will follow later. However, if the researcher has forgotten something and wants to insert it into the data file, the fortuitous inclusion of some blanks will afford the researcher such an opportunity.

Finally, while blanks are troublesome in many software programs, they do not pose a problem for SPSS^x, because this program will disregard any entry or lack of an entry in a column that has not been defined as containing information. The major problem is when SPSS^x finds a code in a column that the researcher has not defined as meaningful for that column. SPSS^x then gets confused and provides a cryptic error message, which says something like "There is an unknown value in your data file." This message does communicate that there is a problem in the data file, but, unfortunately, it *does not communicate where* that problem lies. If a data file contains hundreds of cases, it might take a long time to find the error. Further, if the error is an extra punch, for example, in column 22 and no blanks have been included in the record, information which should be found in column 23 (and all the subsequent columns in this record) will be pushed down one column further than the researcher has told the computer, causing two additional problems. First, the computer may not be able to read subsequent codes because the definitions for, say, column 43 really apply to column 44. Second, and more insidious, the information that is supposed to be in column 37 but is in column 38 will be interpreted using the codes for column 38, while the codes for column 37 will interpret the variable that is supposed to be in column 36. In sum, an extra entry can cause great confusion in one's data file.

By looking at Figure 15.3, one can see that the second line of data is in error. That is, since the final column, which is supposed to have an entry, is blank, then something is wrong in this particular record. You will notice that the next to last grouping of codes has been moved over one space rather than two as in all the other records. Thus, the addition of blanks assists the researcher in *data cleaning,* i.e., eliminating the errors in one's data file.

The Codebook. The codebook for our exercise is located in Appendix C. In this section we concentrate on a number of points about the construction of the codebook. As we argued earlier, the

---

```
/1 001 1330  022890  03  44332 33344  33  1426  111224  28888   48888
/1 002 0955  030190  04  22342 11022  19  1356  111054 28888   48888
/1 003 2030  030290  01  44322 40221  24  1286  111124  28888   48888
```

FIGURE 15.3 Hypothetical Code Sheet Containing Coded Information for Three Individuals, Assuming a Single Record

basic function of the codebook is to clarify the meanings and positions of the various codes contained within the data file.

Title. It is a good idea to put a title on the codebook in order to differentiate it from codebooks for other studies. In our example, the title is "Codebook for 'Opinion Research Study: Spring 1990'."

Headings. There are three headings in this codebook: (1) "Record/Column"; (2) "Variable Name"; and (3) "Variable Label." The heading *Variable Name* contains the names of the variables that will have codes or numerical designations within the data file. SPSS^x requires that these variable names be no longer than eight characters, that the names must begin with a letter, and that there are no spaces within the names.

The "Variable Label" heading contains a string of words that the researcher feels would be more informative than the variable name. In our example, "RECNO" is the variable name of the information contained in columns 3 and 4 of record 1. Since the variable name must be eight characters or less, the variable name may not be meaningful to the reader. Therefore, SPSS^x allows the researcher to generate a variable label, which is more descriptive and informative. This variable label can be up to 120 characters, although most printers will not print all of them. Our VAX system will print only the first 30 characters of the variable label. So, if one's label is 35 characters, the VAX will print the first 30 characters, simply dropping the remaining 5 characters. Therefore, one should check with the computer center at which one will be doing data analysis to determine what the particular requirements are for such items as the variable labels. Again, the variable name may be something such as V14, while the variable label would be, in this case, "Education" (see Appendix C).

Finally, the "Record/Column" heading specifies which row—the record number—and which column or columns are being used for the data codes for any particular variable.

For example, in the codebook notice that the variable name *V11* has a variable label called "Index Score," and the values of V11 are to be found in record 1 (row 1) in columns 39 and 40.

The Codes. Coding is the process of assigning numerical information that either represents actual values for particular variables or represents categories on some variable. In this way, numerical digits replace strings of words within the data file. For example, rather than write "male" and "female" into the data file (see variable V12 in the codebook), the researchers have created codes through which *1* is used to represent male respondents and *2* is used to represent female respondents. This requires less computer space, and the male and female designations can still be printed on the computer's output if we tell the computer to do so and if we have defined the meaning of the codes for the computer.

Sometimes it is not necessary to develop a coding scheme for the data. For example, variable name *V13* whose variable label is "Age" is to be a two-digit code in record 1 in columns 43 and 44. If the respondent is 35, a *3* can be placed in column 43 and a *5* in column 44. In this way, the actual value of the variable is entered into the data file rather than a code whose meaning is different from the numerical designation of the code.

Coding and the Conceptual Model. In this section, we discuss several points to consider when organizing a data file and codebook.

Most of what has been presented pertains to the mechanics of setting up a workable data file. But the formation of a codebook is a serious intellectual exercise as well as one in precision. For example, consider variable *V14* which has the variable label "Education" and which appears in column 45 of record 1. The codebook indicates that there are eight codes representing different degrees of the educational variable. Consider codes *3* and *4,* which stand for "AA degree" and "Some college," respectively.

It is possible for a student to have completed an AA degree at a community college in two years, while another student could have attended a four year college for three years before dropping out to enter the labor force. In our codebook we assigned code *3* to the "AA degree" and code *4* to those persons who had "Some college" but did not complete their degree program—even if they have more hours in the classroom than the person who attained the AA degree. Here the decision was made that the completed AA degree requiring two years of work is more important than having had some college during which the student worked for three years. Why? In this case, your authors believe that the completed two-year AA degree represents an educational attainment that attains closure; i.e., the student not only had some college but also completed the course of study. In the case of the student with three years of study, the degree was not completed and, therefore, was accorded less status. While you may not agree with us, it is obvious that some sort of decision must be made when these two responses occur on the schedule. The point is that coding is not a perfunctory matter. Decisions must be made, and they should have some sort of conceptual reasoning behind them.

When the coding process has been completed and the data entered into the computer, a data file will have been completed that resembles the data base which appears in Appendix D.

Data Cleaning.   Once the data file has been created, one moves on to *data cleaning*. This process is the mechanism through which one locates and revises any data-entry errors. There are two basic strategies one may pursue in doing the data cleaning.

First, one may create a second data file, which is supposedly identical to the first, and then compare the two files, asking the computer to list those records that are not identical.* One would then peruse both records closely along with the original codes on the coding forms to determine where the error or errors are and what the revision or revisions should be. While this data-cleaning procedure is simple, it is time-consuming since one has to enter the entire data base a second time. However, we feel this exercise is superior to asking two people to proofread the data file printout and the original code sheet notations.

Second, one may ask the computer to count various patterns in the data, assuming that such exist. For example, one of your authors has been working with police arrest records. One of the variables indicated the arrested person's age and another indicated the disposition of the charge. Well, the disposition of any juvenile's offense is for the case to be sent to juvenile court. Therefore, if the variable of age was 17 or less and the code in the disposition columns was anything other than Juvenile Court, there was an error in that particular record—either the disposition was wrong or the age was wrong or perhaps both were in error. So it is possible to ask the computer to look for all offenders 17 years of age or less and to print out all the ID (identification) numbers of the offenders whose code is not juvenile court. Of course, one cannot look for patterns if one does not know what possible patterns may exist. Again, the conceptual model may help the researcher with valuable knowledge for methodological purposes.

In sum, there are two basic mechanisms for cleaning one's data: (1) to create a second data file, compare the two data files, and look for mismatches and (2) to look for patterns in the data, which should not exist.

PRELIMINARY MATTERS IN USING THE COMPUTER

A Metaphor

The following metaphor will help you understand what is happening when you use your institution's data processing facilities. Imagine that your computer center is located in a large room containing row after row of filing cabinets. When the center first opened, all the filing cabinets were empty, but through the years various people have gone to the center and asked for a computer account and a certain amount of space in the mainframe's storage. Now, you are about to ask the systems manager for an account and some space to be reserved for you. The manager of the center says that you can have the filing cabinet that is the fifth from the

---

*SPSSˣ will not do this, but the "editor language" in the mainframe will. Ask your systems manager what you need to do in order to accomplish this.

left in row one and that you have been allotted all five filing cabinet drawers for your use. This cabinet will be empty, thereby providing space that you can organize (or configure) in any way that you please. There are stacks of manila file folders on the manager's desk, and one has only to take however many one would like, label them, and put them in whatever drawers one chooses. Of course, one cannot cram more manila folders into the five drawers than the five drawers will accommodate. This, then, is the situation when one goes to the computer center and asks for an account.

Getting an Account Set Up, Logging On, and Logging Off

The mainframe computer user cannot just go into the computer center and start using the mainframe. One must have been allocated space within the mainframe and assigned an account number. The *account number* functions to label your filing cabinets so that the computer will know where to go when you log on, or activate, your account. While the logging-on procedure is usually idiosyncratic to each computer installation, this procedure involves turning on the dummy terminal, which is the monitor and the keyboard, and making sure that your monitor and keyboard are connected into the mainframe CPU.

The account number is a series of keystrokes that sends the CPU to the address (the filing cabinet or cabinets) that has been reserved for you. Additionally, for security reasons, you will be asked to establish a *password*, which functions as a lock on your filing cabinet. After establishing the password, it will be impossible to enter your account without giving the proper password to unlock it. The password, then, functions to protect the privacy of your data and to prevent other people from getting into your data and playing tricks on you. Also, the password prevents someone else from entering your account and doing work, which uses up your computer time. This is a concern because when receiving an account, one is assigned not only space but also a finite connect and computation time span in which to use the space.

In sum, the account number functions to identify your space in the computer, and the password functions as your key to that space. These two items along with the logging-on procedures, which are idiosyncratic to your institution, are the necessary commands to get one started whenever one sits down to do some work on the computer. Similarly, there are logging-off or shutting down procedures which one goes through when one has completed a working session, and these, as well, are idiosyncratic to your institution. After the getting-on and getting-off procedures have been learned, one is ready to do some serious work with the computer.

AN SPSS^x DATA-ANALYSIS PROGRAM

Introduction

In this section we develop an actual SPSS^x data-analysis program. We have chosen the SPSS^x software program because a large number of university computer centers are already equipped with this software package. Further, we will use a mainframe computer, the VAX, which also is found on many campuses. However, it may be that your university has an IBM mainframe or stand-alone computers within the departmental laboratory itself. Therefore, it may be necessary for your instructor to adjust this section to the equipment on your campus.

In sum, we explain the basic strategy and parts of the computer data-analysis package and provide a set of instructions with which you may follow with us and a data file on which to do these and any other calculations that you might want to explore.

Defining the Data File and the Program File

After logging on, the researcher must create a data file that contains the codes of the information that is to be data processed. The nature and appearance of such a data file are indicated in Appendix D. Thus, the data are fed into the computer's memory, record after record, and the data file is given a file name.

The *file name* can contain whatever number of characters that the center has indicated. Usually, the systems designer has configured the system to accept any file name that has a specified number of characters that do not fall below a minimum number or go beyond a maximum number. Additionally, the file name may have an extension, which usually is a period followed by three characters. For all data files, we recommend the use of the extension *DAT,* which easily distinguishes the data file from other types of files that will be created and saved. In our example, then, the data file labeled "DATABASE.DAT" will be used.

One will also be creating another file (discussed in detail in the next subsection) that tells the SPSS^x software what to do with the data file. This second file is the program file; it tells SPSS^x two things: (1) it defines the variable names and the locations of the information contained in the data file and (2) it tells the CPU what data manipulations are to be done on these data. In our example, we will use "DATABASE.PR1" to label the program file. Notice the "PR1" extension, which helps distinguish the program file from the data file, both of which have been saved under our account number within the computer's memory.

When the program is *run,* or executed, the computer essentially is told to go to your account and process the commands contained within your program file on the data contained in your data file.

At this point you have created data and program files and have given them names so that the mainframe can locate them when the mainframe is asked to do so. This information and set of guidelines will always be specific, or customized, to your institution's computer center. Now that we've entered the data into your account and labeled the data file with a name, we need to create the specific SPSS^x commands, which will allow this software program to process the data file.

General Functions of Any Software Data-Analysis Package

Any statistical software package, such as SPSS^x, requires the researcher to perform two tasks: (1)

define the data file for the software package and (2) indicate the statistical procedures on which variables that are to be done.

Finally, as we develop the commands that will drive the SPSS^x software program, you are referred to Appendix E. Appendix E contains a column identified as "Text Ref. Number," which flags the specific command for discussion within the text of this chapter. These numbers are in parentheses, *but one should never actually put these numbers in parentheses within one's SPSS^x program because that will confuse SPSS^x,* causing an error message. Again, they appear only for purposes of connecting the information in Appendix E with the text discussion.

The TITLE Command

The first command that should be developed is the TITLE command. The *TITLE command* can be used to label the printout of the study, so that one will not confuse the printout with a different study on which one may be working simultaneously. As we mentioned earlier in reference to the codebook, it is a good idea to give both the codebook and study printout a common name so that these two parts of the study can be distinguished from other studies. The TITLE command—see text reference number (1) in Appendix E—simply states the word *TITLE* and is followed by whatever one wants to label one's printout, but the title must begin and end with quotation marks, as shown in Appendix E.

The FILE HANDLE Command

At the risk of being redundant, remember that you have already created a data file with its specific label in the mainframe's memory. Therefore, when one wants to work with these data, an *active file* must be created in SPSS^x, which is a file in the CPU where the computations will be performed. This is done through the *FILE HANDLE command*—see text reference number (2). The FILE HANDLE command gives the active file a name, which can be no more than eight characters (no blanks are allowed in the name) and must *begin* with an alphabetic letter.[3] SPSS^x permits the use of marks such as *$, #,* or *@* in the name, but we don't recommend this because the *$* (dollar sign) is also the prompt for the SPSS^x RUN command.

The DATA LIST Command

The FILE HANDLE command is immediately followed by the *DATA LIST command,* which identifies which file is to be obtained and how many records compose each case. The DATA LIST command—see text reference number (3)—should be spaced as it appears in Appendix E. After indenting two spaces and starting on a new line, a forward diagonal immediately followed by a *1* ("/1")—see text reference number (4)—tells SPSS^x that whatever follows are the variable names and column positions of the variables in the first record of each individual case in the data file. For example, note that the variable *IDR1* appears in columns 6, 7, and 8 and that the variable *TIME* appears in columns 10 through 13. (Again, cross reference this information to that which is indicated on the code sheet, Figure 15.2.) Note further that each variable name is followed by a space and the column designation appears followed by another space and then the next variable name.

SPSS^x contains a number of key words[4] which have special predefined meanings to SPSS^x. One of these is the word *TO* which has been used in the DATA LIST command on line 2 of the first record ("/1"). Given the example from Figure 15.2, one will note that *V1* is represented by a code in column 26, *V2* by a code in column 27, *V3* by a code in column 28, *V4* by one in column 29, and *V5* by another code in column 30. Thus, all five variables—*V1* through *V5*—appear in sequence, and they *all* occupy a single column of information. Therefore, when defining these five variables and their location on the DATA LIST command, one can simplify this task by using the keyword *TO*. For example, we could use the more cumbersome form:

V1 26 V2 27 V3 28 V4 29 V5 30

through which *V1* is identified as the code in column 26, *V2* is identified as the code in column 27, and so forth. This can be simplified, however, by using the keyword *TO* as follows:

V1 TO V5 26–30

which says that all the variables between *V1* and *V5* (that is, *V2, V3,* and *V4*) will have codes that are evenly spread out through columns 26 through 30. In this case, there are five such variables and there are five such columns utilized, meaning that each variable has a code that occupies a single column. Further, if one had three variables—*V95, V96,* and *V97*—and if each of them had codes that occupied four columns each—*V95* is coded in columns 10, 11, 12, and 13; *V96* is coded in columns 14, 15, 16, and 17; and *V97* is coded in columns 18, 19, 20, and 21—then one could use the keyword *TO* as follows:

V95 TO V97 10–21

which says to SPSS^x that there are three variables and that they each occupy one-third of the coded values (that is, four each) found in columns 10 through 21. In sum, the keyword *TO* allows one to simplify the DATA LIST command *if* the variables are in sequence and if their respective codes occupy the same number of columns throughout the sequence.

When all the variable names and column positions in record 1 have been used, one moves on to record 2 by starting a new line, indenting two spaces, placing a forward diagonal in column three, and following it with a *2* in column four ("/2"). This tells SPSS^x that the information for record 1 has been completed and that record 2 information is to follow—see text reference number (5).

By writing the TITLE, FILE HANDLE, and DATA LIST commands, one has told SPSS^x what the active file is called, which data file to use, how many records are contained in each case in the data file, and the names and column positions of each of the variables on all of the records. The next command is the VARIABLE LABELS command.

The VARIABLE LABELS Command

Since SPSS^x requires that each variable have a name made up of no more than eight characters, some of the variable names that make sense to SPSS^x may not make much sense to the researcher or the reader of the research report. Therefore, one has the option of creating labels for any or all of one's variables. These labels can be as long as 120 characters, although most mainframe printers will not print that many characters. Therefore, one is urged to create variable labels which will comply with the maximum number of characters the available mainframe is able to print. To create a more meaningful label, one uses the *VARIABLE LABELS command*, which is illustrated in Appendix E as text reference number (6). One simply enters VARIABLE LABELS with two spaces and then lists the variable name followed by a space and the desired variable label, which must be enclosed in apostrophes. For example,

VARIABLE LABELS IDR1 'ID Number'

tells SPSS^x that whenever IDR1—the variable name—appears on the printout, one is to substitute the phrase *ID Number*. There are a couple of additional quirks that must be adhered to when using long variable names. As we argued above, however, the use of long variable names is not recommended, since your computer will not print them anyway.

The VALUE LABELS Command

The next definitional requirement in SPSS^x is the Value Labels requirement. Here, one must distinguish for SPSS^x which numbers are really numbers, such as those found for the variable age, and which are coded numbers, representing other information. The *VALUE LABELS command* functions to tell SPSS^x the meaning of each code that represents some other value. For example, on the variable *SEX*, a *1* does not mean "one" but "male," and a *2* does not mean "two" but "female." How-

ever, *35* does mean 35 on the variable of age. Therefore, one uses the VALUE LABELS command to specify the meanings of the codes so that they can be placed on the mainframe's printouts where these codes are used. For example, look at text reference number (7) on Appendix E.

VALUE LABELS MONTH 01 "January" 02
        "February". . .

Here, one follows the command *VALUE LABELS* with a space and the variable name that was defined in the DATA LIST command, followed by another space, the code, another space, and the true label beginning and ending with quotations marks. In the above example the variable *MONTH* is followed by a space and then the code *01*, another space, and *"January"* in quotation marks. This tells SPSS^x that every time the code *01* is found under the variable *MONTH*, *"January"* is to replace this code.

It is important to remember that when all the codes for *any one variable* have been labeled, one *must* conclude with a forward diagonal (/). This tells SPSS^x that the labels for that variable name have been concluded and it is time to move to the next variable and start the relabeling process for it. For example, after one enters *12 "December"* at the conclusion of the value-labeling process for the variable *MONTH*, the forward diagonal is entered. If this was not done, SPSS^x would move to the next entry which, in this case, is the Variable Name *YEAR* and find that since it is not a numerical code (which it is expecting to find), it is confused and will stop, giving one an error message.[*]

If, however, the numerical codes are real values, e.g., *35* for "35 years of age," any reference to this variable is omitted in the VALUE LABELS command, and SPSSx will treat the code *35* as a real number.

The MISSING VALUES Command

Finally, the *MISSING VALUES command* is used to tell SPSS^x that some codes appear that are not

---

[*]The error message is likely to point to the entry *YEAR* and say something is wrong. In truth, the entry *YEAR* is fine; it is the omitted diagonal, which is supposed to follow the quotation mark after the word *"December,"* that is at fault.

germane to the data analysis. Remember that computers generally do not like to find blanks where they are not supposed to be. For example, what if the researcher forgets to code sex? Instead of finding a *1* to represent "male" or a *2* to represent "female," nothing would be placed here because the interviewer forgot to enter this code. If the information is missing, a common convention is to use the numerical digit *9* to represent missing information. Therefore, there are three possible codes for the variable sex: *1* for "male," *2* for "female," and *9* for "missing information." When the VALUE LABELS command is developed, one accounts for codes *1* and *2*, but not for code *9*. However, code *9* is identified with the MISSING VALUES command—see text reference number (8) in Appendix E. Here, one goes through the entire list of variables and tells SPSS^x which codes represent missing values. The format is as follows:

MISSING VALUES TIME (9999)

where the variable name *TIME* is followed by a space and the code for the missing information enclosed in *parentheses*. Thus, the MISSING VALUES command says, in this example, that whenever four *9*s are found in the columns utilized by the variable *TIME*, SPSS^x is to disregard these *9*s as not meaningful to the analysis. Similarly, some variables may be rendered irrelevant given earlier responses. For example, it doesn't make much sense to ask the ages of the respondent's children if the respondent doesn't have any children. Therefore, given such a contingency, the coder was told to put *8*s in the columns for the ages of the children if the respondent did not have any children. Hence, for the variable *V31*—the age of the first child—one could have gotten no response and, therefore, registered the code *99* or an earlier response that the respondent did not have any children, hence the use of code *88* for irrelevant. The MISSING VALUES command would then be as follows:

MISSING VALUES V31 (88,99)

wherein one tells SPSS^x that either a double *8* or a double *9* code is to be disregarded in the data

analysis. Note that the actual missing values must be placed in parentheses and that if there is more than one set of codes, they must be separated by a comma. Finally, one cannot leave any spaces within the parentheses.

The COMMENT Command

The *COMMENT command* is used when the programmer wishes to insert a statement into the program—see text reference number (9) in Appendix E. Comments are often useful for indicating basic divisions within the program. For example, in Appendix E the COMMENT command has been used to separate that part of the SPSS^x program that is definitional from that part that generates the commands to do the data processing. Thus, insertion of any sort of statement into a program can be done with the COMMENT command. Quite simply, after entering the word *COMMENT,* nothing to the right of this word *on the same line* will be read or executed by SPSS^x.

While COMMENT commands can be placed anywhere, the order of the other data file definitional commands is crucial, and they must be placed in the sequence indicated in Appendix E.

Some SPSS^x Data Processing Commands

Introduction. In this subsection, we continue to develop SPSS^x commands that perform the desired data manipulations on the data file, which has been identified earlier in the FILE HANDLE command. The SPSS^x manual is large and contains an incredible number of commands that will do almost anything the researcher can think to do to a data set. That which follows is the minimum number of commands to illustrate our research-project example.

The RECODE Command. When we entered the data into the file called "DATABASE.DAT," we entered the most detailed and specific numerical information we had available. Since data can always be simplified by transforming it into more general categories, it is recommended that the most detailed information be put into one's data base. To that end we entered, for example, each individual's specific "Index Score" on the variable of positive self-image. While some researchers treat Likert response categories as interval data, we are hesitant to do so for a variety of reasons. Given our orientation, then, the use of a correlation technique like Pearson's r (discussed in Chapter 4) is unwarranted since the data do not have a constant unit of measure. Therefore, and to demonstrate the creation of tables of data, we have elected to group the data into categories and report the results in a table.

The two class I variables in this example are the independent variable of educational attainment and the dependent variable of positive self-image. By collapsing the more specific data available on education, we created two categories: (1) low education, containing those who had graduated from high school or had lesser degrees of education, and (2) high education, containing those who had graduated from college or achieved higher degrees of education. This dichotomization of the variable of education was made because of the widely accepted notion that a college education significantly changes the skill level and attitudinal set of the person compared to these dimensions in those who have achieved a high school diploma or lesser amounts of education.

SPSSˣ contains a *RECODE command*, which allows the researcher to redefine the data in any way deemed appropriate. The RECODE command is operative at the time it is invoked and appears in the calculations within the active file—the file that one creates when one turns on the computer to do a work session. We mention this detail because the RECODE command *will not put the recoded values into the file called "DATABASE.DAT"*; i.e., the RECODE values are only operative during the working session. If such values are to be retained for subsequent working sessions, the RECODE command *must be kept* in one's program.

The RECODE command—see text reference number (10) in Appendix E—takes the following format:

RECODE V14 (1,2=1) (6,7,8=2)

After entering the word *RECODE*, a space is left and the variable name, which in this case is *V14*, is entered. This is followed by another space and within parentheses the old codes followed by an equal sign and the new code. Thus, as shown above, the old codes—*1* for "more than college" and *2* for "college graduate"—are to be combined into a new code *1*, which follows the equal sign. Obviously, there can only be one numeral after the equal sign, and the old codes, which are to be collapsed into the new one, must be separated by commas. In the second set of parentheses, the RECODE command specifies that the initial codes *6, 7*, and *8*—*6* is "high school graduate," *7* is "some high school," and *8* is "less than high school"—are to be combined into the new code *2*. After this command, as far as SPSSˣ is concerned, the active file has only two codes for the variable *V14: 1* and *2*. However, the new variable and these two new codes have not been defined for SPSSˣ, so one has to do so on the second and third lines following the RECODE command.

VARIABLE LABELS V14 'EDUCATION'

VALUE LABELS V14 1 'HIGH' 2 'LOW'

We are now telling SPSSˣ that the variable *V14* is called "Education" and that the new codes are "High" for code *1* and "Low" for code *2*. Notice that these commands are identical to those we used earlier—see text reference number (6)—for the VARIABLE LABELS command and (7) for the VALUE LABELS command in Appendix E.

While the opinion of educational experts, expressed in the literature and based on one's common sense, supports the distinctions made on the variable of education, there is no common body of opinion concerning the range of index scores that we obtained from the composite measure of positive self-image. Should we collapse the self-image scores into two categories—high and low—or should we collapse them into three—high, medium, and low? Why not four or five categories? Since this measuring instrument was constructed specifically for this study, there is no previous experience that might suggest meaningful divisions in the range of responses. Therefore, we are forced into an empirical determination, as discussed in Chapter 14.

Given that the index contains 10 items, each having response categories coded with values from 0 to 4, and that there is no weighting of any of these index items, the theoretical range of values that could be obtained is 0 to 40. One is highly unlikely to obtain such a range in reality. Therefore, the first order of business is to determine the actual, empirical range obtained and the distribution of index scores. SPSS^x can also help one determine this information.

The FREQUENCIES Command (and the VARIABLES, STATISTICS, and HISTOGRAM Subcommands).

The *FREQUENCIES command* is one which will generate a large number of descriptive statistics on any number of variables in the data file. There are measures of central tendency and variation, and one may select information on some or all of them.* In this case, we are interested in the distribution of the values obtained on the variable *V11* (the "Index Score") and the empirical range obtained. The FREQUENCIES command in the box below will generate that information—see text reference number (11) in Appendix E. The FREQUENCIES command requires a number of subcommands. First, the desired frequencies must be specified. The *VARIABLES subcommand* tells SPSS^x that frequencies are desired on some number of variables. The key word *ALL,* if inserted immediately after the equal

sign, would generate the default statistics on all the variables that appear in the data file. But this voluminous output is not needed, so we have specified a particular variable—*V11* ("Index Score")—on which we want certain statistical data. Note that there are no spaces surrounding the equal sign in this command, and a forward diagonal (/) is necessary at the end to tell SPSS^x that the listing of variables on which one wants information is completed.

Second, the *STATISTICS subcommand* tells SPSS^x which specific statistics are requested. Again, the key word *ALL* will generate every statistical datum that SPSS^x has in its repertoire for the FREQUENCIES command. However, we do not want everything, so we specify only those needed. This specification follows the equal sign, and it includes *RANGE, MAXIMUM* (the largest value obtained), and *MINIMUM* (the smallest value obtained). Finally, note that no spaces are placed before or after the equal sign and that this subcommand must end with another forward diagonal (/), which tells SPSS^x that the request for specific statistics has been completed.

What results from the FREQUENCIES command and the VARIABLES and STATISTICS subcommands will be a printout of each of the specific values of the variable *Index Score* (see Figure 15.4). The range, minimum, and maximum values appear at the bottom of the histogram (see Figure 15.5). While this will be helpful in determining the empirical distribution of the index score,

```
FREQUENCIES VARIABLES  = V11/
            STATISTICS  = RANGE MAXIMUM MINIMUM/
            HISTOGRAM  = INCREMENT (1)/
```

---

*Because SPSS^x makes it easy to generate all kinds of statistics—both descriptive and inferential—there is a tendency on the part of some researchers to ask for everything and then mine the results for that which looks interesting. Such a strategy can be useful when doing exploratory research, but when applied to hypothesis testing, mining the results can lead to erroneous conclusions. You will recall from our discussion in Chapter 6 that we work with the probability model in the social sciences. It is possible, through pure chance fluctuation, to occasionally obtain a "significant" result which is *not really significant*. It is simply an error that happens by chance. To routinely call for all possible statistics on all possible variables is tantamount to hunting with a shotgun. If one launches a constant barrage of shot into the skies, one has to hit something sometime by sheer probability, but the duck secured in this fashion does not prove the skill of the hunter. Further, the routine disregard of the assumptions that underlie statistical analysis will generate misleading data, also leading to erroneous conclusions. For these reasons, we have not called for statistical data on all variables, but only those for which we need the information for methodological, conceptual, or analytical reasons.

VALUE LABEL	VALUE	FREQUENCY	PERCENT	VALID PERCENT	CUM PERCENT
	15	5	1.3	1.3	1.3
	16	10	2.5	2.5	3.8
	17	21	5.3	5.3	9.1
	18	35	8.8	8.8	17.9
	19	29	7.3	7.3	25.3
	20	11	2.8	2.8	28.0
	21	5	1.3	1.3	29.3
	23	6	1.5	1.5	30.8
	24	11	2.8	2.8	33.6
	25	22	5.6	5.6	39.1
	26	32	8.1	8.1	47.2
	27	28	7.1	7.1	54.3
	28	11	2.8	2.8	57.1
	29	5	1.3	1.3	58.3
	31	8	2.0	2.0	60.4
	32	8	2.0	2.0	62.4
	33	12	3.0	3.0	65.4
	34	25	6.3	6.3	71.7
	35	37	9.3	9.3	81.1
	36	39	9.8	9.8	90.9
	37	25	6.3	6.3	97.2
	38	11	2.8	2.8	100.0
	Total	396	100.0	100.0	

FIGURE 15.4 SPSS^x Printout of *V11* ("Index Score") to the FREQUENCIES VARIABLES Command*

*Note that there were no index scores equal to 22 or 30 in the data file.

another way of determining this distribution may be instructive as well. This third subcommand is the HISTOGRAM subcommand. The *HISTO-GRAM subcommand* generates a histogram of the variables cited on the VARIABLES subcommand —which in this case is the variable *V11* (the "Index Score"). SPSS^x is already set up to place a maximum of 21 different values on the vertical axis of the histogram, but we will find that we have more than 21 actual values on variable *V11* in DATABASE.DAT.* To keep SPSS^x from col-

lapsing some of these specific values together, we can request that SPSS^x not do any collapsing, which is the purpose of the commands that follow the equal sign on the HISTOGRAM subcommand. The equal sign (without any spaces before or after) is followed by the term *INCREMENT*, a space, and a *1* in parentheses—"(1)"—which tells SPSS^x that one would like the histogram to plot the distribution of the values of the variable *V11* one increment at a time. The number of times any one of these values appears in the data file is reflected on

---

*The reason SPSS^x is defaulted to a maximum of 21 vertical increments is that one could have several hundred different values on a particular variable—e.g., income—and the expenditure of paper and computer time to plot them all would not be warranted. Therefore, SPSS^x will automatically reduce the categories to a maximum of 21.

COUNT	MIDPOINT	ONE SYMBOL EQUALS APPROXIMATELY .80 OCCURRENCES
5	15.50	******
10	16.50	*************
21	17.50	***************************
35	18.50	**
29	19.50	***************************************
11	20.50	***************
5	21.50	******
0	22.50	
6	23.50	********
11	24.50	***************
22	25.50	*****************************
32	26.50	**
28	27.50	**************************************
11	28.50	***************
5	29.50	******
0	30.50	
8	31.50	**********
8	32.50	**********
12	33.50	****************
25	34.50	********************************
37	35.50	**
39	36.50	***
36	37.50	***

```
I .....+ ..... I .....+ ..... I .....+ ..... I .....+ ..... I .....+ ..... I
0        8       16       24       32       40
```

HISTOGRAM FREQUENCY

Range	23.000	Minimum	15.000	Maximum	38.000
Valid cases	396	Missing cases	0		

FIGURE 15.5 SPSS^x Printout of a Histogram of the Values for *V11* ("Index Score") from DATABASE.DAT

the horizontal axis, with the resulting histogram illustrated by Figure 15.5. The range, minimum, and maximum values appear at the bottom of the histogram.

If you carefully study the frequency count (see Figure 15.4) and the histogram (see Figure 15.5), certain characteristics will emerge. First, notice that while the range of values was from 15 through 38, the values of 22 and 30 did not appear in the sample of 396 respondents. Second, the histogram indicates a trimodal pattern—i.e., three peaks at 18.50, 26.50, and 36.50, respectively*—with rather severe drops in frequencies in either direction as one moves away from these three modes. We

---

*The 0.50 attachment to the three values of 18, 26, and 36 represent the midpoints of the intervals in the histogram. SPSS^x assumes that the data entered were continuous and, therefore, gives the midpoint values. The 0.50 may be safely disregarded in this case.

> RECODE V11 (LO THRU 21=3) (22 THRU 29=2) (30 THRU 40=1)
> VARIABLE LABELS V11 'INDEX SCORE'
> VALUE LABELS V11 1 'HIGH' 2 'MEDIUM' 3 'LOW'

would argue that the empirical distribution of values on the variable *Index Score* suggests a three-category truncation of these scores. Therefore, we will operationalize the variable *Index Score* into three categories: (1) *High* with values ranging from 30 to 38; (2) *Medium* with values from 22 through 29; and (3) *Low* with values from 15 through 21. It is in this way that the appropriate number and operationalization of the categories may be determined in any table. This process is entered when logic and the conceptual model are unable to provide the necessary direction. Of course, we will again use the RECODE command in the box above to collapse the values of the variable *Index Score* above into the three desired tabular categories—see text reference number (12) in Appendix E.

At this point, we have used SPSS^x to help us determine the empirical distribution of the variable *V11* through the FREQUENCIES command and the RECODE command to collapse the data from the variables *V11* ("Index Score") and *V14* ("Education") into three and two categories, respectively. We have now prepared these data so that our hypothesis can be tested.

The CROSSTABS   TABLES Command (and the CELLS and STATISTICS Subcommands).
The CROSSTABS command in conjunction with the keyword *TABLES* (thus, *CROSSTABS TABLES* command) allows the researcher to relate a limited number of categories of two or more variables to one another in a tabular format. In this case—see text reference number (13) in Appendix E—the command is as follows:

```
CROSSTABS   TABLES=V14 BY V11
    /CELLS=COUNT ROW
    /STATISTICS=LAMBDA BTAU CTAU GAMMA D
```

The CROSSTABS   TABLES command is immediately followed by an equal sign, the independent variable *(V14)*, a space, the keyword *BY*, a space, and the dependent variable *(V11)*. The first variable mentioned after the equal sign will have its categories represented on the row subheads, while the second variable mentioned will have its categories appear on the column subheads.

Notice that the order of the row subheadings always starts with the category that has been identified with the code *1*. The order of the column subheadings always starts with the category that has been given the code *1*. Therefore, when using the RECODE command, it is important to give the category with the greatest amount of the variable that is being measured (if it is relevant) the code *1*. In so doing, the CROSSTABS   TABLES command will always result in a proper table, which has its major variable subheadings ordered in the conventional manner.

The CROSSTABS   TABLES command also has a *CELLS subcommand,* which allows the researcher to customize the nature of the information that is placed in the table. Along with the cell frequency, we have asked SPSS^x to include the row percentages, which is the third option. Since the independent variable has been placed on the side of the table, the creation of row percentages is proper.

Finally, the CROSSTABS   TABLES command contains the STATISTICS subcommand from which several different measures of association can be generated. In this case, we have chosen Leo Goodman and William Kruskal's lambda, tau,* and gamma; Patricia Kendall's tau-b and tau-c; and Robert Somer's d. Selected characteristics of these statistical measures are summarized

---

*Even though Goodman and Kruskal's tau is not cited as an option in the SPSS^x manual, the program provides this statistic anyway.

in Figure 15.6.* All of these measures have comparable interpretations because they are proportional-reduction-in-error measures (PRE). First, this means that any value of gamma can be compared to any other value of gamma. Thus, if the gamma computed on Table X is 0.3 and the gamma computed on Table Y is 0.6, because the same formula has been used to calculate both gammas and because the gamma statistic is normed (a range of values between 0.0 and 1.0), one may say

---

*All of these statistics possess a number of characteristics. First, they are *proportional-reduction-in-error (PRE)* measures, some of which may be used with nominal data and others that are appropriate to ordinal data. A PRE measure follows the basic definition of measuring association by finding the proportion of error reduction through the establishment of two error rules; PRE measures all use the basic logic of $(E_1 - E_2) / E_1$, where E_1 represents the number of errors made by prediction rule one and E_2 represents the number of errors made by prediction rule two. While different PRE statistics may *define* errors in different ways, they all *calculate* degree of association using the above formula.

Second, they are all *bivariate measures of grouped data,* which means they focus on two variables that have been represented in a cross-tabulation. In the case of ordinal data (where there are ordered categories), the tables must have subheadings ordered as suggested in Chapter 14, i.e., from high to low as one moves across the columns from left to right and as one moves down the rows from top to bottom.

Third, they are all *normed* in that they have been designed so that they have values which range between 0 (zero) and 1 (one). (Note in Figure 15.7 that Kendall's tau-b and tau-c, Goodman and Kruskal's gamma, and Somer's d also indicate the direction—positive or negative—of the measured association. Thus, these statistics range from –1.0 to +1.0). A zero value usually means no association, while a value of one usually means perfect association.

Fourth, some measures are *asymmetric,* which is appropriate when the researcher has chosen to treat one of the associated variables as the independent variable, while others are *symmetric* when neither variable is chosen as the independent variable.

However, while all these statistics are measures of association, they do not define association in the same way. For example, the *lambda statistics* (there are three of them) measure association by focusing on the modal categories in the rows, columns, or both, depending on which of the three lambda statistics is selected. In so doing, however, the lambda statistics neglect the distributional information on the nonmodal categories, a problem which Goodman and Kruskal's tau rectifies, because it measures association through the proportional distribution on the dependent variable given *each* category on the independent variable. Kendall's tau-b incorporates *ties* into its calculation of association, while Goodman and Kruskal's gamma does not, although tau-b can only result in a value of 1.0 *if* the data are reported in a table with two rows and two columns. Kendall's tau-c can achieve the desirable range of 0.0 to 1.0, but it cannot handle ties, which are almost inevitable in a cross-tabulation. Finally, Somer's d includes a correction factor for ties, which gamma and tau-c do not; thereby making Somer's d a more conservative measure of association than gamma or tau-c. [See Gene M. Lutz, *Understanding Social Statistics*, (New York, New York: Macmillan Publishing Co., 1983), pp. 145–190 for a fuller and more leisurely discussion of these statistical dimensions. Also, attention should be given to Leo A. Goodman and William H. Kruskal, "Measures of Association for Cross Classifications," *Journal of the American Statistical Association,* Vol. 49, No. 268 (December 1954), pp. 732–764; Robert H. Somer, "A New Asymmetric Measure of Association for Ordinal Measures," *American Sociological Review,* Vol. 27, No. 6 (December 1962), pp. 799–811; and John H. Mueller, Karl F. Schuessler, and Herbert L. Costner, *Statistical Reasoning in Sociology*, Third Edition, (Boston, Massachusetts: Houghton Mifflin Company, 1977), pp. 183–232.]

The point here is that these statistics all measure association, but they do not use identical definitions of it. In one the focus is on modes, in another the focus is on the proportional distribution on the dependent variable. Gamma totally neglects ties, as does Kendall's tau-c. This problem is compensated for by Kendall's tau-b, although the interpretation of the association value for tau-b is difficult *if* the table is not 2 x 2. And so it goes!

Therefore, because different definitions and variations on a theme are represented here, we have decided to use *all* the statistics furnished by SPSSˣ that are appropriate to our data and that have comparable (normed) values. That is why we restrict our statistics to those that are normed. (Chi-square-based measures—which have been popular statistics in the history of social science data analysis—have been rejected here because they are not comparable from one table to the next. While zero means no association, the chi-square statistics generally have a variable upper limit depending on sample size.)

In sum, we expect a certain consistency in the rank order of the magnitudes of the strength of the associations, even if their differing definitions cannot produce the same values *across* the various statistics. Further, using the same statistic (for example, gamma) allows one to compare relative associational strengths among the five tables that will emerge in this example. Finally, even though there may be small distortions in any one statistic, if they collectively generate similar results, we can have greater confidence in the accuracy of our interpretations.

MEASURE/ CHARACTERISTICS	NORMED[†]	LEVEL OF MEASUREMENT	SIZE OF TABLE	SYMMETRIC OR ASYMMETRIC[‡]	COMMENTARY
Goodman and Kruskal's lambda	Yes	Nominal	Any size	Both	Based on the modal[§] categories of the independent and dependent variables.
Goodman and Kruskal's tau	Yes	Nominal	Any size	Asymmetric	Based on the proportional distribution of the dependent variable, given the independent variable category.
Kendall's tau-b	Yes	Ordinal	Any size	Symmetric	Cannot result in 1.0 unless using a 2 x 2 table; can handle tied[¶] pairs.
Kendall's tau-c	Yes	Ordinal	Any size	Symmetric	Cannot handle ties.
Goodman and Kruskal's gamma	Yes	Ordinal	Any size	Symmetric	Disregards ties, which make interpretations difficult.
Somer's d	Yes	Ordinal	Any size	Both	Includes a correction for ties.

FIGURE 15.6   Comparison of Selected Dimensions of Various Proportionate Reduction in Error Measures[*] of Association for Two Variables Which Are Grouped into Categories in Tabular Data Presentations

[*]See Gene M. Lutz, *Understanding Social Statistics,* (New York, New York: Macmillan Publishing Company, 1983), pp. 145–90 for an excellent discussion and illustration of the notion of a proportionate-reduction-in-error measure.

[†]*Normed* means that the measure has been designed so that it has a range of associational values between 0 and 1, with *0* meaning "no association" and *1* meaning "perfect association" in terms of the *definition of association* for which the associational measure was designed. Some statistics, such as gamma, tau-b, tau-c, and Somer's d, also indicate direction (through the positive or negative sign) as well as the strength of the association. Of course, nominal-level statistics do not indicate direction, because it is meaningless at the nominal level of measurement.

[‡]An *asymmetric* measure is one that measures association, presuming that one of the bivariate variables is an independent variable. A *symmetric* measure means that the researcher does not wish to treat either of the two variables as the independent one; hence, the association value reflects a combination of the results of treating both variables as independent. For example, the symmetric measure *lambda* always has an intermediate value between the asymmetric measures of "lambda a" and "lambda b." See Leo A. Goodman and William H. Kruskal, "Measures of Association for Cross-Classifications," *Journal of the American Statistical Association,* Vol. 49, No. 268 (December 1954), pp. 742f.

[§]The *mode* is a measure of central tendency, which in a cross-tabulation refers to the attribute on both the independent and dependent variables that contains the largest frequency for the particular variable. That is, the mode for the row attributes would be one value, and the mode for the column attributes would be another value.

[¶]In cross tabulations, a *tie* is any pair of cases that have the *same* attributes on one variable but *different* attributes on the other variable. See Lutz, *Understanding Social Statistics,* pp. 168f for an excellent discussion and illustration.

that the association in Table Y is twice that in Table X. Second, if the value of gamma is strong, then we would expect the value of the other PRE measures to be strong as well. The values will not be identical, because each statistic defines association differently, but there should be some rough consensus among them, since they are all normed.

Running an SPSS^x Program

Up to this point we have been creating two types of files in the SPSS^x language: the data file, which contains the coded or numerical information, and the program file, which tells the computer how to manipulate the information which exists in the data file. Once these have been created and saved, one must exit the editor mode of the VAX computer, where all these tasks have been accomplished, and enter the mode for processing these commands.

In our system, when one has finished editing (i.e., working on) a file, one saves this work by holding down the Control [Ctrl] key and hitting the letter Z key once. This automatically saves the file and labels it as one has indicated when starting the file. After holding down the Ctrl key and striking the letter Z key, an asterisk (*) will appear at the bottom of the screen. Type "EXIT" next to the asterisk and hit the Enter key. This provides the exit from the editor mode and returns one to the dollar sign ($) prompt, which is an all-purpose prompt for the VAX system. Remember that the VAX has been configured to operate any number of different software packages, just one of which is SPSS^x. At the dollar sign ($) prompt, one enters the *RUN command,* which tells the VAX to do all the calculations and manipulations that have been programmed and saved in various files. The following is an example:

$ SPSSX/OUTPUT=D-BASE-1.OUT DATABASE.PR1

The programmer is creating an *output file.* In this case, that output file is labeled "D-BASE-1.OUT"—which is another file to be saved containing all the results of the data manipulations

requested from the program (in this case, "DATABASE.PR1") on a data file (in this case, "DATABASE"). The procedure calls for typing "SPSSX" to tell the VAX that one wishes to invoke the SPSS^x software, followed by a forward diagonal [/]. This is followed by the word *OUTPUT,* which tells the VAX that another file is to be created and saved, followed by an equal sign (=) and the file name of the output file labeled "D-BASE-1.OUT." This latter file name can be anything the researcher wants it to be, subject to the limitations imposed by the VAX on file names as discussed earlier. In this example, we have chosen the above, because (1) *D-BASE* refers to the general series of files labeled *"DATABASE"* in the foregoing, (2) *–1* means the first program of instructions (there may be additional programs that the researcher will want to write when the researcher has studied the results of the first program), and (3) the extension *OUT* indicates that this file is an output file (the results of the first program). In sum, this command will tell the VAX to execute the program instructions on the data base that has been created and identified.

At this point, the VAX will inform the user that the job has been started, and it will continue processing the program instructions until "terrible errors" have been found or it gets to the end, at which time it notes that the job has been stopped or completed. Because there are so many different types of errors and difficulties that can happen here, an overview of them is impossible. Suffice it to say, a missed keypunch, an extra blank in the data base, a misspelling of a command, or a missed or improper end mark (e.g., diagonal) will cause the VAX to become confused. One's output file will then contain error messages which more or less tell the researcher where and what the nature of the problem is. This process of responding to the error messages by revising the inaccuracies of one's program is called *debugging* the program.

Once the process of debugging has been completed, the VAX will create an error-free output file containing the results. If it is desirable to see what the results are on the monitor, type at the dollar sign ($) prompt:

$ TYPE D-BASE-1.OUT

The word *TYPE,* which can be in lowercase or uppercase letters, tells the VAX to put the output file onto the monitor. However, when it does so, the program and the results roll by so fast it is difficult to read. However, it is still a good idea to put this on the monitor because when the output file stops scrolling down the monitor at the end of the file, a brief statement about the number of warnings and errors within the program is posted. If there are no warnings or errors, the program was understandable to and executable by the VAX. At this point, it is recommended that the output file be put on *hard copy,* or paper. This is achieved using the *PRINT command,* which will send the output file from the computer to the printer. The format is simply at the dollar sign ($) prompt:

$ PRINT D-BASE-1.OUT

The VAX will note that the print job has been started and will inform you when it has been completed.

The Results

As we argued earlier in a long, substantive footnote, we have decided to report the values of a number of associational statistics for all the cross-tabulations presented in this chapter. The central reason is that each statistic defines association in a different way; to focus on only one statistic may result in the failure to note association, which may be present, simply because that one statistic may not be capable of registering it if it conforms to a different definition. Conversely, if there is association in any table, it should be reflected in several measures, if not in all of them. Therefore, the use of multiple statistics provides a cross-check against an erroneous interpretation based on a single measure. Again, we refer you to Figure 15.6 presented earlier, which summarizes some of the similarities and differences among the measures reported herein.

The class I, explanatory, variables we are developing here are measured at the ordinal level of measurement. Therefore, it would be appropriate to use ordinal-level statistics. However, we have included a couple of nominal-level statistics—Goodman and Kruskal's tau and two lambda statistics, because we encourage you, the reader, to develop a second data-analysis program to probe further the data set on which this example rests. If such is feasible, you could select a variable that has been measured at the nominal level and, therefore, necessitate the use of lambda or tau. In the event that this is done, the lambda and tau values for Tables 15.1 through 15.5 will be available for comparative purposes with the cross-tabulations that you develop, although, strictly speaking, they are not necessary for the analysis presented by your authors.

In those cases where we use an asymmetric statistic, we have chosen to treat the variable *V11* (Index Score) as the dependent variable. Since its attributes are represented as the column subheadings, we percentaged each table across the rows.

Table 15.1 contains the results of the CROSSTABS TABLES command discussed earlier—see text reference number (13) in Appendix E. We have not reproduced the SPSS^x printout exactly, because we feel the table format we suggested in Chapter 14 is preferable. Table 15.1 reports the cross-tabulation between the independent variable of education (V14) and the dependent variable of positive self-image index score (V11). Inspection of the cell percentages reveals little association in Table 15.1. Indeed, all of the values of the PRE measures of association are extremely low or close to zero (no association), with the possible exception of gamma's value of 0.22857. Recall, however, that gamma measures association only among untied pairs, thereby disregarding the ties. Because of this, gamma could well overstate the association; hence, Somer's d might be the better measure to use. Looking at the asymmetric Somer's d shows an association value of 0.15161, which is, of course, weaker than gamma. After inspection of all the associational values presented, we are inclined to conclude that there is little association between educational attainment and positive self-image. But this doesn't make any sense! Knowing what we know about education and self-image in American society,

TABLE 15.1 Number and Percentage of Employed, White, Married Males Sampled by Educational Attainment and by Positive Self-Image Score

EDUC./IMAGE	HIGH	MEDIUM	LOW	TOTAL
HIGH	95 (47.5)	58 (29.0)	47 (23.5)	200 (100.0)
LOW	70 (35.7)	57 (29.1)	69 (35.2)	196 (100.0)
TOTAL	165	115	116	396

STATISTIC	VALUE
Goodman and Kruskal's lambda:	
Symmetric	0.05152
Asymmetric (with V11 dependent)	0.00000
Goodman and Kruskal's tau (with V11 dependent)	0.01051
Kendall's tau-b	0.13233
Kendall's tau-c	0.15159
Goodman and Kruskal's gamma	0.22857
Somer's d:	
Symmetric	0.13111
Asymmetric (with V11 dependent)	0.15161

there should be a positive association between these two variables. Now what do we do?

You will recall that we argued in Chapter 4 that one might use one or more of the modes of elaboration when one obtained "strange" research results. Surely these are strange results. It may be that family debt is a confounding, class III, variable masking the relationship between education and positive self-image. With this in mind, let us turn to the variable *V28* ("Debt"). Let us recode the seven degrees of indebtedness into two categories, "High" and "Low" family debt, as indicated below—see text reference number (14) in Appendix E:

```
RECODE V28 (1 THRU 4=1) (5 THRU 7=2)
VARIABLE LABELS V28 'DEBT'
VALUE LABELS V28 1 'LOW' 2 'HIGH'
```

Creating these two new subcategories for "Debt," we can pursue the mode of elaboration of specification and recalculate the correlation between the variable *V14* ("Education") and the variable *V11* ("Index Score"), holding constant the variable *V28* through the use of the CROSSTABS TABLES commands as shown in the box below—see text reference number (15) in Appendix E:

```
CROSSTABS   TABLES=V14 BY V11 BY V28
        /CELLS=COUNT ROW
        /STATISTICS=LAMBDA BTAU CTAU GAMMA D
```

Notice that the CROSSTABS   TABLES command has changed slightly. In the above command, the keyword *BY* is used a second time, followed by a space, and the variable name *V28* ("Debt"). The variable that follows the second *BY* in this command is treated as a controlled variable, and SPSSˣ will print tables showing the variables *V14* and *V11* for *each of the subcategories of the controlled variable*, i.e., variable *V28* in this case. Since we recoded the variable *V28* into two categories ("High" and "Low"), SPSSˣ will print two tables: (1) one containing the distribution of "Education" and "Index Score" for those

persons with "Low" debt and (2) one containing the distribution of "Education" and "Index Score" for those with "High" debt.

These results appear in Tables 15.2 and 15.3 where an interesting pattern has emerged. All of the statistical measures report very strong associational values. For example, none are below Goodman and Kruskal's tau of 0.44922 (a nominal-level measure, which fails to reflect the ordered nature of these tabular data), and gamma is amazingly 0.96693 (because of the few number of tied pairs in this table). Even the more conservative asymmetric Somer's d is 0.83619. Kendall's

TABLE 15.2   Number and Percentage of Employed, White, Married Males Sampled Who Have Low Family Debt by Educational Attainment and by Positive Self-Image Score*

EDUC./IMAGE	HIGH	MEDIUM	LOW	TOTAL
HIGH	44 (91.7)	3 (6.3)	1 (2.1)	48 (100.1)
LOW	6 (11.8)	11 (21.6)	34 (66.7)	51 (100.1)
TOTAL	50	14	35	99

*The row percentages may not add to a total of 100.0 percent due to rounding error.

STATISTIC	VALUE
Goodman and Kruskal's lambda:	
Symmetric	0.68041
Asymmetric (with V11 dependent)	0.57143
Goodman and Kruskal's tau (with V11 dependent)	0.44922
Kendall's tau-b	0.76302
Kendall's tau-c	0.83542
Goodman and Kruskal's gamma	0.96693
Somer's d:	
Symmetric	0.75984
Asymmetric (with V11 dependent)	0.83619

tau-b which *does* incorporate ties is 0.76302 and would have been stronger for a 2 x 2 table, since this measure cannot achieve a perfect value of 1.0 except for a 2 x 2 table. Although we found virtually no association in Table 15.1, we find a very strong association in Table 15.2. Thus, when the family tends to have low family debt, the association between education and positive self-image is very strong. In Table 15.2 the majority of the cases flow from the upper left-hand cells to the lower right-hand cells. This pattern, along with the order of the subheadings of this table, indicate that the association is a positive one. Additionally,

those measures that are signed—i.e., indicate direction as well as strength—all indicate a positive associational value. In sum, the data presented in Table 15.2 support the original hypothesis, but only under the condition that the family has low indebtedness.

Conversely, the data in Table 15.3, which reflect the association between education and positive self-image for those who have high debt, are very weak at best, even tending toward a negative association rather than a positive one. For example, gamma has fallen to –0.17245 and asymmetric Somer's d to –0.11452. Similarly, all the

TABLE 15.3   Number and Percentage of Employed, White, Married Males Sampled Who Have High Family Debt by Educational Attainment and by Positive Self-Image Score*

EDUC./IMAGE	HIGH	MEDIUM	LOW	TOTAL
HIGH	51 (33.6)	55 (36.2)	46 (30.3)	152 (100.1)
LOW	64 (44.1)	46 (31.7)	35 (24.1)	145 (99.9)
TOTAL	115	101	81	297

*The row percentages may not add to a total of 100.0 percent due to rounding error.

STATISTIC	VALUE
Goodman and Kruskal's lambda:	
Symmetric	0.05199
Asymmetric (with V11 dependent)	0.02198
Goodman and Kruskal's tau (with V11 dependent)	0.00641
Kendall's tau-b	–0.09964
Kendall's tau-c	–0.11446
Goodman and Kruskal's gamma	–0.17245
Somer's d:	
Symmetric	–0.09869
Asymmetric (with V11 dependent)	–0.11452

```
RECODE V26 (LO THRU 19,88=2) (20 THRU HI=1)
VARIABLE LABELS V26 "WIFE'S WORK"
VALUE LABELS V26 1 'HIGH VOLUME' 2 'LOW VOLUME'
```

remaining values show strengths below the gamma value. In view of the weak magnitudes of these values (i.e., values close to zero), it is advisable to refrain from suggesting any direction to these data in Table 15.3.

In short, there appears to be no association between education and positive self-image when the family is characterized by high indebtedness. It may be that the positive association between education and positive self-image is being cancelled by the negative contribution of high family indebtedness. To put this another way, perhaps the husband's perception of high self-worth due to his educational attainment is being counterbalanced by his negative perception of his inability to be the breadwinner or provider within the family. To see if this explanation seems appropriate, we will investigate another variable.

The entries in the data base on the variable *V26* ("Hours/Week") suggest that a substantial number of husbands' spouses are employed outside the home and that some of them are working a considerable number of hours per week. Thinking about people who are employed, we felt that such work can have different meanings, dependent upon the amount of time that is spent working. You will recall we operationalized the variable *V16* (husband's "Work status") with full-time work being that which exacts 35 or more hours per week, part-time work as that on which the employee spends 20 to 34 hours per week, some work as that which involves 10 to 19 hours per week, and occasional work as that which involves less than 10 hours per week. Since all those sampled were full-time employees, each male could perceive himself as a major breadwinner within the family structure. However, the wife's employment may be a threat to her husband's positive self-image, especially if the wife's employment resulted in a major contribution to the family's finances. Further, for those men who have not accepted the concept of the liberated woman, the employed woman may weigh heavily upon the conscience of the husband because his spouse is not performing the traditional wife-mother social role.

Therefore, we decided to recode the variable *V26* ("Hours/Week"), which the wife spent in employment, collapsing the data into two categories: "High volume" and "Low volume." "High volume" was operationally defined as spending 20 or more hours per week in paid employment on the premise that such a time expenditure would place the wife out of the house for a major portion of time. Similarly, low volume was operationally defined as a spouse's working 19 or fewer hours per week. The RECODE command, which appears in the box above, represents the necessary recoding— see text reference number (16) in Appendix E.

Notice another variation in this set of specifications for the RECODE command. The keyword *LO* may be used to tell SPSS^x that the coded values are to start with the lowest one available. Similarly, the keyword *HI* tells SPSS^x to end with the highest value available. The keyword *THRU* tells SPSS^x that one is to recode *all* the values between the lowest and the stated value (19, in the first case) and between the stated value (20, in the second case) and the highest value. Finally, note that we incorporated one additional value (88). The code *88* was originally entered as an irrelevant response, because the respondent had earlier answered that his wife was not employed, thereby making this variable *V26* (Hours/Week) irrelevant. Therefore, in the recoding process, a code *88* means that the wife does not work outside the house and, clearly, falls in the "low volume" category on variable *V26*. The reason for including the code *88* is that we had previously told SPSS^x that the code *88* for the variable V26 was a "missing value." SPSS^x would have disregarded the code *88* in DATABASE.DAT and failed to include in the "low volume" category any person so coded.

After the recoding process has been completed, we did another CROSSTABS TABLES command—see text reference number (17) in Appendix E, identical to the last CROSSTABS TABLES command with the exception that this time we controlled on the variable *V26*. That is, *V26* replaced *V28* in the second CROSSTABS TABLES command, through which we were pursuing the mode of elaboration of specification by controlling *V26*. We used the same CELLS and STATISTICS subcommands. The results appear as Tables 15.4 and 15.5.

Table 15.4 contains data for those males with spouses who were "High volume" employees. The hypothesis here is that these men have their status as breadwinners within the family threatened to a significant degree by the amount of time that their wives spend working outside the home. All the ordinal statistics show negative values ranging from –0.31239 to –0.53410. Again, the strongest association is evidenced by the gamma statistic, which disregards tied pairs, so this statistic (with a value of –0.53410) probably overstates the strength of the association between education and self-image. Indeed, the asymmetric Somer's d value of –0.37743 is more in keeping with the values of Kendall's tau-b and tau-c, which are all quite similar. These data indicate a fairly weak association between education and positive self-image; i.e., the expected strong association seems to have been weakened by the fact that these men had wives who were making substantial time commit-

TABLE 15.4 Number and Percentage of Employed, White, Married Males Sampled with Wives Who have High Volume Employment Experiences by Educational Attainment and by Positive Self-Image Score

EDUC./IMAGE	HIGH	MEDIUM	LOW	TOTAL
HIGH	16 (21.3)	24 (32.0)	35 (46.7)	75 (100.0)
LOW	62 (48.8)	43 (33.9)	22 (17.3)	127 (100.0)
TOTAL	78	67	57	202

STATISTIC	VALUE
Goodman and Kruskal's lambda:	
Symmetric	0.16080
Asymmetric (with V11 dependent)	0.15323
Goodman and Kruskal's tau (with V11 dependent)	0.05719
Kendall's tau-b	–0.31714
Kendall's tau-c	–0.35242
Goodman and Kruskal's gamma	–0.53410
Somer's d:	
Symmetric	–0.31239
Asymmetric (with V11 dependent)	–0.37743

ments to employment opportunities. Indeed, the association is not only weaker, but it has also *changed direction*. The flow of the majority of cases in the cells of Table 15.4 is from the lower left to the upper right, and the statistics that have signed values all report a negative association. This means that as one's education increases, one's self-image decreases. Thus, having a "high-volume" employed wife seems to weaken the association between education and self-image and change the association from a positive to a negative one. If this explanation is creditable, the association between education and positive self-image with wives who are "low-volume" employees

ought to be stronger and also positive. That relationship is presented in Table 15.5.

The values of the ordinal-level statistics for Table 15.5 show reasonably strong associational strength, ranging from a high of 0.84582 for gamma and a low of 0.56641 for the symmetric Somer's d. Recognizing the familiar difficulty with gamma (its disregard of tied pairs), the asymmetric Somer's d indicates a more conservative 0.68186 value. Thus, the strength of the associational values and their indicated directions (for the signed statistics) are consistent with the conceptual model evolving here. That is, for those men whose breadwinner function does not appear to be threatened by their

TABLE 15.5   Number and Percentage of Employed, White, Married Males Sampled with Wives Who have Low Volume Employment Experiences by Educational Attainment and by Positive Self-Image Score

EDUC./IMAGE	HIGH	MEDIUM	LOW	TOTAL
HIGH	79 (63.2)	34 (27.2)	12 (9.6)	125 (100.0)
LOW	8 (11.6)	14 (20.3)	47 (68.1)	69 (100.0)
TOTAL	87	48	59	194

STATISTIC	VALUE
Goodman and Kruskal's lambda:	
Symmetric	0.42045
Asymmetric (with V11 dependent)	0.36449
Goodman and Kruskal's tau (with V11 dependent)	0.21792
Kendall's tau-b	0.57470
Kendall's tau-c	0.62504
Goodman and Kruskal's gamma:	0.84582
Somer's d:	
Symmetric	0.56641
Asymmetric (with V11 dependent)	0.68186

STATISTIC†/TABLE	TABLE 15.1 ZERO-ORDER‡ V14:EDUC/IND¶ V11: S-I/DEP# NO CONTROL	R	TABLE 15.2 FIRST-ORDER§ V14:EDUC/IND V11: S-I/DEP CONTROL V28** LOW DEBT	R	TABLE 15.3 FIRST-ORDER V14:EDUC/IND V11: S-I/DEP CONTROL V28 HIGH DEBT	R	TABLE 15.4 FIRST-ORDER V14:EDUC/IND V11: S-I/DEP CONTROL V26 HIGH VOLUME	R	TABLE 15.5 FIRST-ORDER V14:EDUC/IND V11: S-I/DEP CONTROL V26 LOW VOLUME	R
Lambda symmetric	0.05152	5	0.68041	1	0.05199	4	0.16080	3	0.42045	2
Asymmetric: V11 dependent	0.00000	5	0.57143	1	0.02198	4	0.15323	3	0.36449	2
Goodman and Kruskal's tau Asymmetric: V11 dependent	0.01051	4	0.44922	1	0.00641	5	0.05719	3	0.21792	2
Kendall's tau-b	0.13233	4	0.76302	1	−0.09964	5	−0.31714	3	0.57470	2
Kendall's tau-c	0.15159	4	0.83542	1	−0.11446	5	−0.35242	3	0.62504	2
Gamma	0.22857	4	0.96693	1	−0.17245	5	−0.53410	3	0.84582	2
Somer's d symmetric	0.13111	4	0.75984	1	−0.09869	5	−0.31239	·3	0.56641	2
Asymmetric: V11 dependent	0.15161	4	0.83619	1	−0.11452	5	−0.37743	3	0.68186	2

FIGURE 15.7 Associational Values of Selected Proportionate-Reduction-in-Error Measures (PRE) by Statistic, by Table Measured, and by Comparative Rank (R)*

*The rank is indicated by a single digit under the "R" column and refers to the rank of the associational statistic when compared to the other tables' associational values for the *same* statistic.

†For a brief description and comparison of these specific statistics, see Figure 15.6 and the footnote on p. 355.

‡*Zero-Order* indicates that the association was measured between two class I variables only.

§*First-Order* means that the association was measured between two class I variables while holding a third variable constant as class II.

¶*V14:EDUC/IND* means that one class I variable was V14 or Education and that it is being considered the independent variable.

#*V11: S-I/DEP* means that the other class I variable is self-image score and it is considered dependent.

**Control V28* means that the controlled class II variable was V28 or Debt, and the designation immediately under this refers to the attribute on this variable which was controlled.

wives' employment status, the association between education and positive self-image continues to be positive and strong.

Finally, let us summarize these results by comparing the associational values obtained from these five tables (see Figure 15.7). Figure 15.7 shows that the measures of association between self-image and degree of education in Table 15.1 are very weak. This is a surprising result and cause for further investigation of this relationship. Controlling on degree of indebtedness, Table 15.2, which contains those families who have low indebtedness, reflects the strongest positive correlation between self-image and education. Where the degree of family indebtedness is high (as in Table 15.3), this strong positive correlation is reduced to virtually no association between education and self-image. Exploring further, when controlling on the degree to which the respondent's wife is employed, we find in Table 15.4 that the association between self-image and education is negative for those respondents with wives who are "high-volume" employees, but a strong positive association (Table 15.5) between self-image and education for those men whose wives are "low-volume" employees.

In sum, we would argue from these data that the association between a man's self-image and his educational level is influenced quite strongly by the degree of family indebtedness and by the degree to which his spouse is employed. Low family debt does not appear to threaten the husband's breadwinner status, while high indebtedness apparently does. Further, men experience a positive association between self-image and educational level if their spouses are not significantly involved in employment situations, but when their spouses spend substantial time in outside employment, the association between education and self-image is altered to a negative one, albeit a relatively weak one.

After completing the desired data processing commands, one final command remains. While not obligatory because SPSS^x assumes completion if it does not find any additional commands, it is still a good practice to end with the *FINISH command*—see text reference number (18) in Appendix E.

A Final Note

We have elected to call our first program "DATABASE.PR1." It may be that you would like to experiment by creating a second or third series of programs to analyze DATABASE.DAT differently. If so, we recommend that you call these subsequent programs "DATABASE.PR2" and "DATABASE.PR3" in order to keep them separate from each other.

SUMMARY

In this chapter we illustrated, in an extended example, the importance of having a conceptual model to frame meaningful propositions to be operationalized into hypotheses for testing. We also concentrated on a limited number of descriptive statistics: (1) frequency distribution and histograms to aid in the operationalization of the subheadings, which appeared in the tables where the data were presented and (2) several nominal and ordinal PRE statistics used to measure the degree of association among the class I variables.

Basic attention was also given to the nature of computer data processing, the formation of a codebook, the data-entry mechanism, and a data-cleaning procedure. A computer program was written in SPSS^x to illustrate data redefinition (the FREQUENCIES command, the HISTOGRAM subcommand, and RECODE command), data presentation (the CROSSTABS TABLES command), and data analysis (STATISTICS subcommand).

In sum, this chapter illustrates how the conceptual model, measuring instrument, computer preparation of the data, and computer analysis of the data are separate but integrated pieces of an overall research project.

KEY TERMS

Account number	Floppy disk	Program file
Active file	FREQUENCIES command	Read
Binary code	(SPSS^x)	RECODE command (SPSS^x)
Cathode-ray tube (CRT)	Function keys	Record number
CELLS subcommand (SPSS^x)	Hard copy	Run
Central processing unit (CPU)	Hard disk	RUN command (VAX)
Character	Hard-wired	Software
Codebook	HISTOGRAM subcommand	Software system
Coding	(SPSS^x)	SPSS^x
Coding form	Keyboard	STATISTICS subcommand
COMMENT command (SPSS^x)	Machine language	(SPSS^x)
CROSSTABS TABLES	Mainframe computer	TITLE command (SPSS^x)
command (SPSS^x)	Microcomputer	TYPE command (VAX)
Data cleaning	MISSING VALUES	VALUE LABELS
Data file	command (SPSS^x)	command (SPSS^x)
DATA LIST command (SPSS^x)	Modem	Variable label
Debugging	Monitor	VARIABLE LABELS
Disk drive	Operating system	command (SPSS^x)
Dummy terminal	Output file	Variable name
FILE HANDLE command	Password	VARIABLES subcommand
(SPSS^x)	PRINT command (VAX)	(SPSS^x)
File name	Printer	Write
FINISH command (SPSS^x)		

Following are some comments concerning this list of important terms:

1. Those concepts in uppercase or capital letters are computer software programming commands or subcommands.

2. Those concepts that have "(VAX)" appended to them are commands that drive the VAX mainframe system on our campus, and these commands may be somewhat different on your campus.

3. Those concepts which have "(SPSS^x)" appended to them are commands that tell SPSS^x what to do with the data file or files.

REVIEW QUESTIONS

1. Define the following computer components and characteristics: central processing unit, keyboard, monitor, hard disk, floppy disk drive, data files, program files, and software system. In what ways are these components similar to an audio stereo system?

2. The Statistics Package for the Social Sciences, Version x (SPSS^x) is a prepared software package. List and briefly define the commands necessary to *define a data file* for SPSS^x data processing.

3. What are the three major functions of SPSS^x that were illustrated in the example in this chapter?

4. What is the function of a codebook, what subparts must be included, what is the function of these subparts, and how is the formation of a codebook related to one's conceptual model?

5. If one anticipates entering a large amount of data into a computer, a coding form is required. Discuss the function of blanks on this form.

6. Discuss three ways in which data cleaning can be done on a data file. Which is the best?

7. How may a computer data-analysis program help the researcher operationalize the subheadings in a tabular data-presentation design?

8. In what ways may a computer data-analysis program such as SPSS^x be an impediment to meaningful social research?

9. Make a list of all the *noncomputer related* concepts from throughout the text that are explicitly stated or subsumed in the computer example in this chapter.

CHAPTER 16

ETHICAL CONSIDERATIONS

INTRODUCTION

Some of you may perceive a chapter on ethics as superfluous. After all, most of us see ourselves as ethical in the manner in which we conduct ourselves with others. Nevertheless, there is a current explosion of interest regarding ethical considerations that is affecting a vast array of dimensions, e.g., politics, economics, business, legal decisions, medical issues, and the arenas of research. Ethicists are in great demand as consultants, public speakers, and as members of professional staffs. Indeed, virtually all medical schools now have at least one ethicist on their faculty.

This growth of public interest in ethics has affected the manner in which sociologists plan and conduct their research. While initial concern focused upon biomedical research and the clear potential for harm to those willing to participate in such empirical efforts, the attention has expanded to include any area of research that involves human respondents.

This does not mean that researchers were previously without ethics or concern for human respondents, but such concern has traditionally been passed from generation to generation by word of mouth, mentor to student, and in the classroom.

During the 1960s, however, we witnessed a number of radical movements and subsequent social change within the American society. The civil rights movement continued to expand from the 1954 *Brown* v. *the Topeka Board of Education* desegregation decision, feminism reflected a substantive ideological shift in appropriate-inappropriate social roles for men and women, and the antiwar movement in protest of America's involvement in Vietnam captured the attention and energies of a large segment of the population.

These social issues served as magnets for the interests of sociologists. Specifically, the number of what one might label "radical sociologists" studying these concerns grew dramatically. Significant to this growth was the concurrent idea among such radical sociologists that one should not only study a given phenomena but also register every effort to ameliorate any perceived social injustice, inequality, or pathology.

More traditional sociologists, who had long argued for a more objective stance in sociology, became alarmed at what their radical colleagues were advocating. In response, the traditionalists became primarily responsible for the introduction of the first professional code of ethics endorsed by the American Sociological Association in 1968. A second version of the code, reflecting extensive modification and expansion, was implemented in 1980, and a third edition was introduced in 1989. See Appendix F. Despite the expansion of the conceptualization of ethics, there remains a great deal of ambiguity.

The ethical concerns regarding the relevant parties, i.e., respondent, researcher, sponsor of the research and/or the host institution, and publication expectations regarding the resultant documents are the subject of this chapter. Our purpose is to offer some clarification to the ambiguity and to stimulate your awareness of ethical considerations as they apply to your research formulations and your review of the research of others.

ETHICAL CONCERNS IN THE RESEARCHER-RESPONDENT RELATIONSHIP

It is our position that the volunteer participant within social science research is, and should be, the principal and most significant recipient of an ethical stance. It was generally assumed, prior to the Second World War, that research was value free and, by definition, designed to serve human interests. However, the biomedical experiments conducted within Nazi concentration camps and the research that led to the building of an atom bomb serve as two significant events that clearly communicated the error of this assumption. As a result, researchers have adopted a clearer value orientation and are no longer willing to embrace, without question, the pursuit of knowledge per se. The question of what knowledge is for must be addressed. Consideration of a number of issues relevant to a respondent's participation will facilitate a researcher's decision of whether a proposed project is consistent with contemporary ethical concerns. It is to those issues we now turn.

It should be emphasized that a researcher must consider a number of factors when evaluating the ethical considerations that will govern a research effort. Although we must, by definition, discuss each concern separately, the nature of research precludes rendering final decisions on the basis of a single factor.

Informed Consent

Informed consent is "the procedure in which individuals choose whether to participate in an investigation after being informed of facts that would be likely to influence their decision."[1]

As is the case for ethics in general, concern with informed consent originated in biomedical research. Since human beings are the respondents of social science, it is quite reasonable that ethics

has grown into such a significant issue in social science. Significantly, however, one should not interpret informed consent as a license to violate other ethical considerations.

With the proviso that multiple ethical considerations must be evaluated in formulating one's research design, there are three key elements of informed consent: (1) the respondent should be informed that participation is voluntary, (2) the respondent should be informed of any aspects of the study that might influence the decision to participate, and (3) the respondent should be permitted to exercise continuous free choice of whether to continue participating throughout the study.[2]

Individually, if these guidelines are followed, the respondent's freedom of election to participate and the voluntary assumption of any risks one might encounter is increased. That is, those respondents who fear that some type of harm might occur to them are screened out. On a broader basis, adherence to these key elements will increase general societal trust and respect for science and will probably result in a reduction of legal liability inherent in conducting the research.

Deception

These three elements represent ideal practices regarding informed consent. The realities of research, however, often preclude strict adherence to these guidelines. Human limitations and competing values interrupt a ubiquitous application of these criteria. While informed consent without deception is generally more easily accommodated in studies employing interview or questionnaire data gathering designs because potential participants are informed about the study through cover letters and introductory remarks, many observation studies— particularly those of a field-research nature or those employing unobtrusive measures—could not be adequately or accurately conducted if the researcher followed these criteria to the letter.

When one fails to obtain informed consent from those being studied, by commission or omission, one is guilty of committing *deception.* Since ethics, by definition, is concerned with morality and every moral system known to man has interpreted lying as a violation of the moral code, the researcher is confronted by the real dilemma of whether to inform or deceive the potential participants of the research.

A somewhat mitigating consideration that has recently emerged in ethical debates is the notion of *situation ethics*. A proponent of situation ethics would argue that one should consider the context in which the truth or falsehood is to be offered and the consequences of both alternatives. If lesser harm accrues from the falsehood, then the falsehood is often preferable to the truth. For example, consider a friend of yours who has just purchased a painting for her living room and asks you what you think of it. Your honest opinion is that the painting is ghastly, but you note the obvious excitement and happiness of your friend concerning the "work of art." What is to be gained by offering an honest opinion here? Your friend has not purchased the painting with any intention of treating it as an investment but is intending to enjoy it at home. Under these conditions a polite and reinforcing reply would be appropriate: "Well, I think it is very interesting."

Likewise, in research there are some defensible reasons for not informing the respondent. The most important general guideline is that the researcher should never place a participant in harm's way. This guideline should be interpreted in the broadest of terms. That is, consideration of embarrassment, endangerment of one's home, friendships, and employment should be registered as well as one's physical well being. If this guideline can be followed, a number of potential justifications for failing to attain informed consent can be noted.

This list would include *methodological control*, which might well be forfeited if the researcher was constrained by obtaining informed consent. This would be of particular concern if the project was being conducted in a natural setting. It is almost certain that *reactivity* would become a significant issue and, in all likelihood, would bias somewhat any observations that might be recorded. Similarly, even within a laboratory setting, the

subjects might not be informed of the precise reason they are being studied, the number of fellow respondents, or whether the researcher has incorporated the use of confederates into the study design.

Again, the primary question focuses upon the potential harm to the participant. To argue that respondents should never be subjected to any physical, psychological, or social harm is a dictum easily accepted in theory. In *pragmatic* terms, however, it is almost impossible to realize, as virtually all research carries with it some degree of risk.

Despite the ubiquity of risk, avenues to reduce the degree of harm are present. For example, investigators conducting observational research may elect to utilize unobtrusive measures, the most notable being mechanical recording devices. These can include a variety of audio and/or visual records, e.g., still, moving, or infrared cameras. Informing respondents they were being recorded prior to the data collection would undoubtedly alter behavior. Such informing would preclude the usage of the observational modalities in which the researcher was unknown. Providing access to the recordings following the data collection, however, and affording the participants the opportunity to refuse consent can minimize any risk that might be present. If consent is not given, the researcher has the obligation to destroy any recordings that were made.

Deception, with potential harm for participants, has even been practiced within laboratory environments. We offer two well-known and frequently cited studies to illustrate this danger. The first of these was done by Stanley Milgram.[3] The study assessed the willingness of a small sample of men from divergent social backgrounds to impose physical pain, with the use of electric shock, upon others as a negative sanction for learning errors. Each respondent was paired with another participant who was, in fact, a confederate of the researcher. The respondent was then assigned the role of teacher, allegedly by a random draw, while the confederate was to serve as his student. The teacher and student were placed in separate, but adjacent, rooms. Further, the respondent-teacher was assigned a seat behind a control panel that contained switches, voltage labels, and warning messages such as "Extreme-Intensity Shock," "Danger-Severe Shock," and "XXX."

The respondent-teacher was asked to read a provided list of word pairs to the confederate-learner and then to test the latter's ability to match the terms correctly. Since visual contact was prevented, errors were signaled by a light on the control panel. When the error light was illuminated, the experimenter instructed the teacher-respondent to administer shock to the confederate-learner. Early errors were apparently sanctioned by relatively minor shocks, while continued errors were met with what were thought to be increasingly severe shocks.

Similarly, the confederate-learner, as a part of the study design, reacted to the increased sanctions in a progressively pained manner, asking for mercy and for the experiment to be terminated. Subsequently, the confederate-learner would kick the wall separating the two rooms, and finally registered no reply when read a list of words.

While some of the respondent-teachers voiced concern as the study progressed to the more severe levels of shock, all of the respondents continued to respond to the experimenter's directive to administer such until the confederate-students kicked the wall. At that point, only five refused. Indeed, two-thirds of the 40 respondents continued to follow the experimenter's directions through the entire sequence of the study.

The shocks, of course, were not real, but the respondents were not aware of this deception. Despite obedience to the experimenter's instructions, many of the respondents reported feeling a level of pain consistent with that which they thought they were causing the confederate-students. While the students were asking for the experiment to stop, the teachers were begging the experimenter to let them stop administering the shocks. In general they became anxious, and a few experienced seizures.

While the results of this study are valuable and can assist us in our understanding of blind obedi-

ence to authority (e.g., soldiers following orders of officers to commit atrocities), the respondent's were clearly placed in harm's way.

Another example where volunteer study participants experienced the potential for harm was conducted by Philip Zimbardo and his associates.[4] Unlike the Milgram study, however, Zimbardo's work was not designed to test individual's willingness to place others at risk. Rather, in an effort to understand the importance of social location upon behavior and attitudes, a prison environment was simulated in the basement of the psychology building at Stanford University. Twenty-four male volunteer college students were recruited to participate. The sample was equally divided between those who would act in the capacity of inmates and those who would serve as guards. The study was designed to last two weeks. Unfortunately, these respondents began to identify in an extremely realistic fashion with the roles they had been assigned. Some of the "guards" were brutal and acted capriciously, while others did nothing to interfere with such behavior. Conversely, "inmates" became depressed, docile, begged for release, and turned on one another. The study was canceled after only six days.

STRATEGIES FOR REDUCING RISK

The conscientious and ethical researcher has any number of procedures to select from to minimize the degree of risk inherited by the participant.

Debriefing

The first of these is *debriefing,* whereby the respondents are afforded the opportunity to talk about the research effort and voice any concerns or feelings. Milgram and Zimbardo each elected this alternative and conducted follow-up interviews with their respective respondents to ensure there was an absence of long-range harm. In both cases it was concluded that no permanent damage had occurred to the participants. While debriefing was apparently successful in these two studies, one must be aware that if persons have been selected to participate in a study because they manifest a specific negative trait or characteristic (e.g., alcoholism, drug addiction, adolescent parenthood), caution must be exercised in this process. The emphasis should be placed on the importance of their contribution in order to not further endanger the respondent's self-esteem.

It should be realized that participation in a research project can potentially affect future behavior dramatically, and this realization should have a significant influence upon the nature of the research design and the utilization of human subjects.

Role Playing

A second safeguard to deception is to ask participants in the study to role-play. The idea in *role playing* is to ask subjects to act out some role as if they were participating in real circumstances. The primary difficulty with the use of role playing is achieving an approximation of reality. By definition, there is an intellectual awareness on the part of the respondents that the circumstances of the study are artificial, which can result in behavior that is similarly artificial. The Zimbardo study reminds us, however, that role playing can result in close approximations of reality.

Forewarning

A third alternative to placing human respondents at risk is the *forewarning* of participants that deception may be a part of the study. If this procedure is followed, the researcher can select only those who have previously agreed to participate in deception research. While this only represents an approximation of informed consent, it is superior to ignoring the question altogether.

We should also note an increasing difficulty with introducing deception to research. A great deal of social science research is conducted with students as the respondents. Edward Diener and Rick Crandall cite a number of studies which suggest college and university students do not object to research containing deception.[5] Indeed,

evidence suggests a growing percentage of respondents who *expect* deception to be a part of the study. This, in turn, frequently stimulates the researcher to incorporate greater deception to adequately examine the hypothesis.

Anonymity or Confidentiality

A fourth area in which harm to the respondent has been addressed is providing the respondent with a guarantee of anonymity or confidentiality. You will recall from an earlier discussion that *anonymity* is achieved when it is impossible for the researcher to identify any particular respondent's remarks, while *confidentiality* is achieved when the researcher knows who said what but agrees never to divulge a respondent's identity. Respondents have traditionally been willing, in general, to participate in research if they are comfortable with the promise that their responses will be held in confidence by the researcher. A promise of this nature can be given within the cover letter of a questionnaire or the introductory remarks prior to an interview. Similar commitments can be reinforced through poststudy discussions with participants in observational studies.

It is our opinion that a promise of confidentiality must be honored by the researcher, even if the data were subpoenaed by a court. Unless a proviso that confidentiality of responses would not be honored if requested by a court of law had been included within the original request for informed consent, we believe the researcher has the obligation to go to jail, if necessary, before making the data available.

Anonymity, while more difficult to achieve and/or guarantee, is preferable in that respondents are more likely to register honest and candid behavior and responses. However, anonymity is obviously forfeited within a face-to-face interview or observational research design.

We would note two significant areas the researcher should consider when deciding upon the anonymity-confidentiality commitment to participants of a given study. First, how sensitive are the data that are being requested and recorded? The more sensitive the nature of the data, the more important is the issue of confidentiality. While not everyone will perceive the same dimensions as sensitive, we would recommend pursuit of a conservative orientation. A commitment of confidentiality to respondents in a research effort that is designed to focus upon any social problem area, e.g., drug usage, alcohol consumption, or teenage parenthood, should be especially strong.

Secondly, researchers must be aware of respondent concern regarding storage of data. The contemporary era of computers has made possible the preservation of data for as long as one might want. Respondents may be aware of frightening stories where computer data banks had been accessed by unauthorized persons. If so, it is understandable why high levels of anxiety might be present. The researcher must assure the potential respondents that their responses cannot be traced back to them.

Beyond the safeguards that the researcher might adopt to reduce the degree of risk to participants, funding agencies and the host institutions of investigators are increasingly requiring additional considerations. Funding agencies, both governmental and private, are currently requesting assurance that respondents will not be subjected to any unnecessary risk as a condition of their provision of funds. In some cases, this validation must come from evaluations of the research design by outside or independent persons.

In many instances, the independent evaluation must come from a review board of the host institution. Most universities now employ an administrative person who generally serves as the state attorney general's representative and, thus, carries substantial influence. At this person's directive, a *human-subjects committee* is formed with the responsibility to review every research proposal of study to be conducted on that campus that involves human respondents. Further, the human-subjects committee has access to a number of general guidelines recently enacted into law by the federal government.

Since these are relatively new additions to the research process, they are sometimes troublesome

and their guidelines inappropriately applied. For example, in one situation of which we are aware, the university committee required the reading of a list of every conceivable risk that might apply to human subjects in research, including those that would only be applicable to participants in dental or medical research efforts. Some of these risks can be quite frightening and, no doubt, have discouraged persons from participating in social science research, even though such risks clearly did not exist in the research project they were being asked to join.

Despite this type of overkill on behalf of some, we would argue it is better to err on the side of conservatism. We would note, however, that mistreatment of participants and long-term harm in social science research have been rare.[6] But this absence of deleterious consequences does not minimize the importance of vigilance in examining ethical considerations.

COST-BENEFIT ANALYSIS

Ultimately, the primary agent to determine if a proposed research project will violate acceptable ethical standards is the investigator. The additional checks we have discussed can most accurately be perceived as adjuncts to assist the researcher to remain within acceptable ethical parameters. An area that is helpful in arriving at an eventual decision involves an evaluation of the relative costs of conducting the study in terms of the relative benefits. This is known as a *cost-benefit analysis*. One approach is to argue that if the benefits outweigh the costs, the study is ethical. As Diener and Crandall accurately note, this is simply a more euphemistic way of saying the ends justify the means.[7]

On the surface, it would appear that the potential for making this assessment is reasonably straightforward in biomedical research, but not so easily determined for social science investigations. In fact, it is impossible to weigh the costs or benefits of any proposed intervention prior to data collection and analysis. We would argue, therefore, that some of the suggestions offered in the sampling chapters regarding randomized selection must be reconsidered in light of some types of research.

Permit us to illustrate this complex issue with a longitudinal examination of adolescent parenthood conducted at The Johns Hopkins University School of Medicine.[8] In 1974 an adolescent pregnancy program was established in the Department of Obstetrics and Gynecology at Johns Hopkins. This program resulted from extensive data analysis of The Johns Hopkins Child Development Study begun in 1959. While this study had a sample size of 4,557, only 706 were adolescents (16 years of age or less) at the time of delivery. These mothers and their children were studied at specified intervals over the following seven years. From the resultant observations, a need for education to supplement obstetrical services was recognized.

The resultant program called for any recipient of medical care to also participate in the educational component involving such considerations as nutrition, sex education, and well-baby care. The hospital continued to manage a clinical obstetrical program, which was free of any educational requirements. The question here is whether it is ethical to randomly assign pregnant adolescents to these two treatment modalities in order to maximize satisfaction of an ideal research protocol. In our opinion, and that of The Johns Hopkins University School of Medicine, it was not. It was argued that those participants who wished to participate in the education-treatment group should be permitted to do so, while those who did not should not be forced into such.

While the benefits of exposure to the educational component far outweigh other considerations, to force inclusion also denies the possibility of informed consent. Conversely, but in retrospect, the outcome measures of this program point clearly to the benefits. For example, prior to the development of this obstetrical-educational program, 90 percent of the teenage mothers within the Hopkins catchment area withdrew from school and never returned. This trend has almost been reversed with 87 percent of the teen mothers who experienced this program electing not to leave

school during pregnancy, returning to school following the delivery of their child, or graduating from high school. As one might anticipate, these additional educational credentials have reflected positively upon eventual economic accomplishments. Further, the rate of repeat pregnancy has been dramatically reduced, with only 5 percent becoming pregnant again within the first year and 11 percent within 18 months. Similarly, the incidence of premature delivery has been reduced to below 10 percent. Conversely, the teenage mothers who elected to receive only obstetrical services have continued to reflect high dropout rates, a high rate of unemployment, and a significantly higher incidence of repeat pregnancies.

Clearly, it would not be reasonable to argue these two treatment modalities reflect a classical experimental design. The absence of random assignment to the respective groups eliminates any possibility of representativeness as would be required. However, they do offer the opportunity to gain a general insight into the efficacy of the test stimulus, in this case the educational component. Researchers who elect to use such nonrepresentative samples when addressing the higher ethical question of forced inclusion-exclusion often refer to a *comparison group*. While the comparison group does not provide as accurate a barometer as a control group, it is more ethically acceptable.

While these statistics are impressive, the researchers are open to the question of self-selection. That is, did the more mature and aware adolescents select the program that offered more? Perhaps, but having to respond to this charge seems preferable to arbitrarily denying someone freedom of choice.

A final consideration regarding informed consent is focused upon persons who are unable to responsibly decide for themselves. This primarily includes children and persons who suffer from mental retardation. The researcher is not excused in these circumstances from obtaining informed consent. Consent must be granted by those persons who are legally responsible for the care and supervision of such individuals. In the case of children, informed consent may be attained from parents or guardians. Further, consent from school administrators must also be attained if children are to participate in an investigation as students.

Assuming the investigator has met the general parameters of ethical concern by obtaining informed consent for the participation of dependent persons from parents, guardians, and organizational administrators, we would also argue, if it is possible to do so, for attaining informed consent from the participants as well. For example, children beyond the youngest of age groups are certainly capable of deciding whether or not they wish to be a respondent. It would seem unethical to us to force a child to be an unwilling participant, even though informed consent had been offered by parents, guardians, and/or school administrators.

THE RESEARCHER'S ETHICAL POSTURE

Scientific Integrity

Concern with ethical treatment of the respondent does not conclude the researcher's ethical obligations. The most basic rule an investigator must follow is that "research must be conducted objectively and reported honestly."[9] As we discussed in Chapter 2, science is oriented toward the accumulation of reliable knowledge. Without such knowledge, accuracy in our understanding of the world in which we live cannot be improved.

Although fraudulent or manufactured results are sometimes purposely presented to enhance one's personal reputation or to facilitate receipt of additional funding, we would argue that outright fraud is rare. We are not saying, however, that this necessarily translates into accurately reported results. The need for caution regarding acceptance of results that are reported is underlined if we accept the widely cited idea that scientists are accurate in only half of their predictions.[10] If this is the case for studies in which extensive literature searches have been conducted, it is clear that purported studies in which fabricated results are reported could not possibly register a very impressive accuracy ratio. That is, guessed results cannot compete with properly conducted research in which only one-half of the hypotheses tested are supported.

Interference with accuracy can evolve from a number of directions. Some bias is introduced from the inception of a research project. We have noted earlier that every research effort is stimulated by the existence of a problem. Whether the problem is uniquely perceived by the investigator and is pursued under the rubric of *pure research* or is recognized from a more widespread interest and, therefore, falls under the label of *applied research,* the selection of an area to investigate reflects a value orientation by the researcher by virtue of its selection. This bias is exaggerated by the election of any intervention effort or stimulus to which the respondents are to be exposed.

While we would argue that most scientists do not purposefully misinterpret or misrepresent their data and results, bias can and does enter the picture. The manner in which data are collected can influence the direction or nature of responses. The wording of the items on the schedule used in a questionnaire or interview situation may influence the direction and degree of agreement or disagreement. Subliminal cues provided by the interviewer may also be read by the respondent. Therefore, researchers in contact with respondents should remember to present themselves pleasantly but not to offer their values as a backdrop for the respondents.

Another source by which bias can be introduced is by the deliberate or accidental errors introduced by researchers through carelessness and/or ignorance. This type of bias is most prevalent in the data-analysis stage of a research effort. Appropriate statistical assessments must be selected, and the resultant values must be interpreted accurately. One should request input from knowledgeable sources if unsure of the technique to employ or the interpretation to register. If major policy decisions are to be based upon the results, the financial and human consequences may be considerable.[11]

Sponsorship Concerns

A major area of bias potential has to do with sponsorship of the research. It is always pleasant to receive funding for a research effort one is anxious to undertake. However, there are occasions when the funding comes with too many conditions to be acceptable. These conditions are often presented in a subtle manner so that the researcher must be alert to the possibility of sponsor expectations that would violate his or her ethical code. The researcher may find that a certain result or set of results is expected. This is most likely to occur with private sponsors and particularly those whose primary interest is focused upon a profit motive. We now know we can influence the direction of results by the manner we collect the data, by selecting those from whom we will collect the data, or by suppressing results that might be contrary to the expectations of the sponsor. All of these techniques must be avoided in the maintenance of integrity and preservation of an ethical approach to research.

PUBLICATION SAFEGUARDS

As we have noted, the history of how knowledge from physical, biochemical, and medical research has been used does not permit us to conclude that all research is conducted for our benefit and welfare. While we might argue for efforts to maintain ethical neutrality in social science research, it is not reasonable to assume such neutrality will necessarily be achieved. Indeed, we are not always aware of the bias we take with us into a research effort.

Beyond recognition of potential bias in the conduct of an investigation, researchers are responsible for how and where any knowledge is published and distributed. If one has received funding for a research effort, the funding agency often has proprietary rights to the data and any publication that results. Clearly, the investigator would be aware of this condition at the time the grant or contract was offered. The researcher should evaluate this requirement in terms of what the agency might do with the resultant information. One is well advised to remember that for anything that can be ethically used, the same information can often be employed in an abusive manner. For example, an investigation of a drug subculture might result in some ideas to effectively and humanely combat drug addiction. However, that same information could be used to stage a raid and mass arrest of those persons who have permitted the researcher access to their life-styles.

The researcher can generally feel comfortable in publication efforts with professional journals and governmental agencies. Certainly most readers of these materials are collegial students of the same phenomena and will treat any presented information in an ethical manner.

To further guard against misuse, however, many researchers elect to present data in an aggregate, or grouped, manner. You will recall this approach facilitates insurance of confidentiality of respondents. While aggregation of data does not guarantee against misuse, it does reduce that likelihood by eliminating easy identification of the respondents or the population that they represent. Similarly, the use of pseudonyms for individuals, groups, and places being studied can be helpful. However, the investigator electing this approach must exercise considerable care in the selection of such names, labels, and descriptions. In some cases, researchers using pseudonyms have not adequately disguised their descriptions, and persons and places have been easily identified.

SUMMARY

Concern with ethical standards as they apply to sociological research has grown to such an extent that two of the discipline's journals, *Social Problems* and the *American Sociologist,* have devoted entire issues to them.[12]

In this chapter we have tapped the most significant ethical issues of which the researcher should be aware and address in the formulation of a research strategy.[13] Investigators carry a responsibility to be sensitive to respondents and to the responsibility they shoulder as scientific researchers. The primary responsibility of the scientist is to take precautionary steps to prevent harm and minimize any risk factors that the respondent might encounter as a participant in the research. Ideally, this would represent the elimination of risk, but that is virtually impossible to achieve.

The attainment of informed consent helps ease the responsibility in that those unwilling to assume some risk are afforded the opportunity to withdraw from the study. While concern is registered for any potential participant, special care should be afforded the less enfranchised persons, e.g., children, the mentally retarded, inmates of penal institutions, and less affluent persons.

When informed consent cannot be gained prior to gathering data, for fear of reactivity or data contamination, the researcher should engage in a careful examination of the ethics involved. The study proposal should be reviewed by others, a cost-benefit analysis performed, and a plan for informing and debriefing built into the proposal.

While it is recognized that value-free social science is not a realistic possibility, the researcher is encouraged to constantly be alert to his or her own biases and struggle to prevent their introduction. This obligation continues through the publication phase of the project and demands vigilantly maintaining an alertness to what usage the resultant knowledge is being put.

KEY TERMS

Anonymity	Debriefing	Informed consent
Applied research	Deception	Pure research
Comparison group	Forewarning	Role playing
Confidentiality	Human-subjects committee	Situation ethics
Cost-benefit analysis		

REVIEW QUESTIONS

1. Discuss the concept of respondent reactivity and its relationship to the research strategy of deception. What is the ethical dilemma here?

2. Discuss the strategies for reducing risk or harm. Under what conditions would these be irrelevant or unobtainable?

3. How does a comparison group differ from a control group in an experimental or quasi-experimental data-gathering design?

4. What is the difference between anonymity and confidentiality? Which data-gathering designs permit anonymity and which do not?

5. Discuss the tension between the scientific goal of obtaining unbiased data and the researcher's attempt to design an ethical study.

6. In what ways could an experimental study which has a control group be ethical at the same time?

7. How does the demand to be ethical affect the researcher as a person?

APPENDIX A

A Brief Guide to the Research Proposal

INTRODUCTION

If the preparation of a research proposal is an integral part of your research methods experience, that which follows is a suggested guide to its content, format, and organization. Some proposals may not contain all the items suggested in the guide. Obviously, any real proposal and its subsections will be appropriate to the nature of the particular research topic that is being investigated. We have attempted to include as many of the issues and possibilities involved in a proposal of research as is feasible. There are several omissions, which are really only of interest to those individuals who would be applying for funds from some sponsoring agency: (1) a working guide suggesting the time-line over which the study would be done and the cost of equipment, staff salaries, training research workers, and similar items, and (2) publication or reporting plans.

Since this may be the first formal attempt at conceiving of a research proposal for most of the readers of this book, we have felt under some obligation to attempt to include as many different possibilities as we can practically include. Further, there are crucial interactions between research methodology, on the one hand, and the conceptual model, on the other hand. Therefore, the reader should come to some understanding of the relationships among methodology, conceptualization, and statistical analysis in working through the outline suggested in this Appendix. Indeed, these interactions are important general themes that we have tried to emphasize and illustrate throughout this text.

If all this seems somewhat confusing, realize that sociologists have developed a sequential procedure for *organizing the presentation* of these various ideas. That is, while the *actual process of doing research* is quite varied, the *format for reporting* what one proposes to do or what one has actually done is reasonably well standardized. It is this standardized reporting format that concerns us in this Appendix.

We believe that the proposal is an integral part of the process of doing a scientific study, and several points should be noted. First, the proposal really contains two basic divisions: (1) the conceptual model (Chapters 1 and 2), which is essentially theoretical and says *what* you intend to do and (2) the methodology section (Chapter 3), which tells the reader how you intend to accomplish the investigation. While the conceptual model and the methodology relate to different objectives, these two sections are complementary and interrelated. Second, research and theory do not exist as mutually exclusive subsets of sociology but provide the mutual support that makes possible the generation of new and relevant knowledge. Third, one of the most important considerations in any proposal is that the scientist justify each important decision that is made. Thus, the scientist is not only telling the reader what and how but also why certain decisions are being made. Fourth, a corollary to this third point, and one which is not too obvious, is that the proposal is an exercise in the inherent use of logic. For example, the methodological decision to one-category control a particular variable is contained within the conceptual model that the researcher has constructed to guide the study. Finally, each section of the proposal is either an outgrowth of some previous section and/or a response to the nature of what the scientist believes is necessary for the development of reliable knowledge.

In sum, the proposal functions as an illustration of the organization of thought necessary for the development of scientific knowledge about a research topic as perceived by the sociologist. It deals with specifics and technical items, but it is also an illustration of the underlying logic, rules of evidence, and assumptions demanded by the scientific method. It is hoped that you will come to understand how what may appear to be a number of disparate items really do coalesce into a coherent whole.

With these considerations in mind, we turn to the nature of the research proposal itself. Of course, the first page of any proposal must be the title page, which indicates the general parameters of the proposed study. Also included on this first page of the proposal should be the author's name and institutional affiliation. The next section should be the preface, if one is included. While not obligatory, the preface can function as a place where the author may make some sort of statement that the author wants to include but which is not appropriate at any other place in the proposal.

The table of contents follows, which we offer for illustrative purposes. Note carefully the wording of the chapter titles, what the subsections of each chapter are, and the order in which these items appear.

TABLE OF CONTENTS

CHAPTER 1

Statement of the Problem

Research Topic.   In this subsection, one should present a very brief, general statement in one or two paragraphs of the substantive area of your research interest. Define theoretically only those concepts that need to be so defined.

Rationale.   This subsection should include a justification of the importance of your selected topic. This is the sales part of the first chapter, in which you attempt to convince the reader of the necessity, hence the worthiness, of your projected research. This subsection is normally longer than the first subsection of this chapter, but it still can be kept to two to four paragraphs. Some of the possible justifications which you can make for any study are that (1) the study is timely, because it addresses a strongly felt need in the society; (2) it fills a theoretical void in the existing literature; (3) it addresses a methodological problem; (4) its results will affect a large number of people, such as a study on the consequences of bureaucracy; (5) the results, while appropriate to only a small group, deal with a group that is important (for example, the medical profession) or powerful (for example, the federal government); (6) the results will help to define more clearly a central concept (for example, social structure); and (7) the results will help to broaden the use of a theoretical idea to a larger context (for example, taking labeling theory from the context of delinquency to see if labeling also occurs with reference to drug addicts).[1]

As you can see, the number of possible justifications is large, and we are sure that you can enlarge on the above list if you care to do so. An important consideration to remember here is that one should not overjustify one's study. If you claim too many consequences, you may have trouble living up to your claims in the final draft of your study.

CHAPTER 2

Review of the Literature

Relevant Literature.   In this subsection, you should present a summary of the conceptual model with which you will interpret your research. While a variety of conceptual approaches may have been available, as evidenced by the review of the literature, your task is normally not to inventory this variety. You should summarize the one perspective you have chosen to use. This section will provide a conceptual rationale for the concepts and constructs that you include in your propositions and their particular status (e.g., independent, dependent, or controlled). What is expected here is a

---

*No actual page numbers have been added in this example.
†These sections are only necessary if applying for funds.

grounding of your study in some type of conceptual model that will justify your proposition and facilitate the interpretation of the data that you will collect. This first subsection will be the major part of this chapter and can run from a few pages to a quite lengthy section, depending on the complexity of your conceptual framework.

Proposition(s) to Be Investigated.   In this last subsection of the second chapter, you should state specifically what your proposition or propositions are and theoretically define those concepts and constructs whose meaning would not be clear to the reader. It is here that the independent factor or factors and the dependent factor or factors should be specified as well. This subsection should be quite brief, not extending to more than two short paragraphs.

Indeed, we suggest a rather stylized, yet very clear, format—an example of which follows: "Social class varies positively with income and educational attainment, holding constant race, sex, age, and nature of one's occupation." The above proposition contains seven concepts: social class, income, educational attainment, race, sex, age, and nature of one's occupation. The first three—social class, income, and education—are clearly the class I objects of the researcher's interest, while race, sex, age, and nature of one's occupation have been selected as class II, controlled, factors. In one sentence, the researcher can clearly identify the factors in the study, determine their status, and specify the nature of the relationship among the class I factors. One additional sentence should be included that can define theoretically those concepts or constructs that need to be so defined and that can identify the independent and the dependent factors.

CHAPTER 3

Methodology

Introduction.   The review of the literature is also useful in this chapter of the proposal as well. In the previous chapter, the literature review was used to indicate guidelines on what to do. In this chapter the literature should be used to suggest how others have handled the methodological problems in the previous studies in your

subject area. Citing the professional literature in this chapter is as necessary as in the second chapter.

Research Design.   This subsection provides an overview of the remainder of this chapter. Here you should use several sentences to present an overview of the major methodological decisions that you have made. In other words, is the study cross-sectional or longitudinal? Is the data-collection procedure to be an experiment, case study, observational study, content analysis, secondary analysis, survey, or some combination of different procedures?* If one chooses the survey approach, will this survey take the form of a questionnaire or an interview? If a composite measure is appropriate, will it be an index or a scale? Are the items presented to the respondent going to be general or specific? Are the response categories also going to be structured or unstructured? Will the items take the format of questions, statements, or both? Are the respondents a population or a sample? If a sample is proposed, what kind is it and how is it to be selected? In what form will the data be presented? Finally, what type of statistical analysis (if any) has been chosen to analyze these data?

Below are two sentences that provide an example of the format and the type of answers given to the above questions.

> *This study will be a <u>longitudinal survey</u> employing the <u>questionnaire</u> data-gathering technique using an <u>index</u> with <u>specific questions</u> and with <u>structured</u> response categories on a <u>disproportional stratified</u> sample drawn by a <u>systematic</u> process. These data will be presented in <u>tabular</u> form and analyzed with an <u>associational</u> statistic.*

Each concept underlined in the above illustration represents a decision made by the researcher. Of course, the underlining has been done for the purposes of illustration and should not be done in the actual proposal. We strongly urge you to present some reasonable facsimile as the first paragraph in the research design section. To do so helps the reader to make the transition from the theoretical discussion of the conceptual model to the methodological discussion, which is to follow. Thus, in a couple of sentences, you have presented the reader with the methodological "forest" before plunging into the "trees."

---

*For the purposes of the remainder of this illustration, we will assume that the data-gathering procedure will take the format of a survey, since this data-gathering procedure will maximize the number of issues with which we may deal. Other data-gathering procedures generally do not contain as many issues as does the survey design.

In the succeeding paragraphs of this subsection, one should justify the choices that have been presented in the initial paragraph. Further, it is most logical to present your reasons in the order in which the choices appeared. While it is desirable to say why you are going to do some thing a particular way, it is unnecessary to cite reasons why you failed to choose alternative ways of achieving your objectives. It is assumed that you have looked at all the reasonable alternatives and that the choice you've indicated was the best for the reason cited. Finally, while justifications are necessary, one should not club the reader over the head with a course in research methodology. That is, cite the *one best* reason for any particular choice, rather than multiple justifications, which can be time-consuming and laborious.

Nature of the Sample [Population].   From this point on until you reach the end of the proposal, you will be expanding the general decisions made in the research design subsection of this chapter by specifying the detailed procedures to be followed. In this subsection, the persons, groups, or cases to be analyzed should be discussed. How many people will be selected? Where will you get them? Do you need anyone's help to obtain your respondents? If so, how will this help be solicited? If you ultimately believe that you will be working from a list of people, how will you deal with that list? What is the first thing you will do with or to the list? What comes next? What is the final step to be followed in working with the list? (We refer you back to Chapter 6, where we presented an example of working with an already-formed sampling frame.)

It is important to be very specific. The reader must have enough details so that he or she could do the procedure that you are proposing. Where appropriate, justifications should be given for the decisions made. Finally, you will be proposing to study a sample or a population, but certainly not both.

Operationalization.   It is in this subsection that the content, format, and issues revolving around the actual measuring instrument that you will use should be discussed. If a pilot study is needed, it should be discussed at this point. If a composite measure is to be used, a full explanation of it belongs here. If an index is proposed, what are the specific items, in what order will they be presented, where will they be placed on the page or pages, what response categories are proposed (if any), and where will they be placed? Will any general social or identification items be necessary, and, if so, what are

they and where will they appear? What kind of directions need to be placed on the measuring instrument? If structured response categories are used, how will they be coded? All these questions (and more) are answered and illustrated by the actual construction of a measuring instrument as shown in an appendix (notice the title of appendix A in the illustrative table of contents cited earlier in this Appendix). In the text, you should briefly mention certain descriptive characteristics of the measuring instrument, such as how many total items comprise the composite measure (if that is appropriate) and what the response categories are and how they are coded. Should any of the items in the measuring instrument be weighted, and, if so, what weights should be assigned to which items? Further discussion can focus on such issues as the response set or the acquiescence tendency and how it is to be recognized should your attempts to minimize its occurrence fail. Finally, remember again that you must justify your choices.

Once constructed, the measuring instrument must be tested. First, the pretest functions to eliminate ambiguities, misinterpretations, and similar difficulties. On whom will the pretest be done? How many persons will you select and from where will you get them? Second, the reliability test functions to check the measuring instrument's ability to measure consistently the same phenomenon. How will this test be done? On whom? With which specific test procedure? What results constitute a demonstration of reliability? If such is not obtained, what will you do? Finally, the third test is the validity test, which checks the measuring instrument's capacity to measure what it claims to measure. How is this to be accomplished? On whom? With what desired level of accuracy?

In sum, this subsection addresses the nature of the actual measuring instrument and its formal testing prior to its use on the main or study population or sample. Consideration is also given to the rationales for the decisions made.

Data Collection.   Assuming that the sample has been drawn and the measuring instrument constructed and tested, the researcher must now determine how those persons selected for the study will be contacted. This constitutes a subsection of varying length. Indeed, in some cases this subsection may not be necessary at all.

If a mailed questionnaire is to be used, the cover letter and follow-up letters are mentioned here and suitable examples placed in an appendix (notice the title of appendix B in the illustrative table of contents presented earlier in this Appendix). The mail-back bias and similar issues relevant to mailed questionnaires must be discussed. If an interview is to be done, then the letter introducing the respondent to the study must be presented as well as any other procedures deemed appropriate to the data-gathering process. If some observational technique (e.g., participant observation) is proposed, the specific type and its attending difficulties should be presented. Again, justifications with supporting citations of the literature are necessary for those decisions that are made.

In sum, if one perceives an actual research study in chronological time, the researcher will have concluded the work in the field after carrying out the procedures proposed in this and the preceding subsections of this third chapter.

Data Presentation. At this point, the raw data of the study have been collected. In this subsection, the writer should explain how these data will be manipulated and presented for the reader's perusal. You have a number of possibilities from which to select. For example, you could present individual scores on all the variables in some sort of a matrix, or you could present grouped data in some kind of tabular format. If you elect to present a table or number of tables, then you must decide how to divide your variables into subcategories, how many tables to have, where you will place the independent variable or variables, how you will handle any controlled variables that you might have proposed, and what to put within the cells of the table itself—frequencies, percentages, or both. Your mode of data presentation will be particularly influenced by the choices you presented earlier in the second Chapter in the "Proposition(s) to Be Investigated" subsection, by some choices made in the sampling procedures, and by the actual results obtained from the measuring instrument itself. Again, we stress that while many decisions in the research process may seem somewhat disparate from other decisions, this is not so. Research—or, more properly, good research, is a whole series of different but interlocking and interrelated conscious, rational, and purposeful decisions.

Interpretation of the Results. Finally, some decision relative to the magnitude of the statistical results (suggested in the preceding subsection), which is necessary for rejection or failure to reject the stated hypothesis, is required. Since the facts do not speak for themselves, you must select and state some reasonable minimum

value of your selected statistic that you propose for determining the status of the hypothesis. Any other data interpretation requirements should also be presented in this subsection, which may be only a couple of sentences.

Other Matters. With the conclusion of the "Interpretation of the Results" subsection, your proposal is finished (with the exception of the appendices and a selected bibliography). Therefore, this subsection of the proposal does not normally appear, but we needed to make a couple of additional points, so we added this subsection.

First, you should notice that this guide follows the actual format of a proposal. In other words, the guide itself illustrates the proper chapter titles and subheading titles, the desired order of these items, and similar stylistic points. Of course, your particular university may have some variations on this basic theme. If you are about to write your master's thesis or doctoral dissertation, it is best to check with your institution before embarking. Of course, some alterations in the above suggestions can be made to tailor your proposal to any specific, idiosyncratic need.

Second, the table of contents that appeared earlier in this Appendix exemplifies a format that should be closely followed. In the example given, certain appendixes have been listed which, in reality, do not appear in this particular example of a proposal. This was done to provide an example of the type and of the format of the table of contents that you are likely to need, rather than one that was totally indicative of the material included in this particular Appendix.

Third, appendixes themselves are very useful items. When presenting appendixes, you should present them in the order in which they were referred to in the text. Further, each appendix should have a title and be listed in the table of contents. Also, different appendixes should be used for different material.

Fourth, you may elect (and we strongly recommend that you do) to group all the footnotes in a section called "Appendix (with its appropriate letter): Endnotes" and place it just prior to the selected bibliography.

Finally, in the last item in the proposal, the selected bibliography, you should cite only those works that you have used in the proposal. For most of us, the quantity of citations will rarely influence the reader either positively or negatively. What is, of course, important is the type of use you have made of the literature that you have cited.

APPENDIX   B

Table of Random Numbers

12159	66144	05091	13446	45653	13684	66024	91410	51351	22772
30156	90519	95785	47544	66735	35754	11088	67310	19720	08379
59069	01722	53338	41942	65118	71236	01932	70343	25812	62275
54107	58081	82470	59407	13475	95872	16268	78436	39251	64247
99681	81295	06315	28212	45029	57701	96327	85436	33614	29070
27252	37875	53679	01889	35714	63534	63791	76342	47717	73684
93259	74585	11863	78985	03881	46567	93696	93521	54970	37607
84068	43759	75814	32261	12728	09636	22336	75629	01017	45503
68582	97054	28251	63787	57285	18854	35006	16343	51867	67979
60646	11298	19680	10087	66391	70853	24423	73007	74958	29020
97437	52922	80739	59178	50628	61017	51652	40915	94696	67843
58009	20681	98823	50979	01237	70152	13711	73916	87902	84759
77211	70110	93803	60135	22881	13423	30999	07104	27400	25414
54256	84591	65302	99257	92970	28924	36632	54044	91798	78018
37493	69330	94069	39544	14050	03476	25804	49350	92525	87941
87569	22661	55970	52623	35419	76660	42394	63210	62626	00581
22896	62237	39635	63725	10463	87944	92075	90914	30599	35671
02697	33230	64527	97210	41359	79399	13941	88378	68503	33609
20080	15652	37216	00679	02088	34138	13953	68939	05630	27653
20550	95151	60557	57449	77115	87372	02574	07851	22428	39189
72771	11672	67492	42904	64647	94354	45994	42538	54885	15983
38472	43379	76295	69406	96510	16529	83500	28590	49787	29822
24511	56510	72654	13277	45031	42235	96502	25567	23653	36707
01054	06674	58283	82831	97048	42983	06471	12350	49990	04809
94437	94907	95274	26487	60496	78222	43032	04276	70800	17378
97842	69095	25982	03484	25173	05982	14624	31653	17170	92785
53047	13486	69712	33567	82313	87631	03197	02438	12374	40329
40770	47013	63306	48154	80970	87976	04939	21233	20572	31013
52733	66251	69661	58387	72096	21355	51659	19003	75556	33095
41749	46502	18378	83141	63920	85516	75743	66317	45428	45940
10271	85184	46468	38860	24039	80949	51211	35411	40470	16070
98791	48848	68129	51024	53044	55039	71290	26484	70682	56255
30196	09295	47685	56768	29285	06272	98789	47188	35063	24158
99373	64343	92433	06388	65713	35386	43370	19254	55014	98621
27768	27552	42156	23239	46823	91077	06306	17756	84459	92513
67791	35910	56921	51976	78475	15336	92544	82601	17996	72268
64018	44004	08136	56129	77024	82650	18163	29158	33935	94262
79715	33859	10835	94936	02857	87486	70613	41909	80667	52176
20190	40737	82688	07099	65255	52767	65930	45861	32575	93731
82421	01208	49762	66360	00231	87540	88302	62686	38456	25872
00083	81269	35320	72064	10472	92080	80447	15259	62654	70882
56558	09762	20813	48719	35530	96437	96343	21212	32567	34305
41183	20460	08608	75283	43401	25888	73405	35639	92114	48006

39977	10603	35052	53751	64219	36235	84687	42091	42587	16996
29310	84031	03052	51356	44747	19678	14619	03600	08066	93899
47360	03571	95657	85065	80919	14890	97623	57375	77855	15735
48481	98262	50414	41929	05977	78903	47602	52154	47901	84523
48097	56362	16342	75261	27751	28715	21871	37943	17850	90999
20648	30751	96515	51581	43877	94494	80164	02115	09738	51938
60704	10107	59220	64220	23944	34684	83696	82344	19020	84834
03689	33090	43465	96789	56688	32389	88206	06534	10558	14478
43367	46409	44751	73410	35138	24910	70748	57336	56043	68550
45357	52080	62670	73877	20604	40408	98060	96733	65094	80335
62683	03171	77195	92515	78041	27590	42651	00254	73179	10159
04841	40918	69047	68986	08150	87984	08887	76083	37702	28523
85963	06992	65321	43521	46393	40491	06028	43865	58190	28142
03720	78942	61990	90812	98452	74098	69738	83272	39212	42817
10159	85560	35619	58248	65498	77977	02896	45198	10655	13973
80162	35686	57877	19552	63931	44171	40879	94532	17828	31848
74388	92906	65829	24572	79417	38460	96294	79201	47755	90980
12660	09571	29743	45447	64063	46295	44191	53957	62393	42229
81852	60620	87757	72165	23875	87844	84038	04994	93466	27418
03068	61317	65305	64944	27319	55263	84514	38374	11657	67723
29623	58530	17274	16908	39253	37595	57497	74780	88624	93333
30520	50588	51231	83816	01075	33098	81308	59036	49152	86262
93694	02984	91350	33929	41724	32403	42566	14232	55085	65628
86737	40641	37958	25415	19922	65966	98044	39583	26828	50919
28141	15630	37675	52545	24813	22075	05152	15374	84533	12933
79804	05165	21620	98400	55290	71877	60052	46320	79055	45913
63763	49985	88853	70681	52762	17670	62337	12199	44123	37993
49618	47068	63331	62675	51788	58283	04295	72904	05378	98085
26502	68980	26545	14204	34304	50284	47730	57299	73966	02566
13549	86048	27912	56733	14987	09850	78217	85168	09538	92347
89221	78076	40306	34045	52557	52383	67796	41382	50490	30117
97809	34056	76778	60417	05153	83827	67369	08602	56163	28793
65668	44694	34151	51741	11484	13226	49516	17391	39956	34839
53653	59804	59051	95074	38307	99546	32962	26962	86252	50704
34922	95041	17398	32789	26860	55536	82415	82911	42208	62725
74880	65198	61357	90209	71543	71114	94868	05645	44154	72254
66036	48794	30021	92601	21615	16952	18433	44903	51322	90379
39044	99503	11442	81344	57068	74662	90382	59433	48440	38146
87756	71151	68543	08358	10183	06432	97482	90301	76114	83778
47117	45575	29524	02522	08041	70698	80260	73588	86415	72523
71572	02109	96722	21684	64331	71644	18933	32801	11644	12364
35609	58072	63209	48429	53108	59173	55337	22445	85940	43707

(continued)

81703	70069	74981	12197	48426	77365	26769	65078	27849	41311
88979	88161	56531	46443	47148	42773	18601	38532	22594	12395
90279	42308	00380	17181	38757	09071	89804	15232	99007	39495
49266	18921	06498	88005	72736	81848	92716	96279	94582	22792
50897	22569	48402	80376	65470	19157	49729	19615	79087	47039
20950	65643	52280	37103	66977	65141	18522	39333	59824	73084
32682	51645	11382	75341	03189	94128	06275	22345	86856	77394
72525	65092	65086	47094	14781	61486	61895	85698	53028	61682
70502	57550	29699	36797	35862	90894	93217	96158	94321	12012
63087	03802	03142	72582	44267	56028	01576	69840	67727	77419
16418	07903	74344	89861	62952	49262	86210	65676	96617	38081
67730	17532	39489	28035	13415	83494	26750	01440	01161	16346
27274	98848	59506	28124	33596	89623	21006	94898	03550	88629
44250	52829	22614	21323	28597	66402	15425	39845	01823	19639
57476	33687	81784	05811	66625	17690	46170	93914	82346	82851

Codebook for Opinion Research Study: Spring 1990

"9" = missing and "99" = missing for two digit variable

Record/ Column	Variable Name	Variable Label [Maximum of 20 Characters]
1/ 1–2	[blank]	
1/ 3–4	RECNO	'Record Number' = Code "/1"
1/ 5	[blank]	
1/ 6–8	IDR1	'ID Number' = Code 3 digits
1/ 9	[blank]	
1/ 10–13	TIME	'Time Interview Begun' = in military time 0930 = 9:30 in the morning 1130 = 11:30 in the morning 1515 = 3:15 in the afternoon 2045 = 8:45 at night
1/ 14	[blank]	
1/ 15–16	MONTH	'Month' = See below 01 = January 07 = July 02 = February 08 = August 03 = March 09 = September 04 = April 10 = October 05 = May 11 = November 06 = June 12 = December
1/ 17–18	DATE	'Date' = Code 2 digits

Record/ Column	Variable Name	Variable Label [Maximum of 20 Characters]
1/ 19–20	YEAR	'Year' = Code last 2 digits
1/ 21	[blank]	

1/ 22–23	NAME	'Interviewer' = See below

01	=	Andrew Anderson	06 = Mike Murphy
02	=	Barry Baker	07 = Patrick Perry
03	=	Charles Carter	08 = Ron Rogers
04	=	Frank Felino	09 = Sam Spade
05	=	Larry Luckinbaugh	10 = Tom Thompson

Record/Column	Variable Name	Variable Label
1/ 24–25	[blank]	
1/ 26	V1	'Get along' = See (+) below
1/ 27	V2	'No laugh' = See (−) below
1/ 28	V3	'Hard luck' = See (−) below
1/ 29	V4	'Feel good' = See (+) below
1/ 30	V5	'Happy work' = See (+) below
1/ 31	[blank]	
1/ 32	V6	'Have doubts' = See (−) below
1/ 33	V7	'Level-headed' = See (+) below
1/ 34	V8	'No attention' = See (−) below
1/ 35	V9	'Wrong choice' = See (−) below
1/ 36	V10	'Morning' = See (+) below

Codes for Positive (+) Items	Codes for Negative (−) Items
4 = Strongly agree	0 = Strongly agree
3 = Agree	1 = Agree
2 = No opinion	2 = No opinion
1 = Disagree	3 = Disagree
0 = Strongly disagree	4 = Strongly disagree

Record/ Column	Variable Name	Variable Label [Maximum of 20 Characters]
1/ 37–38	[blank]	
1/ 39–40	V11	'Index Score' = Range: 00 – 40
1/ 41	[blank]	

1/ 42	V12	'Sex'

    1 = Male;   2 = Female

1/ 43–44	V13	'Age' Code = 2 digits (see below)

    Subtract response given from 1990 and record the result.

1/ 45	V14	'Education' = See codes below

    1 = More than college   5 = Technical/trade
    2 = College graduate   6 = High school graduate
    3 = AA degree   7 = Some high school
    4 = Some college   8 = Less than high school

           9 = missing information
           0 = can't remember

1/ 46–47	[blank]	
1/ 48	V15	'Working' = See codes below

    1 = Yes;   2 = No;   9 = No answer

    If not employed, code columns 49 through 53 with "8's".

1/ 49	V16	'Work status' = See codes below

    1 = full-time work (35 or more hours per week)
    2 = part-time work (20 to 34 hours per week)
    3 = some work (10 to 19 hours per week)
    4 = occasional work (under 10 hours per week)
    8 = Not employed and irrelevant (see item 15)

(continued)

Record/ Column	Variable Name	Variable Label [Maximum of 20 Characters]
1/ 50	V17	'Company' = See below

In actuality, there should be only one response: "Social Security Administration". This is because the sample was drawn from the SSA employee files. But this item should be asked to remove any anxiety on the part of the respondent that the SSA is in any way a part of this study.

Code all SSA employees with a "1"

Code all others with a "2", although there should be no such cases. Code those who are unemployed (see item 15) with an "8": irrelevant.

| 1/ 51–52 | V18 | 'Years there' = See below |

23 = 23 years with SSA
00 = less than one year
88 = Irrelevant: not working (see item 15)

Do not be concerned with the new employees who have been with the Social Security Administration less than one year. Code these persons with an "00" as is indicated above.

| 1/ 53 | V19 | 'Occupation' = See below |

1 = Professional (attorney, physician, Ph.D. researcher)
2 = Managerial (department/division head)
3 = Paraprofessional (data analyst, legal secretary)
4 = White collar (clerical, data coder, calculator)
5 = Skilled blue collar (electrician, plumber)
6 = Semi-skilled (carpenter's helper)
7 = Unskilled (janitor, maintenance)

8 = Irrelevant (see item 15)
9 = No response, missing

| 1/ 54–55 | [blank] | |
| 1/ 56 | V20 | 'More school' = See below |

1 = Yes   2 = No (and code columns 57–60 with "8's").

Record/ Column	Variable Name	Variable Label [Maximum of 20 Characters]
1/ 57	V21	'Type' = See below

     1 = Academic school: graduate or professional
     2 = Academic school: college
     3 = Two-year college
     4 = Professional program: nursing, computer
     5 = Trade/specialty: computer repair
     6 = High school or GED program

     8 = Irrelevant (see item 20)
     9 = No response; missing

| 1/ 58–59 | V22 | 'How Long?' = Code 2 digits (see below) |

     04 = 4 years
     00 = Under a year

     88 = Irrelevant (see item 20)

| 1/ 60 | V23 | 'Diploma?' = see below |

     1 = Yes;   3 = No
     2 = Still attending   8 = Irrelevant (see item 20)

| 1/ 61–62 | [blank] | |
| 1/ 63 | V24 | 'Married?' = See below |

     1 = Single   4 = Separated
     2 = Married   5 = Divorced
     3 = Remarried   6 = Other

If the response to this item (V24) is <u>anything</u> other than married (2)
   or remarried (3), code columns 64 through 67 with "8's".

| 1/ 64 | V25 | 'Wife work?' = See below |

  1 = Yes;   2 = No;   8 = Irrelevant (see item 24)

(continued)

Record/ Column	Variable Name	Variable Label [Maximum of 20 Characters]
1/ 65–66	V26	'Hours/Week' = Code 2 digits 07 = 7 hours per week 48 = 48 hours per week 88 = Irrelevant (see item 24)
1/ 67	V27	'Wife's job' = See below 1 = Professional (attorney, physician, Ph.D. researcher) 2 = Managerial (department/division head) 3 = Paraprofessional (data analyst, legal secretary) 4 = White collar (clerical, data coder, calculator) 5 = Skilled blue collar (electrician, plumber) 6 = Semi-skilled (carpenter's helper) 7 = Unskilled (janitor, maintenance) 8 = Irrelevant (see item 15) 9 = No response, missing
1/ 68–71	[blank]	
1/ 72	RECN1	'Record Number' = Code: "1"

---------- RECORD TWO ----------

Record/ Column	Variable Name	Variable Label [Maximum of 20 Characters]
2/ 1–2	[blank]	
2/ 3–4	RECNO	'Record Number' = Code: "/2"
2/ 5	[blank]	
2/ 6–8	IDR2	'ID Number' = Code 3 digits

Record/ Column	Variable Name	Variable Label [Maximum of 20 Characters]
2/ 9–10	[blank]	
2/ 11	V28	'Debt' = See below

1 = Under $10,000   5 = $25,001 – $30,000

2 = $10,000 – $15,000   6 = $30,001 – $50,000

3 = $15,001 – $20,000   7 = Over $50,000

4 = $20,001 – $25,000   8 = No real idea at all

Record/ Column	Variable Name	Variable Label
2/ 12	[blank]	
2/ 13	V29	'Children' = See below

1 = Yes;   2 = No;   8 = Irrelevant (see item 24)

Record/ Column	Variable Name	Variable Label
2/ 14–15	V30	'Number' = Code as 2 digits (if none, "88")
2/ 16–17	[blank]	
2/ 18–19	V31	'Age first' = Code as 2 digits (if none, "88")
2/ 20	[blank]	
2/ 21–22	V32	'Age second' = Code as 2 digits (if none, "88")
2/ 23	[blank]	
2/ 24–25	V33	'Age third' = Code as 2 digits (if none, "88")
2/ 26	[blank]	
2/ 27–28	V34	'Age fourth' = Code as 2 digits (if none, "88")
2/ 29	[blank]	
2/ 30–31	V35	'Age fifth' = Code as 2 digits (if none, "88")

(continued)

```
"9" = missing and "99" = missing for two digit variable
```

Record/ Column	Variable Name	Variable Label [Maximum of 20 Characters]
2/ 32	[blank]	
2/ 33–34	V36	'Age sixth' = Code as 2 digits (if none, "88")
2/ 35–36	[blank]	
2/ 37–38	V37	'At Home' = Code as 2 digits (if none, "88")
2/ 39	[blank]	
2/ 40	V38	'Race' = See below

```
            1 = Black            4 = Oriental

            2 = Hispanic         5 = White

            3 = Native American  6 = Other
```

2/ 41–42	[blank]	
2/ 43–48	V39	'Man's income' = Code answer in 6 digits
2/ 49	[blank]	
2/ 50–55	V40	'Wife's income' = Code answer in 6 digits

If respondent is single, code columns 50–55 with "8's".

| 2/ 56–71 | [blank] | |
| 2/ 72 | RECN2 | 'Record Number' = Code with "2" |

APPENDIX D

The Database for the Study Entitled "Opinion Research"

[If you enter these data into the mainframe computer on your campus, then you may write additional SPSS^x programs to analyze additional variables. If you do so, however, you are warned to enter these data *exactly as they appear here,* since to do otherwise will invalidate some or all of the data definitional commands which appear in Appendix E. The "Column" heading is simply for your convenience in knowing in which positions on the row each keyboard entry is to be made. Obviously, such would not be entered into the mainframe.]

```
Column   10        20        30        40        50        60        70
....|....|....|....|....|....|....|....|....|....|....|....|....|....|
/1 001 1615 051690 01   44424 44442  36 1301   111021   28888   21353    1
/2 001   5 101   03 88 88 88 88 88  01 5  028000 018500                  2
/1 002 1945 051690 02   44232 43433  32 1332   111083   28888   31402    1
/2 002   5 102   07 05 88 88 88 88  02 5  024500 016400                  2
/1 003 1315 051690 05   34443 44342  35 1272   111043   28888   21354    1
/2 003   5 101   04 88 88 88 88 88  01 5  023550 012800                  2
/1 004 1630 051690 03   43343 43331  31 1382   111163   28888   21504    1
/2 004   3 103   14 12 08 88 88 88  03 5  035550 023190                  2
/1 005 2045 051690 04   44344 34441  35 1242   111023   28888   21404    1
/2 005   6 288   88 88 88 88 88 88  88 5  018750 014730                  2
/1 006 2115 051690 07   44444 44441  37 1291   111001   28888   21354    1
/2 006   3 101   06 88 88 88 88 88  01 5  033000 016500                  2
/1 007 1630 051690 06   44444 44442  38 1351   111041   28888   21254    1
/2 007   2 103   10 09 05 88 88 88  03 5  035200 017200                  2
/1 008 1715 051690 08   44344 43431  34 1302   111073   28888   21354    1
/2 008   6 102   07 04 88 88 88 88  02 5  026500 017100                  2
/1 009 2000 051690 09   44344 43443  37 1242   111023   28888   21354    1
/2 009   6 288   88 88 88 88 88 88  88 5  022500 015700                  2
/1 010 1930 051690 10   33443 44231  31 1292   111064   28888   21404    1
/2 010   4 102   06 04 88 88 88 88  02 5  028400 021300                  2
/1 011 1845 051790 01   44444 44442  38 1321   111063   28888   21353    1
/2 011   5 101   09 88 88 88 88 88  01 5  035500 019000                  2
/1 012 2100 051790 02   44343 44241  33 1292   111064   28888   21354    1
/2 012   2 102   06 02 88 88 88 88  02 5  027900 018750                  2
/1 013 2045 051790 03   44343 43431  33 1272   111033   28888   21353    1
/2 013   5 101   05 88 88 88 88 88  01 5  026300 019650                  2
/1 014 2115 051790 04   44434 43442  36 1252   111044   28888   21354    1
/2 014   5 101   07 88 88 88 88 88  01 5  026900 015500                  2
/1 015 2045 051790 05   44344 34433  36 1242   111014   28888   21404    1
/2 015   5 288   88 88 88 88 88 88  88 5  019500 012750                  2
/1 016 1630 051890 07   44234 23340  29 1242   111014   28888   21354    1
/2 016   5 101   01 88 88 88 88 88  01 5  023700 021450                  2
/1 017 1600 051890 06   43423 24220  26 1352   111104   28888   21354    1
/2 017   6 103   12 10 06 88 88 88  03 5  036500 024750                  2
```

```
Column   10        20        30        40        50        60        70
....|....|....|....|....|....|....|....|....|....|....|....|....|....|....|
```

```
/1 018 1615 051890 09   43432 23420   27 1302   111063   28888   21404    1
/2 018    5 101    08 88 88 88 88 88   01 5   028750 020500                2
/1 019 1600 051890 08   34222 32222   24 1262   111023   28888   21354    1
/2 019    5 101    03 88 88 88 88 88   01 5   030000 024500                2
/1 020 1745 051890 10   43422 23421   27 1342   111094   28888   21404    1
/2 020    5 101    11 88 88 88 88 88   01 5   032000 026500                2
/1 021 1800 051890 02   42232 32221   23 1332   111094   28888   21404    1
/2 021    5 102    10 07 88 88 88 88   02 5   034500 029750                2
/1 022 1730 051890 01   24332 22322   25 1482   111244   28888   21354    1
/2 022    1 288    88 88 88 88 88 88   88 5   043700 039000                2
/1 023 1815 051890 03   34243 34221   28 1292   111074   28888   21304    1
/2 023    5 101    03 88 88 88 88 88   01 5   029700 017800                2
/1 024 1850 051890 05   43232 43222   27 1351   111051   28888   21354    1
/2 024    5 102    17 15 88 88 88 88   01 5   045500 023100                2
/1 025 1845 051890 04   43232 31431   26 1332   111044   28888   21403    1
/2 025    5 101    09 88 88 88 88 88   01 5   028750 015500                2
/1 026 1930 051890 08   43322 34131   26 1342   111084   28888   21354    1
/2 026    5 102    11 10 88 88 88 88   02 5   032600 015600                2
/1 027 2000 051890 06   42432 34222   28 1232   111014   28888   21354    1
/2 027    5 288    88 88 88 88 88 88   88 5 016500 012550                  2
/1 028 1915 051890 07   33232 32222   24 1362   111134   28888   21353    1
/2 028    2 103    12 09 05 88 88 88   03 5   028750 024570                2
/1 029 1945 051890 10   24224 23231   25 1382   111153   28888   21354    1
/2 029    5 101    16 88 88 88 88 88   01 5   034400 027300                2
/1 030 2045 051890 09   43333 23330   27 1412   111194   28888   21354    1
/2 030    5 102    17 14 88 88 88 88   02 5   044750 024650                2
/1 031 2100 051890 01   43233 22322   26 1352   111124   28888   21404    1
/2 031    6 104    14 12 07 06 88 88   04 5   039100 018700                2
/1 032 1930 051990 03   43323 24322   28 1382   111083   28888   31352    1
/2 032    5 102    14 10 88 88 88 88   02 5   032450 019500                2
/1 033 1700 051990 02   24224 23322   26 1282   111054   28888   21404    1
/2 033    5 101    05 88 88 88 88 88   01 5   026750 015500                2
/1 034 1815 051990 06   33432 43320   27 1322   111104   28888   21404    1
/2 034    5 102    12 08 88 88 88 88   02 5   032700 023780                2
/1 035 1700 051990 07   32332 32231   24 1492   111263   28888   21354    1
/2 035    6 102    20 15 88 88 88 88   01 5   044560 031200                2
/1 036 1600 051990 04   22422 42322   25 1482   111234   28888   21404    1
/2 036    6 104    25 23 19 12 88 88   01 5   039700 021500                2
/1 037 1930 051990 08   43232 22222   24 1522   111294   28888   21401    1
/2 037    1 103    31 29 25 88 88 88   00 5   047600 069800                2
/1 038 1800 051990 05   32332 32322   25 1392   111154   28888   21304    1
/2 038    5 101    14 88 88 88 88 88   01 5   037690 023850                2
/1 039 1645 051990 09   42332 32222   25 1402   111184   28888   21354    1
/2 039    5 288    88 88 88 88 88 88   88 5   041700 034900                2
/1 040 2000 051990 10   42131 32131   21 1272   111044   28888   21354    1
/2 040    5 101    03 88 88 88 88 88   01 5   024700 019850                2
/1 041 1900 051990 01   31241 13111   18 1392   111144   28888   21404    1
/2 041    5 102    19 17 88 88 88 88   01 5   036800 033200                2
```

```
Column   10        20        30        40        50        60        70
....|....|....|....|....|....|....|....|....|....|....|....|....|....|
/1 042 1945 051990 03  43121 22020  17 1402  111184  28888  21404   1
/2 042  6 103   19 17 10 88 88 88  02 5  039200 038100              2
/1 043 2100 051990 02  41211 32131  19 1412  111174  28888  21353   1
/2 043  5 101   16 88 88 88 88 88  01 5  038700 036100              2
/1 044 2030 051900 04  41311 12111  16 1482  111254  28888  21352   1
/2 044  5 101   24 88 88 88 88 88  01 5  042900 058700              2
/1 045 1750 051990 07  31211 32311  18 1512  111294  28888  21354   1
/2 045  6 103   27 25 21 88 88 88  00 5  051100 049700              2
/1 046 1845 051990 06  31231 21121  17 1392  111164  28888  21354   1
/2 046  5 102   14 13 88 88 88 88  02 5  037900 035800              2
/1 047 2015 051990 05  31231 12321  19 1432  111204  28888  21354   1
/2 047  6 103   18 16 13 88 88 88  03 5  036200 033100              2
/1 048 2015 051990 09  41111 13111  15 1551  111271  28888  21501   1
/2 048  5 102   25 23 88 88 88 88  00 5  059700 063800              2
/1 049 1845 051990 08  32132 32120  19 1382  111154  28888  21354   1
/2 049  5 102   13 09 88 88 88 88  02 5  037600 035100              2
/1 050 1600 052090 01  21323 12211  18 1442  111224  28888  21354   1
/2 050  6 103   22 20 15 88 88 88  02 5  042300 040750              2
/1 051 1700 052090 03  13211 13311  17 1322  111094  28888  21404   1
/2 051  5 101   07 88 88 88 88 88  01 5  029800 027200              2
/1 052 1900 052090 02  23112 12320  17 1492  111264  28888  21404   1
/2 052  6 102   27 23 88 88 88 88  00 5  053900 051500              2
/1 053 1830 052090 06  21312 32130  18 1582  111354  28888  21354   1
/2 053  6 103   33 30 25 88 88 88  00 5  054600 050000              2
/1 054 1615 052090 04  40212 23210  17 1502  111284  28888  21251   1
/2 054  5 101   26 88 88 88 88 88  00 5  051700 052700              2
/1 055 1945 052090 05  42132 12311  20 1462  111244  28888  21354   1
/2 055  6 102   20 16 88 88 88 88  02 5  048700 040100              2
/1 056 1845 052090 07  41132 13111  18 1372  111134  28888  21354   1
/2 056  6 102   14 12 88 88 88 88  02 5  029500 027200              2
/1 057 1630 052090 09  13121 31211  16 1472  111244  28888  21404   1
/2 057  5 101   23 88 88 88 88 88  01 5  043900 041700              2
/1 058 1800 052090 10  31211 31221  17 1532  111304  28888  21304   1
/2 058  6 104   30 27 22 22 88 88  01 5  051900 050800              2
/1 059 1745 052090 06  32322 32211  21 1442  111214  28888  21354   1
/2 059  5 102   17 14 88 88 88 88  02 5  039600 023300              2
/1 060 1830 052190 01  32311 13311  19 1592  111374  28888  21354   1
/2 060  5 103   36 33 31 88 88 88  00 5  053900 041700              2
/1 061 1745 052190 03  13131 22311  18 1512  111234  28888  21354   1
/2 061  5 101   25 88 88 88 88 88  01 5  046700 048200              2
/1 062 1930 052190 05  33122 12121  18 1412  111194  28888  21354   1
/2 062  5 103   16 14 09 88 88 88  03 5  039700 026100              2
/1 063 2030 052190 02  31131 12210  15 1461  111162  28888  21251   1
/2 063  5 101   20 88 88 88 88 88  01 5  063900 068100              2
/1 064 1845 052190 04  32331 12210  18 1452  111234  28888  21354   1
/2 064  5 101   19 88 88 88 88 88  01 5  042700 038900              2
/1 065 1645 052190 09  34311 12211  19 1402  111184  28888  21354   1
/2 065  5 103   13 09 07 88 88 88  03 5  037100 032900              2
```

(continued)

```
Column   10        20        30        40        50        60        70
....|....|....|....|....|....|....|....|....|....|....|....|....|....|....|

/1 066 1700 052190 07   31112 33111   17 1552   111334   28888   21502     1
/2 066   1 288    88 88 88 88 88 88   88 5   042100 049500                  2
/1 067 1800 052190 08   22131 12111   15 1521   111191   28888   21352     1
/2 067   5 102    30 25 88 88 88 88   00 5   041900 052900                  2
/1 068 1830 052190 06   22311 22111   16 1402   111104   28888   21354     1
/2 068   6 101    21 88 88 88 88 88   00 5   027100 031500                  2
/1 069 1700 052190 10   31431 31211   20 1582   111364   28888   21354     1
/2 069   5 102    35 31 88 88 88 88   00 5   049200 031700                  2
/1 070 2130 052190 01   41131 31211   18 1612   111314   28888   21352     1
/2 070   5 101    34 88 88 88 88 88   00 5   048150 049800                  2
/1 071 2130 052190 05   32121 31231   19 1432   111204   28888   21304     1
/2 071   6 104    18 17 15 10 88 88   04 5   038900 032700                  2
/1 072 2100 052190 04   22311 32230   19 1522   111294   28888   21354     1
/2 072   6 103    27 24 23 88 88 88   00 5   051900 042750                  2
/1 073 2015 052190 03   22311 11331   18 1552   111314   28888   21354     1
/2 073   5 102 24 20 88 88 88 88      02 5   053200 047600                  2
/1 074 1745 052190 02   23122 31210   17 1482   111204   28888   21404     1
/2 074   5 101    20 88 88 88 88 88   01 5   039800 038100                  1
/1 075 1645 052290 06   44244 43443   37 1286   111094   28888   21354     1
/2 075   2 101    05 88 88 88 88 88   01 5   021500 016300                  2
/1 076 1700 052290 08   43443 43442   35 1266   111084   28888   21304     1
/2 076   5 102    07 05 88 88 88 88   02 5   019800 015900                  2
/1 077 1715 052290 09   43434 43441   34 1356   111154   28888   21354     1
/2 077   5 102    15 12 88 88 88 88   02 5   024900 018600                  2
/1 078 1630 052290 07   44244 44442   36 1456   111234   13041   21354     1
/2 078   5 101    24 88 88 88 88 88   00 5   033900 024900                  2
/1 079 1815 052290 10   42444 34341   33 1286   111104   28888   21354     1
/2 079   6 103    08 06 03 88 88 88   03 5   017800 010400                  2
/1 080 1745 052290 01   44344 44423   36 1256   111054   13012   31304     1
/2 080   5 101    05 88 88 88 88 88   01 5   013200 009400                  2
/1 081 1645 052290 05   44444 44441   37 1226   111024   28888   21304     1
/2 081   3 288    88 88 88 88 88 88   88 5   010600 009700                  2
/1 082 1815 052290 03   44344 34343   36 1416   111194   28888   21354     1
/2 082   5 102    18 16 88 88 88 88   02 5   026900 020100                  2
/1 083 1730 052290 02   44434 44341   35 1266   111084   28888   21354     1
/2 083   5 102    06 04 88 88 88 88   02 5   014900 010600                  2
/1 084 1815 052290 04   42434 44432   34 1536   111355   28888   21354     1
/2 084   6 105    30 28 24 19 17 88   02 5   037800 023975                  2
/1 085 2015 052290 06   44424 44442   36 1216   111024   28888   21354     1
/2 085   5 288    88 88 88 88 88 88   88 5   016900 012800                  2
/1 086 2030 052290 07   44443 44442   37 1316   111104   28888   31404     1
/2 086   5 101    08 88 88 88 88 88   01 5   022900 012700                  2
/1 087 2100 052290 09   44343 34432   34 1397   111226   16011   31404     1
/2 087   6 102    21 19 88 88 88 88   02 5   028500 033700                  2
/1 088 1930 052290 10   44244 44441   35 1386   111194   28888   21354     1
/2 088   6 101    20 88 88 88 88 88   01 5   024600 019900                  2
/1 089 1945 052290 08   44244 44242   34 1426   111244   28888   21354     1
/2 089   6 102    22 20 88 88 88 88   02 5   033900 030750                  2
```

```
Column    10        20        30        40        50        60        70
....|....|....|....|....|....|....|....|....|....|....|....|....|....|....|

/1 090 2015 052290 01   43434 43343   35 1286   111094   28888   21354    1
/2 090   4 101    07 88 88 88 88 88   01 5   019600 014800                2
/1 091 1915 052390 02   44344 43442   36 1336   111104   28888   21352    1
/2 091   5 102    07 02 88 88 88 88   02 5   018775 014800                2
/1 092 2100 052390 04   34434 43442   35 1226   111036   28888   21302    1
/2 092   5 288    88 88 88 88 88 88   88 5   014800 010600                2
/1 093 2045 052390 07   44144 44441   34 1266   111084   28888   21354    1
/2 093   5 101    07 88 88 88 88 88   01 5   017200 012300                2
/1 094 1930 052390 03   43434 33422   32 1506   111324   28888   21354    1
/2 094   4 102    29 24 88 88 88 88   00 5   039600 036700                2
/1 095 1945 052390 05   44434 34441   35 1386   111204   28888   21352    1
/2 095   5 102    16 12 88 88 88 88   02 5   024800 016700                2
/1 096 2015 052390 08   43444 34343   36 1336   111144   28888   21352    1
/2 096   6 103    12 10 06 88 88 88   03 5   017600 012200                2
/1 097 2045 052390 06   44343 43441   34 1396   111214   28888   21354    1
/2 097   6 102    22 18 88 88 88 88   02 5   032800 018700                2
/1 098 2100 052390 09   44444 44442   38 1256   111074   28888   21402    1
/2 098   5 101    06 88 88 88 88 88   01 5   016900 011850                2
/1 099 1645 052390 10   44444 24441   35 1236   111044   28888   21354    1
/2 099   5 288    88 88 88 88 88 88   88 5   015600 010600                2
/1 100 1715 052390 03   44434 33433   35 1256   111074   28888   21354    1
/2 100   5 101    05 88 88 88 88 88   01 5   017900 010700                2
/1 101 1730 052390 02   43444 43443   37 1296   111114   28888   31404    1
/2 101   6 103    10 07 05 88 88 88   03 5   022250 015600                2
/1 102 1745 052390 01   44424 44442   36 1316   111124   28888   21404    1
/2 102   5 102    12 06 88 88 88 88   02 5   027300 017600                2
/1 103 1845 502390 04   43334 33431   31 1336   111154   12063   21352    1
/2 103   5 101    14 88 88 88 88 88   01 5   030900 031200                2
/1 104 1830 052390 06   43444 34432   35 1276   111094   28888   21354    1
/2 104   5 101    08 88 88 88 88 88   01 5   019200 012900                2
/1 105 1915 052390 05   44343 44441   35 1266   111074   28888   21357    1
/2 105   5 101    08 88 88 88 88 88   01 5   015900 010300                2
/1 106 1615 052390 08   44344 33431   33 1326   111137   28888   21354    1
/2 106   5 101    09 88 88 88 88 88   01 5   020700 019200                2
/1 107 1630 052390 07   44444 44441   37 1206   111014   28888   21354    1
/2 107   5 288    88 88 88 88 88 88   88 5   013900 011200                2
/1 108 1715 052390 09   43443 44442   36 1186   111004   28888   21404    1
/2 108   5 288    88 88 88 88 88 88   88 5   012800 011600                2
/1 109 2000 052390 10   34442 43442   34 1276   111094   28888   21404    1
/2 109   5 101    08 88 88 88 88 88   01 5   019700 017100                2
/1 110 2100 052390 01   44434 44443   38 1226   111044   28888   21407    1
/2 110   5 101    04 88 88 88 88 88   01 5   016800 012100                2
/1 111 1945 052390 02   43433 34432   33 1556   111344   28888   21352    1
/2 111   1 101    31 88 88 88 88 88   00 5   037100 049700                2
/1 112 2000 052490 03   44434 43433   36 1476   111294   28888   21354    1
/2 112   6 104    26 23 19 12 88 88   02 5   033900 024600                2
/1 113 2015 052490 06   24444 44442   36 1296   111107   28888   21352    1
/2 113   5 102    09 06 88 88 88 88   02 5   012800 010750                2
```

(continued)

```
Column   10        20        30        40        50        60        70
....|....|....|....|....|....|....|....|....|....|....|....|....|....|....|

/1 114 1915 052490 05   43444 44442  37 1236   111054   28888   21354   1
/2 114  5 101   03 88 88 88 88 88  01 5  017200 012100                  2
/1 115 1845 052490 04   43434 43422  33 1416   111234   28888   21354   1
/2 115  6 103   19 17 10 88 88 88  03 5  029800 027300                  2
/1 116 1815 052490 09   44434 43443  37 1306   111124   28888   21354   1
/2 116  5 101   10 88 88 88 88 88  01 5  018600 014100                  2
/1 117 1830 052490 07   34344 34432  34 1296   111114   28888   21352   1
/2 117  5 101   06 88 88 88 88 88  01 5  016900 016100                  2
/1 118 1915 052490 08   44444 24441  35 1356   111144   28888   21354   1
/2 118  5 102   16 09 88 88 88 88  02 5  019100 013800                  2
/1 119 2100 052490 10   34443 34343  35 1276   111104   28888   21354   1
/2 119  5 101   07 88 88 88 88 88  01 5  014900 012700                  2
/1 120 1645 052490 01   34434 44442  36 1416   111224   28888   21354   1
/2 120  6 103   18 16 15 88 88 88  03 5  026900 020550                  2
/1 121 1700 052490 04   44443 43343  36 1606   111414   28888   21354   1
/2 121  6 105   38 36 31 29 28 88  00 5  043800 029700                  2
/1 122 1930 052490 03   43444 43432  35 1536   111304   12033   21354   1
/2 122  4 103   31 28 22 88 88 88  00 5  036600 024200                  2
/1 123 1900 052490 02   43424 34242  32 1496   111314   28888   21353   1
/2 123  5 101   25 88 88 88 88 88  00 5  036000 034900                  2
/1 124 1730 052490 05   43444 44443  38 1296   111114   28888   21352   1
/2 124  5 102   09 06 88 88 88 88  02 5  022900 020100                  2
/1 125 1745 052490 07   34344 34321  31 1336   111124   28888   21354   1
/2 125  5 101   11 88 88 88 88 88  01 5  021100 024600                  2
/1 126 1830 052490 06   44244 42441  33 1216   111034   28888   21404   1
/2 126  6 102   03 01 88 88 88 88  02 5  016100 015200                  2
/1 127 1800 052490 08   44444 44441  37 1296   111114   12043   21404   1
/2 127  5 101   06 88 88 88 88 88  01 5  023100 012950                  2
/1 128 1815 052490 09   44444 34443  38 1246   111064   28888   21357   1
/2 128  5 288   88 88 88 88 88 88  88 5  018900 014100                  2
/1 129 1915 052490 10   34443 44441  35 1316   111134   28888   21354   1
/2 129  5 101   12 88 88 88 88 88  01 5  026300 019250                  2
/1 130 2000 052490 01   44424 44441  35 1256   111064   28888   21354   1
/2 130  5 101   05 88 88 88 88 88  01 5  019300 014200                  2
/1 131 1645 052590 03   44424 44442  36 1286   111104   28888   31357   1
/2 131  5 101   08 88 88 88 88 88  01 5  019850 013100                  2
/1 132 1700 052590 04   44444 34442  37 1316   111124   28888   21354   1
/2 132  6 102   10 06 88 88 88 88  02 5  020500 014900                  2
/1 133 1745 052590 06   44444 33442  36 1216   111024   28888   21354   1
/2 133  5 101   02 88 88 88 88 88  01 5  015900 011400                  2
/1 134 1730 052590 05   42444 24442  34 1436   111244   28888   21354   1
/2 134  6 102   23 21 88 88 88 88  00 5  030190 021700                  2
/1 135 1645 052590 07   43444 34443  37 1296   111114   28888   21357   1
/2 135  5 288   88 88 88 88 88 88  88 5  019700 013700                  2
/1 136 1815 052590 09   34424 24441  32 1246   111064   28888   21402   1
/2 136  5 101   05 88 88 88 88 88  01 5  018300 017100                  2
/1 137 1845 052590 08   43434 33434  35 1366   111184   28888   21354   1
/2 137  5 101   14 88 88 88 88 88  01 5  027900 016200                  2
```

```
Column   10        20        30        40        50        60        70
 ....|....|....|....|....|....|....|....|....|....|....|....|....|....|....|

/1 138 1815 052590 10   42242 42240   26 1226   111024   28888   21357    1
/2 138   5 101   02 88 88 88 88 88   01 5   014300 011700                 2
/1 139 1915 052590 02   34243 32420   27 1276   111094   28888   21404    1
/2 139   3 101   06 88 88 88 88 88   01 5   019700 018600                 2
/1 140 1645 052590 01   24232 42231   25 1376   111194   28888   21354    1
/2 140   5 102   16 13 88 88 88 88   02 5   039100 037200                 2
/1 141 1930 052590 01   43422 42320   26 1426   111234   28888   21404    1
/2 141   4 101   19 88 88 88 88 88   01 5   040500 036900                 2
/1 142 2000 052590 03   42342 32241   27 1316   111134   28888   21352    1
/2 142   6 103   12 10 07 88 88 88   03 5   028700 029100                 2
/1 143 2045 052590 02   43443 14330   29 1226   111024   13012   21404    1
/2 143   5 288   88 88 88 88 88 88   88 5   015100 012700                 2
/1 144 1815 052590 06   32323 22322   24 1507   111304   28888   21354    1
/2 144   2 101   26 88 88 88 88 88   00 5   037200 036900                 2
/1 145 1930 052590 05   23232 22322   23 1437   111254   28888   21402    1
/2 145   4 101   23 88 88 88 88 88   01 5   032900 034800                 2
/1 146 1845 052590 07   43342 34221   28 1276   111094   28888   21407    1
/2 146   5 101   06 88 88 88 88 88   01 5   019100 013700                 2
/1 147 1845 052590 04   33422 22332   26 1256   111054   28888   21404    1
/2 147   5 101   04 88 88 88 88 88   01 5   014900 011300                 2
/1 148 1915 052590 09   42233 22432   27 1296   111114   28888   21357    1
/2 148   5 102   09 07 88 88 88 88   02 5   023100 016700                 2
/1 149 2000 052590 08   32323 22233   25 1336   111144   28888   21354    1
/2 149   5 103   14 12 11 88 88 88   03 5   029200 026900                 2
/1 150 2115 052590 10   32343 33330   27 1236   111054   12032   21354    1
/2 150   2 288   88 88 88 88 88 88   88 5   016900 017200                 2
/1 151 1030 052690 10   42322 42222   25 1386   111194   28888   21354    1
/2 151   3 102   15 12 88 88 88 88   02 5   039900 037200                 2
/1 152 1000 052690 08   42232 32242   26 1496   111304   28888   21354    1
/2 152   6 105   28 27 24 18 18 88   03 5   034200 033900                 2
/1 153 1045 052690 09   42323 32441   28 1266   111084   28888   21354    1
/2 153   5 102   07 07 88 88 88 88   02 5   019200 018600                 2
/1 154 1030 052690 07   43232 33340   27 1526   111374   28888   21354    1
/2 154   5 103   33 30 21 88 88 88   01 5   046800 042200                 2
/1 155 1100 052690 02   34223 22322   25 1386   111194   28888   21354    1
/2 155   5 102   15 09 88 88 88 88   02 5   039100 036800                 2
/1 156 1030 052690 06   42224 42420   26 1396   111194   28888   21407    1
/2 156   6 104   18 16 09 09 88 88   04 5   039100 020400                 2
/1 157 1015 052690 01   34224 24320   26 1446   111244   28888   21354    1
/2 157   5 102   20 15 88 88 88 88   02 5   049900 047600                 2
/1 158 1045 052690 03   24222 22322   23 1507   111324   28888   21352    1
/2 158   3 102   26 22 88 88 88 88   00 5   051600 052100                 2
/1 159 1045 052690 05   34244 22322   28 1396   111154   28888   21407    1
/2 159   6 103   19 17 06 88 88 88   03 5   031100 012950                 2
/1 160 1115 052690 04   42332 42340   27 1436   111204   28888   21357    1
/2 160   5 102   16 12 88 88 88 88   02 5   040500 018600                 2
/1 161 1445 052690 10   43233 32411   26 1536   111224   28888   21354    1
/2 161   4 104   30 26 24 15 88 88   01 5   043900 041100                 2
```

(continued)

```
Column   10        20        30        40        50        60        70
....|....|....|....|....|....|....|....|....|....|....|....|....|....|....|

/1 162 1345 052690 09  42232 42231  25 1466  111234  28888  21354  1
/2 162  6 103  23 20 19 88 88 88  02 5  047200 045900            2
/1 163 1315 052690 07  32322 42332  26 1396  111194  28888  21354  1
/2 163  5 101  14 88 88 88 88 88  01 5  039700 035900            2
/1 164 1430 052690 08  42242 23222  25 1466  111224  28888  21354  1
/2 164  5 103  24 20 13 88 88 88  03 5  043800 040050            2
/1 165 1515 052690 04  23233 32321  24 1506  111224  28888  21354  1
/2 165  4 104  31 27 26 19 88 88  01 5  044300 041800            2
/1 166 1415 052690 06  42242 32321  25 1396  111174  28888  21354  1
/2 166  5 102  18 14 88 88 88 88  02 5  036100 032800            2
/1 167 1345 052690 05  34224 23241  27 1296  111104  28888  21354  1
/2 167  5 102  11 07 88 88 88 88  02 5  022900 015800            2
/1 168 1515 052690 02  32341 34231  26 1336  111104  28888  21404  1
/2 168  5 102  10 07 88 88 88 88  02 5  022700 018900            2
/1 169 1415 052690 01  32242 32342  27 1296  111114  28888  21354  1
/2 169  6 104  12 11 08 05 88 88  04 5  023900 018700            2
/1 170 1315 052690 03  32322 32332  25 1486  111204  28888  21354  1
/2 170  5 102  29 27 88 88 88 88  00 5  041500 040900            2
/1 171 1645 052690 10  34222 42232  26 1466  111174  28888  21354  1
/2 171  6 103  23 21 16 88 88 88  03 5  036900 031200            2
/1 172 1715 052690 01  42242 44220  26 1376  111164  28888  21357  1
/2 172  5 104  15 13 09 08 88 88  04 5  033100 029200            2
/1 173 1615 052690 03  43233 42341  29 1236  111044  12032  21354  1
/2 173  5 101  03 88 88 88 88 88  01 5  013700 012100            2
/1 174 1600 052690 02  34232 23232  26 1446  111214  28888  21354  1
/2 174  5 102  20 16 88 88 88 88  02 5  043700 039600            2
/1 175 1700 052690 04  42332 32342  28 1256  111054  12062  21354  1
/2 175  5 101  04 88 88 88 88 88  01 5  014200 011700            2
/1 176 1715 052690 05  22423 42222  25 1476  111224  28888  21354  1
/2 176  6 103  20 17 12 88 88 88  03 5  025900 023700            2
/1 177 1645 052690 06  43224 24230  26 1416  111234  28888  21354  1
/2 177  5 102  28 22 88 88 88 88  01 5  047900 037200            2
/1 178 1715 052690 09  42232 42232  26 1466  111244  28888  21354  1
/2 178  6 104  23 20 18 14 88 88  03 5  049500 042700            2
/1 179 1630 052690 08  34234 33230  27 1276  111074  12062  21354  1
/2 179  5 101  08 88 88 88 88 88  01 5  016100 012200            2
/1 180 1630 052690 07  42342 32420  26 1346  111154  28888  21357  1
/2 180  5 102  13 09 88 88 88 88  02 5  031900 019300            2
/1 181 1330 052790 01  32122 23111  18 1496  111254  28888  21354  1
/2 181  2 102  23 16 88 88 88 88  01 5  042700 046800            2
/1 182 1245 052790 03  23132 11320  18 1516  111306  28888  21354  1
/2 182  2 102  28 24 88 88 88 88  00 5  027900 031600            2
/1 183 1345 052790 05  42121 32200  17 1337  111096  15023  21357  1
/2 183  5 103  15 11 09 88 88 88  03 5  017600 021300            2
/1 184 1400 052790 08  31232 31120  18 1417  111157  28888  21354  1
/2 184  5 104  20 16 14 14 88 88  04 5  024900 023800            2
/1 185 1315 052790 10  31231 31131  19 1406  111154  12053  21354  1
/2 185  3 102  17 13 88 88 88 88  02 5  031300 032900            2
```

```
Column   10        20        30        40        50        60        70
....|....|....|....|....|....|....|....|....|....|....|....|....|....|....|
```

```
/1 186 1430 052790 06   31321 31231   20 1527   111234   12031   21354      1
/2 186   4 103   36 29 24 88 88 88   00 5   047100 046700                   2
/1 187 1415 052790 07   23111 23121   17 1367   111124   12031   21354      1
/2 187   2 101   12 88 88 88 88 88   01 5   026900 028700                   2
/1 188 1300 052790 02   31231 11131   17 1336   111104   12053   21357      1
/2 188   2 102   13 11 88 88 88 88   02 5   021600 020550                   2
/1 189 1330 052790 09   41321 21131   19 1436   111154   28888   21407      1
/2 189   4 102   19 14 88 88 88 88   02 5   031600 028200                   2
/1 190 1400 052790 04   24131 13111   18 1397   111104   16041   21407      1
/2 190   3 103   17 13 08 88 88 88   03 5   022200 018600                   2
/1 191 1500 052790 10   31221 21120   15 1446   111154   12073   21354      1
/2 191   4 104   23 21 16 09 88 88   04 5   031400 036800                   2
/1 192 1630 052790 01   13113 21211   16 1476   111164   12023   21354      1
/2 192   3 102   27 21 88 88 88 88   00 5   033800 031900                   2
/1 193 1515 052790 02   32312 23121   20 1566   111144   12063   21354      1
/2 193   4 104   33 30 22 22 88 88   01 5   032100 029900                   2
/1 194 1645 052790 04   23131 32121   19 1416   111134   28888   21354      1
/2 194   4 101   21 88 88 88 88 88   00 5   027600 024900                   2
/1 195 1530 052790 03   23113 12131   18 1437   111144   16041   21354      1
/2 195   4 102   20 16 88 88 88 88   02 5   029100 027300                   2
/1 196 1630 052790 09   31212 21230   17 1386   111164   12033   21404      1
/2 196   3 103   16 15 08 88 88 88   03 5   034100 036200                   2
/1 197 1630 052790 08   32132 31220   19 1416   111134   12013   21354      1
/2 197   2 288   88 88 88 88 88 88   88 5   027900 026100                   2
/1 198 1545 052790 06   42123 20120   17 1326   111104   12043   21354      1
/2 198   2 103   12 07 05 88 88 88   03 5   022600 023900                   2
/1 199 1500 052790 07   21312 21211   16 1436   111134   28888   21357      1
/2 199   6 105   23 20 16 13 09 88   04 5   027200 026300                   2
/1 200 1545 052790 05   21322 31211   18 1266   111074   12062   21304      1
/2 200   5 103   08 06 03 88 88 88   03 5   017200 018600                   2
/1 201 1900 052790 10   34111 21111   16 1496   111124   12053   21354      1
/2 201   4 102   18 17 88 88 88 88   02 5   026300 031700                   2
/1 202 2015 052790 03   32131 23231   21 1336   111124   28888   21357      1
/2 202   3 103   12 09 05 88 88 88   03 5   026900 020100                   2
/1 203 1715 052890 10   43443 43442   35 1492   111243   28888   22888      1
/2 203   6 102   25 22 88 88 88 88   01 5   051900 000000                   2
/1 204 1815 052890 09   44144 44441   34 1392   111174   28888   31144      1
/2 204   3 102   15 11 88 88 88 88   02 5   038100 010200                   2
/1 205 1745 052890 07   44344 43443   37 1572   111304   28888   22888      1
/2 205   7 103   29 25 23 88 88 88   00 5   057600 000000                   2
/1 206 1730 052890 06   43443 43443   36 1491   111221   28888   22888      1
/2 206   4 103   18 17 12 88 88 88   03 5   051500 000000                   2
/1 207 1800 052890 08   42444 44442   36 1422   111203   28888   31164      1
/2 207   5 103   20 18 04 88 88 88   01 5   046100 012700                   2
/1 208 1830 052890 05   34434 43441   34 1472   111253   28888   21164      1
/2 208   5 102   23 20 88 88 88 88   01 5   055900 007500                   2
/1 209 1830 052890 01   43444 34441   35 1391   111111   28888   22888      1
/2 209   2 101   09 88 88 88 88 88   01 5   072200 000000                   2
```

(continued)

```
Column  10        20        30        40        50        60        70
....|....|....|....|....|....|....|....|....|....|....|....|....|....|....|

/1 210 1730 052890 02  44444 44442  38 1502  111274   28888   21104    1
/2 210  5 102  26 24 88 88 88 88  00 5  057100 000000              2
/1 211 1700 052890 03  43434 43441  34 1432  111204   28888   21144    1
/2 211  5 103  19 14 08 88 88 88  03 5  043900 010100              2
/1 212 1800 052890 02  44344 34442  36 1262  111044   11042   22888    1
/2 212  5 101  02 88 88 88 88 88  01 5  019300 000000              2
/1 213 1945 052890 01  44244 44441  35 1392  111174   28888   21144    1
/2 213  2 101  14 88 88 88 88 88  01 5  037900 012200              2
/1 214 1930 052890 03  43434 43411  31 1362  111144   28888   31184    1
/2 214  5 103  17 09 07 88 88 88  02 5  032900 026300              2
/1 215 1900 052890 07  34424 44342  34 1592  111374   28888   21184    1
/2 215  1 102  36 31 88 88 88 88  00 5  059900 000000              2
/1 216 2015 052890 02  43444 34343  36 1442  111204   28888   22888    1
/2 216  5 102  23 19 88 88 88 88  00 5  047200 000000              2
/1 217 2045 052890 04  43443 34433  35 1482  111254   28888   21104    1
/2 217  5 103  25 21 16 88 88 88  01 5  054700 000000              2
/1 218 2000 052890 06  34342 34432  32 1372  111153   28888   21144    1
/2 218  5 102  13 08 88 88 88 88  02 5  037300 019900              2
/1 219 1930 052890 05  44444 44441  37 1522  111282   28888   31104    1
/2 219  2 102  25 24 88 88 88 88  00 5  064900 000000              2
/1 220 2045 052890 09  44343 34442  35 1402  111174   28888   21064    1
/2 220  3 102  16 12 88 88 88 88  02 5  038900 005500              2
/1 221 2015 052890 08  44444 24442  36 1451  111192   28888   22888    1
/2 221  5 101  23 88 88 88 88 88  00 5  049200 000000              2
/1 222 1900 052890 10  14444 44441  34 1392  111174   28888   21144    1
/2 222  3 102  15 10 88 88 88 88  02 5  035200 007500              2
/1 223 1700 052990 01  42444 24442  34 1412  111193   28888   21144    1
/2 223  2 101  16 88 88 88 88 88  01 5  043600 024900              2
/1 224 1715 052990 02  24424 42442  32 1532  111274   28888   22888    1
/2 224  3 102  29 25 88 88 88 88  00 5  057600 000000              2
/1 225 1800 052990 05  44444 44441  37 1572  111304   28888   32888    1
/2 225  3 102  17 13 88 88 88 88  02 5  063800 000000              2
/1 226 1730 052990 04  34444 34442  36 1402  111183   28888   21104    1
/2 226  2 101  15 88 88 88 88 88  01 5  041200 006850              2
/1 227 1715 052990 06  44343 42441  33 1492  111234   28888   21184    1
/2 227  5 102  25 21 88 88 88 88  00 5  048900 029700              2
/1 228 1845 052990 09  44344 43441  35 1382  111164   28888   21164    1
/2 228  5 101  14 88 88 88 88 88  01 5  044100 009500              2
/1 229 1700 052990 07  34344 43443  36 1452  111214   28888   32888    1
/2 229  6 103  20 17 14 88 88 88  03 5  044900 000000              2
/1 230 1800 052990 08  43444 44443  38 1542  111304   28888   22888    1
/2 230  5 104  31 27 25 22 88 88  00 5  061300 000000              2
/1 231 1730 052990 03  43443 43442  35 1592  111332   28888   22888    1
/2 231  5 102  27 23 88 88 88 88  00 5  068700 000000              2
/1 232 1815 052990 10  43442 44342  34 1372  111154   28888   21064    1
/2 232  5 102  13 08 88 88 88 88  02 5  036300 004550              2
/1 233 1930 052990 10  44242 42441  31 1512  111284   28888   21181    1
/2 233  3 102  27 25 88 88 88 88  00 5  057100 039200              2
```

```
Column   10        20        30        40        50        60        70
....|....|....|....|....|....|....|....|....|....|....|....|....|....|....|

/1 234 2045 052990 09   44444 44422   36 1262   111053   11032   22888   1
/2 234    5 102   03 01 88 88 88 88   02 5   025900 000000                2
/1 235 1945 052990 03   44434 44442   37 1542   111304   28888   21124   1
/2 235    3 102   29 24 88 88 88 88   00 5   063100 004200                2
/1 236 2030 052990 01   43443 43432   34 1372   111154   28888   21164   1
/2 236    4 103   13 09 06 88 88 88   03 5   033900 010200                2
/1 237 2000 052990 08   43434 34334   35 1462   111204   28888   21104   1
/2 237    5 102   20 16 88 88 88 88   02 5   041300 000000                2
/1 238 2100 052990 06   34444 34442   36 1382   111163   28888   22888   1
/2 238    4 103   11 08 03 88 88 88   03 5   041300 000000                2
/1 239 2115 052990 05   24414 44441   32 1332   111104   11052   32888   1
/2 239    1 102   04 01 88 88 88 88   02 5   026900 000000                2
/1 240 1945 052990 07   44342 43441   33 1482   111234   11023   21164   1
/2 240    3 102   14 11 88 88 88 88   02 5   047100 019900                2
/1 241 2030 052990 02   44444 43442   37 1532   111284   28888   22888   1
/2 241    4 102   29 24 88 88 88 88   00 5   057600 000000                2
/1 242 2045 052990 04   34344 34431   33 1422   111204   28888   21164   1
/2 242    5 104   18 16 13 07 88 88   04 5   043800 018750                2
/1 243 1745 053090 10   44344 43441   35 1292   111083   11062   21144   1
/2 243    5 102   06 02 88 88 88 88   02 5   027600 008700                2
/1 244 1700 053090 08   34344 44343   36 1392   111174   28888   21104   1
/2 244    3 101   15 88 88 88 88 88   01 5   036100 006200                2
/1 245 1715 053090 06   34344 34432   34 1492   111233   28888   32888   1
/2 245    5 104   29 26 12 08 88 88   02 5   049200 000000                2
/1 246 1800 053090 07   44444 24441   35 1412   111163   28888   22888   1
/2 246    4 102   16 09 88 88 88 88   02 5   037200 000000                2
/1 247 1830 053090 09   42434 43422   32 1292   111083   11023   21144   1
/2 247    5 101   07 88 88 88 88 88   01 5   023100 010500                2
/1 248 1730 053090 05   34343 43342   33 1352   111134   28888   21144   1
/2 248    5 102   09 07 88 88 88 88   02 5   028600 011700                2
/1 249 1745 053090 01   44444 24442   36 1442   111214   28888   22888   1
/2 249    6 102   19 14 88 88 88 88   02 5   043500 000000                2
/1 250 1800 053090 02   34444 34443   37 1542   111294   28888   22888   1
/2 250    1 101   32 88 88 88 88 88   00 5   059100 000000                2
/1 251 1800 053090 04   44444 44441   37 1442   111184   28888   22888   1
/2 251    6 102   19 13 88 88 88 88   02 5   037100 000000                2
/1 252 1730 053090 03   42444 44441   35 1362   111144   28888   21144   1
/2 252    5 101   13 88 88 88 88 88   01 5   032500 009200                2
/1 253 1945 053090 01   34333 43431   31 1492   111234   28888   22888   1
/2 253    7 105   23 19 15 13 07 88   05 5   049300 000000                2
/1 254 1915 053090 02   34343 44433   35 1432   111183   28888   22888   1
/2 254    3 102   15 09 88 88 88 88   02 5   043100 000000                2
/1 255 1930 053090 05   43444 44432   36 1462   111194   28888   21164   1
/2 255    5 102   23 20 88 88 88 88   01 5   039900 000000                2
/1 256 1915 053090 07   44244 42442   34 1552   111314   28888   22888   1
/2 256    5 103   30 26 23 88 88 88   02 5   059800 000000                2
/1 257 1900 053090 03   34444 44442   37 1411   111111   28888   22888   1
/2 257    2 101   11 88 88 88 88 88   01 5   061000 000000                2
```

(continued)

```
Column    10        20        30        40        50        60        70
....|....|....|....|....|....|....|....|....|....|....|....|....|....|....|
  /1 258 2000 053090 04   34434 44433  36 1372   111163   28888   21164    1
  /2 258   5 102   12 07 88 88 88 88  02 5  038100 009150                  2
  /1 259 2015 053090 06   43434 44443  37 1482   111234   28888   22888    1
  /2 259   4 103   22 18 12 88 88 88  02 5  048700 000000                  2
  /1 260 1930 053090 10   34344 44432  35 1332   111123   28888   21144    1
  /2 260   5 101   08 88 88 88 88 88  01 5  029300 007400                  2
  /1 261 1900 053090 08   34442 34442  34 1362   111143   28888   32888    1
  /2 261   5 103   16 06 02 88 88 88  02 5  035900 000000                  2
  /1 262 1900 053090 09   43444 44431  35 1442   111214   28888   21124    1
  /2 262   4 102   20 13 88 88 88 88  02 5  043900 005600                  2
  /1 263 1900 053190 01   44424 44442  36 1522   111294   28888   22888    1
  /2 263   1 101   30 88 88 88 88 88  00 5  059900 000000                  2
  /1 264 1700 053190 05   43432 43431  31 1402   111174   28888   21184    1
  /2 264   5 103   16 13 07 88 88 88  03 5  036700 004200                  2
  /1 265 1715 053190 03   44444 44442  38 1532   111244   28888   22888    1
  /2 265   1 288   88 88 88 88 88 88  88 5  047100 000000                  2
  /1 266 1830 053190 02   44444 44441  37 1472   111254   28888   22888    1
  /2 266   4 102   23 19 88 88 88 88  02 5  049200 000000                  2
  /1 267 1745 053190 06   44434 44443  38 1462   111214   28888   21184    1
  /2 267   4 102   18 13 88 88 88 88  02 5  043900 000000                  2
  /1 268 1800 053190 09   44344 43442  36 1382   111164   28888   21184    1
  /2 268   5 102   14 10 88 88 88 88  02 5  035200 009450                  2
  /1 269 1815 053190 08   34344 43443  36 1432   111204   28888   21144    1
  /2 269   4 101   19 88 88 88 88 88  01 5  041900 009200                  2
  /1 270 1700 053190 04   44442 44441  35 1482   111214   28888   21124    1
  /2 270   4 102   24 16 88 88 88 88  01 5  043600 007100                  2
  /1 271 1730 053190 10   44441 44441  34 1432   111184   28888   21184    1
  /2 271   4 101   19 88 88 88 88 88  01 5  038400 000000                  2
  /1 272 1730 053190 07   34444 34443  37 1292   111073   11052   22888    1
  /2 272   5 102   04 01 88 88 88 88  02 5  029900 000000                  2
  /1 273 1900 053190 10   34344 34432  34 1502   111244   28888   21184    1
  /2 273   1 101   23 88 88 88 88 88  01 5  049100 005000                  2
  /1 274 1945 053190 09   44244 42442  34 1462   111224   28888   21184    1
  /2 274   2 102   20 14 88 88 88 88  02 5  045100 004200                  2
  /1 275 2015 053190 06   44343 44342  35 1432   111204   28888   21144    1
  /2 275   4 102   20 15 88 88 88 88  02 5  042300 007900                  2
  /1 276 2000 053190 08   44444 24442  36 1462   111234   28888   21124    1
  /2 276   4 102   24 20 88 88 88 88  01 5  047900 006300                  2
  /1 277 2000 053190 07   34443 34433  35 1392   111173   28888   21184    1
  /2 277   5 101   13 88 88 88 88 88  01 5  042700 009800                  2
  /1 278 1945 053190 02   44444 43442  37 1572   111314   28888   21184    1
  /2 278   6 103   25 23 19 88 88 88  01 5  058600 003400                  2
  /1 279 2015 053190 01   43444 43442  36 1502   111284   28888   21184    1
  /2 279   4 103   29 27 22 88 88 88  00 5  057100 003200                  2
  /1 280 2030 053190 04   34344 44343  36 1442   111214   28888   21184    1
  /2 280   4 101   20 88 88 88 88 88  01 5  044600 009800                  2
  /1 281 2015 053190 05   43444 34441  35 1382   111163   15041   21184    1
  /2 281   5 102   15 09 88 88 88 88  02 5  043100 008200                  2
```

```
Column   10        20        30        40        50        60        70
....|....|....|....|....|....|....|....|....|....|....|....|....|....|....|
  /1 282 1700 060190 01   34243 24320   27 1312   111093   15061   21184    1
  /2 282  5 102   08 05 88 88 88 88  02 5  027600 007200                    2
  /1 283 1730 060190 03   43231 32431   26 1402   111174   28888   21184    1
  /2 283  5 102   15 13 88 88 88 88  02 5  037100 014200                    2
  /1 284 1800 060190 05   32432 34242   29 1302   111083   15031   21144    1
  /2 284  5 101   07 88 88 88 88 88  01 5  028600 010900                    2
  /1 285 1715 060190 09   24233 24240   26 1422   111204   28888   21184    1
  /2 285  6 102   17 16 88 88 88 88  02 5  042900 012900                    2
  /1 286 1800 060190 07   22423 42231   25 1352   111123   15041   21144    1
  /2 286  5 102   10 06 88 88 88 88  02 5  036600 007800                    2
  /1 287 1700 060190 08   43333 23330   27 1392   111163   15061   21184    1
  /2 287  5 102   14 10 88 88 88 88  02 5  040100 012300                    2
  /1 288 1745 060190 04   42322 33232   26 1362   111134   28888   21184    1
  /2 288  5 102   10 06 88 88 88 88  02 5  029800 012900                    2
  /1 289 1715 060190 06   32322 33232   25 1372   111124   15013   21144    1
  /2 289  6 101   23 88 88 88 88 88  01 5  027300 009300                    2
  /1 290 1800 060190 02   32313 32321   23 1352   111114   11023   21184    1
  /2 290  5 103   12 08 03 88 88 88  03 5  027600 014300                    2
  /1 291 1930 060190 01   42324 42321   27 1432   111194   11051   21144    1
  /2 291  5 101   19 88 88 88 88 88  01 5  041400 006500                    2
  /1 292 1945 060190 03   42232 23232   25 1362   111154   28888   21104    1
  /2 292  5 102   12 07 88 88 88 88  02 5  033100 009100                    2
  /1 293 1930 060190 02   42334 31231   26 1392   111144   28888   21184    1
  /2 293  5 103   15 11 07 88 88 88  03 5  029700 012700                    2
  /1 294 2015 060190 06   43243 42321   28 1432   111214   28888   21104    1
  /2 294  6 102   19 12 88 88 88 88  02 5  043500 000000                    2
  /1 295 2000 060190 05   42322 32432   27 1402   111184   28888   21164    1
  /2 295  5 101   16 88 88 88 88 88  01 5  039100 007500                    2
  /1 296 1930 060190 04   42223 22422   25 1392   111184   28888   21184    1
  /2 296  5 103   16 12 10 88 88 88  03 5  039100 013100                    2
  /1 297 2045 060190 07   32342 32232   26 1362   111123   11041   21144    1
  /2 297  5 102   12 07 88 88 88 88  02 5  039100 012300                    2
  /1 298 2000 060190 09   42232 23222   24 1402   111144   28888   21184    1
  /2 298  5 102   16 11 88 88 88 88  02 5  029100 018600                    2
  /1 299 2015 060190 08   43243 24230   27 1442   111214   28888   21144    1
  /2 299  6 103   20 15 10 88 88 88  03 5  045900 000000                    2
  /1 300 0945 060290 09   42334 23311   26 1392   111164   28888   21184    1
  /2 300  5 101   15 88 88 88 88 88  01 5  035200 000000                    2
  /1 301 1000 060290 07   42232 23222   24 1432   111204   11023   21184    1
  /2 301  6 103   20 18 12 88 88 88  03 5  042100 015900                    2
  /1 302 1000 060290 06   42322 42231   25 1412   111174   28888   21184    1
  /2 302  5 101   15 88 88 88 88 88  01 5  036100 013900                    2
  /1 303 1015 060290 08   43423 42321   28 1432   111204   28888   21104    1
  /2 303  6 103   19 15 12 88 88 88  03 5  041300 000000                    2
  /1 304 1030 060290 03   42342 34220   26 1372   111153   15061   22888    1
  /2 304  5 104   14 09 07 07 88 88  04 5  043200 000000                    2
  /1 305 0945 060290 05   34224 24231   27 1392   111164   28888   21164    1
  /2 305  5 101   15 88 88 88 88 88  01 5  035100 012900                    2
```

(continued)

```
Column   10        20        30        40        50        60        70
....|....|....|....|....|....|....|....|....|....|....|....|....|....|....|
/1 306 1030 060290 04   42323 24232  27 1412  111173  14021  21184     1
/2 306  5 102   16 12 88 88 88 88  02 5  043900 013600              2
/1 307 1015 060290 01   42232 32232  25 1362  111123  14031  21144     1
/2 307  5 101   10 88 88 88 88 88  01 5  029900 009500              2
/1 308 1000 060290 02   32323 32320  23 1432  111184  11023  21184     1
/2 308  5 103   19 15 10 88 88 88  03 5  037200 015600              2
/1 309 1200 060290 09   32322 32322  24 1442  111204  11013  21184     1
/2 309  5 103   20 16 07 88 88 88  03 5  042600 013900              2
/1 310 1345 060290 07   42224 32322  26 1412  111184  28888  21104     1
/2 310  5 102   16 10 88 88 88 88  02 5  039100 000000              2
/1 311 1230 060290 05   43333 32330  27 1402  111143  28888  22888     1
/2 311  5 102   13 09 88 88 88 88  02 5  040300 000000              2
/1 312 1300 060290 06   43423 24321  28 1432  111203  28888  22888     1
/2 312  6 104   19 15 12 04 88 88  04 5  053900 000000              2
/1 313 1300 060290 08   32323 32231  24 1352  111123  11023  21144     1
/2 313  5 103   11 07 03 88 88 88  03 5  034900 007800              2
/1 314 1415 060290 04   42422 24240  26 1392  111164  11013  21184     1
/2 314  5 102   15 11 88 88 88 88  02 5  034100 012900              2
/1 315 1400 060290 01   42343 23240  27 1411  111113  28888  21184     1
/2 315  5 101   10 88 88 88 88 88  01 5  039800 009800              2
/1 316 1230 060290 03   41231 21311  19 1302  111073  28888  21144     1
/2 316  5 102   06 04 88 88 88 88  02 5  024300 009000              2
/1 317 1300 060290 02   42231 12200  17 1282  111064  11042  21184     1
/2 317  6 103   07 04 01 88 88 88  03 5  017900 008300              2
/1 318 1615 060290 05   31212 23121  18 1262  111033  11042  21184     1
/2 318  5 102   04 02 88 88 88 88  02 5  022500 007350              2
/1 319 1630 060290 03   42231 31211  20 1332  111103  28888  21184     1
/2 319  5 103   11 08 04 88 88 88  03 5  031900 006300              2
/1 320 1700 060290 02   23113 11321  18 1312  111094  28888  21184     1
/2 320  5 102   06 03 88 88 88 88  02 5  021400 014300              2
/1 321 1600 060290 04   32132 12311  19 1292  111044  28888  21184     1
/2 321  5 102   05 01 88 88 88 88  02 5  019200 008600              2
/1 322 1630 060290 01   32312 22130  19 1262  111044  11042  21184     1
/2 322  5 101   03 88 88 88 88 88  01 5  015600 009200              2
/1 323 1545 060290 06   32111 31221  17 1292  111064  28888  21144     1
/2 323  5 102   05 03 88 88 88 88  02 5  018100 010500              2
/1 324 1700 060290 09   41121 13111  16 1332  111104  28888  21187     1
/2 324  6 103   09 07 05 88 88 88  03 5  022900 007000              2
/1 325 1800 060290 08   41311 21311  18 1242  111014  11012  22888     1
/2 325  6 102   02 02 88 88 88 88  02 5  014100 000000              2
/1 326 1500 060290 07   32112 13231  19 1302  111084  28888  22888     1
/2 326  6 103   06 05 01 88 88 88  03 5  022300 000000              2
/1 327 2000 060290 02   31322 32120  19 1282  111044  11042  21184     1
/2 327  5 101   04 88 88 88 88 88  01 5  017900 009100              2
/1 328 1000 060390 01   44424 44442  36 1216  111035  28888  21187     1
/2 328  5 101   03 88 88 88 88 88  01 5  012100 007100              2
/1 329 1015 060390 03   34443 43442  35 1277  111097  28888  21187     1
/2 329  5 101   06 88 88 88 88 88  01 5  019300 006800              2
```

```
Column   10          20          30          40          50          60          70
....|....|....|....|....|....|....|....|....|....|....|....|....|....|....|....|
/1 330 1000 060390 05   43424 44432   34 1226   111044   14042   21187      1
/2 330   5 288    88 88 88 88 88 88   88 5   014200 007200                   2
/1 331 1030 060390 07   34444 44443   38 1256   111074   12052   21144      1
/2 331   5 101    06 88 88 88 88 88   01 5   019100 006400                   2
/1 332 1045 060390 09   44343 34341   33 1377   111167   28888   21184      1
/2 332   6 104    17 14 12 07 88 88   04 5   025200 008200                   2
/1 333 1100 060390 10   44444 44242   36 1246   111064   12052   21184      1
/2 333   5 101    04 88 88 88 88 88   01 5   017500 006200                   2
/1 334 1200 060390 06   44344 34443   37 1397   111144   16031   21187      1
/2 334   5 101    16 88 88 88 88 88   01 5   023900 009900                   2
/1 335 1000 060390 04   44344 44432   36 1216   111034   12012   21187      1
/2 335   5 101    03 88 88 88 88 88   01 5   012700 008800                   2
/1 336 1015 060390 08   34242 34230   27 1317   111104   16041   21147      1
/2 336   6 103    11 08 06 88 88 88   03 5   019100 008200                   2
/1 337 1100 060390 02   42342 24230   26 1356   111144   28888   21187      1
/2 337   6 104    15 11 08 05 88 88   04 5   022400 007900                   2
/1 338 1300 060390 01   34234 32420   27 1296   111104   28888   21147      1
/2 338   5 103    09 07 05 88 88 88   03 5   017900 006800                   2
/1 339 1300 060390 03   24223 42231   25 1336   111094   28888   21187      1
/2 339   3 102    12 07 88 88 88 88   02 5   018100 009900                   2
/1 340 1330 060390 07   32423 24341   28 1276   111084   13051   21187      1
/2 340   5 102    07 05 88 88 88 88   02 5   019900 007500                   2
/1 341 1315 060390 04   42342 23241   27 1256   111074   13061   21187      1
/2 341   5 101    04 88 88 88 88 88   01 5   018200 005900                   2
/1 342 1400 060390 02   32432 34131   26 1266   111084   12062   21147      1
/2 342   5 102    07 05 88 88 88 88   02 5   019300 007600                   2
/1 343 1415 060390 06   32222 42231   23 1336   111144   28888   21184      1
/2 343   6 104    14 11 09 06 88 88   04 5   020800 004300                   2
/1 344 1300 060390 05   43243 43220   27 1236   111034   12022   21184      1
/2 344   2 101    03 88 88 88 88 88   01 5   014300 006400                   2
/1 345 1300 060390 09   34242 24230   26 1286   111093   28888   21187      1
/2 345   5 102    07 05 88 88 88 88   02 5   019200 007100                   2
/1 346 1200 060390 08   42342 42321   27 1296   111103   12072   21184      1
/2 346   5 101    09 88 88 88 88 88   01 5   023900 008300                   2
/1 347 1330 060390 10   24232 32421   25 1256   111054   12062   21184      1
/2 347   5 101    06 88 88 88 88 88   01 5   015900 009200                   2
/1 348 1500 060390 05   32232 32232   24 1346   111157   28888   21184      1
/2 348   5 104    15 13 10 06 88 88   04 5   020500 012300                   2
/1 349 1600 060390 08   33422 33342   29 1326   111134   12082   22888      1
/2 349   5 103    10 06 02 88 88 88   03 5   022900 000000                   2
/1 350 1800 060390 01   23213 21311   19 1386   111157   28888   21187      1
/2 350   6 104    19 17 13 09 88 88   04 5   024600 009200                   2
/1 351 1930 060390 08   31211 32131   18 1426   111164   12073   21147      1
/2 351   5 103    17 12 10 88 88 88   03 5   029100 007300                   2
/1 352 1815 060390 06   31413 12131   20 1447   111224   16021   21187      1
/2 352   6 104    20 16 13 09 88 88   03 5   029800 007600                   2
/1 353 1845 060390 05   31213 21121   17 1267   111057   16013   21107      1
/2 353   5 102    04 02 88 88 88 88   02 5   016300 004900                   2
```

(continued)

```
Column   10        20        30        40        50        60        70
....|....|....|....|....|....|....|....|....|....|....|....|....|....|....|....|

/1 354 1900 060390 02   23213 21320   19 1406   111154   28888   21147      1
/2 354    5 103   19 16 10 88 88 88   03 5   027800 006300                   2
/1 355 1815 060390 03   41131 13121   18 1396   111164   28888   21184      1
/2 355    5 103   17 15 09 88 88 88   03 5   029100 008300                   2
/1 356 1815 060390 04   23113 21131   18 1257   111077   28888   22888      1
/2 356    5 103   05 03 01 88 88 88   03 5   015900 000000                   2
/1 357 1830 060390 07   41131 21321   19 1297   111074   16021   22888      1
/2 357    3 102   10 06 88 88 88 88   02 5   018200 007300                   2
/1 358 1900 060390 10   42311 32131   21 1257   111074   16021   21187      1
/2 358    5 103   07 05 02 88 88 88   03 5   019900 007800                   2
/1 359 1945 060390 09   13132 31221   19 1286   111094   28888   22888      1
/2 359    5 103   08 04 01 88 88 88   03 5   021300 000000                   2
/1 360 1230 060490 06   31213 21131   18 1326   111104   28888   21147      1
/2 360    3 102   07 04 88 88 88 88   02 5   022900 006400                   2
/1 361 1445 060490 02   21312 13121   17 1306   111114   28888   21187      1
/2 361    4 103   10 07 04 88 88 88   03 5   024600 005900                   2
/1 362 1230 060490 05   32132 21320   19 1416   111164   28888   21187      1
/2 362    6 102   21 18 88 88 88 88   00 5   029300 009200                   2
/1 363 1500 060490 03   13122 31211   17 1387   111167   28888   21184      1
/2 363    4 104   16 13 08 08 88 88   04 5   023800 011900                   2
/1 364 1415 060490 04   23121 13110   15 1437   111177   16033   21184      1
/2 364    6 105   21 19 16 15 10 88   04 5   026100 013200                   2
/1 365 1515 060490 01   42131 21231   20 1246   111044   12032   22888      1
/2 365    2 102   05 01 88 88 88 88   02 5   015900 000000                   2
/1 366 1630 060490 09   31213 21321   19 1366   111144   28888   21187      1
/2 366    3 103   15 12 08 88 88 88   03 5   023600 012900                   2
/1 367 1315 060490 08   31221 13221   18 1317   111124   16031   21187      1
/2 367    5 103   11 06 04 88 88 88   03 5   019200 008200                   2
/1 368 1400 060490 10   23113 41221   20 1266   111084   12052   21187      1
/2 368    2 102   06 02 88 88 88 88   02 5   019900 009100                   2
/1 369 1500 060490 07   41212 30220   17 1317   111117   16023   21184      1
/2 369    2 102   10 07 88 88 88 88   02 5   017200 009900                   2
/1 370 1700 060590 04   21311 31121   16 1497   111307   28888   21184      1
/2 370    5 105   27 23 22 14 08 88   01 5   032100 012800                   2
/1 371 1715 060590 02   21321 12121   16 1406   111154   28888   21144      1
/2 371    4 102   18 13 88 88 88 88   02 5   029200 013100                   2
/1 372 1745 060590 01   31113 21221   17 1376   111154   12043   21184      1
/2 372    5 103   14 11 06 88 88 88   03 5   030900 009800                   2
/1 373 1700 060590 03   31213 21131   18 1216   111044   12023   21184      1
/2 373    2 101   02 88 88 88 88 88   01 5   015200 009200                   2
/1 374 1615 060590 05   31211 41131   18 1356   111124   28888   21144      1
/2 374    5 102   12 08 88 88 88 88   02 5   024100 013200                   2
/1 375 1700 060590 10   13223 11321   19 1266   111074   12062   21184      1
/2 375    2 102   06 03 88 88 88 88   02 5   016100 010100                   2
/1 376 1830 060590 08   31322 23120   19 1427   111154   16041   21184      1
/2 376    6 104   24 18 15 11 88 88   03 5   030900 009200                   2
/1 377 1600 060590 09   21311 31231   18 1326   111114   28888   21184      1
/2 377    3 102   11 06 88 88 88 88   02 5   022300 011300                   2
```

```
Column   10        20        30        40        50        60        70
....|....|....|....|....|....|....|....|....|....|....|....|....|....|
  /1 378 1600 060590 06   31214 13131   20 1256   111094   12032   22888      1
  /2 378    5 102   05 02 88 88 88 88   02 5   019100 000000                  2
  /1 379 1645 060590 07   31212 21331   19 1277   111094   16033   22888      1
  /2 379    5 103   10 06 03 88 88 88   03 5   017200 000000                  2
  /1 380 1930 060590 02   31121 21131   16 1396   111134   12043   21184      1
  /2 380    5 103   19 14 11 88 88 88   03 5   024700 014700                  2
  /1 381 1945 060590 01   23113 12131   18 1356   111104   12013   31184      1
  /2 381    5 104   17 16 06 03 88 88   02 5   019200 010900                  2
  /1 382 1930 060590 03   23112 31121   17 1306   111104   12033   21184      1
  /2 382    3 102   10 06 88 88 88 88   02 5   021600 012900                  2
  /1 383 1900 060590 08   32122 31121   18 1276   111064   28888   21187      1
  /2 383    5 101   07 88 88 88 88 88   01 5   018100 007900                  2
  /1 384 1945 060590 05   23113 21231   19 1236   111054   12042   22888      1
  /2 384    5 102   04 01 88 88 88 88   02 5   015900 000000                  2
  /1 385 2000 060590 09   41113 21131   18 1286   111074   12062   21147      1
  /2 385    5 103   08 07 04 88 88 88   03 5   019200 000000                  2
  /1 386 2000 060590 02   32123 21331   21 1256   111064   12042   22888      1
  /2 386    5 102   05 02 88 88 88 88   02 5   017900 000000                  2
  /1 387 2015 060590 01   31132 13121   18 1316   111104   12033   21187      1
  /2 387    3 101   10 88 88 88 88 88   01 5   019900 004200                  2
  /1 388 1900 060590 07   23113 21231   19 1297   111117   28888   21187      1
  /2 388    5 102   17 13 88 88 88 88   02 5   018700 006900                  2
  /1 389 1945 060590 10   31112 31321   18 1407   111167   16023   21147      1
  /2 389    5 103   18 15 09 88 88 88   03 5   026300 007200                  2
  /1 390 1700 060690 10   21311 23131   18 1366   111144   28888   31184      1
  /2 390    3 102   14 04 88 88 88 88   01 5   026900 008200                  2
  /1 391 1830 060690 07   23112 32131   19 1506   111274   12033   21147      1
  /2 391    6 103   28 24 21 88 88 88   00 5   032900 005900                  2
  /1 392 1715 060690 06   23124 12311   20 1256   111064   12062   22888      1
  /2 392    5 102   05 01 88 88 88 88   02 5   015900 000000                  2
  /1 393 1700 060690 01   21311 23131   18 1356   111144   12023   21144      1
  /2 393    5 103   15 11 07 88 88 88   03 5   026900 007200                  2
  /1 394 1800 060690 03   14113 21131   18 1317   111064   16021   31107      1
  /2 394    5 103   15 05 02 88 88 88   02 5   015900 005100                  2
  /1 395 1845 060690 05   32213 21230   19 1386   111174   28888   21187      1
  /2 395    5 104   16 15 13 10 88 88   04 5   029300 005100                  2
  /1 396 2000 060690 04   42113 21231   20 1226   111034   12022   21187      1
  /2 396    3 101   03 88 88 88 88 88   01 5   013900 006800                  2
```

APPENDIX E

SPSS^X Program Called "DATABASE.PR1" for the Computer Manipulation of the Data File Labeled "DATABASE.DAT"

Text Ref. Number	Actual Command
(1)	TITLE "OPINION RESEARCH STUDY: SPRING, 1990"
(2)	FILE HANDLE=DATABASE/NAME='DATABASE.DAT'
(3)	DATA LIST FILE=DATABASE RECORDS=2
(4)	/1 IDR1 6–8 TIME 10–13 MONTH 15–16 DATE 17–18 YEAR 19–20 NAME 22–23 V1 TO V5 26–30 V6 TO V10 32–36 V11 39–40 V12 42 V13 43–44 V14 45 V15 TO V17 48–50 V18 51–52 V19 53 V20 56 V21 57 V22 58–59 V23 60 V24 63 V25 64 V26 65–66 V27 67 RECN1 72
(5)	/2 IDR2 6–8 V28 11 V29 13 V30 14–15 V31 18–19 V32 21–22 V33 24–25 V34 27–28 V35 30–31 V36 33–34 V37 37–38 V38 40 V39 43–48 V40 50–55 RECN2 72
(6)	VARIABLE LABELS IDR1 'ID Number'
	TIME 'Time Interview Begun'
	MONTH 'Month'
	DATE 'Date'
	YEAR 'Year'
	NAME 'Interviewer'
	V1 'Get along'
	V2 'No laugh'
	V3 'Hard luck'
	V4 'Feel good'
	V5 'Happy work'
	V6 'Have doubts'
	V7 'Level-headed'
	V8 'No attention'
	V9 'Wrong choice'
	V10 'Morning'
	V11 'Index Score'
	V12 'Sex'
	V13 'Age'
	V14 'Education'
	V15 'Working'
	V16 'Work status'
	V17 'Company'
	V18 'Years there'
	V19 'Occupation'
	V20 'More school'

Text Ref. Number	Actual Command
	V21 'Type' V22 'How Long?' V23 'Diploma?' V24 'Married?' V25 'Wife work?' V26 'Hours/Week' V27 "Wife's Job" V28 'Debt' V29 'Children' V30 'Number' V31 'Age First' V32 'Age Second' V33 'Age Third' V34 'Age Fourth' V35 'Age Fifth' V36 'Age Sixth' V37 'At Home' V38 'Race' V39 "Man's Income" V40 "Wife's Income"
(7)	VALUE LABELS MONTH 01 "January" 02 "February" 03 "March" 04 "April" 05 "May" 06 "June" 07 "July" 08 "August" 09 "September" 10 "October" 11 "November" 12 "December"/ YEAR 90 "1990"/ V1 4 "Strongly Agree" 3 "Agree" 2 "No Opinion" 1 "Disagree" 0 "Strongly Disagree"/ V2 TO V3 4 "Strongly Disagree" 3 "Disagree" 2 "No Opinion" 1 "Agree" 0 "Strongly Agree"/ V4 TO V5 4 "Strongly Agree" 3 "Agree" 2 "No Opinion" 1 "Disagree" 0 "Strongly Disagree"/ V6 4 "Strongly Disagree" 3 "Disagree" 2 "No Opinion" 1 "Agree" 0 "Strongly Agree"/ V7 4 "Strongly Agree" 3 "Agree" 2 "No Opinion" 1 "Disagree" 0 "Strongly Disagree"/ V8 TO V9 4 "Strongly Disagree" 3 "Disagree" 2 "No Opinion" 1 "Agree" 0 "Strongly Agree"/

(continued)

Text Ref. Number	Actual Command
	V10 4 "Strongly Agree" 3 "Agree" 2 "No Opinion" 1 "Disagree" 0 "Strongly Disagree"/
	V12 1 "Male" 2 "Female"/
	V14 1 "More than college" 2 "College graduate" 3 "AA degree" 4 "Some college" 5 "Technical/trade" 6 "High school graduate" 7 "Some high school" 8 "Less than high school"/
	V15 1 "Yes" 2 "No"/
	V16 1 "Full-time work" 2 "Part-time work" 3 "Some work" 4 "Occasional work"/
	V17 1 "SSA" 2 "Other"/
	V18 00 "Less than one year"/
	V19 1 "Professional" 2 "Managerial" 3 "Paraprofessional" 4 "White collar" 5 "Skilled blue collar" 6 "Semi-skilled" 7 "Unskilled"/
	V20 1 "Yes" 2 "No"/
	V21 1 "Academic: grad/prof" 2 "Academic: college" 3 "Two-year college" 4 "Professional program" 5 " Trade/specialty" 6 "High school"/
	V22 00 "Under a year"/
	V23 1 "Yes" 2 "Still attending" 3 "No"/
	V24 1 "Single" 2 "Married" 3 "Remarried" 4 "Separated" 5 "Divorced" 6 "Other"/
	V25 1 "Yes" 2 "No"/
	V27 1 "Professional" 2 "Managerial" 3 "Paraprofessional" 4 "White collar" 5 "Skilled blue collar" 6 "Semi-skilled" 7 "Unskilled"/

Text Ref. Number	Actual Command
	V28 1 "Under $10,000" 2 "$10,000 – $15,000" 3 "$15,001 – $20,000" 4 "$20,001 – $25,000" 5 $25,001 – $30,000" 6 "$30,001 – $50,000" 7 "Over $50,000" 8 "No real idea"/ V29 1 "Yes" 2 "No"/ V38 1 "Black" 2 "Hispanic" 3 "Native American" 4 "Oriental" 5 "White" 6 "Other"/
(8)	MISSING VALUES TIME (9999) MONTH TO NAME (99) V1 TO V10 (9) V11 (99) V12 (9) V13 (99) V14 (9) V15 (8,9) V16 (8,9) V17 (8,9) V18 (88,99) V19 (8,9) V20 (9) V21 (8,9) V22 (88,99) V23 (8,9) V24 (9) V25 (8,9) V26 (88,99) V27 (8,9) V28 (9) V29 (8,9) V30 TO V37 (88,99) V38 (9) V39 (999999) V40 (888888,999999)
(9)	** COMMENT The commands above are those used to define the COMMENT data file for the SPSS^x software package. Those COMMENT which follow are the ones which will do the desired COMMENT recalculations (such as the RECODE command) and the COMMENT desired data calculations and manipulations from COMMENT which the researcher will basically draw COMMENT substantive conclusions. **
(10)	RECODE V14 (1,2=1) (6,7,8=2) VARIABLE LABELS V14 'EDUCATION' VALUE LABELS V14 1 'HIGH' 2 'LOW'

(11)	FREQUENCIES VARIABLES=V11/
	            STATISTICS=RANGE MAXIMUM MINIMUM/
	            HISTOGRAM=INCREMENT (1)/

(12)	RECODE V11 (LO THRU 21=3) (22 THRU 29=2) (30 THRU 40=1) VARIABLE LABELS V11 'INDEX SCORE' VALUE LABELS V11 1 'HIGH' 2 'MEDIUM' 3 'LOW'

(13)	CROSSTABS TABLES=V14 BY V11
	        /CELLS=COUNT ROW
	        /STATISTICS=LAMBDA BTAU CTAU GAMMA D

(continued)

Text Ref. Number	Actual Command
(14)	RECODE V28 (1 THRU 4=1) (5 THRU 7=2) VARIABLE LABELS V28 'DEBT' VALUE LABELS V28 1 'LOW' 2 'HIGH'

(15)	CROSSTABS TABLES=V14 BY V11 BY V28
	    /CELLS=COUNT ROW
	    /STATISTICS=LAMBDA BTAU CTAU GAMMA D

(16)	RECODE V26 (LO THRU 19,88=2) (20 THRU HI=1) VARIABLE LABELS V26 "WIFE'S WORK" VALUE LABELS V26 1 'HIGH VOLUME' 2 'LOW VOLUME'

(17)	CROSSTABS TABLES=V14 BY V11 BY V26
	    /CELLS=COUNT ROW
	    /STATISTICS=LAMBDA BTAU CTAU GAMMA D

(18)	FINISH

APPENDIX F

Code of Ethics of the American Sociological Association

PREAMBLE

Sociologists recognize that the discovery, creation, transmission, and accumulation of knowledge and the practice of sociology are social processes involving ethical considerations and behavior at every stage. Careful attention to the ethical dimensions of sociological practice, teaching, and scholarship contributes to the broader project of finding ways to maximize the beneficial effects that sociology may bring to humankind and to minimize the harm that might be a consequence of sociological work. The strength of the Code, its binding force, rests ultimately on the continuing active discussion, reflection, and use by members of the profession.

Sociologists subscribe to the general tenets of science and scholarship. Sociologists are especially sensitive to the potential for harm to individuals, groups, organizations, communities and societies that may arise out of the incompetent or unscrupulous use of sociological work and knowledge.

Sociology shares with other disciplines the commitment to the free and open access to knowledge and service, and to the public disclosure of findings. Sociologists are committed to the pursuit of accurate and precise knowledge and to self-regulation through peer review and appraisal, without personal and methodological prejudice and without ideological malice. Because sociology necessarily entails study of individuals, groups, organizations and societies, these principles of access and disclosure may occasionally conflict with more general ethical concerns for the rights of clients and respondents to privacy and for the treatment of clients and respondents with due regard for their integrity, dignity, and autonomy. This potential conflict provides one of the reasons for a Code of Ethics.

The styles of sociological work are diverse and changing. So also are the contexts within which sociologists find employment. These diversities of procedures and context have led to ambiguities concerning appropriate professional behavior. The clarification of ethical behavior in diverse context provides a second reason for this Code.

Finally, this Code also attempts to meet the expressed needs of sociologists who have asked for guidance in how best to proceed in a variety of situations involving relations with respondents, students, colleagues, employers, clients and public authorities.

This Code establishes feasible requirements for ethical behavior. These requirements cover many—but not all—of the potential sources of ethical conflict that may arise in research, teaching and practice. Most represent *prima facie* obligations that may admit of exceptions but which should generally stand as principles for guiding conduct. The Code states the Association's consensus about ethical behavior upon which the Committee on Professional Ethics will base its judgments when it must decide whether individual members of the Association have acted unethically in specific instances. More than this, however, the Code is meant to sensitize all sociologists to the ethical issues that may arise in their work, and to encourage sociologists to educate themselves and their colleagues to behave ethically.

To fulfill these purposes, we, the members of the American Sociological Association, affirm and support the following Code of Ethics. Members accept responsibility for cooperating with the duly constituted committees of the American Sociological Association by responding to inquiries promptly and completely. Persons who bring complaints in good faith under this Code should not be penalized by members of the Association for exercising this right.

Printed with the permission of the ASA.

I. *The Practice of Sociology*

A. *Objectivity and Integrity*

Sociologists should strive to maintain objectivity and integrity in the conduct of sociological research and practice.

1. Sociologists should adhere to the highest possible technical standards in their research, teaching and practice.

2. Since individual sociologists vary in their research modes, skills, and experience, sociologists should always set forth *ex ante* the limits of their knowledge and the disciplinary and personal limitations that condition the validity of findings which affect whether or not a research project can be successfully completed.

3. In practice or other situations in which sociologists are requested to render a professional judgment, they should accurately and fairly represent their areas and degrees of expertise.

4. In presenting their work, sociologists are obligated to report their findings fully and should not misrepresent the findings of their research. When work is presented, they are obligated to report their findings fully and without omission of significant data. To the best of their ability, sociologists should also disclose details of their theories, methods and research designs that might bear upon interpretations of research findings.

5. Sociologists must report fully all sources of financial support in their publications and must note any special relations to any sponsor.

6. Sociologists should not make any guarantees to respondents, individuals, groups or organizations—unless there is full intention and ability to honor such commitments. All such guarantees, once made, must be honored.

7. Consistent with the spirit of full disclosure of method and analysis, sociologists, after they have completed their own analyses, should cooperate in efforts to make raw data and pertinent documentation collected and prepared at public expense available to other social scientists, at reasonable costs, except in cases where confidentiality, the client's rights to proprietary information and privacy, or the claims of a fieldworker to the privacy of personal notes necessarily would be violated. The timeliness of this cooperation is especially critical.

8. Sociologists should provide adequate information and citations concerning scales and other measures used in their research.

9. Sociologists must not accepts grants, contracts or research assignments that appear likely to require violation of the principles enunciated in this Code, and should dissociate themselves from research when they discover a violation and are unable to achieve its correction.

10. When financial support for a project has been accepted, sociologists must make every reasonable effort to complete the proposed work on schedule, including reports to the funding source.

11. When several sociologists, including students, are involved in joint projects, there should be mutually accepted explicit agreements at the outset with respect to division of work, compensation, access to data, rights of authorship, and other rights and responsibilities. Such agreements may need to be modified as the project evolves and such modifications must be agreed upon jointly.

12. Sociologists should take particular care to state all significant qualifications on the findings and interpretations of their research.

13. Sociologists have the obligation to disseminate research finding, except those likely to cause harm to clients, collaborators and participants, or those which are proprietary under a formal or informal agreement.

14. In their roles as practitioners, researchers, teachers, and administrators, sociologists have an important social responsibility because their recommendations, decision, and actions may alter the lives of others. They should be aware of the situations and pressures that might lead to the misuse of their influence and authority. In these various roles, sociologists should also recognize that professional problems and conflicts may interfere with professional effectiveness. Sociologists should take steps to insure that these conflicts do not produce deleterious results for clients, research participants, colleagues, students and employees.

B. *Disclosure and Respect for the Rights of Research Populations*

Disparities in wealth, power, and social status between the sociologist and respondents and clients may reflect and create problems of equity in research collaboration. Conflict of interest for the sociologist may occur in research and practice. Also to follow the precepts of the scientific method—such as those requiring full disclosure—may entail adverse consequences or personal risks for individuals and groups. Finally, irresponsible actions by a single researcher or research team can eliminate or reduce future access to a category of respondents by the entire profession and its allied fields.

1. Sociologists should not misuse their positions as professional social scientists for fraudulent purposes or as a pretext for gathering intelligence for any organization or government. Sociologists should not mislead respondents involved in a research project as to the purpose for which that research is being conducted.
2. Subjects of research are entitled to rights of biographical anonymity.
3. Information about subjects obtained from records that are opened to public scrutiny cannot be protected by guarantees of privacy or confidentiality.
4. The process of conducting sociological research must not expose respondents to substantial risk of personal harm. Informed consent must be obtained when the risks of research are greater than the risks of everyday life. Where modest risk or harm is anticipated, informed consent must be obtained.
5. Sociologists should take culturally appropriate steps to secure informed consent and to avoid invasions of privacy. Special actions may be necessary where the individuals studied are illiterate, have very low social status, or are unfamiliar with social research.
6. To the extent possible in a given study sociologists should anticipate potential threats to confidentiality. Such means as the removal of identifiers, the use of randomized responses and other statistical solutions to problems of privacy should be used where appropriate.
7. Confidential information provided by research participants must be treated as such by sociologists, even when this information enjoys no legal protection or privilege and legal force is applied. The obligation to respect confidentiality also applies to members of research organizations (interviewers, coders, clerical staff, etc.) who have access to the information. It is the responsibility of administrators and chief investigators to instruct staff members on this point and to make every effort to insure that access to confidential information is restricted.
8. While generally adhering to the norm of acknowledging the contributions of all collaborators, sociologists should be sensitive to harm that may arise from disclosure and respect a collaborator's wish or need for anonymity. Full disclosure may be made later if circumstances permit.
9. Study design and information gathering techniques should conform to regulations protecting the rights of human subject, irrespective of source of funding, as outlined by the American Association of University Professors (AAUP) in "Regulations Governing Research On Human Subjects: Academic Freedom and the Institutional Review Board," *Academe,* December 1981: 358–370.
10. Sociologists should comply with appropriate federal and institutional requirements pertaining to the conduct of research. These requirements might include but are not necessarily limited to failure to obtain proper review and approval for research that involves human subjects and failure to follow recommendations made by responsible committees concerning research subjects, materials, and procedures.

II. Publications and Review Process

A. Questions of Authorship and Acknowledgment

1. Sociologists must acknowledge all persons who contribute to their research and to their copyrighted publications. Claims and ordering of authorship and acknowledgments must accurately reflect the contributions of all main participants in the research and writing process, including students, except in those cases where such ordering or acknowledgment is determined by an official protocol.
2. Data and material taken verbatim from another person's published or unpublished written work must be explicitly identified and referenced to its author. Citations to ideas developed in the written work of others, even if not quoted verbatim, should not be knowingly omitted.

B. Authors, Editors and Referees Have Interdependent Professional Responsibilities in the Publication Process

1. Editors should continually review the fair application of standards without personal or ideological malice.
2. Journal editors must provide prompt decisions to authors of submitted manuscripts. They must monitor the work of associate editors and other referees so that delays are few and reviews are conscientious.
3. An editor's commitment to publish an essay must be binding on the journal. Once accepted for publication, a manuscript should be published expeditiously.

4. Editors receiving reviews of manuscripts from persons who have previously reviewed those manuscripts for another journal should ordinarily seek additional reviews.
5. Submission of a manuscript to a professional journal clearly grants that journal first claim to publish. Except where journal policies explicitly allow multiple submissions, a paper submitted to one English language journal may not be submitted to another journal published in English until after an official decision has been received for the first journal. Of course, the article can be withdrawn from all consideration to publish at any time.

C. Participation in Review Processes

Sociologists are frequently asked to provide evaluations of manuscripts, research proposals, or other work of professional colleagues. In such work, sociologists should hold themselves to high standards of performance in several specific ways:

1. Sociologists should decline requests for reviews of work of others where strong conflicts of interest are involved, such as may occur when a person is asked to review work by teachers, friends, or colleagues for whom he or she feels an overriding sense of personal obligation, competition, or enmity, or when such requests cannot be fulfilled on time.
2. Materials sent for review should be read in their entirety and considered carefully and confidentially. Evaluations should be justified with explicit reasons.
3. Sociologists who are asked to review manuscripts and books they have previously reviewed should make this fact known to the editor requesting review.

III. Teaching and Supervision

The routine conduct of faculty responsibilities is treated at length in the faculty codes and AAUP rules accepted as governing procedures by the various institutions of higher learning. Sociologists in teaching roles should be familiar with the content of the codes in force at their institutions and should perform their responsibilities within such guidelines. Sociologists who supervise teaching assistants should take steps to insure that they adhere to these principles.

A. Sociologists are obligated to protect the rights of students to fair treatment.

1. Sociology departments should ensure that instructors are qualified to teach the courses to which they are assigned. Instructors so assigned should conscientiously perform their teaching responsibilities.
2. Sociologists should provide students with a fair and honest statement of the scope and perspective of their courses, clear expectations for student performance, and fair, timely, and easily accessible evaluations of their work.
3. Departments of Sociology must provide graduate students with explicit policies and criteria about conditions for admission into the graduate program, financial assistance, employment, funding, evaluation and possible dismissal.
4. Sociology departments should help students in their efforts to locate professional employment in academic and practice settings.
5. Sociology departments should work to insure the equal and fair treatment of all students, by adhering both in spirit and content to established affirmative action guidelines, laws, and policies.
6. Sociologists must refrain from disclosure of personal information concerning students where such information is not directly relevant to issues of professional competence.
7. Sociologists should make all decisions concerning textbooks, course content, course requirements, and grading solely on the basis of professional criteria without regard for financial or other incentives.

B. Sociologists must refrain from exploiting students.

1. Sociologists must not coerce or deceive students into serving as research subjects.
2. Sociologists must not represent the work of students as their own.
3. Sociologists have an explicit responsibility to acknowledge the contributions of students and to act on their behalf in setting forth agreements regarding authorship and other recognition.

C. Sociologists must not coerce personal or sexual favors or economic or professional advantages from any person, including respondents, clients, patients, students, research assistants, clerical staff or colleagues.

D. Sociologists must not permit personal animosities or intellectual differences vis-a-vis colleagues to fore-close student access to those colleagues.

IV. Ethical Obligations of Employers, Employees, and Sponsors

No sociologists should discriminate in hiring, firing, promotions, salary, treatment, or any other conditions of employment or career development on the basis of sex, sexual preference, age, race, religion, national origin, handicap, or political orientation. Sociologists should adhere to fair employment practices in hiring, promotion, benefits, and review processes. The guidelines outlined below highlight some, but not all, ethical obligations in employment practices. Clear specification of the requirements governing practices of fair and equal treatment are stated in the guidelines of the U.S. Equal Employment Opportunity Commission and the AAUP. Employers, employees, and sponsors should abide by these guidelines and consult them when a more complete description of fair employment practices is needed.

A. Employment Practices and Adherence to Guidelines

1. When acting as employers, sociologists should specify the requirements for hiring, promotion, and tenure and communicate these requirements thoroughly to employees and prospective employees. Voting on tenure and promotion should be based solely on professional criteria.
2. When acting as employers, sociologists should make every effort to ensure equal opportunity and fair treatment to all persons at all levels of employment.
3. When acting as employers, sociologists have the responsibility to be informed of fair employment practices, and to attempt to change any existing unfair practices within the organization or university.
4. All employees, including part-time employees, at all levels of employment, should be afforded the protection of due process through clear grievance procedures. It is the obligation of sociologists when acting as employers, to communicate these procedures and to protect the rights of employees who initiate complaints. They should also communicate standards of employment, and provide benefits, and compensation.

B. Responsibility of Employees

1. When seeking employment sociologists should provide prospective employers with accurate information on their relevant professional qualifications and experiences.
2. Sociologists accepting employment in academic and practice settings should become aware of possible constraints on research and publication in those settings and should negotiate clear understandings about such conditions accompanying their research and scholarly activity. In satisfying their obligations to employers, sociologists in such settings must make every effort to adhere to the professional obligations contained in this Code.
3. When planning to resign a post, sociologists should provide their employers with adequate notice of intention to leave.

C. Sponsor's Participation in Employment Processes

1. In helping to secure employment for students and trainees, sociologists should make every attempt to avoid conflicts of interest. When a conflict of interest does arise, full disclosure of potential biases should be made to job seekers.

V. Policies and Procedures

The Committee on Professional Ethics (COPE) appointed by the Council of the American Sociological Association, shall have responsibility for: interpreting and publicizing this Code, promoting ethical conduct among sociologists, receiving inquiries about violations of the Code, investigating complaints concerning the ethical conduct of members of the American Sociological Association, mediating disputes to assist the parties in resolving their grievances, holding hearings on formal charges of misconduct, and recommending actions to the Council of the American Sociological Association.

A. The Committee shall:

1. At any time, not necessarily in the context of the investigation of a particular case, advise the Council of the Association of its views of general ethical questions, which the Council may elect to publish in appropriate publications of the Association;

2. Receive complaints of violations of the Code of Ethics, and endeavor to resolve them by mediation, and if mediation is unsuccessful, proceed to a hearing. If, after a hearing, the Committee determines that an ethical violation occurred, it should so notify the parties and prepare a report for Council, which may or may not recommend one of the following actions:

    a. Apply no sanctions

    b. Suspend the membership and attendant privileges of a member (e.g., participation in the Annual Meeting for a period to be recommended by the Committee)

    c. Request the resignation of a member; or,

    d. Terminate the membership of a member.

B. The Council of the Association shall receive case reports and recommendations from the Committee, and from the Review Board hereinafter provided, and take appropriate action.

C. The following are the rules and procedures under which the Committee operates:

1. Except as hereinafter provided, all formal actions of the Committee shall be adopted at a meeting at which a quorum is present, by a majority vote of the members present and voting. A quorum shall consist of a majority of members of the Committee. Members of the Committee with conflicts of interest as outlined in "COPE's Guidelines for Committee Conduct" will be excluded from Committee deliberations and will not be included in determining a quorum.

2. All inquiries about violations of the Code of Ethics should be directed to the Executive Officer of the Association, who shall determine whether the alleged violator is a member of the Association. A person making an inquiry should be sent a copy of the Code and requested to specify in writing the Section(s) of the Code that is (are) believed to have been violated. After receipt of this formal and specific complaint, the Executive Officer shall notify the Chair of the Committee of the inquiry. The Chair, in conjunction with the Executive Officer, shall determine whether or not the complaint is in fact covered by the Code. If so determined, the complainant will be notified of the acceptance by the Committee of the Complaint. The Executive Officer shall then communicate the entire complaint to the person or persons accused, together with a copy of the Code and an explanation of the composition and purpose of the Committee (by registered mail with return receipt requested) and request a response within 90 days.

    a. The Committee shall consider complaints received from both members and non-members of the Association against members of the Association.

    b. In order to be considered by the Committee, complaints must be received within eighteen months of the alleged violation or, if received later, must be certified for Committee consideration by the ASA Council.

    c. The Executive Officer shall acknowledge receipt of the complaint, shall send a copy of the Code, and, where necessary, advise the complainant that a formal complaint must include specification of the time, place, persons, and events constituting the alleged violation and cite the paragraph(s) of the Code alleged to be violated.

3. In cases in which negotiation between the parties is deemed proper, the Chair of COPE will designate members of the Committee to cooperate with the Executive Officer in trying to find an informal and satisfactory solution to the problem.

4. The Executive Officer shall send copies of the complaint, responses and supporting documents to all members of the Committee and to the complainant and the alleged violator. After deliberation, the Committee shall decide by majority vote whether (1) the case should not be pursued further, (2) further information is needed, (3) mediation should be attempted, or (4) the case should not come to a hearing.

    a. If the Committee decides there should be no further pursuit of the case, the Chair shall communicate the decision and the reasons therefore to the Executive Officer, who should notify all parties.

    b. If the Committee decides that further investigation of the case is necessary, it may direct inquiries through the Executive Officer to either the complainant or the alleged violator, with copies of the request and responses thereto in every instance to the other party.

    c. If the Committee decides to attempt mediation, it shall appoint a mediator from among members of the Association, acceptable to both parties. The mediator shall in due course notify the Committee that the matter has been resolved by written agreement of the parties, or if no such resolution has been achieved, the mediator may (1) recommend that the matter be dropped, or (2) recommend that the case proceed to a hearing.

d. If the Committee decides that a hearing is appropriate, either upon the recommendations of a mediator, or upon its own initiative, it shall advise the complainant and the alleged violator that a hearing will be conducted, giving at least 90 days notice of time and place. The alleged violator, as well as the complainant, should be advised of their rights to introduce witnesses and evidence in their behalf, to cross-examine witnesses, and to have the assistance of professional or other counsel at the hearing. All documentary evidence to be introduced by the complainant, and the names of all witnesses to be offered in support of the changes shall be supplied to the alleged violator at least 80 days prior to the hearing. If either complaint or alleged violator refuses to participate in the hearing, the Committee may elect to continue without their participation.

e. At the hearing, the evidence in support of the complaint shall be presented by the complainant, by complainant's lawyer or by a representative of the ASA Council, and the alleged violator shall have full opportunity to answer factual questions.

f. The Committee shall record the proceedings of the hearing. The alleged violator shall have the right to be present either in person or, with the consent of all parties, through a conference telephone hook-up at all evidential sessions of the hearing and to have a transcript at cost. Every attempt will be made to conduct hearings at one time and place so as to reduce travel costs of the parties involved in the dispute.

g. Unless the alleged violator requests and the Committee grants a public hearing, the hearing of the complaint shall be private. All persons except those necessary for the conduct of the hearing shall be excluded.

h. At the conclusion of the introduction of all evidence, the alleged violator, counsel for the alleged violator, or both shall be permitted to argue against or in mitigation of the complaint.

i. Thereafter, the Committee shall conduct its further discussion in private.

j. If the Committee finds that no ethical violation has occurred, the parties, organizations and individuals contacted during the investigation shall be so notified by the Executive Officer and the case closed.

k. If the Committee finds that an ethical violation has clearly occurred, it shall prepare a report of the case summarizing its findings and recommendations. A copy of that report shall be sent to the alleged violator and complainant who shall have an opportunity to prepare written comments within 30 days as part of the appeals process.

l. When the Committee has followed the procedure set forth in paragraph "k", the findings shall be automatically appealed to a Review Board composed of three past Presidents of the Association appointed by the current President. The Review Board shall consider the written record alone, and by majority vote shall recommend to the Council that the findings of the Committee be upheld, reversed or modified. Copies of the recommendations of the Review Board shall be sent to the complainant, the alleged violator, and the Committee on Professional Ethics, all of whom shall have 30 days to comment in writing before the recommendation is forwarded to Council.

m. The Council, after examination of the Committee's and the Review Board's recommendations and comments thereto, shall make a final determination of the case on behalf of the Association, and either dismiss the case or take appropriate action.

D. The effective date of these procedures is August 14, 1989.

ENDNOTES

Chapter 1

1. See Thomas S. Kuhn, *The Structure of Scientific Revolutions,* Second Edition, Enlarged (Chicago, Illinois: The University of Chicago Press, 1970).

2. Robert K. Merton, "The Self-Fulfilling Prophecy," *Social Theory and Social Structure,* 1968 Enlarged Edition (New York, New York: The Free Press, 1968), p. 475.

3. Carlo L. Lastrucci, *The Scientific Approach: Basic Principles of the Scientific Method* (Cambridge, Massachusetts: Schenkman Publishing Company, Inc., 1963), p. 6.

4. Ibid., p. 11.

5. Ibid., p. 12.

6. Dagobert D. Runes, ed., *The Dictionary of Philosophy* (New York, New York: Philosophical Library, Inc., n.d.), p. 94.

7. Lastrucci, *The Scientific Approach,* p. 29.

8. Ibid., p. 30.

9. Ibid., p. 31.

10. Ibid., pp. 31f.

11. See ibid., p. 13.

Chapter 2

1. See Hubert M. Blalock, Jr., "The Measurement Problem: A Gap between the Languages of Theory and Research," *Methodology in Social Research,* Hubert M. Blalock, Jr., and Ann B. Blalock, ed. (New York, New York: McGraw-Hill Book Company, 1968), pp. 5–27.

2. See Lastrucci, *The Scientific Approach,* p. 77.

3. See ibid.

4. See ibid., p. 110 (taken with revision).

5. See ibid., p. 111.

6. Ibid., p. 115.

7. Max Weber, *The City,* Trans. and ed. by Don Martindale and Gertrud Neuwirth (New York, New York: Collier Books, 1962), p. 88.

8. See ibid., pp. 71–249.

Chapter 3

1. See Leslie Kish, "Some Statistical Problems in Research Design," *American Sociological Review,* Vol. 24, No. 3 (June 1959), pp. 328–338.

2. See Merton, "Manifest and Latent Functions," *Social Theory and Social Structure,* 1968 Enlarged Edition, pp. 73–138.

3. See Lastrucci, *The Scientific Approach,* pp. 110ff.

4. See Robert McGinnis, "Randomization and Inference in Sociological Research," *American Sociological Review,* Vol. 23, No. 4 (August 1958), pp. 408–414.

5. See John Ross and Perry Smith, "Orthodox Experimental Designs," *Methodology in Social Research,* Hubert M. Blalock, Jr., and Ann B. Blalock, ed. (New York, New York: McGraw-Hill Book Company, 1968), pp. 337f and 344f.

Chapter 4

1. L. H. C. Tippett, *Statistics* (London, England: Oxford University Press, 1943), p. 94.

2. Ibid., pp. 94f.

3. See William J. Goode and Paul K. Hatt, *Methods in Social Research* (New York, New York: McGraw-Hill Book Company, 1952), p. 74.

4. See ibid., p. 75.

5. See ibid., p. 76.

6. Philip Babcock Gove, ed., *Webster's Third New International Dictionary of the English Language Unabridged* (Springfield, Massachusetts: G. & C. Merriam Company, Publishers, 1971), p. 1772.

7. See Lastrucci, *The Scientific Approach,* pp. 202f.

8. See ibid., pp. 201f.

9. See Hubert M. Blalock, Jr., *Social Statistics,* Second Edition (New York, New York: McGraw-Hill Book Company, 1972).

10. See Sanford Labovitz and Robert Hagedorn, *Introduction to Social Research,* Third Edition (New York, New York: McGraw-Hill Book Company, 1981), pp. 7f.

11. See ibid., p. 8.

12. See Patricia L. Kendall and Paul F. Lazarsfeld, "Problems of Survey Analysis," *Continuities in Social Research,* Robert K. Merton and Paul F. Lazarsfeld, ed. (New York, New York: Arno Press, 1974), pp. 133–196.

13. See Morris Rosenberg, *The Logic of Survey Analysis* (New York, New York: Basic Books, Inc., Publishers, 1968).

Chapter 5

1. See Gerhard E. Lenski, "Status Crystallization: A Non-Vertical Dimension of Social Status," *American Sociological Review,* Vol. 19, No. 4 (August 1954), pp. 405–413.

2. See Gerhard E. Lenski, "Social Participation and Status Crystallization," *American Sociological Review,* Vol. 21, No. 4 (August 1956), pp. 458–464.

3. See Peter L. Berger, *Invitation to Sociology: A Humanistic Perspective* (Garden City, New York: Doubleday Anchor Books, 1963).

4. See Merton, "Manifest and Latent Functions," *Social Theory and Social Structure,* 1968 Enlarged Edition, pp. 73–138.

5. See Talcott Parsons, *The Social System* (New York, New York: The Free Press, 1951).

6. See Chauncy D. Harris and Edward L. Ullman, "The Nature of Cities," Paul K. Hatt and Albert J. Reiss, Jr., ed., *Cities and Society: The Revised Reader in Urban Society* (New York, New York: The Free Press of Glencoe, Inc., 1957), pp. 237–247.

7. See ibid.

8. See ibid.

9. See Robert Merton, "The Bearing of Sociological Theory on Empirical Research" and "The Bearing of Empirical Research on Sociological Theory," *Social Theory and Social Structure,* 1968 Enlarged Edition (New York, New York: The Free Press, 1968), pp. 139–171.

10. Ibid., p. 171.

11. See Denton E. Morrison and Ramon E. Henkel, *The Significance Test Controversy: A Reader* (Chicago, Illinois: Aldine Publishing Company, 1970).

12. See Theodore D. Sterling, "Publication Decisions and Their Possible Effects on Inferences Drawn from Tests of Significance or Vice Versa," *Journal of the American Statistical Association,* Vol. 54, No. 285 (March 1959), pp. 30–34.

Part II

1. See Leslie Kish, *Survey Sampling* (New York, New York: John Wiley & Sons, 1965).

Chapter 6

1. See Gene M. Lutz, *Understanding Social Statistics* (New York, New York: Macmillan Publishing Company, 1983), p. 75.

2. Ibid., p. 117.

3. Ibid., p. 125.

4. Ibid., p. 124.

5. See Bernard Lazerwitz, "Sampling Theory and Procedures," *Methodology in Social Research,* Hubert M. Blalock, Jr., and Ann B. Blalock, ed. (New York, New York: McGraw-Hill Book Company, 1968), p. 287.

6. See, for example, ibid.

7. See ibid.

8. See Blalock, Jr., *Social Statistics,* Second Edition, pp. 529f and Lazerwitz, "Sampling Theory and Procedures," pp. 287f.

9. See William L. Hays, *Statistics for Psychologists* (New York, New York: Holt, Rinehart, and Winston, 1963), p. 195.

10. See Lutz, *Understanding Social Statistics,* pp. 242–249.

11. See Lazerwitz, "Sampling Theory and Procedures," pp. 280f.

12. Kish, *Survey Sampling,* p. 7.

13. See ibid., pp. 384–439.

Chapter 7

1. See, for example, Kenneth D. Bailey, *Methods of Social Research,* Third Edition (New York, New York: The Free Press, 1987), pp. 87f; James A. Black and Dean J. Champion, *Methods and Issues in Social Research* (New York, New York: John Wiley & Sons, 1976), p. 276; Blalock, Jr., *Social Statistics,* Second Edition, p. 143; and Richard L. Scheaffer, William Mendenhall, and Lyman Ott, *Elementary Survey Sampling,* Second Edition (North Scituate, Massachusetts: Duxbury Press, 1979), p. 33.

2. See, for example, Morris James Slonin, *Sampling: A Quick Reliable Guide to Practical Statistics* (New York, New York: Simon and Schuster, 1960), p. 16 [Originally published as *Sampling in a Nutshell*]; Lutz, *Understanding Social Statistics,* p. 253; and Hays, *Statistics for Psychologists,* pp. 210 and 216.

3. See Lutz, *Understanding Social Statistics,* p. 254.

4. See, for example, Bailey, *Methods of Social Research,* Second Edition, pp. 87f; Black and Champion, *Methods and Issues in Social Research,* p. 276; and Sheldon Olson, *Ideas and Data: The Process and Prac-*

tice of Social Research (Homewood, Illinois: The Dorsey Press, 1976), p. 276.

5. See, for example, John H. Mueller, Karl F. Schuessler, and Herbert L. Costner, *Statistical Reasoning in Sociology,* Third Edition (Boston, Massachusetts: Houghton Mifflin Company, 1977), pp. 371ff; Blalock, Jr., *Social Statistics,* Second Edition, p. 143 and, particularly, p. 513; and Kish, *Survey Sampling,* p. 38.

6. Kish, *Survey Sampling,* p. 38.

7. Blalock, Jr., *Social Statistics,* Second Edition, p. 513.

8. See Kish, *Survey Sampling.*

9. Hays, *Statistics for Psychologists,* p. 215.

10. Ibid., p. 217.

11. Lutz, *Understanding Social Statistics,* p. 308.

12. Kirk W. Elifson, Richard P. Runyon, and Audrey Haber, *Fundamentals of Social Statistics* (Reading, Massachusetts: Addison-Wesley Publishing Company, 1982), p. 347.

13. See Lutz, *Understanding Social Statistics,* p. 254.

14. Blalock, Jr., *Social Statistics,* Second Edition, pp. 514f.

15. See Mueller, Schuessler, and Costner, *Statistical Reasoning in Sociology,* Third Edition, p. 379.

16. Scheaffer, Mendenhall, and Ott, *Elementary Survey Sampling,* Second Edition, p. 179.

17. See, for example, Herbert J. Rubin, *Applied Social Research* (Columbus, Ohio: Merrill Publishing Company, 1983), p. 151.

18. See, for example, Scheaffer, Mendenhall, and Ott, *Elementary Survey Sampling,* Second Edition, p. 182.

19. Blalock, Jr., *Social Statistics,* Second Edition, p. 516.

20. Ibid., p. 517.

21. See also Mueller, Schuessler, and Costner, *Statistical Reasoning in Sociology,* Third Edition, p. 375.

22. See Slonim, *Sampling: A Quick Reliable Guide to Practical Statistics,* p. 53.

23. See Mueller, Scheussler, and Costner, *Statistical Reasoning in Sociology,* Third Edition, p. 375.

24. Scheaffer, Mendenhall, and Ott, *Elementary Survey Sampling,* Second Edition, p. 60.

25. See Black and Champion, *Methods and Issues in Social Research,* p. 288.

26. See Kish, *Survey Sampling,* pp. 77–80.

27. See Louise H. Kidder, *Selltiz, Wrightsman and Cook's Research Methods in Social Relations,* Fourth Edition (New York, New York: Holt, Rinehart and Winston, 1981), p. 434.

28. Blalock, Jr., *Social Statistics,* Second Edition, p. 520.

29. Olson, *Ideas and Data: The Process and Practice of Social Research,* p. 278.

30. See Kish, *Survey Sampling.*

31. See Lazerwitz, "Sampling Theory and Procedures," pp. 298f.

32. Scheaffer, Mendenhall, and Ott, *Elementary Survey Sampling,* Second Edition, p. 142.

33. See Blalock, Jr., *Social Statistics,* Second Edition, p. 524.

34. Ibid., p. 527.

35. See Black and Champion, *Methods and Issues in Social Research,* p. 312.

36. Ibid., p. 312.

37. Ibid., p. 313.

38. Mueller, Scheussler, and Costner, *Statistical Reasoning in Sociology,* Third Edition, p. 409.

39. Hays, *Statistics for Psychologists,* pp. 203–206.

40. See Bailey, *Methods of Social Research,* Third Edition, p. 96.

41. Ibid.

42. See Lazerwitz, "Sampling Theory and Procedures," pp. 284f.

43. See Olson, *Ideas and Data: The Process and Practice of Social Research,* p. 274.

44. Black and Champion, *Methods and Issues in Social Research,* p. 314.

Chapter 8

1. See Richard S. Rudner, *Philosophy of Social Science* (Englewood Cliffs, New Jersey: Prentice-Hall, Inc., 1966), pp. 4–9.

2. Earl R. Babbie, *The Practice of Social Research,* Fifth Edition (Belmont, California: Wadsworth Publishing Company, 1989), p. 400.

3. See Erving Goffman, *Presentation of Self in Everyday Life* (Garden City, New York: Doubleday & Co., Inc., 1959).

Chapter 9

1. See Mueller, Schuessler, and Costner, *Statistical Reasoning in Sociology,* pp. 18ff.

2. See Blalock, Jr., *Social Statistics,* Second Edition, pp. 361–393.

3. See Leo A. Goodman and William H. Kruskal, "Measures of Association for Cross Classifications," *Journal of the American Statistical Association,* Vol. 49, No. 268 (December 1954), pp. 732–764.

4. See Babbie, *The Practice of Social Research,* Fifth Edition, pp. 390ff.

5. Harry S. Upshaw, "Attitude Measurement," *Methodology in Social Research,* Hubert M. Blalock, Jr., and Ann B. Blalock, ed. (New York, New York: McGraw-Hill Book Company, 1968), p. 96.

6. Ibid., p. 93.

7. See Andy B. Anderson, Alexander Basilevsky, and Derek P. J. Hum, "Measurement: Theory and Techniques," *Handbook of Survey Research,* Peter H. Rossi, James D. Wright, and Andy B. Anderson, ed. (New York, New York: Academic Press, 1983), p. 259.

8. See ibid., p. 264.

9. Ibid., p. 247.

10. See William J. Goode and Paul K. Hatt, *Methods in Social Research* (New York, New York: McGraw-Hill Book Company, 1952), pp. 145ff.

11. Ibid., p. 147.

12. See ibid., pp. 235f.

13. See Lutz, *Understanding Social Statistics,* pp. 206ff.

14. See Goode and Hatt, *Methods in Social Research,* p. 236.

15. Ibid., p. 236.

16. See ibid., pp. 237f.

17. See ibid., p. 238.

18. See Bernard S. Phillips, *Social Research: Strategy and Tactics,* Third Edition (New York, New York: Macmillan Publishing Co., 1976), pp. 139f.

19. See Claire Selltiz, Lawrence J. Wrightsman, and Stuart W. Cook, *Research Methods in Social Relations,* Third Edition (New York, New York: Holt, Rinehart and Winston, 1976), pp. 172–178.

Chapter 10

1. See Goode and Hatt, *Methods in Social Research,* pp. 176ff.

2. See Don A. Dillman, *Mail and Telephone Surveys: The Total Design Method* (New York, New York: John Wiley & Sons, 1978), pp. 166–172.

3. Ibid., p. 162.

4. See Raymond L. Gorden, *Interviewing: Strategy, Techniques, and Tactics,* Fourth Edition (Homewood, Illinois: The Dorsey Press, 1987), pp. 139–150.

5. See Dillman, *Mail and Telephone Surveys,* pp. 172f.

6. Ibid., pp. 163f.

7. See ibid., p. 164.

8. See Babbie, *The Practice of Social Research,* Fifth Edition, p. 241.

9. See ibid., p. 242.

10. See Bailey, *Methods of Social Research,* Third Edition, p. 169.

11. See David Nachmias and Chava Nachmias, *Research Methods in the Social Sciences,* Third Edition (New York, New York: St. Martin's Press, 1987), p. 235.

12. See Dillman, *Mail and Telephone Surveys,* p. 21.

13. See ibid.

14. See Raymond L. Gorden, *Interviewing: Strategy, Techniques, and Tactics,* Fourth Edition.

15. See William Foote Whyte, *Street Corner Society* (Chicago, Illinois: The University of Chicago Press, 1943).

16. See William R. Klecka and Alfred J. Tuchfarber, "Random Digit Dialing: A Comparison to Personal Surveys," *The Public Opinion Quarterly,* Vol. 42, No. 1 (Spring 1978), pp. 105–114.

17. Personal communication with an employee of the telephone company.

Chapter 11

1. See Goode and Hatt, *Methods in Social Research,* p. 76.

2. See Donald T. Campbell and Julian C. Stanley, *Experimental and Quasi-Experimental Designs for Research* (Chicago, Illinois: Rand McNally College Publishing Company, 1963), p. 25.

3. See Fritz J. Roethlisberger and William J. Dickson, *Management and the Worker* (Cambridge, Massachusetts: Harvard University Press, 1939).

4. See Richard L. Solomon, "Extension of Control Group Design," *Psychological Bulletin,* Vol. 46, No. 2 (March 1949), pp. 137–150.

5. See ibid. and see Richard L. Solomon and Michael S. Lessac, "A Control Group Design for Experimental Studies of Developmental Processes," *Psychological Bulletin,* Vol. 70, No. 3, Part 1 (September 1968), pp. 145–150.

6. See Campbell and Stanley, *Experimental and Quasi-Experimental Designs for Research.*

7. See Thomas D. Cook and Donald T. Campbell, *Quasi-Experimentation: Design and Analysis Issues for Field Settings* (Chicago, Illinois: Rand McNally College Publishing Company, 1979).

Chapter 12

1. Bernard Berelson, *Content Analysis in Communication Research* (Glencoe, Illinois: The Free Press, 1952), p. 18.

2. See Bailey, *Methods of Social Research,* Third Edition, p. 290 and pp. 301f.

3. Ole R. Holsti, *Content Analysis for the Social Sciences and Humanities* (Reading, Massachusetts: Addison-Wesley Publishing Company, 1969), p. 95.

4. See Fred N. Kerlinger, *Foundations of Behavioral Research,* Second Edition (New York, New York: Holt, Rinehart and Winston, 1973), pp. 524–535.

5. See Bailey, *Methods of Social Research,* Third Edition, pp. 289–315.

6. Holsti, *Content Analysis for the Social Sciences and Humanities,* p. 116.

7. See ibid., pp. 116–119.

8. See ibid., pp. 123f.

9. See Allen Edwards, *Techniques of Attitude Scale Construction* (New York, New York: Appleton-Century-Crofts, 1957), pp. 83–117.

10. See Bailey, *Methods of Social Research,* Third Edition, pp. 302–306.

11. Herbert H. Hyman, *Secondary Analysis of Sample Surveys: Principles, Procedures and Potentialities* (New York, New York: John Wiley and Sons, Inc., 1972), p. 1.

12. Ibid., p. 2.

13. Ibid., p. 1.

14. Ibid., p. 26.

15. See Janet G. Hunt and Larry L. Hunt, "Secondary Analysis: A Personal Journal," *Readings for Social Research,* Theodore C. Wagenaar, ed. (Belmont, California: Wadsworth Publishing Company, 1981), pp. 317–323.

16. See Walter Lippmann, *Public Opinion* (New York, New York: The Macmillan Company, 1922), pp. 3–32.

17. Hyman, *Secondary Analysis of Sample Surveys: Principles, Procedures and Potentialities,* p. 11.

18. See ibid., p. 8.

19. See ibid., p. 9.

20. See Catherine Hakin, *Secondary Analysis in Social Research: A Guide to Data Sources and Methods with Examples* (London, England: George Allen and Unwin, 1982), p. 1.

Chapter 13

1. See John I. Kitsuse and Aaron V. Cicourel, "A Note on the Uses of Official Statistics," *Social Problems,* Vol. 11, No. 2 (Fall 1963), pp. 131–139.

2. See Goffman, *Presentation of Self in Everyday Life.*

3. See W. I. Thomas and Dorothy Swaine Thomas, *The Child in America* (New York, New York: Alfred Knopf, 1928), p. 572.

4. See Buford H. Junker, *Fieldwork: An Introduction to the Social Sciences* (Chicago, Illinois: The University of Chicago Press, 1960).

5. See Roethlisberger and Dickson, *Management and the Worker.*

6. See Robert F. Bales, *Interaction Process Analysis: A Method for the Study of Small Groups* (Cambridge, Massachusetts: Addison-Wesley Publishing Company, 1950).

7. See Solomon E. Asch, "Studies of Independence and Conformity: A Minority of One against a Unanimous Majority," *Psychological Monographs,* Vol. 70, No. 416 (complete), 1956.

8. See Whyte, *Street Corner Society,* pp. 279–358.

9. See Muzafer Sherif, *The Psychology of Social Norms* (New York, New York: Harper & Row, 1936).

10. See Solomon E. Asch, "Effects of Group Pressure upon the Modification and Distortion of Judgments," E. E. Maccoby, T. M. Newcomb, and E. L. Hartley, ed., *Readings in Social Psychology,* Third Edition (New York, New York: Holt, Rinehart and Winston, 1958).

11. See Robert F. Bales, *Interaction Process Analysis.*

12. See Eugene J. Webb, Donald T. Campbell, Richard D. Schwartz, Lee Sechrest, and Janet Belew Grove, *Nonreactive Measures in the Social Sciences,* Second Edition (Boston, Massachusetts: Houghton Mifflin Company, 1981), p. 1.

13. See Jay Stanley, "An Empirical Study of Aggression and Parental Roles" (Unpublished M.A. Thesis, University of Tennessee, Knoxville, 1963).

14. Norman K. Denzin, *The Research Act: A Theoretical Introduction to Sociological Methods,* Third Edition (New York, New York: McGraw-Hill Book Company, 1988), p. 260.

15. See Eugene J. Webb et al., *Nonreactive Measures in the Social Sciences,* Second Edition.

16. See ibid., pp. 4–33, 78–143, 197–240, and 241–274.

17. See ibid., pp. 31ff.

18. See ibid., pp. 197–240.

19. See ibid., pp. 222.

20. See Kerlinger, *Foundations of Behavioral Research,* Second Edition, p. 406.

21. See James P. Spradley, *You Owe Yourself a Drunk: An Ethnography of Urban Nomads* (Boston, Massachusetts: Little Brown & Co., 1970).

Chapter 15

1. See Emile Durkheim, *Suicide: A Study in Sociology* (New York, New York: The Free Press, 1951).

2. See Max Weber, *The Protestant Ethic and the Spirit of Capitalism* (New York, New York: The Free Press, 1958).

3. See *SPSS-X User's Guide,* Third Edition (Chicago, Illinois: SPSS Inc, 1988), p. 10.

4. See Ibid., p. 11.

Chapter 16

1. See Edward Diener and Rick Crandall, *Ethics in Social and Behavioral Research* (Chicago, Illinois: The University of Chicago Press, 1978), p. 34.

2. See ibid.

3. See Stanley Milgram, "Behavioral Study of Obedience," *Journal of Abnormal and Social Psychology,* Vol. 67, No. 4 (1963), pp. 371–378 and "Some Conditions of Obedience and Disobedience to Authority," *Human Relations,* Vol. 18, No. 1 (February 1965), pp. 57–76.

4. See Philip G. Zimbardo, "Psychology of Imprisonment," *Society,* Vol. 9 (April 1972), pp. 4–8.

5. See Diener and Crandall, *Ethics in Social and Behavioral Research,* pp. 78f.

6. See ibid., p. 7.

7. See ibid., p. 24.

8. See Janet B. Hardy, Doris W. Welcher, Jay Stanley, and Joseph R. Dallas, "Long Range Outcome of Adolescent Pregnancy," *Clinical Obstetrics and Gynecology,* Vol. 21, No. 4 (December 1978), pp. 1215–1232.

9. Diener and Crandall, *Ethics in Social and Behavioral Research,* p. 151.

10. See ibid., p. 158.

11. For a more in-depth discussion of bias concerns, see Diener and Crandall, *Ethics in Social and Behavioral Research,* pp. 151–162.

12. See *Social Problems,* Vol. 27, No. 3 (February 1980), and *American Sociologist,* Vol. 13, No. 3 (August 1978), pp. 128–177.

13. We have leaned heavily upon the suggestions and guidelines of Edward Diener and Rick Crandall, *Ethics in Social and Behavioral Research* (Chicago, Illinois: The University of Chicago Press, 1978) in a number of segments of this chapter. In summarizing our discussion of ethical considerations, we can do no better than to refer to the guidelines offered by Diener and Crandall at the conclusion of their volume, pp. 215–217.

Appendix A

1. See Delbert C. Miller, "An Outline Guide for the Design of a Social Research Problem," [Adapted from Russell L. Ackoff, *The Design of Social Research* (Chicago, Illinois: The University of Chicago Press, 1953)], *Handbook of Research Design and Social Measurement,* Delbert C. Miller, ed., Fourth Edition (New York, New York: Longman, Inc., 1983), p. 3.

GLOSSARY

The number or numbers that appear following each entry refer to the chapter or chapters in which the principal discussion of the concept appears. Any concept in capital letters is a computer command. If it is followed by *(SPSS^x)*, it is relevant to SPSS^x software; if it is followed by *(VAX)*, it is a VAX software command.

Abscissa   the horizontal axis in a two-dimensional graph; also called the *X axis*; compare with the term *ordinate*. (6)

Absolute hypothesis   an analytical statement in the language of hypothesis testing that contains a minimum of two class I variables and *only* class I objects of the research. (3)

Accidental sample   also called *haphazard* and *availability,* a type of nonprobability sample for which the sampling elements are selected because of their accessibility and convenience. (7)

Account number   the address in the computer's memory where the researcher's data, program, and output files are stored. (15)

Accretion measure   a subcategory of a physical-trace unobtrusive measure indicating evidence of deposits to objects or the environment over time, e.g., cigarette butts in a hidden part of the high school property or fingerprints on a museum exhibit. (13)

Acquiescence tendency   the tendency of some respondents to reply on a survey measuring instrument negatively or positively to all or almost all of the items given in an index; synonymous with the term *response set*. (8)

Active file   in SPSS^x, the file that one creates when one logs onto the computer for a working session. (15)

After-groups design   a quasi-experimental research design in which one after measures two groups, only one of which has been exposed to the experimental stimulus. (11)

Analytical proposition   a statement in the language of conceptualization that suggests some sort of relationship between two or more concepts or constructs. (2)

Anonymity   the construction of the research design in such a way that the identities of the participants in the study are impossible to determine. (10 and 16)

Antagonistic question   an abrasive question that is likely to aggravate or embarrass the respondent and that is highly likely to generate a socially desirable response or vehement denial (e.g., how often do you beat your spouse?). (8)

Applied knowledge   information that is perceived to be of benefit to society or knowledge that is believed to help alleviate some sort of human problem. (1)

Applied research   research that is designed to lead to applied knowledge (see previous term, *applied knowledge*); compare with the term *pure research*. (16)

Arbitrary collapse of data   the grouping of data into categories on the basis of the investigator's own personal judgment; since no other principle or source of information is utilized, this is an unacceptable mechanism for operationalizing tabular categories. (14)

Arbitrary zero point   one of the characteristics of the interval level of measurement wherein a zero amount is that point that scientists have decided to call zero; there can be quantities smaller than zero or negative numbers (e.g., Celsius temperature), compare with the term *nonarbitrary zero point*. (9)

Archive   a repository for public and private written, video, and audio documents, which constitute a subcategory of unobtrusive or nonreactive measures. (13)

Associational relationship   one in which a change in the amount or direction of one or more factors is accompanied by a change in the amount or direction of one or more different factors; the idea of association is synonymous with the concept of *correlation*. (2)

Assuming (embarrassing) question   a survey question that is assuming because of the way it is posed to the respondent and embarrassing because of its content (e.g., "Everyone has problems in a marriage. When was the last time you and your spouse had a fight?"). (10)

Asymmetric measure a statistical procedure designed for use when the researcher has selected one or more variables as the independent variables; compare with symmetric measure. (15)

Attitude of skepticism the scientific attitude that recognizes the negative aspects of the scientific epistemology and that stresses caution in evaluating the results of scientific research. (1)

Attribute a characteristic that is a subcategory of a more general dimension (e.g., male and female are attributes of the dimension of sex). (2)

Authority a person who is believed to be a source of the truth because he or she is an expert or highly respected. (1)

Basic knowledge knowledge that has no practical utility except that it satisfies the researcher's desire to know; knowledge for knowledge's sake emerges from basic, or pure, research. (1)

Basic research a study devoted to the investigation of a research problematic designed to generate basic knowledge; synonymous with the term *pure research;* compare with the term *applied research.* (5)

Before-and-after design a quasi-experimental research design in which one before and after measures a single group that has been exposed to some experimental stimulus; synonymous with the terms *panel design* and *succession design.* (11)

Bias in sampling, a general category of errors that do not cancel out but tend to accumulate, or mount up (e.g., the tendency among older respondents to underreport their ages). (6)

Binary code a series of zeroes and ones into which information, as we know it, is translated and through which a computer is able to do mathematical calculations and reproduce alphabetic characters; synonymous with the term *machine language.* (15)

Bivariate analysis investigation into the nature of the relationships between two variables. (Preface)

Bivariate measure a statistical procedure that measures some characteristic between two variables. (15)

Block variable control a separation of the cases to be analyzed into two or more relevant subcategories or attributes on the variable or variables that are controlled as a class II variable or variables. (3)

Body the total number of cells in any given table, not including the descriptive headings, the marginals, or the grand total. (14)

Cathode-ray tube (CRT) the televisionlike screen that functions to provide a computer user with a visual image of what has been typed on the keyboard; synonymous with the term *monitor.* (15)

Causal relationship a relationship in which one or more independent factors are believed to determine, be responsible for, or create one or more other dependent factors. (2)

Causation the process or mechanism in which one set of factors called the independent factors are responsible for the establishment of a second set of factors called the dependent factors. (4)

Cell any one of the divisions in a table identified by a specific attribute of the row variable and a specific attribute of the column variable. (14)

CELLS subcommand (SPSSˣ) a subcommand of the CROSSTABS TABLES command that allows one to customize the content of the cross-tabulation or table that SPSSˣ has been asked to produce. (15)

Central limit theorem a statistical principle that says that the sampling distribution from repeated samples of large size will be nearly normal in shape even though the characteristic being measured is not normally distributed within the population. (6)

Central processing unit (CPU) the part of the computer hardware that receives input, analyzes it according to specific programming instructions, and stores the results either internally on hard disk or externally on a floppy disk. (15)

Central tendency a category of descriptive statistics or descriptive parameters that suggests that a single value is typical of a whole set of such values, e.g., statistical mean, median, or mode. (6)

Chance the variation from what is expected to happen due to factors that the scientist either has not been able to measure or has not been able to discover. (4)

Character when using a computer, any single keystroke, whether it is a number, letter, or single mark, such as the dollar sign ($). (15)

Class I variable an explanatory variable that is an object of the research and treated as either an independent variable or a dependent variable. (3)

Class II variable an extraneous variable that has been controlled by the researcher so that the effects of this variable either do not fluctuate within the context of the study or fluctuate in known ways. (3)

Class III variable an extraneous variable whose effect on one or more of the objects of the research has not been controlled and which is affecting one or more of the class I variables in a differential way. (3)

Class IV variable an extraneous variable that is not an object of the research, is not controlled, and is assumed to have no effect on one or more of the class I variables. (3)

Classical experimental design the experimental research design that incorporates Mill's method-of-difference canon for the demonstration of causality involving one experimental group, which is before and after measured and exposed to the experimental stimulus, and one control group, which is before and after measured but not exposed to the experimental stimulus. (11)

Close-ended response categories predetermined response categories from which the survey respondent must choose in response to a question or statement, e.g., "yes" or "no" and "strongly agree" to "strongly disagree"; synonymous with the term *structured response categories*. (10)

Cluster sampling a probability type of sampling that involves the selection of *groups* of persons and which can be done without an accurate listing of the sampling frame. (7)

Codebook a document that functions to tell the coder how to translate schedule responses into numerical codes in the data file, to tell the keyboard operator which symbols to input, and to explain where the coded information is to be found in the data file. (15)

Coding the process of assigning numerical values to responses for the purposes of easier data manipulation through machine processing. (8 and 15)

Coding error a data preparation error in which a designated numerical value for one attribute is used for a different attribute. (6)

Coding form any number of sheets of paper that are organized into blank rows and columns on which data codes are placed prior to their entry into a data file. (15)

Coefficient of reproducibility a statistical formula that measures the scalability of a Guttman scale, with any value less than 0.90 considered too small to guarantee reasonable success in interpreting the Guttman measure as having a true intensity order. (9)

COMMENT command (SPSS^x) a command that is not processed or read by the computer and that allows the researcher to enter any type of statement desired; if the statement runs for more than one line, each line must begin with "COMMENT"; useful in documenting one's program file. (15)

Commonsense proposition a statement of a relationship that the general public believes to exist as an empirical reality; a notion shared widely by the general public. (5)

Comparison group the group that is exposed to the normal or naturally occurring environmental conditions, when it would be unethical to withhold the experimental stimulus from the research subjects, thereby preventing the use of a control group; e.g., the experimental group is given a new medical drug, while the comparison group is given the conventional medical treatment. (11 and 16)

Complex issue a statement or question that contains more than one issue and that is likely to confuse or frustrate the respondent into making an inappropriate and unusable response. (8)

Composite measure a measuring instrument containing more than one item and which can take the form of an index or scale; examples are the Likert, Thurstone, and Guttman measures and the semantic differential. (9)

Computer-assisted telephone interviewing (CATI) a relatively new data-gathering design in which many of the advantages of a face-to-face interview can be achieved over the telephone without the great costs of time and money that usually accompany interviews in the field; if done with the aid of a computer, this technique can greatly simplify both the data-entry and data-analysis processes. (10)

Concept a general idea or abstraction that refers to a whole category of tangible, or concrete, items, e.g., chair, table, occupation. (2)

Conceptual model a partial explanation of some phenomenon written in the language of conceptualization. (2, 4, and 5)

Concurrent criterion validity one of two criterion-validity techniques through which one compares the results from a measure to be validated with the results of a well-accepted measure, expecting a very strong positive correlation between the two measures. (9)

Confederate a person who plays a predetermined role in a research project; e.g., in Asch's experiments on group influence on the individual, several people were told to respond in certain ways prior to the experimental situation on the reactions of a single experimental subject. (13)

Confidence interval a statistical concept through which one can create, using the standard normal distribution, a range of values around a selected estimate of some characteristic within which one can be confident, to some predetermined degree, that the true population value falls. (6)

Confidentiality a situation in which the researcher agrees to keep the identity of the respondents secret so that the respondents will be known to only the researcher. (10). [Second definition: in Junker's discussion of marginality in observational research, a stage at which the researcher is made privy to information without knowing the source. (13 and 16)]

Constant a factor that never changes or that has been manipulated by the researcher so that it does not have a differential effect on any of the class I variables. (3)

Construct a general idea or abstraction that refers to a whole category of intangible or nonconcrete items, e.g., dreams, feelings, attitudes. (2)

Construct validity the most elusive and difficult validity test in which one looks for a number of concrete measures to correlate with the abstract construct and in which one expects consistency of direction but not necessarily very strong correlations. (9)

Content analysis a basic data-gathering procedure that involves the sampling and analysis of usually written or verbal communication sources. (12)

Context unit in content analysis, the selection of a larger unit rather than the desired recording unit in order to assess not only the frequency of occurrence of certain words but also the degree of favorableness, indicated when the recording unit is found. (12)

Continuum a line or scale on which the occurrence of various values of a variable are represented. (14)

Contrived observation data gathered through audio or visual mechanical recording devices, which function to fill observational voids created when the observer is not able to perceive what is happening. (13)

Control group the group that is not exposed to the stimulus or treatment in any experimental or quasi-experimental data-gathering design. (11)

Correlational consistency one of two additional criteria which strengthen Mill's method of concomitant variation canon of evidence for causality in which the direction (either positive or negative) of the associational values is repeatedly found to exist when the same variables are correlated in a variety of different research contexts or a variety of samples composed of people with different characteristics. (4)

Correlational magnitude one of two criteria that strengthens the scientist's causal interpretation of an associational relationship and that refers to the strength of the associational value. (4)

Correlational relationship one where a change in the amount or direction of one or more factors is accompanied by a change in the amount or direction of one or more different factors; the idea of a correlation is synonymous with the concept of *association*. (2)

Cost-benefit analysis an ethical criterion in which the researcher compares the advantageous aspects against the detrimental aspects of the research; the study is deemed ethical if the advantages outweigh the disadvantages; your authors believe that this is not the soundest criterion. (16)

Cover letter   the researcher's first contact with the respondent in a mailed questionnaire data-gathering study; it should contain an intriguing first sentence, the nature of the study and who is sponsoring it, why the respondent was selected, a statement of anonymity or confidentiality (if applicable), a rationale for the study, and any other relevant items. (10)

Cover sheet   the first page of a measuring instrument, usually in schedule format, that contains essentially administrative information (such as the title of the study) and material to orient and direct the respondent. (8)

Covert role   the role played by the researcher when it is decided to withhold from the persons studied that they are part of an observational research study; while this leads to more natural behavior on the part of the sample, it is not an ethical stance for the researcher to take; compare with the term *overt role*. (13)

Criterion validation   a general validity strategy involving the comparison of the results of the to-be-validated measure with the results of some already valid well-accepted standard; two specific forms exist: *predictive validity* and *concurrent criterion validity*. (9)

Cross-lagging   a technique for determining which of two variables is independent and which is dependent, involving the comparative analysis of two associational statistics between two variables, measured two times on the same sample of cases. (4)

Cross-sectional design   a quasi-experimental data gathering design involving two groups: (a) an experimental group that is exposed to the stimulus, or treatment, and after measured and (b) a control group that is only before measured. (11)

Cross-sectional study   one in which the required data are gathered for any one person or case at a *single* point in time; appropriate for comparing one variable with another, but not appropriate for measuring change; compare with *longitudinal study*.

CROSSTABS TABLES command (SPSS^x)   a command that allows the relationship of a limited number of categories of two or more variables to one another in tabular format; it is used often with the CELLS subcommand to customize one's data output and with the STATISTICS subcommand to generate various statistical values. (15)

Cross-tabulation   the distribution of the frequency or percentage of cases that jointly possess specified attributes on two or more dimensions. (14)

Data cleaning   any one of a number of computer mechanisms for determining the accuracy of one's data file; an essential process necessary to debug one's data file. (15)

Data file   any computer file that contains the coded information that is to be stored and subsequently analyzed according to the instructions provided by a program file. (15)

Data-gathering design   the procedure or strategy through which the social scientist intends to collect the information needed for the study; among the strategies subsumed here are surveys, both questionnaires and interviews; experiments; observational strategies; secondary analysis; the use of official statistics; and unobtrusive measures (see Part III). (8)

DATA LIST command (SPSS^x)   a command that identifies which data file is to be used, the number of records that are contained, and the column location and variable name of each variable that appears within the data file. (15)

Debriefing   one of several ways to defuse or reduce any harmful consequences that accrue to the research participant; it entails further explanation of the research that could not have been divulged prior to the execution of the study and allows for the participant to voice any negative feelings, which can be dealt with by the research team. (16)

Debugging   the process of responding to a computer's list of errors by revising the inaccuracies within the program and data files. (15)

Deception   an ethical difficulty which involves deliberately misleading the research participant for the purpose of producing more natural or unbiased research results. (16)

Deduction   rational thinking in which one moves from a general idea to a more specific one. (1 and 3)

Dependent variable   (a) class I, explanatory, variable, which is caused by one or more other class I, independent and explanatory, variables; or (b) one whose value is to be predicted. (3)

Descriptive knowledge information that communicates the distribution or occurrence of a given variable. (1)

Descriptive proposition a statement in the language of conceptualization that suggests the occurrence or the distribution of a single concept or construct; e.g., all physicians are wealthy or the national debt is growing. (2)

Descriptive statistic any one of several basic types of mathematical measures of samples that summarizes or condenses empirical data, e.g., mean, median, mode, standard deviation, range, and associational values. (6)

Determinism the idea that nothing happens in nature without natural causes and the additional notion that cause-and-effect relationships are inevitable. (1)

Dimension the word that refers to the sum or totality of all its logically related attributes or subcategories; e.g., sex is the dimension to the attributes of male and female. (2)

Disembodied posturing an unobtrusive subtype of expressive movement, which is a subtype of simple observation and which occurs when one's body language communicates a different or contradictory message than one's verbal behavior. (13)

Disk drive a computer structure within the central processing unit, which functions to take off or put data or program instructions on a floppy disk. (15)

Disproportional stratified sample a type of probability sampling procedure in which strata on some variable are first created and then different sampling fractions are used in selecting elements from these strata resulting in percentages of the sample strata that differ from the percentages of the strata in the sampling frame; best when one is investigating differences among strata and when there are radically different numbers of elements within the strata. (7)

Distribution based on statistical requirements an unacceptable strategy for determining the operational definition of tabular categories, which involves combining subcategories of data for the sole purpose of achieving a statistically acceptable minimum number of cases for statistical analysis; this problem can be eliminated by the preparation of a research proposal and the inclusion of a disproportional stratified sampling design. (14)

Double-blind experiment an experimental design in which neither those who are the study subjects nor those who are conducting the evaluation know who is exposed to the experimental stimulus in the experimental group and who is not exposed to it in the control group. (11)

Dummy terminal a keyboard and a monitor (CRT) that are connected to a central processing unit (CPU); the dummy terminal cannot process program instructions since it is only capable of receiving output or sending input to the CPU. (15)

Ecological fallacy a logical error that involves attributing a value of some variable derived from one unit of analysis to a different unit of analysis. (6 and 11)

Embodied posturing an unobtrusive subtype of expressive movement, which is a subtype of simple observation and which occurs when one's body language and verbal behavior communicate an identical message. (13)

Empirical determination a strategy for determining the operational definitions of tabular attributes (when the previous literature fails to present such information), which involves plotting the empirical results of one's study on a continuum and looking for naturally occurring groupings of cases. (14)

Empirical model a partial simulation or laboratory replication, which contains concrete examples of some aspects of the real world. (3)

Empiricism the idea that sense experience is the only reliable source of knowledge. (1)

Epistemology the branch of philosophy that investigates the origin, structure, methods, and validity of knowledge systems. (1)

Equal probability of selection one of the two criteria for a simple random sample where each element in the sampling frame has the *same probability* of selection as any other element throughout the sampling process; this means sampling with replacement. (7)

Erosion measure a subcategory of a physical trace unobtrusive measure indicating evidence of wear or use of objects or the environment over time, e.g., floor tiles that are more worn at one museum exhibit than another. (13)

Experiment   a data-gathering strategy that maximizes the researcher's control in that the researcher is able to determine randomly how the experimental subjects are assigned to the experimental and control group or groups and can control the intensity and timing of the before measure, the exposure to the experimental stimulus, and the after measure. (11)

Experimental group   the group that will be exposed to the experimental stimulus, treatment, or intervention. (11)

Explanation   one of the modes of elaboration that involves the selection of a test factor, which is antecedent to both the supposed independent and dependent variables. (4)

Explanatory knowledge   information that provides acceptable answers to the questions scientists raise about their subject matter. (1)

Explanatory proposition   a statement of a relationship of very broad scope or applicability, a type that is probably beyond the empirical information currently available to the social and behavioral scientist; compare with the term *middle range proposition*. (5)

Explanatory variable   a class I variable, which is an object of the research and which is either an independent or dependent variable; synonymous with *Class I variable*. (3)

Exploratory research   the first research one does when there is a lack of descriptive data and, probably, no conceptual model to direct one's efforts; the main objective of exploratory research is to complete one's study with a set of hypotheses for more systematic testing. (13)

Expressive movement   a type of simple observation unobtrusive measure which is more popularly known as body language. (13)

Extraneous variable   a variable that is not the object of the research and that can be controlled (class II), uncontrolled and confounding (class III), or uncontrolled and assumed irrelevant (class IV). (3)

Face validity   the selection of items that the researcher determines to be valid because they seem logically to be related to the variable being measured. (8 and 9)

Face-to-face interview   one type of survey data-gathering design in which the interviewer reads the schedule, or guide, items and copies down the replies, while the respondent replies in a setting in which both persons are physically able to see and hear one another. (10)

Factor   a basic dimension in science containing either the attribute of concepts or constructs or the attribute of variables. (2)

Factorial design   an experimental design that allows the researcher to test the effects of two or more experimental treatments or stimuli singularly and in combination through the use of multiple experimental groups and a single control group. (11)

Falsified answer   a nonsampling error in which the respondent purposely provides an untrue response. (6)

Field research   research that takes place in its natural setting and that makes maximum demands on the researcher's observational capacities because of the lack of control that can be exercised over the research setting; compatible with the term *natural setting*. (13)

FILE HANDLE command (SPSS^x)   the command that gives the active file a name when one wishes to work on the computer; this is different from data, program, or output files, which can be stored within the computer. (15)

File name   the label given to any computer file that is to be stored so that it can be called upon and found later. (15)

Filter question   a schedule question that functions to separate those who should respond to subsequent items from those for whom those items are inappropriate; synonymous with the term *sieve question*. (8)

FINISH command (SPSS^x)   the final command given at the end of the program file that tells the computer that one has concluded the desired set of program instructions. (15)

Finitely conditional hypothesis   an analytical hypothesis in which some of the extraneous variables have been controlled as class II variables. (3)

First-order variable   any census measure that deals with fertility (birth rates), mortality (death rates), and migration (movement to and from a specified area). (12)

Floppy disk   a somewhat flexible, flat, magnetized disk on which computer files may be stored; compare with *hard disk*. (15)

Follow-up mailings   any one of usually three mailings in a questionnaire data-gathering design that are subsequent to the initial mailing and are designed to increase the response rate of the sample. (10)

Forewarning   a mechanism for dealing with the harmful or potentially harmful aspects of a research study, which involves intentionally telling the potential participant that some degree of deception is a part of the proposed study; this affords the potential participant the opportunity to refuse to participate. (16)

FREQUENCIES command (SPSSˣ**)**   a command that generates a number of descriptive statistics on any number of specified variables contained within a data file. (15)

Frequency   in general terms, the total number of cases possessing some attribute; in specific terms, the number of cases within a cell in tabular presentations that jointly share specific attributes on two or more dimensions. (14)

Frequency distribution control   a matching technique that involves the equation of *groups* of persons in terms of the overall distribution of a series of variables. (3)

Function key   a single keystroke or limited number of keystrokes that are built into a piece of software and that cause the central processing unit to perform various data manipulations. (15)

General item   a measuring instrument question or statement that is broad or global in its scope and that allows the respondent to mention whatever the respondent happens to have in mind; compare with the term *specific item*. (8)

Genuine test stimulus   a stimulus given to the experimental group in a double-blind experiment using a placebo. (11)

Guide   one of two survey measuring instruments that contains a general list of topics the researcher wants asked; it is usually used in interview data-gathering designs and in the context of exploratory research rather than in hypothesis testing, compare with *schedule*. (8)

Guttman scale   a composite measure that possesses an internal intensity order among the items con-

tained within it and that reflects not only the respondent's intensity of feeling but also the exact pattern of feeling as well. (9)

Hard copy   a printout on paper of the requested computer input or output. (15)

Hard disk   a permanently installed, internal structure within the central processing unit of a computer in which data, program, and output files are stored. (15)

Hard-wired   having a connection between a dummy terminal and a mainframe central processing unit so that one is in immediate communication with the mainframe after turning on the dummy terminal. (15)

Hawthorne effect   the alteration by respondents of their behavior simply because of the *presence* of the researcher; this effect argues for the researcher's assuming a participant and covert role. (11 and 13)

Heterogeneity   in sampling, diversity of one's population on a number of variables of interest to the researcher; one needs a larger size sample for representativeness than if the population was homogeneous. (6)

Heuristic research   research which is particularly important, not only for what it says, but also for its characteristic of stimulating additional inquiry. (5)

HISTOGRAM subcommand (SPSSˣ**)**   a subcommand that requests histograms on the variables identified on the FREQUENCIES command. (15)

Homogeneity   in sampling, similarity of one's population on a number of variables of interest to the researcher; one needs a smaller size sample for representativeness than if the population was heterogeneous. (6)

Human subjects committee   an internally based committee (within the university, funding agency, or research firm) whose responsibility is to evaluate science research proposals to ensure that they meet ethical standards. (16)

Hypothesis   a statement written in the language of hypothesis testing containing variables that have been operationally defined and that can be empirically tested. (3)

Ideal type   Max Weber's notion of the characteristics found in a pure case of the phenomenon one

wishes to describe; this concept is both a theoretical and a methodological notion. (2)

Idiographic explanation   a total accounting of the
variables involved and their relationships as they
relate to a single situation. (1)

Inaccurate answer   a nonsampling error in which the
respondent unintentionally provides an incorrect
response. (6)

Inclusivity   any type of classification that is designed
to result in the categorization of all the empirical
cases studied, with each case falling into one and
only one category. (8 and 14)

Incompleteness   a difficulty of content analysis in
which the data have segments missing (e.g., some
meetings not covered) or in which pertinent information has been left out (e.g., the committee
voted, but no specific vote count is presented).
(12)

Independence of choice   one of two criteria for a
simple random sample in which each selection
from the sampling frame is made completely
separately from every other selection. (7)

Independent variable   a class I, explanatory, variable, which is responsible for causing another
variable or series of variables in a causal relationship or a variable whose value is known and
will be used to predict another variable. (3)

Index   one of two basic types of composite measures
that contains more than one item, has no internal
intensity order, and whose items are usually
thought to measure the underlying variable
equally. (8 and 9)

Indicator   a multidimensional measure that includes
two or more indexes, or scales. (9)

Induction   rational thinking in which one infers from
a specific situation to a more general one. (Preface and 3)

Inferential statistic   a statistic that functions to measure the likelihood that some descriptive statistic
of a sample is also true within a selected degree
of error of the population parameter; it is also
called an *inductive statistic*. (6)

Infinitely conditional hypothesis   an analytical hypothesis in which *all* of the extraneous variables
have been controlled as class II variables; this is
a theoretical, rather than an empirical, possibility
at the present time. (3)

Informed consent   a basic requirement for an ethical
research study, which requires that the potential
participant explicitly tell the researcher that he or
she is willing to participate after having been
honestly and completely told about the nature of
the research situation; one concentrates here on
those factors considered harmful to the participant. (16)

Initial mailing   the first mailing in a mailed questionnaire survey data-gathering design, which should
include the schedule, a cover letter, and a stamped,
return envelope (and, under some conditions, a
return postcard) for the respondent to return the
completed schedule. (10)

Interaction   the idea that the combined effect of two
or more variables may be more or less than the
simple sum of their individual contributions (3);
see also Solomon's use of the term in experimental data-gathering designs. (11)

Internal intensity order   the format of a composite
measure in scale form in which the arrangement
of the items is in a definite order that is reflective
of different degrees of the variable and each item
extrinsically identifies a different point in this
order. (9)

Interpretation   one of the modes of elaboration. It
involves the selection of a test factor, which is an
intervening variable between the independent and
the dependent variable. (4)

Interval level of measurement   one of four levels of
measurement that has two characteristics: a constant unit of measure (e.g., an inch, pound) and
an arbitrary zero point. (9)

Interview   one of two survey data-gathering designs
in which there is a face-to-face (or telephone)
conversation between an interviewer and a respondent for the purposes of eliciting information; compare with *questionnaire*. (8 and 10)

Intuition   the very strong feeling that what one believes is true. (1)

Item   (a) any single statement or question found in an
interview guide or questionnaire schedule that is
thought to adequately measure a single variable
of interest or that is a part of a composite measure (9); (b) in content analysis, an entire document, be it a book, film, or television program.
(12)

Item analysis a technique used to select appropriate items for inclusion in a composite measure in which the coded value of the specific item in question is correlated with the entire composite score; if the correlation value is not strongly positive, the item is rejected. (9)

Item misinterpretation a nonsampling error in which the respondent provides an inaccurate response because the respondent misunderstands the survey item being asked. (6)

Judgmental sample a type of nonprobability sample in which the researcher is free to select any element that the researcher's judgment and expertise identify as a typical element; synonymous with the term *purposive sample*. (7)

Jury opinion validity a technique for testing a measure's validity in which a number of persons believed to be experts in the area being measured are asked to examine and report their assessment of the to-be-validated measure. (9)

Key respondent those persons sampled who have specialized or particularly insightful knowledge. (10)

Keyboard a typewriterlike structure with additional function keys that allows one to input data and programming instructions into the central processing unit of a computer. (15)

Known-groups validity an empirical validity test of a measure in which two groups already known to be at the extremes of the continuum being measured are given the to-be-validated measure with the expectation that both those that are high or possess a lot of the variable being measured and those that are low or possess little of the variable will so indicate this. (9)

Known nonparticipant one of four modalities in observational research in which the researcher tells the respondents that he or she is a researcher (the overt role) and will not take an active part in the study group's activities. (13)

Known participant one of the four modalities in observational research in which the researcher tells the respondents that he or she is a researcher (the overt role) and will be taking an active part in the activities of the study group. (13)

Laboratory setting the setting for a controlled experimental design, i.e., not in the field or a natural setting where the interaction normally occurs. (13)

Lack of availability a difficulty in content analysis in which certain existing records cannot be used by the researcher because of the guarantee of confidentiality, national security concerns, or similar reasons. (12)

Language behavior one type of unobtrusive, simple observation measure that involves noting the substance and tone of verbal utterances. (13)

Language of conceptualization one of the two languages of science, which contain concepts, constructs, theoretical definitions, propositions, theories, and conceptual models and which scientists use to communicate with one another. (2)

Language of hypothesis testing one of the two languages of science, which contain variables, operational definitions, hypotheses, simulations, and empirical models and which scientists use to empirically test their ideas. (2)

Latent content in content analysis, the essential or underlying implication or meaning in any particular communication; this is very hard to objectively determine. (12)

Letter of introduction functions in the interview data-gathering survey much like the cover letter in a questionnaire data-gathering survey by informing the interviewee that he or she has been selected for study and by encouraging the interviewee's participation; compare with the term *cover letter*. (10)

Levels of measurement one of several important prerequisites for the legitimate use and interpretation of statistical formulas; generally, four levels are recognized: nominal, ordinal, interval, and ratio. (9)

Likert response categories usually an ordinal series of five response categories (strongly agree, agree, don't know, disagree, strongly disagree) developed by Rensis Likert, not to be confused with a Likert scale that uses the Likert response categories. (8)

Likert scale a composite measure in index format that not only contains the Likert response categories but also has been framed by taking only those items that have been selected through the item analysis procedure. (9)

Linear association   the association where one unit of change in one or more factors is accompanied by a constant unit of change in one or more other factors. (4)

Logical reasoning   thinking in a reasonable fashion, using deduction and induction. (1)

Longitudinal study   a research design that involves a minimum of two measurements of the same subject matter at a minimum of two times; compare with *cross-sectional study*. (4)

Machine language   a series of zeroes and ones representing letters of the alphabet, numbers in the base ten system, and other characters in a form that can be electronically manipulated within the central processing unit of a computer; synonymous with the term *binary code*. (15)

Mailed questionnaire   a survey data-gathering design in which the schedule, or guide, to which the respondent is to respond is sent to the respondent and returned to the researcher through the postal system; its major advantages are in money and time savings. (10)

Mainframe computer   a large capacity computer with a number of dummy terminals connected to it; because it processes information so quickly, it allows more than one person to work on it at the same time. (15)

Manifest content   content analysis that is focused on what is explicitly presented in verbal and written communications, e.g., counting the frequencies of the appearance of selected words, themes, or sentence fragments. (12)

Marginal   the *subtotals* found in any row or column of a tabular presentation; does not include the grand total. (14)

Marginality   in observational research, according to Junker, the degree to which the researcher is excluded from full knowledge of the subject matter; Junker identified four degrees of marginality: public, confidential, secret, and private. (13)

Masking   the alteration of the respondent's behavior in an observational research study from what it would normally be due to the presence of the researcher who is a known participant (playing an overt research role) within the group being studied. (13)

Matching control   the adjustment of an experimental or quasi-experimental data-gathering design so that a number of groups or cases have been equated on a limited number of variables. (3)

Matrix format   the separation of items from response categories and the alignment of the response categories to reduce respondent error and to efficiently use schedule space. (8)

Method of agreement   one of Mill's canons of evidence for causality which can be subdivided into the *positive canon of agreement* and the *negative canon of agreement*. (4)

Method of concomitant variation   one of Mill's canons of evidence for causality, which states that if two factors are causally related, a change in one factor will be accompanied by a change in the other factor; of the four canons presented, this one is the most frequently used in the social and behavioral sciences. (4)

Method of difference   one of Mill's canons of evidence for causality, which states that when one has but two situations and they are exactly the same with the exception that one situation contains two factors and the other does not contain the two factors, there is a causal relationship between the two factors; the logic of this canon underlines the classical experimental design. (4 and 11)

Method of residues   one of Mill's canons of evidence for causality, which assumes more than one independent variable and which says that if one knows all the independent factors causing a situation, if one knows the total consequence of all the factors, and if one knows the contribution of all the factors except one to this consequence, one can determine the last factor's contribution; this canon assumes more information about cause and effect relationships than the social and behavioral scientist has at this time. (4)

Microcomputer   a completely self-contained computer unit that can accommodate only one user at a time; also called a *stand-alone computer*. (15)

Middle-range proposition   a statement of a relationship of modest, rather than gradiose, scope which Merton, and your authors, believe appropriate at the current stage of conceptual development of the social and behavioral sciences; compare with the term *explanatory proposition*. (5)

MISSING VALUES command (SPSS^x)   a command that is used to identify those data file codes that are not to be processed because they are not germane to the analysis. (15)

Modem a peripheral device that connects a dummy terminal or microcomputer to a mainframe computer through telephone wires. (15)

Modes of elaboration a data-analysis strategy involving the recomputation of the association between two class I variables after controlling on a test factor to determine the test factor's influence; pioneering technique by Kendall and Lazarsfeld and significantly expanded by Rosenberg. (4)

Monitor the televisionlike screen that functions to allow the user to see the input into or output from the computer; synonymous with the term *cathode-ray tube* (CRT). (15)

Multidimensionality an indicator that assesses more than one characteristic in which more than one item is used to tap into each of the characteristics represented. (8 and 9)

Multiple-forms reliability a reliability assessment in which two different forms of the same measure are given to the same sample of persons and the summed scores of the two forms are correlated with the expectation of a strongly positive correlation for reliability. (9)

Multistage cluster sample a type of probability sample involving the successive creation and sampling of ever smaller groupings of elements until the sample contains a reasonable number and distribution of elements. (7)

Multivariate analysis the investigation of the nature of the relationships among three or more variables. (Preface)

Mutual exclusiveness a property of structured re sponse categories that refers to the fact that no one category overlaps with any of the remaining categories, resulting in the classification of any one person or case once and only once. (8 and 14)

Natural setting a nonlaboratory context for research, synonymous with the notion of a *field study;* a study done in the setting in which the research topic normally occurs; compatible with the term *field research*. (13)

Necessary condition assuming a causal relationship between an independent and a dependent variable, a criterion for causality that suggests that the independent variable must happen prior to the dependent variable; must be used in conjunction with a *sufficient condition*. (4)

Negative association an increase in one or more factors that is accompanied by a decrease in one or more different factors; i.e., when one set of factors increases, a different set of factors decreases; compare with the term *positive association*. (2)

Negative canon of agreement one of two subtypes of Mill's method-of-agreement canon for causality, which suggests that if an independent factor is the cause of another dependent factor, when one of these factors is absent, the other will be absent; compare with the term *positive canon of agreement*. (4)

Nominal level of measurement one of four levels of measurement that involves sorting items into discrete categories or labeling each item with a distinctive number. (9)

Nomothetic explanation a partial explanation of the variables involved and their relationships, which seeks to maximize the explanatory power of a limited number of factors relative to some category of situations; also called the *rule of parsimony* or *Occam's razor*. (1)

Nonarbitrary zero point a true zero point, meaning that recording 0 represents the least amount of the variable possible; this is one of two characteristics of the ratio level of measurement; compare with the term *arbitrary zero point*. (9)

Nonmailed questionnaire a survey data-gathering design in which the schedule or guide to which the respondent responds is hand delivered and picked up by the researcher, e.g., an examination given to students in the classroom. (10)

Nonparticipant the researcher who does not want to have any role related to the subject matter being studied except that of observer; compare with the term *participant*. (13)

Nonprobability sample a sample in which the likelihood of selecting any element from the sampling frame is not known and cannot be determined. (7)

Nonreactive measure any measurement procedure that can be done without the knowledge or conscious participation of the group that is the subject matter; there are four types: physical traces, archives, simple observation, and contrived observation; synonymous with the term *unobtrusive measure*. (12)

Nonresponse error   an error due to the fact that the person sampled either refuses to participate in the study or cannot be located for participation; there are two types of nonresponse error: (a) selective and (b) total. (6)

Nonsampling error   the difference between the value of the descriptive statistic of the sample and the true population parameter, which is due to reasons *other than* sampling errors. (6)

Normal science   the usual progression of science involving the accumulation of knowledge under the current reigning scientific paradigm. (1)

Normed statistic   any statistical measure of association that has been designed to generate values between 0 and 1; additionally, if the statistic indicates the direction of the association, the values will range from –1 to +1. (15)

Objective phenomena   those phenomena that can be understood through the use of one's senses (sight, hearing, smell, touch, and taste); compare with the term *subjective phenomena*. (1)

Objectivity   a scientific value with which the scientist is thought to be able to analyze relationships and data in an unbiased, dispassionate way. (1 and 12)

Observational differentiation   a strategy for operationalizing the subcategories in a table in which the researcher uses his or her own years of observation and knowledge to determine meaningful divisions on the key tabular variables. (14)

One-category control   one technique for controlling class II variables that involves relegating all the cases studied to a single attribute on the controlled dimension. (3)

Open-ended response category   one in which the researcher allows the respondent to respond to the survey items using the respondent's own words; synonymous with the term *unstructured response category*. (10)

Operating system   a computer's internal system of instructions, which relates all the hardware components together and which tells the computer how to manage program, data, and output files. (15)

Operational definition   the definition of a variable presented in terms of empirically observable char-

acteristics; it is a statement of how a variable is to be scientifically measured. (2)

Ordinal level of measurement   one of four levels of measurement in which items are ranked with respect to the degree of some common characteristic that the items all possess. (9)

Ordinate   the vertical axis in a two-dimensional graph; also called the *Y axis*; compare with the term *abscissa*. (6)

Origin   the point at which the abscissa (*X axis*) and the ordinate (*Y axis*) meet in a two-dimensional graph; this point represents the zero point on both axes. (6)

Output file   a file created by a VAX command that contains the results of a computing session and that can be outputted to the monitor or to the printer and saved as a file in the computer's storage facility. (15)

Overt role   the role played by the researcher when it is decided to inform the persons studied that they are part of an observational research study; while this may lead to certain reactivity responses, such as masking behavior and the socially desirable response on the part of the sample, it is an ethical stance for the researcher to take; compare with the term *covert role*. (13)

Paired comparison technique   a strategy developed by Thurstone for determining the rank order of items by explicitly comparing every possible pair of stimuli to determine their higher or lower rank on a preselected dimension. (12)

Panel design   a quasi-experimental research design in which one before and after measures a single group that has been exposed to some experimental stimulus; synonymous with the terms *before-and-after design* and the *succession design*. (11)

Paradigm   a general set of ideas, assumptions, concepts, and relationships of broad scope that helps the scientist to focus attention on the subject matter being studied. (1)

Paradigmatic shift   the emergence of a new scientific paradigm that leads to the abandonment of the previous paradigm. (1)

Paragraph   a rarely used unit of analysis in content analysis in which the researcher focuses on the entire paragraph. (12)

Participant   the researcher who decides to pursue an active role related to the subject matter in an observational study; compare with the term *non-participant*. (13)

Password   a computer security device which, when established and attached to a computer account, functions to prevent those who do not know it from entering. (15)

Pearson product-moment correlation   a parametric, descriptive (usually) statistic which measures the association between two variables which have been measured at the interval or ratio levels of measurement; synonymous with the term *Pearson's r*. (4)

Pearson's r   see *Pearson product-moment correlation*. (4)

Percentage   the number of cases possessing some characteristic divided by the total number of cases that could have had the characteristic multiplied by 100. (14)

Percentaging tables   in a tabular data presentation, the marginal frequencies of the independent variable should be used as the base on which to compute cell percentages; however, if the percentages are to be purely descriptive of the tabular distribution, they should be determined using the grand total as the base. (14)

Perceptual acuity   an essential characteristic of the researcher doing a secondary analysis, which focuses on the person's ability to use imagination and creativity in selecting appropriate operationalized measures for the variables of interest from already existing data bases and survey results. (12)

Physical exterior sign   in unobtrusive observational research, a subcategory of simple observation in which the researcher observes the outwardly visible characteristics of the subject matter, e.g., nature of adornment (jewelry or protest buttons), form of dress (casual or formal), and hair length and style. (13)

Physical-location analysis   in unobtrusive observational research, a subcategory of simple observation that focuses on the subject matter's placement vis-à-vis other competing and simply different subject matters; e.g., who goes to the library, who goes to the university union, or who sits with whom in a classroom setting. (13)

Physical trace   in unobtrusive measurement, a directly observable piece of nonreactive evidence from which relevant data may be taken; there are two principal types: accretion measures (such as finger prints) and erosion measures (such as wear on linoleum tiles). (13)

Placebo   a bogus stimulus or treatment given to the control group that has no effect on the dependent variable; it is used in conjunction with the double-blind experimental research design. (11)

Population   the total number of elements (cases or people) that are of interest to the researcher; practically speaking, this usually means the total number of elements which are *available to the researcher,* or the sampling frame. (6)

Population distribution   the relative frequency within which the true values of the universe fall into a value or category of values from among all the theoretically possible values on some measurement. (6)

Population parameter   a descriptive mathematical value that summarizes empirical data collected from a population; a vast array of statistical formulas, usually represented by Greek letters. (6)

Positive association   an increase (or decrease) in one or more factors that is accompanied by an increase (or decrease) in one or more different factors; i.e., both sets of factors must change, when they do, in the same direction; compare with the term *negative association*. (2)

Positive canon of agreement   one of two subtypes of Mill's method of agreement canon for causality, which suggests that if an independent factor is the cause of another dependent factor, when one of these factors is present, the other will be present; compare with the term *negative canon of agreement*. (4)

Post hoc fallacy   a fallacious argument that some factor which occurs before some other factor must be the cause of the second factor. (4)

Pragmatism   the notion that the ultimate value of an idea is its usefulness in the solution of practical problems. (1)

Precision   the degree of closeness or congruency between the measured value of some variable and the variable's true value. (9)

Precision control   a technique for controlling on class II variables in an experimental or quasi-experimental data-gathering design, which involves the pairing (if two groups are desired) of individuals on a limited number of variables and their subsequent random assignment to two different groups. (3)

Predictive criterion validity one of two criterion measures of validity in which forecasts from the to-be-validated measure are compared with the actual future empirical evidence gathered later. (9)

Predictive knowledge information that permits one to make a reasonably accurate forecast of future events. (1)

Pretest the full dress rehearsal of the anticipated research design for the purpose of detecting bugs or errors within the design. (9)

Primary sampling unit in a multistage cluster sampling design, the first set of groups that were selected before subsequent groupings were created and sampled. (7)

Primary source any verbal or written communication that has been formulated by the person who is performing a content analysis. (12)

PRINT command (VAX) a command that sends the output file to the printer for printing onto paper or hard copy. (15)

Printer a computer component that prints output onto paper. (15)

Private personal information concerning individuals; one of Junker's four stages of marginality; to be able to determine private information, the observer must have significantly reduced marginality. (13)

Probability the likelihood that some event may occur; probability theory was developed on mathematical principles and functions importantly to measure chance occurrences. (4)

Probability sample a sampling design in which the likelihood of including any element in the sampling frame is known or can be determined; this property is a vital one in the proper use of statistical reasoning, particularly the use of inferential statistics; synonymous with the term *random sample*. (7)

Probe question a neutral question used in interviewing situations that encourages the respondent to elaborate about the topic being discussed and that communicates the interviewer's interest in the respondent's ideas. (8 and 10)

Problem a perceived difficulty whose negative consequences one seeks to lessen, if not eliminate. (1)

Problematic a research question that is motivated solely by the scientist's desire to seek an answer to it. (1)

Program file a computer file containing statements that identify the location and nature of the data in the data file, instructions on how these data are to be manipulated, and instructions on how the results are to be organized and reported. (15)

Proof evidence sufficient to establish the credibility of that which has been proven for all time; relationships that have been proven are called laws in science. (3)

Proportional stratified sample a type of probability sampling design in which one divides the sampling frame into strata and then samples using a probability process within each of the strata using the same sampling fraction, thereby guaranteeing that the selected sample contains the same proportions on the stratification variable or variables as does the sampling frame. (7)

Proportionate-reduction-in-error (PRE) measure any of a number of statistical procedures which calculate the proportion of error reduction through the establishment of two error rules using the formula $(E_1 - E_2) / E_1$, where E_1 are the number of errors made by prediction rule 1 and E_2 are the number of errors made by prediction rule 2. (15)

Proposition a statement written in the language of conceptualization that functions substantively to suggest a relationship between or among concepts and constructs or that functions to suggest the distribution or occurrence of a single concept or construct. (2)

Public in observational research, information that any conscientious observer can determine; it is the first stage in Junker's notion of marginality, which indicates high separation of the researcher and the subject matter. (13)

Pure research research in which the researcher seeks to study some phenomenon simply because the researcher is driven by his or her own curiosity for basic knowledge; a study which has no applied benefit at the time which it is done; compare with the term *applied research*. (16)

Purposive sample   a type of nonprobability sample in which the researcher is free to select any element that the researcher's judgment and expertise identify as a typical element; synonymous with the term *judgmental sample*. (7)

Quantitative   data which has been described by some meaningful numerical value. (12)

Quasi-experiment   any one of a number of data-gathering procedures that are lacking one or more of the necessary components found in the classical experimental design, i.e., a minimum of two randomly assigned groups, a minimum of two measurements each, and only one group exposed to the test stimulus. (11)

Quaternary sampling unit   in a multistage cluster sampling design, the fourth set of groups that were selected before subsequent groupings were created and sampled. (7)

Question   an interrogatory item used in various data-gathering procedures, which is directed toward eliciting information about the respondent's behavior or actions; compare with *statement*. (8)

Question format   one of two item formats found in schedules and guides, which is appropriate to the measurement of one's behavior or actions. (8 or 9)

Questionnaire   one of two survey data-gathering designs in which the respondent is responsible for both reading the directions and the items and entering the responses on the measuring instrument; compare with *interview*. (8 and 10)

Quota sample   a type of nonprobability sample in which the researcher tries to replicate the same proportions of theoretically important categories as exist in the sampling frame; this is done through the exercise of the researcher's ability to select typical cases. (7)

Radical empiricist   one who seems only to be interested in testing hypotheses with little, or no, thought to their conceptual or theoretical significance; compare with the term *significant generalizer*. (5)

Random digit dialing (RDD)   a computerized random sampling process that is used in conjunction with a telephone interview survey data-gathering design. (10)

Random error   those errors that tend to cancel one another out (a popular notion with which your authors disagree). (6)

Random sample   synonymous with the term *probability sample*. (7)

Random start   the initial point that is determined by pure chance within the first sampling interval in a systematic probability sampling design. (7)

Randomization   a technique for controlling class II variables that involves the selection of cases in a single sample or the distribution of cases in the formation of multiple groups for an experimental data-gathering design on the basis of pure chance; its success can be measured using probability theory. (3)

Ratio level of measurement   one of the four levels of measurement that contains two characteristics: a constant unit of measure (e.g., an inch, pound) and a nonarbitrary, or absolute, zero point. (9)

Rationale   (a) the justification for doing a research study (Appendix A), or (b) the reasons for participating in the scientist's study (10); these are important sections in both the research proposal and the survey data-gathering designs.

Rationalism   the epistemology in which one believes that rational thinking and the power of the mind are sufficient to discover the truth. (1)

Raw data   the values of the data that have been collected prior to their manipulation in the data-analysis phase of the study. (6)

Reactive effect   synonymous with *reactivity*. (11)

Reactivity   any one of a number of changes in the respondent's behavior or attitude due to the fact that the subject knows he or she is the focus of a research project, e.g., the Hawthorne effect, the socially desirable response, and masking. (13)

Read   to take data or instructions off some computer storage component such as a hard or floppy disk. (15)

RECODE command (SPSS^x)   a command that allows the researcher to redefine the data in any way deemed appropriate; the results of the recode command are present only in the active file. (15)

Record number   any one row of data within a single case in a data file. (15)

Recording unit synonymous with the term *unit of analysis,* as it applies in the context of content analysis. (12)

Referral sample a type of nonprobability sample in which persons sampled identify other persons for the researcher to contact; synonymous with the term *snowball sample.* (7)

Relevant literature that portion of the researcher's review of the literature that is used to construct the conceptual model which provides the basis for the researcher's study. (5 and Appendix A)

Reliable knowledge accurate scientific knowledge that functions to describe, to predict, or to explain the subject matter of interest. (1)

Reliability a desirable characteristic of a measure that produces the same value when repeatedly applied to the same subject matter, assuming that subject matter is stable. (9)

Replication a general characteristic of scientific methodology that suggests that any study should be sufficiently explained so that one's colleagues could repeat the study as it was originally done; more specifically, replication has been associated with experimental data-gathering designs because of the latter's attention to detail and the element of control. (11)

Representativeness a desirable characteristic of a sample in which the sample accurately reflects the population distribution on the variables of interest to the researcher. (6)

Research design (1) the sum total of all the methodological decisions pertinent to a research study; compare with the term *conceptual model* (5); or the introductory subsection to the methodology chapter of a research proposal or finished report which presents an overview of the more specific decisions and rationales which follow. (Appendix A)

Research topic the researcher's area of interest which takes the form of a problematic or topic, which, if answered, leads to basic knowledge and functions to satisfy the researcher's curiosity or which takes the form of a problem or topic, which, if answered, leads to applied knowledge or knowledge which is believed to be beneficial to society. (5)

Respondent the sampled person who participates in an interview or questionnaire data-gathering survey design. (10)

Respondent sensitivity the degree to which an after measure is affected by the administration of the before measure in an experimental or quasi-experimental data-gathering design; the function of the control group in the classical experimental design is to measure respondent sensitivity. (11)

Response category any one of a number of possible ways in which the researcher wishes the respondent to reply; these can be structured (specific) or they can be unstructured (open-ended). (8 and 10)

Response rate the proportion (percentage) of sampled persons who respond to any guide or schedule in an interview or questionnaire survey data-gathering research design; as a rule, early returners of the measuring instrument have different characteristics than later respondents to mailed questionnaire designs. (10)

Response set the tendency of some respondents to reply on a survey measuring instrument negatively or positively to all or almost all of the items given in an index; synonymous with the term *acquiescence tendency.* (8)

Response variation one of the criteria for the design of an appropriate item in a measuring instrument that suggests that any item should elicit a range of responses. (8 and 9)

Revelation the belief that the information is correct because it comes to us from some supernatural source. (1)

Robustness a characteristic of some statistics that indicates that the measure is relatively impervious or unaffected by violations of the requirements for its use, e.g., an improperly drawn sample, or violations of the levels of measurement assumptions. (5)

Role playing one of several alternatives to deception in which the research participants are asked to act out some behavior as if they were participating in a real circumstance; difficulties involve creating a realistic role-playing situation and minimizing the participant's intellectual awareness of the artificial nature of the research setting. (16)

Run to execute the computer instructions contained in one's program file on the specified data file. (15)

RUN command (VAX) a command that tells the computer to execute a program file or a data file and identify and save the result as an output file. (15)

Sample some portion of the population (more accurately, the sampling frame); hopefully its key characteristics are sufficient size and representativeness. (6)

Sample distribution the frequency with which the actual scores from those persons sampled fall into certain values or categories from among all those values possible. (6)

Sample mortality the drop out in one's sample, which occurs from the beginning to the completion of the study. (4)

Sample statistic a mathematical value derived from a sample. (6)

Sampling the process through which the researcher selects a lesser number of elements from the population (or sampling frame) for inclusion in the study. (6)

Sampling bias (a) see *bias*; (b) in content analysis, a bias caused by the fact that the written document is not usually directed to those persons with little formal education or low socioeconomic status; therefore, even simple random samples of written documents will minimize the feelings and attitudes of these persons. (12)

Sampling design the particular sampling strategy that the researcher selects for drawing the sample. (7)

Sampling distribution a theoretical distribution of all the possible combinations of values of a particular descriptive statistic for a sample of some specified size that was drawn in some specified way which could have occurred by pure chance. (6)

Sampling element an actual element that is selected for study. (6)

Sampling error the difference between the value of the descriptive statistic derived from the sample and the value of the true population parameter, which is due *solely* to the fact that the sample is *not* representative of the population. (6)

Sampling fraction in a stratified sampling design, the proportion of the stratum that will be sampled; different sampling fractions are used in disproportional stratified sampling and the same sampling fraction is used in proportional stratified designs. (7)

Sampling frame the actual list of elements available to the researcher from which the sample will be selected. (6)

Sampling interval the number of elements contained within any one grouping of a sampling frame that has been prepared for a systematic sampling design; its size is determined by dividing the total numbers of elements in the sampling frame by the desired sample size. (7)

Sampling with replacement a crucial characteristic in the creation of a simple random sample that is guaranteed when the researcher adheres strictly to the criteria of equal probability of selection and independence of choice. (7)

Scale a composite measure that has an internal intensity order or an arrangement of the items in a definite order, which reflects the degree of the variable's being measured. (9)

Schedule one of two types of survey measuring instruments in which the items are designed to elicit information on specific variables found in predetermined hypotheses; compare with the term *guide*. (8 and 10)

Science an objective, logical, and systematic method of analysis of phenomena devised to permit the accumulation of reliable knowledge. (1)

Scientific fact a verified hypothesis. (3)

Scoring unit in content analysis, the scoring unit is often the same as the unit of analysis; however, they sometimes differ (e.g., newspapers may be the unit of analysis but the number of times a specific community or metropolitan area is mentioned may be the scoring unit); synonymous with the term *unit of enumeration*. (12)

Second-order variable any type of census data which does *not* deal with fertility, mortality, or migration. (12)

Secondary analysis a data-gathering design that uses a quantitative inventory of already existing data, e.g., census data or data bases from previously gathered surveys (SRC). (12)

Secondary sampling unit in a multistage cluster sampling design, the second set of groups that were selected before subsequent groupings were created and sampled. (7)

Secondary source a data source compiled by a person who was *not* an eyewitness to the event the data reflects. (12)

Secret information that is only available to members of the in-group and about which efforts are made to prevent its distribution outside the group; one of Junker's four stages of marginality. (13)

Selective nonresponse   a type of nonresponse error through which the respondent refuses to answer one or more, but not all, of the items in a survey measuring instrument. (6)

Selective survival   a difficulty in content analysis when documents are missing; this can be due to a number of factors, such as the decomposition of old documents or the purging of more ancient files to make room for current ones. (12)

Semantic differential   a multidimensional measure in which the researcher seeks to measure the respondent's feelings on a number of different dimensions on a single variable. (9)

Sentence   a rarely used unit of analysis in content analysis in which the researcher focuses on the entire sentence. (12)

Sieve question   a schedule question that functions to separate those who should respond to subsequent items from those for whom those items are inappropriate, and those respondents who are knowledgeable from those who are not; synonymous with the term *filter question*. (8)

Significant generalizer   one whose propositions-to-be-investigated are of such a high level of abstraction that their translation into the language of hypothesis testing is impossible; justified by the proponents as theoretically important; compare with the term *radical empiricist*. (5)

Simple observation   a subcategory of unobtrusive measurement that refers to those data that can be collected through the conscientious perception of the researcher of which there are five types: physical exterior signs (bruises), expressive movement (body language), physical-location analysis (sitting in the front of the class), language behavior ("You turkey!"), and time duration (student visits to professors just prior to exams). (13)

Simple random sample   a type of probability sample in which two criteria are maintained: (1) each element in the sampling frame must have an equal likelihood of being selected and (2) every element must be chosen independently of every other element; this type of sample is assumed in most elementary statistics texts. (7)

Simulation   the replication, usually within the laboratory, of a concrete example of all of the dimensions of the real-world situation; simulations are not found in the social sciences at the present time. (3)

Single-cell design   a quasi-experimental research design involving the after measurement only of a single experimental group which has been exposed to a stimulus or treatment; because of the lack of control in the selection of the subjects and in the manipulation of the experimental stimulus, it is only recommended for exploratory research purposes. (11)

Single-stage cluster sample   the initial selection of a number of groups of sampling elements and the subsequent study of all elements within the selected groupings. (7)

Single word   one of a number of popular units of analysis used in content analysis in which the researcher quantifies the number of times a particular word is used in a document; it is the least subjective unit of analysis that can be used. (12)

Singularity   a difficulty that emerges when the researcher only uses a single technique to measure a variable; almost all social science measurement strategies possess some disadvantages, which tend to somewhat bias the results; compare to the term *triangulation*. (13)

Situation ethics   a strategy similar to the cost-benefit analysis of the ethics of a situation in which the evaluator believes that few moral principles are absolute and that deception is sometimes permissible if the benefit outweighs the cost and the situation is right; this is tantamount to someone who argues that everything has its time and place. (16)

Snowball sample   a type of nonprobability sample in which persons sampled identify other persons for the researcher to contact; synonymous with the term *referral sample*. (7)

Socially desirable response   the type of response that the respondent feels will "please" the researcher or believes is the appropriate response which other "respectable" persons would give. (8, 10, and 11)

Software   a set of computer programming instructions, which are not part of the hardware intrinsically and which are designed to execute specified functions. (15)

Software system   see *software*. (15)

Solomon's three-group design   an experimental design that adds a second control group (which is not before measured but is exposed to the stimulus or treatment) to the classical experimental design. (11)

Solomon's four-group design   an experimental data-gathering design that adds two control groups to the classical design   where neither is before measured, both are after measured, and one is exposed to the experimental stimulus or treatment. (11)

Spearman-Brown prophecy formula   an adjustment to the split-half reliability correlation value, which takes into consideration that the correlation value is affected by differing numbers of items. (9)

Specific item   a question or statement in a measuring instrument that focuses on a narrow context and directs the respondent's attention to limited variables; compare with the term *general item*. (8)

Specification   one of the modes of elaboration in which the researcher indicates the conditions under which different attributes of the test factor cause increases or decreases in the values of the association between the dependent and independent variables. (4)

Split-half reliability   a reliability test involving the submission of the measure once to a single sample of people, the division of the results into two equal halves, and the correlation of summed scores of both halves to obtain a correlation value, which is adjusted by the Spearman-Brown prophecy formula. (9)

SPSS^x   the Statistics Package for the Social Sciences, Version x, which is a preprogrammed or canned set of data definition, input, analysis, output, and storage instructions. (15)

Spurious correlation   a bogus or nonmeaningful association between two variables, which is due to the fact that these variables are both in a causal relationship with a third independent variable. (4)

Standard deviation   a statistical concept defined as the square root of the arithmetic average of the sum of the squared deviations around the mean in a distribution. (6)

Standard normal distribution   the *one* normal curve the researcher would get *if* the mean were zero and the standard deviation were one. (16)

Statement   a declarative sentence that states a single idea and that is used to evaluate the respondent's feelings about some situation; compare with *question*. (8)

Statement format   one of two possible formats for items in a measuring instrument; it is the desired format when soliciting information on an attitude or feeling. (8 or 9)

Statistical distribution determination   one of the strategies for operationalizing tabular subheadings that involves determining meaningful divisions on a variable through legitimate statistical analysis; e.g., if the variable is normally distributed, one would use standard deviation to determine the limits of categories. (14)

Statistical formula control   an actual statistical formula for controlling on class II variables through the mathematical computations contained within the formula itself. (3)

Statistical mean   the sum of all the individual scores on some variable for all the elements studied divided by the total number of values. (6)

Statistical significance   a research result which has a high probability of *not* happening through the fluctuation of pure chance; compare with the term *substantive significance*. (5)

STATISTICS subcommand (SPSS^x)   (a) a subcommand used in conjunction with the FREQUENCIES command that allows one to select from a wide range of descriptive statistics, and (b) a subcommand used in conjunction with the CROSSTABS TABLES command that allows one to select from various measures of association that are appropriate to one's particular tabular data. (15)

Stratified sampling   separating the sampling frame into some number of conceptually relevant subcategories that are relatively homogeneous and then sampling within each subcategory using a probability process; there are two types: (1) proportional stratified and (2) disproportional stratified. (7)

Structured items   specifically designed schedule items that function to obtain information on predetermined variables so that hypothesis testing can be achieved; compare with the term *unstructured items*. (10)

Structured response categories predetermined categories framed by the researcher from which the respondent must choose; synonymous with the term *close-ended categories*. (8)

Structured schedule interview an interview data-gathering design in which the measuring instrument elicits information on specific variables so that predetermined hypotheses can be tested. (10)

Stub the upper left-hand portion of any table where one identifies the row and column variables, whose attributes compose the subheadings. (14)

Study population all those elements that really exist and from which the actual sample will be drawn; this is what most researchers mean when they use the word *population*. (6)

Subheading the attributes or subcategories that identify the columns and rows in a table. (14)

Subjective phenomena those phenomena that one could *not* understand directly through the use of one's senses; compare with the term *objective phenomena*. (1)

Substantive goal an objective that pertains to the subject matter under investigation. (Preface)

Substantive significance a research result which is meaningful to one's conceptual model or to the decision-making apparatus that accompanies applied research; compare with the term *statistical significance*. (5)

Succession design a quasi-experimental research design in which one takes a before and an after measure of a single group that has been exposed to some experimental stimulus; synonymous with the terms *panel design* and the *before-and-after design*. (11)

Sufficient condition assuming a causal relationship between an independent and a dependent variable, a condition that suggests that the independent variable will always be followed by the dependent variable; must be used in conjunction with a *necessary condition*. (4)

Survey a general data-gathering strategy that can take the form of a self-administered questionnaire or a face-to-face or telephone interview; the survey is appropriate when large numbers of persons need to be studied and when the researcher is interested in measuring an attitudinal variable. (10)

Symbol a popular unit of analysis in content analysis that is virtually synonymous with the notion of the single-word unit of analysis; it can also refer to a short phrase that contains one idea, e.g., the National Rifle Association or a liberal Democrat. (12)

Symmetric measure a statistical procedure designed for use when the researcher has not selected an independent variable; compare with asymmetric measure. (15)

Systematic proceeding in an orderly fashion; not random or in a haphazard fashion; an essential, general characteristic of science and, more specifically, in content analysis, it means to apply the procedures chosen to each and every data source in the same way. (1 and 12)

Systematic sample the selection of every nth element from a sampling frame after having determined the sampling interval and the initial random start in the first interval. (7)

Telephone interview an interview data-gathering procedure using the telephone; compare with *face-to-face interview*. (10)

Tertiary sampling unit in a multistage cluster sampling design, the third set of groups that were selected before subsequent groupings were created and sampled. (7)

Test factor any class II, controlled, variable, which *must be* coupled with one or more of the modes of elaboration analytical strategies. (4)

Test-retest reliability a reliability procedure involving a variation on the classical experimental design in which the experimental group is given the measure twice at the before and after period and the control group is given the measure only during the after period. (9)

Theme in content analysis, a unit of analysis that refers to the overall purpose, aim, or goal of a document. (12)

Theoretical definition the definition of a concept or construct that is given in terms of other concepts or constructs and that is found in the language of conceptualization. (2)

Theoretical, or conceptual, differentiation one of several strategies for determining the attributes of tabular variables through the direction offered by one's conceptual model. (14)

Theory a generalized, synthetic, explanatory statement which interrelates a set of other more specific propositions. (2)

Thurstone equal-appearing interval scale a scale formed by expert judges, who are asked to sort a large number of items for a composite measure into different piles representing equidistant points along a continuum of the variable being measured. (9)

Time duration one of the subtypes of unobtrusive simple observation measures available to the observational researcher, which focuses upon the chronology of the subject matter. (13)

Time-series design an extension of the successional quasi-experimental data-gathering design in which a single experimental group is measured more than once prior to the introduction of the stimulus and more than once after the treatment; this permits the measurement of change over a number of measurement periods. (11)

Title a crucial part of any table that should identify the nature of the data within the cells, the major explanatory variables whose attributes appear in the rows and columns, the controlled variables in the study (if any), and the nature of the sample from whom the tabular data were taken. (14)

TITLE command (SPSS^x) a command that permits labeling of the computer printout that one will eventually wish to generate. (15)

Total error the square root of the sum of the squares of the sampling error and the nonsampling error. (6)

Total nonresponse a type of nonresponse error in which the respondent selected for participation in the study either refuses totally to participate or cannot be located. (6)

Triangulation the process of comparing the measurements of the same variable from a variety of measuring instruments; this strategy greatly improves the confidence that the researcher may have in the accuracy and validity of the results. (13)

TYPE command (VAX) a command that tells the computer to place the output file on the monitor or cathode-ray tube (CRT). (15)

Unidimensionality a criterion for the proper design of an index or scale, which focuses on the measure's ability to assess only one characteristic of the situation. (8, 9, and 12)

Unit of analysis (1) in content analysis, a reference to any one of many units, such as a single word, symbol, theme, sentence, paragraph, or item (synonymous with the term *recording unit*); and (2) more generally, in any scientific study, the entity that is to be studied. (12 and 6)

Unit of enumeration in content analysis, one that may not be the unit in which the researcher is interested; e.g., the number of times a certain word appears in a publication may be the scoring unit or the unit of enumeration, while the unit of analysis may be the entire publication; synonymous with the term *scoring unit*. (12)

Univariate analysis the investigation of the distribution or occurrence of a single variable. (Preface and 15)

Universe a theoretical notion containing *all* the particular elements that have ever been, are, and will be that can be subsumed under some general conceptual heading. (6)

Unknown nonparticipant one of the four modalities in observational research in which the researcher declines to take an active role in the subject matter and decides to play a covert role as a researcher. (13)

Unknown participant one of the four modalities in observational research in which the researcher elects an active role within the group being studied and declines to tell the group that he or she is there for research purposes; this obviously has ethical drawbacks. (13)

Unobtrusive measure a measurement strategy that neither requires the subject matter to participate nor affects the subject matter in any way; synonymous with the term *nonreactive measure*. (12 and 13)

Unstructured items schedule or guide items which are general in nature and which allow the respondent maximum latitude to respond in ways which are of interest to the respondent; such items are appropriate in exploratory research; compare with *structured items*. (10)

Unstructured response category one in which the researcher asks the respondent to reply to the schedule items in the respondent's own words;

synonymous with the term *open-ended response category*. (8)

Validity   a characteristic of a measuring instrument that truly measures what it claims to measure. (9)

Value   any specific category or number descriptive of the degree to which a variable possesses some attribute. (3)

VALUE LABELS command (SPSSˣ)   a command that tells the computer the meaning of a data file code that represents some other value; usually this means an alphabetical label of some type. (15)

Variable   a factor in the language of hypothesis testing that can change either through time or from case to case. (3)

Variable label   the label that the researcher wishes any variable to have when the variable is placed on the computer output; it is usually more informational than the variable name. (15)

VARIABLE LABELS command (SPSSˣ)   the specific command that is used to identify any variable to SPSSˣ; the command with which a limited number of characters are assigned to each of one's variables. (15)

Variable name   the name given to any variable by which SPSSˣ will identify it; software limita-

tions often truncate this name to a limited number of characters, necessitating the use of a variable label. (15)

VARIABLES subcommand (SPSSˣ)   a subcommand used to identify the specific variables to which the FREQUENCIES command is to apply. (15)

Variation   the degree to which the values of some variable differ from one another among the elements being studied; this is the spread or dispersion in a set of measurements. (6)

Verification   the collection of sufficient objective evidence so that the scientist believes that the hypothesis being tested can be considered a scientific fact. (3)

Weighting   (a) in sampling, the adjustment of each stratum's values so that each proportionally mirrors that stratum's proportion in the population (7); and (b) in operationalization, the occasional practice of giving some item in an index a differential amount of impact than the remaining items have. (8)

Write   to put a data, program, or output file on a hard or floppy disk. (15)

Selected bibliography

Anastasi, Anne. *Psychological Testing*. Fifth Edition. New York, New York: Macmillan Publishing Co., 1982. Pp. 552–555.

Anderson, Andy B., Alexander Basilevsky, and Derek P. J. Hum. "Measurement: Theory and Techniques." *Handbook of Survey Research*. Peter H. Rossi, James D. Wright, and Andy B. Anderson, ed. New York, New York: Academic Press, Inc., 1983. Pp. 231–287.

Asch, Solomon E. "Effects of Group Pressure upon the Modification and Distortion of Judgments." *Readings in Social Psychology*. Third Edition. E. E. Maccoby, T. M. Newcomb, and E. L. Hartley, ed. New York, New York: Holt, Rinehart and Winston, 1958.

——. "Studies of Independence and Conformity: A Minority of One against a Unanimous Majority." *Psychological Monographs*. Vol. 70, No. 416 (complete), 1956.

Babbie, Earl. *The Practice of Social Research*. Fifth Edition. Belmont, California: Wadsworth Publishing Company, 1989.

Bailey, Kenneth D. *Methods of Social Research*. Third Edition. New York, New York: The Free Press, 1987.

Bales, Robert F. *Interaction Process Analysis: A Method for the Study of Small Groups*. Cambridge, Massachusetts: Addison-Wesley, 1950.

Bart, Pauline, and Linda Frankel. *The Student Sociologist's Handbook*. Fourth Edition. New York, New York: Random House, 1986.

Berelson, Bernard. *Content Analysis in Communication Research*. Glencoe, Illinois: The Free Press, 1952.

Berger, Peter L. *Invitation to Sociology: A Humanistic Perspective*. Garden City, New York: Doubleday Anchor Books, 1963.

Black, James A., and Dean J. Champion. *Methods and Issues in Social Research*. New York, New York: John Wiley & Sons, 1976.

Blalock, Jr., Hubert M. "The Measurement Problem: A Gap between the Languages of Theory and Research." *Methodology in Social Research*. Hu-

bert M. Blalock, Jr., and Ann B. Blalock, ed. New York, New York: McGraw-Hill Book Company, 1968. Pp. 5–27.

——. *Social Statistics*. Second Edition. New York, New York: McGraw-Hill Book Company, 1972.

Bradburn, Norman M. et al. *Improving Interview Method and Questionnaire Design*. San Francisco, California: Jossey-Bass, 1979.

Campbell, Donald T., and Julian C. Stanley. *Experimental and Quasi-Experimental Designs for Research*. Chicago, Illinois: Rand McNally College Publishing Company, 1963.

Catton, Jr., William R. "The Development of Sociological Thought." *Handbook of Modern Sociology*. Robert E. L. Faris, ed. Chicago, Illinois: Rand McNally & Company, 1964. Pp. 912–950.

Cochran, William G. *Sampling Techniques*. Third Edition. New York, New York: John Wiley & Sons, 1977.

Cook, Thomas D., and Donald T. Campbell. *Quasi-Experimentation: Design and Analysis Issues for Field Settings*. Chicago, Illinois: Rand McNally Publishing Company, 1979.

Denzin, Norman K. *The Research Act: A Theoretical Introduction to Sociological Methods*. Third Edition. New York, New York: McGraw-Hill Book Company, 1988.

Diener, Edward, and Rick Crandall. *Ethics in Social and Behavioral Research*. Chicago, Illinois: The University of Chicago Press, 1978.

Dillman, Don A. *Mail and Telephone Surveys: The Total Design Method*. New York, New York: John Wiley & Sons, 1978.

Durkheim, Emile. *Suicide: A Study in Sociology*. New York, New York: The Free Press, 1951.

Edwards, Allen L. *Techniques of Attitude Scale Construction*. New York, New York: Appleton-Century-Crofts, 1957.

Elifson, Kirk W., Richard P. Runyon, and Audrey Haber. *Fundamentals of Social Statistics*. Reading, Massachusetts: Addison-Wesley Publishing Company, 1982.

Farmer, Robert, and Ron Blum. *TACS User Manual.* Towson, Maryland: TSU Academic Computer Service, 1988.

Frankel, Martin. "Sampling Theory." *Handbook of Survey Research.* Peter H. Rossi, James D. Wright, and Andy B. Anderson, ed. New York, New York: Academic Press, 1983. Pp. 21–67.

Franklin, Jack L., and Jean H. Thrasher. *An Introduction to Program Evaluation.* New York, New York: John Wiley & Sons, 1976.

Goffman, Erving. *Presentation of Self in Everyday Life.* Garden City, New York: Doubleday & Co., Inc., 1959.

Goode, William J., and Paul K. Hatt. *Methods in Social Research.* New York, New York: McGraw-Hill Book Company, 1952.

Goodman, Leo A., and William H. Kruskal. "Measures of Association for Cross Classifications." *Journal of the American Statistical Association.* Vol. 49, No. 268 (December 1954). Pp. 732–764.

Gorden, Raymond L. *Interviewing: Strategy, Techniques, and Tactics.* Fourth Edition. Homewood, Illinois: The Dorsey Press, 1987.

Gouldner, Alvin W. "Anti-Minotaur: The Myth of a Value-Free Sociology." *Sociology on Trial.* Maurice Stein and Arthur Vidich, ed. Englewood Cliffs, New Jersey: Prentice-Hall, Inc., 1963. Pp. 35–52.

Gove, Philip Babcock, ed. *Webster's Third New International Dictionary of the English Language Unabridged.* Springfield, Massachusetts: G. & C. Merriam Company, Publishers, 1971.

Hakin, Catherine. *Secondary Analysis in Social Research: A Guide to Data Sources and Methods with Examples.* London, England: George Allen and Unwin, 1982.

Hardy, Janet B., Doris W. Welcher, Jay Stanley, and Joseph R. Dallas. "Long Range Outcome of Adolescent Pregnancy." *Clinical Obstetrics and Gynecology.* Vol. 21, No. 4 (December 1978). Pp. 1215–1232.

Harris, Chauncy D., and Edward L. Ullman. "The Nature of Cities." Paul K. Hatt and Albert J. Reiss, Jr., ed. *Cities and Society: The Revised Reader in Urban Society.* New York, New York: The Free Press of Glencoe, 1957. Pp. 237–247.

Hays, William L. *Statistics for Psychologists.* New York, New York: Holt, Rinehart and Winston, 1963.

Holsti, Ole R. *Content Analysis for the Social Sciences and Humanities.* Reading, Massachusetts: Addison-Wesley Publishing Company, 1969.

Hunt, Janet G., and Larry L. Hunt. "Secondary Analysis: A Personal Journal." *Readings for Social Research.* Theodore C. Wagenaar, ed. Belmont, California: Wadsworth Publishing Company, 1981. Pp. 317–323.

Hyman, Herbert H. *Secondary Analysis of Sample Surveys: Principles, Procedures, and Potentialities.* New York, New York: John Wiley and Sons, Inc., 1972.

Junker, Buford H. *Fieldwork: An Introduction to the Social Sciences.* Chicago, Illinois: University of Chicago Press, 1960.

Kendall, Patricia L., and Paul F. Lazarsfeld. "Problems of Survey Analysis." *Continuities in Social Research.* Robert K. Merton and Paul F. Lazarsfeld, ed. New York, New York: Arno Press, 1974. Pp. 133–196.

Kerlinger, Fred N. *Foundations of Behavioral Research.* Second Edition. New York, New York: Holt, Rinehart and Winston, Inc., 1973.

Kidder, Louise H. *Selltiz, Wrightsman and Cook's Research Methods in Social Relations.* Fourth Edition. New York, New York: Holt, Rinehart and Winston, 1981.

Kish, Leslie. "Some Statistical Problems in Research Design." *American Sociological Review.* Vol. 24, No. 3 (June 1959). Pp. 328–338.

———. *Survey Sampling.* New York, New York: John Wiley & Sons, Inc., 1965.

Kitsuse, John I., and Aaron V. Cicourel. "A Note on the Uses of Official Statistics." *Social Problems.* Vol. 11, No. 2 (Fall 1963). Pp. 131–139.

Klecka, William R., and Alfred J. Tuchfarber. "Random Digit Dialing: A Comparison to Personal Surveys." *The Public Opinion Quarterly.* Vol. 42, No. 1 (Spring 1978). Pp. 105–114.

Kuhn, Thomas S. *The Structure of Scientific Revolutions.* Second Edition, Enlarged. Chicago, Illinois: The University of Chicago Press, 1970.

Labovitz, Sanford, and Robert Hagedorn. *Introduction to Social Research.* Third Edition. New York, New York: McGraw-Hill Book Company, 1981.

Lastrucci, Carlo L. *The Scientific Approach: Basic Principles of the Scientific Method.* Cambridge, Massachusetts; Schenkman Publishing Company, Inc., 1963.

Lazerwitz, Bernard. "Sampling Theory and Procedures." *Methodology in Social Research*. Hubert M. Blalock, Jr., and Ann B. Blalock, ed. New York, New York: McGraw-Hill Book Company, 1968. Pp. 278–328.

Lenski, Gerhard. "Social Participation and Status Crystallization." *American Sociological Review*. Vol. 21, No. 4 (August 1956). Pp. 458–464.

———. "Status Crystallization: A Non-Vertical Dimension of Social Status." Vol. 19, No. 4 (August 1954). Pp. 405–413.

———. "Status Inconsistency and the Vote: A Four Nation Test." *American Sociological Review*. Vol. 32, No. 2 (April 1967). Pp. 298–301.

Lippmann, Walter. *Public Opinion*. New York, New York: Macmillan Publishing Company, 1922.

Lutz, Gene M. *Understanding Social Statistics*. New York, New York: Macmillan Publishing Company, 1983.

McGinnis, Robert. "Randomization and Inference in Sociological Research." *American Sociological Review*. Vol. 23, No. 4 (August 1958). Pp. 408–414.

Merton, Robert K. "Introduction." *Social Theory and Social Structure*. Revised and Enlarged Edition. New York, New York: The Free Press of Glencoe, 1957. Pp. 3–16.

———. "Manifest and Latent Functions." *Social Theory and Social Structure*. 1968 Enlarged Edition. New York, New York: The Free Press, 1969. Pp. 73–138.

———. "The Bearing of Sociological Theory on Empirical Research." *Social Theory and Social Structure*. 1968 Enlarged Edition. New York, New York: The Free Press, 1968. Pp. 139–155.

———. "The Bearing of Empirical Research on Sociological Theory." *Social Theory and Social Structure*. 1968 Enlarged Edition. New York, New York: The Free Press, 1968. Pp. 156–171.

———. "The Self-Fulfilling Prophecy." *Social Theory and Social Structure*. 1968 Enlarged Edition. New York, New York: The Free Press, 1968. Pp. 475–490.

Milgram, Stanley. "Behavioral Study of Obedience." *Journal of Abnormal and Social Psychology*. Vol. 67, No. 4 (1963). Pp. 371–378.

———. "Some Conditions of Obedience and Disobedience to Authority." *Human Relations*. Vol. 18, No. 1 (February 1965). Pp. 57–76.

Miller, Delbert C. *Handbook of Research Design and Social Measurement*. Fourth Edition. New York, New York: Longman, Inc., 1983.

Morrison, Denton E., and Ramon E. Henkel, ed. *The Significance Test Controversy: A Reader*. Chicago, Illinois: Aldine Publishing Company, 1970.

Mueller, John H., Karl F. Schuessler, and Herbert L. Costner. *Statistical Reasoning in Sociology*. Third Edition. Boston, Massachusetts: Houghton Mifflin Company, 1977.

Nachmias, David, and Chava Nachmias. *Research Methods in the Social Sciences*. Third Edition. New York, New York: St. Martin's Press, 1987.

Olson, Sheldon. *Ideas and Data: The Process and Practice of Social Research*. Homewood, Illinois: The Dorsey Press, 1976.

Parsons, Talcott. *The Social System*. New York, New York: The Free Press, 1951.

Payne, Stanley L. *The Art of Asking Questions*. Princeton, New Jersey: Princeton University Press, 1951.

Phillips, Bernard S. *Social Research: Strategy and Tactics*. Third Edition. New York, New York: Macmillan Publishing Co., 1976.

Roethlisberger, Fritz J., and William J. Dickson. *Management and the Worker*. Cambridge, Massachusetts: Harvard University Press, 1939.

Rosenberg, Morris. *The Logic of Survey Analysis*. New York, New York: Basic Books, Inc., Publishers, 1968.

Rosenthal, Robert, and Ralph L. Rosnow. *Essentials of Behavioral Research: Methods and Data Analysis*. New York, New York: McGraw-Hill Book Company, 1984.

Ross, John, and Perry Smith. "Orthodox Experimental Designs." *Methodology in Social Research*. Hubert M. Blalock, Jr., and Ann B. Blalock, ed. New York, New York: McGraw-Hill Book Company, 1968. Pp. 333–389.

Rubin, Herbert J. *Applied Social Research*. Columbus, Ohio: Merrill Publishing Company, 1983.

Rudner, Richard S. *Philosophy of Social Science*. Englewood Cliffs, New Jersey: Prentice-Hall, Inc., 1966.

Runes, Dagobert D., ed. *The Dictionary of Philosophy*. New York, New York: Philosophical Library, Inc., n. d.

Scheaffer, Richard L., William Mendenhall, and Lyman Ott. *Elementary Survey Sampling*. Second Edition. North Scituate, Massachusetts: Duxbury Press, 1979.

Selltiz, Claire, Lawrence J. Wrightsman, and Stuart W. Cook. *Research Methods in Social Relations*. Third Edition. New York, New York: Holt, Rinehart and Winston, 1976.

Sheatsley, Paul B. "Questionnaire Construction and Item Writing." *Handbook of Survey Research*. Peter H. Rossi, James D. Wright, and Andy B. Anderson, ed. New York, New York: Academic Press, Inc., 1983. Pp. 195–230.

Sherif, Muzafer. *The Psychology of Social Norms*. New York, New York: Harper & Row, 1936.

Singleton, Jr., Royce, Bruce C. Straits, Margaret M. Straits, and Ronald J. McAllister. *Approaches to Social Research*. New York, New York: Oxford University Press, 1988.

Slonin, Morris James. *Sampling: A Quick Reliable Guide to Practical Statistics*. New York, New York: Simon and Schuster, 1960.

Solomon, Richard L. "Extension of Control Group Design." *Psychological Bulletin*. Vol. 46, No. 2 (March 1949). Pp. 137–150.

Solomon, Richard L., and Michael S. Lessac. "A Control Group Design for Experimental Studies of Developmental Processes." *Psychological Bulletin*. Vol. 70, No. 3, Part 1 (September 1968). Pp. 145–150.

Somer, Robert H. "A New Asymmetric Measure of Association for Ordinal Variables." *American Sociological Review*. Vol. 27, No. 6 (December 1962). Pp. 799–811.

Spradley, James P. *You Owe Yourself a Drunk: An Ethnography of Urban Nomads*. Boston, Massachusetts: Little Brown & Co., 1970.

Stanley, Jay. "An Empirical Study of Aggression and Parental Roles." Unpublished M. A. Thesis.

Knoxville, Tennessee: University of Tennessee, 1963.

Sterling, Theodore D. "Publication Decisions and Their Possible Effects on Inferences Drawn from Tests of Significance or Vice Versa." Journal of the American Statistical Association. Vol. 54, No. 285 (March 1959). Pp. 30–34.

Sudman, Seymour. *Applied Sampling*. New York, New York: Academic Press, 1976.

Thomas, W. I., and Dorothy Swaine Thomas. *The Child in America*. New York, New York: Alfred Knopf, 1928.

Tippett, L. H. C. *Statistics*. London, England: Oxford University Press, 1943.

Upshaw, Harry S. "Attitude Measurement." *Methodology in Social Research*. Hubert M. Blalock, Jr., and Ann B. Blalock, ed. New York, New York: McGraw-Hill Book Company, 1968. Pp. 60–111.

Walker, Helen M., and Joseph Lev. *Statistical Inference*. New York, New York: Holt, Rinehart and Winston, Inc., 1953.

Webb, Eugene T., Donald T. Campbell, Richard D. Schwartz, Lee Sechrest, and Janet Belew Grove. *Nonreactive Measures in the Social Sciences*. Second Edition. Boston, Massachusetts: Houghton Mifflin Company, 1981.

Weber, Max. *The City*. Trans. and ed. by Don Martindale and Gertrud Neuwirth. New York, New York: Collier Books, 1962.

———. *The Protestant Ethic and the Spirit of Capitalism*. New York, New York: The Free Press, 1958.

Whyte, William Foote. *Street Corner Society*. Chicago, Illinois: University of Chicago Press, 1943.

Zimbardo, Philip G. "Psychology of Imprisonment." *Society*. Vol. 9 (April 1972). Pp. 4–8.

———. *American Sociologist*. Vol. 13, No. 3 (August 1978). Pp. 128–177.

———. *Social Problems*. Vol. 27, No. 3 (February 1980).

———. *SPSS-X User's Guide*. Third Edition. Chicago, Illinois: SPSS Inc., 1988.

INDEX

Note: Page numbers followed by *n* indicate material in footnotes.

model
Modem, 330
Modes of elaboration, 69–75
  concluding comments on, 74–75
  of explanation, 71–72
  of interpretation, 70–71
  of specification, 72–74
  test factor and, 69–70
Monitor, computer, 330
Multiple correlation, 22
Multiple forms reliability, 199–200
  critique of, 200
  described, 199–200
Multiple nuclei theory, 92
Multistage cluster sampling, 142–143
Mutual exclusiveness, 171, 180, 267
  of table subheadings, 311

Nachmias, Chava, 221
Nachmias, David, 221
National Institute of Health, 216
National Science Foundation, 216
Natural settings, 288
  known nonparticipant and, 291–292
  loss of control in, 252–253
Necessary conditions, 57–58
Negative association, 23, 93
Negative canon of agreement, 59–60
Negative items, coding of, 165–166
Newton, Sir Isaac, 2
Nominal level of measurement, 179–180
Nomothetic explanation, 13–14, 40
Nonarbitrary zero point, 182
Nonmailed questionnaires, 215
Nonparticipant
  defined, 286
  known, 291–292
  unknown, 292–293
Nonprobability sampling
  sample size in, 146–149
  sampling frame in, 125
  types of, 143–145
    accidental, 144
    judgmental (purposive), 144–145
    quota, 144
    referral (snowball), 145
Nonreactive measures, 273, 280, 294–300
Nonresponse errors, 111
Nonsampling error
  defined, 110
  examples of, 111–114
    coding error, 112, 113
    falsified answer, 111
    inaccurate answer, 111–112

item misrepresentation, 111
nonresponse, 111
relationship to sampling error, 113–114
types of, 112–113
  bias, 112
  random error, 112–113
Normal science, 2
Normed statistics, 355*n*
Northrop, F. S. C., 17

Objective phenomena, 8–9, 19
  concepts and, 19–20
Objectivity, 3–4, 6
  in content analysis, 262
Observation, 67, 284–294
  contrived, 299–300
  degree of conceptual structure in, 289
  degree of control in, 288
  degree of disclosure in, 288
  degree of involvement in, 286–288
  design correlation and, 289
  in differentiating between independent and dependent variables, 66–67
  introduction, 284–285
  nature of research setting in, 288
  reactivity and, 294
  research modalities for, 289–293
    with known nonparticipant, 291–292
    with known participant, 289–291, 301
    with unknown nonparticipant, 292–293
    with unknown participant, 291, 301
  simple, 296–299
  singularity and, 293–294
  sociological, 285–286
  unobtrusive measures and, 273, 294–300
Observational differentiation, 318–319
Official records, 265
Olson, Sheldon, 141, 148
One-category control, 43
Open-ended responses, 156, 162, 215
  spacing of, on schedules, 173
  summarizing, 228
Operating systems, computer, 338
Operational definitions, 29
  equating with theoretical definitions, 33–34
  example of, 29–30
Operationalization, 328–329
  of secondary analysis, 278

of table subheadings, 315–322
Ordinal level of measurement, 181, 184, 190
Ordinate, 117
Origin, 117
Original research, 80
Osgood, Charles, 195
Ott, Lyman, 133, 138
Outgoing mailing, 219–220
Output file, 357
Overt role, 288, 289–291

Paired comparison technique, 272
Panel design, 254
Paradigmatic shifts, 2
Paradigm, 2
Paragraphs, in content analysis, 269
Parsons, Talcott, 90, 91–92
Partial correlation, 22
Participant
  defined, 286
  known, 289–291, 301
  unknown, 291, 301
Password, 345
Pearson, Karl, 63–64
Pearson product-moment correlation, 63–64, 69, 182, 190, 199, 350
Percentage, cell, 311–312
Percentaging tables, 313–315
Perception, defined, 279
Perceptual acuity, secondary analysis and, 279
Periodic characteristics, 134
Permission, 89, 294, 300
Personal documents, 264–266
Phenomena, 8–9
  causation and. *See* Causation
  subjective, 8–9, 19, 20
Physical exterior signs, 296–297
Physical-location analysis, 298
Physical traces
  accretion measures, 295
  defined, 295
  erosion measures, 295
Placebo, 240
Police departments, 225
Population, 54
  defined, 104, 121
  making inferences from sample to, 109–120
  mean of, 55
  parameters of, 54, 106
  sample vs., 104
  size of, and need for sampling, 104–105, 146–149
  standard deviation of, 107–109
  study, 121